W9-CZA-483

LINES OF
Communication

**BAR CODE AND DATA COLLECTION
TECHNOLOGY FOR THE 90S**

by Craig K. Harmon

Helmers Publishing, Inc.
174 Concord Street, Peterborough, NH 03458-0874

Table of Contents

Foreword

When *Reading Between the Lines* was originally penned in 1983, I had no idea of the success that the text would realize—hopes possibly, but no real expectations of *Lines* being utilized as a college text, required reading for new employees at various bar code technology companies, pre- and post-seminar handouts by a wide range of speakers; generating sales of tens of thousands of copies over several editions; and referred to as "the classic" in the industry. To all of the readers of *Lines I* I would like to express my heartfelt appreciation and the hope that they will find *Lines of Communication—Lines II* as beneficial as the previous work.

One of the underlying philosophies in *Lines I* was a sense that for an industry to be successful, standards must be developed. I felt the proliferation of symbologies only served to inhibit standardization which, in turn, caused the text to focus on Universal Product Code (U.P.C.) and Interleaved 2 of 5 in the retail community and Code 39 elsewhere. Possibly due to naivete, I felt that U.P.C. was a static issue and that if organizations would give up the multitude of proprietary symbol structures in favor of this symbol trinity, many of the problems associated with data collection would go away. I still feel that U.P.C., Interleaved 2 of 5, and Code 39 may well be the best set of symbols on which organizations should focus, but related and additional issues need discussion and understanding for bar code technology to truly realize the potential available for inter- and intra-organizational communications.

This text expands on some of the basics that *Lines I* addressed. But *Lines II* also speaks to the issues of common coding structures, common labeling structures, data collection control systems, electronic communications between trading partners, the implications of global standards, some of the newer symbology entrants in the bar code market, and advances that have occurred in printing, reading, verification, and data collection systems. *Lines II* also provides many applications that readers may find similar enough to their own applications to be helpful and stimulating.

One of the things that I believe made *Lines I* successful was periodically releasing new editions with updated applications and more current insights into the various technologies involved. *Lines II* is intended to provide a similar format, because as times change so change the technologies to support the times.

Over the past decade I have had the opportunity to work with many standards development activities and from each I have had the benefit of substantial education. I have learned not only about technology, but also about human nature: vested interests, long-range attitudes (or the lack thereof), primary and secondary agendas, and proactive/reactive perspectives in the adoption of global standards. I am thought of by some as the "industry gadfly," or as "a bothersome, irksome fellow." This is not a reference that I find to be particularly offensive since I do challenge opinions. In the establishment of industry, national, and global standards, if one's perspective cannot be defended, it may, in fact, not be correct. I have had the president of an industry trade association of technology manufacturers tell me, "It is *our* (the manufacturers') industry, *we* will control it!" I believe technology is the users' industry, not the manufacturers', and I will strive to continue to challenge those who attempt to use industry standards development for their own interests as opposed to the interests of the user. I have also become aware that some have searched for ways to negate my activity in, or influence over, standardization. To those I simply respond, "I am a consultant whom organizations and individuals retain to keep them abreast of the changes in technology and standards relating to technology. The easiest way to negate my involvement in standards work is to adopt, and then live by, a common set of standards for all industries and markets." Short of that, I and my son (presently age 12) will have employment throughout our lifetimes.

It should not be thought, however, that the data collection technology marketplace is fraught with conspiring evildoers, for a vast majority of those involved in standards setting activities are genuinely concerned, forward-thinking, user-oriented individuals. I would like to express my appreciation to some of those individuals: Allan Gilligan—AT&T, Gary Ahlquist—Kodak, Bert Moore—IDAT, Chuck Biss—PSC, Marty Hileman—Standard Register, Sprague Ackley—Intermec, Tom Mitchell and David Reeves—Graphic Systems, Frank Oglesby—DuPont, Bruce Philpot—Uniform Code Council, Bill Sibley—Sibley & Associates, Jack Kindsvater and Karen Longe—Zebra Technologies, David Allais, Harry Burke, George Wright, Margarita Queralt, Rob Durst, and Jo Martell. Because of them the bar code technology marketplace is a better place.

I would also like to thank Theo Pavlidis, Jerome Swartz, Ynjiun Wang, and Richard Bravman of Symbol Technologies for their insights into two-dimensional symbologies and their generous permission to utilize a considerable amount of their scholarly contributions to the field of automatic identification. Further, I would like to thank Tom Mitchell and David Reeves of Graphic Systems, Charlie Sellberg of Diagraph, and the folks at Zebra Technologies for their generous permission to utilize their work on printing systems. I also want to express my appreciation to the people of Black Box Corporation for permission to use their work in data communications and local area networks. I must also thank the industry associations that permitted various sections of their standards and publications to be utilized in this work. Most notably I would like to thank the Uniform Code Council, International Article Numbering Association, Federation of Automated Coding Technologies, National Electrical Manufacturers Association, United States Postal Service, National Office Products Association, The Microcomputer Industry Association, Book Industry Systems Advisory Committee, Automotive Industry Action Group, and the Automatic Identification Manufacturers. Without the cooperation of these organizations this text would be far less complete.

I would also like to thank my wife Marsha for her understanding and invaluable assistance with this text. Finally, I would like to express my thanks to my son Matthew to whom I dedicate *Lines of Communication—Lines II,* for without him this text might not have been necessary.

Craig K. Harmon
June, 1993

CHAPTER 1

Technology Overview

E ver since 1890, when Dr. Herman Hollerith invented what today has become almost universally known as the IBM card, attempts have been made to automate the manual collection of data and subsequent tabulation of that collected data. From the sliding entry (pantographic) and keypunch systems of the 1950s which embraced punched cards and punched tape, the 1960s and 1970s brought the data entry industry magnetic tape encoders, various key-to-cassette, key-to-tape, key-to-diskette, and key-to-disk systems.

Today's computer systems process data at literally millions of instructions per second (MIPS). While such processing power is truly mind-boggling, what is even more mind-boggling is the rate at which computers traditionally receive data input from key-entry. The skilled key-entry operator is able to key data at rates of two to five characters per second. So, with computers processing at speeds in MIPS—with each instruction consisting of several characters—and data entry constrained to unitary characters per second, it is not difficult to see where the data processing bottleneck is located. These transcriptive forms of data collection—where data is prepared on documents at their source and then transcribed to another medium capable of being read and interpreted by a computer—represent as much as 80 percent of the total cost of data processing.

In addition to being costly—by virtue of being labor intensive—such data collection methods are highly error prone. A typical key-entry operator experiences approximately 1 undetected error in every 300 characters entered. Conservatively, the cost of an error to U.S. Industry is $27 per error (a 1988 study at 3M estimated the cost of an error at $138). Methods of data collection available today are able to realize error rates of one error in literally trillions of characters entered.

Finally, traditional methods of data collection deny management the opportunity of employing "control systems" to manage moment-to-moment and day-to-day activities. Instead, management must rely upon accounting systems that report operations activities days after the activity occurs. Today, data collection systems exist that enable data collection equipment to be taken "where the action is": on the production line, in the truck, on the forklift, to the patient bedside, in the hands of quality control inspectors, with maintenance personnel, with salespersons (or in the hands of the customer), and to the check-out clerk. Oftentimes, advanced data collection technologies can even be employed in unattended operations such as warehouse conveyor systems.

Studies show the non-keyboard data collection market to be worth more than $2 billion. This market is forecasted to grow at a rate of approximately 25 percent per year with bar code technology and portable data entry terminals maintaining the lion's share of the market through the end of the century. While the markets for bar code technology, portable data entry terminals, transponders, and smart cards are expected to enjoy growth rates in excess of 35 percent per year, optical character recognition (OCR) may not grow that much by the year 2000, and magnetic stripe and magnetic ink character recognition (MICR) technologies will actually decrease.

Data collection systems are comprised of three elements, namely, the machine readable media, the terminal configuration, and the software that supports the data collection techniques.

Optical Character Recognition (OCR)

Optical character recognition systems employ special fonts readable by both human and machine. OCR is a more reliable method of data entry than key-entry, but is invariably less reliable than bar code technology. The problems associated with optical character recognition as a data entry tool for reading fields of data can easily be characterized by the early experiences of some of the more prestigious mass merchandise stores. The clerk makes several passes of the reading device over the OCR characters, becomes frustrated, and eventually keys the information into the terminal. The reading difficulty is the result of the technology employed in OCR. Optical character recognition characters are read by either software templating techniques, feature extraction, or a combination of both.

OCR-A (FULL ALPHA)

NUMERIC	0123456789
ALPHA	ABCDEFGHIJKLMNOPQRSTUVWXYZ
SYMBOLS	>$/-+-#"
MEDIA ONLY	Space, Period (Std.), Comma (Std.)

E13B

NUMERIC	1234567890
Special Symbols	⑈ ⑊ ⑉ ⑇
MEDIA ONLY	Space

Figure 1. 1: Examples of OCR-A Alpha and Numeric Fonts

While OCR is significantly better than key entry, its data integrity increases only to approximately 1 error in 10,000 characters entered. OCR is used to advantage where pages of data must be input to a computer system. Optical page readers are either pre-programmed to recognize specific font styles, or can be "taught" the character set contained in the document.

These techniques require each character to be physically unique from other characters in the character set. For machine recognition the most popular OCR font is that of OCR-A. One other drawback of optical character recognition is that the OCR reader must be precisely oriented to the symbol being read, much more precisely than the orientation required by bar code reading techniques. When long strings of information are read, it is difficult to maintain precise placement of the reading instrument over the entire string, since the scanning motion is not really a straight line but more of an arc. Further, optical character recognition is far more sensitive to the velocity and acceleration of the operator's hand during scanning than is bar code reading. Finally, OCR systems cannot easily read information from moving objects. To do so requires, for example, a strobe light synchronized with the object's movement. While OCR is significantly better than key entry, its data integrity increases only to approximately 1 error in 10,000 characters entered.

An advantage of bar code over optical character recognition is that the bar code reader interprets information by measuring only width. Further, the bar width has vertical redundancy. This vertical redundancy permits the bar/space pattern to be read with less precise orientation of the reader as well as providing improved tolerance for localized printing defects. Unlike OCR, bar codes have a repeating pattern that exists in every character. (Code 39 has nine elements, three of which are wide; Interleaved 2 of 5 has five elements, two of which are wide.) Bar codes can be checked at the character level by examining each character to establish the presence of a certain pattern of bars and spaces, wide elements and narrow elements, or a defined parity pattern. OCR must be read by identifying features of the isolated characters. Optical character recognition techniques identify the horizontal and vertical strokes, curves, and endings peculiar to each character in the character set. The absence of vertical redundancy and repeating character patterns causes OCR to be less resistant to errors caused by the printing process.

OCR is a viable technology where pages of data must be input to a computer system. Optical page readers are similar to office copiers and facsimile terminals in that an entire page is scanned before the next page is presented to the reader. The optical page reader is either pre-programmed to recognize a set of specific font styles and sizes or can be "taught" the character set contained in the document by identifying a specific character structure in the document and telling the reader "this is an A, this is a B," etc.

OCR was initially adopted in 1975 by the National Retail Merchants Association (NRMA), now known as the National Retail Federation (NRF), as the standard font for automatically entering merchandise identification, credit authorization, and inventory control. After having experienced poor manufacturer compliance in providing source-marked tags bearing OCR symbols and mixed performance with front-end reading equipment, the NRMA announced in 1986 that in the future it would support bar code symbols for source marking of general merchandise.

Magnetic Ink Character Recognition (MICR)

Magnetic ink character recognition was developed in 1956 and has been widely embraced by the banking community. It is a stylized OCR font, printed with a magnetic ink to permit readability after being overprinted with postmarks, cancellation marks, smudges, and the like. MICR is generally employed when reading smaller documents such as checks, money orders, and credit card applications, which are typically between 2 3/4 by 6 inches and 3 2/3 by 8 3/4 inches. But like OCR page readers, magnetic ink character recognition readers require precise registration and orientation.

Magnetic Stripe

Magnetic stripe technology, as employed by financial institutions, is attractive in that it is difficult to reproduce without expensive machinery. Depending upon which of three possible tracks is read, recording densities per inch are available from 79 alphanumeric characters (Track 1) to 40 numeric characters (Track 2) to 107 numeric characters (Track 3). This may sound impressive, but data integrity is achieved by repeating the character string several times on a single track, yielding a recording media whose density is not vastly superior to that of bar codes. The media must be read by a device that is in contact with the magnetic stripe; the technology is quite expensive; and the recorded information is susceptible to being altered or erased when exposed to fairly weak magnetic fields (300 gauss or less). Magnetic stripe technology does have good application potential with limited-life type media, such as transit passes and airline boarding passes, where the expected life of the media is anticipated to be no longer than 24 hours.

Voice Recognition (VR)

For the past several years voice recognition systems suffered from the inability of the technology to live up to users' expectations. Today, however, voice technology is being intelligently packaged and applied to useful applications. A primary attraction of these systems, which understand spoken words, is that speech is possibly the most natural communication means for humans. Voice input as a data collection medium frees the user from the need to understand computer systems. Training can be minimized, and in industrial settings the use of VR with wireless microphones frees the user from the constraints of a keyboard. The user's hands and eyes are freed, permitting object manipulation and quality checks in jobs requiring hand and eye coordination.

Voice recognition systems come in two distinct types: speaker-dependent and speaker-independent systems. Most recognition systems are the speaker-dependent variety. They are trained by the user to recognize a vocabulary of words as they are spoken by each speaker. Each user recites each vocabulary word to be used one or more times so that the VR system recognizes how the user says the word. The voice recognition system stores a computer image of each utterance and then later compares incoming words to these computer images. Matching the incoming image to the stored image provides the recognition. The system can be adjusted to determine how closely the incoming word must match the stored word before a valid recognition is made. Speaker-dependent systems provide for the larger vocabulary and most accurate recognition. Many commercial speaker-dependent systems provide 50 to 100 words in their active vocabularies. Skillful programming can provide application-dependent vocabularies that are, for all practical purposes, infinite. The real promise for voice recognition technology rests in systems that do not require speakers to train the system. Speaker-independent systems have used recognition templates from large memories of previously recorded images, allowing a user who has never worked with voice recognition systems before to use the system. The templates within these database memories represent speech patterns from northern and southern dialects and those of both male and female speakers. The commercially available speaker-independent systems are presently restricted to vocabularies that include digits and a few words, while existing data entry applications typically require active vocabularies of 30 to 80 words to be effective.

In addition to speaker-dependence and speaker-independence, a distinction can be made among commercial voice recognition systems on the basis of whether a system supports discrete word recognition or continuous word recognition. Discrete word VR systems require a pause between utterances. Continuous VR systems permit speech at a normal rate, with natural breaks after word groupings. Most state-of-the-art voice recognition systems support continuous speech, but some still do not.

RF Tags: Transponders and Surface Acoustic Wave (SAW)

Most data collection applications will, through the remainder of this century, focus on bar code media. There are some applications, however, that are not well-suited to optically read media. These applications have hostile environments, such as a surface that is oily, dirty, or painted over. Other applications include those where data must not only be read *from*, but must also be written *to* the media. Still other applications include those where a need exists to identify animals. For these applications, RF tag technology should be considered. RF identification systems use a tag that interacts with a radio signal from the scanner, revealing the identity. SAW technology is an RF tag version of bar code, in that a fixed identification message is built into the tag when it is manufactured.

Transponder technology is based on the use of a small radio transmitter and receiver encased in a tag. The receiver is either powered by an internal battery (active) or by the energy received from a polling reader (passive). The reader transmits a radio signal that is received by the tag's radio receiver triggering the tag's transmitter to transmit a unique coded message, which in turn is received by the reader's receiver. The transponder information can be transmitted up to 1000 feet, decoded, and then passed on to the computer system. Transponder technology is available in a variety of forms. Some are capable of storing up to 16,000 bytes of data and can be read from and written to. Such systems could track a tote throughout a manufacturing application, instructing the operators at each station as to the procedures to be undertaken on the components within the tote, and record the completion of the procedure, (including who completed it, when it was started, and when it was completed). At the last station in the production process, the entire tag could be read, providing a detailed history of the manufacturing operation.

Another transponder system is capable of identifying vehicles at speeds of up to 100 miles per hour and is a logical replacement choice for the failed bar code system adopted by the railroad industry in 1967. Information other than simple identity could also be included, i.e., contents, weight, consignee, shipper, value, and special handling instructions. Another application currently in place at several automotive manufacturing facilities is the identification of specific engine, model, color, and optional components for a vehicle under construction.

Other credit-card sized transponder systems are in use to identify packages and pallets, and to provide access control to secure areas. A recently introduced transponder system is the size of a coin and can be given an initial monetary value. When a retail transaction occurs, the value of the purchased item is debited from the transponder coin, which then has a value equal to the initial value minus the debited amount. Such devices are under consideration for cashless theme parks and coin-operated machines. Another recently introduced transponder system is used for automatic recognition and billing of charges for frequent users of toll roads.

Lower cost surface acoustical wave-based systems use a low power transmitter that transmits a microwave signal to the SAW tag. Electronic identification occurs when a signal transmitted from a reader strikes a tag attached to the object being identified. The tag consists of a small antenna and a man-made lithium niobate crystal. The antenna captures the signal transmitted from the reader and propagates it across the surface of the crystal. The piezoelectric properties of the lithium niobate crystal generate a surface acoustic wave effect analogous to the propagation of a wave created by dropping a stone into a calm pond. A layer of metalization on the crystal interrupts the propagation of the surface wave as it scatters across the crystal. These interruptions create the phase-modulated encoding characteristics unique to each tag, forming the equivalent of a binary number. A high-resolution photolithographic masking process is used to deposit the layer of metalization, creating the individual codes at the time of manufacture of the tag. The same antenna then returns the modified signal to the reader. Such SAW systems can operate at up to six feet from the reader.

One surface acoustical wave system is small enough (³/₈-inch long and the thickness of mechanical pencil lead—0.5 mm) to be subcutaneously implanted in an animal using a standard 12-gauge veterinarian syringe. This form of identification has been proven superior to branding, lip tattoos, and face markings to identify thoroughbred horses, other registered animals, and pets. Such a system is also in use to replace the banding of fish.

In 1992 and 1993 several industries began the process of standardization of RFID applications. Most notably the American Trucking Associations (ATA) issued its standard for RFID, the U. S. Military working with the ANS X3T6 committee has nearly completed its recommendations for RFID, the Federal Aviation Administration (FAA) has issued an RFID standard for baggage tracking (and potentially sortation), and the Automotive Industry Action Group (AIAG) has completed its recommendations for RFID applications. Regrettably, each of these efforts has evolved independently, creating a lack of standardization for both format and recommended RFID technology.

Smart Cards

Smart cards are credit card-sized plastic packages with one or more microchips embedded within. A typical smart card has an 8-bit microprocessor with storage capability of up to 8,000 characters and 8 gold-plated contacts in the upper left-hand corner of the front surface of the card. Smart cards employ personal identification numbers (PINs) to prevent unauthorized use. If three successive false PINs are entered, the smart card locks up, rendering it useless to the unauthorized user.

As a result of successful trials conducted by MasterCard, a detailed proposal for an international standard for a financial transaction card has been submitted. The card could be used as a credit card, debit card, or prepaid cash card anywhere in the world. Meanwhile, Visa, through its French organization, Carte Bleue, has developed a super smart card having its own keyboard, LCD display, and internal battery. In addition to functioning as a credit/debit/pre-paid cash card, the super smart card will function as a clock, calendar, calculator, currency converter, and memo pad.

Other smart cards employ a digitized photograph of the authorized user and biometric measurements such as fingerprints, signature, or other personal features to ensure an unprecedented level of security. Combined with a substantial amount of electronic storage, this technology delivers a very small, very personal computer system.

Table 1 shows some of the comparative characteristics of various data collection techniques.

Characteristic	Key-Entry	OCR	Bar Code	Magnetic Stripe	MICR	Voice Recognition	Transponder & SAW	Smart Card
Speed (12 char)	6 seconds	4 seconds	.3 to 2 seconds	4 seconds	Machine read	12 seconds	2 seconds	2 seconds
Error Rate	1 character error in 300 characters	1 character error in 10,000 characters	1 character error in 15,000 to 36 trillion characters	Low	Medium	High	Low	Low
Advantages	Human	Human-readable	Low Error Rate Low Cost High Speed Can be read at a distance	Data can be changed High data density	Human-readable	Hands-off operation	Media does not need to be visible	High data density
Disadvantages	Human High cost High error rate Inflexible	Low speed Moderate error rate Cannot read moving object without special equipment	Requires education of user community	High cost of equipment Contact Data affected by magnetic fields and abrasion	Expensive Inflexible reading equipment	Human operator High error rate Most systems required to be trained for different operators	Expensive media Inflexible reading equipment	High reader cost Moderate media cost

Table 1: Comparative Characteristics of Data Collection Technologies

CHAPTER 2

Bar Code Technology

===

W hat began as a system to improve productivity within retail supermarkets has blossomed into what many have come to view as a "new revolution" in factory data collection. The concept began back in 1949 when N.J. Woodland filed the first patent relating to this new technology. It is now embraced by most, if not all, segments of industry including automotive, health care, primary metals, graphics, pulp and paper, electronics, air transport, government, warehousing, and retail. This new technology is termed automatic identification (or automated data collection) and, more specifically, bar code technology.

Year	Name	Use
1949	Circular	First Bar Code (N.J. Woodland & B. Silver)
1962	ACI	Railroads
1971	Plessey	European Libraries
1972	Codabar	Blood Banking ('77) & Federal Express ('78)
1972	ITF	Fixed Content Shipping Container ('81)
1973	U.P.C.	United States Retail
1974	Code 39	Variable Length, Alphanumeric
1977	EAN	International Retail
1980	PostNet	United States Postal Service
1981	Code 128	Serialized Shipping Container (UCC) ('88)
1987	Code 49	High Density (Two Dimensional)
1988	Code 16K	High Density (Two Dimensional)
1989	Codablock	High Density (Two Dimensional)
1989	PDF417	High Density (Two Dimensional)

Table 2.1: A Brief History of Bar Code Technology

Bar code technology is data communications reduced to a printed form. A computer generates a printed image of a bar code symbol on paper or other graphic medium. This symbol is then presented to a scanning device or bar code reader. The bar code reader illuminates a bar code symbol and examines successive segments of the symbol to determine whether the detected area is highly reflective (a space) or non-reflective (a bar). As the detector is moved from the leading quiet zone through the printed symbol and into the trailing quiet zone, the transitions from light to dark and dark to light are detected. The length

9

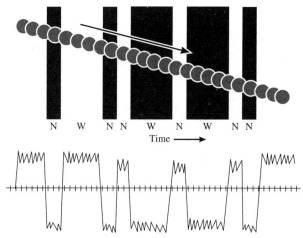

Figure 2.1: Principles of Bar Code Scanning

A scanning detector successively looks at points on a bar code symbol on some path through the symbol (top). An electronic signal (bottom) is generated corresponding to the wide (W) and narrow (N) spaces and bars. The width N of a narrow bar or space is commonly referred to as the X Dimension, or simply X.

of time the detector "sees" a light or dark area between transitions is converted into a digital representation (ones and zeros) of the printed bar code message as perceived by the detection method of the scanner. This digital representation is then translated into the original character code message that generated the bar code symbol in the first place. Figure 2.1 illustrates the essential principles of bar code scanning.

The narrowest element width of a bar code is conventionally called "X" in the specifications of bar codes. In two-width symbologies, the ratio of wide (W) to narrow (N) spacing is specified as a range from 2.4:1 to 3.2:1 with recommended value of 3.0:1. Wider bars are readable at greater distance. The typical narrow bar in open systems (where different organizations are expected to read the symbol), should not be smaller than X = 0.010 inch; a narrow bar dimension of from X = 0.013 to X = 0.017 inch is recommended.

Figure 2.2 shows a typical bar code symbol. Each symbology specifies a required quiet zone, which should typically be 10 times the narrow element width (X) or 0.25 inch, whichever is greater. The symbol height should typically be a minimum 15 percent of symbol length; many symbology specifications recommend a minimum 0.5 inch. The greater the symbol height, the easier it will be to read in the face of the inevitable noise from dirt and "wear and tear" defects.

The American National Standards Institute defines *bar code symbol* as "an array of rectangular bars and spaces which are arranged in a predetermined pattern following specific rules to represent elements of data that are referred to as characters. A bar code symbol typically contains a leading quiet zone, start character (pattern), data character(s) including a check character (if any), stop character (pattern), and a trailing quiet zone." Symbology is the language of bars and spaces in a printed symbol. Today there are over 50 different symbologies, but only four (U.P.C./EAN, Code 39, Code 128, and Interleaved 2 of 5) merit consideration in today's retail, materials management, and manufacturing applications. At mid-

Figure 2.2: Recommended Parameters of a Bar Code Symbol

The narrowest element width of a typical bar code symbol is noted X. Wide elements are shown here as 3X. The symbol specifications require a blank (commonly white) quiet zone on either end, shown here as the shaded regions.

year 1993 PDF417, DataMatrix, and Code 6 appear to be the leading contenders in the transportation, automotive, chemical, and electronics industries. PDF417 leads in applications where high data density and handheld scanning are required. DataMatrix leads in applications where symbols are laser etched, e.g., small part marking. Code 6 is beginning to make inroads into sortation-style applications.

To encode data, each symbology uses a unique set of rules which determines the type of information (numerics only, alpha and numeric characters together, or other special purpose characters), and the patterns of wide and narrow bars and spaces *(elements)* that represent the information. The rules also determine whether the *message length* is fixed or variable and affect how densely the data can be packed in a given length.

For instance, *Code 39*, the original *alphanumeric bar code symbology*, requires five bars and four spaces (three are wide and six narrow) to represent a single character. Alphanumeric *Code 128*, on the other hand, displays a character in three bars and three spaces of multiple widths. Different symbologies have different relative character densities (the number of characters able to be compacted into a unit of area).

Quiet zones positioned at the beginning and end of each symbol (see Figure 2.2) provide a reference point for the optoelectronic detector mechanism within the scanner. This reference point permits the device to "see" what a space is going to look like and in contrast what the lightest bar should look like.

A *start character* or *start pattern* immediately following the first quiet zone gives the scanner specific reading instructions, such as reading direction, element widths, and in the case of "auto-discrimination," symbology definition. Positioned at the other end of the symbol prior to the final quiet zone, a *stop character* or *stop pattern* contains instructions to conclude the symbol's message.

Bar code symbologies are said to be either *continuous* or *discrete*. Each character in a discrete bar code symbology begins with a bar and ends with a bar and has an *intercharacter space* between all characters. This intercharacter space can vary in width within certain ranges, usually between 1 and 5.3 times the width of the narrow bar. Except for mechanical printing on forms, this width is generally equal to the width of the narrow element. Code

39, Codabar, and 2 of 5 Code are discrete bar code symbologies. Continuous codes, on the other hand, have no intercharacter space. U.P.C./EAN, Interleaved 2 of 5, and Code 128 are continuous bar code symbologies.

Bar code systems will dramatically improve the error rates associated with data entry from a key-entry level of 1 in 300 characters entered, to better than 1 error in a million characters entered. As much as we would like to believe that everyone is going to be scanning next year, some will continue to key data—whether the key-entry is a result of scanner failure, label failure, system failure, or simply a result of some company not using bar codes. Prudent systems designers may wish to at least consider whether it is desirable to add an additional *check character* or symbol length to accommodate a dramatic reduction in key-entry errors. Check characters are mathematical computations of values assigned to each character in a symbol's message. Traditionally appearing as the last character preceding the stop character, check characters can virtually eliminate any form of data errors, scanned or keyed. Check characters are discussed further in the data collection portion of this test; popular check character algorithms are included within the Appendix E.

In order to be read reliably bar code symbols should have a specific secure stucture that the symbols can be compared with. This structure ensures that a single printing defect in the symbol will not cause the character with the defect to be transposed into another valid character within that symbology. This feature is referred to as *self-checking*. Code 93 is not self-checking at the character level but does provide two check characters within the structure in order to enhance data integrity. Bar codes should also be readable by devices with variable scanning speeds. Light pens, for example, can range widely between 3 and 30 inches per second, and even moving beam lasers exhibit some variation in speed. To be read reliably, the number of bars and spaces per character and the relative widths of the bars and spaces within the character must be constant. Such symbols are referred to as *self-clocking,* designed for reading with a single aperture reader over a range of velocities, with reasonable allowances for change in velocity after reading has commenced.

Symbology is further defined as, "A set of rules for encoding information in a bar code symbol." But before we delve into how a user of bar code technology goes about choosing a specific symbology, it is only prudent that the reader understand the differences between a "code" and a "symbol."

It is somewhat regrettable that, many years ago, the name "bar *code* technology was chosen." But just as those who preceded the technology opted for names such as Morse Code, our contemporaries have chosen to perpetuate the confusion with names like Code 39, Code 49, Code 93, and Code 128. A more precise term would have been "bar symbol technology."

Simply stated, a *code* is a system of letters, numbers, and special characters used in sending messages or representing elements of data. A Social Security Number is a *code* to uniquely identify an individual. A product *code* is intended to identify one's product with uniqueness to distinguish that product from any other product. Further, a manufacturers identification *code* will uniquely identify that manufacturer from any other manufacturer.

Symbols, on the other hand, are employed to represent *codes*. H_2O is the chemical *symbol* for that "colorless, transparent liquid occurring on earth as rivers, lakes, oceans, etc., and falling from the clouds as rain" —or in other words "water." In today's technology, the feature of "autodiscrimination" in bar code readers may eliminate some of the concern regarding the *symbols* used to represent data, for a computer does not care what bar code *symbol* is being read so much as about the convention of the *code* transmitted from the bar code reader to the computer.

A computer is concerned only with what part number is being read, e.g., 123456, and not whether the part number is symbolized in Code 39, Code 49, Code 93, Code 128, Codabar, Interleaved 2 of 5, or one of the two-dimensional symbologies.

There are two basic ways of encoding information into traditional bar code symbols. In one scheme we assign each bit to a bar or a space and make that element wide if the bit is "1" and narrow if the bit is "0." Although these codes are commonly referred to as "binary codes," this text refers to them as "width codes" because the term more properly describes the scheme (and because of the broad meaning of "binary" in computer literature).

The second method employs the division of the bars and spaces into an interval (or sub-division) referred to as a "module." Modules defined as "1s" form the bars, and modules defined as "0s" define the spaces. Individual bars and spaces may be constructed from many modules. This method is referred to as delta encoding; the code is referred to in this text as a "delta code." Figure 2.3a shows encoding the binary string 11001010 as a width code. Figure 2.3b shows encoding the same binary string as a delta code. As can be seen from Figures 2.3a and 2.3b, delta codes (U.P.C., Code 93, Code 128, Code 16K, Code 49, and PDF417) have a higher density than width codes (Code 39, Interleaved 2 of 5, Codabar, and MLC 2D).

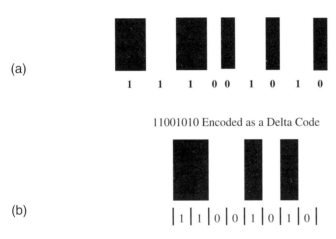

(a)

1   1   1   0 0   1   0   1   0

11001010 Encoded as a Delta Code

(b)

| 1 | 1 | 0 | 0 | 1 | 0 | 1 | 0 |

Figure 2.3: Width versus Delta Encoding

Here we show width (a) and delta (b) encoding of the binary data 11001010.

Let us begin to explore the various bar/space conventions popularly used in industry today. If the bar code symbols you intend to apply and read are for your internal use only, the selection made is less critical as long as the symbol selected meets your needs. Quite often the term "closed system" is used to describe symbols intended only for internal issue with no intent or desire for those symbols to be read outside the walls of one's own organization. If, however, the bar code symbols applied are intended for use among trading partners (buyers, sellers, transporters, and intermediaries), adherence to industry standards is paramount. Such systems are often referred to as "open systems."

For the purposes of this text, bar code symbols will be classified along three lines. The first group is retail symbols, aimed primarily at aiding the retail community in point-of-sale, receiving, and inventory control applications. Included within this category are

U.P.C. and EAN (International Article Numbering), Interleaved 2 of 5 in a U.P.C. shipping container configuration, and Code 128 in UCC/EAN-128 formats. These structures are discussed in Chapter 3.

Chapter 4 focuses on the second group, materials management symbols, and specifically on uses of Code 39 with Federation of Automated Coding Technologies (FACT) data identifiers. Chapter 5 discusses some other code structures that have and will continue to have pockets of influence in the 1990s. Chapter 6 provides some insights into the future, where the third group, two-dimensional symbols, will enable us to print substantial amounts of data in a minimum amount of space. It is incumbent upon the prudent systems designer to be far-sighted when configuring data collection file structures and to plan to accommodate those symbols and coding structures that can be expected to be read in a specific system.

C H A P T E R 3

UCC/EAN Symbologies

U.P.C.: The Universal Product Code

By far, the most ubiquitous of all bar code symbols is the U.P.C. Symbol. Seen on more than 99 percent of items sold in U.S. grocery stores, this bar code convention is increasingly being seen on office, software, hardware, mass merchandise, pharmaceutical, book, magazine, and electrical products. Formally adopted in 1973 by the U.S. grocery industry, this symbol has been expanded to encode supplemental information, such as the 1976 two-digit issue date add-on for magazines.

The basic U.P.C. symbol consists of a six-digit U.P.C. manufacturer ID number assigned by the Uniform Code Council (UCC), a five-digit item code assigned by the manufacturer, and a modulus 10 check digit which is computed from the prior 11 digits. One of the most valuable services provided by the UCC is the controlled assignment of the six-digit U.P.C. manufacturer ID number. For a nominal one-time fee, based on the applicant's U.S. sales, the UCC will ensure that the six-digit code assigned to the applicant is never issued to another applicant. While the UCC controls and maintains the U.P.C. manufacturer ID number, it does not control *or maintain* listings of the *item codes* assigned by the manufacturers. Various database services are currently in the process of assembling listings, but at the current time it is incumbent upon manufacturers to communicate their item codes and U.P.C. manufacturer ID numbers to their trading partners. This may be best accomplished through EDI communications of the Price/Sales Catalog (ANS X12 "832" or UN/EDIFACT "PRICAT"). See Chapter 12 for more information on EDI.

In 1992, the plumbing industry notified the UCC that "UPC" was a registered service mark (Office of Patents and Trademarks) meaning Uniform Plumbing Code. Therefore, all current references to this symbol is now shown with periods after each letter, i.e., "U.P.C."

Manufacturers wishing to bar code with U.P.C. symbols, should follow these steps:

• Copntact the UCC and request an application for a manufacturer identification code.

• Assign a five-digit number to each of the manufacturer's products.

• Communicate U.P.C. numbers to trading partners.

• Include U.P.C. symbols on product packaging. Symbols can be post-applied to printed packaging with pressure sensitive labels, or film masters can be secured to incorporate symbol marking in the packaging printing process.

• Establish a quality control program to ensure that the printed symbols meet the requirements of the U.P.C. printing specifications.

UNIFORM CODE COUNCIL
8163 Old Yankee Road • Suite J
Dayton, OH 45458
Telephone: (513) 435-3870
Facsimile: (513) 435-4749
Publications:

- *U.P.C. Coupon Code Guidelines - U.P.C.*
- *U.P.C. Film Master Verification Manual*
- *U.P.C. Guidelines*
- *U.P.C. Industrial and Commercial Guidelines*
- *U.P.C. Symbol Specification Manual*
- *U.P.C. Symbol Location Guidelines*
- *U.P.C. Shipping Container Code and Symbol Specification Manual - ITF*
- *Application Specification for UCC-128 Serial Shipping Container Code (with Symbol and Shipping Label Guidelines) - Code 128*
- *Commercial & Industrial Application of the Uniform Industrial Code - U.P.C., ITF*
- *UCC/EAN-128 Application Identifier Standard (1993)*
- *U.P.C. Marking Guidelines for General Merchandise and Apparel*
- *U.P.C. Data Communications Guidelines for General Merchandise and Apparel*
- *VICS Implementation Guidelines for EDI*

Table 3.1: Uniform Code Council (UCC), Inc. Publications

The Uniform Code Council, Inc., is the organization responsible for U.P.C. symbology specifications, registration of manufacturers, and details of related symbologies and codes.

Establishing U.P.C. Item Codes

One of the biggest problems that many manufacturers run into when trying to set up or convert a numbering system lies in the attempt to define the scheme under which the products will be numbered. Oftentimes a manufacturer is tempted to group its numbering into "product family codes," e.g., all fasteners begin with a "1," all binders with a "2," etc. After "family codes" have been established, sizes, colors, or base material may be chosen to further define "standardized codes" for product numbering. While on its face such numbering appears quite sensible, definite hazards exist. The U.P.C. numbering structure is divided into three components: a six-digit manufacturer identification code (assigned by the UCC); a five-digit item code (assigned by the manufacturer); and a one-digit derived checksum digit. Of these 12 digits, only 5 are assigned by the manufacturer. Five digits afford 100,000 possible permutations (00000 to 99999). Assigning any degree of significance to the positions of the digits dramatically reduces the permutations possible. A simple example illustrates the point. Assume that a company manufactures wood products, metal products, and plastic products. Having a possible 100,000 numbers, management decides that it will encode, for U.P.C. purposes, all wood products to begin with a "1," all metal products to begin with a "2," and all plastic products to begin with a "3." Assigning that first character position has

16

reduced the number of permutations from 100,000 to 30,000. And then we have color (there are more than 10 colors) and sizes. We see that adding any intelligence to the code will quickly reduce the number of products able to be coded in five digits. Almost any numbering system that is devised will someday be violated as a product's family members exceed the numbering range of the product category. Since the numbering scheme will eventually be violated, it may be better to acknowledge this at the front end and to design a random numbering system. A random five-digit decimal number can encode 100,000 products before duplication would necessitate a second manufacturer identification code. Numbering on the basis of any non-significant, e.g., alphanumeric, sort of existing descriptions or the date of introduction of the product may best serve the present and future needs of the manufacturing organization. Since some manufacturers might feel uneasy about numbering a product 00001, any other starting point could be considered, e.g., 25001.

U.P.C. was originally established for the benefit of the supermarket industry, to facilitate automatic scanning of item numbers with associated price look-up files at point of sale. According to the UCC, there were approximately 130,000 U.P.C. manufacturer codes issued as of June, 1993. In its 1992 Annual Report EAN International estimated over 140,000 scanning stores (100,000 identified in Japan) with nearly 160,000 companies participating in the EAN system through the network of the EAN Numbering Organizations spanning some 47 countries.

Retailers such as Kmart, Wal-Mart, and Toys 'R' Us insist on U.P.C./EAN marking as a condition of doing business with suppliers. In 1986, the National Retail Merchants Association, now known as the National Retail Federation, abandoned its recommendation for optical character recognition (OCR-A) in favor of U.P.C.

The Design of U.P.C.

The structure of the U.P.C. symbol and the reasons for selecting such a structure are best explained by reviewing some of the explicit and implicit criteria leading to its selection. A primary criterion was to enable packaging companies to print the U.P.C. symbol directly on product packages along with text and promotional materials without increasing the printing cost. Product packages are printed by a variety of printing processes, including offset lithography, flexography, letterpress, gravure, and silkscreen. Some of these processes are inherently more precise and controllable than others. A further objective was to choose a symbol that could be scanned in an omnidirectional fashion at the point of sale. Omnidirectional scanning allows any package orientation, provided the symbol faces the scanner. Other objectives included the capacity for the symbol to be scanned by a light pen and to be printed by specialized in-store equipment. Additional guidelines included the capability of a 99 percent first-read rate with a slot scanner and a substitution error rate at the scanner not to exceed one in 10,000 symbols scanned.

Printing presses are subject to ink spread, such that the width of printed lines generally exceeds the corresponding line width on the printing plate. The amount of ink spread depends upon press conditions, amounts and viscosity of ink, and other factors which are difficult to control precisely. IBM proposed a technique called delta distance, whereby a bar code symbol is made insensitive to uniform ink spread. This property, as embodied in the U.P.C. symbol, is illustrated in Figure 3.1. Dimension T_1 is taken from the leading edge of the first bar to the leading edge of the second bar, while dimension T_2 is from the trailing edge of the first bar to the trailing edge of the second bar. Dimension C is the distance from the leading edge of the character to the leading edge of the adjacent character. Such mea-

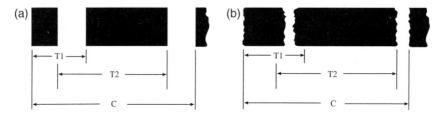

(a)

(b)

T1

T2

C

Figure 3.1: Delta Distance Decoding Technique of U.P.C.

At (a) we see a portion of some bars as represented in the master of some printing process. At (b) we see bars containing an exaggerated representaton of uniform ink spread.

surements are unaffected by uniform ink spread. If ink spread is excessive, however, some spaces become too small for the scanner to resolve, and the symbol will be unreadable.

A complete U.P.C. Version A symbol is shown in Figure 3.2. The longer bars at the center (center guard bars) divide the symbol into a left half and a right half. Point-of-sale slot scanners are constructed with orthogonal beams (the simplest format being two beams that cross at a 90-degree angle), such that at least one beam will pass through each half symbol, regardless of orientation. The bars in each half-symbol are sufficiently taller (referred to as being "over-square") than the half-symbol width so that the omnidirectional scanning feature can operate reliably while the symbol moves rapidly over the scanner.

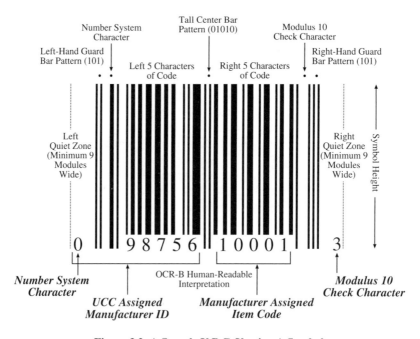

Figure 3.2: A Sample U.P.C. Version A Symbol

The captions identify various key details of the symbol. The basic bar or space unit in U.P.C. terminology is the "module" which has a width "X," the minimum element width. For further explanation of the terms shown in this diagram, see text.

U.P.C./EAN Physical Dimensions

The U.P.C./EAN symbol physical dimensions begin with a "standard size symbol" which is referred to as the "nominal size" or 100 percent magnification. U.P.C. and EAN symbols are then scaled between 80 percent and 200 percent of the nominal symbol. The dimensions associated with a 200 percent symbol, then, are twice those of the nominal (100 percent) symbol, and the dimensions associated with an 80 percent symbol are 8/10 those of the nominal (100 percent) symbol. This rule holds true for all dimensions except for the right-hand column in Table 3.2, insofar as the bar/space tolerance for U.P.C. is expressed as $\pm(X - 0.009)$ for $X <= 0.013$ inch and additionally $\pm(0.47X - 0.00216)$ for $X > 0.013$. The length of a U.P.C./EAN symbol can be calculated as follows:

$$L = (95 \cdot X) + 2 \cdot Q$$
where:
L=length of symbol, excluding quiet zones
X=width of the narrow element (X dimension)
Q=width of the quiet zone.

Truncation

Some manufacturers market products whose packaging design would be affected by a standard size U.P.C. symbol. Often these manufacturers solve the problem by truncating, or reducing, the overall height of the symbol. The effect of truncation is that the half-symbols are no longer over-square and the orthogonal beams are no longer able to pass through each half-symbol, except when the package is precisely positioned over the slot scanner. Figure 3.3 shows a truncated symbol. Symbol truncation reduces the first-pass read rate of the scanning system; both U.P.C. Location Guideline #3 and U.P.C. Symbol Specification, Appendix E, advise against its use.

Figure 3.3: Truncated U.P.C. Version A Symbol

Some manufacturers reduce the length of bars in a U.P.C. symbol to achieve a better fit to available area on packages. As noted in text, this practice is not recommended by UCC due to its effects on the scannability of the symbol.

U.P.C. Symbol Location—Individual Items

The Uniform Code Council recommends that the U.P.C. symbol be placed on the packaging in such a fashion that it can be easily found in retail point-of-sale scanning applications. This placement is often the bottom of the container. Obviously, many different types of packages might be scanned in a retail point-of-sale setting. Specific placement recommendations can be found in the *U.P.C. Symbol Location Guidelines* and in the *U.P.C. Marking Guidelines for General Merchandise and Apparel* available through the Uniform Code Council.

Magnification	Minimum Element (Bar or Space) Width "X" Dimension in mils (0.001")	Bar/SpaceWidth Tolerance (±) in mils (0.001")	U.P.C.-A/EAN-13 Symbol Height with Margins in Inches	U.P.C.-A/EAN-13 Symbol Width with Margins in Inches	U.P.C.-A/EAN-13 with 5-digit add-on Width with Margins in Inches
0.80	10.4	1.4	0.816	1.175	1.750
0.85	11.1	2.0	0.867	1.249	1.859
0.90	11.7	2.7	0.918	1.322	1.969
0.92	12.0	3.0	0.938	1.351	2.013
1.00	**13.0**	**4.0**	**1.020**	**1.469**	**2.188**
1.08	14.0	4.4	1.102	1.587	2.363
1.10	14.3	4.6	1.122	1.616	2.406
1.15	15.0	4.9	1.173	1.689	2.516
1.20	15.6	5.2	1.224	1.763	2.625
1.23	16.0	5.4	1.255	1.807	2.691
1.30	16.9	5.8	1.326	1.910	2.844
1.31	17.0	5.8	1.336	1.924	2.866
1.38	17.9	6.3	1.408	2.027	3.019
1.40	18.2	6.4	1.428	2.057	3.063
1.46	19.0	6.8	1.489	2.145	3.194
1.50	19.5	7.0	1.530	2.204	3.281
1.54	20.0	7.2	1.571	2.262	3.369
1.60	20.8	7.6	1.632	2.350	3.500
1.62	21.1	7.7	1.652	2.380	3.544
1.69	22.0	8.2	1.724	2.483	3.697
1.70	22.1	8.2	1.734	2.497	3.719
1.77	23.0	8.7	1.805	2.600	3.872
1.80	23.4	8.8	1.836	2.644	3.938
1.85	24.1	9.1	1.887	2.718	4.047
1.90	24.7	9.4	1.938	2.791	4.156
1.92	25.0	9.6	1.958	2.820	4.200
2.00	26.0	10.1	2.040	2.938	4.375

Table 3.2: U.P.C./EAN Symbol Dimensions and Tolerances

This table shows U.P.C./EAN physical dimensions for various "magnifications" of the "nominal size" symbol.

U.P.C. Character Construction

Individual U.P.C./EAN characters are constructed from combinations of two bars and two spaces. They occupy a total of seven modules, as illustrated in Figure 3.4. Dark modules are associated with binary one and light modules with binary zero, so that the sum of these bits equals the number of dark modules in the character. Characters on the left side of the center guard pattern have an odd number of dark modules (either three or five) and are referred to as having odd parity. Characters on the right side of the center guard pattern have an even number of dark modules (either two or four) and are referred to as having even parity (see Table 3.3). Twenty possible left-hand and 20 possible right-hand characters can be constructed using these rules, though for U.P.C. Version A only 10 right-hand characters and 10 left-hand characters are valid. As seen in Figure 3.2, each U.P.C. half-symbol contains a total of six digits, with the last digit in the right half being a check digit (modulus 10) computed from the preceding 11 information digits. U.P.C. Version A symbols have two levels of checking. The first is a parity check of individual characters within the half-symbol. The second is the symbol check digit. The calculations for the U.P.C. modulus 10 check digit are included in Appendix D. The scan direction of U.P.C./EAN is determined from character parity rather than from start/stop characters.

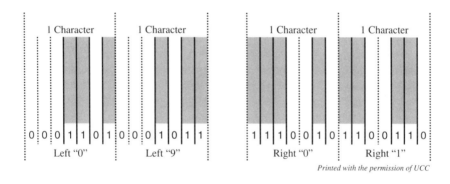

Figure 3.4: U.P.C./EAN Character Structure

Each character consists of 7 "modules" comprising two bars and two spaces, encoding even or odd parity versions of the digits 0 through 9. As shown here, light modules have a binary "0" value and dark modules have a binary "1" value. Odd parity characters have an odd number of dark modules and are used on the left side of the symbol. Even parity characters have an even number of dark modules and are used on the right side of the symbol. (See also Figure 3.2.)

U.P.C. Version E

A shorter U.P.C. Version E encodes six digits of data, shown in Figure 3.5 as "300955" and is similar to the left-hand Version A symbol. Only symbols using Number System "0" manufacturer identification codes can be encoded in the Version E symbol, represented below by the leading "0." Version E symbols use the character encodation patterns shown in Table 3.4(a).

Character Value	Left Characters (Odd Parity)	Right Characters (Even Parity)
0	0001101	1110010
1	0011001	1100110
2	0010011	1101100
3	0111101	1000010
4	0100011	1011100
5	0110001	1001110
6	0101111	1010000
7	0111011	1000100
8	0110111	1001000
9	0001011	1110100

Printed with the permission of UCC

Table 3.3: U.P.C./EAN Character Encodation

Each decimal digit has an odd and even parity encodation. In U.P.C. Version A, the odd parity encodations are used on the left side of the center guard bands, and even parity encodations are used on the right. Binary "0" corresponds to a light module; binary "1" corresponds to a dark module.

0 300955 0

Figure 3.5: Sample U.P.C. Version E Symbol

Version E U.P.C. symbols represent six decimal digits in a fashion similar to the left-hand side of a U.P.C. version A symbol, but using a different encodation as shown in Tables 3.4(a) and 3.4(b).

No explicit character encoding for the modulo check character is in U.P.C. Version E: Its value is derived from the parity permutation of the six encoded characters as shown in Table 3.5. The six explicit characters are derived from the U.P.C. code as follows:

Case 1: If a manufacturer number ends in 000 or 100 or 200, the company has available to it 1,000 item numbers between 00000 and 00999. The six characters are obtained from the first two characters of the manufacturer number followed by the last three characters of the item number, followed by the third character of the manufacturer number.

Case 2: If a manufacturer number ends in 300, 400, 500, 600, 700, 800, or 900, it has available 100 item numbers between 00000 and 00099. The six characters are obtained from the first three characters of the manufacturer number followed by the last two characters of the item number, followed by "3."

(a)	Character Value	Odd Parity	Even Parity
	0	0001101	0100111
	1	0011001	0110011
	2	0010011	0011011
	3	0111101	0100001
	4	0100011	0011101
	5	0110001	0111001
	6	0101111	0000101
	7	0111011	0010001
	8	0110111	0001001
	9	0001011	0010111

Printed with the permission of UCC

(b) Check Character Value	Character Position					
	1	2	3	4	5	6
0	E	E	E	O	O	O
1	E	E	O	E	O	O
2	E	E	O	O	E	O
3	E	E	O	O	O	E
4	E	O	E	E	O	O
5	E	O	O	E	E	O
6	E	O	O	O	E	E
7	E	O	E	O	E	O
8	E	O	E	O	O	E
9	E	O	O	E	O	E

Printed with the permission of UCC

Table 3.4: U.P.C. Version E Encodation and Parity

*(a) is a table of U.P.C.Version E odd and even parity encodations of the decimal digits.
(b) is a parity pattern table for the the six digits showing its relation to the encodation of
the check character.*

Case 3: If a manufacturer number ends in 10, 20 ,30, 40, 50, 60, 70, 80, or 90, it has available 10 item numbers between 00000 and 00009. The six characters are obtained from the first four characters of the manufacturer number followed by the last character of the item number, followed by "4."

Case 4: If a manufacturer number does not end in zero, then five item numbers between 00005 and 00009 are available. The six characters are obtained from all five characters of the manufacturer identification number, followed by the last character of the item number.

In the example shown in Figure 3.5, the Version E code is "03009550." The first character "0" is the number system character (Version E is valid only for number system 0 manufacturer ID codes). The last digit "0" is the derived check character. This leaves "300955." The last digit in "300955" is not a "0," "1," or "2" (Case 1), nor a "3" (Case 2), nor a "4" (Case 4). This implies that the manufacturer ID code is "030095" and the item code is

"00005." When transmitted to a receiving point-of-sale or computer system this code should be transmitted as "0300955000050" *not as* "*0300950*", enabling the database to clearly identify the manufacturer and the manufacturer's item code.

The check character (shown above as the "0" to the right of the symbol) determines whether the characters in the individual character positions are encoded in odd parity or even parity. Table 3.4(b) shows how individual characters are assigned either odd or even parity depending upon their character position in the code.

In the U.P.C. Version E shown in Figure 3.5, the manufacturer has a U.P.C. manufacturer identification code of "030095" and five products encoded under it that are capable of being encoded in U.P.C. Version E. The specific product (or item) code in Figure 3.5 assigned by manufacturer "030095" is "00005" with a full code number of "03009500005." The modulo check character is calculated as follows:

1. Add the odd positions (left to right) $0 + 0 + 9 + 0 + 0 + 5 = 14$
2. Multiply this sum times "3" $14 \cdot 3 = 42$
3. Add the even positions (left to right) $3 + 0 + 5 + 0 + 0 = 8$
4. Add Step 2 to Step 3 $42 + 8 = 50$
5. Subtract from modulus multiple $50 - 50 = 0$
6. Resulting check character value $= 0$
7. Parity assignment—use the "zero" line of Table 3.4(b)
8. Character-by-character encodation table choices (from Table 3.4(a))
   "3" (Even)
   "0" (Even)
   "0" (Even)
   "9" (Odd)
   "5" (Odd)
   "5" (Odd)

U.P.C. Number System Characters

The Number System Character in U.P.C. serves as a means to identify which of the many types of retail symbols is being read. These number system characters are defined in Table 3.5.

"0"	Assigned to standard retail and nonretail items
"1"	Reserved for future use by the Uniform Code Council
"2"	Assigned to random-weight items symbol-marked at store level or by a vendor
"3"	Assigned for encoding National Drug Code (NDC) and National Health Related Items Code (NHRIC) items in FDA controlled 10-digit code lengths
"4"	Assigned by retailer for internal use
"5"	Assigned for use on coupons
"6"	Assigned to standard retail, nonretail, and Uniform Industrial Code items
"7"	Assigned to standard retail, nonretail, and Uniform Industrial Code items
"8"	Reserved for future use by the Uniform Code Council
"9"	Reserved for future use by the Uniform Code Council

Table 3.5: U.P.C. Number System Characters

The U.P.C. number system character assignments are contained in the leading digit of the full U.P.C. code. These are the current assignments as of publication date, with number systems 1, 8, and 9 reserved for future assignment.

U.P.C. Number System 2—Random Weight

U.P.C. Number System 2 is assigned to items sold by weight, e.g., fish, poultry, meat, cheese, or produce. The format for this symbol follows:

$$2_{NS}\ P_1\ X_1X_2X_3X_4\ K_P\ \$_1\$_2\$_3\$_4\ K_S$$

where,

2_{NS}	is Number System 2	
P_1	is the packager code	(0,1,2,3 indicate retailer marked)
		(4,5,6,7,8,9 indicate vendor marked)
$X_1X_2X_3X_4$	is the item ID	
K_P	is the price check digit	
$\$_1\$_2\$_3\$_4$	are the price digits	
K_S	is the modulus 10 symbol check digit	

Printed with the permission of UCC

Calculations for the price check digit can be found in U.P.C. Guideline #11 available from the UCC. A representative U.P.C. Version A—Number System 2 symbol (marked by the retailer for a product costing $19.95) is shown in Figure 3.6.

2   00827   71995   0

Figure 3.6: Sample U.P.C. Version A—Number System 2 Symbol

This number system is used for retail items sold by weight. The typical retailer uses on-demand printing based on data from a digital scale to produce a symbol which contains four digits of price information.

U.P.C. Number System 3— Pharmaceuticals and Health Devices

The National Drug Code (NDC) and the National Health Related Items Code (NHRIC) are ten-digit codes and are administered by the Food and Drug Administration (FDA). NDC and NHRIC numbers have a U.P.C. Number System 3 code in order to uniquely identify drugs and related items. The formats currently authorized for these numbering systems follow:

NDC	NHRIC
3**O**XXX-XXXX-XX (4-4-2)	38**XXX-XXXXXX** (4-6)
3**DXXXX-XXXX-X** (5-4-1)	39**XXXX-XXXXX** (5-5)
3**DXXXX-XXX-XX** (5-3-2)	

National Drug Code structures have three formats. The D positions in the NDC structures are the digits 1 through 7 as defined by the FDA Drug Listing Branch. If the first character following the "3" is a "0," it is an NDC 4-4-2 format. If the first character following the "3" is one of the digits 1 through 7, it is either an NDC 5-4-1 format or an NDC 5-3-2 format. If the first character following the "3" is an "8," it is an NHRIC 4-6 format. If the first character following the "3" is a "9," it is an NHRIC 5-5 format.

The first four or five digits of these formats are the numbers assigned by the Food and Drug Administration to identify manufacturers. The term "Labeler Code" is the official name for this part of the code. The next three to six digits of these formats are the numbers assigned and controlled by the labelers to identify their product/package designations. The representative symbol shown in Figure 3.7 is an NDC 4-4-2 symbol with Number System 3, an FDA-assigned labeler code of "0172," product code "1234," and package designation "01."

Until July 1990 the Uniform Code Council attempted to encourage some companies to utilize a separate UCC manufacturer ID instead of their FDA-assigned code in a U.P.C. Version A format because many earlier point-of-sale systems stored the U.P.C. structure as a ten-digit number (five digits for manufacturer and five digits for item). Consequently, in the example shown in Figure 3.7, a labeler code of 0172 could have been confused with ten possible manufacturer identification codes beginning 0172X. U.P.C. Bulletin #1 issued in February 1989 and U.P.C. Bulletin #2 issued in June 1989 strongly suggested that the U.P.C. product field be extended to at least 13 digits to address Number Systems 3, 6, and 7 and International Article Numbering (EAN) symbols. Number Systems 6 and 7 and EAN symbols are described later in this text. In order to accommodate future systems, the U.P.C. product field should, I believe, be extended to support at least 14 digits.

Figure 3.7: Sample U.P.C. Version A—Number System 3 Symbol

Number System 3 is used for marking pharmaceuticals with National Drug Code (NDC) digits, and health devices with National Health Related Items Code (NHRIC) digits.

U.P.C. Number System 4—Retailer Marking

In some cases a retailer may wish to encode items locally, either product codes locally applied, product codes printed on point-of-sale menus, or various customer service applications such as check cashing authorizations, frequent purchaser programs, or for consumer research purposes. In these cases, the retailer has the availability of Number System 4 for local marking. U.P.C. Number System 4 is *not* to be used by labelers (manufacturers/distributors) for source-marked items.

A hypothetical example of the difference between Number System 0 and Number System 4 coding is shown below. The QED Pen Company has the same UCC assigned manufacturer identification number, namely "098756." The QED Pen Company manufac-

(a) 0 98756 50001 1   (b) 4 98756 50001 9

Figure 3.8: Use of U.P.C. Version A Number System 0 and 4 Symbols

Number System 4 is used for locally generated markings by retailers as in this example: (a) is a typical Number System 0 U.P.C. source marked symbol supplied on a carton of some items as received from the manufacturer. (b) is a corresponding Number System 4 symbol applied by the retailer for in-store marking of individual items from that carton.

tures a black pen known as "220S Black" whose randomly assigned item number, for U.P.C. purposes, is "50001." The symbol in Figure 3.8(a) is the U.P.C. symbol that appears on a box of 12 "220S Black" pens.

When the retailer removes one 220S Black pen from the box to sell, the individual pen might be marked with the locally generated Number System 4 symbol of Figure 3.8(b).

Note that the only differences between Number System 0 and Number System 4 symbols are the first digit, which in the former case is a "0," and in the latter a "4," and the check digit that changed because the first digit changed.

Another option exists for retailers using a U.P.C. Guideline #23—Local Assigned Code. It is intended that the local assigned code option would exist only for those products marked at the store level, which would not be sold in another store. Coding scheme for the local assigned code (LAC) follows:

Version A LAC

$0_{NS} \; 0 \; X_2 X_3 X_4 X_5 \; 0 \; 0 \; 0 \; 0 \; X_{10} \; K_S$

Version E LAC

$0 \; X_2 X_3 X_4 X_5 X_{10}$

where,

0_{NS}	is Number System 0
X_2	is restricted to the numbers 1 through 7
$X_3 X_4$	can range from 0 through 9
X_5	can range from 0 though 9 and in Version E LAC is used to obtain a specific check digit when a fixed parity pattern is used
X_{10}	is restricted to the numbers 5 through 9
K_S	is the modulus 10 symbol check digit

Printed with the permission of UCC

The combination the 7,000 numbers available with $X_2 X_3 X_4 X_5$ and the five numbers available with X_{10} gives 35,000 numbers for in-store use. Further information on local assigned codes is detailed in the U.P.C. Guidelines Manual available through the Uniform Code Council.

U.P.C. Number System 5—Coupons

The purpose of the U.P.C. Number System 5 Coupon Code is to aid in the development of systems to automate coupon handling at point of sale. These systems permit coupon validation, where coupons can be scanned and matched against the items purchased, verifying that the coupon was redeemed for the purpose intended. Once validated, the customer's register can be credited for the coupon, and the issuer of the coupon can be assured that the coupon was properly redeemed. Misredemption of coupons is a multimillion-dollar problem for manufacturers. Bar code marked coupons can aid in the reduction of misredemptions.

U.P.C. Number System 5 identifies:
- The symbol is a coupon
- The issuer of the coupon
- The family (families) of products for which the discount is offered
- The value of the coupon

The format for this symbol follows:

$$5_{NS}\ M_1M_2M_3M_4M_5\ F_1F_2F_3\ \$_1\$_2\ K_S$$

where,

5_{NS}	is Number System 5
$M_1M_2M_3M_4M_5$	is the U.P.C. manufacturer ID number without number system character (5 digits)
$F_1F_2F_3$	s the family code
$\$_1\$_2$	is the value code
K_S	is the modulus 10 symbol check digit

Printed with the permission of UCC

The coding structures for specific family codes and value codes can be found in the U.P.C. Coupon Code Guidelines Manual available from the Uniform Code Council. Since a five-digit U.P.C. manufacturer ID is implied, organizations not having a Number System 0 U.P.C. manufacturer ID (e.g., companies using Food & Drug Administration labeler IDs (NDC/NHRIC) or those whose U.P.C. manufacturer ID begins with Number Systems 6 or 7), should contact the UCC for additional guidelines on coupon coding. Figure 3.9 shows a U.P.C. Coupon Code. In the example shown, the company's U.P.C. manufacturer ID is "098756," the coupon is valid for any product in the consumer's order bearing the U.P.C. manufacturer ID "098756" (family code "000"), and the value of the coupon is $0.95.

Number Systems 6 and 7

In 1976, Distribution Codes Incorporated (DCI)—which was founded in 1971 by the National Association of Wholesaler-Distributors—issued its DCI code and symbol specification for industrial manufacturers, wholesalers, and distributors. Distribution Codes Incorporated issued tens of thousands of codes to organizations involved in bar code marking where those bar code symbols were not intended to be scanned in a retail point-of-sale environment. In 1984 a merger took place between DCI and the Uniform Code Council, with the UCC accepting administration of the DCI system. Since the DCI coding structure involved a six-digit manufacturer code and a five-digit product code, the two structures merged nicely.

5 ‖‖‖ 98756‖00095 ‖‖ 0

Figure 3.9: Sample U.P.C. Version A Number System 5 Symbol

Number System 5 is used for representing a coupon code in a U.P.C. symbol in order to control coupon redemptions in a grocery retail situation.

All DCI numbers began with either a "6" or a "7." When administration of the prior DCI coding was taken over by UCC, the structure became known as the U.P.C. Industrial Code (UIC); in May of 1984, the UCC (then known as the Uniform Product Code Council) issued its U.P.C. Industrial Code Guidelines Manual. Anticipating a need for more codes than were available in Number System 0, the UCC informed scanner manufacturers in 1986 that future scanners should have the ability to scan U.P.C. symbols beginning with Number System 6 and 7. In June 1989 the UCC issued U.P.C. Bulletin # 2 informing retailers that scanning equipment needed to be capable of reading these new number system codes by December 1, 1989. In December 1989 and January 1990 the UCC began issuing to organizations U.P.C. manufacturer ID codes that did, in fact, begin with Number System 6 or Number System 7. Coding in Number Systems 6 and 7 is identical to Version A—Number System 0, except for the change of the Number System character (see Figure 3.2).

In 1992 the UCC released the *U.P.C. Industrial and Commercial Guidelines,* which signaled the UCC's commitment to pursuing the industrial and commercial marketplaces with vigor. The essence of these guidelines was for manufacturers in the commercial and industrial market segments to begin using U.P.C. for item marking, ITF-14 for standard multipacks, and UCC/EAN-128 for secondary symbols (see discussion that follows in the Code 128 section of this chapter).

U.P.C. Symbol with Two-Digit Add-on for Periodicals

Developed by George Wright, the U.P.C. with a two-digit add-on (Version A 12-digit or Version E 6-digit, plus 2-digit issue code) is used in the marking of most commercial periodicals, where the distributor or wholesaler, and in select applications the retailer, wishes to track which issue of a given periodical is being sold. Most often wholesalers, distributors, and rack jobbers place periodicals in stores on a consignment basis. That is, the store is charged only for issues sold. Those controlling the periodical racks within the stores need to ensure that current issues are available and dated issues are returned for credit. Most point-of-sale systems do not read the two-digit supplemental code, identifying only the publisher and title for pricing purposes. Specialized scanners are employed by those controlling the racks to record both the publisher/title and the issue date for billing and returns issues. Weeklies are numbered 1 through 52, semi-monthlies 1 through 24, and monthlies 1 through 12. In the Version A example in Figure 3.10(a), the publisher is identified as "098756" and the title as "10001," and in the case that this title is a monthly, the issue date is August. Further information on two-digit add-ons, including the parity and character construction of the two-digit add-ons, is identified in Appendix D of the U.P.C. Symbol

Specification Manual available from the Uniform Code Council.

The Version E example in Figure 3.10(b) shows a publisher of "30095," a title of "0005," and, if a monthly periodical, an issue date of August.

Figure 3.10: U.P.C. Symbol with Two-Digit Add-on for Periodicals

This variation is used by distributors of newsstand periodicals to encode the issue, as an aid in crediting unsold copies. (a) shows a Version A symbol with the two-digit add-on. (b) shows a Version E symbol with the add-on digits.

International Article Numbering (EAN)

In 1976 non-U.S. interests adopted International Article Numbering (EAN), founded on the principles of U.P.C.. The basic difference between U.P.C. and EAN is that U.P.C. is a 12-digit number, while EAN is a 13-digit code. The terminology EAN-13 refers to this full 13-digit code. Figure 3.2 shows a representative U.P.C. symbol. The first digit of the symbol is referred to as the Number System character. U.S. applications permit this digit to assume any of the ten values identified by the Uniform Code Council. The first two or three digits of the EAN symbol (Figure 3.11) represent the "number systems" of the international coding authorities of EAN. It is often stated that U.P.C. and EAN are compatible symbologies and scanners capable of reading one are also capable of reading the other. A confusion develops when you consider that U.P.C. is a 12-digit symbol and EAN-13 is a 13-digit symbol. In fact, U.P.C. is really a subset of EAN-13. Consider for a moment lining up 100 persons and asking each to count off, from 0 to 99. The first ten persons would have a single digit num-

---

EAN INTERNATIONAL (EAN)
Rue Royale 29
B-1000 Bruxelles (Belgium)
ATTN: Reinhold Van Lennep, Secretary General
Telephone: 011.32 2 218.76.74
Telefax: 011.32 2 218.75.85
Publications:
  • *General Specifications for the Article Symbol Marking*
  • *EAN Prefix List*

Table 3.6: EAN International (EAN)

EAN International (EAN) in Belgium is the organization responsible for administering the U.P.C.-derivative EAN-13 symbology specifications. Among other functions, this agency coordinates international standards and assigns country codes. The acronym EAN stands for "European Article Numbering," reflecting the original European orientation of this U.P.C. extension in the mid-1970s.

Figure 3.11: A Sample EAN-13 Symbol

The EAN symbols are maintained by the International Article Numbering Agency (see Table 3.6). EAN symbologies are generalizations of the original U.P.C. symbology to a more global context than the original US/North American grocery retail application of U.P.C..

ber (0 through 9) while the remaining 90 persons would have two-digit numbers (10 through 99). Such is the issue with U.P.C. and EAN. The United States was the first to implement this specific coding structure and took the digits 0 through 9 as its "number system characters." Most U.P.C./EAN scanning systems store U.P.C. as a 13-digit field and store U.P.C. number system characters as 00 through 09. Additional information on International Article Numbering activities can be secured by contacting the address in Table 3.6, which also lists two EAN publications.

Scanning systems in U.S. retail environments are supposed to be able to scan International Article Numbering symbols, and all EAN scanning environments are able to scan U.P.C. symbols. The true problems arise when retailers choose to store manufacturer codes as less than the seven-digit numbers required in EAN. It is unreasonable (and provincial) for retailers to insist that non-U.S. suppliers re-mark their EAN source-marked product with U.P.C. symbols to accommodate ill-conceived designs of retail software packages. System designers should enable Country Codes 10 through 99, as well as U.P.C. Number Systems 0 through 9 (00 through 09).

With the numbers of countries that exist on Earth, even two-digit country code numbering is somewhat inadequate. Starting in 1981, EAN manufacturers could employ a three-digit country identifier and employ only four digits to identify the manufacturer, as opposed to the U.P.C. convention of 00 through 09 for country designation and five digits to identify the manufacturer. In the international counterpart to U.P.C., namely International Article Numbering, the first two or three digits are the country code, some of which are listed in Table 3.7.

As described in Chapter 2, bar code technology is made up of both codes and symbols. The symbology of U.P.C./EAN is two bars and two spaces over seven modules (see Figure 3.4), with left-hand and right-hand guard patterns of 101, and a center guard pattern, separating the left and right halves, of 01010 (1=a narrow bar, 0=a narrow space). The code structure of U.P.C. is 12 digits; the code structure of EAN is 13 digits. However, both U.P.C. and EAN symbols have 30 bars and 29 spaces. Table 3.3 shows the bar/space encoding patterns of the left and right halves of U.P.C. symbols. The right-hand characters of EAN (positions $X_6X_5X_4X_3X_2X_1$ read right to left with X_1 representing the check character) are encoded the same as the right-hand characters of U.P.C.. The left-hand characters $X_{12}X_{11}X_{10}X_9X_8X_7$ of EAN-13 symbols are constructed similarly to U.P.C. Version E. The 13th (leftmost) digit of any EAN-13 symbol defines the character parity pattern of X_7 through X_{12} (see Table 3.8).

00 - 09	United States of America
10 - 19	Reserved (U.S. if UCC joins EAN)
20 - 29	EAN Retailers (similar to U.P.C. Number System "4")
30 - 37	France
40 - 43	Germany
440	Germany
460 - 469	USSR
471	Taiwan
489	Hong Kong
49	Japan
50	United Kingdom & Ireland
520	Greece
529	Cyprus
54	Belgium & Luxembourg
560	Portugal
569	Iceland
57	Denmark
590	Poland
599	Hungary
600 - 601	South Africa
611	Morocco
619	Tunisia
64	Finland
70	Norway
729	Israel
73	Sweden
750	Mexico
759	Venezuela
76	Switzerland
770	Colombia
773	Uruguay
775	Peru
779	Argentina
780	Chile
789	Brazil
80 - 83	Italy
84	Spain
850	Cuba
859	Czechoslovakia
860	Yugoslavia
869	Turkey
87	Netherlands
880	South Korea
885	Thailand
888	Singapore
90 - 91	Austria
93	Australia
94	New Zealand
955	Malaysia
959	Papua New Guinea
977	Periodicals (ISSN)
978 - 979	Books (ISBN)
98 - 99	Coupon Numbers

Table 3.7: EAN Country Prefix Codes

(a)	Character Value	Number Set A	Number Set B	Number Set C
	0	0001101	0100111	1110010
	1	0011001	0110011	1100110
	2	0010011	0011011	1101100
	3	0111101	0100001	1000010
	4	0100011	0011101	1011100
	5	0110001	0111001	1001110
	6	0101111	0000101	1010000
	7	0111011	0010001	1000100
	8	0110111	0001001	1001000
	9	0001011	0010111	1110100

(b)	Value of 13th Digit	Parity Number Sets of Digits 7 through 12					
		12	11	10	9	8	7
	0	A	A	A	A	A	A
	1	A	A	B	A	B	B
	2	A	A	B	B	A	B
	3	A	A	B	B	B	A
	4	A	B	A	A	B	B
	5	A	B	B	A	A	B
	6	A	B	B	B	A	A
	7	A	B	A	B	A	B
	8	A	B	A	B	B	A
	9	A	B	B	A	B	A

Table 3.8: EAN-13 Character Sets and Parity Map

(a) Binary codes of the decimal digits defined for the three EAN character sets. (b) Map of number set usage in EAN-13 digits 7 through 13 versus the decimal value of digit 13.

EAN Parity Number Set B is the same as U.P.C. Version E (even parity); EAN Parity Number Set A is the same as U.P.C. Version A left characters; and EAN Parity Number Set C is the same as U.P.C. Version A right characters. Since U.P.C. Number Systems 0 through 9 are interpreted by EAN scanners as 00 through 09, it can be seen from Table 3.8 that the implied 13th digit in U.P.C. Version A (*00* through *09*) is constructed in EAN scanners as an EAN Parity Number Set A/U.P.C. Version A left character. Therefore, when a 12-digit number is scanned and stored in a 13-digit memory field (right justified/zero-filled to the left) EAN scanners have no difficulty reading U.P.C. symbols. Two examples are shown here. The first example, Table 3.9(a), is the EAN symbol code structure shown in Figure 3.11. The second, Table 3.9(b), is the U.P.C. symbol shown in Figure 3.2.

EAN-8

EAN-8 is an eight-digit code comprised of the two leftmost digits representing the assigned prefix of EAN International Coding Authority and the rightmost digit signifying the modulus 10 check digit of the prior seven digits. The remaining five digits are assigned jointly between the EAN Coding Authority and the manufacturer of the product. Insofar as only 100,000 products can be coded with the EAN-8 symbol within any single country code, the EAN-8 symbol is restricted to those products where insufficient area exists for the

(a) Character Position	13	12	11	10	9	8	7	6	5	4	3	2	1
Parity Number Set		A	A	B	B	B	A	C	C	C	C	C	C
Character	3	0	9	8	7	5	6	1	0	0	0	1	0

(b) Character Position	13	12	11	10	9	8	7	6	5	4	3	2	1
Parity Number Set		A	A	A	A	A	A	C	C	C	C	C	C
Character	0	0	9	8	7	5	6	1	0	0	0	1	3

Table 3.9: Contrasting Symbol Code Parity Structures

At (a) is the EAN-13 symbol code structure of the symbol in Figure 3.11. At (b) is the symbol code parity structure of the U.P.C. symbol shown in Figure 3.2. The letter codes in each digit character position correspond to character sets A, B, and C as defined in table 3.8(a) .
Character 1 in both EAN-13 and U.P.C. is the modulus 10 check digit.
Characters 2 through 6 in EAN-13 and U.P.C. are the manufacturer-assigned item code.
Characters 7 through 11 for EAN-13 are the EAN Coding Authority-assigned (fabricator) manufacturer ID number.
Characters 7 through 12 for U.P.C. are the UCC-assigned U.P.C. manufacturer ID number (including the Number System Character in position 12).
Characters 12 and 13 for EAN-13 are the EAN Coding Authority prefix digits.
Character 13 in the U.P.C. interpretation is the filled high order "0" of 13-digit interpretation of a 12-digit number.

printing of an EAN-13 symbol. Table 3.10 shows the parity structure of an EAN-8 symbol (also see Table 3.8(a) for parity number set definition).

In U.P.C. formats, Number System 4 is reserved for retailer use. In EAN-13, country flags 20 through 29 are reserved for identical purposes. The shortened EAN-8 format can be used for retailer use. Retailers wishing to employ EAN-8 would encode character position 8 in Table 3.10 as a "2." As in all other EAN structures, character position 1 is the modulus 10 check character, leaving character positions 2 through 7 for retailer assignment. Care should also be used when employing U.P.C. Number System 4, EAN-13 country flags 20 through 29, and EAN-8 structures where character position 8 is a "2" to ensure that these symbols are not employed outside of the retailer's store, since other retailers may assign different meaning to the same code structure.

Character Position	8	7	6	5	4	3	2	1
Parity Number Set	A	A	A	A	C	C	C	C
Character	3	7	6	5	4	3	2	0

Table 3.10: Symbol Code Parity Structure for EAN-8 Symbols

EAN-8 is a short form EAN symbol used where the full EAN-13 symbol would occupy too much area on a package, analogous to Version E of U.P.C.. The letter codes in each digit character position correspond to character sets A, B, and C as defined in table 3.8(a).
Character position 1 is the modulus 10 check digit.
Character positions 2 through 6 are the item code assigned jointly by the EAN Coding Authority and the manufacturer of the product.
Character positions 7 and 8 are the country code of the International Article Numbering (EAN) Coding Authority.

34

Bookland EAN

The International Standard Book Numbering System is an internationally accepted system for uniquely numbering all books and related information-carrying items, such as audio and video cassettes and software. The key element in the system is the International Standard Book Number, usually referred to as simply the "ISBN." The purpose of the ISBN system is to reduce the costs of both identification and distribution of published products by improving the accuracy and speed of these operations. The International Standard Book Number provides unique identification of title, edition, binding, and packaging (boxed sets, for example). All titles in *U.S. Books in Print* have ISBNs assigned to them, either by the publisher or by the U.S. International Standard Book Number Agency.

The ISBN system, developed out of the book numbering system introduced into the United Kingdom in 1967, became known as an American National Standard (ANS Z39.2—1980) and was accepted as an international standard in 1973. The U.S. standard has been revised to reflect usage experience and reaffirmed as a standard.

In November 1985, the Book Industry Systems Advisory Committee (BISAC) voted unanimously to recommend that book publishers print the bar code symbology known as the "Bookland EAN" in the lower right-hand corner of the back cover and of the dust jacket of all their publications. This code should appear below the ISBN in OCR-A font, as recommended by BISAC in November 1978.

Since the International Standard Book Number is an international number in its own right, with its own language designator, the EAN prefixes "978" and "979" were set aside as a prefix to indicate that the product is one of the country "Bookland." Only the prefix "978" is now in use. Bookland EAN encoding of an ISBN consists of 13 digits, "978" to signify the country "Bookland," the first nine digits of the ISBN (the tenth digit of a non-Bookland EAN ISBN is a mathematically derived modulus 11 check digit which is dropped prior to being encoded in a Bookland EAN symbol), and the EAN mod 10 check digit, which verifies all preceding numbers (including the "978").

A Bookland EAN ISBN is made up of the parts shown in Figure 3.12:

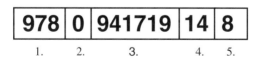

    1.   2.   3.   4.   5.

Figure 3.12: Fields of the Bookland EAN-13 ISBN

This diagram shows the five fields of the 13-digit Bookland EAN ISBN code. "Bookland" is the mythical country code 978 assigned to all ISBNs. The fields are:
1. Bookland EAN identifier (country prefix "978"—see Table 3.7)
2. Group identifier (i.e., national, geographic, language, or other convenient group)
3. Publisher identifier
4. Title identifier
5. EAN check digit

The group identifier (2) is allocated by the International Standard Book Number Agency. Group identifiers assigned in English-speaking countries are either "0" or "1."

The publisher identifier (3) is allocated in the U.S. by the U.S. ISBN Agency. The publisher identifier varies in length according to the title output anticipated by the publisher.

(a)	If the 2nd & 3rd Digits Are in the Range	Publisher & Title Lengths Are	
	00-19	2 digit publisher	6 digit title
	20-69	3 digit publisher	5 digit title
	70-84	4 digit publisher	4 digit title
	85-89	5 digit publisher	3 digit title
	90-94	6 digit publisher	2 digit title
	95-99	7 digit publisher	1 digit title
(b)	If the 2nd, 3rd, 4th & 5th Digits Are in the Range	Publisher & Title Lengths Are	
	0000-5499	Reserved for Future Use	
	5500-8697	5 digit publisher	3 digit title
	8698-9989	6 digit publisher	2 digit title
	9990-9999	7 digit publisher	1 digit title

Table 3.11: Determining ISBN Field Lengths

The publisher (3) and title (4) fields of an EAN ISBN (see Figure 3.12) have lengths totaling 8. The method of allocating these eight digits to the two fields depends on the group identifier (2) of the ISBN and on the data of the ISBN. If the group identifier is "0," then table (a) determines field lengths based on data in the first two digits of the combined publisher and title fields. If the group identifier is "1," then table (b) specifies the lengths of these fields based on data in the first four digits of the publisher field.

The length of the title identifier (4) is determined by subtracting from "9" the length of the group and publisher identifiers that precede it.

Consider the ISBN part of the Bookland EAN code to be 9 digits in length [(2), (3), and (4) above]. If the first digit is "0," Table 3.11(a) can be used to determine the respective lengths of publisher and title numbers. If the first digit is "1," Table 3.11(b) can be used.

The Bookland EAN is usually followed by the optional add-on symbol representing the suggested retail price (referred to as Bookland EAN/5). A sample of a Bookland EAN symbol with an EAN/5 add-on is shown in Figure 3.13. The U.K. Machine-Readable Coding Joint Working Party has assigned a lead digit "0" to the British pound and "5" to the U.S. dollar. Other English-speaking countries will be assigned as requested. It is also possible that the 10-digit ISBN code can be converted to the 13-digit Bookland EAN (known as Bookland EAN/1) without the 5-digit price code add-on. In this case, the first three digits are always "978," the next nine digits are the first nine digits of the ISBN (with hyphens deleted since U.P.C./EAN can encode only the digits 0 through 9), and the thirteenth digit is the computed EAN check digit.

While the Book Industry Systems Advisory Committee and the National Association of College Stores have endorsed Bookland EAN, certain mass market paperbacks carry a symbol which may on the surface look similar—having the five-digit add-on—but in actuality is a U.P.C. symbol with a five-digit add-on. Known as Price-Point U.P.C. and placed on the back cover of mass market paperbacks, this symbol consists of the six-digit U.P.C. Manufacturer ID Number plus a five-digit price code. The five-digit add-on code incorporates the last five digits of the title portion of the ISBN, with zeros preceding any number that has fewer than five digits. The Bookland EAN symbol may also be printed on the

Figure 3.13: Sample Bookland EAN Symbol

This sample shows the Bookland country prefix of 978 followed by the ISBN 0 394 56979 in this EAN-13 symbol with check digit 6. The add-on EAN/5 symbol 51995 at the right specifies a suggested price of $19.95; the add-on's leading digit, 5, specifies a monetary unit of U.S. dollars.

inside front cover (cover 2) of mass market paperbacks for use by retailers who wish item-specific codes and symbols and/or by publishers for returns processing.

The National Association of College Stores also recommends, for books that are not traditionally pre-priced and on which the publisher uses Bookland EAN, that the five-digit add-on contain a number from the portion of the "90000" range designated by the Book Industry Systems Advisory Committee for publisher "internal" use. This Bookland EAN format is known as Bookland EAN/9. Publishers may use any number in the range 90001 through 98999. If the publisher does not encode the five-digit add-on for internal purposes, it is recommended that the number "90000" be used. The National Association of College Stores has specified the add-on "99990" for used books (applied locally by the retailers), and if a publisher or retailer wishes to designate a complimentary desk copy, the five-digit add-on should be "99991." Table 3.12 shows the possible code formats that may need to be supported by book retailers. For specific technical guidelines on the symbol and parity structures for the five-digit add-ons, see Appendix D of the U.P.C. Symbol Specification Manual available from the Uniform Code Council.

In July 1992, the Association of American Publishers (AAP) Paper Publishing Division Heads of House Council finalized their decision to change the bar code symbologies on mass market paperbacks effective with those carrying a February, 1994 publication date (distributed in January, 1994). As of that date, mass market paperback books will carry the Bookland EAN on both cover 2 and cover 4.

Symbol Designation	Primary Symbol	Add-on	OCR-A
Bookland EAN/1	978 EAN	None	Yes
Bookland EAN/2	978 EAN	5XXXX	No
Bookland EAN/5	978 EAN	5XXXX	Yes
Bookland EAN/9	978 EAN	9XXXX	Yes
Price-Point U.P.C.	U.P.C.-A	ISBN Title	Yes
Standard U.P.C.	U.P.C.-A	None	Optional

Table 3.12: Retail Book Formats

Systems for book retailers need to support several variations of EAN symbology and coding as shown here.

U.P.C. Shipping Container Symbol (Interleaved 2 of 5)

The Evolution of Interleaved 2 of 5 from the 2 of 5 Code

The 2 of 5 Code was developed by Gerry Woolf of Identicon Corporation in 1968. Its historic uses are found in warehouse inventory handling, identification of photofinishing envelopes, airline ticket marking, and baggage/cargo handling. The design of the 2 of 5 Code is such that all information is contained in the widths of the bars, with the spaces serving only to separate the individual bars. Bars can be either narrow or wide; conventionally, the wide bars are three times the width of the narrow bars. In each 2 of 5 Code symbol characters have five elements, two of which are wide. (Thus, the name of the code comes from the fact that two of five bars are wide.) Spaces may be any reasonable width. Typically, they are the width of the narrow bars. Narrow bars are identified as a binary 0 and wide bars as a binary 1. The format of the 2 of 5 Code is shown in Figure 3.14. Coding conventions for 2 of 5 are shown in Table 3.13.

Figure 3.14: Sample 2 of Five Code Symbol

The 2 of 5 code is a numeric, discrete character code in which all the information is carried in the widths of the bars, and the spaces contain no encoded information. The 2 of 5 character encodations are found in Table 3.13.

The code structure associated with the bar positions from left to right is weighted 1, 2, 4, 7, and parity. So a "5" is represented by a wide bar in the "1" and in the "4" weighting position (1 + 4=5). Exceptions to this are the character zero, the start, and the stop.

The 2 of 5 Code is a discrete code, beginning with a bar and ending with a bar, with an intercharacter space between characters. Discrete codes are easily printed by formed font printing devices, such as letterpress numbering heads. This gives rise to the historic popularity of the 2 of 5 Code's utilization on business forms where until recently the principal printing devices were rotary numbering heads.

The 2 of 5 Code has lost some popularity with the availability of electronic forms printing that permits form marking with more flexible and higher density bar code symbologies.

In October 1972 Intermec proposed certain bar code printing equipment to Computer Identics. In this context a problem arose over the low density of the 2 of 5 Code, coupled with a limitation on bar height imposed by the printing equipment. The use of 2 of 5 Code would have resulted in a long, slender bar code symbol, which was deemed unsuitable for laser scanning in a warehouse. As a solution to this problem, Dr. David Allais, then of Intermec, proposed the Interleaved 2 of 5 symbology.

Interleaved 2 of 5 has been widely accepted as the numeric bar code symbol in the marking of multipack containers. Recommended in 1981 by the Distribution Symbology Study Group for printing on corrugated and adopted by the Uniform Code Council in the same year, Interleaved 2 of 5 has developed wide acceptance by the retail community and many nonretail markets for the marking of containers having more than one of the same product.

The encoding technique for Interleaved 2 of 5 is the same as for the 2 of 5 Code with one

Character	Binary Code 1248P
0	00110
1	10001
2	01001
3	11000
4	00101
5	10100
6	01100
7	00011
8	10010
9	01010
Start	110
Stop	101

Table 3.13: 2 of 5 Encodation Convention

The 2 of 5 code contains 10 possible discrete data character encodations plus the over-head symbols of a start and a stop code. In this table, the binary codes represent a wide bar as a "1" and a narrow bar as a "0". The name "2 of 5 Code" comes from the fact that every possible digit has two wide bars out of a total of five bars.

exception—bars *and* spaces both carry information. The odd number character position (left to right) digits are represented in the bars, while the even number character position digits are represented in the spaces. The start character to the left of the symbol consists of the following sequence: narrow bar, narrow space, narrow bar, narrow space. The stop character to the right of the symbol consists of a wide bar, narrow space, narrow bar. A sample two-digit Interleaved 2 of 5 symbol is shown in Figure 3.15.

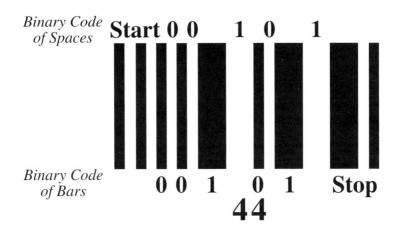

Figure 3.15: A Sample Interleaved 2 of 5 Symbol

This symbol encodes the decimal digits "44." Interleaved 2 of 5 "interleaves" pairs of two of five encoded digits, using bars for the first digit of the pair and spaces for the sec-ond digit of the pair, with the 2 of 5 encodations shown in Table 3.13. The Interleaved 2 of 5 start and stop codes are marked on this sample. Unlike 2 of 5, Interleaved 2 of 5 is a continuous code and requires an even number of digits.

The specification for Interleaved 2 of 5 requires the symbol to contain an even number of digits. For applications where a code consists of an odd number of digits, a leading zero is added to the data prior to encoding. Interleaved 2 of 5 is self-checking, but is continuous rather than discrete like 2 of 5 Code. It is recommended that the nominal width ratio of wide elements to narrow range between 2.5:1 to 3:1. The U.P.C. Shipping Container Symbol specifies a 2.5:1 wide-to-narrow ratio.

Interleaved 2 of 5, in and of itself, is not a very secure bar code symbol. A problem that is experienced in Interleaved 2 of 5 is a phenomenon known as a "short scan." Documented in 1983 by Malcom Beers of Eastman Kodak, a short scan occurs when the symbol is scanned in a diagonal fashion. Particularly of concern when handheld laser scanners are employed, short scans do not intersect all bars and spaces but find embedded strips of data within the symbol. The construction of the symbol characters and the start/stop codes permits scanners to pass incorrect "decoded data" back to the computer system when a diagonal scan occurs. The probability of such mis-scans increases as the length of the symbol increases.

Three solutions exist to eliminate the problems associated with short scans. First, a modulus 10 check digit added to the symbol and checked by either the decoding equipment or by the application's software will increase the reliability of the decoded message by a factor of ten (the number of possible values that can be derived from a modulus 10 computation). Note that when a check digit is added, the check digit becomes part of the decoded message. If the Interleaved 2 of 5 code has an even number of digits prior to the incorporation of the check digit, the addition of the check digit causes the number of digits encoded to be odd. Since Interleaved 2 of 5 requires an even number of digits, an additional leading zero may be required. The use of a modulus 10 check digit with all Interleaved 2 of 5 symbols is recommended.

The second solution to the short-scan phenomenon is to fix the length of the code in the applications or decoding software. If the application or decoder is expecting a specific number of digits and a smaller number of digits is received, the decoded value is disregarded and the symbol is rescanned. The fixing of the length of the code expected in the applications or decoding software (preferably, the decoding software) is strongly recommended.

The third solution is adding a bearer bar perpendicular to the bars in the bar code symbol both above and below the printed symbol. These bearer bars should physically connect with the bars of the symbol. The width of the bearer bar should minimally be the width of the wide bar and is recommended to be four times the width of the narrow bar. The structure of the Interleaved 2 of 5 symbol is such that the start character begins with a narrow bar and the stop character concludes with a narrow bar. The presence of a bearer bar (at least equal to the width of the wide bar) above and below the symbol will not permit a valid start or stop pattern to be decoded by the scanner, so short scans can be rejected by the scanner.

While bearer bars prevent short scans, they also provide an additional valuable feature when printing with wet-ink processes in which a printing plate creates the image of the bar code symbol, namely, providing support for the printing plate so as not to unduly spread the ink when the ink bearing plate comes in contact with the label or an intermediate print roll. When the Interleaved 2 of 5 symbol is printed with a wet-ink process, the bearer bar should circumscribe the symbol as shown in Figure 3.16. When the Interleaved 2 of 5 symbol is printed by means other than wet ink, e.g., electrostatic, direct thermal, thermal transfer, or dot-matrix impact, the bearer bar need be present only at the top and the bottom of the symbol, as shown in Figure 3.17(b).

In 1981 the Uniform Code Council adopted the use of the Interleaved 2 of 5 symbol in a 14-digit format (ITF-14) for the marking of shipping containers. Table 3.15 shows the various dimensional considerations I recommend. The *U.P.C. Shipping Container Code and Symbol Specification Manual* available through the UCC recommends that for direct printing on multipack containers, the ITF-14 symbols should be printed at 100 percent magnification, and in no case should be smaller than the 70 percent magnification shown in Table 3.14. Printing on labels is limited to no smaller than 62.5 percent. Certain industries, most notably the office products and electrical industries, have inner packs and shelf packs that cannot accommodate symbols three inches long and one inch high which are rough approximations of the ITF-14 symbol printed at 62.5 percent magnification. It is for their benefit and those with like interests that magnifications below 62.5 percent are provided in Table 3.14. In no case should "shipping containers" be direct-printed below 70 percent or labels printed below the 62.5 percent magnification recommended by the UCC. The length of an Interleaved 2 of 5 symbol can be calculated as follows:

$$L = (((D \cdot (2 \cdot N + 3) + (6 + N)) \cdot X) + 2 \cdot Q$$

where:
L=Length of symbol, excluding quiet zones
D=Number of numeric digits
N=Wide-to-narrow ratio
X=Width of the narrow element (X dimension)
Q=Width of the quiet zone

Table 3.14 contains an anomaly beginning at the magnification of 70 percent for bar and space tolerance. *U.P.C. Shipping Container Code and Symbol Specification Manual* calculates element tolerance at 0.012 inch times the magnification factor. However, the *U.P.C. Shipping Container Code and Symbol Specification Manual* recommends that in no case should the narrow element be smaller than 0.020 inch. For this reason, the tolerances shown for 70 percent and 62.5 percent magnification are the narrow element width less the 0.020 inch minimum. Tolerances shown for magnifications below 62.5 percent are calculated at 0.012 inch times the magnification factor, which also concurs with the published tolerances in the Uniform Symbology Specification for Interleaved 2 of 5.

The rationale behind this minimum requirement relates to the scanning of U.P.C. Shipping Container Symbols with conveyor mount scanners. A 62.5 percent symbol has a narrow bar width of 0.025 inch. Assuming a helium-neon scanner mounted on the conveyor, the U.P.C. Shipping Container Symbol with a 0.025 inch narrow element is designed to be read at distances roughly up to three feet away from the scanner. Reduction in the magnification reduces the width of the narrow elements and, consequently, the distance from which the symbol can be read. Symbols with narrow elements smaller than 0.025 inch, i.e., those below the 62.5 percent magnification, are envisioned to be read by handheld devices, not devices mounted on the side of conveyors.

A representative ITF-14 symbol is shown in Figure 3.16. Consisting of a packaging indicator, U.P.C. manufacturer identification number, manufacturer assigned item code, and modulus 10 check digit, this symbol is designed to be used on shipping containers.

Prior to 1987, shipping containers in compliance with UCC specifications were permitted to be encoded in one of three ways. What is shown in Figure 3.16 as the packaging indicator was previously known as the assortment indicator. An assortment indicator of "0" was

Table 3.14 ITF-14 (U.P.C. SCS) Values Below 0.625 are Not Sanctioned by the UCC

Mag	N	W	Tolerance	Quiet Zone	Bearer Bar	Symbol Length	H-R C1-C1	Min Height	Bearer to HR	H-R Height	Σ Symbol Height
1.20	0.048	0.120	±0.0144	0.480	0.190	7.124	0.180	1.500	0.048	0.225	2.153
1.10	0.044	0.110	±0.0132	0.440	0.190	6.562	0.180	1.375	0.044	0.225	2.024
1.00	0.040	0.100	±0.0120	0.400	0.190	6.000	0.180	1.250	0.040	0.225	1.895
0.90	0.036	0.090	±0.0108	0.360	0.190	5.438	0.180	1.125	0.036	0.225	1.766
0.80	0.032	0.080	±0.0096	0.320	0.190	4.876	0.180	1.000	0.032	0.225	1.637
0.70	0.028	0.070	±0.0080	0.280	0.190	4.314	0.156	0.875	0.028	0.200	1.483
0.625	0.025	0.063	±0.0050	0.250	0.075	3.663	0.156	0.781	0.025	0.200	1.156
0.60	0.024	0.060	±0.0072	0.250	0.072	3.536	0.156	0.750	0.024	0.200	1.118
0.55	0.022	0.055	±0.0066	0.250	0.066	3.283	0.117	0.688	0.022	0.150	0.992
0.50	0.020	0.050	±0.0060	0.250	0.060	3.030	0.117	0.625	0.020	0.150	0.915
0.45	0.018	0.045	±0.0054	0.250	0.054	2.777	0.117	0.563	0.018	0.150	0.839
0.40	0.016	0.040	±0.0048	0.250	0.048	2.524	0.078	0.500	0.016	0.100	0.714
0.35	0.014	0.035	±0.0042	0.250	0.042	2.271	0.078	0.438	0.014	0.100	0.636
0.30	0.012	0.030	±0.0036	0.250	0.036	1.018	0.078	0.375	0.012	0.100	0.559
0.25	0.010	0.025	±0.0030	0.250	0.030	1.765	0.078	0.313	0.010	0.100	0.483

Table 3.14: Some Dimensions for ITF-14 Shipping Container Symbols

This table several shows magnifications in the range from 1.2 (120 percent) to .25 (25 percent) of the nominal ITF-14 symbol used for shipping containers. All dimensions shown are in inches. Given the magnification, the other dimensions and tolerances are determined: N is the narrow element width specification. W is the wide element width specification. H-R refers to the various human-readable text specifications measured from the center (centerline C-I) of one character to the centerline of an adjacent character.

Figure 3.16: Sample U.P.C. Shipping Container Symbol

This 14-digit Interleaved 2 of 5 (ITF-14) symbol with bearer bars and check digit is applied to packages containing U.P.C./EAN marked retail goods. The 14 digits include information from the U.P.C. codes on items contained within.

employed where the item code portion of the shipping container was different from the item code portion of the U.P.C. Version A symbol marked on the individual items inside the shipping container. An assortment indicator of "1" was used where the item code portion of the shipping container was the same as the item code portion of the U.P.C. Version A symbol marked on the individual items inside the shipping container. An assortment indicator of "9" was employed where the item code portion of the shipping container was the same as the item code portion of the U.P.C. Version A symbol marked on the individual items inside the shipping container and a trailing variable quantity symbol followed the ITF-14 symbol (see Figure 3.18). The 20-digit coding structure is sometimes called ITF-20. Assortment indicators of 2 through 8 were left undefined and reserved for future use by the UCC.

The publication of the *U.P.C. Shipping Container Code and Symbol Specification Manual* in 1987 recognized that many products had intermediate levels of packaging where specific identification of those intermediate packs and the quantities associated with those inner packs would be beneficial in material handling applications. It was also recognized that maintaining the U.P.C. manufacturer identification number and manufacturer assigned item code across the various levels of packaging would be beneficial.

The *U.P.C. Shipping Container Code and Symbol Specification Manual* makes no recommendations for the assignment of packaging indicators 1 through 7 except that they could assume one of these values where the item code on the shipping container was the same as the item code marked on the individual items in a U.P.C. Version A symbol. Through the National Office Products Association's and my efforts, a rationale was created for the assignment of meaning to values 1 through 7 (as shown in Table 3.15). The first digit in the coding structure shown in Figure 3.16 is the packaging indicator, shown in this example as "5." The U.P.C./EAN packaging indicators recommended by the National Office Products Association and me for marking packages containing quantities of U.P.C. marked product are listed in Table 3.15.

"0" Used to indicate that the manufacturer identification number/item number combination on the unit of sale contained within the shipping container is *different* from the manufacturer number/item number combination on the shipping container. It is to be used for these circumstances in all levels of shipping carton identification. "0" is also used when the shipping container holds only one retail unit of sale. In this case the manufacturer identification number/item number combination on the unit of sale contained within the shipping container is *the same* as the manufacturer number/item number combination on the shipping container.

"1" Used to identify packaging above the "each" level and below the inner packs of *like* product (when the manufacturer number/item number is the same on the unit of sale as on this packaging).

"2" Used as an alternative means to identify packaging above the "each" level and below inner packs of *like* product (alternative code for "1").

"3" Used to identify the inner packs of *like* product.

"4" Used as an alternative means to identify packaging above the "each" level and below shipping containers of *like* product (alternative code for "3").

"5" Used to identify shipping containers of *like* product.

"6" Used as an alternative means to identify shipping containers of *like* product (alternative code for 5).

"7" Used to identify a pallet of *like* product.

"8" Reserved for future use by UCC.

"9" Used to represent a variable content shipment. The "9" indicates to the scanner that a mandatory variable content add-on (five-digit quantity plus check digit) symbol follows the primary symbol.

Table 3.15: U.P.C./EAN Packaging Indicators

Packaging indicators used as the ITF-14 U.P.C. shipping container symbol's leading digit. Packaging indicators 1 through 7 comply with the U.P.C./EAN recommendations although specific recommendations have been made thus far only by the author and the National Office Products Association.

Use of the Packaging Indicators

The purpose of the packaging indicator is to define the quantity of product being scanned to accurately update a computer file. The number "7" should be used as the packaging indicator to identify unit loads or pallets. A packaging indicator of "5" should be the initial standard identifier for shipping containers. The number "3" should be used as the packaging indicator for an inner pack within a shipping container. Note: It is incumbent on the labeler to communicate to its customer base how the packaging indicator is used for the labeler's product lines, packaging practices, and the quantity of individual items contained within the packaging.

Example

To illustrate this case, a hypothetical example is useful. The QED Ring Binder Company's assigned U.P.C. manufacturer identification number is "098756." The QED Ring Binder Company manufactures a blue three-ring binder whose stock number is 461BL. Its item number for U.P.C. purposes is "10001." On each binder the QED Ring Binder Company would place the U.P.C. symbol shown in Figure 3.17(a).

(a)

0 98756 10001 3

(b)

3 00 98756 10001 4

(c)

5 00 98756 10001 8

(d)

7 00 98756 10001 2

Figure 3.17: An Example of U.P.C. and Shipping Symbol Usage

Refer to Table 3.15 and the discussion in text. (a) is a U.P.C. Version A symbol applied to some product. (b) is the ITF-14 shipping container symbol with packaging indicator digit 3 which is recommended for placement on an inner pack of several of these products. (c) is the ITF-14 shipping container symbol with packaging indicator digit 5 which is recommended for placment on shipping containers of like product, and (d) is the ITF-14 shipping container symbol with packaging indicator digit 7 to identify a whole pallet of like product.

On the QED Ring Binder Company's inner carton of 25 blue ring binders, the symbol seen in Figure 3.17(b) would appear.

On its shipping container of four inner cartons of blue ring binders (a total quantity of 100) would be the symbol shown in Figure 3.17(c).

If the QED Ring Binder Company were to ship a pallet of these blue ring binders (45 cases or a total quantity of 4,500), and were to mark the pallet, its ITF-14 symbol would appear as demonstrated in Figure 3.17(d).

Changes in Packaging Quantities

If the quantity of items within a package or carton changes without any physical change to the item itself, the labeler should assign a new item code to the package, or employ the unused packaging indicators in that numbering. When the unused packaging indicators are employed, it is recommended that they be used as follows:

"2"   Alternative structure for packaging indicator "3"
"4"   Alternative structure for packaging indicator "5"
"6"   Alternative structure for packaging indicator "7"

Let's use the QED Ring Binder Company as an example again. If its marketing department decided to begin shipping two inner cartons of 50 blue ring binders per shipping container, they might choose to mark each inner carton with an ITF-14 shipping container symbol with the packaging indicator 2 instead of 3 as used in our Figure 3.17(b) example. Because the quantity in the shipping container has not changed, its symbol would remain as it was before.

Prior to the use of the ITF-14 symbol with packaging indicators, if a manufacturer wanted to put bar code symbols on the intermediate packaging, it would have had to use an assortment indicator of "0" and then change the item code portion of the ITF-14 symbol. It was felt by many that it would be beneficial to have the same item code on individual items, inner packs, and shipping containers. ITF-14 with packaging indicators appears to solve this problem.

The emergence of wholesale clubs, discount stores, and super stores added a new wrinkle to the issue. The Uniform Code Council recommends that an item be marked with U.P.C. Version A, U.P.C. Version E, EAN-13, or EAN-8 symbols if it is to be scanned at point of sale. These new retailers have adopted a novel way of selling their product—they sell individual items, inner packs, and shipping containers. Since they need to scan these products at point of sale, they pointed to the UCC specifications that these packages should also be marked with the U.P.C. Version A, U.P.C. Version E, EAN-13, or EAN-8 symbols (some did not even permit the EAN symbols). These inner pack symbols would need to have item codes different from those on the individual items to differentiate the quantity (and subsequently the price) within each package.

Manufacturers seldom know to whom a specific package is going to be sent until the order is received and the item is picked from stock. Not knowing the ultimate destination of an individual package at the packaging line, where the symbols are most often applied, creates a dilemma for the manufacturer. Five solutions are available. The first is to convince these wholesale clubs, discount stores, and super stores to modify the software in their point-of-sale systems to also accept the codes within the ITF-14 symbols. Most of the scanning devices manufactured since 1987 have the ability to read both U.P.C./EAN and ITF-14. These retailers prevailed upon the Uniform Code Council to strictly interpret the UCC specifications that ". . . if a [multipack] container were also offered for sale at the consumer level, that consumer unit should carry a different U.P.C. Consumer Package Code (Version A/E symbol)" (*U.P.C. Guideline #7*).

A second option is that the inner packs and shipping containers could carry both the ITF-14 symbol—to be utilized for shipping, receiving, and inventory control applications—and a unique U.P.C. Version A symbol for point-of-sale applications. This option would create multiple codes for the same product and violates UCC specifications: "Manufacturers should not assign a different U.P.C. (11-digit, all numeric code that will identify the consumer package and/or the shipping container) to the same product " (*U.P.C. Guideline #3*).

A third option would be that packaging indicator "0" could be used for the ITF-14 symbol, and the item code portion of the ITF-14 symbol would be the same as the item code portion of the U.P.C. Version A symbol on the shipping container. This would appear to violate the spirit of the *U.P.C. Shipping Container Code and Symbol Specification Manual*, which states, "The expanded use of the packaging indicator ... will support improvements in distribution operations of the future."

The fourth option is for the manufacturer to package the product based upon the ultimate destination of the product. The concepts of changes in the packaging lines and segregation of inventory—based upon the type of customer the product is ultimately destined for—have not been favorably received by the manufacturer.

The fifth option, and the one many manufacturers/distributors have reluctantly adopted, starts with printing the ITF-14 on inner packs and shipping containers. When the item is picked for sale to a retailer who may sell the inner pack or shipping container at point of sale, the manufacturer then overlabels the ITF-14 symbol with a label encoding a unique item code in a U.P.C. Version A symbol. This fifth option unduly burdens the manufacturer/distributor with additional handling and labeling costs, which ultimately may be passed on to the retailer.

I believe that the best option for all segments of industry—manufacturer, wholesaler/distributor, and retailer—is for wholesale clubs, discount stores, and super stores to modify the software in their point-of-sale systems to also accept the codes within the ITF-14 symbols. Once the retailers begin to utilize receiving systems that address both case quantities and less than case quantities, the code structure contained within the ITF-14 symbol will be of substantial benefit to the retailer. Further, manufacturers and distributor/wholesalers can use the same structures in their operations. This common coding among all trading partners will best serve the entire market channel.

Variable Content U.P.C. Shipping Container Symbol

A similar situation existed in the electrical industry until 1990 when the National Electrical Manufacturers Association, National Association of Electrical Distributors, and National Electrical Manufacturers Representatives Association recommended the use of the Variable Content U.P.C. Shipping Container Symbol, as shown in Figure 3.18.

9   00   98756   10001   6   00100   7

Figure 3.18: Variable Content U.P.C. Shipping Container Symbol

This form of a shipping container symbol consists of an ITF-14 symbol and an additional six-digit (five data plus check digit) trailer for quantity information. This symbol was developed for the needs of the electrical equipment manufacturing industry by its industry organizations.

Again, the same issues developed. Historically, packaging had been designed for the distribution channel. Retailers looked for U.P.C. on the item and until recently were not concerned with shipping containers. Electrical distributors, on the other hand, wanted to be able to identify the quantity in the bar code symbol as shown in Table 3.16(a). An electrical component manufacturer had to decide which market it would conform with and which one it would alienate.

Specifically, the 1987 Electrical Industry Bar Code Application Guidelines recommend that shipping containers for non-retail and retail points of sale be encoded as shown in Tables 3.16(a) and 3.16(b), respectively.

(a) Description	Qty	Pack Ind	Country Code	Mfr No.	Item Number	Check	Trailer Code Qty	Check
20 Amp XYZ	1	1	0	098756	00001	x	None	
20 Amp XYZ	10	9	0	098756	00001	x	00010	x
20 Amp XYZ	100	9	0	098756	00001	x	00100	x

(b) Description	Qty	Mfr No.	Item Number	Check
20 Amp XYZ	1	098756	00001	x
20 Amp XYZ	10	098756	00002	x
20 Amp XYZ	100	098756	00003	x

Table 3.16: Electrical Industry Shipping/Point of Sale Codes

The 1987 Electrical Industry Bar Code Application Guidelines recommendations for ITF-14 symbols. (a) shows shippping container/non-retail point of sale recommendations. (b) shows shipping container/retail point of sale recommendations.

In 1990 the National Electrical Manufacturers Association approved the rewriting of its bar code labeling guidelines to no longer provide preferential support of variable quantity ITF-14, but to provide support for packaging indicators. For product that could be sold in either marketplace, I recommend the use of the U.P.C. Version A on individual items and ITF-14 coding structures with packaging indicators on containers with a quantity greater than one. This solution meets the needs of all members of the distribution channel. Quantity can and should be included on the labels in human-readable form. One justification for a variable content symbol is that the content of a container can be truly variable, as when packaging meat, poultry, or other items sold by weight. A second justification might be packaging that contains a differing quantity and an inconsistent size from purchase to purchase. Additionally, to scan a variable content ITF-14, most scanners on the market have to read the primary structure in one scan and the quantity in a second scan and might read the wrong symbol at the wrong time.

The 1992 release of the U.P.C. Industrial and Commercial Guidelines provided a better method to deal with truly variable containers. Packaging indicator "1" is used to indicate that the quantity associated with the ITF-14 symbol must be subsequently entered, either through key entry or by scanning a UCC/EAN-128 symbol with an AI of "30."

In the above discussion referring to ITF-14, the term "coding structure" was referenced as opposed to ITF-14 specifically. The reason for this is the fact that other industries are considering utilizing the ITF-14 coding structure, but in another symbology, namely, Code 128, which is described in the next section.

Shipping Container Symbol Location

The Uniform Code Council recommends that the U.P.C. shipping container symbol be located on all four vertical panels of the shipping container when it is pre-printed. When the symbol is printed on labels and then post-applied to the shipping container, it should appear on two adjacent panels. The label should be positioned so that the bottom of the lower bearer bar is 1.25 inch from the natural bottom of the container. Further, the leading edge of the beginning quiet zone should be no closer than 0.75 inch from the left edge of the panel, and the trailing edge of the ending quiet zone, no closer than 0.75 inch from the right edge of the panel. The rationale for specific placement is to position the symbol in such a fashion that the symbol can be read by a fixed-position scanning device located on the side, above, or below a conveyor system. Specifying the position at a certain distance from the natural bottom ensures that all shipping containers, regardless of physical height, can be read once on the conveyor. The rationale for the symbol placement at least 0.75 inch from the edge of the panel is to make the symbol readable, even if some crushing occurs to the edge of the container.

Figure 3.19 shows the recommended placement for the U.P.C. shipping container symbol. Further details on placement can be found in the *U.P.C. Shipping Container Code and Symbol Specification Manual* available through the Uniform Code Council.

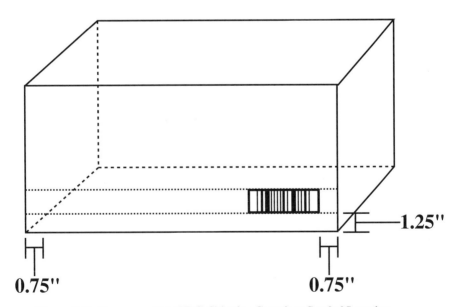

Figure 3.19: Recommended U.P.C. Shipping Container Symbol Location

The shipping container symbol should be placed so that it can be read by a fixed position scanning device in proximity to a conveyor system. The location shown here is relative to the natural bottom surface of the container, ensuring that all shipping containers can be processed regardless of height.

Code 128

Developed by Ted Williams, then of Computer Identics, Code 128 was introduced in the fall of 1981 in response to the need for a compact alphanumeric bar code symbol that could be used to encode complex item identification. The fundamental requirement called for a symbology capable of being printed by existing data processing printers (primarily dot-matrix impact printers). The ability to print identification messages between 10 and 32 characters in length on existing forms and labels was deemed an important requirement.

Code 128 was designed with geometric features to improve scanner read performance, to be self-checking, and to provide data message management function codes.

As shown in Table 3.17, Code 128 encodes the complete set of 128 ASCII characters without adding extra symbol elements. Code 39 and Code 93 also have an extended capability, beyond the encodation of alphabetic and numeric characters, of encoding the ASCII character set, but it is accomplished by utilizing two bar code characters for each ASCII character. Code 128 is designed as a variable length symbology and has the ability to link one message with another for composite message transmission FNC2 (Message Append). In symbols representing fields of numeric data, Code 128 can encode pairs of numeric digits (00 through 99) in place of alphanumeric characters (Code C). This cuts in half the required space for encoding numeric data. When six or more digits of adjacent numeric data exist in a message, coding can be done in numeric pairs to double the density. Code 128 is decoded and checked at several levels. First, it is checked at the individual character level using character self-checking parity. Second, bar/space decode values are compared with the edge-to-similar-edge values. Third, it is checked as a complete message using the calculated end-of-message check character.

Code 128 follows the general bar code format rules of quiet zone, start code, data, check digit, stop code, and quiet zone. The "X" dimension can be selected to suit either the printer used or the optical requirements of the scanner. I recommend that no "X" dimension be smaller than 0.010 inch and preferably no smaller than 0.013 inch. Characters in Code 128 consist of three bars and three spaces such that the total character width is 11 modules. Bars and spaces may be one, two, three, or four modules wide. There are 103 different 11-module bar/space combinations (sometimes called codewords) representing each character on the Code 128 character set, plus three different start codewords and a stop codeword. The choice of start code selects one of three possible character sets, so that the ASCII 128 character set can be represented. Character set Code C provides that each codeword represents two decimal digits, thus doubling the density for numeric-only data. Various control, function, and shift codewords are defined to allow switching between character sets within a symbol. The length of a Code 128 symbol can be calculated as follows:

$$L = (((5.5D + 11C + 35) x X)) + 2Q$$

where:

L=Length of symbol, excluding quiet zones
D=Number of digits in numeric fields (see note)
C=Number of characters not included in D, plus the number of
function and shift characters required
X=Width of the narrow element (X dimension)
Q=Width of the quiet zone

Note: If the numeric field contains a string of six or more digits, shifting to Code Set C

50

Table 3.17: The Code 128 Character Set

Codeword	Code A	Code B	Code C	B	S	B	S	B	S
0	SP	SP	00	2	1	2	2	2	2
1	!	!	01	2	2	2	1	2	2
2	"	"	02	2	2	2	2	2	1
3	#	#	03	1	2	1	2	2	3
4	$	$	04	1	2	1	3	2	2
5	%	%	05	1	3	1	2	2	2
6	&	&	06	1	2	2	2	1	3
7	'	'	07	1	2	2	3	1	2
8	(	(	08	1	3	2	2	1	2
9	)	)	09	2	2	1	2	1	3
10	*	*	10	2	2	1	3	1	2
11	+	+	11	2	3	1	2	1	2
12	,	,	12	1	1	2	2	3	2
13	-	-	13	1	2	2	1	3	2
14	.	.	14	1	2	2	2	3	1
15	/	/	15	1	1	3	2	2	2
16	0	0	16	1	2	3	1	2	2
17	1	1	17	1	2	3	2	2	1
18	2	2	18	2	2	3	2	1	1
19	3	3	19	2	2	1	1	3	2
20	4	4	20	2	2	1	2	3	1
21	5	5	21	2	1	3	2	1	2
22	6	6	22	2	2	3	1	1	2
23	7	7	23	3	1	2	1	3	1
24	8	8	24	3	1	1	2	2	2
25	9	9	25	3	2	1	1	2	2
26	:	:	26	3	2	1	2	2	1
27	;	;	27	3	1	2	2	1	2
28	<	<	28	3	2	2	1	1	2
29	=	=	29	3	2	2	2	1	1
30	>	>	30	2	1	2	1	2	3
31	?	?	31	2	1	2	3	2	1
32	@	@	32	2	3	2	1	2	1
33	A	A	33	1	1	1	3	2	3
34	B	B	34	1	3	1	1	2	3
35	C	C	35	1	3	1	3	2	1
36	D	D	36	1	1	2	3	1	3
37	E	E	37	1	3	2	1	1	3
38	F	F	38	1	3	2	3	1	1
39	G	G	39	2	1	1	3	1	3
40	H	H	40	2	3	1	1	1	3
41	I	I	41	2	3	1	3	1	1
42	J	J	42	1	1	2	1	3	3
43	K	K	43	1	1	2	3	3	1
44	L	L	44	1	3	2	1	3	1
45	M	M	45	1	1	3	1	2	3
46	N	N	46	1	1	3	3	2	1
47	O	O	47	1	3	3	1	2	1
48	P	P	48	3	1	3	1	2	1
49	Q	Q	49	2	1	1	3	3	1
50	R	R	50	2	3	1	1	3	1
51	S	S	51	2	1	3	1	1	3
52	T	T	52	2	1	3	3	1	1
53	U	U	53	2	1	3	1	3	1
54	V	V	54	3	1	1	1	2	3
55	W	W	55	3	1	1	3	2	1
56	X	X	56	3	3	1	1	2	1
57	Y	Y	57	3	1	2	1	1	3
58	Z	Z	58	3	1	2	3	1	1
59	[	[	59	3	3	2	1	1	1
60	\	\	60	3	1	4	1	1	1
61	]	]	61	2	2	1	4	1	1
62	^	^	62	4	3	1	1	1	1
63	_	_	63	1	1	1	2	2	4
64	NUL	`	64	1	1	1	4	2	2
65	SOH	a	65	1	2	1	1	2	4
66	STX	b	66	1	2	1	4	2	1
67	ETX	c	67	1	4	1	1	2	2
68	EOT	d	68	1	4	1	2	2	1
69	ENQ	e	69	1	1	2	2	1	4
70	ACK	f	70	1	1	2	4	1	2
71	BEL	g	71	1	2	2	1	1	4
72	BS	h	72	1	2	2	4	1	1
73	HT	i	73	1	4	2	1	1	2
74	LF	j	74	1	4	2	2	1	1
75	VT	k	75	2	4	1	2	1	1
76	FF	l	76	2	2	1	1	1	4
77	CR	m	77	4	1	3	1	1	1
78	SO	n	78	2	4	1	1	1	2
79	SI	o	79	1	3	4	1	1	1
80	DLE	p	80	1	1	1	2	4	2
81	DC1	q	81	1	2	1	1	4	2
82	DC2	r	82	1	2	1	2	4	1
83	DC3	s	83	1	1	4	2	1	2
84	DC4	t	84	1	2	4	1	1	2
85	NAK	u	85	1	2	4	2	1	1
86	SYN	v	86	4	1	1	2	1	2
87	ETB	w	87	4	2	1	1	1	2
88	CAN	x	88	4	2	1	2	1	1
89	EM	y	89	2	1	2	1	4	1
90	SUB	z	90	2	1	4	1	2	1
91	ESC	{	91	4	1	2	1	2	1
92	FS	|	92	1	1	1	1	4	3
93	GS	}	93	1	1	1	3	4	1
94	RS	~	94	1	3	1	1	4	1
95	US	DEL	95	1	1	4	1	1	3
96	FNC3	FNC3	96	1	1	4	3	1	1
97	FNC2	FNC2	97	4	1	1	1	1	3
98	SHIFT	SHIFT	98	4	1	1	3	1	1
99	CODE C	CODE C	99	1	1	3	1	4	1
100	CODE B	FNC4	CODE B	1	1	4	1	3	1
101	FNC4	CODE A	CODE A	3	1	1	1	4	1
102	FNC1	FNC1	FNC1	4	1	1	1	3	1
103	START (CODE A)			2	1	1	4	1	2
104	START (CODE B)			2	1	1	2	1	4
105	START (CODE C)			2	1	1	2	3	2
STOP				2 3 3 1 1 1 2					

Code 128 is a continuous code with three bar/space pairs per codeword. Each bar or space can have one of four widths in multiples of X, the narrow element width or module. Bar or space widths are denoted in this table by integers 1, 2, 3, and 4. The sum of all the bar and space widths for any codeword in the table is 11 modules. There are three widths for each codeword in the table. There are three variations of the Code 128 character set, Code A, Code B, and Code C. Code A is an upper case subset of ASCII including most of the non-printable ASCII control characters. Code B is an upper/lower case ASCII subset without control characters. Code C is used to represent numeric information from 00 to 99. Overhead includes function and control characters to allow switching between character sets, as well as start characters for each character set choice.

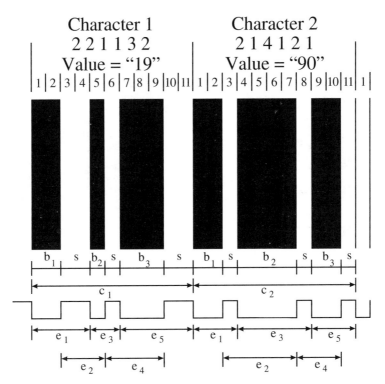

Figure 3.20: Code 128—Layout of Typical Characters

This figure shows the bar patterns of two characters from the Code C character set of Code 128, "19" and "90." The character widths are 11 modules, modules are numbered 1 through 11. Each character contains three bars and three spaces. The edge-to-similar-edge method of decoding the pattern is described in the text.

will realize a shorter symbol length. If an odd number of digits exists in the string, the last digit in the string would be coded in either Code Set A or Code Set B. For length calculation purposes the even number of digits would be calculated in D, above, and the last digit would be included in C, above.

The correct method of decoding Code 128 begins with the preferred edge-to-similar-edge measurements to decode each character. Figure 3.20 shows the dimensional features and decode measurements for two Code 128 characters. Using the edge-to-similar-edge measurements for decoding each Code 128 symbol involves the following steps:

1. Scan the symbol with an optical device measuring the reflectance changes between bars and spaces. The output of this scanning system will be an analog waveform measuring the perceived width of each bar and space.

2. Digitize the analog waveform to a square wave as shown below the characters in Figure 3.20.

3. Decode each character based upon its bar/space pattern, evaluating each character for correct black and white parity.

4. Confirm that the number of elements (bars and spaces) equals six times the number of decoded characters plus one (to account for the additional bar in the stop code).

5. Calculate the widths e_1, e_2, e_3, e_4, and e_5 and convert the values e_1, e_2, e_3, e_4, and e_5 to nearest whole integer E1, E2, E3, E4, and E5.

6. Decode the character using the five values E1, E2, E3, E4, and E5 as the key. In the example in Figure 3.20 the first character decoded value is "221132" and if correctly printed the measured value of E1=4, E2=3, E3=2, E4=4, and E5=5. These measured values can then be compared with the decoded value by summing adjacent elements, i.e, 2 + 2=4 (E1), 2 + 1=3 (E2), 1 + 1=2 (E3), 1 + 3=4 (E4), and 3 + 2=5 (E5).

7. The final step is to calculate and compare the encoded end-of-message modulus 103 check character.

Using the same bar/space configuration as shown in Figure 3.20, one can change the start pattern to Start A (Codeword 103), Start B (Codeword 104), or Start C (Codeword 105) shown in Table 3.17, causing different information to be passed by the decoder to the computer system. Figure 3.21(a) shows the above data characters preceded by a Start A code. The decoded value of this Code 128 symbol is "3 (Sub)" (3 followed by the ASCII "Substitute" character).

Figure 3.21(b) shows the same data characters when preceded by a Start B code. Note that the only differences are the start code and the modulus 103 check character which is changed because of the different start code.

Figure 3.21(c) shows the same data characters preceded by a Start C code.

Figure 3.21: Three Interpretations of Code 128

(a) is a representation of the bars and spaces of Figure 3.20 following the Start A pattern, which is decoded as the two Code A characters "3" and "(SUB)." (b) is the same bar data preceded by the Start B pattern, which causes it to be decoded using Code B as the two characters 3 and z. (c) is the same bar/space pattern, but preceded by the Start C pattern, causing it to decode via the Code C character set as the two character pairs "19" and "90" (the decimal string of four digits, 1, 9, 9, and 0).

UCC/EAN-128 Serialized Shipping Container Symbol

Not all retailers receive shipping containers of like product. Apparel retailers may receive the same style of a given article of clothing, but these styles may appear in many colors and numerous sizes, each of which the retailer will want to monitor for inventory and reorder purposes. As the variety of colors, sizes, and styles is packed into the shipping case, each is scanned and recorded by the manufacturer. When the carton is full, a bar code label is printed with the manufacturer identification code and a nine-digit serial number. This bar code label is then affixed to the carton and the label scanned, relating the carton's serial number to the codes on each article of clothing inside. A computer file containing that package serial number (and related articles) and the other serial numbers in the shipment is transmitted to the customer. When the customer receives the shipment, scanning of each carton serial number will disclose the contents without manual reconciliation and re-packing.

In 1988 the Uniform Code Council adopted Code 128, reserving the FNC1 character in Code 128 symbols to identify structures approved by the UCC. This symbol and code format is referred to as UCC/EAN-128.

This coding structure has been adopted by the general merchandise and apparel industries, through the Voluntary Inter-industry Standards Committee, in a Code 128 symbology. The code within the UCC/EAN-128 symbol is in the following format:

$$\text{S}^c \text{F}_1\ \mathbf{Q_1 Q_2\ T_1\ N_1 N_2\ M_1 M_2 M_3 M_4 M_5\ S_1 S_2 S_3 S_4 S_5 S_6 S_7 S_8 S_9\ K_{10}}\ \text{K}_{103}\ \text{S}_p$$

Bold characters appear in human-readable form; all characters are encoded in the UCC/EAN-128 symbol.

00 0 00 98756 000000011 7

Figure 3.22: Sample U.P.C./EAN-128 Serialized Shipping Container Symbol

The UCC/EAN-128 serial shipping container symbol is used to represent a packaging code, EAN numbering authority code, a manufacturer idenfication number, and a nine-digit serial number that together reference the shipping container to the orders for the goods within the container .

S_C is the symbol start code ("Start C" for DD Numeric)
F_1 is the UCC/EAN-128 function code ("FNC 1")
Q is an Application Identifier of "00" indicating a serialized shipping container code
T is a packaging type ("0") for serialized carton code
N is for number system/numbering authority code
M is the manufacturers ID code
$S_1...S_9$ are the nine-digits of the license plate
K_{10} is a check character for the human-readable data
K_{103} is a check character for the entire symbol
S_p is the stop code of the symbol

A UCC/EAN-128 symbol encoding the serialized shipping container symbol is shown in Figure 3.22. The first two digits of the serialized shipping container code are referred to as Application Identifiers (AIs), which identify the nature of the code, i.e., serial number, etc.

To date only a few dozen UCC/EAN-128 application identifiers have been approved by the UCC and EAN. Table 3.19 shows those application identifiers approved as of June 1, 1993.

In the example shown in Figure 3.22 positions 1 and 2 represent the specific application identifier. The third code position is known as "packaging type." Those approved by the UCC are shown in Table 3.18.

---

0 = Serial number shipping case or carton identification
1 = Serial pallet (larger than case/carton)
2 = Serial container (larger than pallet)
3 = Undefined packaging type
4 = Internally defined shipping container code (intracompany)
5 = Mutually defined between trading partners
6-9 = Reserved for future use

Printed with the permission of UCC

Table 3.18: U.P.C./EAN-128 Serial Shipping Container Packaging Types

The third decimal digit of the U.P.C./EAN-128 serial shipping container symbol specifies the packaging type from this UCC/EAN approved list

The UCC/EAN-128 symbol is also capable of encoding the standard U.P.C. shipping container symbol which historically has been encoded in the Interleaved 2 of 5 symbol (ITF-14). This UCC/EAN-128 encodation of the code portion of the ITF-14 symbol is to be used only when concatenating (combining) the shipping container symbol with another data field such as expiration date or lot number. The UCC/EAN Application Identifier Standard dated January 1993 specifically states that the U.P.C. Shipping Container Symbol should only be encoded in UCC/EAN-128 if the data structure is being concatenated with another data structure.

If a purchase order number of "110780' was to be encoded in UCC/EAN-128 that data would be represented as follows:

(400) 110780

When actually encoded in UCC/EAN-128, the data in the symbol would be as shown below. Note that only the bolderized positions are shown in the human-readable interpretation of the symbol.

$$S_C \; F_1 \; \mathbf{A_1 A_2 \; A_3 \; D_1 \; D_2 \; D_3 \; D_4 \; D_5 \; D_6} \; K_{103} \; S_p$$

where

S_C is the symbol start code ("Start C" for double density numeric see Table 3.17)
F_1 (Function 1)is the reserved identifier to identify UCC/EAN-128
A_1 - A_3 is the Application Identifier (AI) for purchase order "400"
S is the Subset Identifier ("0") for purchase order formats
D_1 - D_6 is the actual purchase order number
K_{103} is the modulus 103 check character used in all Code 128 symbols
S_p is the stop code of the symbol.

AI	Data Content	Format
00	Serial Shipping Container Code	n2+n18
01	Shipping Container Code	n2+n14
10	Batch or Lot Number	n2+an...20
11 (*)	Production Date (YYMMDD)	n2+n6
13 (*)	Packaging Date (YYMMDD)	n2+n6
15 (*)	Best Before/Sell By Date (YYMMDD)	n2+n6
17 (*)	Sell By/Expiration Date (Safety)(YYMMDD)	n2+n6
20	Product Variant	n2+n2
21	Serial Number	n2+an...20
22	HIBCC—Quantity, Date, Batch, and Link	n2+an...29
23 (**)	Lot Number (Transitional Use)-	n3+n...19
240	Secondary Product Attributes	n2+an...30
250	Secondary Serial Number	n2+an...20
30	Quantity each	n2+n...8
310 (***)	Net Weight, kilograms	n4+n6
311 (***)	Length or First Dimension, Meters	n4+n6
312 (***)	Width, Diameter, or 2nd Dimension, Meters	n4+n6
313 (***)	Depth, Thickness, Height or 3rd Dimension, Meters	n4+n6
314 (***)	Area, Square Meters	n4+n6
315 (***)	Volume, Liters	n4+n6
316 (***)	Volume, Cubic Meters	n4+n6
320 (***)	Net Weight, pounds	n4+n6
330 (***)	Gross Weight, Kilograms	n4=n6
331 (***)	. Length or 1st Dimension, Meters Logistics	n4+n6
332 (***)	Width, Diameter, or 2nd Dimension, Meters Logistics	n4+n6
333 (***)	Depth, Thickness, Height or 3rd Dimension, Meters Logistics	n4+n6
334 (***)	Area, Square Meters Logistics	n4+n6

Table 3.19 continued on next page

Table 3.19 continued

335 (***)		Gross Volume, Liters Logistics	n4+n6
336 (***)		Gross Volume, Cubic Meters Logistics	n4+n6
340 (***)		Gross Weight, Pounds	n4+n6
400		Customer Purchase Order Number	n3+an...30
410		Ship To (Deliver To) Location Code Using EAN-13 or DUNS Dun & Bradstreet) Number with Leading Zeros	n3+n13
411		Bill To (Invoice To) Location Code Using EAN-13 or DUNS (Dun & Bradstreet) Numbers with Leading Zeros	n3+n13
412		Purchase From (Location Code of Purchasee) Location Code Using EAN-13 or DUNS Number with Leading Zeros	n3+n13
420		Ship To (Deliver To) Postal Code within a Single Postal Authority	n3+an...9
421		Ship To (Deliver To) Postal Code with 3-digit ISO Country Code Prefix	n3+n3+an...9
8001		Roll Products—Width,Length,Core Diameter, Direction, and Splices	n4+n14
8002		Electronic Serial Number for Cellular Mobile Telephones	n4+an...20
90		FACT Data Identifiers (Internal Applications)	n2+an...30
91	-	Internal Use—Raw Materials, Packaging, Components	n2+an...30
92	-	Internal Use—Raw Materials, Packaging, Components	n2+an...30
93	-	Internal Use—Product Manufacturers	n2+an...30
94	-	Internal Use—Product Manufacturers	n2+an...30
95	-	SCAC+Carrier PRO Number	n2+an4+an...16
96	-	SCAC+Carrier Assigned Container ID	n2+an4+an...16
97	-	Internal Use—Wholesalers	n2+an...30
98	-	Internal—Retailers	n2+an...30
99	-	Mutually Defined Text	n2+an...30

(*) To indicate only year and month, DD can be filled with "00"
(**) Plus one digit for length indication
(***) Plus one digit for decimal point indication

Date Value Representation:

a	alphabetic characters	n	numeric characters
an	alpha-numeric characters	n3	3 numeric characters, fixed lenfgth
an3	3 alpha-numeric characters, fixed length	n...3	up to 3 numeric characters
a...3	up to 3 alphabetic characters	an...3	up to 3 alpha-numeric characters

Table 3.19: UPC/EAN Application Identifiers

This is a complete list of the U.P.C./EAN application identifiers defined for UCC/EAN-128 serial shipping container symbols at the time of publication.

CHAPTER 4

Code 39 and FACT Data Identifiers

T he discussion in Chapter 3 dealt with the family of UCC/EAN symbols. As we noted there, UPC/EAN and ITF-14 are specifically related to identifying:

1. Manufacturer

2. Product code

3. Quantity

UCC/EAN-128's primary emphasis to date has been in an electronic data interchange (EDI) trading relationship where the package serial number in the serial shipping container symbol provides an identity to a quantity of mixed product. This identity is then telecommunicated by the supplier to the recipient of the container marked with the UCC/EAN-128 serial shipping container symbol, which permits the recipient to simply scan the symbol on the incoming container and then to reference that code with the code previously telecommunicated by the supplier.

The international community—through the efforts of the Uniform Code Council (UCC), and EAN International (EAN)—has begun to establish new uses for the UCC/EAN-128 symbol, many of them only recently adopted by the UCC. The initial focus of the UCC was the grocery industry. For a long time even the grocery industry's use of U.P.C. has been concerned only with "price file lookup." Here scanning the U.P.C. symbol can access a price file in a retailer's computer system, permitting the retailer to avoid pricing errors at check-out. The elimination of these errors can easily contribute an additional three to five percent to the retailer's bottom line—possibly doubling profit. Some retailers are beginning to realize even more efficiencies by using the ITF-14 serial shipping container symbol in receiving operations, and a few are beginning to establish quick response relationships with their suppliers by utilizing the U.P.C. serial shipping container symbol and electronic data interchange.

Many other applications exist for bar code technology. Likewise, not many EDI trading relationships exist between suppliers and retailers. Some supplier/retailer relationships need to communicate more than manufacturer/product/quantity:

- The computer industry would like to establish serial number traceability for computer equipment to track warranty data and to minimize "gray-market" trading of product.
- The aerospace, transportation, and government segments would like to track specific lots of supplied product to ensure that the batches tracked meet specific performance criteria.

- The transportation industry would like to use bar codes applied by the supplier to assist in the routing of shipments by including destination postal codes on shipments.
- In the absence of EDI trading relationships, customers would like to be able to identify the purchasing authority (purchase order) under which the received product was ordered.
- Physical inventory taking and cycle counting can be far more accurate and less time-consuming if product identification and product storage location can be scanned instead of key-entered.
- In the health care industry, identification of the product administered and to whom the product was administered could reduce errors and save lives as well as money.
- Time and attendance applications could benefit from not having to key-enter the timecards after the employee has clocked in and out. Scanning an employee badge could substantially reduce the cost associated with labor reporting.
- Bar code marked subassemblies matched to bar code marked specific work orders can improve the product flow in manufacturing operations.
- Batches of chemicals and pharmaceutical products can be marked with bar code symbols to aid in the traceability of these items both internally and between trading partners.
- Documents and files can be more easily controlled through bar code markings that identify who has which file.
- Company assets and tools can be accounted for more easily by identifying the asset and who has it or where it is located.

Many of these applications may require code structures that need more than five digits for a specific tracked item or the use of both alphabetic and numeric data. The 1991 approval of the UCC/EAN-128 application identifiers shown in Table 3.18 provides solutions to many of the prior limitations of the U.P.C. and Interleaved 2 of 5 data structures.

For the future, we can expect use of U.P.C./EAN, ITF-14, and UCC/EAN-128 in materials management and other internal applications in manufacturing, warehousing, distribution, and retail settings—for in many situations these symbols and coding structures form the base for product identification. The discussions that follow in this chapter relate to symbols other than what traditionally have been thought of as "retail symbols."

Code 39

The most common bar code symbology that is used for identifying objects in many of the applications listed above is that of Code 39.

Code 39 (previously known as Code 3 of 9 and 3 of 9 Code) was developed in 1975 by Dr. David Allais and Ray Stevens of Interface Mechanisms (now Intermec). The name Code 39 is a descriptor of both its original character set of 39 characters (currently Code 39 has 43 characters) and the structure of the code, namely, that three of the nine elements per character are wide, with the remaining six being narrow. Each character in Code 39 is represented by a group of five bars and four spaces. The complete character set is shown in Table 4.1 and includes a start/stop character (conventionally represented as an asterisk, "*") and 43 data characters consisting of the 10 digits, the 26 letters of the alphabet, space, and the six symbols, −, ., $, /, +, and %.

The strong self-checking property of Code 39 provides a high level of data security. With properly designed scanning equipment along with very good symbol printing, one

Char.	Pattern	Bars	Spaces	Char.	Pattern	Bars	Spaces
1		10001	0100	M		11000	0001
2		01001	0100	N		00101	0001
3		11000	0100	O		10100	0001
4		00101	0100	P		01100	0001
5		10100	0100	Q		00011	0001
6		01100	0100	R		10010	0001
7		00011	0100	S		01010	0001
8		10010	0100	T		00110	0001
9		01010	0100	U		10001	1000
0		00110	0100	V		01001	1000
A		10001	0010	W		11000	1000
B		01001	0010	X		00101	1000
C		11000	0010	Y		10100	1000
D		00101	0010	Z		01100	1000
E		10100	0010	-		00011	1000
F		01100	0010	.		10010	1000
G		00011	0010	SPACE		01010	1000
H		10010	0010	*		00110	1000
I		01010	0010	$		00000	1110
J		00110	0010	/		00000	1101
K		10001	0001	+		00000	1011
L		01001	0001	%		00000	0111

Table 4.1: Code 39 Character Encodations

This table shows definitions of the graphic characters, graphic bar/space patterns, and binary patterns for bars and spaces of the Code 39 character set. In the binary patterns, a "0" represents a narrow element, "1" represents a wide element.

might reasonably expect only one substitution error out of several million characters scanned.

In 1991 the Center for Automatic Identification at Ohio University under the sponsorship of AIM-USA and the Health Industry Business Communications Council (HIBCC) conducted a bar code symbology test, which examined, among other things, the reliability of Code 39 and U.P.C.-A bar code symbologies when scanned under uniform controlled circumstances and with autodiscrimination.

SUMMARY

Symbology	Worst Case (95% Confidence Level)	Best Case (95% Confidence Level)
Code 39 w/Check Char	1 error in 2,500,000	1 error in 34,000,000
Code 128	1 error in 2,800,000	1 error in 37,000,000
U.P.C.-A	1 error in 394,000	1 error in 800,000

A couple of noteworthy items became clear from these tests. The first is that Code 39 with a check character appears to have performed a bit less than one might have anticipated without a check digit. Further, the reliability of U.P.C.-A would appear to be considerably better than previously stated. With U.P.C.-A showing error rates between 1 in 394,000 and 1 in 800,000 without comparison to a price look-up file, supporters of U.P.C.-A should be

Figure 4.1: Significant Dimensional Parameters for a Code 39 Symbol

*This is a sample Code 39 symbol with the message "*QED*." Refer to Appendix C for tables showing values for these parameters for selected narrow element and wide-to-narrow element width ratios for Code 39 messages of various lengths*

pleased. The addition of the price look-up file database would lessen the probability of point of sale errors by several orders of magnitude.

Since the error rates associated with bar codes is so much better than that of key entry, the use of a check character may appear superfluous. A strong incentive for the inclusion of a check character, especially a weighted check character, exists when for some reason the scanner is not able to read the symbol and back-up manual entry is required. Code 39's traditional check character assigns a modulus value to each character in the character set. The sum of the symbol's character modulus values is divided by 43 and the remainder is the modulus value of the symbol's check character. This simple summation would give the same check character assignment for the character strings 123456 and 123546, namely "21" or "L," which is represented as 123456L and 123546L. The traditional modulus 43 check character will not catch any rearrangement of the data. The transposition of characters is a common substitution error for key-entry, especially as the length of the character string increases. Therefore, a method of "weighting" adjacent characters is necessary so that a transposed message will be rejected by the decoder. Information regarding both standard and weighted modulus 43 check character calculation is contained in Appendix D.

Code 39 is a variable-length code whose maximum length depends upon the reading equipment used. Code 39 characters are discrete, with a range of intercharacter gaps permitted. Code 39 is bidirectional, meaning it can be scanned from left to right or right to left. The size of Code 39 is variable over a wide range, lending itself to light pen, handheld laser, and fixed-mount scanner reading. A unique character, conventionally represented as an asterisk (*), is used exclusively for both a start and stop character. A Code 39 symbol consists of a leading quiet zone, a start character, appropriate data characters, an optional check character, a stop character, and a trailing quiet zone, as shown in Figure 4.1.

Q   Quiet Zone—.25 inch or 10 times the X-value, whichever is greater
L   Total symbol length including quiet zone

H	Bar height
S	Start and stop code asterisk (*)
C	Character width
I	Intercharacter gap which is within a range from 1X to a maximum of 5.3X
W	Wide bar or space width. Wide-to-narrow ratio is 3:1
X	The X-value, which is the narrowest bar or space of a bar code

The characters "QED" are shown in Figure 4.1 as a Code 39 symbology message, *QED*. The various elements of that message are labeled and described in the caption. The length of a Code 39 symbol can be calculated as follows:

$$L = (((C+2)\bullet(3\bullet N+6)\bullet X)+((C+1)\bullet I))+2\bullet Q$$

where:

L = Length of symbol, excluding quiet zones
C = Number of data characters
X = Width of the narrow element (X dimension)
N = Wide-to-narrow ratio
I = Intercharacter gap width
Q = Width of the quiet zone

While some industry standards permit the wide-to-narrow ratio to vary between 2:1 and 3:1, I suggest a wide-to-narrow ratio of 3:1 (in no case would I recommend a ratio below 2.5:1). The significant parameters of a Code 39 symbol are shown in Appendix B, Tables B.1 through B.5. These tables show recommended printing tolerances, symbol widths, quiet zones, and symbol heights for coded messages from 4 to 22 data characters with narrow bar and space dimensions calculated for both 3:1 and 2.5:1 ratios. Table 4.1 shows the Code 39 character set, with its bar/space and bit configurations.

The significant parameters of Code 39 are the nominal width of the narrow elements and the nominal ratio of wide-to-narrow elements. The minimum nominal width of the narrow element ("X" dimension) should be 0.025 inch for direct printing on corrugated board. Otherwise, the minimum nominal width of the narrow element ("X" dimension) should be 0.013 inch; I recommend no X dimension smaller than 0.010 inch. The nominal width of the various elements and the nominal ratio of the width of wide-to-narrow elements should not change within a given Code 39 symbol.

The 3:1 ratio for Code 39 permits the printing at smaller "X" dimensions for increased character density while affording the maximum in read-reliability. The minimum of 0.025 inch for direct printing on corrugated is fixed only to permit an increased depth of field for a fixed-mount scanner mounted on a conveyor system. A 25-mil "X" dimension will permit approximately a 3-foot depth of field. To permit uniform fixed-mount scanning, a minimum 0.025-inch "X" dimension is recommended for direct printing on corrugated.

Open systems within the channels of distribution must establish some common minimum for "X" dimensions that may move within those distribution channels. 10 mils has been established as that minimum by ANS MH10.8M—1993. Smaller "X" dimensions are acceptable in "closed system" applications, as long as there is a match between the "X" dimension of the printed symbol and the resolution of the reader. Users are cautioned not to attempt to read open system symbols with closed system ultra-high resolution scanners.

Single-detector scanners represent the past and present art of bar code reading equipment. In these systems the diffuse reflection of a small spot of light, typically having a diameter of 0.010 inch (matched to a 0.013-inch narrow element width), is observed with a

(a) $N_1\ N_2\ N_3N_4\ N_5\ N_6\ N_7\ N_8\ N_9N_{10}\ N_{11}\ N_{12}\ N_{13}$

where

N_1 through N_{13} represent the 13-character contract number and for national stock numbers

---

(b) $S_1\ S_2\ S_3\ S_4\ C_1\ C_2\ N_1\ N_1\ N_3\ N_4\ N_5\ N_6\ N_7\ N_4\ N_7$

where

S_1 through S_4 represent the four-character supply classification code

C_1 and C_2 represent the two-character National Classification Bureau code

N_1 through N_7 represent the seven-character national item identification number

---

Table 4.2: MIL-STD-129 Required Markings

This standard was developed by the Department of Defense for the Standard Defense Symbology of MIL-STD-1189. It refers to required bar code marking for individual containers, inner packs, and shipping containers with 13-digit Code 39 symbols for (a) the 13-digit contract number N_1 through N_{13} or (b) the national stock number of the item.

single detector. Consequently, as the magnitude of printing defects begins to approach the limits established in ANS X3.182-1990, distortion of the received signal may adversely affect readability.

In 1981 the United States Department of Defense issued *The Final Report of the Joint Steering Group for Logistics Applications of Automated Marking and Reading Symbols (LOGMARS).* This report concluded a four-year study of the use of bar code technology in a wide range of defense logistics operations. Immediately following this report came military standard MIL-STD-1189, defining the official Standard Defense Symbology. The department also revised MIL-STD-129 which required all suppliers of defense logistics material (more than 25,000 of them) to commence marking all individual containers, inner packs, and shipping containers with a bar code representation of the national stock number assigned to the product. Unfortunately, no organization other than the U.S. government uses national stock numbers. Additionally, MIL-STD-129 also required that each shipping container contain the code, in the standard defense symbology, of the contract number under which the material was procured. These coding structures are shown in Table 4.2. Shortly thereafter, the General Services Administration (GSA) followed suit with the issuance of a revision of FED-STD-123 requiring that all products being shipped to GSA also follow the marking requirements detailed in MIL-STD-1189 and MIL-STD-129. This defense standard symbology was Code 39.

Also in 1981, the Distribution Symbology Study Group issued its report, *Recommended Practices for Uniform Container Symbol—UCS/Transport Case Symbol/TCS,* following a similar four-year effort regarding the direct printing of bar codes on corrugated containers. This UCS/TCS report recommended that two bar code symbologies were strong candidates for direct printing on corrugated. These were Interleaved 2 of 5 and Code 39. The Interleaved 2 of 5 section of the UCS/TCS report ultimately became the U.P.C. shipping container symbol (ITF-14) adopted by the retail industry, and Code 39 became the favorite of many other industries, primarily due to its variable-length and alphanumeric capabilities.

AUTOMOTIVE INDUSTRY ACTION GROUP (AIAG)
26200 Lahser Road, Suite 200
Southfield, MI 48034
Telephone: (313) 358-3570

Publications:
- ARF-1—General Parameters for Automotive Radio Frequency Identification Systems
- B-1—Bar Code Symbology Standard
- B-2—Vehicle Identification Number Label Application Standard
- B-3—Shipping/Parts Identification Label Standard (to be replaced by B-10)
- B-4—Individual Part Identification Application Standard
- B-5—Primary Metals Identification Tag Application Standard (to be replaced by B-10)
- B-6—Data Identifier Dictionary Standard (withdrawn in 1993 - replaced with FACT-1)
- B-7—Vehicle Emissions Application Standard
- B-8—Bar Code Evaluation Guidelines
- B-9—Gas Cylinder Identification Labe
- B-10—Shipping Label Standard (Draft 1993 to replace B-3 & B-5 in ANS MH10.8M-1993 format)

Table 4.3: Automotive Industry Action Group (AIAG) Publications

The Automotive Industry Action Group is the organization responsible for administering the numerous standards relating to communications between trading partners in the automotive industry.

FACT Data Identifiers

At the same time as the LOGMARS and UCS/TCS reports were being published, a non-profit trade association group of North American automobile manufacturers and suppliers was being formed with the stated objective of increasing industry-wide productivity and competitiveness through a cooperative effort between manufacturers and suppliers. Named the Automotive Industry Action Group (AIAG), this group has published numerous standards relating to communications between trading partners. A list of these standards publications is shown in Table 4.3.

The Automotive Industry Action Group formally adopted Code 39 as its Bar Code Symbology Standard (AIAG-B-1) in March of 1984 and in December of the same year adopted the AIAG Shipping/Parts Identification Label Standard (AIAG-B-3). Prior standards of other industries used one bar code symbol to identify a unique item or container of items. The Automotive Industry Action Group, recognizing the need to identify a wide range of "things" for a wide range of applications, utilized AIAG-B-3 not only to specify label format, location, and protection but also to introduce the concept of "Data Identifiers." A data identifier is a specified character (or string of characters) that defines the general category or intended use of the data that follows. In the AIAG standards and subsequent standards that were issued by other organizations, data identifiers are positioned as the first character(s) immediately following the start code of the Code 39 symbol.

When B-3 was first published, 12 data identifiers were defined. By 1987, with the prior issuance of AIAG-B-2 Vehicle Identification Number Label Standard (1985), AIAG-B-4 Individual Part Identification Label Standard (1986), AIAG-B-5 Primary Metals Identification Tag Application Standard (1986), and internal applications identified by Automotive Industry Action Group members, this list had extended to 32 data identifiers as published in AIAG-B-6 Data Identifier Dictionary Standard. In 1993 the AIAG concluded that since ANS FACT-1-1991 was an accepted American National Standard and since the AIAG data identifiers were included in the FACT-1 standard, the maintenance of a separate list for the automotive industry was unnecessary. Consequently AIAG withdrew its B-6 standard in 1993.

Three problems faced the automotive industry and its suppliers:

1. There was no industry-wide common method of identifying suppliers. This led to the second problem.

2. In the absence of a common supplier identity, each customer specified that the shipping labels and individual parts encode the customer's part number (not the supplier's). Even within the same company, different plants had different part numbers for the same product from the same supplier. In one example, a supplier to one of the major automotive companies shipped the same product to 13 different plants, each requiring that the items being shipped be labeled with the part numbers unique to that plant.

3. The automotive industry standards were designed by and for the automotive manufacturers. Companies that considered themselves part of other industries, e.g., the electrical and chemical industries, adopted their own standards independent and sometimes different from those of some of their customers (the automotive industry). The Automotive Industry Action Group had no interest in administering the standards of all of their suppliers' industries. Nor was it likely that these other industries would want AIAG to administer their standards.

A specific case in point was that of the electrical industry. In addition to variable content 20-character Interleaved 2 of 5 structures shown in Chapter 3 (e.g., Figure 3.18), the 1987 standard of the National Electrical Manufacturers Association (NEMA) also permitted the use of Code 39 with data identifiers for product labeling, which conflicted with most of those assigned by AIAG. Then it came time for an electrical manufacturer to ship product to the automotive industry. Since the automotive company was the customer, it might appear straightforward to those wearing sales/marketing hats that the manufacturer simply mark the product the way the customer wants to receive it. This denies two important considerations of communications between trading partners.

1. The concept of trading partners presumes that both parties, customer *and* supplier, will benefit from adopted standards—not simply that the supplier benefits from securing the customer's business. Shipping labels are obviously applied after the order is picked and the customer is known. But individual parts are most cost-effectively marked on the packaging line before the customer is known. If the supplier is to benefit from bar code marking, bar code structure on individual parts needs to encode the supplier's product-specific data.

2. Software designed for the supplier's shipping area will likely utilize the data identifiers for edit checking to ensure that the correct symbol is being read. Scanning an AIAG customer assigned product ID symbol may be interpreted by the shipping software as a NEMA purchase order. Scanning an AIAG master label symbol may be interpreted by the shipping software as a NEMA manufacturer ID.

In November 1987, the Federation of Automated Coding Technologies (FACT) invited individuals representing various standards-making activities to attend a January 1988 meeting to discuss issues related to cross-industry commonality of data identifiers used in automatic identification technologies.

The increasing popularity of data identifiers (also called "field identifiers") in industry-wide bar code standards had begun to create conflicts between data identifiers in various industries. This situation carried the potential of adversely impacting the further development of industry-wide standards and threatened the integrity of existing ones.

Prior to this meeting, the major burden of coordinating data identifiers (DIs) had been borne by the Automotive Industry Action Group. Working with industries that had contacted them for advice, the AIAG managed to guide the development of a number of standards that could coexist with established AIAG DI assignments. The Automotive Industry Action Group was not, however, a national DI clearing house and requested that the Federation of Automated Coding Technologies (FACT) assume this responsibility.

FACT recognized the importance of the work done by the AIAG and the appropriateness of FACT's assuming this responsibility. A Data Identifier Work Group was formed to examine existing standards and to produce materials that would provide guidance to standards-writing industries in order to permit coexistence of standards from all industries.

The FACT Data Identifier Standard was prepared by FACT, with Bert Moore of the Automatic Identification Manufacturers serving as the FACT DI Chairman and Craig K. Harmon of Q.E.D. Systems serving as Editor. FACT maintained contact with the following standards-making groups in the development of the FACT Data Identifier Standard:

Aerospace Industries Association, Air Transport Association, American National Standards Institute, American Trucking Association, Association of Home Appliance Manufacturers, Automotive Industry Action Group, Book Industry Systems Advisory Committee, Chemical Industry Data Exchange, Department of Defense, Electronics Industry Association, Federation of Automated Coding Technologies, Furniture Industry Bar Code Task Force, General Merchandise & Apparel Implementation Council, Health Industry Business Communications Council, Industry Bar Code Alliance, International Air Transport Association, Motor Equipment Manufacturers Association, National Electrical Manufacturers Association, National Motor Freight Traffic Association, National Office Products Association, National Welding Supply Association, Telecommunications Industry Forum, Uniform Code Council.

The data identifiers recommended within the FACT DI Standard were developed to provide guidance to organizations considering the development of standardized data element identifiers within a specific firm, organization, or industry. The FACT DI Standard is intended to provide guidelines for the development of application standards. In 1991, the American National Standards Institute (ANSI) formally approved ANS FACT-1-1991 Data Identifier Standard as an American National Standard.

American National Standards Institute

In 1983 the American National Standards Institute (ANSI) published ANS MH10.8M—1983, *American National Standard for Materials Handling—Bar Code Symbols on Unit Loads and Transport Packages*. This standard assimilated much of the work that had been accomplished by the Department of Defense LOGMARS project, as well as the work of the Distribution Symbology Study Group. ANS MH10.8M-1983 also technically defined the symbology and printing characteristics of three bar code symbologies for unit loads and transport packages, namely, Interleaved 2 of 5, Code 39, and Codabar. We have already discussed Interleaved 2 of 5 and Code 39; Chapter 5 contains a discussion of Codabar. ANSI procedures require that standards such as ANS MH10.8M-1983 be reviewed every five years and either approved as is, modified, or withdrawn.

In May, 1992, the theretofor sponsor of FACT, AIM-USA, decided to no longer fund administrative support for the FACT organization effective December, 1992. The ANSI MH10 SBC-8 subcommittee agreed to undertake the stewardship of the FACT-1 document and its revisions.

ANS X3.182-1990 Bar Code Print Quality

In 1985 the MH10.8 committee joined with another ANSI committee, X3A1.3, to develop a procedure for measuring quality parameters of printed bar code symbols. In 1990, ANSI released this standard, *American National Standard Guidelines for Bar Code Print Quality*, (ANS X3.182-1990). In 1989 ABCD—The Microcomputer Industry Association published its *Bar Code Label Print Quality & Label Specification*, patterned after the recommendations of the ANS X3 and MH10.8 Project. Copies of ANS X3.182-1990 are available from the American National Standards Institute.

Many of the individuals involved in the rewrite of ANS MH10.8M were also actively involved in the ANS X3.182 effort. For this reason, the American National Standards Institute granted a waiver on the five-year requirements for the review and rewrite of ANS MH10.8M until the Bar Code Print Quality standard was completed.

FACT Common Label

Once the FACT DI Standard was completed and submitted for ANSI review, FACT began working on the development of a standard label format to serve as an acceptable alternative for suppliers to multiple industries, each of which has its own unique marking requirements, and as guidance to industries that have not yet established industry standards. Efforts for the development of the FACT Standard Label began in July 1989. In November 1989 the FACT Standard Label Work Group merged its effort with that of the group responsible for updating the American National Standard for Bar Code Marking of Transport Packages and Unit Loads (ANS MH10.8M-1983). It has continued as part of the SBC8 Subcommittee of ANSI MH10 since that time.

ANS MH10.8M-1993 for Materials Handling—
Bar Code Symbols on Unit Loads and Transport Packages

ANS MH10.8M-1993 incorporates present standards for Code 39, FACT Data Identifiers as well as UCC/EAN formats and UCC/EAN-128 Application Identifiers. MH10.8M-1993 further incorporates the ANS X3.182-1990 Print Quality Standard and the FACT Common Label. MH10 also provides recommendations for marking to meet the needs of supplier, customer, and carrier as well as guidance for symbol order on labels. Narrow bar width minimums have been recommended at 0.010 inch (0.0254 cm) to 0.017 inch (0.0432 cm) printed at a 3:1 wide-to-narrow ratio, within a 2.4:1 to 3.2:1 range. Standardized segment titles have been established.

Non-U.S. Standards

In addition to the efforts of American National Standards committees, several non-U.S. organizations are adopting standards quite similar to the MH10.8M standard. In Europe, the Comite Europeen Normalisation (CEN) has established Technical Committee 225 (CEN TC225). TC225 performs many of the same functions as has the MH10, FACT, and AIM-USA standards activities. The CEN TC225 Work Group is responsible for the development of symbology standards, in much the same way AIM-USA has functioned in the U.S. CEN TC225 Work Group is responsible for the European adoption of the FACT Data Identifiers. Finally, CEN TC225 Work Group has developed the Multi-Industry Transport Label (M.I.T.L.) modeled after the MH10 standard. The CEN TC225 and ANSI committees have worked closely to ensure that standards developed for one continent can function on the other.

Other European organizations that have adopted the CEN/ANSI standards include the Electronic Data Interchange Forum for Companies with Interests in Computing and Electronics (EDIFICE) and the Organization for Data Exchange by Tele Transmission in Europe (ODETTE). EDIFICE is the European equivalent of the Electronic Industries Association (EIA) in the U.S. while ODETTE serves a similar role for the European automotive industry as does the AIAG in the U.S.

The Asia-Pacific geographic region has been far less active in regional and global standardization than have Europe and North America. Australia's forum is mainly through the Australian Product Numbering Association (APNA), its UCC equivalent. The same can be said for New Zealand through the New Zealand Product Numbering Association (NZPNA). Japan has two active groups for standardization. The first is the Japanese UCC counterpart, Distribution Code Center (DCC), and the second is EIA-J, who under the guidance of the Japanese EDI Center is developing standards for the Japanese electronics industry. A close working relationship exists between EIA-J, EDIFICE, and the North American electronics industry.

Both ODETTE and EDIFICE in Europe as well as EIA-J in Japan suffer from the same ailment of using customer part numbers as opposed to supplier part numbers. While this is less of a concern at the shipping level (the customer is now known) such philosophy may encourage customers to ask for their part numbers on individual items.

Since the customer is not known at the time of packaging, the individual items should be marked with the supplier's part number. EDI, and specifically the X12 832 Transaction Set or PRICAT EDIFACT Message (Price Catalog) can be well utilized to provide a cross reference between the customer's part number and that of the supplier.

Further, if the customer is not capable of receiving price catalog information electronically, both the customer's part number cross-referenced to the supplier's U.P.C. item number could be included on the shipping label in a two-dimensional bar code (See Chapter 6).

The Uniform Code Council's Standards—
For Identification of General Trade Products

The UCC is a nonprofit organization responsible for the administration of the Universal Product Code (U.P.C.) initially designed to serve the retail and distribution environments. The UCC system enables unique identification on a global basis for industries providing products for general distribution. Based on the requirements of its global constituency, the UCC and its international counterpart, EAN International (EAN), jointly released expanded sets of Application Identifiers (AIs) in 1990 and 1991 (see Chapter 3), thereby permitting encodation of a wider range of secondary information within UCC/EAN-128 applications.

The U.P.C./EAN system is the identification standard for general trade products where the same product in the same packaging is sold to multiple trading partners in multiple industries. FACT Data Identifiers are analogous to the UCC/EAN AIs and have been implemented by the automotive and other industries for internal use and where unique product is manufactured for and shipped to a specific customer. It is expected that both standards will coexist for the near term.

Which Identifiers Should a Manufacturer Use? UCC/EAN AIs or FACT DIs?

Some manufacturers sell product only to industries embracing FACT DIs. Other manufacturers sell product only to industries embracing the UCC/EAN standard. Such product should be appropriately marked. Manufacturers selling specific products to both industries should consider migration toward the UCC/EAN AI standard.

All industries should carefully consider the efficiencies and data format simplicity of the U.P.C./EAN/ITF-14 Primary Identification coding structures. The exchange of customer part numbers via electronic data interchange and machine-readable data encoded with the supplier's part number should be carefully considered by any standards development work anticipating a recommendation for customer part numbers on individual products. New standards for products that are supplied to multiple customers in multiple industries would be best served by using the UCC/EAN-128 AIs for Product Specific Secondary Symbols. Existing standards for products supplied to multiple customers in multiple industries should likewise consider migration to AIs. The AIs listed in Chapter 3, Table 3.19 represent the assignments made through April 1993. Those wishing further information should contact either the Uniform Code Council or EAN International for the most current list of AI assignments and relevant standards.

CHAPTER 5

Other Symbologies

W hen *Reading Between the Lines* (*"Lines I"*) was written, I listed 48 different bar code symbologies that were known by various names. The list exemplified the numerous methods used to encode data in bars and spaces. I will not repeat that list here, but will briefly examine four of those symbologies—Codabar, Code 93, Plessey, BC412 and BC309, and Postnet. These four symbologies are selected because they are representative of symbologies that have pockets of influence in commercial settings. Codabar is presented because of its wide use by Federal Express and the blood banking community. Code 93 is discussed because Code 128 was extensively discussed in Chapter 3, and, when encoding alphanumeric information, Code 93 has a higher density than Code 128 (in strictly numeric applications Code 128 is higher density). Plessey is discussed because some retailers utilize bar code markings on shelf tags, which until recently have been the province of Plessey Code and its derivations. BC412 and its companion BC309 are discussed because BC412 has been adopted as a standard for the marking of semiconductor wafers. Postnet is present- ed because it is used by the U.S. Postal Service. Two-Dimensional (2-D) Codes are present- ed in Chapter 6; they represent the wave of the future for encoding significant amounts of information.

Codabar

Codabar was developed around 1972 by the Monarch Marking Systems division of Pitney Bowes for use in retail price-labeling systems. When the grocery industry was eval- uating symbols between 1970 and 1973, a variant of Codabar was unsuccessfully proposed. (The symbology that was finally selected has come to be known as U.P.C..) Codabar's retail marking efforts continued until the National Retail Merchants Association adopted OCR-A for department store marking. Following other unsuccessful attempts in retail, efforts to market Codabar were redirected to industrial markings.

In 1977 Codabar was formally adopted by the Committee for Commonality in Blood Banking Automation (CCBBA) for the marking of blood product bags. Each blood product collecting/processing bag label provides a code for the solution contained in the unfilled bag, e.g., anticoagulant, as well as a code for its intended contents, e.g., whole blood cells. Four other labels are post-applied to the bag label, providing a unique unit number, blood product code, collection date, and group type information. Unit number labels are also used to identify the donor, donor documents, test tubes, and satellite bags. Each of the four labels utilizes a unique combination of Start/Stop codes, as shown in Table 5.1, to identify the specific label type. Codabar has four bar code characters that can be represented as either Start or Stop codes. These multiple start/stop codes yield 16 different possible combinations that can be used to uniquely identify different types of data fields in much the same way as the "data identifiers" were explained in Chapter 4. CCBBA combined the Start and Stop Codes with up to one additional identifier (following the Start Code and preceding the Stop Code) to identify the uses shown in Table 5.1.

Further information on CCBBA's use of Codabar can be found by contacting the American Blood Commission whose address appears in Appendix A.

Codabar is a variable length, discrete, self-checking code, with each of 16 characters represented by a stand-alone group of four bars and three intervening spaces. Codabar's character set and start/stop codes are shown in Table 5.2, and a representative Codabar symbol appears in Figure 5.1. The 12 principal characters (0 through 9, –, and $) are constructed as a 2 of 7 code, seven elements of which two are wide; each of these principal characters has one wide bar and one wide space. The four additional characters (:, /, ., and +) and four start/stop codes are constructed as a 3 of 7 code, seven elements of which three are wide. The wide-to-narrow ratio can range between 2:1 and 3:1 (I recommend a 3:1 wide-to-narrow ratio). Each of the additional characters and start/stop codes will increase the respective character width by the narrow element width ("X") times the wide-to-narrow ratio. The USS (Uniform Symbology Specification)/Codabar document of the Automatic Identification Manufacturers (AIM) specifies that the X dimension should be a minimum of 0.0075 inch. I recommend a minimum X dimension of 0.013 inch. The intercharacter

Start/ Control Code	Data	Stop/ Control Code	Used on
a0	7-digit FDA Registration Number	1b	Bag Label
a1	7-digit FDA Registration Number	1b	Bag Label
a$	3-digit Julian Date	d	Collection Date Label
a0	5-digit Blood Product Code	2b	Bag Label
a0	5-digit Blood Product Code	3b	Product Label
d	2-digit Package/Anticoagulant Code	$b	Bag Label
d	2-character Blood Typing Codes	0b	Grouping Label
d	7-digit Unit Number	d	Unit Number Label
b0	7-digit Patient Identification	0a	Patient Wristband
b1	7-digit Patient Identification	0a	Blood Sample Tube
b2	7-digit Patient Identification	0a	Blood Bag (Cross-match Recipient)
a9	Program Identification Number	$b	Program's Lightpen Terminals
a9	Personnel Identification Number	0b	Personnel I.D. Cards
a9	Hospital Number	1b	Hospital's Lightpen Terminals

Table 5.1: CCBBA's Use of Codabar Start/Stop Codes

The Codabar symbology has four different start/stop codes, symbolically shown here as a, b, c, and d. CCBA combines the Codabar Start and Stop Codes with optional control codes (following the Start Code and preceding the Stop Code) to identify the type of data and its use.

CHARACTER SET

0 1 2 3 4 5 6 7 8 9 - $: / . +

START/STOP CODES

a b c d

Table 5.2: Rationalized Codabar Character Encodations

(a) The Rationalized Codabar symbology encodes the ten decimal digits and six other data character choices. (b) Codabar uses one of four start/stop characters to begin its messages, and one of four start/stop characters to end its messages. As noted in text, the choices of start and stop characters can be used to encode additional information.

a 0 9 8 7 5 6 b

Figure 5.1: A Sample Rationalized Codabar Symbol

This symbol shows the digits 098756 with the "a" start code and "b" stop code.

space for Codabar can range from 1X up to 5.3X. Since Codabar is a discrete bar code, it can be printed on forms with mechanical numbering heads. If Codabar or any bar code symbol is printed with mechanical numbering heads, it is recommended that the interchar-acter space be set at its maximum of 5.3X.

The original specifications for Codabar defined each bar width within each character to optimize the performance of certain early printing and reading equipment. Unfortunately, these bar and space dimensions were not even multiples of units—to the point where Codabar had 18 different bar and space widths, a nightmare for printers. The AIM USS-Codabar specification refers to "Rationalized Codabar," whose specifications are identified above. Comprehensive works, such as those by Stephen Stewart of Federal Express, sug-gest that Rationalized Codabar's two-element widths (wide and narrow) would have equal or better performance because of the superficial nature of traditional Codabar's 18 different printing widths. Traditional Codabar with its 18 different widths is not recommended for any new bar code systems. Therefore, additional discussion of traditional Codabar is omit-ted from this book.

Codabar sometimes employs a modulus 16 check character to improve key-entry data accuracy when the bar code symbol is not scannable. Modulus 16 check character calcula-tions are shown in Appendix D.

The single largest user of bar code technology is Federal Express. It scans more symbols, uses more labels, and uses more sequentially bar code printed forms than anyone else in the world. A discussion of the Federal Express system is contained in Chapter 14 of this text. Federal Express uses Codabar. Federal Express also employs a modulus 7 DSR check character in its symbol coding structure. The calculations for a modulus 7 DSR check character are shown in Appendix D.

Code 93

Code 93 was introduced by Intermec in 1982 as a competitive symbology to Code 128 and to provide a complementary character set to that of Code 39. (Code 128 had been introduced in 1981 due to a perceived need to encode data at higher densities than Code 39.) Each character consists of nine modules arranged into three bars and three spaces. With an arrangement of three bars (and associated three spaces) over nine modules, Code 93 would be capable of encoding 56 possible characters. The character set shown in Table 5.3 encodes only 48 of these 56 characters—43 of them coincide with the Code 39 character set, and four are used for control characters when encoding the full ASCII character set in Code 93's expanded mode.

Code 93 is a variable-length, continuous code but is not self-checking. The symbol uses two modulus 47 check characters to provide data security. Bar and space widths may be one, two, three, or four modules wide. Its structure uses edge-to-similar-edge decoding techniques, making the symbol immune to uniform ink spread.

Char.	Value	Pattern	Encoding	Char.	Value	Pattern	Encoding
			1	2	3	4	5	6	7	8	9						1	2	3	4	5	6	7	8	9		
0	0		100010100	O	24		100101100
1	1		101001000	P	25		100010110
2	2		101000100	Q	26		110110100
3	3		101000010	R	27		110110010
4	4		100101000	S	28		110101100
5	5		100100100	T	29		110100110
6	6		100100010	U	30		110010110
7	7		101010000	V	31		110011010
8	8		100010010	W	32		101101100
9	9		100001010	X	33		101100110
A	10		110101000	Y	34		100110110
B	11		110100100	Z	35		100111010
C	12		110100010	-	36		100101110
D	13		110010100	•	37		111010010
E	14		110010010	SPACE	38		111001010
F	15		110001010	$	39		101101110
G	16		101101000	/	40		101110110
H	17		101100100	+	41		110101110
I	18		101100010	%	42		100100110
J	19		100110100	(S)	43		111011010
K	20		100011010	(%)	44		111010110
L	21		101011000	(/)	45		100110010
M	22		101001100	(+)	46		101011110
N	23		101000110	□			

Table 5.3: Code 93 Character Encodings

Code 93 is a variable length, continuous symbology which directly encodes uppercase alpha-numeric data and a limited set of special characters shown here. A full ASCII encodation using shift characters is not detailed here.

If Code 39 is printed at a 2:1 wide-to-narrow ratio, an individual bar code character would be 12 X dimensions, or 12 modules, wide. Additionally, since Code 39 is a discrete code, it has an intercharacter space, which, if fixed at 1X, would realize a character width of 13 modules.

Code 128, on the other hand, is a continuous symbol with no intercharacter space, and each character is 11 modules wide. Code 93, also a continuous code with no intercharacter space, is but nine modules wide and is, therefore, more efficient for alphanumeric data. However, when Code 128 is in its double-density numeric mode, each pair of numeric characters is represented by one bar code character, yielding an effective "number of modules per character" of 11 modules divided by 2 characters, equaling 5.5 modules per character. Thus, when encoding strictly numeric data, Code 128 is a more efficient code than Code 93 (5.5 modules per character vs. 9 modules per character). But when encoding alphanumeric data, Code 93 is a more efficient code than Code 128 (9 modules per character vs. 11 modules per character). As of this writing, no national or international industry organization has adopted Code 93.

Plessey

Plessey Code and its variants (MSI Code, Telxon Code, and Anker Code) all find their origins in the pulse width modulated (PWM) code developed by Plessey Company Limited of Dorset, England. It has been widely used for shelf marking in grocery stores. Pulse

"0" Bit ▌		"1" Bit ▐	
|1|2|4 8|		|1|2|4|8|	
0	0 0 0 0	8	0 0 0 1
1	1 0 0 0	9	1 0 0 1
2	0 1 0 0	A	0 1 0 1
3	1 1 0 0	B	1 1 0 1
4	0 0 1 0	C	0 0 1 1
5	1 0 1 0	D	1 0 1 1
6	0 1 1 0	E	0 1 1 1
7	1 1 1 0	F	1 1 1 1

Table 5.4: Plessey Code Character Encodations

Plessey Code is a "pulse width modulated" continuous code that encodes the ten decimal digits plus six additional characters, A, B, C, D, E, and F. The bars and spaces of characters encode four bits of data with binary weighting shown.

width modulated codes represent each bit of information by a bar/space pair. A zero bit consists of a narrow bar followed by a wide space, while a one bit consists of a wide bar followed by a narrow space.

Each decimal digit is represented by a binary code decimal (BCD) character consisting of four bits as formatted in Table 5.4. Pulse width modulated codes are not self-checking and employ a variety of check characters. The MSI Code employs a modulus 10 check; Plessey Code employs a polynomial-based cyclic redundancy check; and Anker employs an inverted cyclic redundancy check. For start and stop characters, Plessey and Anker employ a 1101 (B) and previously used a 0101 (A). MSI employs a single bit pair of 1 as a start code and a single bit pair of 0 as a stop symbol. Telxon employs a right and left bar pattern (start and stop code) of 010. MSI and Telxon reverse the 1-2-4-8 BCD pattern, shown in Table 5.4, for bit pair weighting to 8-4-2-1. Pulse width modulated codes for individual digits range in length from 12 times the width of the narrow nominal element width for MSI and Telxon to 20 times the nominal width for Plessey and Anker.

Plessey is not a self-checking coding structure, has no inherent strengths that would cause it to be considered over more widely used structures, and, with but a few pockets of influence, is not seen except in older grocery and library applications.

Postnet Code

The Postnet bar code was developed by the U.S. Postal Service (USPS) to provide a system of encoding on letter mail ZIP Code information that can be read reliably by relatively inexpensive bar code sorters. The first specification for Postal Numeric Encoding Technique (Postnet) was prepared by Mason Lilly of the U.S. Postal Service's Systems Development Branch in 1980. The code is made up of binary elements printed in the lower right corner of the mail piece as tall and short bars representing the ZIP Code or ZIP + 4 code. Bar/half bar symbologies like Postnet were first tried commercially in the late 1960s but were soon dropped due to lack of adequate scanning technology, among other reasons. Newer technologies of wide area scanning have made these codes practical.

The USPS has developed optical character recognition systems that have been tested and verified to read 25 different type styles. Further, the National Composition Association has identified 46 additional type styles that are considered equivalent to the tested and verified 25. At the origin postal center optical character recognition systems scan human-readable addresses at speeds of up to ten pieces of mail per second. Once an address is read, the Postnet symbol is printed on the piece in a precise location. This symbol is then used at intermediate and destination postal centers to route the mail by lower-cost, high-speed bar code sorters. Symbols may also be printed by the sender with qualified printing devices; in the case of preprinted business reply mail, preprinted symbols may also be employed.

The ZIP + 4 Postnet bar code is comprised of nine digits plus a check digit. Each digit of the ZIP + 4 code is represented by five bars, which comprise various positional arrangements of two tall bars and three short bars. A tall bar represents the binary value "1"; a short bar represents the binary value "0." The coding structure of Postnet, shown in Table 5.5, is an even parity structure similar to inverted values of the 2 of 5 Code.

A complete ZIP + 4 Postnet code consists of 50 bars representing the nine digits of the ZIP + 4 Code and the check digit, plus a framing bar at each end of the string for a total of 52 bars. The check digit for the ZIP + 4 Code is a simple sum modulus 10 check digit subtracted from the modulus. For example, a check digit for the ZIP + 4 Code 52403-2140 is calculated by summing $5 + 2 + 4 + 0 + 3 + 2 + 1 + 4 + 0 = 21/10 = 2$ with a remainder of 1 subtracted from the modulus 10 (check digit "9"). The coding structure for this ZIP + 4 is illustrated in Figure 5.2.

Individual bars, which make up the Postnet bar code, should be printed so that the height of the tall bars is 0.125 inch ± 0.010 inch, and the height of the short bars is 0.050 inch ± 0.010 inch. The width of the bars should be 0.020 inch ± 0.005 inch. The pitch of the bars should be 21 ± 1 bars per inch. The spacing between the centerlines of adjacent bars should be within the range of 0.045 inch to 0.050 inch. Specifications for the Postnet bar codes and FIM patterns, including printing, ink, and paper considerations, type styles, permitted tilt and offset, and location guidelines are available by ordering Publication 25 from local postmasters or from U.S. Postal Service Headquarters whose address appears in Appendix A.

a.   b.   c.   d.

Figure 5.2: USPS Facing Identification Mark (FIM) Patterns

The FIM patterns are used by business mailers on preprinted mailing pieces for compatibility with various USPS automatic sortation systems. (a) FIM-A used on Courtesy Reply Mail with preprinted Postnet symbology in the address. (b) FIM-B used on Business Reply, Penalty, and Franked mail with no preprinted Postnet image. (c) FIM-C used on Business Reply, Penalty, and Franked mail with preprinted Postnet image. (d) FIM-D used on OCR Readable Mail without preprinted Postnet symbology.

Character	Code 8421P
0	11000
1	00011
2	00101
3	00110
4	01001
5	01010
6	01100
7	10001
8	10010
9	10100

Table 5.5: Postnet Character Encodings

The Postnet code is a bar/half bar code consisting of four bars and a parity bar per character. In this table, a long bar is represented by a binary "1" and a short bar is represented by a binary "0."

Beyond the optically read characters, two types of indicia are employed by the USPS. These are the Postnet bar code symbols and Facing Identification Mark (FIM) patterns. The FIM is a 9-position bar/no-bar pattern. There are four FIM patterns (A, B, C, and D) for specific use by business mailers. These patterns are shown in Figure 5.3, as are FIM defini-

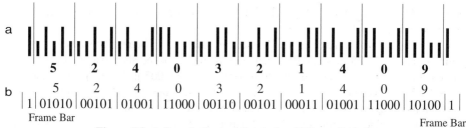

a ... **5 2 4 0 3 2 1 4 0 9**

b 5   2   4   0   3   2   1   4   0   9
| 1 | 01010 | 00101 | 01001 | 11000 | 00110 | 00101 | 00011 | 01001 | 11000 | 10100 | 1 |
Frame Bar
Frame Bar

Figure 5.3: A Sample Postnet Symbol and Binary Pattern

This figure shows a typical Postnet ZIP + 4 representation of a nine-digit ZIP + 4 code, "52403-2140," as it might be placed in the address area of a mailing piece (a) and in its equivalent binary representation (b). The Postnet code contains nine digits of data plus a check digit (in this example, "9"). Each five-bit code consists of four BCD data bits plus an individual parity bit for that digit, as shown in Table 5.5.

tions and uses. The Postal Service will provide camera-ready FIM and Postnet bar code positives to business mailers or their suppliers upon request and without charge. Requests for the positives should be made through local account representatives or postmaster.

The height of FIM bars should be 0.625 inch ±0.125 inch. The width of FIM bars should be 0.031 inch ±0.008 inch. The pitch of bars is a nominal 1/16 inch. Tilt of the bars measured relative to a line perpendicular to the top edge of the envelope should be ± 5°.

Effective March 21, 1993, the Postal Service began requiring that all mail submitted for bar code marking discounts include not only the ZIP+4 but an additional 2 digits as well to identify the specific delivery point (Delivery Point Bar Codes - DPBC); usually the last two digits of a residential address. The Postnet bar code has three varieties. The first, shown in Figure 5.4 below, is the standard 11-digit 62-bit configuration printed to allow further sorting down to the carrier delivery point. The second is a standard 5-digit, 32-bit ZIP code used for coding a mail piece on which there is not enough information to encode a 9-digit ZIP+4 or 11-digit DPBC. The third is the standard 9-digit 52-bit ZIP+4, shown in Figure 5.3 above, used whenever a non-bar code marked mail piece is to be encoded and sufficient information is available in the address block to determine the full 9-digit code.

A complete recommended ZIP+4+2 Postnet code consists of 60 bars representing the 11 digits of the ZIP+4+2 Postnet code and the check digit, plus a framing bar at each end of the string for a total of 62 bars. The check digit for the ZIP+4+2 Postnet code is a simple sum Modulus 10 check digit subtracted from the Modulus, e.g., a check digit for the ZIP+4+2 code 52403-21406<u>3</u> (the address is 39<u>63</u> Highlands Lane, SE) is calculated by summing 5+2+4+0+3+2+1+4+0+6+3 = 30/10 = 3 with a remainder of 0. The check digit is 0 since nothing need be added to reach a multiple of 10. The coding structure for this ZIP+4+2 is as illustrated in Figure 5.4 below:

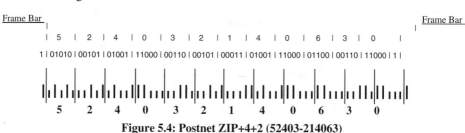

Frame Bar   Frame Bar

| 5 | 2 | 4 | 0 | 3 | 2 | 1 | 4 | 0 | 6 | 3 | 0 |

1 | 01010 | 00101 | 01001 | 11000 | 00110 | 00101 | 00011 | 01001 | 11000 | 01100 | 00110 | 11000 | 1 |

5 2 4 0 3 2 1 4 0 6 3 0

Figure 5.4: Postnet ZIP+4+2 (52403-214063)

BC412

Semiconductor Equipment and Materials International (SEMI) has published a draft standard, which is expected to be adopted in 1993 for marking the back surface of silicon wafers. The draft standard describes a bar code symbol called BC412, which is a variant of the FIM bar/no bar patterns. Where the FIM patterns in Postnet have nine positions in which there is either the presence or absence of a bar, BC412 similarly has 12 positions. In BC412 there are always 4 bars.

Single width bar codes, that is, codes in which all bars are marked with the same width, are ideal for semiconductor wafer identification applications where the serial numbers are scribed on wafers by pulsed lasers. Compared to conventional multiwidth bar codes, single-width bar codes offer better marking quality, require less scribing time, yield higher density, and provide better readibility rates for processed wafers that have a low contrast ratio.

Multiwidth bar codes, Code 39 for example, would pose several problems in such applications. Pulsed laser scribers do not produce high-quality bars when the bar widths exceed the dot's diameter. Code density and scriber throughput rates are additional problems. The most serious deficiency is the poor readibility associated with discriminating between narrow and wide bar widths when wafers have been exposed to numerous.types of process conditions.

SEMI's Standard

The relatively new BC412 single-width bar code was developed by Computer Identics and IBM in 1988. Used to mark the serial numbers on semiconductor wafers, the code has the following features:

- •35 alphanumeric characters can be encoded,
- •12 modules per character,
- •4 bars per character,
- •8 spaces per character,
- •timing bar in the first module location of each character,
- •a space in the second and the last modules.

The inherent timing bars for synchronization in scanning of code symbols provides the self-clocking features, in contrast to the Postnet bar code that uses separate timing marks. Bi-directional reading ability is provided by a start symbol (bar-space-space) and a stop symbol (bar-space-bar) of the BC412 definition (see Figure 5.4). In June 1992, SEMI approved BC412 as an industry standard, and published BC412 as SEMI Spec 1934B in SEMI Standards in 1993.

Three wafer suppliers, (MEMC, SEH, and Wacker) scribe the 125 mm and 200 mm wafers as defined in IBM engineering specifications. Four bar code reader vendors, Computer Identics, Control Module Inc., Kensington Labs, and Opticon, are qualified to provide high readability rates. The small, low-cost readers are integrated into the IBM process, metrology, and logistic equipment to provide automated wafer identification and control. Readability rates on the wafers exceed 99.99 percent.

A check character is added to verify the data integrity based on a module 35 checking algorithm. The check character can also be used to recover a nonreadable character. A character may be nonreadable for a number of reasons, for example, if the number of bars in the 12-module symbol is not exactly 4, or if the first module is not a bar, or if the last module is not a space. An error correction algorithm is available to reconstruct the character when the

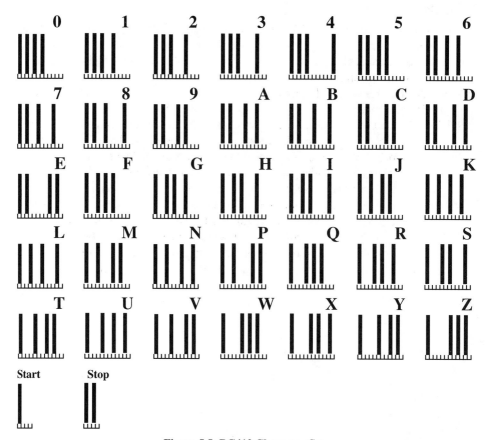

Figure 5.5: BC412 Character Set

Wafers are scribed with BC412 at the silicon foundries prior to the polish and anneal operations. The BC412 font parameters are specified based on the current YAG laser scribing practices coupled with the optical resolution of conventional bar code reader technologies. the code is marked on the wager's back surface to avoid front side process films that would jeopardize high-performance readability.

location of the nonreadable character is identified.

With its special features and excellent operational results, the new bar code BC412 has been successfully applied to wafer identification in the semiconductor industry. Other areas of potential BC412 use are CD-ROM, metals, or glass, where only a small area is available for scribing data. And BC412 is only one member of the single-width bar code family. Various other codes can be tailored to accommodate specific applications.

Where applications require only numeric data, a similar symbology called BC309 can be utilized. Where BC412 has four bars over 12 modules, BC309 has three bars over nine modules. The BC309 character set is shown in Figure 5.6.

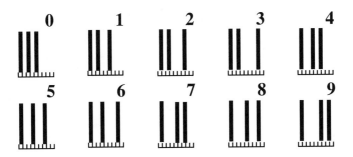

Figure 5.6: BC309 Character Set

BC309 is a variation of BC412, used in applications requiring numeric data only. Where BC412 has four bars over twelve modules, BC309 has three bars over nine modules.

CHAPTER 6

Putting More Information in a Smaller Space

I n recent years there has been an increasing demand for storing more information in a bar code symbol. Most bar code applications utilize a "license plate" approach to coding design: The bar code is used as a simple item identifier; all information regarding that item is stored in a database record; and the license plate is used as a key for information retrieval.

A familiar example of the license plate approach is the use of the Universal Product Code (UPC) symbol in retail settings. The 12-digit code identifies the manufacturer and product, while the product description, price, taxability, inventory information, and other data are stored in the store's computer system in a database typically referred to as the "price/inventory file." When an item is scanned at check-out, the description and price are looked up in the price/inventory file and forwarded to the point of sale to complete the purchase transaction.

The license plate scheme offers two important advantages:
- The ability to refer to large amounts of information using a relatively short code and symbol; and
- The ability to change the data associated with an item without reprinting the bar code.

This approach cannot be used in applications where it is either impractical to store needed information about the item in a database, or where that database is not accessible when and where the information is to be referenced by the bar code. This might be the case because the item has moved to a remote location, without access to the host computer on which the database resides.

An alternative to the license plate approach would be the use of a longer bar code to store all of the relevant information, such as the name of the product, manufacturer, price, weight, expiration date, etc. This portable data file could be retrieved without access to a data base. Price lookup files are necessary and convenient in a retail setting. This may not be the case, however, at a distribution center receiving goods from and shipping goods to remote warehouses or overseas depots, or in certain hospital patient/specimen applications, or when encoding information on small semiconductor components and assemblies.

The EDI Connection

One solution to the problem of access to information stored in remote databases involves the use of electronic data interchange (EDI) techniques to exchange information between computers. The idea is that information from a remote computer can be transferred to a local computer, using standardized protocols and formats, so that it can be accessed when required.

The problem with this approach is that full EDI connectivity has proven to be an elusive goal in many industries. Standards are just now emerging. Smaller trading partners lack the technical resources to implement electronic data interchange support. Remote mobile sites cannot be accommodated by current technology. Transportation services are just barely being considered as "trading partners" having need for product and shipment data. Third-party networks providing translation and mapping functions are becoming another utility much the way telephone, electric, gas, and water companies have. In short, 1992 finds full EDI often still being referred to in the future tense. Similarly, smartcard technology is still generally judged to be impractical for the application of portable data files, mainly due to the cost involved in the medium.

Requirements of a Bar Code Symbol

The basic problem we face is that of encoding information on some medium using low-cost encoding technology. We will presume for the moment that the medium is a printed symbol. Recall our discussions in Chapter 2 regarding the differences between codes and symbols. Any such encoding has these conflicting requirements:

- The symbol should have a high density of information.
- The symbol should be able to be read reliably.
- The symbol should be able to be created (printed) at relatively low cost.
- The symbol should be able to be read by relatively low-cost equipment.

For the remainder of this chapter, what has been traditionally thought of as a bar code character—as distinguished from its English equivalent—is referred to as a "codeword." This permits discussions of those cases where, dependent upon usage, a specific arrangement of bars and spaces in a specific symbology can mean different things, such as Code 128's use of the same bar/space pattern to represent different data when that bar/space pattern is used in Code 128's Subset A, B, or C (see Table 3.17 and Figures 3.21 for examples). With regard to data density this text shall concern itself with the basic types of bar codes, namely, width codes and delta codes shown in Figure 2.3.

Within each codeword for width codes, such as Interleaved 2 of 5, Code 39, and Codabar, is a specific number of elements (m) of which a specific number are wide (w). Code 39, for example, has nine elements of which three are wide and can be expressed in "(m,w)" terms as "(9,3)." Table 6.1 shows some of the characteristics of these width codes. In Table 6.1, it is assumed that the wide-to-narrow ratio for the symbol is 2.5:1. Information content is a function of modules per codeword and the number of codewords that can be generated. For a technical discussion of information content of bar codes see *Fundamentals of Bar Code Information Theory* by Theo Pavlidis, Jerome Swartz, and Ynjiun P. Wang. Also see *Two-Dimensional Bar Codes* by Theo Pavlidis and Ynjiun P. Wang. These papers are available from Symbol Technologies, 116 Wilbur Drive, Bohemia, NY 11716.

Within each codeword for delta codes, such as U.P.C., Code 49, Code 93, Code 128, Code 16K, and PDF417, is a specified number of modules and bar/space combinations—Code 93, for example, has nine modules and three bar/space combinations. Delta codes are also referred to as "(n,k)" codes where "n" is the number of modules and "k" is the

(m,w)	Number of Codewords Possible	Number of Codewords Used	Total Width (in modules)	Information Content	Related Code Name
5,2	10	10	8	0.415	Interleaved 2 of 5
9,3	84	44	13.5	0.404	Code 39
7,2	21	16	10	0.400	Codabar

Table 6.1: Characteristics of Some Width Codes

Shown here are some parameters of several "width code" symbologies, specified by (m,w), where "m" is the number of elements and "w" is the number of wide elements.

number of bar/space combinations. The number of possible codewords, "C," that can be constructed from *n,k* codes is calculated from a variation of the algebraic formula for the number of combinations of "n" items taken "k" at a time. The expression for C, the number of codewords, appropriate for (n,k) codes is:

$$C = \frac{(n-1)!}{(2k-1)!\,(n-2k)!}$$

Presume for a moment that we are interested in finding out how many bar/space combinations exist with U.P.C.. We know from Figure 3.4 that U.P.C. is constructed from seven modules arranged as two bars and two spaces. U.P.C. is thus an (*n,k*) code where n = 7 and k = 2, denoted (7,2). We can evaluate each parenthesized expression in the above expression with these values:

$$(n-1)! = (7-1)! = 6! = 6 \cdot 5 \cdot 4 \cdot 3 \cdot 2 \cdot 1 = 720$$

$$(2k-1)! = (2 \cdot 2 - 1)! = (4-1)! = 3! = 6$$

$$(n-2k)! = (7-2 \cdot 2)! = (7-4)! = 3! = 6$$

Plugging these results into the C expression above, we find that for U.P.C. there are:

$$C = \frac{720}{6 \cdot 6} = 20$$

combinations available for codewords. With 20 codewords available in U.P.C., 10 of the codewords are employed in the left half of the symbol and 10 of the codewords are employed in the right half of the symbol. Table 6.2 shows some of the characteristics of these delta codes or (*n,k*) codes.

As noted above, readers are referred to the technical discussion of information content of bar codes in two papers available from Symbol Technologies, *Fundamentals of Bar Code Information Theory* and *Two-Dimensional Bar Codes* by Theo Pavlidis et al.

(n,k)	Number of Codewords Possible	Number of Codewords Used	Total Width (in modules)	Information Content	Related Code Name
7,2	20	20	7	0.617	U.P.C./EAN
9,3	56	48	9	0.645	Code 93
11,3	252	106	11	0.725	Code 128
16,4	6,435	4,802	16	0.791	Code 49
11,3	252	106	11	0.725	Code 16K
17,4	11,440	929	17	0.793	PDF417

Table 6.2: Characteristics of Some Delta Codes

Shown here are some parameters of several "delta code" symbologies, specified by (n,k), where "n" is the number of modules and "k" is the number of bar/space combinations.

Stacked Codes

Four techniques have been proposed for increasing the information density in bar code symbols. The first is to develop new one-dimension (width) symbol structures using delta coding techniques to encode more information in less space. Delta coding techniques have given rise to codes such as Code 128 and Code 93. These delta codes have improved the density over width codes by approximately 43 percent assuming the same module widths. Code 128 further improves its density by allowing double-density numeric encodation within one of its subsets (Subset C) as described in Chapter 3 of this text.

Reducing the widths of the modules (smaller X dimensions) is the second technique. Reduction of the X dimension also reduces the printing tolerance, making the requirements for creation of the symbols more precise and, consequently, more expensive.

The third technique is to reduce the height of the bars and then stack the symbols on top of one another, as do MLC 2D, Code 16K, and to some extent Code 49 (though Code 49 has also introduced newer delta code techniques). One drawback to stacking is that the inclusion of separator bars between the stacked rows has an adverse effect on the amount of information that can be printed in a given amount of space. Without the separator bars, however, interference is induced between the rows.

The fourth method is to develop an encoding technique that is scannable across the rows without separator bars and then to be able to "stitch" together information from partial scans. This technique, as used by PDF417, requires more powerful computational processing but is still within the limits of today's technology.

The Portable Data File Solution

The availability of symbol structures accommodating large data fields presents an attractive solution to the problem of increasing symbol information content. Using a two-dimensional symbology capable of storing hundreds of characters of data, detailed item and shipment information can be printed directly on the product and shipping labels, minimizing the need for access to remote databases. It is not believed that printed portable data files will necessarily replace electronic purchase orders, invoices, or catalogs, but much product-specific and shipment-specific information can, with *today's* technology, be available without distributed databases.

Under this scheme, the bar code becomes, in effect, a portable data file. This portable data file might be printed as part of an item label or on associated paperwork. The key is that low-cost direct access to detailed information is provided wherever and whenever it is required. Many believe that the portable data file concept will prove to be of fundamental importance to the development of distributed applications in the 1990s.

MLC 2D

In 1989, the German company ICS Identcode introduced three versions of its Codablock MLC (Multi-line Code) two-dimensional coding structures. One version, called Codablock A, is Code 39 structures stacked upon one another with shortened bars encoding up to 1320 characters in 1 to 22 rows. Another, Codablock F utilizes Code 128 internally, and provides its full alphanumeric and double-density numeric capabilities. A variation of Codablock F, Codablock E utilizes the UCC/EAN-128 symbology, with function code f1 in the first position to indicate that the data is a UCC/EAN-128 structure. And finally, Codablock N, is Interleaved 2 of 5 stacked upon one another with shortened bars encoding up to 600 numeric characters in 1 to 10 rows.

Each symbol has a parent symbology start and stop code and two character row indicators per row. Each Codablock version offers an optional weighted modulus 43 check character

MLC 2D Code	Encodable Character Set	Non-Stacked Base Symbology	Code Type	Maximum Data Character Density	Maximum Data Characters per Symbol
Codablock A	Upper case alphanumerics, –, ., Space, $, /,+, and %	Code 39	Discrete	Determined by undefined bar height	1320 in 1 to 22 rows
Codablock F	Full alphanumeric, double-density numerics 3 Start, 1 Stop Codes 4 Control Codes	Code 128	Continuous	Determined by undefined bar height	420 in 1 to 7 rows
Codablock N	Numeric digits 0-9	Interleaved 2 of 5	Continuous	Determined by undefined bar height	2728 in 1 to 62 rows

Characteristics Applicable to all MLC-2D variations:
Character Self-Checking: Yes
Symbol Size: Variable
Bidirectional Decoding: Yes
Number of Row Indicator Characters Required per Row: 2
Smallest Nominal Element Width: Limited only by the printing technology and reading technology. Current bar code industry print technology limits print width to 0.0075
Smallest Recommended Nominal Element Height: 0.010 inch

Table 6.3: Summary of MLC 2D Characteristics

MLC 2D is a set of three stacked symbologies that provides a record frame structure for several rows of data in a conventional symbology but with shortened bar heights.

Figure 6.1: Sample Codablock A Symbol

for symbols. The size of the symbol is dictated by the printing and reading equipment. The ICS Identprint MLC 2D printing program offers a 0.007-inch narrow bar with wide-to-narrow ratios of 2:1 and 3:1 and a bar height of 0.118 inch. Other offered X dimensions include 0.010 inch and 0.005 inch with user selectable wide-to-narrow ratios and bar height. In Codablock A there can be from 2 to 61 codewords per row. MLC 2D's characteristics are summarized in Table 6.3; an example of a Codablock A symbol is shown in Figure 6.1.

Codablocks have many of the characteristics of a unique symbology. Even moreso than Code 16K, they were designed to take advantage of the existing encode and decode tables of symbologies already resident in most bar code printers and scanners. Like Code 49 and Code 16K, Codablock is scanned and decoded row by row, and the data structure recovered by use of row indicators. Primary applications have been in medical and electronics labeling, and potential applications include EAN unit transport labels, and portable database applications such as medical identification and chemical ingredient labels.

Code 16K

In 1988 Laserlight Systems introduced Code 16K. Code 16K can have from 2 to 16 rows with Row "1" at the top of the symbol. Rows 1 to 8 have sequential start patterns derived from U.P.C./EAN Number Set A (0 to 6 and 9) and sequential stop patterns derived from U.P.C./EAN Number Set C (0 to 6 and 9). See Table 3.8(a). Rows 9 to 16 have sequential start patterns derived from U.P.C./EAN Number Set A (0 to 6 and 9) and sequential stop patterns derived from U.P.C./EAN Number Set C (4 to 6, 9, 0 to 3). This pattern structure also provides for row numbering.

Each row has a leading quiet zone of width 10X, a start pattern (7 modules), a synchronization bar (1X), 5 codewords from an inverted Code 128 character set (11 modules each), a stop pattern (7 modules), and a trailing quiet zone (minimum 1X) for a total row length of 70X, plus 11X for the quiet zones. Symbols having two to ten rows have a minimum row height of 8X. No symbol should have a height of more than 80X to enable that code to be scannable by a two-dimensional scan head, e.g., a matrix charge-coupled device array. The last row has two modulus 107 check characters, which decreases the number of available codewords for the last row by two. Modulus 107 check character calculations are shown in Appendix D.

Encodable Character Set:
Code Set A—Upper Case ASCII Alphabetics, Numerics, Punctuation, and
Control Characters
Code Set B—Upper and Lower Case ASCII Alphabetics, Numerics, and
Punctuation Characters
Code Set C—Double-Density Numeric

Code Type: Continuous

Character Self-Checking: Yes

Symbol Size: Variable

Bidirectional Decoding: Yes

Number of Row Indicator Characters Required per Row:
2 included in start/stop pattern

Smallest Nominal Element Width:
Limited only by the printing technology and reading technology. Current bar code
industry print technology limits print width to 0.0075 inch

Smallest Nominal Element Height: 0.010 inch (0.254mm)

Maximum Data Character Density:
Character sets A and B (Alphanumeric Modes)—117 ASCII characters
per square inch
Character set C (Numeric Mode)—234 numeric characters per square inch

Maximum Data Characters per Symbol:
Character sets A and B (Alphanumeric Modes)—78 Characters
(Extended Option Concatenating 107 symbols = 8,025 ASCII characters)
Character set C (Numeric Mode)—158 Numeric Characters
(Extended Option Concatenating 107 symbols = 16,050 numeric characters)

Non-Data Overhead: Two ASCII characters per symbol

Additional Feature: Edge-to-Edge Decodable

Table 6.4: Code 16K Characteristics

This is a summary of various features of Code 16K. For a more detailed technical discussion of Code 16K see AIM-USA USS-16K, available from AIM-USA and Laserlight Systems, Inc.

Figure 6.2: Sample Code 16K Symbol

The character set for Code 16K includes all of the 103 Code 128 characters, plus codewords for "pad," set specific "shift," "double shift," and "triple shift" for a total of 107 codewords. The set specific shift, double shift, and triple shift codewords permit the shifting to another code set for the following 1, 2, or 3 characters, respectively, and then transferring back to the original code set. While the Code 128 character set is used, the bar/space patterns are inverted, i.e., if the Code 128 bar pattern of a character is B S B S B S, then in Code 16K the bar pattern is S B S B S B. Code 16K's characteristics are summarized in Table 6.4; Figure 6.2 shows a sample Code 16K symbol.

Code 49

Designed by Dr. David Allais and introduced by Intermec in 1987, Code 49 was one of the first codes to take advantage of the high capacity (n,k) coding in a stacked structure. Code 49 encodes 49 characters (0 to 9, A to Z, –, ., space, $, /, +, %, Shift 1, Shift 2, F1, F2, F3, and Numeric Shift (ns)). The use of the Shift 1 and Shift 2 characters permits Code 49 to encode the entire ASCII character set. Code 49 can have from 2 to 8 rows. Each row contains 18 bars and is 70 modules long. The start pattern is two modules wide and the stop pattern four modules wide. Each row is separated by a one-module separator bar. The minimum bar height is 8X.

Each row contains four codewords. Each codeword contains two characters. The last character in each row is a modulus 49 check character for the prior seven characters in that row. If the symbol encodes a number of characters and does not fill out the last row, the row is padded with trailing "ns" characters. Code 49 also encodes the row number of each row through unique parity patterns assigned to each row. Table 6.5 shows the parity pattern assigned to each codeword based upon the rows in which the codeword appears. Observe that the designator for the row after Row 7 is not Row 8. Last Row is the parity pattern for the last row in the symbol, regardless of whether the symbol contains 2, 3, 4, 5, 6, 7, or 8 rows.

	Codeword 1	Codeword 2	Codeword 3	Codeword 4
Row 1	Odd	Even	Even	Odd
Row 2	Even	Odd	Even	Odd
Row 3	Odd	Odd	Even	Even
Row 4	Even	Even	Odd	Odd
Row 5	Odd	Even	Odd	Even
Row 6	Even	Odd	Odd	Even
Row 7	Odd	Odd	Odd	Odd
Last Row	Even	Even	Even	Even

Table 6.5: Code 49 Row Designator Parity Patterns

Each row of the Code 49 symbol has four codewords encoded in from 2 to 8 rows using odd or even parity according to this map. The pattern labeled "Last Row" is used for the last row of the symbol instead of the pattern shown here, regardless of the actual number of rows.

For symbols having fewer than seven rows, the Last Row contains two modulus 2401 check codewords. For symbols with seven and eight rows the Last Row contains three modulus 2401 check codewords. Modulus 2401 check character calculations for Code49 are given in AIM USS-49 available from AIM and Intermec, as well as in Appendix F of *The Bar Code Book* by Roger Palmer, published by Helmers Publishing, Inc. The next-to-last character in the Last Row designates the number of rows in the symbol and the symbol mode.

Code 49 offers seven modes. In its regular alphanumeric mode (Mode 0) two characters are mapped onto one codeword. In its regular numeric mode (Mode 2) ten digits are mapped onto three codewords. With one check character at the end of each row and two to three checkwords within each symbol, Code 49 is a very secure code. Code 49's characteristics are summarized in Table 6.6; an example of a Code 49 symbol is shown in Figure 6.3.

Encodable Character Set:
    Normal Mode: 0 to 9, A to Z, −, ., Space, $, /, +, %, Shift 1, Shift 2, F1, F2, F3,
        and Numeric Shift (ns)
    ASCII Mode: All 128 ASCII Characters (Shift 1 and Shift 2)
    Numeric Mode: 100 Numeric Values
Code Type: Continuous Character
Self-Checking: No
Symbol Size: Variable
Bidirectional Decoding: Yes
Number of Row Indicator Characters Required per Row: Row Indicator Derived from
    Row Parity Pattern
Smallest Nominal Element Width: Limited only by the printing technology and
    reading technology. Current bar code industry print technology limits print
    width to 0.0075 inch
Smallest Recommended Nominal Element Height: 0.010 inch
Maximum Data Character Density:
    Alpha Mode or ASCII: 93.3 Alpha/ASCII characters per square inch
    Numeric Mode: 81 Numeric Characters
Non-Data Overhead: Equivalent of one ASCII character per row, plus 4 to 6 per symbol
Additional Features:
    Edge-to-edge decodable
    Concatenation ability
    Rows may be scanned in any order
    High data security

Table 6.6: Code 49 Characteristics

This is a summary of various features of Code 49. For a more detailed technical discussion of Code 49 see The Bar Code Book: Reading, Printing, and Specifications of Bar Code Symbols *by Roger C. Palmer, available from Helmers Publishing, Inc. Also see* AIM-USA USS-49, *available from AIM-USA and Intermec.*

Figure 6.3: Sample Code 49 Symbol

PDF417

PDF417 is a two-dimensional bar code symbol capable of encoding information at about one thousand bytes per symbol. However, the maximum number of ASCII characters that can be encoded in a symbol is a function of the data compression scheme. There are 12 data compression schemes, referred to as *modes,* in PFD417. Two of them are default modes, called the *printable ASCII mode* and the *Binary mode.* The remaining 10 modes are *user modes,* which can be defined by the user according to specific applications. Each user mode can encode 900 different entities (English words, part numbers, etc.). These modes can change within a symbol according to the requirements of an application.

In the printable ASCII mode, the maximum number of ASCII characters in a symbol is 1,848. In the Binary mode, it is 1,108 characters. In the user-defined modes, the maximum number of ASCII characters in a symbol is much higher than in the printable ASCII mode. If the amount of data exceeds the maximum capacity of a symbol, several individual symbols can be concatenated to form a data file, called *macro PDF417,* which has no logical limit on capacity (although practical considerations tend to keep the number of symbols as small as possible).

Every PDF417 symbol is composed of a stack of rows. Each row consists of several codewords. Each codeword is constructed of 17 modules arranged into four bars and four spaces. The whole set of codewords is partitioned into three mutually exclusive subsets, called clusters, each of which encodes the 929 PDF417 codewords with distinct bar/space patterns so that one cluster cannot be confused with another. Each row uses only one of the three clusters to encode data, with the same cluster repeated sequentially every third row. Because any two adjacent rows use different clusters, the decoder can stitch partial scans while decoding a very high density PDF417 symbol.

The first and last codewords in each row of a PDF417 symbol are row indicators. There are two checksums for a PDF417 symbol. In addition, every PDF417 symbol has a user-defined error correction capability of up to 510 codewords. PDF417's characteristics are summarized as follows in Table 6.7; Figure 6.4 shows an example of a PDF417 symbol.

In Table 6.7, the smallest nominal element width is a limitation imposed by the printing processes used in the bar code industry, not a limitation of the PDF417 symbology. It is possible to print a PDF417 symbol as small as the printing equipment can produce and the reading equipment can resolve. For example, in the application of marking IC wafers, the nominal element could be 10 μm or less, presuming that the reading equipment could resolve such a narrow element.

The smallest recommended nominal element height is based on the assumption of using handheld laser scanners, not on a limitation of the PDF417 symbology. If another type of reader is used, such as a charge-coupled device (CCD) camera, nominal height can be as small as the nominal element width.

The maximum data character density is calculated by assuming that the smallest nominal element width (0.0075 inch) and the smallest nominal element height (0.010 inch) are used.

The number of concatenating symbols of a macro PDF417 is limited by the host buffer size. For example, a host with a disk-swapping operating system might have some 80 megabytes of free disk space. Thus, the buffer size may be as big as 80 megabytes, and the maximum number of symbols in a macro PDF417 message can be 80,000—with each containing up to approximately 1 kilobyte.

The reader of PDF417 symbols can be a laser scanner or a CCD camera. In 1992 Symbol Technologies announced its PDF1000 scanner, which equipped with a 15 million instruc-

Encodable Character Set: All 128 ASCII characters and binary data
Code Type: Continuous Character
Self-Checking: Yes
Symbol Size: Variable
Bidirectional Decoding: Yes
Number of Row Indicator Characters Required per Row: 2
Minimum Number of Rows per Symbol: 3
Maximum Number of Rows per Symbol: 90
Minimum Number of Data Columns: 1
Maximum Number of Data Columns: 30
Number of Symbol Length Descriptors Required: 1
Smallest Nominal Element Width: 0.0075 inch (0.191mm)
Smallest Recommended Nominal Element Height: 0.010 inch (0.254mm)
Maximum Data Character Density:
       BINARY Mode: 686 bytes per square inch (106.2 bytes per square centimeter)
       Printable ASCII Mode: 1,144 ASCII characters per square inch (177.2 ASCII characters per square centimeter)
Maximum Data Characters per Symbol:
       BINARY Mode: 1,108 bytes
       Printable ASCII Mode: 1,848 bytes
Non-Data Overhead: Four codewords per row plus three codewords per symbol
Additional Features:
       Edge-to-edge decodable
       Partial scans stitchable
       Error correction capability

Table 6.7: PDF417 Characteristics

This is a summary of various features of PDF417. For a more technical discussion of PDF417 see AIM-USA USS-PDF417 available from AIM-USA and the PDF417 Specification available from Symbol Technologies.

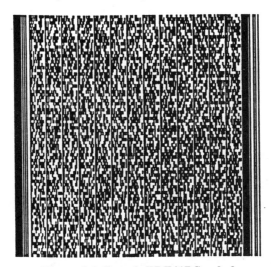

Figure 6.4: Sample PDF417 Symbol

tions per second (MIPS) processor raster, scans a PDF417 symbol at a speed of 560 scans per second. The PDF1000 laser scanner can decode a PDF417 symbol within a quarter second (including error correction).

The PDF417 symbol can use the same printing equipment as linear bar codes. The handheld laser scanner can read both PDF417 symbols and linear bar codes. Furthermore, a linear bar code reader with a modified decoder can read PDF417 symbols, although with slower performance.

Code 1

Code 1 is a public domain two-dimensional checkerboard code. It can encode the full ASCII 128-character set in addition to the same function characters of Code 128 and Code 16K. There are seven different sizes of the symbol containing 160 checkerboard squares in the smallest size up to 16,320 in the largest. The largest symbol, Code 1H, can encode 2,182 alphanumeric characters or 3,493 digits while correcting up to 2,240 bit errors.

Symbol Structure

Code 1 includes eight symbol versions used to encode different data lengths. The versions are Code 1A, B, C, D, E, F, G, and H, where A is the smallest and H is the largest symbol.

Each symbol consists of data segments which contain a two-dimensional checkerboard pattern representing the encoded data. The number of data segments are six for Code 1A, B, C, D, and E, and 16 for Code 1F, G, and H. Each symbol version has a unique pattern of bars running the center of the symbol, called the center bar pattern. This pattern divides the symbol into upper and lower half sections.

Pairs of vertical adjacent bar and spaces called the vertical reference patterns are used to separate data segments. Code 1F, G, and H also have horizontal reference patterns to separate data segments. Each vertical and horizontal reference pattern is terminated with a short perpendicular line segment called a cap, which is used to measure the extent of the symbol for decoding.

Symbol Versions

Each Code 1 Version A through H has an increasing number of checkerboard squares and symbol bytes. The number of horizontal and vertical squares and symbol bytes are:

Code 1 Version	Horizontal	Vertical	Bytes
A	16	10	20
B	20	14	35
C	28	20	70
D	36	30	135
E	48	42	252
F	68	60	510
G	92	88	1,012
H	136	120	2,040

Symbol Character Encodation

Each checkerboard square encodes one bit of data. A white square is a "zero" and a black square is a "one." The squares are used to encode 8-bit bytes of data in a rectangular array of two rows of four squares each. The most significant bit in the byte is in the top left corner of the rectangle, proceeding left to right through the upper row and then the lower row, to the least significant bit in the bottom right corner of the rectangle.

The data byte rectangles are split vertically into two 4-wide by 1-high segments by the center bar pattern and the horizontal reference patterns for some Code 1 versions. The vertical reference patterns can also split the rectangles vertically.

The symbol character bytes are ordered left to right and then top to bottom. Thus, the first byte is in the top left corner of the symbol and the last byte is in the bottom right corner.

Table 6.8: Code 1 Characteristics

Encodable Character Set: All 128 ASCII characters, 4 Function Characters, and 1 Pad Character

Code Type: Continuous
Character Self-Checking: Yes
Symbol Size: Variable
Bi-directional Decoding: Yes
Number of Segments per Symbol: 1-16
Number of Required Check Characters: 10 to 560
Current bar code industry print technology limits print width to 0.0075"[1]
Smallest Recommended Nominal Element Height: 0.010 inch[2]
Maximum Data Character Density
• Numeric Mode: 1,403 numeric characters per square inch[3]
• Alphanumeric Mode: 877 alphanumeric characters per square inch[3]
Maximum Bytes per Symbol[4]
• Code 1A = 10 data bytes and 10 check bytes
• Code 1B = 19 data bytes and 16 check bytes
• Code 1C = 44 data bytes and 26 check bytes
• Code 1D = 91 data bytes and 44 check bytes
• Code 1E = 182 data bytes and 70 check bytes
• Code 1F = 370 data bytes and 140 check bytes
• Code 1G = 732 data bytes and 280 check bytes
• Code 1H = 1,480 data bytes and 560 check bytes
Additional Features:
• Edge-to-Edge Decodable
• Error Correction Capability

---

1 This is a limitation imposed by the printing processes used in the bar code industry, not a limitation of the symbology. One can print a Code 1 symbol as small as the printing equipment can produce and the reading equipment can resolve. For example, in the application of marking IC wafers the nominal element could be 10 μm or less, presuming that the reading equipment could resolve such a narrow element.
2 This is a recommended value assuming the use of a CCD scanner, and not a limitation of the symbology.
3 These numbers are calculated by assuming that the smallest nominal element width (0.0075") and the smallest nominal element height (0.0075") are used.
4 The number of concatenating symbols of a macro Code 1 is limited by the host buffer size.

Figure 6.5
Sample Code 1C

Other 2D Symbols

Only Code 49, Code 16K, PDF417, MLC2D, and Code 1, of the 2D symbols, have comprehensive published specifications. Five others, Vericode, DataMatrix, ArrayCode, Phillips Dot Code, and Code 6 may be published in the future.

Vericode

In 1990 Carl, Robert Anselmo, and David Hooper were awarded U.S. Patent No. 4,924,078, filed in 1987, on what is today known as Vericode. Vericode is a rectilinear array of data cells as shown in Figure 6.6. Except for the border (the black cells shown below), each cell can take the value of "on" ("1") or "off" ("0"). The external data cells (shown outside the border) can be used for orientation, timing, or symbol identification. The internal data cells (shown inside the border) is where the data of the symbol is encoded. Figure 6.6 shows an internal matrix of data cells of 15 columns by 15 rows which permits 2224 (exp. 224) different symbols.

Using the same size symbol, one can vary the density of the data in the data array by changing the size of the data cell. Conversely one can hold the density constant and vary the size of the symbol. The symbol can be as large as optically readable. Due to the binary nature of the data cell, parity bits can be added to ensure the correct reading of the data under adverse conditions. Redundancy can also be built into the symbol allowing up to 50 percent of the symbol to be obliterated with no loss of data. The missing data is reconstructed with the aid of a computer and specific algorithm.

A complete Vericode symbol encoding 22 characters is shown in Figure 6.7. Note that the upper left, upper right, and lower left corner cells are "off" and that the lower right corner cell is "on." Vericode symbols can be positioned anywhere within a 360° orientation and through the location and status ("on" or "off") of the corner cells the symbol can be accurately decoded. Vericode symbols can be formatted to encode anywhere from 1 to 5,000 characters.

Figure 6.6
Vericode Matrix Array

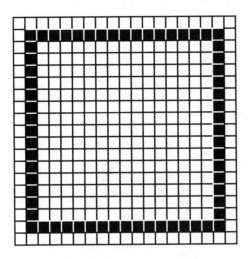

What is shown in Figure 6.7 is referred to as "MacroVericode" since the sides are greater than 0.75". Such symbols might be used where increased reading distance may be needed. Standard Vericode symbols range from 0.375" to 0.625" on a side. Such applications might include products, packaging, and documents. "MicroVericodes" range from 0.25" down to 0.0625" on a side. Applications for such symbols include electronic components, printed circuit boards, tools, tooling, and metal parts. In 1988, Veritec produced the smallest (to date) machine-readable symbol measuring 6 microns on a side containing 16 characters of data. Presently, there are no "public domain" published detailed specification for the encodation of Vericode.

Figure 6.7
Vericode Symbol Encoding 22 characters

DataMatrix

DataMatrix, f.k.a., Datacode was developed in 1989 by International DataMatrix of Clearwater, Florida. Where Vericode emphasizes security through secrecy, DataMatrix emphasizes storage of information. As shown in Figures 6.6 and 6.7 Vericode traditionally employs a border of "on" bits. DataMatrix, on the other hand, employs a frame half of which is solid and the other half alternating black and white cells, as shown in Figure 6.8.

Figure 6.8

DataMatrix Symbol Encoding 20 characters

The frame allows some self-clocking since it can be used to estimate label orientation and cell size. Symbol size can range from 0.001 inch per side to 14.0 inches per side. DataMatrix can encode from 1 to 2,000 characters in any language. 500 characters can be encoded with a 24-pin dot-matrix printer in a 1.0 inch square for numeric-only data to a 1.40 inch square for Full ASCII data.

DataMatrix has been adopted to identify surgical instruments in Japan and was adopted in 1993 as the format for the SEMI (Semiconductor Equipment and Materials International) standard for identifying silicon wafers (SEMI T2-93). Allegran Medical Optics is using DataMatrix in the robotic manufacture of interoccular lenses. IBM Toronto is laser etching a 2mm square DataMatrix symbol on PC boards containing 12 to 16 characters of information.

On August 21, 1992 announcement was made that Veritec had filed suit in Tampa Federal Court charging International DataMatrix with Patent Infringement as well as violations of other rights of Veritec.

ArrayTag

ArrayTag technology has been under development for the past four years. Development started at the University of Victoria (British Columbia) but is now driven by the spin-off company ArrayTech Systems. Forest products company MacMillan Bloedel Ltd., has supported the development of prototype ArrayTag systems for identifying logs and packages of lumber. The symbol can take many different forms and can be optimized for particular applications. Tagging of logs has been accomplished with an octagonal symbol while Figure 6.9 shows a generic rectangular ArrayTag symbol suitable for many applications.

The octagonal system for forest products applications contains 32 inner data cells and 16 contrasting border cells. The 32 data cells encode 24 bit binary identification numbers and 8 check bits including 7 cyclical redundancy code (CRC) bits. The octagonal symbol is well suited for affixing to near-circular logs.

ArrayTag is said to be more area efficient than that of any other published commercial code. While Figure 6.9 shows the encodation of 38 data cells, a symbol of 15 rows and 15 columns would realize 165 data cells for encodation. The encoding of data on ArrayTags may be binary, decimal, or alphanumeric and may include as many error detection and error correction cells as desired. Standards for such encodation and error detection/correction are presently being formatted.

Figure 6.9
ArrayTag Symbol Encoding 38 bits of Data

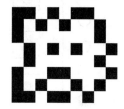

The rectangular symbol shown in Figure 6.9 uses "N" rows and "M" columns for encoding data for a contrasting border and for 4 cells (corner cells) that specify symbol orientation. The number of data cells is (N-2)(M-2)-4. The contrasting border of the ArrayTag defines an invariant closed contour using minimal symbol area, that is used by the image processing software to locate the symbol images. Such a border enables ArrayTag symbol images to be located on any background without the need for a quiet zone surrounding a symbol. Because the invariant closed contour is formed with contrasting cells, the resultant effect is a robust system that is relatively insensitive to lighting levels, shadows, and reflections. ArrayTag symbols may be well suited for applications requiring low-cost identification that must be read from a long distance, that must be read within a substantial depth-of-field and field-of-view, or that require reading many tags simultaneously. Such applications include the automatic tracking and sorting of objects such as logs, lumber, airline baggage containers, packages, paper rolls, and vehicles. ArrayTech also points to applications where large amounts of information must be stored within a small symbol, such as integrated circuits and electrical and mechanical components.

Phillips Dot Code

Phillips of Eindhoven, The Netherlands, has developed a 2D code known as Phillips Dot Code. Phillips developed this code for labeling small parts and not for storing large amounts of data on a label. A symbol consisting of a 8 by 8 matrix is shown in Figure 6.10. The four corner dots are always present. A dot in the second position of the first row and one in the first diagonal position indicate the start corner for decoding.

Dot Code symbols are square array of dots, from 6 by 6 to 12 by 12 in size, fitting the basic format shown in Figure 6.10. Ten of the dot locations constitute the "finder" pattern:
  • The four corner dots, all printed, clearly mark the symbol's boundaries
  • The four locations diagonally inward, with only the upper left one printed with a dot

and the other three left clear, indicate symbol orientation

• The two locations adjacent to the upper left dots, with only one printed distinguish the symbol from its mirror image.

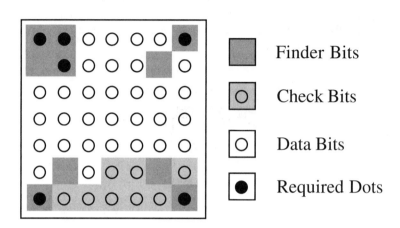

Figure 6.10
Phillips Dot Code

The remaining dot locations constitute a single, long, binary string working from left-to-right in rows from the top row to the bottom, with a printed dot signifying a "1" and a missing dot signifying a "0." Regardless of symbol size, the final 8 bits in the binary string are the check bits, a cyclical redundancy check on the preceding binary string.

Thus the number of data bits is the number of dot locations in each square array less the 18 overhead bits (10 finder and 8 check). The smallest 6 by 6 Dot Code encodes 36-18 = 18 bits, which may be thought of as a numeric value between 0 and (218 - 1) or 256,143. The largest 12 by 12 Dot Code encodes 144 - 18 = 126 bits which may well be interpreted as a string of characters (18 data characters in ISO 646 7-bit encodation).

The Dot Code specification calls for the dots to be roughly round, with a clear region between them equal in width to their diameter. The surrounding quiet zone is also one dot diameter wide. Thus the area required for an N by N Dot Code is (2N+1)X square, where "X" is the resolution of the print technology.

Dot Code may be printed as dark dots on a light substrate as illustrated in Figure 6.10. Alternately, it may be embossed, drilled, hot stamped, laser etched, or molded into parts as long as its image to a camera is an array of separated, relatively dark marks. Phillips has demonstrated a wide variety of installed applications ranging from laundry tags to serial numbers on small parts.

Lastly, the minimal quiet zone requirements make it possible for a larger Dot Code symbol to contain a completely valid smaller symbol. For this reason, sizes should not be mixed within an application and readers should be set to recognize only the exact size of Dot Code being used.

Code 6

Code 6, formerly known as UPSCodeSM, was specifically designed for the package distribution environment. A Code 6 label is a portable database that is applied to a package and carries with it all the information necessary for sorting, tracking and billing. Sophisticated image processing techniques are used to compensate for tilted or warped labels and to decode the label at any orientation.

Symbology Specifications
- High information density exceeding a hundred characters per square inch of paper
- Over-the-belt, omni-directional, unmanned reading
- Acquisition belt speeds exceeding 500 feet per minute
- Acquisition depth of field of 36 inches
- Acquisition belt width of 42 inches
- Label throughput exceeding 5000 labels per hour
- Very high decode rates
- Significant error correction capability

A Code 6 label is approximately one inch by one inch square and is comprised of a two dimensional honeycomb array of hexagons. Each of the hexagons represents one bit of information and can be either black or white. Located in the geometric center of the label are six alternating black and white concentric rings which constitute the bulls-eye pattern. This pattern allows the label to be located omni-directionally at high speeds. The hexagons are ordered in a grid consisting of 33 rows by 30 columns yielding a total of 990 hexagons. Accounting for the area occupied by the rings, this results in a total usable number of about 888 hexagons. Each hexagon is about 35 mils in size.

The data content of the label is represented partly in binary and partly as characters depending on context. Each character is represented by 6 bits of information. A total of 148 characters can be encoded if the entire message is represented as characters. A significant number of these characters are used for error correction.

The label information content is divided into a high priority message and a low priority message. The high priority message contains information needed frequently in the package handling process. The low priority message is accessed relatively infrequently. The high priority message is provided with about twice the error correction capability as the low priority message. Since label damage tends to occur at the outer edge or corners of the label, the high priority message is placed near the center of the label.

For a given sensor resolution, this symbology offers the maximum information encoding density of any other one dimensional or two dimensional symbology currently available. For example, an equivalent label printed in PDF417 symbology with the smallest element comparable to the dimension of one Code 6 hexagon will require a label surface approaching four times that of a Code 6 label for the same amount of data and error correction capability.

The Code 6 error correction process provides redundancy to allow full message recovery despite possible label deterioration in the shipping process. The label encoding process constructs the label using the Code 6 error correction encryption algorithms. The final stages of the decode process use an error correction decryption algorithm to extract the message.

Technology Components
Along with the development of the symbology, the Code 6 technology development consists of the following components:

(1) Over the Belt Reader

The over the belt reader consists of a line scan CCD camera with a high speed focusing mechanism. A 4096 element CCD array provides the required resolution over 42 inches of belt width. The camera box provides a folded optical path and holds the image acquisition and processing electronics. The illumination system consists of high pressure sodium lamps located in a specially designed reflector that yields uniform illumination across the belt. The level of illumination varies with height and is compensated for in software. Package height is measured using a light curtain system.

As packages flow past the reader, the package height is sensed and is used to focus the camera to the label surface. Pixel data acquired by the camera is converted to digital form and is amplified and compensated for any uneven illumination. The bulls-eye detector identifies the label location. Software correlation verifies the presence of the bulls-eye and identifies the precise center of the label. Image processing operations described earlier are performed on this image to locate the label direction and identify the centers of the hexagons. This process is followed by label reconstruction, error correction and decoding.

(2) Handheld Reader

A hand held reader can be used in those areas of the package handling operations where package speeds are limited. A handheld reader could also allow shippers to use the Code 6 symbology for their internal needs.

Label acquisition in the handheld reader is performed by means of a standard video area CCD array providing a resolution of 100 pixels per inch over the label image. Since the label is assumed to be in the field of view, the handheld reader does not require the high speed bulls-eye location circuitry of the over the belt reader. Instead, identification of the bulls-eye is performed in software. The rest of the decoding steps are similar to those in the over-the-belt case.

Two Dimensional Summary

All matrix symbols require 2-dimensional CCD scanners or 2D CCD video cameras and cannot be read easily by laser scanners due to the fact that the laser beam cannot intersect easily all of the cells without some level of skewing. If the applications for Matrix 2D symbols permit stationary scanners, the Matrix 2D symbols may provide a solution. Handheld 2D CCDs are not yet commercially available. Further, handheld 2D CCDs will need to overcome issues such as "jitter" to be commercially viable. Finally, there exists a patent issue with the handheld CCD scanner patent holder, Norand Corporation.

DataMatrix was the first with a standard in SEMI T2-93 even though Veritec is claiming that DataMatrix infringes on the Vericode patent.

We have established the data security for four (Code 49, Code 16K, PDF417, and DataMatrix) of the 2D symbologies. In 1992 The Center for Automatic Identification (CAI) at Ohio University published studies that demonstrated that Code 49 had 0 errors in over 15.9 million characters scanned and the Code 16K had 0 errors over 16.2 million characters scanned. In 1993, CAI conducted studies over PDF417 and DataMatrix. It was demonstrated that for these two symbologies where over 35 million symbols were scanned for each symbology 0 errors were reported.

AIM-USA has published uniform symbol specifications for Code 49 and Code 16K, PDF417 is in process, and the Code 1 Uniform Symbol Specification has just begun. With regards to data density, one must evaluate the type of reader to be used in scanning. Code

49, Code 16K, and PDF417 can be read by handheld laser scanners. These six symbologies can, and Code 1 must, be read by CCD scanners. Most laser scanners have licensed technology from the patent holder (Symbol Technologies). No CCD scanners have licensed technology from the patent holder (Norand Corporation).

Laser scanners require the height of the symbol element to be greater than the symbol element width. The USSs for Code 49 and Code 16K specify the height of the element to be 8 times the width of the element. The specification for PDF417 specifies the height of the element to be 3.00 times the element width. CCD scanners permit the symbol element height to be equal to its width. Consequently, making an apples-to-apples comparison of the symbol's data density can be a bit tricky. In July 1993, the American National Standards Institute MH10 SBC-8 Committee and the Automotive Industry Action Group published the results of a study of the various sizes of 2D symbols. Code 1, DataMatrix, PDF417, and Vericode were all able to put anywhere from 20 to 10,000 characters in appreciably similar surface areas. In under 100 characters, UPS sample codes additionally fared well. ANSI MH10 and AIAG also asked that to be considered in future standards Veritec (Vericode) and ID Matrix (DataMatrix) had to resolve their lawsuits by September 1993.

So given the need or desire to the maximum amount of information in the smallest amount of space, PDF417 and Code 1 are better candidates that Code 49 and Code 16K. And until matrix CCD scanners are the commonplace, PDF417 may be the better choice.

CHAPTER 7

Industry Standards

Appendix A to this text lists the various organizations involved in standards setting activities. It seems as if every association or industry group is in the process of writing a standard for its membership, with the result that we have far too many conflicting standards. All industries are interwoven and consequently must subscribe to a common set of standards

There are four primary types of bar code standards for product marking today: the UCC/EAN standards, Customer Part Numbers in Code 39 with FACT DIs (Data Identifiers), Supplier Part Numbers in Code 39 with FACT DIs, and a handful of other standards. Table 7.1 shows to which standards each of these industries subscribe.

UCC/EAN	Code 39 FACT DIs Customer Part #	Code 39 FACT DIs Supplier Part #	Other
Grocery	AIAG	CIDX	SEMI
Genl Merchandise	EIA-556-A	Microcomputer	ISBT
Mass Merchandise	EIA-J	Furniture	Graphics Industry
Electrical	EDIFICE	Fabric/Textiles	Health Care
EIA CEG	Telecommunications		U.S. Government
ATA	Primary Metals		NATO
Microcomputer	ODETTE		French Pharmaceutical
Telecommunications	CEFIC		
Published Products			
Office Products			
Furniture			
Plumbing			
HVAC			
Fluid Power			
Power Transmission			
Pharmaceutical			

Table 7.1: Industry Standards

It may also be instructive to learn that telecommunications is moving to the UCC/EAN standards, and for nonproduction parts and for general trade products, the automotive industry is also considering movement towards UCC/EAN.

Why Would a Supplier Not Wish to Use the Customer's Part Number?

The most cost effective point at which to mark a product is on the production line. At any other point in the distribution of the product, containers must be opened, and the individual items must be labeled as well as the shipping container. The point at which the customer is known is at order fulfillment, not at the packaging line. Some, though very few organizations manufacturer items to order, but most in this century will continue to build to stock. To use the customer's part number when marking product, concludes that marking will occur only when the customer is known. To wait until the customer is known, in most cases, denies the supplier the opportunity to take advantage of machine-readable markings between the packaging line and order fulfillment. Marking product at order fulfillment means a post-production process which is far more costly than marking product on the packaging line.

Why Would a Customer Not Wish to Use the Supplier's Part Number?

Supplier part numbers have historically been variable length, alphanumeric, with embedded significant special characters. Customers know what they call an inbound product, because they ordered it. However, they may not know how the supplier identifies this product. Regrettably most EDI conventions first implement the Purchase Order (850) not the Catalog (832); therefore the customer orders based on their stock keeping unit (SKU) code, not the supplier's. To employ supplier part numbers may mean that all product code fields in a product database would need to be equal in length to the longest part number; and while memory may be cheap, memory management is not cheap. Additionally, supplier A may have one part number and supplier B the same part number.

The most desirable product codes for all trading partners are fixed-length, numeric, check-digit protected product codes which includes the identity of the manufacturer. That system already exists; it is called U.P.C. and EAN.

Supplier vs. Customer Product Codes

Two types of product coding structures are typical. The first product code is one that is for general trade. General trade products are those where multiple customers receive the same product. The second variety of product code is one that is unique to a specific customer, i.e., a custom product. A third type of coding structure is one which includes process information, using supplier coding, and is accepted by all trading partners.

Manufacturer's with product destined for the general trade should mark their products with the manufacturer's product code. Either the manufacturer's product code or the customer's product code could appear on custom product. Mutual agreement between the trading partners should dictate which product code to use for custom product.

Some customers may request unique marking of product shipped to that customer. If the product is unique to that customer, such requests are reasonable. Suppliers should endeavor to provide bar code markings consistent with reasonable industry standards. Suppliers should communicate their part numbers and supplier identification to their customers. ANS X12 EDI (Transaction Set 832 - Price/Sales Catalog) or UN/EDIFACT (Message PRICAT - Price-Sales Catalog) may best serve this trading partner communication. Customers requesting customer-specific marking of general trade should become aware of the supplier's cost of marking product specifically for that customer. These costs include the additional cost for handling, labels, ribbon, amortization of equipment, label application, and profit margin. Since in all likelihood the customer is not known for general trade product at the point of packaging, supplier product codes are the only cost effective method of bar code marking.

Figure 7.1 shows an example of the problems associated with customer-specific marking. Each of the four suppliers sells one product to each of the four customers. If the trading channel uses supplier product codes, there are four codes. If the trading channel uses customer product codes, there are 16 codes. Customers who have an internal number to identify the product may establish an alias to identify that product. The database can have two indices, supplier code and internal code (alias). The input of either number can access and update the status of the physical product. The use of supplier product codes, internally and within the trade channel, limits the number of codes to the number of products in the channel. Establishing customer aliases doubles the number of codes. The use of customer product codes arithmetically raises the number of codes used within the channel linearly by the number of customers within the channel.

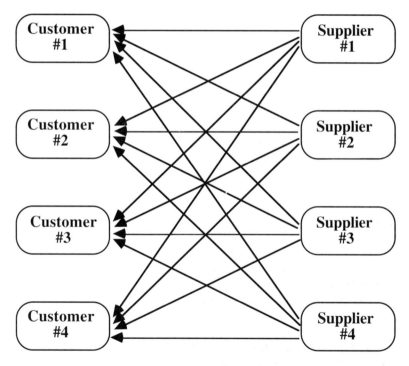

Figure 7.1

Alphanumeric vs. Numeric Product Codes

Coding structures can be either numeric or alphanumeric. The rationale for most alphanumeric structures is to establish some form of intelligence within the coding structure (Significant Coding). This intelligence may provide a specific meaning for a character string in given positions. Alternately, the intelligence may require more than the 10 possibilities for any given character position available with numeric coding. Oftentimes, the claim is that this intelligence provides human understanding of the elements of the code. Most alphanumeric systems have good intentions. As time passes, the needs of the enterprise violate these "coding systems." Invariably, instead of violating the coding system, the enterprise increases the length of the field by one or more positions. It is such practices that give rise to product codes of such a length as to be unreasonable. Such modification requires all persons within the enterprise, working with product codes, to re-learn the structure.

The coding structures designed for the 21st Century will be codes that reference a computer database. Companies using alphanumeric part numbers may not need to abandon them. People may still care to use them. Many contemporary systems now employ codes that reference a computer database. The intelligence of the code exists within the computer system. Computer databases can contain alternate part numbers, or "aliases." A numeric code "key" can provide the benefits of numeric coding without requiring any change to information exchanged between humans. Coding therefore may be nonsignificant. A common form of nonsignificant coding is that of sequential numbering. When manually entered, fewer errors occur with keying numeric structures than with alphanumeric structures. Keyboards for numeric entry are simpler, easier to use, and less costly. Processing of numeric strings of data is more efficient for computer systems than are alphanumeric strings of data.

Fixed Length vs. Variable Length Product Codes

Computer systems which utilize variable length product codes (product codes from numerous suppliers) must establish data field lengths that can support the longest code which may be input to the computer. Oftentimes, the maximum field length supports only one or a few products. Efficiency in memory management suffers when a majority of the data fields must support unused character positions. Editing fixed length fields, to ensure the correct number of characters were entered, is easier than editing variable length fields. Data manipulation of fixed length fields by computer systems is more efficient than variable length fields.

Determining When Product Codes Should Change

Product code changes should occur only when the change in a product is significant. If a change involves minor differences, and the new product is a replacement of the old, and the production of the old product ceases, the product code does not change. However, if the customer expects to be able to distinguish the new product from the old (such as a new version of software) and order accordingly, the enterprise should assign a new product code to the product.

Duplicate Product Codes Among Multiple Suppliers

Product codes may not be unique. Several suppliers may use the same code for different product. This can create major problems for distribution and end-user systems. To ensure uniqueness, the product code should include the identification of the supplier. Each industry conceivably could establish an agency to administer supplier identification schemes. This would presume that vertical industries truly exist and that there would be no crossover of product between industries. At this point in time, there are few, if any, vertical industries. Electronics suppliers ship to health care product manufacturers, automotive industry manufacturers, computer system manufacturers, and to other electronic industry manufacturers. The same multi-industry shipments also exist in chemical, primary metals, office products, computer products, media/supplies, sanitary products, furniture/furnishings, taping, adhesives, institutional foods, telecommunications, and graphics. To establish independent industry supplier identification agencies would require, at a minimum, a yearly investment in excess of $100,000.00 per year. Insofar as such assignment agencies already exist, this duplication of effort and expense will only drive up the cost of distribution in all industries. The most widely accepted supplier identification agencies in North America, Europe, Asia-Pacific, South America, and Africa are the Uniform Code Council (UCC) and the EAN International affiliates.

Product Code Recommendations for the 21st Century

- Unique Product Code,
- Supplier Product Code,
- Numeric Product Code,
- Non-significant Product Code,
- Fixed Length Product Code, and
- Product Code Includes Unique Identity of Manufacturer.

The UCC/EAN Standards for Identification of General Trade Products

The UCC is a not-for-profit organization responsible for the administration of the Universal Product Code (U.P.C.). Initially designed to serve the retail and distribution environments, the UCC system enables unique identification on a global basis for industries providing products for general distribution. Based on the requirements of its global constituency, the UCC and its international counterpart, EAN International, jointly released expanded sets of AIs (Application Identifiers) in 1990 and 1991, thereby permitting encodation of a wider range of secondary information within UCC/EAN-128 applications.

The U.P.C./EAN system is the identification standard for general trade products where the same product in the same packaging is sold to multiple trading partners in multiple industries. FACT Data Identifiers (DIs) are analogous to the AIs and have been implemented by the automotive, electronics, chemical, and other industries for internal use and where unique product is manufactured for and shipped to a specific customer. It is expected that both standards will coexist for the near term.

Uniform Code Council (UCC) and EAN International (EAN) coding provide for bar code symbols that serve the purposes of primary and secondary identification.

UCC Primary Product Identification

Primary identification is a coding structure which identifies the supplier of the product and a code for item identification. Primary identification at the item level has been achieved in industries which support the UCC/EAN standards through either a 12-digit U.P.C. symbol or a 13-digit EAN symbol. Primary identification at the multipack level has been achieved in these industries through a 14-digit Interleaved 2 of 5 symbol (ITF-14) for standard count multipacks of the same product.

The fixed length, numeric U.P.C., EAN, and ITF-14 structures have become bar code standards in many industries where the same product is shipped to many customers in multiple industry sectors. If the manufacturer ships product in grocery, mass merchant, general merchandise, home improvement, or any other retail distribution channel the UCC/EAN standards may be used for both primary identification and secondary identification. Increasingly, the industrial and commercial (nonretail) channels are adopting UCC/EAN standards.

The UCC/EAN standards for item and shipping container identification emphasize the supplier's product number, so product ID may be consistent and independent of the receiving trading partner and the industry or industries in which they participate. With very few exceptions, such as "Ship To: " and "Purchase Order Number" AIs, customer-specific information is looked up or cross referenced at the receiving end. This enables the supplier to mark one way for all trading partners.

UCC Secondary Product Identification

The Uniform Code Council (UCC) developed a Code 128-based serialized shipping container standard and supplementary identification coding architecture. This standard and associated architecture includes all-numeric qualifiers—Application Identifiers (AIs)—analogous to the alphanumeric FACT DI approach. The Application Identifiers (AIs) are an integral part of the U.P.C./EAN structure. The UCC/EAN Application Identifier standard provides for non-numeric fields where required (such as, customer purchaser order number).

UCC/EAN secondary identification is a coding format which identifies additional product or order information. Secondary identification information is printed in UCC/EAN-128 (A subset of Code 128) containing all numeric Application Identifiers (AIs) which define the structure, format, and intended use of the data which follows. Product specific information is information known at the time of manufacture and includes serial number, lot/batch number, and expiration date. Order specific information is information known at the time of order fulfillment and includes purchase order number, ship to location, carrier-assigned PRO number, and Serialized Shipping Container Code.

The fixed-length, numeric U.P.C., EAN, and ITF-14 symbols for primary product identification have become the bar code standards in many industries shipping the same product to many customers in multiple industries. Since their introduction in 1990, UCC/EAN-128 AIs for secondary identification have become the standard for a number of industries currently using U.P.C. and EAN for primary product identification.

FACT DIs for Custom-Engineered Product

Variable-length, alphanumeric product and shipment coding structures in the bar code symbology Code 39 have become standard in situations where a unique product is manufactured for and shipped to a specific customer. In this environment, the FACT DIs serve the customer specific identification needs very well.

FACT DIs for Serial Numbers

Many industries serialize their product and include bar code markings which encode the product serial number. Historically, these serial numbers have been variable length, alphanumeric, and encoded in Code 39. It is anticipated that many manufacturers may migrate their serial number encodation to the Code 128 symbology over time. When Code 39 is used, it is recommended that the FACT Data Identifier "S" be used to identify a serial number. When Code 128 is used, UCC/EAN-128 with the Application Identifier "21" is recommended for the same purpose. Retailers and non-retail distributors of serialized product should be able to scan both symbologies and make use of both the DI and AI options for product serial numbering.

Industrial Raw Materials

For raw materials used in a single industry, particularly where process information is important to the customer, industries may develop their own specifications for identifying items produced, shipped, stored, or consumed. Industries should collaboratively take requirements of each stage in the distribution chain, particularly the end-user, into account in developing these specifications. They may result in a structure or approach different from the product coding recommendations listed above, but the principles of supplier rather than customer identification still apply. Where industrial raw materials may also be offered in the general trade or retail marketplaces, industries should consider the UCC/EAN structures described above.

FACT DIs for Internal Applications

There are many more identification schemes than the simple identification of product, which must also be addressed. There are structures for returnable containers, storage locations, employee identification, and many of the other identification formats which have been addressed in the FACT Data Identifier Standards. It is for the benefit of lower cost software products to aid in the data collection process that these internal structures must be addressed. In a spirit of cooperation at a March 1993 joint UCC and EAN meeting, a new committee was established—the International Data Application Standards Committee. At is second meeting in March 1993, this committee agreed to the use of a UCC/EAN Application Identifier ("90") for internal applications. The preferred use of this AI is with the coding structures identified by the FACT Data Identifier Standard. Therefore, a new cooperative spirit exists between FACT and the UCC/EAN agencies.

Customer Databases Which Require Customer Part Numbers

It is recognized that many existing databases and application programs require that the data presented must reference the customer's part number. One possibility would be to provide the product with the supplier's part number. On the master carton label or shipping label a label could exist which would contain the customer's part number(s) for the product contained within the carton as well as the associated supplier part number. The part numbers could be distinguished from one another by either FACT Data Identifiers or Product ID Qualifiers in ANSI X12 (DE 235) or UN/EDIFACT (UNTDED DE EN 27372 7020) formats. Substantial label space could be eliminated if this associated information was encoded in PDF417.

Which Structures Should a Manufacturer Use? UCC/EAN or Code 39/FACT DIs?

Some manufacturers sell product only to industries embracing FACT DIs. Other industries sell product only to industries embracing the standard of the UCC and EAN. Such product should be appropriately marked. Manufacturers selling specific products to both industries should consider migration toward the UCC/EAN standards.

Those implementing data collection standards should seriously consider what information is known when various coding structures are assigned, e.g., a batch number is known at the packaging line where a purchase order number is not known until order fulfillment. Further, a supplier's part number is known at the packaging line while a customer's part number is not known until order fulfillment, except where the product is manufactured in a unit-level-specific build-to-order environment. Customer receiving areas would like each product received to have the customer's part number on the product. This may, in effect, either deny the supplier the opportunity to use the machine-readable coding within their own pre-order fulfillment operations or increase the cost for labeling product with the customer's part number. Information cross-referencing supplier and customer part numbers may be best served through the use of an electronic data interchange purchase order or price/sales catalog process.

All industries should carefully consider the efficiencies and data format simplicity of the U.P.C./EAN/ITF-14 Primary Identification coding structures. The exchange of customer part numbers via electronic data interchange and machine-readable data encoded with the supplier's part number should be carefully considered by any standards development work anticipating a recommendation for customer part numbers on individual products. New standards for products which are supplied to multiple customers in multiple industries should carefully weigh the benefit of the UCC/EAN-128 AIs for Product Specific Secondary Symbols. Existing standards for products which are supplied to multiple customers in multiple industries should seriously consider a migration to UCC/EAN-128 AIs for Product Specific Secondary Symbols.

C H A P T E R 8

Bar Code Reading Technology

Scanner Development

When Woodland and Silver applied for their circular bar code patent in 1949, a device to read the symbol was also proposed. This bar code scanner became the first of many designs to read bar code markings. The first industrial scanning system was installed by General Atronics (now Accu-Sort Systems) in 1960 at Scott Paper Company. It used a duo photocell system to scan a double row bar code designed for carton diverting purposes.

When the first retail system was installed in 1974 at Marsh's Supermarket in Troy, Ohio, it employed a scanning device designed by Spectra Physics Retail Systems. This system read the Universal Grocery Products Identification Code, now known as U.P.C., the specification for which had been released in 1972.

In industry, the wand scanner or light pen was developed and used with portable data collection devices, in contrast to the stationary devices used in supermarkets. The Railroad Retirement Board and the US Patent Office were the first major users of wand scanners, beginning around 1976. For nearly a decade the slot scanner and bar code wand reigned alone.

In 1980, the first handheld helium-neon (He-Ne) gas laser scanner was introduced by Symbol Technologies. It went through several engineering steps to become basically the same gas laser scanner used today. In 1986 the first generation of laser diode scanners appeared. These are solid-state devices, smaller, less expensive, rugged, and using less power than the He-Ne gas laser scanners. The second generation of laser diode scanners, or third generation of laser scanners, was introduced in 1988. These use visible light laser diode technology to eliminate the problems that arose when the inks or paper caused the codes to be invisible to infrared diode scanning devices.

In 1990 Symbol Technologies introduced its 8500 ALR reader capable of reading symbols that have a narrow element width of 0.015 inch from distances of two to eight feet. This same device is capable of reading lower density symbols (approximately 0.040-inch X dimension) at distances of up to 15 feet.

In 1990 Symbol Technologies introduced its PDF1000 handheld scanner specifically designed to read two-dimensional symbologies while at the same time providing enhanced reading of one-dimensional symbols that have localized printing defects.

In 1981 Norand Corporation produced the first handheld charge-coupled device (CCD) scanner. Norand's device used a xenon tube to create a flash of light to illuminate the symbol. A linear CCD element, employing a line of over a thousand detectors, was used to take a "snapshot" of the entire symbol. Each element of the linear CCD either observes a reflective area (a space) or an absorptive area (a bar). A second generation of CCD scanners uses banks of high-power visible light LEDs (light-emitting diodes) for illumination.

A third generation of charge-coupled device scanning was introduced in 1990 by Symbol Technologies to handle higher resolution codes and includes integral decoding. This device employs a matrix CCD similar to the elements in CCD video cameras, as opposed to the linear devices mentioned above. This CCD area detector is a matrix of photodetectors. Such devices are able to overcome problems associated with spots, voids, and bar edge roughness and permit the scanning of ultra-high density (very narrow bars), low density (wide bars), and new two-dimensional symbols with the same device. Matrix CCDs can be either fix-mounted or handheld.

Components of a Bar Code Reader

Scanner

Bar code reading devices are often called bar code readers or scanners. This definition is imprecise insofar as the scanner is an integral part of the reading system. The true term for the system is a bar code reader. Literally, the bar code *scanner* illuminates the symbol and examines the reflectance from the symbol. Areas of high reflectance are considered to be spaces and areas of low reflectance (absorption) are considered to be bars.

All bar code readers use an *electro-optical system* to read bar codes. The hardware components common to all bar code readers include a light source, optics, photodetector, and signal processing circuitry. To see the bars and spaces of a bar code symbol, the scanner's *optics* direct the internal *light source* onto the symbol which reflects light back into the *photodetector*. The photodetector measures and maps the reflected light (illuminated spaces reflect more light than do illuminated black bars) and converts the data to an electrical signal. The *signal processing circuitry* transmits signals to a decoder which translates the data into useful information.

Decoder

While individual manufacturers rely upon proprietary techniques to decode a bar code symbol, the function of the decoder is similar across all types of decoders.

Once the photodetector has converted the reflected pattern of bars and spaces to an electrical signal, this signal is then digitized. The digitization process occurs as the circuitry and decoder software measure the strength of the reflected optical signal from the scanner. If the reflectance is higher than a certain threshold, the signal is considered to be a space, and if lower than yet another threshold, considered to be a bar. The decoder then assigns the correct *binary assignment ("0" or "1")* to the signal. By translating all signals received from a single symbol, the decoder builds a complete message.

The decoder performs several functions in the decode process. First, the decoder determines the width of each bar and space. A scanner that uses a moving beam measures width as a length of time. The width measurement is accomplished by determining the length of time that the scanner observes low reflectance (bars) or high reflectance (spaces). Alternately, the decoder may clock the length of time between transitions from light to dark and dark to light. Second, the decoder ensures that valid quiet zones exist at both ends of the symbol. Third, the decoder maps the number of widths seen (quantizing) to the number of widths within the symbology. Code 39, Interleaved 2 of 5, Codabar, and MLC-2D have two widths. U.P.C./EAN, Code 128, and Code 16K have four widths. Code 93 has five widths. Code 49 and PDF-417 have six widths. Fourth, the decoder ensures that the number of element widths is consistent with the encoding rules for the symbology. Finally, the decoder compares the bar width and space patterns to a table of stored values to determine the data within the symbol.

Figure 8.1 shows three stages in the scanning of the Code 39 symbol, *$M*, leading to the digitization of the reflectance scan profile and assignment of binary values to the wide and narrow bars and spaces. These binary values are then compared to the table of stored values in the decoder, converting the binary values to the appropriate ASCII characters corresponding to the scanned symbol.

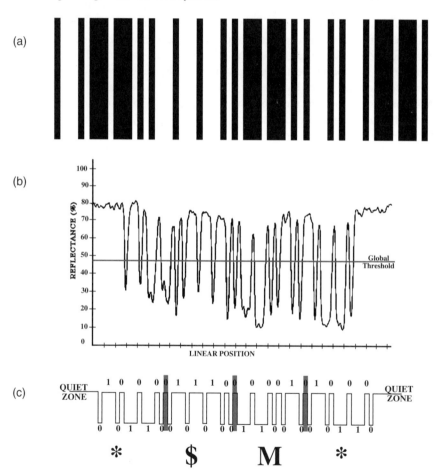

Figure 8.1: Scanning the Code 39 Symbol "*$M*"

This example shows three stages in the decoding of a simple bar code message: (a) illustrates the Code 39 symbol to be decoded; (b) shows a profile of the observed reflectivity versus linear position across the symbol; and (c) shows the resulting digitization of the reflectivity profile as a binary value "0" or "1" for each linear position within the scan. Linear position is measured by time displacement of a scanning spot or by actual position on a linear or area CCD sensor.

In some readers, the decoder may have to decide which of several bar code symbols is being read. *Autodiscrimination* is an automatic process that determines the specific symbology of the bar code symbol. Decoders are available that can autodiscriminate up to a dozen bar code symbologies. Increasing the number of algorithms to be employed in decoding a specific symbol increases the mathematical possibility that a printing defect in the symbol may cause it to be interpreted as a valid symbol in another symbology. I recommend that when autodiscrimination is employed, the number of symbol options activated within the reader be only those symbols with which the bar code reader would likely be confronted.

Most symbologies are bidirectional, which means they can be scanned from left to right or from right to left. Generally, the direction of the scan can be determined by the start and stop pattern of the symbol. As an example, the start/stop pattern of a Code 39 symbol is NB WS NB NS WB NS WB NS NB ("N" is narrow, "W" is wide, "B" is bar, and "S" is space). If the pattern seen by the decoder is in the above sequence, the decoder knows the symbol has been read left to right. If, on the other hand, the sequence is reversed, the decoder knows the symbol has been read right to left. Once the direction of the scan has been determined, the data is stored in a buffer as if the symbol were read left to right.

Moving-beam systems provide the opportunity to view a symbol many times in one second and can offer an additional check, known as a *voting algorithm*, where two or more scans of the same symbol are made, decoded, and compared. Only when three adjacent decodes agree does the device recognize the signal as a valid bar code symbol and pass along the data.

The output of the decoder is a binary signal which must then be presented to some form of data collection device. Most decoders have a variety of output options including transistor-to-transistor logic (TTL) and RS232C. The coding format could be binary coded decimal (BCD), asynchronous ASCII, or extended BCD interchange code (EBCDIC) (see Chapter 11's discussion of Data Collection).

Symbology Identifiers

In 1990 Automatic Identification Manufacturers adopted a set of symbology identifiers that decoders would pass to applications software to signal the software as to which bar code was read and with what options. Such identifiers would also enable applications software to determine whether the entry was scanned or key-entered. It is imperative that if the UCC/EAN systems are to work as they were intended, symbology identifiers must be incorporated in all reading equipment. These symbology identifiers are fully listed and explained in Appendix C to this text.

Illumination Sources

All types of bar code scanners have a light source which illuminates the printed symbol and whose reflectance from the printed symbol is evaluated by a photodetector. Either the illumination from the light source is highly focused through lensing between the light source and the symbol, or the lensing system in front of the photodetector tightly focuses the reflected light from the symbol back to the photodetector.

Today's bar code scanners typically illuminate symbols with either infrared light sources (in the 900 nanometer wavelength range—B900) or visible-red light sources (in the 600 nanometer to 700 nanometer wavelength range—B670). Scanners employing helium-neon laser illumination operate at 632.8 nanometer. Visible light-emitting diodes (LEDs) employed in wand scanners operate in the 670 nanometer to 700 nanometer range, most typically at approximately 670 nanometer. Infrared LEDs (also employed in wand scanners) operate in the 800 nanometer to 950 nanometer range. Infrared laser diodes employed in noncontact fixed-beam and moving-beam readers generally operate in the 900 nanometer range. Newer introduced visible light laser diodes operate in the 670 nanometer to 680 nanometer range.

Most commonly, bar code applications stipulate a visible-red light source. In such applications poor symbol contrast will result if the bars are printed with ink colors having red pigmentation. Bars printed in red, yellow, orange, reddish-purple, or reddish-brown, for example, will not appear sufficiently different from the white spaces when viewed by a red light source, such as that used in He-Ne, visible red laser diodes, and many wand scanner reading devices.

Another common contrast problem results when the symbol is to be read by a scanner having an infrared light source. A printed bar with an ink that has a low carbon content will be unseen by the scanner, though to the human eye this symbol may appear totally acceptable. Further, a popular method of thermal printing is with organic papers. Most organic papers cannot be read with an infrared reading device.

Many solid-state devices—lasers, light-emitting diodes, even light-sensitive transducers—work most effectively with infrared light, generally well above 900 nanometers in wavelength. Unfortunately, many commonly used inks are blind to infrared. That is, many of the inks observable by the human eye cannot be seen by infrared scanners. Therefore, if an infrared scanner is to be used, bar code messages must be printed with a carbon-based ink.

Carbon inks are not as physically stable as other popular inks. Carbon inks may cause problems—smears, wear on the print mechanisms, and the like—resulting in higher costs. The main economic issue, however, lies in the cost of putting bar coded messages on an item—packages, documents, etc. If the machine-readable label is to be printed with a special ink, every item must be processed twice—once for the text, artwork, etc., and a second for the bar code. If a labeler wants to use carbon inks, it would be perfectly acceptable since carbon inks can be read at visible-red wavelengths. However, present technology makes it just as easy to design suitable hardware for scanning visible red.

It may be that the better approach is to use visible-red reading equipment in all applications. Otherwise, systems that try to use scanning devices that operate only in the infrared portion of the spectrum will not be able to capitalize on some of the coming printer innovations. These include ink-jet, thermal-transfer, and electrostatic printers; printing inks capable of standing high temperatures; and inks that diffuse into substrates to give very reliable, long-life labels.

In supermarket scanning implementations, many aluminum cans have the shiny metallic surfaces showing through white, red, or yellow "bars." Since we generally consider the bars to be the printed area, it appears that what is being printed is the bars when in reality it is the spaces. One would presume that a shiny surface has more reflective qualities than a white surface. Here we must draw the distinction between "specular reflection" and "diffuse reflection." Specular reflection is "the reflection of light from a surface at an equal but opposite angle to the angle of incidence, mirrorlike reflection qualities." Diffuse reflection is "the process by which incident flux is redirected over a range of angles." The specular reflection quality of shiny surfaces causes the incident light to be redirected away from the light source and detector in the scanning system, unless the detector is in the plane of the reflected light, e.g., a wand scanner held exactly perpendicular to a symbol surface.

Consequently, little reflected light reaches the detector, as if the detector were receiving light from a dark bar. The white printed spaces operate as white spaces always do, and the shiny bars reflect the light away from the detector causing the shiny bar to appear as a dark bar.

To be certain that bar code symbols can be read by virtually all bar code scanning devices presented to the scanner, it is best to evaluate the printed symbol in the infrared spectrum. To be certain that bar code scanning devices can read virtually any symbol presented to the scanner, it is best to utilize visible-red scanning devices.

Types of Bar Code Scanners

Bar code scanning devices can be categorized in terms of the scanning process, namely, whether movement is provided by the scanning device or by some motion of the object to which the bar code symbol is attached. (Is the device fixed beam or moving beam?) A third category of scanner is an imaging device that functions similarly to that of a video or photographic camera. The entire symbol is illuminated by a light source—xenon flashtube, light-emitting diode (LED), incandescent, or laser diode—and the image is reflected back to a photosensitive semiconductor component referred to as a charge-coupled device (CCD). Table 8.1 categorizes these devices.

Fixed Beam	Moving Beam		Charge-Coupled Device (CCD)	
	X-Axis	*Raster*	*Linear Array*	*Matrix Array*
Handheld (Wand/Gun)	Handheld Laser	Handheld Laser	Handheld CCD	Handheld
Conveyor	Conveyor	Conveyor	Conveyor	Conveyor
Integrated	Desk Top	Slot (P-O-S)		Scan Lamp

Table 8.1: Types of Bar Code Scanners

This table shows a brief summary of the types of bar code scanners. Fixed-beam and moving-beam types move a sensitive spot across the object being scanned by either moving the object or moving the spot. The linear array and matrix array CCD scanners use some form of flood illumination with measurement by an array of sensitive photodetectors that are picture elements, with the key scanning done electronically using the image obtained.

Fixed-Beam Scanners

A fixed-beam scanner depends upon external motion to read the symbol. This motion can be provided by an operator moving the scanner across the symbol or by providing movement to the symbol in front of the scanner. The following section discusses the various types of fixed-beam readers: wand scanners, handheld noncontact scanners, conveyor fixed-beam scanners, and fixed-beam scanners integrated into other devices.

Wand Scanners

One of the more common and popular bar code scanning devices is the handheld wand scanner, sometimes referred to as a "light pen." Its popularity stems from its portability and low cost. Here the operator provides the scanning motion by moving the wand scanner across the symbol in a smooth sweeping motion, traversing the leading quiet zone across all of the bars and spaces and through the trailing quiet zone. Oftentimes when unable to successfully decode a bar code symbol with a wand scanner, an operator will attempt to scan more slowly. In most cases, the operator would be well advised to try to scan a little

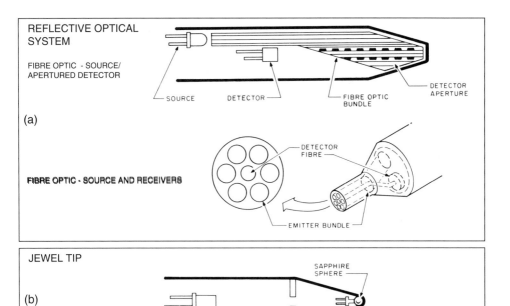

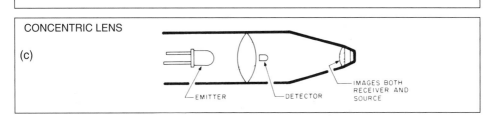

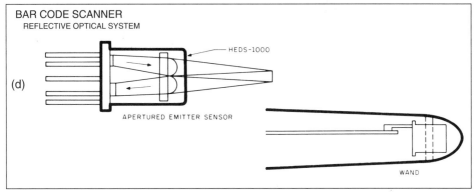

Figure 8.2: Typical Wand Scanners

The least expensive and most common form of scanner is the handheld wand scanner, sometimes called "light pen." Whatever variation is used, the scanning is provided by the movement of the human hand and arm, using a smooth sweeping motion traversing the leading quiet zone, across all the bars and spaces, and on through the trailing quiet zone. In most cases the optics are set up so that the tip of the wand must be in contact with the symbol being scanned. At (a) we see a fiber optic bundle version; (b) is a jeweled tip version; (c) is a version that uses a lens assembly; and (d) is an apertured emitter/sensor version.

(a)

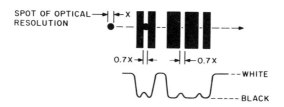

(b)

Matrix Printer characteristic defects

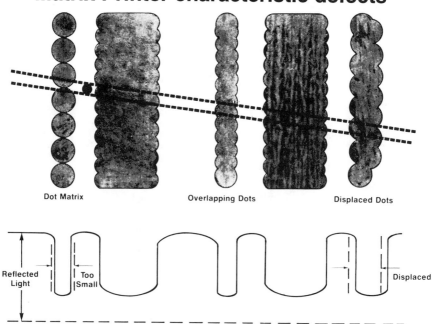

Figure 8.3: Effects of Relative Aperture Size

For all bar code scanning processes, the sensitive aperture of the scanning spot must be matched to the symbol being read. (a) If the aperture is too large, more than one adjacent bar or space may contribute to the effective image. (b) If the aperture is too small, printing defects may dominate over the real data of bars and spaces.

faster—not slower. Increasing the speed at which the wand scanner is moved across the symbol also tends to minimize the amount of jerking motion associated with slower scanning, for it is often this jerking motion that causes difficulty in reading bar code symbols. Most wand scanners respond to a wide range of different sweep velocities and accelerations. However, these velocities and accelerations cannot change significantly over the sweep through the symbol. With manual scanning shorter symbols are recommended because it is hard to maintain a relatively uniform velocity over longer symbols. The longer the symbol, the greater the difference in velocity at the end of the scan versus the beginning of the scan. Wand scanners are generally rated as being able to support scanning speeds of 3 to 30 inches per second.

A wand scanner consists of a pen-shaped housing and a light source that emits a specific wavelength through either a fiber-optic bundle version (Figure 8.2(a)), a jeweled tip (Figure 8.2(b)), a lens assembly (Figure 8.2(c)), or an apertured emitter/sensor (Figure 8.2(d)). As the operator moves the wand scanner across the symbol, the reflectance differences between bars and spaces are detected by a photoreceptor. The receptor converts these differences to an analog signal (see Figure 8.1(b)), which is then passed on to the decoder.

Wand scanners are referred to as contact scanners since they generally require physical contact with the symbol. Most wand scanners, however, allow the tip to be lifted slightly, to accommodate protective coatings of films on the symbol. The distance that the tip of the wand scanner can be from the symbol is no more than 0.05 inch and is referred to as depth of field.

The aperture width is more important in wand scanners than in laser-based scanning systems. The aperture width of the wand scanner should be approximately the same size as the

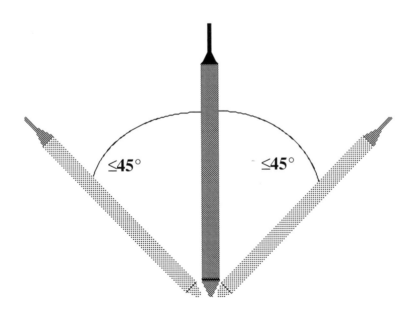

Figure 8.4: Permissible Tilt Angles of Wand Scanners

The optics of wand scanners are designed for a certain range of tilt angles relative to the plane of the symbol being scanned. While a ±45° range as shown here is typical, some wand scanners have a tighter tilt angle specification, such as ±25°.

narrow bar it is expected to read. If the aperture width is significantly larger than the X dimension of the symbol (as shown in Figure 8.3(a)), the wand scanner may find adjacent bars in the "scanning window" at the same time, reducing signal strength and rendering the symbol harder to read. If the aperture size is too small and confronts poorly printed symbols (as shown in Figure 8.3(b)), the scanner may erroneously see a printing defect as a bar or space where none exists.

Wand scanners are appropriate tools for scanning symbols on a smooth, flat, rigid surface where the wand scanner can be maintained within a range of angles perpendicular to the symbol. Irregular surfaces cause a bouncing effect in the wand scanner, producing reflectance signals which incorporate the bounce. This works against easy scanning. Pliant surfaces, such as a loaf of bread, also cause problems, since the sinking of the wand scanner into the surface adds a jerky motion to the scanning process. Curved surfaces and symbols that are much below or above the operator's torso yield yet another problem. Wand scanners are designed to function within a certain range of angles from perpendicular to the surface of the symbol, as is shown in Figure 8.4. When these angles are exceeded, insufficient reflectance is received by the scanner to properly process the signal from the symbol.

Some wands are designed for optimum performance when used at an angle of 25° from vertical. Wand scanner angle attitude may cause the spot of light to grow so that the spot of light exceeds a small multiple of the X dimension of the symbol. Too large a spot may cause a low first-read rate.

When reading through transparent films of any kind, some wand scanners cannot focus on the symbol surface at right angles because the surface reflections obscure anything beneath the surface. Designers of fiber optic wand scanners have attempted to circumvent this issue by having the symbol illuminated at a prescribed angle to the wand axis while the reflected light is sensed along the wand axis. Apertured emitter/sensors (such as HP HEDS sensors—Figure 8.2(d)) provide cross lighting while concentrating energy in an illuminated spot. Such a design permits reading through transparent media of at least a hundredth of an inch at any angle plus or minus 45° from vertical.

A wand scanner should be able to successfully read the bar code symbols in the application at least 85 percent of the time with the first pass of the wand scanner. This is referred to as an 85 percent first pass read rate. If operators experience first pass read rates substantially below this 85 percent level, frustration occurs and the bar code data collection application suffers. Where first pass read rates do fall below 85 percent it is recommended that the quality of the printed symbol, condition of the wand scanner, and operator use be checked immediately.It should be noted that many application specifications consider 85 percent too low; 95 percent is the current target for first pass read rate.

Wand scanners have a number of benefits and limitations of whichthe purchaser of scanning devices should remain aware. These considerations are listed in Table 8.2.

General Considerations
- Aperture should match X dimension of symbols
- Degree of tilt permitted
- Light source wavelength

Advantages
- Low cost
- Low power consumption
- Compact and lightweight

- Proven technology
- Rugged design

Drawbacks
- Operator training required
- Requires flat, smooth, rigid surface
- Reads long symbols with difficulty
- Lower first-read rate: higher frustration factor than lasers
- Abrades symbol
- Tip needs periodic replacement

Table 8.2: Wand Scanner ("Light Pen") Selection Considerations

When considering the use of a handheld wand scanner for bar code acquisition, this list of issues should be addressed.

Fixed-Beam, Noncontact, Handheld Scanners

Incorporating laser diode technology along with handheld, fixed-beam scanning produces what is known as a handheld, fixed-beam, noncontact scanner. These scanners still rely upon the operator to provide the scanning movement, but permit the operator to scan the symbol at a greater distance from the symbol. Many of these handheld, fixed-beam, noncontact scanners employ an infrared light source unable to be seen by the human eye. Since these devices are noncontact, a visible aiming light is often provided within the scanner to facilitate positioning.

In spite of the benefits of lower cost than moving-beam systems, expanded depth of field over wand scanners, and improved field of view over moving-beam readers and linear arrays (limited only by a consistent, smooth, sweeping stroke across the bar code symbol by the operator), existing handheld, fixed-beam readers are an "intermediate technology." In my opinion, more promise exists with moving-beam readers embracing the visible-red spectrum.

Fixed-Beam, Fixed-Mount, Noncontact Scanners

In some conveyor applications and present mail sorting operations scanning is accomplished by moving the bar code symbol past the scanning aperture(s) so that the movement is able to present each bar and space or short bar and tall bar before the scanner.

In applications where the symbol is moved past the scanner, a single opportunity is provided to the scanning device to decode the signal. Fixed-beam conveyor scanning devices typically have a limited depth of field. Oftentimes an additional photosensor detects the presence of the object bearing the bar code symbol and if the symbol is not read correctly, the object is diverted to a recirculation route or manual handling exception area. The principal advantage of fixed-beam scanners is that they are less expensive and have no moving parts, as compared to their moving-beam counterparts. The principal disadvantages are that the bar code symbol must be relatively close to the scanner, and the distance, as well as the location of the symbol, must be tightly controlled. As we will see in our following discussions of moving-beam scanners, better readability occurs when the symbol is in a stepladder configuration rather than in a picket fence orientation relative to the object's direction of travel past the scanner. If this is the case, then why do standards for shipping containers require symbol orientation in the picket fence manner? When many of the standards for shipping containers were being developed, fixed-beam systems were a dominant form of

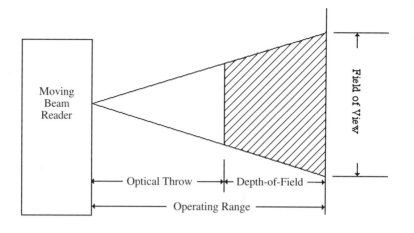

Figure 8.5: Scanner Distance Terminology

All scanners—wand, moving-beam, fixed-beam, and handheld—have a common distance termi-
nology shown here. Focal distance is the optimum distance for optical focus at the scanner's detec-
tor. Depth of field is the range of distances centered on the optical focal distance at which the
scanned symbol is sufficiently in focus to be read without error. Optical throw is the minimum dis-
tance from scanner to symbol. Operating range is the maximum distance from scanner to symbol.
For a moving-beam scanner, the field of view is the maximum length of a scannable symbol, a limit
that depends on distance to the symbol and the limits of the beam's movement.

Figure 8.6: A Fixed-Beam Scanner Component

Fixed-beam scanner components such as this can be integrated into transport systems of equip-
ment in order to read bar codes on objects as they pass by.

Figure 8.7: A Moving-Beam Scanner

Moving-beam laser scanners permit an expanded depth of field, thus yeilding greater operating ranges, and they presently provide the greatest benefit to the industrial and commercial community.

conveyor scanning. When these types of readers are mounted on the side of a conveyor, the symbol must be in the picket fence orientation. Once these standards were in effect, changes to stepladder configurations would have been disruptive to the material handling process.

In any optical system, focus is paramount to the crispness and clarity of the reflected image. An out-of-focus photograph is fuzzy, and the outlines of its subjects are indistinct. Fuzzy and indistinct lines distort the reflection of bars and spaces to a point where the transition between bar and space cannot be discerned. The range of distances in which a bar code symbol will be in focus is called depth of field (DoF). (DoF is the range between the maximum and minimum distance at which a bar code symbol can be read.) One method of determining this range is to define the optimum distance (or focal point) from the symbol to the scanner, and then define the range of distances on both sides of the focal point where the target will be in sufficient focus for the system's signal conditioning circuitry to acquire the bar/ space pattern of the symbol. An example would be a scanner whose optical focal point is three inches with a one-inch depth of field. A second method is to define the depth of field as ±0.5 inch. Both methods yield the same result, namely, that the scanner will be able to resolve a bar code symbol that is between 2.5 inches and 3.5 inches away.

For wand scanners, the depth of field is defined as the maximum distance that the wand scanner tip could be from the symbol and still achieve a good scan. This differs from noncontact scanners, where the focal point of the scanner is extended further in space through lens assemblies or the use of coherent light sources, e.g., lasers. As with a camera, a target could be too far away or too close. The distance from the reader to the near edge of the depth of field is referred to as optical throw. The combination of optical throw and depth of field is known as a bar code scanner's operating range, as illustrated in Figure 8.5.

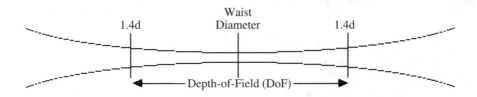

Figure 8.8: Laser Beam Waist and Optical Resolution

As a laser beam projects out of a laser scanner, it is a tightly focused, pencil-like beam of some transverse diameter. A characteristic of such beams is that the transverse diameter depends upon the distance from the source. The beam's diameter starts out at some value at the source. It shrinks with distance until a minimum transverse diameter called the "waist diameter" is reached at the focal distance L, after which the transverse diameter grows again with increasing distance from the source. The √2d points on either side of focal distance L define the depth of field limits (DoF$_{LIM}$) for the laser beam.

A fixed-beam reader is capable of reading a symbol moving in front of it at speeds ranging from 2 to 200 inches per second (10 to 1000 feet per minute) when the width of the narrow element is 0.01 inch. Symbols with narrow elements need to move more slowly than symbols with wider elements. Fixed-beam readers usually operate at transport speeds of 18 inches per second (90 feet per minute).

Integrated Fixed-Beam Scanners

Fixed-beam scanners may often be integrated into some form of transport mechanism. Such a mechanism may be in the form of a mail sortation system or a medical diagnostic device transport system having bar code symbols on test tubes within the transport. Additionally, fixed-beam scanners may be integrated into time and attendance terminals to serve as bar code badge readers. These types of devices are quite compact which aids in easy integration with the rest of the system. An example of such a fixed-beam scanning device is shown in Figure 8.6.

Moving-Beam Scanners

Most moving-beam scanners (see Figure 8.9) in today's environment are laser scanners. Laser technology is the science that deals with the generation of coherent light in small but powerful beams. The word laser is an acronym for Light Amplification by the Stimulated Emission of Radiation. Laser light has unique properties. A laser beam is one color, or monochromatic. If the light is one color, then it is also of one wavelength. If the wavelengths are stimulated so that they are in phase, the beam is coherent. Incoherent light is illustrated by an ordinary light bulb, which emits white light. White light is incoherent because it has all visible colors and some that are not visible. It is therefore called panchromatic. It is also transmitted in all directions from the light source and cannot be concentrated or controlled. Laser light can be controlled because the beams are of the same wavelength and in phase with one another.

All bar code scanning devices have a specified depth of field (as shown in Figure 8.5). The directional and coherent nature of laser light permits an expanded depth of field; the concentrated power of laser light can improve the laser scanner's optical throw. This combination yields a greater operating range. Laser scanners further focus the light source

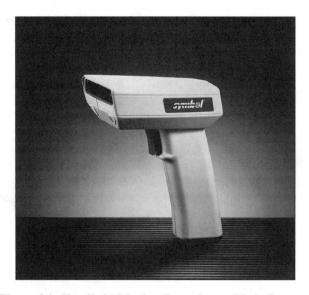

Figure 8.9: Handheld Moving-Beam Laser Diode Scanner

while most other scanners focus the reflected light. Combining this focused light with the coherent nature of laser light, a narrow band optical filter tunes the received signal to only that specific wavelength of the laser. This provides greater immunity to ambient lighting conditions, leading to improved signal quality and generally better scanning.

In my opinion, laser scanners provide the greatest benefit to the industrial and commercial community where rapid and accurate data acquisition is required. The coherent, monochromatic laser light exists in a focused spot, generally less than a hundredth of an inch in diameter. The light source illumination is focused through a set of optics onto a moving mirrored surface which makes the illuminated "spot" appear to be a continuous "line of light." The movement of the mirrored surface can be rotating in nature, as in the case of a polygonal mirror, or reciprocating in nature, as in the case of a "flipper mirror" (left-to-right-to-left, etc.). A reciprocating mirror may be controlled by a reversing motor or by an electromechanical resonance, as with a tuning fork. The reversing motor may be ill-favored due to the inertial force applied to the motor as reversing occurs, lessening the operational life of the motor.

The light in a laser beam is extremely directional. It is focused by a lens into a narrow cone and projected in one direction. The direction of the laser beam is the result of optics at the ends of the laser light source. The laser, when focused to a fine, hairlike beam, can concentrate all of its power into the beam. If the beam were allowed to spread out, it would lose power. Confinement of large amounts of power into a narrow beam permits focus over a greater depth of field. With a greater depth of field, not so much precision is required in presenting the symbol to the scanner.

Figure 8.10 shows some of the specific features of a laser beam. The beam's focal length (L) is the center of its depth of field. At this point the transverse diameter of the beam is smallest; the beam's waist is the transverse diameter at its focal length. At the $\sqrt{2d}$ points in Figure 8.10, the beam loses its collimation and begins to diverge (and lose illumination

Figure 8.10: Desktop Moving-Beam Scanner

power). To reliably read a bar code, the maximum diameter of the beam cannot exceed $\sqrt{2}$ times the minimum bar width. The smaller the X dimension, the less the available depth of field. Remember, however, that the depth of field can be extended into space by increasing its optical throw.

To calculate the depth of field of a laser scanner, we need to define two variables:

1. The laser spot diameter at the waist.
2. The wavelength of the light source.

The $\sqrt{2d}$ points in Figure 8.8 are where the laser beam transverse diameter has increased to $\sqrt{2}$ times the waist diameter. This is defined as the limits of the depth of field.

Depth of field is calculated:

$$\frac{\pi(d^2)}{2\lambda}$$

where:

$\pi = 3.1415927\ldots$
d = Waist diameter
λ = Wavelength of light source
      633 nanometers = $24.92 \cdot 10^{-6}$ inch (red light)
      900 nanometers = $35.43 \cdot 10^{-6}$ inch (infrared light)

Using the above formula, Table 8.3 shows depth of field values for visible-red (633-

"X" Dimension	Optimized Spot Size @ √2d Points (Depth of Field$_{LIM}$)	Depth of Field @ 633 nm	Depth of Field @ 900 nm
0.002	0.0028	0.252	0.177
0.004	0.0057	1.009	0.709
0.006	0.0085	2.269	1.596
0.008	0.0113	4.034	2.837
0.010	0.0141	6.303	4.434
0.012	0.0170	9.077	6.384
0.014	0.0198	12.355	8.690
0.016	0.0226	16.137	11.350
0.018	0.0255	20.423	14.365
0.020	0.0283	25.213	17.734
0.022	0.0311	30.508	21.458
0.024	0.0339	36.307	25.537
0.025	0.0354	39.396	27.710

Table 8.3: "X" Dimension versus Depth-of-Field

For a given symbol's narrow element width X, this table shows the optimal beam diameter (spot size) at the depth of field limits (DoF$_{LIM}$) and the corresponding depth of field values at two common wavelengths. All table values are expressed in inches.

nanometer) and infrared (900-nanometer) light sources for various X dimensions.

Table 8.3 shows that with an X dimension of 0.008 inch, a laser scanner with a spot size of 0.008 inch, and an optical throw of 14 inches, we could expect the symbol to be readable within a range of 14 to 18 inches from the reader.

The grocery industry has established a minimum X dimension of 0.025 inch for the U.P.C. Shipping Container Symbol. This dimension is specified for both labels and direct printing on shipping containers. A reader optimized for a 0.025-inch X dimension permits the symbol to be located within a 39-inch depth of field.

Lasers and other moving-beam scanners have another important feature: Field of View (see Figure 8.5). Field of view defines the length of the bar code that can be scanned at a given distance from the scanner. The oscillated spot has a defined travel, both to the left and to the right, that is indicated by the length of the line of light. For moving-beam scanners to read a bar code symbol, the entire symbol typically must be illuminated during one scan. Consequently, if the bar code symbol is longer than the line of light, the symbol exceeds the field of view of the scanner, and the symbol will not be readable. As the distance between scanner and symbol becomes greater, the field of view also increases. Beyond the limits of the depth of field, the line of light continues to grow longer, but the symbol is unreadable due to its being out of focus and the reduced irradiance from the illumination.

Handheld Moving-Beam Scanners

Handheld moving-beam readers, an example of which appears in Figure 8.9, are often viewed in terms of the light source that they employ for illumination, namely, incandescent (infrequent implementations), helium-neon (He-Ne) laser, and laser diode.

A primary consideration regarding light source is the amount of power required to generate the light source, especially in battery-powered configurations. Early suppliers of handheld moving-beam readers employed a helium-neon plasma tube to generate monochromatic, coherent light. The lasing process requires the application of approximately 1,000 volts or more to the cathode of the plasma tube. This is not generally a problem with commercial AC power supplies, but a significant challenge is presented when battery power is used. To transform a 5- to 12-volt DC to the 1,000 volts needed requires a specialized power transformer. The plasma tube and power supply represent nearly 65 percent of the bill-of-material costs of the handheld laser bar code reader.

The replacement of the plasma tube with a laser diode operated at 5 to 12 volts substantially diminishes the cost and, ultimately, the price. Due to the attractiveness of such cost reductions, the industry is presently witnessing a migration from He-Ne lasers to semiconductor lasers, or laser diodes. Laser diodes are relatively new devices, however. As with the first wand scanner diodes, the first laser diodes employed an infrared emitter—limiting the potential applications for their use to pigment/dye-based inks. Visible-red laser diodes have entered the marketplace and are now the light source of choice.

The appeal of visible red exists for both the wider variety of printing inks permitted and the ability to see the line of light for positioning purposes. Designers of scanners with infrared laser diodes have approached the human interaction problem in various novel ways. One way is to generate a parallel, visible tracer beam. Another scheme is to use a pair of visible marker lights, between which the invisible infrared beam scans back and forth. Such approaches are, in my opinion, less-than-optimal attempts to overcome the limitation of invisibility to the human eye. Many users who are looking for lower cost moving-beam readers elected to wait for the commercial availability of visible-red laser diodes.

One of the largest industrial applications for handheld bar code scanners is long-range scanning in warehouse environments. The typical requirement is to read symbols that are from 2 to 3 inches to 10 to 15 feet away from the operator. It is a demanding requirement which presents a challenge for scanner designers.

There are three major problems facing a long-range scanner designer. First, the amount of signal reflected back from the bar code and received by the scanner is very small. The signal received from the bar code located 10 feet away is about 1/150 of the signal received by a regular scanner from a bar code located 10 inches away. The weakness of the received signal imposes certain requirements on the laser power output, efficiency of the laser focusing optics, and the size of the light collecting optics. Existing visible laser diodes with 5 to 10 milliwatt output power can do the job.

The second task is to provide a huge depth of focus. The symbol can be located anywhere within 2 to 15 feet from the operator. Fortunately, in warehouse applications, only low-density symbols are being used at the present time. Typically, the narrowest element width is 40 to 55 mils. An optimally designed laser focusing system can provide for the required depth of focus. The trend in industry is to put more information in bar codes. This will require higher density symbols. In order to read higher density symbols within the same depth of focus range, the system will have to use unconventional optical elements or simple and fast zoom systems as part of the laser focusing system.

Another important parameter of a long-range scanner is the visibility of the laser light. It should be sufficiently bright to be seen by the operator when scanning at 15 feet. The easiest way to enhance visibility is to use shorter wavelength (shorter than existing 670-nanometer) laser diodes. There are commercially available laser diodes with a wavelength of 650 nanometers, but they remain too expensive. There are also reports of laboratory experiments involving laser diodes with a wavelength of 633 nanometers (wavelength of HeNe lasers). Meanwhile, scanner manufacturers are using different means to improve visibility.

One of the methods is the so-called "aim-and-scan" mode. It usually requires a two-position trigger. When the trigger is pulled to the first position, the angular scan amplitude is much smaller and, as a result, the scan line is much shorter and visibility much higher. As soon as the operator aims at the symbol, he/she pulls the trigger to the second position and the angular scan amplitude returns to the normal mode, which allows the symbol to be read.

In 1990 Symbol Technologies introduced its 8500 ALR scanner able to read a 0.015-inch X dimension symbol at distances ranging from two to six feet; the same scanner can read a 0.050-inch X dimension symbol at up to eight feet. Another version of the long-range scanner can read a 0.055-inch X dimension symbol at up to 15 feet. At Scan-Tech in 1992 PSC demonstrated a scanner that could read a 100 mil symbol from over 100 feet away.

Field of view can be an issue with handheld moving-beam scanners. Handheld moving-beam readers may have too wide a field of view for traveler and menu symbols not anticipating handheld moving-beam readers. Traveler and menu symbols may be closely positioned to each other. When attempting to read one of the symbols on the traveler, transaction menu, or character menu (paper scannable keyboard), adjacent symbols may appear in the scan path. In such cases the operator may not be able to establish which of the symbols was being read.

Stationary Moving-Beam Scanners for Conveyors

Stationary moving-beam scanners are, as the name implies, fixed in position and location. These devices are hardwired to both a power source and a data communications channel. An inherent feature of stationary scanners is the need to bring the bar code marked material to the scanner system in order for the bar code information to be read. Typically, the transport mechanisms to get the material to the scanner include:

- Product sortation systems
- Gravity fed conveyors
- Constant speed powered conveyors
- Carousels
- Automatic guided vehicle systems (AGVS)
- Robotic arms
- Human guided vehicle systems

These scanners are able to scan the bar code symbol as it moves through their scan paths. The symbol could contain the material's product code, lot number, serial number, expiration/ manufactured date, destination code, or an internally assigned code unique to a specific material or combination of materials. The symbol content is read and the read data is passed on to some form of computer system.

Product sortation and product routing typically occur as follows:

- The symbol read contains a product or lot code. The code is matched to a data file having that code's sortation lane which is transmitted to the diversion equipment, changing the path of the material. This alternative requires a communications channel from the reader to the computer system, a data base management system to access files, application files, and a communications channel from the computer to the diverting equipment.
- As an alternative, the storage location for the finished product can be defined be-

fore the production process begins. A pressure-sensitive label contains the storage location to which the finished product is to be sent. A local workcenter without a data base management system could faithfully effect the correct storage of the finished product by reading the label and routing the material based on the label storage location bar code marking.

Stationary Moving-Beam Scanner Issues

Stationary scanners require that the symbol be brought to the reader. Consequently, these scanners must be positioned within the material flow path. Moving-beam scanners oscillate a spot of light at speeds of 40 scans per second and higher. This oscillation causes the moving spot of light to appear as a continuous line. For a bar code to be successfully read by one of these devices, all bars and spaces must be intersected by the same scan path, as shown in Figure 8.11.

In addition to the simple "line-of-light," some scanning systems will create a pattern to enable the reading device to be more tolerant of the symbol's orientation and placement. Some of these patterns are shown in Figure 8.11.

Moving-beam conveyor scanners are generally mounted on the side of a conveyor with the symbol in an industry standard picket fence configuration as shown in Figure 8.12. Industry standards were originally written to support one of the technologies involved at the time the standards were written, namely, fixed-beam scanning systems. The movement of the symbol through the scanning beam effected a successful read. With moving-beam systems, a picket fence configuration with side mount scanners is not the most efficient orientation but the standards are already written.

In the example shown in Figure 8.12, if the scan rate is assumed to be 200 scans per second and both symbols are traveling at 180 feet per minute, the stepadder symbol is in view for 108 milliseconds (21 scans) while the picket fence symbol is in view for 60 milliseconds (11 scans). At 200 scans per second (sps),1 scan occurs in 5 milliseconds; at 180 feet per minute (fpm), 1 inch of symbol passes the scanner in 36 milliseconds.

Internal applications should employ stepladder symbol orientation if the scanner is going to be side mounted. If the scanner is going to be mounted above or below the conveyor, reading the approaching side panel, picket fence orientation should be used so that the symbol can be drawn through the beam.

Since moving-beam scanners are dependent upon the symbol being brought to the reader, the manner in which the label is presented to the scanner is also important. If the label is skewed from the normal way in which symbols are usually presented, a no-read would occur. Consequently, symbol orientation is a critical matter to stationary readers. The problem of orientation can be overcome by flooding the symbol area with a starburst pattern (see Figure 8.11(c)) that could accommodate any orientation. This is a rather neat solution to the problem, except for its expense. Of all the stationary scanners presently produced, the starburst pattern scanner is by far the most expensive. Another possible alternative would be to ensure that the bar code symbol always appears in the same position relative to the scan path (in many situations a specific distance from the natural bottom of the material bearing the symbol). This alternative would require automatic application of the bar code symbol to the material. See the discussion of print/apply systems at the end of Chapter 9. Accuracy of placement with print/apply systems can easily be within 1/32 inch. Further symbol skew, prevalent in human-applied labels, is for all intents and purposes eliminated.

In Figure 8.13 Symbol (a) represents a properly printed bar code symbol. Symbol (b)

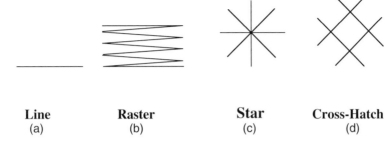

Line	Raster	Star	Cross-Hatch
(a)	(b)	(c)	(d)

Figure 8.11: Moving-Beam Scanner Patterns

(a) The oldest and least sophisticated scanning pattern to generate in a moving-beam scanner is the line pattern. (b) By adding mechanical motion in a perpendicular direction, the line scan becomes a raster scan which covers more of the area of the symbol than the simple line, covering the symbol redundantly with different paths until one free of defects gives a correct read. On the same principle of increasing the number and variety of paths across the symbol, the starburst (c) and crosshatch (d) are more expensive patterns developed to improve chances of a successful read.

represents a printed bar code symbol with substantial printing defects. Symbol (c) represents a properly printed symbol oriented in a stepladder fashion to accommodate a conveyor-side mounted moving-beam reader. Symbol (d) represents the same reader scan lines (shaded vertical lines) positioned over the poorly printed symbol.

Moving-beam scanners often have voting algorithms, able to take several views of the symbol as it moves before the reader. A voting algorithm requires that any symbol

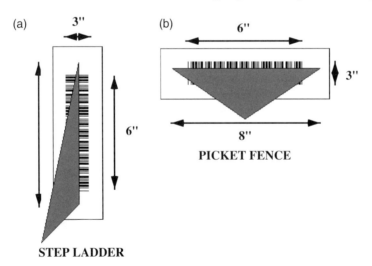

Figure 8.12: Orientation of Scanning Beam and Object Motion

There are two orientations of symbols relative to the motion of tagged objects in a conveyor system. (a) If the direction of motion is perpendicular to the bars of the bar code, the orientation is called "picket fence." (b) If the direction of motion is parallel to the bars of the bar code, the orientation is called "stepladder." For historical reasons, many standards specify the picket fence orientation which was optimum at the time the standards were written—even though modern moving-beam scanners read stepladder orientation labels more effectively.

observed in a given scan line agree with subsequent observations—usually one or two subsequent observations. If the observations agree, the information contained in the symbol patterns would be transmitted from the scanner. This minimizes the possibility of detecting an erroneous data structure when reading poorly printed symbols (data content of subsequent symbols would not agree unless the data content were correct).

A second issue can be found in the combined variables of the speed of the conveyor, the scanning speed, and the height of the bar code symbol. (In Figure 8.13 the height of the bars of Symbols (a) and (c) would be the left-to-right dimension.) This relationship is shown in Table 8.4.

Since just about every system has some tilt, pitch, or skew deviation from perfect picket fence or stepladder orientation, the effective width (including the quiet zone) of the symbol is calculated as it appears to the scanner. Figure 8.16 provides examples of symbol tilt, pitch, and skew. If more than one factor (tilt, pitch, or skew) is present in the system, each calculation needs to be made separately and the resultant values are additive (positive or negative).

$$E_W = E_L(COS\ \Phi) - (S_L + Q)(SIN\ \Phi)$$

where
Φ = Symbol tilt, pitch, or skew angle
E_W is the element width
E_L is the element length
S_L is the symbol length
Q is one quiet zone

A	B	C	D

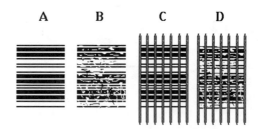

Figure 8.13: Raster Scanning and Improved Readability of Poor Quality Symbols

At (a) we see a properly printed bar code. At (b) we see the same bar code with substantial defects. At (c) we see a raster grid of scan trajectories applied to the good symbol, as might be the case with a moving-beam scanner. At (d) we see the same raster grid applied to the defective symbol. The superiority of a raster pattern—whether generated by the moving-beam scanner itself or by motion of the target symbol in front of a simple moving-beam scanner's line pattern—is that it increases the number of times the reader can possibly obtain a correct read in the face of visual noise of a poorly printed or damaged symbol.

Point-of-Sale Slot Scanners

No discussion of bar code scanners would be complete without addressing retail slot scanners. These systems employ a moving-beam laser or laser diode with similar characteristics and benefits as all moving-beam scanners, except one. Where industrial and other commercial implementations of laser bar code readers employ a single line of light and in some cases a raster pattern, slot scanners produce a light pattern to optimize the symbol being read, namely, a U.P.C. symbol. This pattern is usually either a crosshatch or starburst pattern, permitting the left side of the U.P.C. symbol to be read by one line and the right side by another, lending to the concept of rotational omnidirectionality. For illustration purposes, Figure 8.14(a) shows the orthogonal pattern of a simple slot scanner scanning the left side with one beam and the right side with a second beam. Figure 8.14(b) shows the adverse effects of symbol truncation requiring that the symbol be moved through one beam to effect scanning, since the intersection of the two orthogonal beams would not read the symbol.

LINE Feet/min	50	75	100	125	150	200	250	300
SPEED Inches/sec	10	15	20	25	30	40	50	60
SCAN Inches of bar length SPEED needed (5 scans)								
45/sec	1.04	1.61	2.24	2.78	3.33	4.40	5.55	6.66
90/sec	.52	.80	1.12	1.39	1.66	2.20	2.77	3.33
180/sec	.26	.40	.56	.69	.83	1.10	1.39	1.66
360/sec	.13	.20	.28	.35	.42	.55	.69	.83
720/sec	.07	.10	.14	.18	.21	.28	.35	.42

Table 8.4: Relationship of Symbol Size to Conveyor and Scanner Speed

In this table, for several conveyor line speeds in feet per minute (columns), we see across the rows the number of inches of bar length needed to acccomplish five complete scans at selected scanning speeds.

Rotational omnidirectionality implies that a U.P.C. symbol could be oriented face down toward the scanner, rotated in any direction with the face remaining toward the scanner, and still be decoded.

Slot scanners have become substantially lower in cost over the past five years. Earlier slot scanners required that the counter be modified to place the scanner within the counter. Newer point-of-sale slot scanners such as those shown in Figure 8.15 provide for placement on the counter, oriented in either a horizontal or vertical fashion.

CCD Image Scanners

Each of the preceding scanning technologies has employed a light source and a single photodetector. By the application of movement, from either the operator (wand scanners and handheld fixed-beam scanners), the symbol (fixed-beam readers), or the light source (moving-beam readers), the single photodetector produced a signal proportional to the reflected light, varied by the presence of a space or a bar.

The technology employed in charge-coupled device (CCD) scanners, an example of which is shown in Figure 8.16, operates similarly to that of a conventional photographic camera. The symbol is illuminated by a light source (photoflash—Xenon or incandescent or laser diode). Where the image in a photographic system is reflected onto photosensitive film, CCD scanners focus the reflected image onto a photosensitive semiconductor component. In a linear photodiode array, between 1,024 and 4,096 tiny photodiodes measuring less than 25 microns, or 0.001 inch in width, detect the reflected signal. When the reflected image of the bar code symbol is projected onto the photodiodes, the spaces saturate the diodes (representing the presence of a high amount of reflected light) and the darker bars fail to saturate the photodiodes, representing the presence of a relatively low amount of reflected light.

The pixels are sampled by a microprocessor to determine the levels of saturation of each, with the output of the entire array producing a signal nearly identical to the symbol being read. Then, as with all bar code scanners, the output signal is conditioned, digitized, and decoded.

As with all focused image scanners, as opposed to focused light source scanners, such as lasers and laser diodes, the depth of field of these devices is limited to less than a few inches. Further, with most CCDs the field of view is limited by the number of pixels in the CCD which precludes their use with longer bar code symbols. In 1991 charge-coupled

(a)

Full Size U.P.C. Symbol Being Scanned with Orthogonal Lines — One beam scans the left side and another the right. Scanner software properly reassembles both side to decode data.

(b)

Truncated U.P.C. Symbol Being Scanned with Orthogonal Lines — One beam must used to scan both right and left sides to successfully decode data. Truncated symbols require more time to scan.

Figure 8.14: Orthogonal Beams and U.P.C. Symbols

(a) Orthogonal beams from a slot scanner, shown over a proper height U.P.C. symbol. The data from one beam covers half the symbol; data from the other beam can fill in the rest of the symbol. (b) If the U.P.C. symbol is printed with abbreviated bars so it is not full height, there is no way that orthogonal beams can together pass every bar and space in the symbol.

Figure 8.15: Typical Point-of-Sale Scanner

device scanners were introduced that permitted an expanded depth of field and a greater field of view. Generally, CCD scanners are used in a retail setting reading U.P.C. symbols. The number of pixels in the scanner also determines the resolution achievable. Multiple pixels are required for each symbol element, with the higher the number of pixels, the smaller the bar code element that is able to be resolved.

Charge-coupled device scanners are available in fixed-mount, handheld, and most recently, desktop configurations. The handhelds are priced between wand scanners and laser diode readers. Fixed-mount charge-coupled device readers are currently price-competitive with lower priced laser scanners. The new desktop CCD scanners employ a laser diode as the illumination source and a matrix array with more than a single line of photodiodes, permitting the scanner to compensate for printing defects which may be present along a single scan line.

Determining Which Scanner to Use

The first step in selecting the right scanner for your application requires understanding how your application operates today and your goals for the future. While there is probably no single, all-inclusive list of questions to answer, here are some to get you started.

- Will the scanner be in an automated or non-automated system;
- Will the scanner be handheld or fixed position;
- For wand scanners does the aperture size match the "X" dimension of the symbols to be scanned;
- How will the bar codes be printed;
- Does the light source wavelength match the requirements of the printed symbol;
- What are the environmental conditions (temperature, light level, humidity, abuse, dirt levels) at the scanner station;
- What types of surfaces are to be scanned;

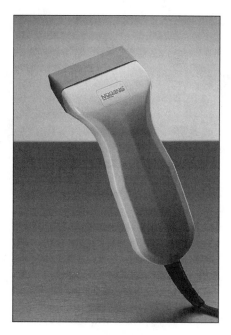

Figure 8.16: A CCD Image Scanner

- Is it practical or desirable to touch the scanner to the bar code;
- How many symbols will be scanned per unit of time and of what size are the symbols;
- How do the items carrying bar codes travel past the scanner and at what speed;
- Is the position of the bar code consistent from item to item;
- What is the angular range between scanner and symbol;
- What are the minimum and maximum distances of the scanner to the symbol;
- What are the height, length, and orientation of the bar code;
- How quickly must decisions about the item be made and action taken after the bar code is read;
- If the scanner cannot read a bar code, what happens to the item;
- What is the cost and size of the scanner and associated decoding logic; and
- What is the mean time between failure (MTBF), the maintenance cost, and the mean time to repair (MTTR) of the scanning equipment.

I recommend that the following types of scanners be considered for specific types of applications.

- For desk or clipboard environments—wand scanners;
- For low volume point-of-sale environments—handheld visible light laser diodes (VLDs) and charge-coupled devices (CCDs);
- For moderate volume point-of-sale environments—stationary VLDs;
- For file tracking and scanning symbols on documents—stationary VLDs;

- For conveyor applications—stationary, raster scanning VLDs;
- For greasy or oily locations—handheld infrared laser diodes (IRLDs);
- For material handling applications—handheld VLDs; and
- For all portable and field computer applications, seriously consider scanners that are functionally integrated to the portable device.

Table 8.5 provides a comparative look at the capabilities of the types of scanners discussed in this chapter.

Scanners

	Scanning Mode	Light source wavelength in nanometers	Depth of field	Portable	Weight	Tolerance to Label Skew	Price
Handheld Contact							
Wand	Manual	660-940	Limited	Yes	Low	High	Low
Charge-coupled device	Manual	660-900	Limited	Yes	Low	High	Low
Handheld Noncontact							
Fixed-beam gun	Manual	633-820	Great	Yes	Medium	High	Medium
Moving-beam gun	LED	Manual	660-940	Limited	Yes	Medium	High
Medium							
Helium-neon laser	Manual	633	Great	Yes	Medium	High	Medium
Infrared laser diode	Manual	720-820	Great	Yes	Medium	High	Medium
Visible laser diode	Manual	670-690	Great	Yes	Medium	High	Medium
Fixed-Position Contact							
Card reader	Manual	660-940	Limited	Yes	Medium	Low	Low
Fixed-Position Noncontact Beam							
Single moving	Automatic	633-820	Great	No	High	Medium	High
Raster moving	Automatic	633-820	Great	No	High	Medium	Higher
Omnidirectional	Automatic	633	Great	No	High	High	Highest
Desktop							
CCD/VLD	Manual	660-900	Great	Yes	Medium	High	Medium
Helium-neon laser	Manual	633	Great	Yes	Medium	High	Medium
Infrared laser diode	Manual	720-820	Great	Yes	Medium	High	Medium
Visible laser diode	Manual	670-690	Great	Yes	Medium	High	Medium

Table 8.5: An Overview of Scanner Capabilities

A qualitative overview of the capabilities of various types of bar code scanning technologies is provided by this table.

CHAPTER 9

Bar Code Printing Technologies

===============

When you are selecting a printing method, the first question to be answered is whether the content of the bar code symbols will be known in advance of their use, or whether they will not be known until the actual time of use. In other words, can the bar code symbols be preprinted or do they need to be generated on demand? If the symbols can be preprinted, what types of symbols are needed—static, consecutive, or variable data content? If static codes are required, traditional commercial means using film masters may provide the most economical and accurate results for large runs. If consecutive codes are needed, large runs (over 5,000 symbols) will usually employ either rotary numbering machines or electronic imaging on the press or other on-press/off-line encoder methods of generating symbols. For shorter runs and/or for producing variable content bar codes, computer-controlled machines such as laser phototypesetters, electrostatic printers, dot-matrix impact, ink jet, and erosion techniques may be the best alternative. Short runs of consecutively bar code marked forms also may be generated by forms manufacturers with an off-line encoder. For demand situations, the user of bar code marked labels must determine whether the volume dictates a higher speed printer in a central location or whether multiple printers at the points of use are needed. Here the user can choose between electrostatic, thermal/thermal transfer printers, and dot-matrix impact printers. Electrostatic and dot-matrix impact printers can be used for other printing needs as well as bar code production.

In all cases, the minimum nominal narrow element of the printed bar code is a consideration. Often the space limitations on the label or form will dictate the density needed to encode the message that is desired. In general, the higher the density, the narrower the width of the nominal narrow element. Commercial printing techniques offer high to low density symbols (label printing—high, corrugated printing—low). Dot-matrix impact formed symbols offer a wide range of densities from very high (electrostatic, thermal transfer, and thermal printers) to medium and low (impact and some ink-jet).

Direct Printing of Static Symbols

For the purposes of this section "source marked symbols" are considered to be bar codes that are created through traditional commercial printing processes employing printing plates and are applied at the source of product packaging. While preprinted labels could be considered in this section, they are discussed elsewhere in this text. Further, the bar code markings on many forms are either printed when the form is initially printed with local information or when the form graphics are printed by the forms manufacturer. Bar code marked forms are also discussed elsewhere in this text. Finally, bar code symbols could be printed at the source through demand printing systems, and the symbols could be applied to an item automatically. Discussions of demand printing systems and print/apply systems appear later in this chapter.

First, let's turn our attention to the printing techniques that are considered in the production of static symbols. Static symbols are those where the same symbol is printed repeatedly, such as in the cases of UPC symbols and shipping container symbols. Static symbols employ "film masters" and are generally printed in runs of hundreds or thousands or more. These techniques are not used to produce consecutively numbered or variable content codes. These production methods include:

- Offset Lithography
- Flexography
- Silkscreen
- Hot Stamping
- Letterpress
- Intaglio (or Gravure)

Commercial printing methods are used to produce static bar codes in high volume. Because of the economies of scale involved in typical commercial runs, these printing processes often prove to be the least expensive means of producing bar codes. Several issues are common to most static symbol production, namely, film masters, bearer bars, and who calculates the check digits. These are discussed below.

Film Masters

The heart of all of the commercial printing techniques is the master image on the printing plate. This image must be extremely accurate. The plate production technique begins with a very precise film master of the bar code symbol. The accuracy of the film master must be controlled within a range of 0.0002 to 0.0005 inch. Depending upon the printing technique, the film master can be produced as either a film positive or negative and with the emulsion side up or down. The printed bars of the bar code can vary significantly from the bars on the film master. This variance is caused by any combination of factors, such as mold shrinkage, over- or under-etching of metal masters, amount of printing plate/substrate impression, and ink viscosity. Mold shrinkage and improper metal master etching can be controlled through a quality control program that checks the bar dimensions during plate production. Printing plate/substrate impression and ink viscosity variations are a result of the printing process. Dimensional variations can be controlled to provide fairly consistent printing. The bars normally show a uniform increase in size with an associated uniform decrease in the size of the intervening spaces. The approximate increase in bar width size, or print gain, can be established for each printing press operation.

Since the print gain for a specific press can be established, the film master manufacturer can reduce the size of the bars on the film master to compensate for the bar gain during printing. This amount, called bar width reduction (BWR), should be determined for each printing press, with specific attention given to bar width reduction when producing bar code symbols with an X dimension approaching the minimum for a particular printing process. The amount of bar width reduction is a function of many variables, including printing technique, printing press, printing plate material, ink viscosity, substrate, printing impression, and press operation. Table 9.1 provides some basic guidelines for bar width reduction for various printing processes. It is incumbent upon the supplier of bar code marked packaging to work with the film master maker to determine the specific bar width reduction for the supplier's set of circumstances.

Printing Process	Printing Plate Type	Minimum "X" Recommended	Recommended Bar Width Reduction
Flexography	Magnesium Engraving	9	2
	Plastic Matrix	9	3
	Photopolymer	9	3
Offset Lithography		8	2.5
Letterpress	Metal	9	2
	Magnesium (non-etched)	9	3
	Photopolymer	9	3
Gravure		8	1
Screen	Review individually with attention to the transfer of the emulsion to the screen and the viscosity of the ink.		

Table 9.1: Bar Width Reduction Guidelines

Each printing process, and each specific printing press using that process, has a characteristic and measurable print gain, the expansion of bar widths due to effects like ink viscosity and flow. In order to compensate, film masters must be generated with a "bar width reduction" to compensate for the print gain. This table shows recommended bar width reduction for the typical X dimension (minimum element width) used in several printing processess. All values are in mils (thousandths of an inch).

A close working relationship is required by the bar code printer and the film master maker. It is recommended that the user select a reputable bar code film master maker and receive recommendations from the maker as to qualified bar code printing vendors in the user's geographic area. The film master maker works with numerous printers and is best qualified to recommend a printer for a specific application.

Bearer Bars on Film Masters

Bearer bars should be ordered on all film masters where flexographic printing is to be used on a corrugated surface. The bearer bar consists of a rectangular bar pattern circumscribing the code horizontally and vertically and intersecting the bars at the top of the bar code symbol (see Figure 3.17(c)). The purpose of the bearer bar is to provide printing plate support at critical areas near the symbol and to enhance read reliability by assisting in the reduction of the probability of misreads which may occur when a skewed scanning beam enters or exits the symbol through the top or bottom edge. Rounded corners may be utilized on the bearer bar if the film maker can supply such a feature. The dimensions for bearer bars on the ITF-14 symbol are shown in Table 3.14; placement of the bearer bar is illustrated in Figure 3.19 of this text. For processes printing directly onto corrugated that do not use printing plates, the vertical bearer bars may be eliminated (see Figure 3.17(b)). If the ITF-14 symbol is not printed directly on the corrugated packaging material, the bearer bar need be only two times the width of a narrow element. The portions of the bearer bar above and below the symbol should butt directly against the top and bottom of the symbol bars.

Check Characters on Film Masters

Some bar code symbols employ a check character. It is strongly recommended that the user provide only the basic data to the film master maker and have the film master maker compute the check character. Computations by the film master maker are under computer control and more reliable than manual computations at the user level. The film master maker should presume that no check character has been calculated in the data given by a user.

Flexography

Flexography is used most often for rotary tag and label presses. It is an inexpensive and simple printing process heavily used in decorative and packaging printing. Flexography employs a flexible rubber or photopolymer plate onto which the image has been etched in relief. These plates wrap around a cylinder and squeeze the paper against a rubber impression roller, as shown in Figure 9.1, to produce the image.

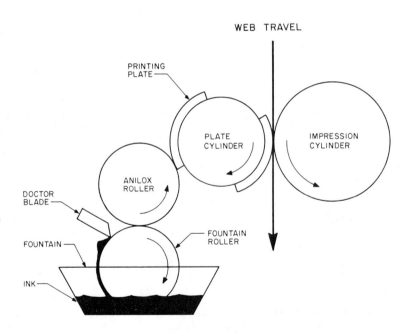

Figure 9.1: Flexographic Press Operation

Flexography is a mass printing technique in which images are prepared on a "web" of paper. Ink is transferred from a "fountain" reservoir via the "anilox" roller up to the image etched in relief on a flexible rubber or photopolymer printing plate wrapped around its cylinder. The plate cylinder is pressed against the moving web which picks up a direct impression of the image on the plate. The web is backed up by the rubber impression roller.

144

With flexography (also referred to as "flexo"), the trade-off is between versatility of substrate selection and print quality. Since rubber plates distort and compress, it is necessary to employ special techniques to compensate for stretch and shrinkage of the rubber during printing, thus assuring faithful reproduction. The advantage of flexography is its ability to print bar codes on an extremely variable selection of materials. Flexography is used to print the shipping container symbols directly on corrugated boxes. The flexographic process is very versatile and well established as a method of printing for business forms, labels, tags, folding cartons, and corrugated boxes, as well as foils and the various cellulosic and plastic films. Since many applications requiring static bar codes call for labels, flexography is probably the most widely employed technique for the commercial production of bar codes. Bar codes printed on a flexo press can be printed either "with the web" or "across the web" as shown in Figure 9.2. Because of the distortion mentioned above and the distortion introduced by the plate being attached to a cylinder, it is usually advisable to print bar codes "with the web."

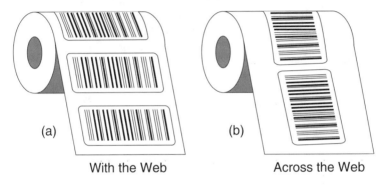

(a)	(b)
With the Web	Across the Web

Figure 9.2: Printing "With" and "Across" the Web

When using flexo or similar web printing techniques, there are two possible orientations of bar code symbols relative to the web. (a) shows a series of bar code symbols aligned "with the web." (b) shows a series of bar code symbols aligned "across the web." Distortions caused by the wrapping of these symbols around the plate cylinder cause the bar widths and spacings to be more subject to error when printing across the web than when printing with the web.

The flexographic press permits maximum widths to range from 3 inches to more than 100 inches. Each printing plate can vary in size and be mounted with a matching die-cutting cylinder. Such flexibility permits length, width, and shape of the labels to vary greatly. Due to the rapid drying of flexo inks, printing on foils and the various cellulosic and plastic films (nonabsorbent materials) may be more practical by flexography than by offset or letterpress.

Flexographic Printing Plates

Flexographic printing plates are commonly made of either rubber or photopolymer. Rubber plates are created using the following steps:
- A film master negative is used to create a metal engraving of zinc, magnesium, or copper.
- A mold or matrix is then created from the engraving.
- The rubber plate is vulcanized from the mold or matrix.

More recently developed photopolymer plates are created by exposing a photosensitive polymer masked with the film master negative to high intensity ultraviolet light. The area exposed to the ultraviolet radiation hardens and the area protected by the blacked parts of the negative are washed away.

Offset Lithography

Offset lithography (commonly referred to as "offset") provides the highest quality bar codes and can do so on a wide range of stocks. Its primary advantage is its ability to produce a clear image on a number of materials, no matter how rough or smooth the surface.

Offset relies on the surface physics of the prepared printing plate interacting with the oil-based ink. The image and non-image areas are etched on the surface of a thin metal plate using a special plate preparation process. The printing image is made oil receptive and water repellent, while the non-image areas are water receptive and oil repellent. Inks employed in offset lithography are oil based. The plate is wrapped around a pickup (or dampening) roller for wetting and cleaning. The ink is picked up by the image areas of the plate, and the image is printed on an intermediate image carrier (blanket cylinder).

The term "lithography" refers to the process of printing with the oil receptive/water repellent image; in Figure 9.3 the term "offset" refers to the two-step image transfer

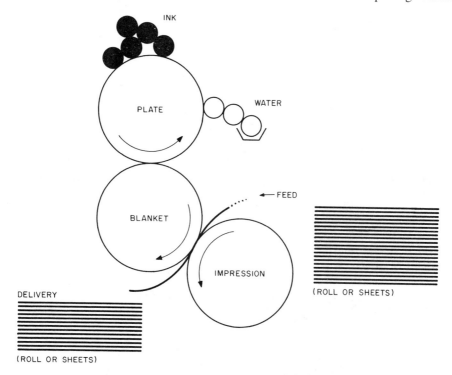

Figure 9.3: Offset Lithography Printing Process

Offset lithography is a mass printing technique. Offset presses are available with either cut sheet or web feed. An oil-based ink is applied to a photographically produced master plate whose pre-wetted image pattern selectively accepts the ink. Instead of direct transfer to the web, the inked image is transferred to the "blanket" roller, then to the web. This indirect, "offset" process gives rise to the name.

146

process: plate-to-blanket, then blanket-to-paper. Technically, the offset principle can be used with all commercial printing processes, but its nearly exclusive usage in combination with lithography has made the term "offset" and "offset lithography" synonymous.

For bar code printing, the significance of offset lithography is its widespread use on presses of all sizes, speeds, and configurations (sheet fed and rotary web), and its ability to produce fixed codes of the highest quality and high density.

Printing plates employed in offset lithography include paper for short runs, polymer for medium runs, and metal for long runs. In general, metal plates or some of the newer polymer plates would be recommended for bar code printing. And while this printing plate composition may be the most expensive, the quality of the printed image with bimetal plates and the new polymers is superior. Bimetal plates are usually constructed of an aluminum base material with copper or brass electroplated to the image areas, with the copper or brass being ink-receptive and the aluminum base material, water-receptive.

Silkscreen Printing

The silkscreen printing process consists of forcing ink through a porous stenciled screen, usually consisting of mylar, dacron, or stainless steel. The screens are photographically reproduced, so that the image areas are porous and the non-image areas are non-porous. In its simplest form, a paste-like ink is forced through the screen onto the substrate by a rubber squeegee, as illustrated in Figure 9.4.

Silkscreen printing can be used successfully on a variety of surfaces, such as wood, glass, and fabric. By incorporating various jigs and fixtures, it is possible to print on irregular surfaces of bottles and other product containers.

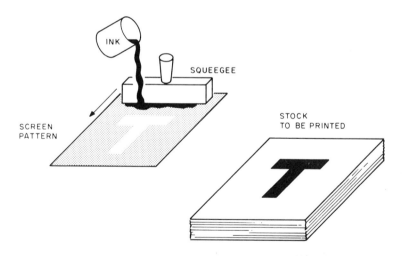

Figure 9.4: The Silkscreen Concept

In its simplest form, silkscreen is a manual process in which ink is forced through a screen using a squeegee. The screen is prepared so that the image areas are porous and allow the ink to pass. Production jigs and machinery allow this basic process to be used to apply images to a variety of materials and surface shapes.

Gravure/Intaglio Printing

The terms gravure and intaglio are frequently used interchangeably, although intaglio refers to the process, while gravure refers to the printing press or cylinder on which the image created by intaglio resides. A gravure press can be either sheet fed or web fed (rotogravure). The rotogravure printing station consists of an ink fountain, an etched cylinder partially submerged in ink, a doctor blade for maintaining film thickness, and an impression cylinder for controlling impressions and supporting the substrate. An illustration of the rotogravure press operation is shown in Figure 9.5.

The printing plate or cylinder for gravure printing has the image to be printed etched below the surface, forming an array of microscopic cells. The ink used for this process is very fluid and flows into the cells when rolled over the plate. The surface of the plate, which is the non-printing area, is wiped clean of ink by a doctor blade before the paper is brought into contact with the plate. When the paper comes into contact with the printing plate, the cells dump their contents, forming the printed image.

While intaglio/gravure is used in such diverse applications as the printing of packaging materials, as well as currency and stock and bond certificates, the process yields a bar code of lower quality than those produced using flexo and offset printing presses. The lower quality is due to the cell pattern, which creates fine toothlike edges on the bars.

Letterpress Printing

Letterpress is the original method of printing with type. It is still used by commercial printers and business forms manufacturers. The process employs metal, rubber, and pho-

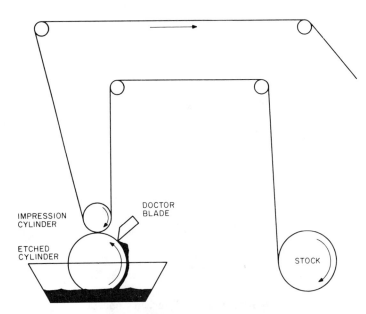

Figure 9.5: Rotogravure Printing Process

In rotogravure printing the printing plate, on the surface of a cylinder, is uniformly inked with a very fluid ink. The ink flows into an array of microscopic cells etched in the printing plate that correspond to the image being printed. The inked image is transferred directly to the moving web under the mechanical pressure of the impression cylinder.

topolymer plates with the image surfaces raised. The process differs from flexographic printing basically because paste inks are used, as opposed to the fast-drying liquid inks used in flexo. The letterpress printing station consists of inking rollers that transfer the ink to the printing plate, a plate cylinder for mounting the printing plate, and an impression cylinder for controlling impressions and supporting the substrate. Letterpress is used in rotary numbering machines and is capable of printing accurate bar code images if care is taken to maintain the printing equipment.

Letterset Printing

The letterset process utilizes rubber or photopolymer plates with raised image surfaces. A typical letterset printing station consists of inking rollers, plate cylinders for mounting the printing plate, an offset rubber blanket cylinder for transferring the printed image from the plate to the substrate, and an impression cylinder to control the impression and support the substrate. The printing stocks and the inks are similar to those used with letterpress, except that stronger ink pigments may be required.

Each of the above printing processes involves the transfer of an image to a substrate by application of wet ink. Film master-based processes and set-type processes are well suited in situations requiring thousands of copies of the same image. Product package labeling is a good example of the success of such printing processes in the printing of bar code symbols. All of the above printing processes have another common characteristic as well: The bar code printing is done off-site, away from the location where the symbol is used or applied. But wet ink/film master systems share off-site printing with other technologies as well.

Hot-Stamp Printing

Hot stamping uses a dry carbon ribbon with predetermined ink thickness, thus eliminating certain wet ink problems. Closely akin to letterpress, hot stamping requires a separate metal plate for every legend desired. Since these plates are etched from photographic film masters, they are very accurate. Bar widths having an X dimension of 0.010 inch are possible with consistent quality. Print quality is superb and the first-read rate is high. Hot stamping, however, is expensive relative to other printing methods. It is used primarily for high quality multi-color labels. The hot stamp technique is illustrated in Figure 9.6.

HOT STAMP TECHNIQUE

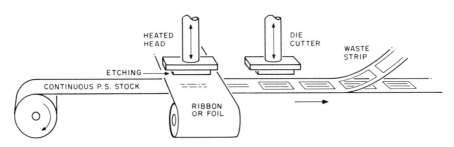

Figure 9.6: Hot Stamp Printing Process

This figure illustrates the concept of hot stamp printing in a typical case of producing pressure sensitive labels on a continuous web of laminated label stock.

149

Corrugated Printing

A broad range of printing processes may be applied to the printing of bar code symbols. Compliance with symbol requirements and printing tolerances for the symbology should be verified for each process.

Extensive studies by the Distribution Symbology Study Group (DSSG) recommend that plates for the symbol be 30-durometer natural rubber, synthetic rubber, or photopolymer.

Metal Engravings

The DSSG study incorporated tests and studies on manufacturing techniques of metal engravings to optimize printing plate quality for bar code printing when employing molded rubber or synthetic materials. Recommendations that originated with DSSG presume the use of two printing plate thicknesses, i.e., 0.250 inch and 0.125 inch:

- Code graphics should be etched individually or in a flat of code graphics near the middle of the bath.
- The shoulder angle should range from 20° to 25°.
- If topping is removed after etching, care should be taken not to round off the edges of the face of the bar.
- Care should be exercised to ensure that the bath temperature is appropriate for etching.
- The final etching should be checked for accuracy against the specification with the use of a minimum 40-power optical instrument by checking various areas of the engraving. The maximum bar width loss in the final engraving should be 0.002 inch (0.05 mm).
- These engraving recommendations are presented as a starting point for testing individual plant operating procedures and to assist in the development of a production specification.

Photopolymer Plates

Manufacture of photopolymer printing plates is a more precise process than that used in producing rubber plates from metal-etched engravings. A photopolymer plate is a close duplicate of the film master and, therefore, unaffected by normal manufacturing variances.

Preprint Procedures

Corrugated converters and engravers have to acquire film masters of the symbol to be printed. The film master supplier has the capability to reduce all bar widths from the designated dimensions to compensate for print gain. The reduction of bar widths on the film master is called bar width reduction. Tests to determine the amount of print gain and its consequent bar width reduction requirement for the printer should require at least two steps.

1. Order film master for the size symbol required for packaging needs while ensuring the symbol meets the requirements of the symbol and application specification. Film masters should be ordered so that the film master supplier calculates the required check characters, if any, of the code through computer assistance. Based on the printing process employed, determine whether the film master should be provided as:

    a. Positive or negative.
    b. Right reading emulsion down or right reading emulsion up.

After the film masters have been received, make printing plates using the standard plate-making processes as detailed above.

2. The effects of different printing processes (flexographic, letterpress), press size, and press operating practices may combine to produce small but significantly different bar width print gains. To obtain ideal reproduction of the desired bar size, bar width print gain should be studied for each press operation. Starting with the recommended bar width reduction of the film master, actual bar width print gain should be measured for two or three consecutive runs. The amount of variance from the desired nominal bar width should then be used to adjust the bar width reduction so that the desired bar width can be reproduced on subsequent runs.

Press Operation

Accurate symbol printing on corrugated board requires proper printing press operation. This section covers some of the general practices that should be followed when mass printing bar code symbols. The following practices are only recommendations and should not be substituted for first-hand experience.

Printing Plate Mounting

The symbology plate and the remaining printing plates should be premounted on a carrier sheet. The mounting should be preproofed to assure uniform height throughout. Make-ready should be used to elevate low spots. Once a symbology plate is mounted on a carrier sheet, it should be left intact. Removing and remounting can affect the quality and accuracy of the plate. Printing plates mounted on compressed backing material have provided excellent printed symbols.

Flexo Press Operation

To assure uniform pressure adjustment, both printing and impression cylinders should be clean (free of any ink buildup). All rolls in the printing train should be in parallel. Printing pressures should be adjusted carefully to avoid excessive squeeze or crush. Maintain kiss impression between anilox roll and printing plate and the printing plate to board surface. Printing pressure should be the minimum amount required to transfer the full image to the board surface. Excessive squeeze will cause excessive bar width distortion (growth) or haloing. Anilox roll should be free of any circumferential damage that might affect ink transfer and show up as excessive striation. Ink viscosity control is vital to maintain adequate ink coverage and uniform quality throughout the run. Initial viscosity should be high enough to obtain good solid coverage while still maintaining adequate drying for the desired run speed. Avoid ink viscosities that are too high, as this will cause excessive ink buildup on the printing plate and possible fill-in between bars. If excessive line width growth occurs at high speeds, try printing with a lower viscosity ink. Heavier ink film thicknesses occur on the anilox roll with increased speed and with increased ink viscosity on a two-roll (rubber metering roll) fountain. Lower ink viscosity should produce lower ink film thickness.

Letterpress Printing on Corrugated

There are at least three main points requiring attention for successful symbol printing. They are press condition, accompanying printing plates, and ink adjustment. As with flexo printing, minimum plate impression is required so as not to distort the print. Unlike flexo presses, letter press print cylinders are mostly wood or plastic covered. These coverings are often out of round, creating more difficulty in adjusting for the minimum plate impression required to obtain the desired bar width dimension. Make-ready should be used to raise low spots in the plate that otherwise would require excessive pressure to obtain full coverage. Unlike flexo printing, letter presses require different ink film thickness for printing large solids as compared to fine type. Satisfying the heavy ink film requirements of the solids may flood the fine type. (A symbol printing plate would be classified as fine type.) Therefore, it is imperative that the artwork on the corrugated complement the ink required for the symbology plate.

Photocomposition

Bar codes created by photocomposition come as film masters and various paper, plastic, metal, and tag media that are produced on specialized phototypesetting equipment. Such equipment uses a photographic process that exposes characters on photographic film or paper. Character sets are stored electronically as digital, or bit, patterns. Composed images are drawn in raster fashion on a CRT at resolutions of up to 7000 lines per inch. (To put this in perspective, consider that a commercial television rasters at from 9 to 21 lines per inch.) The image passes through a lens and is projected onto the photographic medium. These phototypesetters have several characteristics that make them ideally suited for producing bar codes. The first is high output speed. Most CRT typesetters are capable of creating bar code symbols at speeds of 2000 characters per second. Second, they can contract or expand bar code elements, in increments as fine as 0.0002 inch. Bar width can be easily adjusted, matching the master image created to the press, ink, and substrate being used. Thus, phototypesetters are widely employed to produce bar code film masters for offset printing, flexo printing on corrugated containers, and finished labels on photographic paper.

To produce labels on photographic paper, the individual labels are exposed on photographic paper, which is chemically processed to develop and fix the images. Next, the back of the paper is coated with an adhesive. A waxed backing sheet is attached, and the paper is die-cut into individual, adhesive-backed labels. For heavy usage and hostile environments, various types of transparent polymer laminates can be applied on the top of the label to provide greater durability.

CRT typesetters are naturally suited for computer-controlled production. The resultant labels may contain data taken from a computer tape supplied by the customer, or the encoded information may consist of sequential numbers created by a computer program. These sequential labels are a common application for photocomposed symbols. Typically, the user can specify the starting number and the amount by which to increment the count. Any check character can also be generated under computer control.

Photocomposed labels offer a unique combination of advantages. The first is quality. With the high print resolution common to these devices, they can produce labels with a precision and clarity available from few other printing technologies. Miniaturization of the label is an important secondary benefit of high print resolution. Photocomposed high density bar codes can fit on extremely small labels and can support all of the newer symbologies, such as Code 49, Code 16K, DataMatrix, and PDF417.

The second advantage of photocomposition is durability. The photo development process creates an image that is resistant to moisture, chemical change, abrasion, or temperature variations. The third benefit is flexibility. Label adhesives, protective laminations, and packaging of the finished product can be customized for special label applications to maximize utility, durability, and ease of use. The fourth advantage is the variability available with computer control of input.

Forms Printing

Commercial printing techniques are satisfactory if the bar code user knows in advance what information is to be printed. When a grocery manufacturer packages a product, a predetermined code that identifies the manufacturer and the product is printed on the packaging. Since many thousands of the same item are manufactured, a printing technique that employs film masters, printing plates, and high speed presses is the most cost-effective. Likewise, a business forms manufacturer needs to number printed forms sequentially. Here, printing plates for the graphics and numbering machines for the sequentially bar coded numbers may be the most cost-effective means of printing long runs of such business forms.

A manufacturer or distributor may wish to provide bar code marked order books for customers or salespersons. A user may wish to label shelves that contain inventory. The content of the bar code symbols in these cases is known in advance. No variable information is required. Commercial printing techniques are again probably the most cost-effective means of producing these bar codes.

Bar code markings on forms could be produced commercially or through demand printing. This section addresses the commercial printing of bar code marked forms. An overview of the technologies to produce bar code symbols on forms can be grouped into four major divisions, namely, impact, ink-jet, toner, and thermal.

Impact

Rotary Numbering Machines

The rotary impact numbering technology is a viable production method that has proven its worth in the business forms industry. Though quite inflexible, this method has the least impact on the forms manufacturer, in terms of both initial investment and production throughput considerations. The current delivery requirements for this technology are approximately six months.

Sequentially numbered bar codes on forms are economically printed using special rotary numbering heads and the letterpress technique. Figure 9.7 shows a typical numbering machine that could be used on a printing press, on the collator of the press, or as an off-line encoder—for adding the bar code as a subsequent operation. The numbering wheels within the tower have the engraved images of the bar code and human-readable characters and are advanced in sequence to the next number after the entire symbol is printed. The actuating mechanism (or pawl) in the numbering machine is located between the character engravings. This process is limited to discrete bar codes, such as Code 39. This is due to the spaces between the engraved images of the bar code (intercharacter gaps) on the numbering head being fixed, which means they cannot be varied in width as the symbol is advanced sequentially. Therefore, only discrete codes that have intercharacter gaps in their symbology can be printed by this technique. These codes exclude Interleaved 2 of 5, UPC, Code 93, and Code 128. Code 39 and Codabar are the most common codes printed with this technique.

Bar code numbering heads are, because of the strict tolerances required in their produc-

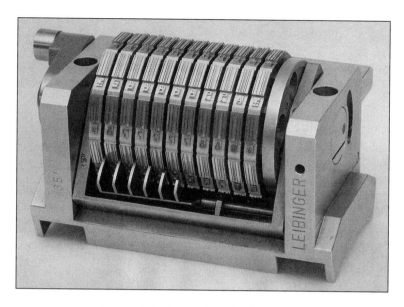

Figure 9.7: Rotary Numbering Head

The rotary numbering head, composed of several numbering wheels, is an adaptation that allows a mass printing method such as letterpress to include variable information with each impression. Several numbering wheels in such a head are used with an auto-incrementing mechanism to create a multidigit sequence of numbers. The numbering wheels can include discrete character bar code symbology patterns corresponding to the digits being printed.

tion, quite expensive. However, the production speeds are high, and there are no other special requirements necessary to create high quality consecutively numbered bar codes. Bar code numbering heads can also print a human-readable equivalent with the bar code.

Multipart forms often receive a crash-imprinted bar code on the collator or on an off-line encoder. The internal parts, with carbon impression bar codes, are generally not scannable. The purpose of crash imprinting here is to produce an eye-readable equivalent on all parts.

If the internal parts of a multipart form are to be scanned, the bar code must be added to each part separately, indicating a press numbering operation. If the form is to be carbon interleaved, the design must prevent the bar code from coming in contact with the carbon paper. Carbon smudges on a bar code reduce its readability. Solutions to this problem include the use of die cut or pattern carbon.

While the use of numbering heads has been the predominant method of printing bar codes on a forms press, the industry can expect to see the following technologies emerging in the next several years, and eventually surpassing mechanical numbering head systems.

Check character calculation is accomplished either mechanically or electromechanically. A modulus 43 check character employed in some industries is a challenge for rotary numbering heads, but can be accomplished. Since each of the 43 Code 39 characters must occupy a separate face on each wheel, the print wheel is substantially larger and has more mass than those associated with numeric (10-face) wheels. This increased mass means that the printing press will have to run more slowly, which will marginally increase the cost of printing.

Commercially available rotary numbering heads require an intercharacter gap of 46 mils when printing a face of 0.76 inch (divided between the height of the bar, the human readable character height, and the space between bar code and human readable). For symbols which have a height (including bar, human readable characters, and the space between them) exceeding these dimensions, an intercharacter gap of 66 mils is required. Using these intercharacter gap values implies an "X" dimension of between 9 and 12 mils for a 46-mil intercharacter gap. Greater "X" dimensions require a 66-mil intercharacter gap. This increased intercharacter gap reduces the overall character density of the bar code symbol. If a user is attempting to squeeze the most information into the smallest amount of space, rotary numbering machines may not be a viable alternative. However, in many applications the increased length of the symbol does not cause any hardships. In such applications rotary numbering machines may prove to be the most cost effective way to print the symbol.

The final issue on rotary numbering machines to be considered by a potential user is whether the symbols to be printed are sequential or random. Rotary numbering systems work best for sequential numbering and may not be cost effective for random symbol generation. As rigid mechanisms for creation of sequences, all the typical rotary numbering system can do is perform operations such as sequential numbering and check character calculation.

Random sequences are created under computer control in a typical interactive application. The emerging electronic printing technologies can potentially provide higher resolution randomly generated (on demand) bar symbols at reduced costs over numbering machine bar code printing.

Impact Encoders

This type of equipment is basically a stand-alone impact numbering device. The technology is designed for lower volumes and shares the inflexibilities of rotary numbering equipment. Though some brands of this equipment are direct inking, others suffer from lower print quality as a result of the image being transferred via ribbon.

Forms Printing with Ink Jet

Ink jet is a prevalent technology in the business forms industry and is used extensively for personalization of direct mail and for meeting unique numbering and encoding requirements. Though this technology has been used for some time, it is undergoing a resurgence of advanced growth. The major drawback of this method of printing is poor resolution at 120×120 dots per inch, which prevents it from meeting many bar code specifications. As of this writing (mid-1993), one company is projecting dot resolution of 240×240 dots per inch within the next twelve months.

In addition, ink formulations require development: Current fluid products are not scannable in the infrared spectrum. Also, print contrast and ink spread are directly related to the ink/substrate combination. Clear over-coating is normally required to protect the image from abrasion and environmental damage. Substrate considerations become very important with ink jet when using ultra-thin carbonless stocks that are now part of many business forms.

There are basically two methods of applying ink jet: on-line and off-line. The standard of the industry for off-line has a high initial cost, approaching $1.2 million, but this off-line system would allow beneficial rotary press production rates up to 1,000 feet per minute and is not press cylinder size dependent. This unit may be adapted to a rotary forms press in an on-line configuration, but results in higher costs per printed unit because of slower press speeds and bundled equipment complexities. The leading on-line system is currently limited to a one-inch wide pattern with the web and can be mounted either on a rotary forms press or collator. The width constraint requires that the bar code be imaged in a ladder format only. This system costs approximately $100,000 per ink jet imaging head.

Toner-Based Imaging Systems

Toner-based imaging systems meet the printing resolution and print contrast reflectance requirements of quality bar code printing. In general, these systems suffer from reduced production throughput, image permanence considerations such as toner flaking, and high pressure and heat damage to certain substrates, such as carbonless stocks. However, this is a young industry that produces technological advancements frequently. To date, toner-based technologies have been favored by the printing industry for label press imaging of variable data with very good results. As a rule, these toner images must be clear over-coated to protect the toner from abrasion damage. It is important to realize that a great variety of toner fusing systems in this general category produce varied results, and this should be considered apart from the image formation on the transfer drum.

Magnetography

This process has excellent flexibility that meets quality bar code printing standards. The high cost of producing this technology has limited the vendor base to a handful of suppliers. Equipment costs approach $1.2 million per off-line unit for installation.

High-resolution images are available in this technology at 240 × 240 dots per inch. Newer equipment has reported throughput speeds of 250 feet per minute, and web widths range from 18 to 20 inches. Most substrates used with this method do not require over-coating of the image, as a very strong bond is formed between the toner and the substrate. The low-pressure fusing requirements (as opposed to the pressure of ion deposition) allow the imaging of some carbonless papers, including self-contained stock. The major implementation of this dry magnetic mono-component toner technology is on off-line equipment.

Ion Deposition

Currently, most commercially available ion deposition units are based on the Delphax print engine, and cost upwards of $150,000 per installed unit. This imaging method is also capable of printing at 240 × 240 dots per inch. Speeds run currently at 200 feet per minute and are increasing as the technology improves.

This process does meet the requirements for quality bar code printing standards, but its flexibility is restricted by a rather narrow image width of 8.5 inches and poor toner fusion to the substrate. High-pressure fusion causes capsule damage when imaging carbonless stocks. Two additional bar code considerations are that (1) the formation of the toner dots across the form web results in a skewing effect of a straight line by 0.031 inch every 12 linear inches, and (2) the high pressure fusing of the toner dots results in an unequal growth which is greater across the web and which could adversely affect the "X" dimension in the picket fence format. Because of speed considerations, this technology is not well suited for on-line application with a rotary forms press. However, it should be speed-compatible with collator production speeds.

	Ink Jet	Magnetography	Ion Deposition	Rotary Engraved Print Wheels
Dots Per Inch	120 X 120	240 X 240	240 X 240	N/A
Nominal Dot Size	0.00833"	0.00417"	0.00417"	N/A
Measured Dot Size	0.010"	0.0055"	0.0080"	N/A
Smallest "X"	1 dot + gain = 0.010 to 0.0125" 2 dots + gain = 0.020"	3 dots + gain = 0.014" to 0.015"	1 dot + gain = 0.008"	0.013"
Wide:Narrow Ratio	2.66:1	2.4:1	2.5:1	2.8:1
18-digit length Codabar	2.6"	3.67"	2.16"	3.431"
Interleaved 2 of 5	2.91"	2.18"	1.27"	N/A
Aspect Ratio	Off-line > 100 percent	>100 percent	>100 percent	0.520" Across Web

Table 9.2: Feature Comparison of Bar Code Printing

This table lists some of the features of the major methods of printing variable information during print runs of business forms on mass printing equipment. The first of such technologies to be introduced, rotary printing wheels, is still used but has largely been replaced by modern, electronically controlled graphic techniques. Note: The 18-digit length for Codabar assumes an intercharacter space of 1X in all cases except rotary print wheels, where the 18-digit length was calculated using an intercharacter space of 0.053 inch.

Electrophotography and Electrography

Electrophotography is a mature printing technology evolving from the photocopier industry and is widely used to generate high-speed data processing output. Numerous suppliers are actively involved in this general category. Specific subgroups include LED and laser imaging techniques, which make use of a dry, two-component reversal toner/developer system to produce the final image.

High heat and pressure need to be considered, as do web path problems. While, theoretically, throughput speeds approach 190 feet per minute with at least one model, this portion of the industry has not involved itself to date with the forms printing industry. So, even though such factors as 240 X 240 dots per inch are impressive, it would appear that these processes are impractical for the high-volume forms printer.

Electrography printing systems require a special dielectric printing paper for imaging and are normally found in such applications as facsimile, medical diagnostic and monitoring recorders, and geological data recorders. The only high-speed data processing printer to utilize this process was produced in the early 1970s, and remains in very limited use because of its special substrate requirements.

Thermal Printing

This non-impact printing method produces high quality bar code images and is a fast-growing technology. The two major subgroups are thermal transfer, which requires the use of resistive thermal transfer ribbons, and direct thermal, which requires special thermal dye-coated substrates.

These approaches have relatively slow throughput; the special ribbon/substrate requirements preclude the use of current forms materials. Thermal printing has not yet been integrated with business forms manufacturing equipment.

Off-Site Printing

Benefits of Off-Site Printing

Selecting an external source for bar code printing gives you several distinct advantages over having the labels printed on site. Listed below are some of these advantages, some of which apply to one process more than another.

Print Direct—In some cases, notably glass, metal, and high-density polymer containers, the printer can print the bar code directly on the surface of the container. This eliminates the cost of printing and applying labels. By incorporating bar code printing in the press run, the printer can accurately position the bar code on the container.

High Volume—Some of the printing processes can print labels at speeds of 1000 feet per minute. In instances where a large quantity of bar code labels is required, there can be substantial savings in cost per label.

Expertise—Some printers have been printing bar code symbols on packaging for more than 15 years. They have acquired considerable expertise in bar code printing, enabling them to assist their clients in selecting proper substrates, ink colors, and bar code dimensions to comply with the standards of the industry.

Graphics—The off-site printer can print additional graphics and color combinations to provide the aesthetic appeal required in some label and direct printing applications. Some presses allow printing of up to eight different colors.

Responsibility—The control and responsibility for complying with standards and producing scannable bar codes can be centralized. Vendors can be selected based upon their expertise in producing bar codes and their familiarity with quality assurance requirements of the standards and guidelines.

Quality—The nature of the technology employed in many off-site printing processes produces bar codes of very high quality.

Limitations of Off-Site Printing

Just as there are advantages to off-site production of bar code symbols, there are also limitations. Listed below are some of these limitations, some of which apply to one process more than another.

Timeliness—Once an order for bar code labels is placed, it is not unusual to have a delay of two weeks before they can be received.

Flexibility—In addition to the order/receipt delay associated with off-site printing, another delay will be experienced before receipt of the new symbols if the coding structure of a product is changed after an order is placed. (The original symbols will have to be replaced.)

Material Inventory—When labels or containers are preprinted and received, dedicated inventory space is required for each unique symbol structure. Blank or color-coded labels without item descriptions can be stored in mass storage, and bar code can be marked when required in demand printing situations.

On-Site Printing

It may not always be possible to predefine the codes that are needed. Even if such definition is possible, it may be too labor-intensive to maintain an inventory of the desired labels. Applications often require random information, such as lot/batch number and expiration dates. And labels are frequently unique, prohibiting their purchase ahead of time. These labels must be produced on-site and in real time. Such unique labels can be produced using demand printers. These printers operate under microprocessor control and can create unique labels as they are needed.

There exist three basic varieties of creating symbols on demand, namely:

- Intelligent controller
- Intelligent printer
- Host software

The first of these, an intelligent controller, is a hardware solution that incorporates a microprocessor-based graphics controller between the computer system and the printer. An application's program resident on the host computer system creates a series of escape sequence messages (e.g., QMS Code V Version II) to the graphics controller that in turn controls the horizontal and vertical placement of dots to create various size human-readable characters; various height, narrow bar width, and wide-to-narrow ratio bar code symbols; and other graphic symbols. Intelligent graphics controllers are supplied either by the manufacturer of the printer or by a third party. Suppliers include QMS, Printronix, and Analog Technology Corporation.

The intelligent printer (notably thermal and thermal transfer printers) incorporates the controller intelligence within the printing device. Formatted ASCII or EBCDIC character strings (e.g., Zebra Technologies ZPL) are transmitted to the printer to create the bar code symbol, text, and graphics.

Host Software systems permit the user to create the format—often in a WYSIWYG (What You See Is What You Get) manner—on the screen, defining the text, bar code symbol, and graphics fields. These fields can be incremented/decremented under computer control and can also access database information to dynamically change the data within the fields. Host Software systems often create a bit-mapped graphic format and transmit this format directly to the printer.

Demand printing systems use one of three methods: character-by-character impact, serial dot-matrix, or linear array technologies. These categories are expanded upon in Table 9.3.

CHARACTER-BY-CHARACTER IMPACT PRINTERS
     Drum
     Belt
     Typewriter Element
     Rotary Encoders
SERIAL DOT-MATRIX PRINTERS
     Impact
     Laser (Toner and Drum)
     Matrix Thermal
     Thermal Transfer
     Ink-jet
LINEAR ARRAY PRINTERS
     Line Impact
     Linear Array Thermal
     Linear Array Thermal Transfer

Table 9.3: On-Site Printing Technologies

This table enumerates several of the demand printer technologies used for on-site bar code printing.

Until 1985, electrostatic printing was either sheet fed or cost over $200,000. Laser printers in sheet-fed varieties are presently available for well under $5,000. There has also been an introduction of medium-speed continuous-form laser printers for under $60,000. In 1991 three vendors introduced lower-speed continuous-form laser printers at a cost of approximately $5,000.

Typewriter element printers do not presently provide an adequate aspect ratio (bar code height to symbol length) to be applicable in most bar code applications. The applications for this obsolete technology are extremely limited.

Rotary encoders (movable type on a printing wheel with wet ink) have few suppliers and require special inks. The quality of print also leaves much to be desired.

Consequently, we'll consider only the major forms of demand printers useful in bar code applications: drum printers, thermal and thermal transfer printers, belt printers, ink jet printers, and electrostatic printers.

Drum Printers

Character-by-character drum printers, an example of which is shown in Figure 9.8(a), work much like standard office typewriters and generally print high-density, discrete bar

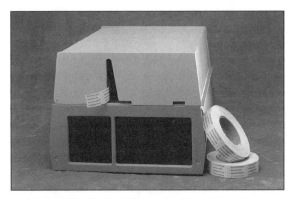

Figure 9.8: Serial Character Drum Printer

A typical serial character drum printer forms a bar code symbol by sequentially selecting fully formed character/bar code images on a rotating drum or wheel.

codes. The characters are etched or engraved in reverse on a drum. Paper, vinyl, or mylar label stock and a dry carbon ribbon pass between the rotating drum and a hammer, as shown in Figure 9.8(b). Operated by an electromagnet, the hammer forces the paper and ribbon against the drum, causing the image to be transferred from the drum through the ribbon to the label. Each hammer stroke forms a complete character.

Around the base of the drum are timing marks counted by a LED/photo-eye unit. When the count equals that associated with the correct character, the microprocessor causes the hammer to strike the label and ribbon against the drum. The drum rotates continually at about 500 revolutions per minute, and the hammer actuates at a speed of approximately 5 milliseconds, so there is virtually no relative motion between the hammer and drum.

The machine is considered to be a dedicated bar code printer, and label format is limited to the symbols engraved on the drum. One to ten lines of human-readable text may be provided, but the basic purpose of the machine is to provide a bar code symbol. However, various fields within the format can be changed randomly, allowing each label to be different.

Character-by-character printers use label stock which comes in rolls. The stock is either die-cut to size or continuous, in which case it is cut after printing. The media is available in either plain or preprinted (logo, color code, company name, etc.) form. It can be backed by an adhesive that meets the particular application need. Character-by-character impact printing uses a one-time, high-quality, carbon-based printing ribbon, providing instant-dry, smear-resistant prints. Typical narrow bar widths are about 0.007 inch. Production speed depends on label length and content. Typically 40 to 60 labels per minute can be produced. Accessories are available to laminate, butt cut, cut off, stack, rewind, and apply the labels. The size of the printer is small enough so that it can be used almost anywhere.

Bar-by-bar printers operate in a manner that is very similar to the character-by-character drum printers, except that each bar, wide or narrow, is printed with the strike of a single hammer, and the sequence of wide or narrow bars/spaces is determined through programming. This process enables the printing of discrete or continuous bar codes. Bar-by-bar drum printers are generally used for medium- to low-density bar codes.

Character-by-character and bar-by-bar drum printers have a specific engraved format on the drums provided by the bar code printer manufacturer. Consequently, to change the format (the number of human-readable lines of text) or the symbology requires a separate drum. Character-by-character and bar-by-bar printers typically cost less than $10,000.

Formed character impact printing was the preferred method to print bar code in the original LOGMARS report published by the Department of Defense in 1981. Only about 10 percent of bar code users still print on site with formed character impact printing. Formed character printing was rated in the 1981 LOGMARS report as the most cost-effective form of bar code printing. Today, this is no longer the case. The machines are more expensive than dot-matrix and thermal printing systems and are similar in price to laser and thermal transfer printers. Since the symbols are etched on the drum, it is more difficult to change symbologies, and the printer is limited to printing fixed data for discrete symbologies like UPC.

Belt Printers

The technology involved in belt printers is very similar to that of character-by-character drum printers, except that the characters are resident on a metal or rubber belt instead of the drum. Since the belt must travel a greater distance than the circumference of the drum, its speed—in inches per second—is faster than a drum to accomplish the same print speed. This increase in speed causes the bar code characters to slew (or become distorted). This distortion causes the bars to grow and the spaces to shrink, producing a bar code of less than optimal quality.

The Dot-Matrix Printing Process

A dot-matrix printer produces images using a pattern of dots arranged in a vertical and horizontal grid referred to as a matrix. Within the matrix grid, bar codes, graphics, and alphanumeric text characters can be constructed. Figure 9.9 illustrates a typical text character within a matrix grid.

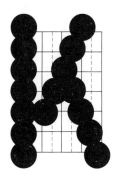

Figure 9.9: Text Characters within a Matrix Grid

Modern electronically controlled printing methods uniformly use a dot matrix grid to lay out the "pixels" of a symbol. This electronic flexibility allows such printers to print text characters and graphics (line and, to a limited extent, half-tone), as well as bar codes. This diagram shows how a typical character image is laid out by selecting which pixels of a rectangular grid will be printed. Each printer technology employs a different method to cause a given pixel to be formed and retained on the output media.

This figure was reproduced with permission of AIM USA from its publication Matrix Impact Printing *which is available in its entirety from AIM USA.*

Ink Jet Printing

Since the introduction of large character ink jet printers in the United States in 1980, there has been a proliferation of manufacturers entering the market. This can create confusion regarding functionality and result in potential system users thinking that all ink jet systems function the same and utilize the same design technology. This is an easy assumption to make since the end result, the creation of a character formed by dots, is the same for all printheads. There are, however, different printhead technologies to match application needs with printhead technology that is best suited to meet those needs.

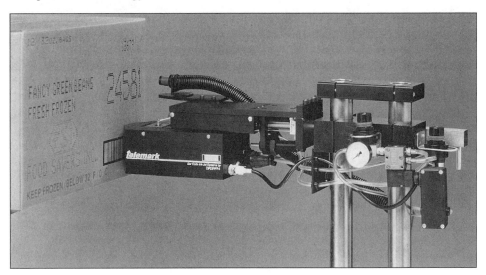

Figure 9.10: Ink Jet Printer

This is a typical large character ink jet printer, used to spray a printed symbol on media such as corrugated cartons.

This figure was reproduced with permission of AIM USA from its publication Matrix Impact Printing which is available in its entirety from AIM USA.

Printhead Technologies

The printhead is the heart of an ink jet system. While the printhead cannot function independently (without other components), the overall system performance is directly related to the printhead's capabilities. The four printhead technologies discussed here share some common characteristics. They all utilize a pressurized fluid, normally ink, in order to create an image. All technologies utilize an electromagnetic solenoid that activates a plunger to control the ink propelled from the orifices. These orifices are arranged vertically so that one activation of each solenoid creates one vertical column of dots. As the substrate moves horizontally, the valves are selectively opened or closed to create a specified character. This is called drop-on-demand technology. In spite of these basic similarities, the design of each of the four technologies is dramatically different from the others. Figures 9.11(a) through 9.11(d) illustrate the four types of printheads, which are presented in approximately chronological order of their development and market introduction in the United States.

Type A operates by bringing pressurized fluid into an ink manifold. Out of this manifold, individual fluid tubes connect to an inlet port of the solenoid valve. Inside the solenoid, the ink enters a chamber containing a plunger and spring. The plunger seals a second valve

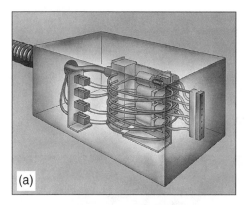 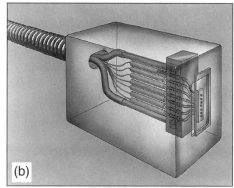

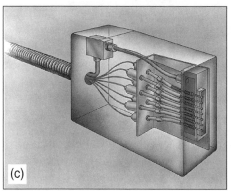 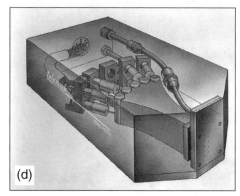

Figure 9.11: Ink Jet Printheads

The evolution of ink jet printing technology has brought with it improved printhead designs. (a) Type A Ink Jet Printhead. (b) Type B Ink Jet Printhead. (c) Type C Ink Jet Printhead. (d) Type D Ink Jet Printhead. As explained in the text, these four types represent a series of improved designs for "drop-on-demand" ink jet printheads as the distance from the flow control mechanism to the orifice is shortened.

opening where small tubing connects this opening to the printhead orifices. A dot is created by energizing the coil of the solenoid, thus retracting the valve plunger. Pressurized fluid flows through the tubing and out the orifices. When the solenoid is de-energized, the spring returns the plunger to stop the flow of fluid.

Type B operates in a slightly different manner. In this technology pressurized fluid is brought into a manifold by a single fluid tube. The manifold also has an exit line that allows fluid to pass through the main ink manifold chamber. Inside the ink manifold, fluid is captured in a main chamber and allowed to enter a secondary chamber that contains the back end of the valve plunger. The coil of solenoid is wrapped around this chamber. The sealing end of the plunger is held in position by a spring. For each valve plunger, a tube carries the fluid from the ink manifold to the orifices.

To form a dot, the coil of the solenoid is energized, retracting the plunger which allows the ink to flow through the tube and out through the orifices. When the solenoid coil is de-energized, the spring returns the plunger to a sealed position, stopping the flow of fluid.

Type C has a single fluid entry line into an ink manifold similar to Type B. As in Type

B, ink is allowed into a secondary chamber containing the valve plunger. The solenoid, however, is located at the end of this chamber. Inside the manifold, a spring holds the sealing end of the plunger against a channel opening that leads to the orifices.

To form a dot, the solenoid is energized, retracting the plunger. Pressurized fluid enters the channel and is pushed out through the orifice. When the solenoid is de-energized, the spring returns the plunger to a sealed position, stopping the fluid flow.

Type D has a single fluid entry line that brings pressurized ink into an ink manifold. The manifold also has a fluid to pass through the ink manifold. The ink is captured in the ink manifold by a flexible membrane and a front plate that contains the orifice openings. A piston presses against the flexible membrane to seal the orifices in the front plate. A wire connects the piston to a solenoid. To form a dot, the solenoid is energized, the piston retracts, and the pressurized fluid pushes the membrane back allowing the fluid to flow into the orifice. When the solenoid is de-energized, the piston returns to a "rest" position, sealing the membrane against the orifice and stopping the fluid flow.

These four drop-on-demand ink jet technologies have progressed in three important evolutionary steps, resulting in improved performance. The most important progression is the reduction of the length of the column of fluid between the flow control mechanism (plunger) and the orifice opening. This reduction improves fluid control between the plunger and the orifice, resulting in more precise drops that require less ink and produce a more legible image, especially at high speeds. A second improvement is the separation of mechanical components from contact with the fluid. This protects the mechanical valve components from corrosive effects of the ink and from sticking caused by ink drying on the valve parts. The third improvement is the elimination of secondary fluid chambers. This allows thorough and complete cleaning of the valve cavities that come in contact with the fluid.

Ink Performance

Just as the printhead is the heart of an ink jet system, the fluid or ink is the lifeblood of an ink jet system. Application requirements and printhead performance must be matched to ensure reliable operation of the system. As such, the following application needs must be defined in order to effectively evaluate the printhead's ability to fulfill these demands:

1. Legibility Requirements
2. Drying Time Requirements
3. Adhesion Requirements
4. Water/Chemical Resistance
5. Light Fastness
6. Agency Approvals
7. Ink Color

Within the printhead, all components that come in direct contact with the ink must be absolutely compatible with the ink's ingredients. This is especially true when marking on a non-absorbent substrate, such as plastic bags, that require the use of aggressive solvents in order to adhere to the substrate. When a pigmented ink is used, some method of keeping the solid colorant in suspension in the fluid while in the printhead is required. In addition, with any ink used, there should be a convenient way of cleaning all components that come in direct contact with the ink.

Image Quality

There are three basic categories into which printheads can be divided based on the number of orifices that produce dots. The image quality is directly related to dot density, the number of dots vertically and the horizontal distance between the dots.

Seven-Dot and Nine-Dot Printheads: The vertical distance between the bottom dot and the top dot ranges from 5/16 to 1-1/2 inches. A seven-dot printhead can produce a single stroke and a double stroke bold font. The nine-dot printhead can not only produce single stroke and double stroke fonts, it can also vary the character height by printing with nine dots or seven dots in the same horizontal line.

16-Dot and 18-Dot Printheads: The vertical distance between the bottom dot and the top dot of these printheads ranges from 1-1/4 to 2 inches. These printheads are basically like two printheads in a single housing. As a result, the printhead can print an extremely bold character utilizing all 16 or 18 dots or two separate 7-dot characters. In addition, an 18-dot printhead can print separate 7-dot and 9-dot characters for improved character definition and highlighting of information.

32-Dot and 42-Dot Printheads: The vertical distance from the bottom dot to the top dot of these printheads ranges from 2-3/4 to 6 inches; the 32-dot printhead is the same as four 7-dot printheads in a single housing. The 48-dot printhead is the same as having six 7-dot printheads in a single housing. Like the 16-dot and 18-dot printheads, these printheads can produce a single character 2-3/4 to 6 inches tall and four to six separate lines of messaged text.

The user has to match the legibility requirements of the application with the printhead capabilities. Consideration must be given to factors such as the print area available; the horizontal position of each message line of text; and the legibility requirements for each line of text. It is important to keep in mind that character height alone will not create a highly legible image. The character must have a proportional width to complement the height.

Line Speed

A complement to legibility is the ability of a printhead to produce a quality mark at high line speeds. Most printhead technologies can accommodate up to 100 feet per minute, with another group of printheads effectively printing at 200 feet per minute, and a few that operate at over 250 feet per minute. Beyond the obvious need to produce a crisp circular dot without splatter or tails, it is important that the printhead produce a character that has a proportional width-to-height ratio that fits in the designated surface print area. Some technologies merely spread the distance between vertical columns of dots in order to obtain higher speeds.

Environment

It is important to define the environment with respect to temperature, humidity, and dust levels. The printhead should be chosen based on its ability to withstand the given environmental conditions, or steps must be taken to modify the environment. Some simple environmental modifications are: utilizing a heat source as simple as a heat lamp in a cold environment; providing an air source that blows particulates from the front plate periodically in a dusty environment; and either covering or removing the printheads during the washdown process in a wash-down environment.

Preventive Maintenance

It is imperative that a preventive maintenance strategy be developed and implemented conscientiously in order to keep the printhead operating at peak performance. At the very minimum, this should include cleaning the front plate of the printhead with a cleaner on a daily basis. Each month all of the valve and tubing areas that come in contact with ink should be thoroughly cleaned. Some manufacturers offer preventive maintenance and service contracts.

Operating Costs

Operating costs include the cost of consumables (the ink), the cost to initialize or make the system ready for operation on a daily basis, and the cost for service.

The design of the printhead can dramatically influence the amount of consumable fluid used. In general, the more precise the control of fluid flow, the better the fluid consumption. The best measurement of this is to establish a measurable and controlled test to determine ink economy.

Determining the cost of repairs can be extremely difficult. Such costs as replacement parts, maintenance personnel time, and the cost of production line downtime must be considered. However, a thorough evaluation can determine which printhead design is most likely to succeed in a well-defined application based on the criteria previously presented. In addition, look for helpful design considerations such as quick disconnect electrical and fluid line fittings. Features such as these can greatly affect the speed and efficiency of maintenance or repairs.

Some ink-jet systems claim the ability to be able to print "scannable" bar code symbols, and some vendors will even supply a bar code reader by which to "scan" the symbol. "Scannability" by one bar code reader does not qualify the bar code symbol. A bar code symbol must be able to be repeatedly "verified" as at least a "C"-quality symbol when measured with a 0.020-inch aperture under standards such as ANS X3.182-1990 to be acceptable. As of this writing, few in-line ink-jet systems were commercially available that met the requirement of "verification." R&D labs of various companies have systems on the drawing boards that provide four-, six-, and eight-inch printheads with resolutions of 150 dots per inch and better, permitting the printing of an entire side of a carton with all applicable information, bar code symbols, and other graphics. Once perfected, this technology will achieve high print resolution, low cost, relatively high speed, and quality printing.

Dot-Matrix Impact

Of all of the types of printers presently employed in bar code printing, the most common is the serial dot-matrix impact printer. The popularity of dot-matrix impact printing is due to its ability to produce both text and graphics in varying sizes on many types of printing stock. Drum printers are quite acceptable for printing labels up to a certain size, but they do not possess the text and graphics capabilities of dot-matrix impact systems.

A dot-matrix impact print element consists of a series of pins (or styli) arranged in an array or in a line. On some printers the printhead is fixed and the label stock moves. Other systems use a moving printhead and stationary stock. The pins strike an inked ribbon against the label stock to form the desired characters. The pins are typically 12 to 14 mils in diameter or larger. When these pins strike an inked nylon ribbon, the thickness of the ribbon and the bleeding of the ink can cause a wire of 12 to 14 mils to create a dot that is about 14 to 16 mils in diameter.

A narrow bar in a bar code is created by printing a row of overlapping dots, and a wide bar is produced by printing a series of overlapping narrow bars. Overlapping can occur either by single vertical half-space form movement or by multi-pass printing, or a combina-

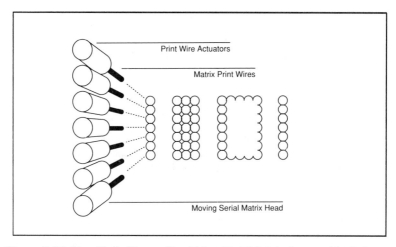

Figure 9.12: Bar Code Formation Using Dot-Matrix Impact Techniques

A narrow bar is created by printing overlapping dots, and a wide bar is produced by printing a series of overlapping narrow bars. Overlapping dots result in bar edges not so well defined as those printed by formed character printers.

tion of both. The use of overlapping dots, as shown in Figure 9.12(a), results in bar edges that are not so well defined as those edges of bar codes printed by formed character printers. Some of the problems associated with this overlapping are shown in Figure 9.12(b). Further, notice in Figure 9.12(a) that there is a small space at the intersection of four dots. A bar code reader of sufficient resolution could see this "void" as a space and cause a no-read situation. By reducing the size of the dot and using the proper overlapping techniques, edge distortion can be minimized.

Dot-matrix impact printers fall into two major categories, serial matrix printers and matrix line printers. The serial matrix printer consists of a printhead with 7 to 24 pins as shown in Figure 9.13(a). With serial matrix printers the printhead travels across the printer and selected pins are fired to create the desired image as shown in Figure 9.13(b).

Matrix line printers on the other hand utilize a bank of hammers as shown in Figure 9.14(a). The printhead shuttles back and forth across the printer, as shown in Figure 9.14(b), with each of the pins in the printhead able to fire simultaneously, creating an entire row of dots in a single pass. The paper is then advanced to accomplish subsequent printing on a line-by-line basis down the page. Due to their larger printheads, matrix line printers are generally faster than their serial matrix counterparts.

Dot-band printers, which have a revolving band of raised dots fire against the print surface by stationary hammers, are considered matrix line printers.

One of the issues relating to dot-matrix impact printers is the speed at which they can print bar code symbols. Historically, if you had a 600 line per minute printer, such a rating was identified in a text mode, not a graphics mode. Bar code symbols are created in the graphics mode and were significantly slower (200 to 300 lines per minute) than the rated speed. Recent developments in some of the controller software and hardware, most notably QMS Magnum Code V, Version 2.0, permit bar code printing speeds even higher than the rated speed of the printer.

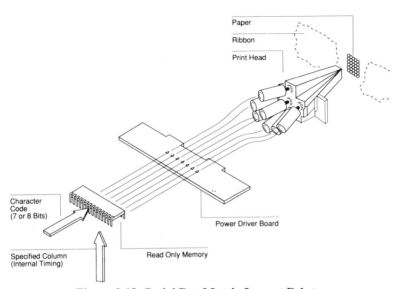

Paper

Ribbon

Print Head

Character
Code
(7 or 8 Bits)

Power Driver Board

Specified Column
(Internal Timing)

Read Only Memory

Figure 9.13: Serial Dot-Matrix Impact Printer

(A typical serial dot matrix impact printhead that has from 7 to 24 pins in a vertical row, actuated by a solenoid as the head is moved across the media.

This figure was reproduced with permission of AIM USA from its publication Matrix Impact Printing which is available in its entirety from AIM USA.

Electrophotographical

Laser Printing (Electrophotographical—EPG)

Electrostatic printing techniques (laser, LED, and ion) create a charged area either on the label or form to be printed or on a dielectric cylinder which holds a latent image until the image is transferred to the label or paper media. EPG printing is most familiar in copying and reproducing machines as opposed to data output printers. Exceptions are the electronic imaging systems which have the ability to print data and forms at the same time.

Most often, non-impact computer printers employ dot-matrix impact character and graphics formation. In electrophotographical printing techniques, a latent image is created by making use of the photoelectric characteristics of the material being used to coat an image transfer drum. A typical EPG system might employ a Helium-Neon (He-Ne) laser whose circuitry permits the He-Ne to be scanned in a raster pattern and pulsed under the control of resident software. The pattern of laser on/off signals corresponds to the dot-matrix pixels of the information to be printed. The laser beam causes the electrostatic image consisting of charged and uncharged areas to be formed on the surface of the cylindrical drum. A toner consisting of small, black, electrically charged particles is brought near the surface of the drum, and the toner particles adhere by electrostatic attraction to the charged areas of the drum image. Next, the medium is brought near the drum and a charge is applied to its back to attract toner particles away from the drum and onto it. The medium is then moved to a heater/fusing station to fix the toner permanently to the medium. The final step of the process restores the drum to its original condition. The laser spot is generally focused to approximately 5 mils (and in some systems currently down to 3 mils), generating a print spot of 5.5 mils in diameter. EPG systems can print 45 pages per minute,

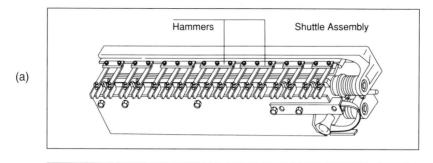

(a)

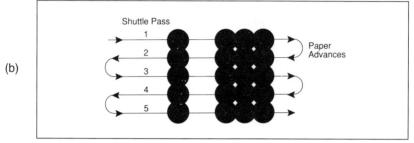

(b)

Figure 9.14: Dot-Matrix Impact Line Printer Details

(a) represents a typical dot-matrix impact line printer hammer bank and shuttle.
(b) shows the construction of a bar code using dot matrix line printing technology.

This figure was reproduced with permission of AIM USA from its publication Matrix Impact Printing which is available in its entirety from AIM USA.

placing high-quality images anywhere on the page.

EPG techniques have attempted to capitalize on the office automation marketplace and until recently have disregarded the need for low-cost, continuous-stock systems over sheet-fed stock systems. For mounting of labels using automatic applicators, the stock must be continuous form. Recently, several companies have introduced continuous stock printing systems at dramatically lower cost compared to their $275,000 to $450,000 predecessors. Such a system is shown in Figure 9.15.

LED Printers (Electrophotographical—EPG)

A new form of EPG replaces the laser as a light source with a linear array of photodiodes which extend across the dielectric cylinder. Under computer control, selective diodes are illuminated to form the image on the cylinder. As the cylinder rotates, the complete image of the document or label is formed. LED printers have fewer moving parts than flying spot lasers. Fewer moving parts generally means better durability. Other than the difference in light source, LED printers and laser printers operate similarly.

Advantages of EPG Printing Systems

Electrophotographical printing systems provide the user with a high-quality image as well as capabilities for document printing. The small dot size, ranging from 300 to 600 dots per inch, permits narrow and wide bars to be formed with extremely fine width increments of .0033 inch and .0016 inch, respectively. Taking the example of a 300 dots per inch printer, bar codes could be printed with a narrow bar of 3 dots wide (approximately equal to 0.010 inch) and a wide bar of 9 dots wide (approximately 0.030 inch) for a 3:1 wide-to-nar-

Figure 9.15: Continuous Form Laser Printer

The continuous form laser printers currently being introduced allow creation of on-demand bar code labels in contemporary applications of bar code technology.

row ratio. Similarly, a Code 39 symbol with a narrow bar of 4 dots wide (approximately 0.013 inch) and a wide bar of 10 dots wide (approximately 0.033 inch) could realize a 2.5:1 wide-to-narrow ratio. Unlike dot-matrix impact, EPG dots are not made to overlap. Electrophotographical systems can print on the widest range of substrates (from label stock to plain paper) any symbology, and any computer-controlled structure of sequential, random, and static code structures. These printers can print not only text and bar codes but any bit-mapped graphic as well. Under computer control, the text, bar code symbols, and graphics can be rotated to any orientation. Accessories are available from some manufacturers to laminate, cut, and apply adhesives to output from EPG systems.

Disadvantages of EPG Printing Systems

Some electrophotographical printers are disadvantaged by the type of photosensitive technology employed in the generation of the image. As of 1991, two types of photoreceptive surfaces exist. The first and oldest is that of the selenium metal coated drum. While the element selenium does possess some of the best imaging qualities, selenium is also highly carcinogenic, which introduces risk in handling and environmental issues of disposal. Copiers and laser printers with replaceable drum/toner cartridges are designed so that the drum is not handled. Many of the newer laser printers employ an organic coating to the imaging drum. The organic drum does not possess the same negative qualities of handling and environmental risks, but as of yet has not been able to achieve the resolutions possible with selenium. The organic drum does provide sufficient quality for many bar code printing requirements.

Many EPG systems also employ heat and pressure in the imaging process. For some pressure-sensitive label stocks this process may liquify the adhesive, jamming the printer. Ensure that any pressure-sensitive stock introduced to EPG systems employing heat and pressure is rated for such printers.

Recent developments in laser printing technology eliminate the heat and pressure imaging in favor of flash fusing which heats only the toner for a brief instant. Figure 9.16 shows a mid-range, high-speed laser printer which employs both flash fusion and organic cylinder construction.

Ion Deposition

Ion deposition printing is a patented electronic imaging process similar to laser and LED EPG printing. Instead of creating the image on the dielectric cylinder with photons (light), electrically charged particles known as ions are projected onto the dielectric cylinder through a matrix addressed print cartridge (see Figure 9.17). Ion deposition systems employ a cold fusion system whereby the toner is affixed to the substrate utilizing only pressure.

Figure 9.16: Flash Fusion Printer

Newer laser printers such as this one employ "flash fusion" techniques which operate at lower continuous temperature and lower pressure, thus allowing faster operation. This printer also uses an organic toner drum technology.

Thermal Printers

Thermal printers use heated printheads and special heat activated paper. Two types of direct thermal printers are available. One employs a printhead similar in design to those of dot-matrix impact printers. The printhead consists of rectangular or round styli that are selectively heated and cooled under microprocessor control. The heated styli cause chemicals in the paper to turn brown or black or to burn off a top coating. The dot-matrix impact pattern can vary from a 5-by-7 to a 16-by-20 array and is selectable by CRT or computer input. The second variety of thermal printer employs a single bar, much in the same way bar-by-bar drum printers operate. Instead of striking a ribbon, the bar is heated and cooled as the paper stock moves across the head. This creates the wide and narrow bars that form the bar code symbol.

Thermal printheads are primarily available in one of two technologies, thin film or thick film. Figure 9.18 presents a cross-sectional view of a typical thin film head.

Thick film heads differ from thin film heads fundamentally in the resistive elements. A coating protects the resistive elements effectively enough to give the thermal head a typical life expectancy in excess of 2,000,000 inches of printing.

There are few moving parts in thermal printers, so the printers are inexpensive, quiet, and ideally suited to environments such as libraries and hospitals. Production speed is between 10 and 60 labels per minute. The matrix and bar-by-bar character formation permit these printing systems to compose either discrete or continuous bar code symbols with human-readable data in varying sizes. The minimum element size is approximately 4.5 mils. Edge definition of bars is superior to either dot-matrix impact or formed character impact printing.

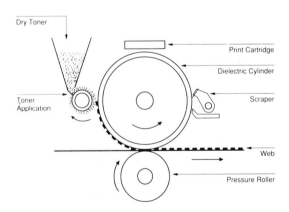

Figure 9.17: Ion Deposition Print Station

Ion deposition printers are toner-and-drum printers similar to laser printers. The graphic pattern of electrostatic charges is painted on the drum using a controlled beam of electrically charged ions. As in the laser printer, the charged pattern attracts particles of toner, which are then transferred to the print medium and fused—in this case with pressure alone.

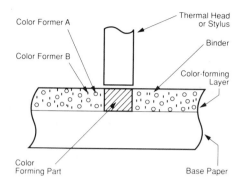

Figure 9.18: Thin Film Direct Thermal Printhead

Here is a diagram of a typical thin film direct thermal printhead, used to selectively heat surface areas in contact with the special paper medium, thus changing the paper's color and making an image.

This figure was reproduced with permission of AIM USA from its publication Direct Thermal Printing *which is available in its entirety from AIM USA.*

Today's thermal papers form a dark image when heat is applied to the surface. When heat is applied, a chemical reaction occurs in which two colorless chemicals combine to form the darkened image. These chemicals are bound to the surface of the paper.

Typical thermal papers in use today fall into two categories—organic and inorganic. The organic type of paper is generally not infrared absorbing, making it impractical to use with infrared readers. The background color for organic papers is generally white. Some of these papers are coated with a protective layer which serves to increase the moisture and chemical resistance. See the discussion of labels and adhesives later in this chapter.

Inorganic papers use a different chemistry to form an image. The chemical employed forms a reduced metal which has a black color and is infrared absorbing, producing an image compatible with infrared readers. The inorganic papers also are more resistant to moisture, chemicals, and ultraviolet radiation than organic papers. Inorganic papers are slightly more expensive and more abrasive to printheads than are organic papers; many of these papers are beige instead of white.

Thermal printers have two disadvantages. First, since the label stock is heat sensitive, label quality may deteriorate over time if the labels are stored in a warm environment. Further, these same label stocks are quite often sensitive to ultraviolet radiation, e.g., sunlight, which may affect label quality. Second, many thermal labels do not provide adequate contrast when scanned by infrared light sources (band B900). Since earlier scanning systems might use light sources in the infrared band, the labels may not read reliably. When thermal labels are used, the user must ensure that the stock is rated for infrared readability or that only visible red light sources are employed. Printing stocks do exist for thermal printers to achieve adequate contrast in the infrared spectrum, to be less sensitive to ultraviolet radiation, and to be more resistant to elevated temperatures.

Thermal printing is a popular method for producing high-quality, free-format, random, on-demand labels. The technology has the advantage of low equipment costs, low mainte-

(a)   (b)

Figure 9.19: Typical Direct Thermal Portable Printers

At (a) is a handheld thermal printer. (b) shows a typical portable thermal printer.

nance costs, and high image quality, particularly for bar codes. Some typical thermal printers are shown in Figure 9.19.

You can expect to replace printheads after 1,000,000 to 2,000,000 inches of printing. However, this variable is dependent on paper characteristics and overall printer design methodology

Some approximate life expectancies of thermal labels are given in Table 9.4. As with any printed image, label life is adversely affected by rough or frequent use of contact-scanning equipment. It is recommended that a protective laminate be used when a label is subject to abuse or very long service life with frequent contact scanning.

Thermal Transfer

Thermal transfer printers are similar to thermal printers. Both use selective heating of elements to produce the bar code image. But thermal transfer printers use a thin-film or paper-based ribbon impregnated with a waxy coating. Instead of changing the color of a

	Inorganic Paper	Coated Organic Paper
Expected Life		
Archival (e. g., file cabinet)	10+ years	5+ years
Indoor (Office, Warehouse)	5+ years	2+ years
Outdoors	4 weeks	4 weeks

Table 9.4: Thermal Paper Life Expectancies

This table shows life expectancies for images printed on the two styles of direct thermal printer paper. In order to achieve these lifetimes, ambient temperature must be kept under 140° Fahrenheit, or the papers will uniformly blacken, obliterating the printed image.

chemical in the paper stock, the elements melt the wax coating and the pigment in the coating flows onto the paper.

Ordinary paper stock, including continuous roll for labeling, can be used in thermal transfer printers, such as the one shown in figure 9.20. Some units also can handle thermal ribbon with different color pigments and can print in colors. However, these color thermal printers often print black bar code symbols by building the symbol up from equal amounts of cyan, magenta, and yellow. These symbols will not scan under infrared readers.

Common thermal transfer printers can print bar code with a resolution of about 150 dots-per-inch (an X-dimension of about 6 mils), but the ribbon must be matched to the label stock. Label printing speed is less than most laser printers. Labels produced with thermal transfer printers are not as prone to wear as are laser printed labels. That's because the wax-based ink chemically bonds to the paper. See the discussion of labels and adhesives later in this chapter.

Thermal Transfer Ribbons

Thermal transfer ribbons consist of three elements: a polyester film, ink, and a protective back treatment or coating. The polyester film for thermal transfer ribbons is chosen for smoothness, low coefficient of printing, high melting point, good thermal conductivity, high tensile strength, and chemical resistance.

During thermal transfer printing, the uncoated surface of the ribbon is heated by the printhead to raise the temperature of the ink layer. As the ink melts, gaining fluidity, it

Figure 9.20: Typical Thermal Transfer Printer

adheres to the print surface through a combination of pressure and capillary action.

The film must simultaneously exhibit enough heat resistance (to prevent its melting), heat conductivity (to allow the ink to melt), tensile strength (to prevent ripping and tearing), and smoothness (to prevent sticking or slipping) to print high-quality bar codes and graphics. It also requires a sufficiently low coefficient of friction to prevent printhead abrasion.

Films typically come in two thicknesses, 5.7 and 4.5 microns. The 5.7-micron film has become the standard and offers some cost savings, but the newer 4.5-micron film offers distinct advantages and is becoming less expensive due to economies of scale.

The 4.5-micron film permits more film to be available on a roll, saving time for roll change-over. It also takes less energy to melt ink through a 4.5-micron film, making the film ideal for use in high-speed printing systems.

Thermal transfer ink formulations consist of several components: a pigment, a wax, a dispersing agent to carry the pigment, and varying amounts of resin to provide adhesion properties within the ink itself. Other components, such as plasticizers and film-formers, may be added to disperse the pigment and ensure the uniformity of coating, or to improve adhesion of the ink to the facestock.

The main components of a traditional wax-based thermal transfer ink and their effects are listed in Table 9.5. This represents a generic formula which provides a good idea of ink's components.

To be optimized for a specific application, the above "recipe" is adjusted for color, binding, softening, etc. Obviously, this can't be done for a "generic" one-formula-fits-all thermal transfer ribbon. For example, for an especially durable formulation, you might need a solvent-coated ink which consists of:

- A binding layer on top to enhance the surface binding of the ink pigment to the facestock. This layer is an adhesive-like formulation, high in resins.
- The pigment layer, containing the coloring compound or carbon black used to form the image.
- An under-coating layer which transfers onto the top of the printed image, used to protect the pigment surface. This enhances the image and adds scratch and smear resistance. An additional function of this layer can be to control and enable release of ink from the polyester ribbon film.

Due to the technological evolution in printing technology, average users cannot be expected to optimize the ink for their applications. Once the label material and expected environ-

Material	Effect	Percent by Weight
Pigment	Colorant	20
Carnauba Wax	Binder	20
Ester Wax	Binder	40
Oils	Softener	10
Others	Additives	10

Table 9.5: Components of Thermal Transfer Inks

Thermal transfer ribbon is a tough polyester film with a thin coating of transfer ink. The ink is a wax-like substance that can be quickly melted and transferred to the paper or other media in the thermal transfer printer, thus making an image. Listed here are the typical components of this film and relative percentages.

mental conditions have been defined, the thermal transfer ribbon supplier can best formulate the ink for that application.

Thermal transfer printing is best suited for applications needing a quiet printer for producing very high- to medium-density labels (up to 6 mils X dimension). These units can print small circuit board labels at rates up to 40,000 labels per hour. They are ideal for high-density, continuous-form, label printing applications.

Demand Printer Recommendations

In assessing which print technology to employ for demand label generation, print quality, print speed, narrowest "X" dimension achievable, and text/graphics flexibility should be carefully matched to the needs of the application and the reading equipment employed. Table 9.6 summarizes present demand printing technology.

Printing Process	Image Formation Technique	Minimum "X"	Typical "X" Provided
Electrolithography	Dielectric Cylinder	3.3	10.0
Formed Character Impact	Engraved Face	6.0	7.5
Dot-Matrix Impact	Matrix Printhead	14.5	16.0
Dot-Matrix Impact	Line Printer	12.0	16.0
Thermal	Matrix Printhead	5.0	10.0
Thermal	Linear Printhead	5.0	10.0
Thermal Transfer	Linear Printhead	5.0	10.0
Ink Jet	Linear Printhead	8.3	40.0
Photocomposition	Photographic Process	3.0	7.5

Table 9.6: Demand Printer Technology

This table summarizes image formation techniques and narrow element width ("X") values in mils achievable with contemporary bar code demand printers.

Print/Apply Systems

Preprint/apply systems employ commercially printed labels that are supplied to the user in roll form for use on a label application device. This section reviews some of the savings possible in automatic applicators and addresses some specific advantages of print/apply systems over preprint/apply systems.

Major savings can accrue at manufacturer and distributor levels with automatic application of the symbol to the container or packaging. Assuming that a packaging employee was hired to hand-apply each bar code symbol, the company could expect to spend at least $25,000 per year in wages and fringe benefits. Further, the company can expect the "Monday Morning/Friday Afternoon Syndrome" with the employee either trying to readjust from the weekend or anxiously awaiting the same. If the label is expected to be read downstream by a fixed-station reader, uniform orientation and placement are quite important. Within a two-year period the cost of automatic application equipment would pay for itself versus the direct labor component of applying the labels by hand. Further, placement by the application equipment is uniformly accurate, generally within 1/64 inch, dramatically lessening the need for manual intervention when labels are unreadable due to manual misalignment.

Print/apply systems do exactly what their name implies. A roll of blank or standard format pressure-sensitive labels is automatically unwound. The labels progress to a printing station (today the predominant printing method is either dot-matrix impact or thermal transfer). The variable information is printed on the label which then progresses to a station where the label is removed from its adhesive release liner and applied to the packaging. Since the printing is accomplished by a demand printer, variable information such as lot codes and expiration dates can be easily modified from an integral control console which can prompt the operator to enter the variable fields and stipulate the quantity of each format to be printed. The console could have a locked protective cover and be accessed only by quality control/quality assurance (QC/QA) personnel who would enter the information to be printed. Since the label content would be entered by QC/QA personnel and since the label quantity could be set—with QC/QA intervention required before more of the same labels could be printed—a print/apply scenario, such as that shown in Figure 9.21, could negate the need for many functions of "label control rooms."

In addition to the bar code symbols, with the associated human-readable representations, other text such as product description, "Expiration Date:," "Reorder Number:," and "Lot Number:" could also be printed. Further, since the information is being printed with dot-matrix graphics, the information on one label could be varied with respect to font size and font style.

Print/apply systems can be mounted to packaging equipment, can stand alone on a dedicated conveyor system, can be activated manually, or can be activated electronically through a pressure switch or electronic sensor. When mounted on automated packaging

Figure 9.21: Print/Apply System

A print/apply system first prints a self-adhesive label, then physically attaches it to the package being labeled. Such systems achieve uniform and reliable label placement, a factor in improved readability of the labels in automatic equipment systems.

equipment, such as form, fill, and seal machines, the printing cycle is keyed to the packaging cycle. In one example, the packaging machine cycles at 13 cycles per minute and seals 6 packages in one cycle (6 packages across the web of the machine) for a total of 78 packages per minute. The print/apply system employed prints two Code 39 symbols with extensive other text on the label at a rate of 48 per minute. Having two printheads on the packaging machine satisfies the need of 78 labels per minute. Considerable liaison is required between the systems designer, the print/apply manufacturer, the label supplier, and the packaging equipment vendor to ensure that all components work together.

Print/apply systems are said to print "so many up" (number of labels printed in advance of applying the first label printed). A system said to print "one up" prints and applies the same label. Care should be exercised with print/apply systems to ensure that the correct number of labels is printed and applied when print/apply systems print other than "one up."

Print/apply systems apply the labels in one of two ways: The labels are "blown on" or "tamped on." A system that blows on the label removes the pressure-sensitive label from its release liner by suction, holds the label on the applicator head by reverse pressure until it moves to the application station, and then blows the label on with a specified amount of air pressure. Systems in which the labels are tamped on may remove the label with either reverse pressure, static charge, or an "adhesive" arm, and then press the label onto the packaging. Both "blown on" and "tamped on" label applicators can be equipped with a roller and arm to apply a single label onto two adjacent sides of a container. Here the content of the label is printed in its entirety twice, once on the left side of the label and once on the right with a substantial margin in the middle. The left side of the label is applied to one corner of the container, and the roller then applies the right side onto the adjacent panel of the corner.

Print/apply systems represent one of the best ways for manufacturers and distributors to realize the benefits of variable content bar code symbols.

Labels and Adhesives

Beyond the issues of equipment selection addressed earlier, and print quality, discussed in Chapter 10, careful attention should be paid to the selection of the label on which the symbol will be printed, the selection of the imaging material (ink or ribbon), and the conditions to which the label will be subjected.

Labels consist of three basic elements: facestock, adhesive, and release liner. Some label materials also have an optional top-coating.

The release liner serves four functions. It carries the label through the production and printing processes, protects the adhesive, provides for a base in die-cutting, and releases when the label is peeled for application to a surface.

The adhesive must be able to hold the release liner to the facestock through the production, die-cutting, and printing processes, be able to properly release from the release liner depending on the label application technique employed, and remain adhered to the product or item for a specified period of time under specified environmental conditions. Adhesives possess various properties, namely, tack, shear, peel, and adhesion. Tack defines the initial "grabbiness" of the adhesive to the surface on which it is to be applied. Shear defines internal cohesive strength of the adhesive permitting it to remain bound to the release liner. Peel is the force required to remove the adhesive from the release liner. Adhesion is the force required to remove the adhesive from the labeled surface after initial application and after the adhesive has had an opportunity to "set." Some adhesives permit repositioning of a label immediately after application though a permanent bond is created between the facestock and the labeled surface after the adhesive has set. To select the proper adhesive for a label, the user must be aware of several factors:

- The environment in which the label will be used;
- The expected life of the label;
- The surface to which the label will be applied;
- The technique used to print the label; and
- The manner in which the label will be applied (manual or mechanical).

The facestock is the medium onto which printing is applied to create a label, providing information to the user when reading the label. Common facestocks include paper and polymer-based materials. The least initially expensive facestock is paper, but the polymer facestocks offer improved durability and aesthetics.

Top coating may provide an aesthetic, protective, or functional property to the label. Top coats can provide a clear, glossy, or matte finish. They are able to provide resistance to abrasion, chemicals, humidity, and other environmental conditions. They also provide a base so that inks may adhere to facestocks. Top coats will vary depending upon whether the printing is being accomplished through a wet-ink process, e.g., flexo, offset, silkscreen, or letterpress; a dot-matrix impact process; or a thermal transfer process, permitting the printed image to bond to the facestock.

Facestocks

Some of the more frequently employed polymers for facestocks include polypropylene, polyester, polyethylene, polystyrene, polyimide, and polyvinyl.

Polyvinyl is moderately priced and retains its shape through repeated use. Polyvinyl is smooth, glossy, highly tear-resistant, and is stable with prolonged exposure to ultraviolet light. Dimensionally, polyvinyl is not very stable, and its lack of stiffness makes it difficult to use with automatic applicators. Polyvinyl labels also shrink over time. Since the adhesives do not shrink along with the polyvinyl, an adhesive ring may appear, rendering its appearance aesthetically unpleasing. The shrinkage may also induce an adhesive failure.

Polyester is dimensionally stable, retaining its shape over time. While polyester is tear-, heat-, and abrasion-resistant, as well as providing for UV stability, polyester is also more expensive than vinyl. Because of polyester's durability, converters may require special dies to cut the material, leading to higher converting costs. Polyester does not accept ink well and may require a top coating or chemical treatment to permit the printing of bar codes, graphics, and human-readable information.

Polypropylene offers dimensional stability and tear-, chemical-, and abrasion-resistance at a lower cost than polyester. Disadvantages of polypropylene include low ultraviolet stability and lower heat-resistance than polyester. Polypropylene may be a good alternative facestock for polyester where the label will not have outdoor exposure and exposure to excessive heat is not a problem. Polypropylene also suffers from the same requirements for special cutting dies as does polyester, leading to higher converting costs.

Polystyrene is rising in popularity. Polystyrene is very low in cost, dimensionally stable, easy to die-cut, and stretch-resistant. The absence of plasticizers in polystyrene means no migration of contaminants to inks, adhesives, and substrates. Polystyrene has a low resistance to ultraviolet light, heat, tearing, abrasion, and solvents, so it also is best used for labels in indoor environments.

Polyimides are very resistant to heat and chemicals, but at a price. The primary use of polyimides is in the labeling of printed circuit boards where the wave-solder process may experience temperatures up to 600° and the post-solder process involves a chemical bath.

Adhesives

Adhesives are presented in four major categories: solvent rubber, solvent acrylic, water acrylic, and hot melt. The choice and thickness of the adhesive will depend upon the face-stock and release liner employed, the material onto which the label will be applied, and the environment in which the label is expected to survive.

Solvent rubber adhesives are made from natural or synthetic rubber-tackifying resins. They tend to be difficult to remove, are not very resistant to humidity, provide only medium shear strength, suffer from low resistance to plasticizer migration, and provide little resistance to ultraviolet light. Typically they do not become brittle (moderate "wet-out") and range in cost from low to moderate.

Solvent acrylics are high-performance adhesives ranging in cost from moderate to high. They provide for easy die-cutting, offer very good wet-out, and provide for good resistance to humidity. Depending upon their specific chemical make-up, solvent acrylics can be purchased with the full range of adhesion properties—removability, shear, and tack.

Water acrylic adhesives have historically not been so versatile as their solvent acrylic counterparts, but in low-performance applications provide an economically superior alternative. They provide fair ultraviolet resistance. R&D efforts currently under way will dramatically improve this versatility. Water acrylic adhesives have poor wet-out, humidity resistance, shear strength, and resistance to plasticizer migration.

Hot-melt adhesives, used in high-volume, low-performance applications are the least expensive of the adhesives. The heat-activated gum is typically not sticky at room temperature, but converts to an adhesive state at temperatures above 135° F. Hot-melt adhesives are usually used in high-speed printing press applications. They suffer from poor wet-out, heat aging, and poor humidity resistance. Typical removability is poor, shear is medium, and tack is high.

Release Liners

Paper release liners provide the lowest cost alternative, can be printed on the back side, provide thermal stability and low static, and can be handled more efficiently on press and in dispensing due to the friction available from the paper back. Paper release liners suffer from poor caliper (thickness) consistency, do not release facestock/adhesives easily, and are not very dimensionally stable, potentially causing curling which can be problematic when printing with laser printers.

Polyester release liners provide for improved tensile strength, tear resistance, caliper consistency, releasability, and adhesive smoothness. Polyester release liners are more costly than paper, are difficult to handle on press and in dispensing, and are prone to static buildup.

Polypropylene's pricing is positioned between that of paper and polyester; it offers the same qualities as polyester.

Recently introduced polymer/paper release liners may prove to be the release liners of choice in the near future. Polymer/paper release liners offer improved tensile strength and caliper profile over their paper counterparts. Polymer/paper liners provide for facestock/adhesive release similar to their polymer counterparts but at a lower cost. Polymer/paper release liners also borrow from paper the ability to be printed on the back side, better thermal stability, and low static; they can be handled more efficiently on press and in dispensing due to the friction similar to paper's.

Table 9.7 provides an analysis of applications, facestocks, and adhesives to be considered in a thermal/thermal transfer selection process.

Determining Which Printer to Use

The first step in selecting the right printer for your application requires understanding how your application operates today and your goals for the future. While there is probably no single, all-inclusive list of questions to answer, here are some to get you started.

- Define the desired output speed of the desired size labels
- What is the minimum "X" dimension desired and the required ratio of the wide elements to the narrow ones
- What is the unit cost and unit size
- What consumables (labels, ribbons/toner) are required and what are their costs
- What is the duty cycle of print element
- What graphics capabilities are available and how are these graphics capabilities controlled (programming)
- How are the printed labels designed
- What additional software or hardware is required to make the unit functional in the intended environment
- Will information for the printed symbols come from a database, and can the software accommodate the database to be used
- What parts are user serviceable, what is the Mean Time Between Failure (MTBF) for the equipment, and what are the maintenance costs
- What is the Mean Time To Repair (MTTR)
- On what type of media can the equipment print (pressure sensitive, TyVek®)
- Do any environmental issues exist with regard to disposal of the print media, toner, or print element

I recommend that the following types of printers be considered for specific types of applications.

- For combined forms and pressure sensitive labels—cold fusion, organic, continuous feed laser or sheet-fed ion deposition
- For on-demand one label at a time—thermal transfer
- Where an employee will be charged with the singular responsibility of applying the labels—in-line print/apply system.

CHAPTER 10

Verifying the Printed Symbol

W hen *Reading Between the Lines* was published, the methods of establishing print quality were taken either from the U.P.C. Symbol Specification Manual—which is still successful and in use today—or from ANS MH10.8M-1983, which did little more than caution printers of bar code symbols not to have excessive holes in the middle of bars nor excessive dirt in the spaces and quiet zones. Numerous devices were supplied to the market that claimed to be able to verify that the printed symbol met these print quality standards. However, ANS MH10.8M-1983 did not evaluate the symbol in the same way that a bar code reader would read the symbol. Rather, it was an honest attempt to describe under what circumstances a symbol absolutely would not be readable.

In 1990 the American National Standards Institute (ANSI) published ANS X3.182-1990—Bar Code Print Quality. The effort that concluded with the publication of this standard was undertaken by some of the better scientific minds in the bar code reading, bar code printing, bar code verification, and user communities. Further discussions of ANS X3.182-1990 can be found below.

For a bar code symbol to be read successfully, the optical sensor in the reader must be able to discern the transitions between the bars and spaces in the symbol. The resolution of the optical sensor should be nearly equivalent to or smaller than the width of the narrowest bar in the symbol that the scanner will be expected to read. The sensor must also be presented with a bar code whose dimensions do not deviate significantly from the predetermined pattern of the symbology. To be successfully and reliably read, the printed symbol must have sufficient optical contrast between the bars and the spaces. Ideally, the printed bar should be observed as perfectly black and the non-printed spaces should be perfectly white. In practice, however, this condition is not met. Bar codes are printed on a wide range of substrates and in numerous colors, for consistency with the existing artwork on the package.

Factors Influencing Quality Printing

In a bar code printing setting, continued rigor is recommended to ensure that printing devices employed are of high quality. Demand printers require periodic maintenance. Ribbons that are new may provide excessive print coverage, while older, worn ribbons may not provide sufficient print coverage.

Poor first-read rates are a function of the printed symbol and operator technique, including those cases where the nominal narrow elements are too narrow for the spot size of the reader or where the spectral characteristics of the printed symbol do not match the light source of the reader.

The print mechanism, the media (or substrate), and the inking process together determine the quality of the printed symbol. Some of the major factors influencing quality are:

- Ink spread/shrinkage
- Ink voids/specks
- Ink smearing
- Nonuniformity of ink coverage
- Contrast between the dark and light elements
- Bar/space width tolerances
- Edge roughness

All of these factors are potential sources of both systematic and random errors. These errors must be closely controlled to ensure that the symbol will be easily scanned.

The primary problems associated with thermal and thermal transfer printing are: a mismatch between the printer and label stock; misalignment of the print or heating elements; and inadequate voltage applied to the printing mechanism. In thermal transfer printing an additional source of error is a mismatch between the thermal transfer ribbon and the media/print mechanism.

Ink jet printing errors are generally classified as problems of nozzle alignment, ink composition mismatch to media composition, and clogged nozzles. Electrostatic printing problems include toner composition, dielectric cylinder wear, improper voltage to the fusing station, cylinder recycling problems, and wear of the motors driving the dielectric cylinder or the rotating mirror (in the case of laser-based electrostatic printing).

The amount of ink spread or shrinkage that occurs in impact printing techniques is determined by the condition of the ribbon, the hammer (or styli) pressure, and the porosity, thickness, and impressibility of the substrate onto which the print is applied. Ink spread results in wider bars and narrower spaces, whereas ink shrinkage has the opposite effect. Both ink spread and shrinkage may cause degradation in the bar edge definition.

Ink voids are characteristic of any printing process. If the ink void or speck is large enough, it is possible for the scanner to recognize the transition across the void/speck as a space or bar. The effects of ink voids and specks will be minimal if they are small relative to the narrow element width.

Ink smearing and nonuniform inking may also lead to poor read rates. Ink smearing is a problem because it may cause a narrow bar to appear wide or a wide space to appear narrow.

The various inking errors, combined with the characteristics of the print mechanism, determine the bar/space width tolerances that can be maintained when printing bar codes. The deviation from nominal print widths of sample symbols can be determined by using a toolmaker's microscope, an optical comparator, or by using a diagnostic verifier. A larger percentage of errors occurs if the element width is near the largest available for the printing technique. This could lead to a more severe degradation in performance than if a smaller element size is used. It is important to overall system performance that the printing tolerances be maintained within the limits specified by the symbology.

Edge roughness is caused by the combined effects of inking, substrate smoothness/porosity, and the printing technique. Edge roughness is one of the factors determining

186

bar/space width tolerances. In effect, the scanner senses a different bar width depending upon which part of the bar it passes over. Bar edge roughness is a common error in symbols printed with some dot-matrix impact printers. For many dot-matrix impact printers the narrow element width is large enough to make this error small. Other dot-matrix impact printers have a sufficiently small dot size and dot overlap to cause virtually no degradation in the symbol's readability.

In bar code applications using scanners with a visible red light source, poor symbol contrast will result if the bars are printed with ink colors having red pigmentation. Bars printed in red, yellow, orange, reddish-purple, or reddish brown, for example, will not appear sufficiently different from the white spaces when viewed by a red light source, such as that in Helium-Neon lasers, visible light laser diode scanners, and many wand scanner reading devices.

As stated in Chapter 8, to be certain that bar code symbols can be read by virtually all bar code scanning devices presented to the scanner, it is best to evaluate the printed symbol in the infrared spectrum. To be certain that bar code scanning devices can read virtually any symbol presented to the scanner, it is best to utilize visible-red scanning devices.

The type of finish and its effects on the reflectance of light is also important. A dull or matte finish is preferred over a glossy finish because it spreads the reflected light (diffuse reflection) and ensures successful scanning over a wide range of orientations of the reading device. This is especially important when a bar code is being read by a handheld scanner. Different operators will orient the scanner to the bar code at different angles.

The translucency of the medium being used is also important. If there is back printing or a darker sheet or background behind a translucent sheet, the inherent reflectivity of the translucent sheet will be decreased. Translucent sheets should be avoided. If they are not, a white background should be placed behind the sheet before reading is attempted.

Another phenomenon, media bleed, occurs when a transparent or translucent medium is used (as is the case with plastic containers, such as bottles, fluid bags, etc.). This phenomenon is caused by the scattering of incidental light rays within the medium or from the underlying surface of the container contents. Some of the scattered light will be detected by the scanner, thereby adding to the light reflectivity from the medium's surface. However, as the scanner approaches the edge of a bar, some of this scattered light is absorbed in the ink before it can be reflected back to the detector. As a result, the reflectivity of the medium begins to drop off before the bar edge is reached. This optical effect tends to make the bars appear larger and the spaces appear narrower than they were actually printed.

The systematic error introduced by media bleed is relatively constant in magnitude for a specific medium. Its effects are more pronounced when narrow element bar codes are used, because the error will be a larger percentage of the module width. This is particularly true for some photographic papers commonly used to print high density (small element width) symbols with photocomposition techniques. In general, factors that influence media bleed are rag content, the type of binder used, the thickness of the medium, and the medium's transparency. Media bleed, in the case of papers, can be minimized by using heavyweight stock with a high rag content.

Another consideration in the selection of the medium for contact scanners is durability, or how many times the wand scanner can be moved across the surface without degrading the reflectivity of media, smearing the bars, or abrading the symbol. When evaluating the media durability required by the application, the user should consider the number of times the symbol will be scanned by contact scanning devices during its lifetime and the severity of the environment to which the symbol will be exposed. If the expected number of scans is few and the environment is clean and dry, heavyweight paper with a smooth surface texture is acceptable. In applications where the symbol will be exposed to adverse environments such as dirt, grease, temperature extremes, and weather, or the label will be scanned many times by contact devices, the symbol should be protected by a thin transparent coating.

A frequently used method of printing bar code symbols is on pressure-sensitive labels. The typical pressure-sensitive label includes a face stock, an adhesive back, and a carrier, or release sheet. Pressure-sensitive labels come in all shapes and sizes, on many facing stocks (paper, vinyl, polyester, and mylar), in special die cuts and perforations, and with numerous adhesives. Asset tags may require a combination of stock and adhesive that makes the label permanent once it is applied, so that it is impossible to remove without destroying the label. The stock and adhesives may have to resist environments of varying temperatures, humidity, pressure, and atmospheric content. The environment in which the label must survive is an important consideration in the development of any bar code system that uses pressure-sensitive labels.

The texture of the medium is another consideration. Non-contact scanning systems are especially sensitive to media texture. The reflected light signal in a bar code reader is evaluated using a concept known as a signal-to-noise ratio. The higher the ratio, the better the quality of signal. Textured surfaces introduce additional noise into the scanning system, lowering the signal-to-noise ratio. Further, the smaller the spot diameter, in relation to texture parameters, the greater the noise in relation to the area being examined and the poorer the performance. An excellent example of a textured surface lowering the signal-to-noise ratio is provided by TyVek®. The "threads" running through the medium that give it

Symbology	Bar or Space	Edge to Similar Edge	Pitch
U.P.C./EAN ($X \leq 0.013$)	$\pm(X - 0.009)$	$\pm 0.147X$	0.29X
U.P.C./EAN ($X > 0.013$)	$\pm(0.47X - 0.0022)$	$\pm 0.147X$	0.29X
Interleaved 2 of 5	$\pm((18N - 21) / 80)X$	N.A.	N.A.
Code 128	$\pm(0.40X - 0.0005)$	$\pm 0.20X$	0.20X
Code 39	$\pm 0.148(N - 0.667)X$	N.A.	N.A.
Codabar (USS)	$\pm((5N - 8) / 20)X$	N.A.	
Code 93	$\pm(0.45X - 0.001)$	$\pm 0.20X$	+/-0.20X
Code 16K	$\pm(0.40X - 0.005)$	$\pm 0.20X$	0.20X
Code 49 ($0.0075 \leq X \leq 0.020$)	Greater of 0.0056 or 0.65X	$\pm 0.20X$	0.20X
Code 49 ($X > 0.020$)	Greater of 0.013 or 0.55X	$\pm 0.20X$	0.20X
PDF417	$\pm(0.40X - 0.005)$	$\pm 0.20X$	0.20X
Postnet (Bars)	0.020 ± 0.005	N.A.	N.A.
Postnet (Spaces)	0.0475 ± 0.0025 (CL to CL)	N.A.	N.A.

Table 10.1: Printing Tolerance

Tolerance formulas are shown here for bar or space widths, and, where applicable, edge-to-similar-edge distance and pitch. In this table, the symbol "X" is the width of the narrow element (bar or space) of the symbology; "N" is the ratio of the wide element to narrow element width. The abbreviation N.A. means not applicable.

strength also generate noise. This noise will affect the modulated signal in the scanning and verification processes.

Printing Tolerances

The tolerances listed in a specification indicate how far the bars and spaces may expand or contract and still be within specification or *printing tolerances*. Each bar code symbology has an absolute breakdown tolerance; normally, approximately 60 percent is allocated to the printer (printing tolerance) and 40 percent to the scanner. When these *printing tolerances* are exceeded, part of the scanner's tolerances are consumed, increasing the possibility of a no-read or a substitution error. It is, therefore, quite important that the quality of the bar code symbol be within the specifications for the symbology. Table 3.2 shows the print tolerances for selected magnifications of the U.P.C./EAN Symbols. Table 3.14 shows the print tolerances for ITF-14. Appendix B consists of a set of tables that show selected narrow and wide bar widths for Code 39, as well as their associated printing tolerances. Table 10.1 shows the formulas for computation of printing tolerances for the major bar code symbologies.

Durability of Image

The print medium can affect the durability of the printed image. Print media factors include the ribbons/ink used, the paper, and the label environment. These factors should be considered based on:

1. The number of times the bar code is expected to be scanned;
2. The environment to which the bar code is subjected (outdoors, temperature, etc.);
3. The length of time the bar code is expected to be functional; and
4. The processes the bar code will be subjected to (solvents, water, etc.).

Generally, the bar code symbol can be printed on a low-cost uncoated stock using general office environment ribbons if only a few scans, short life, and no severe environmental or process factors are involved. However, if frequent scanning, long life, or severe conditions are expected, a "premium" ribbon should be used to print on polyester- or vinyl-based materials. In addition to resistance to abrasion and heat, these ribbons have high fade resistance to direct sunlight if ink and substrate are properly matched.

Verifying the Quality of the Printed Symbol

There are several schools of thought regarding quality control of the printed symbol. One assumes that if a symbol can be read by one bar code reader, it can be read by any other reader. This theory disregards the differences in bar code scanner aperture size, waveshaping/decoding software, and light source wavelength—and is thus quite incorrect.

A second theory concludes that if the bar code reader's aperture size and light source are matched to the specifications of the printed symbol, another bar code reader of the same light source and aperture size could correctly read the bar code. In the vast majority of cases, this theory is correct. But it assumes that bar code reader manufacturers share common, well-designed circuitry and decoding software, a reasonable assumption to make. In practice, however, each manufacturer has its own unique decode algorithm, wave-shaping circuitry, and signal conditioning techniques.

A third school of thought contends that to be absolutely certain that the printed symbols will be readable requires a routine sampling and analysis of print quality, or *verifi-*

cation of the printed symbol. Verification involves the checking of the following elements of a bar code symbol:

- Edge Determination
- Symbol Contrast
- Modulation of the Signal
- Symbol Defects
- Decode Algorithm Employed
- Decodability
- Observance of Quiet Zone
- Porosity, Smoothness, Gloss, Grain, and Opacity of the Substrate
- Opacity, Optical Effects of Gloss, and Physical Effects of Smoothness of any Over-laminate

Quality Audit Concept

To achieve successful readability of bar code symbols produced, unknown changes must be kept from creeping into the bar code printing operation. An example of such a change might be a purchasing department selecting a new ribbon vendor without testing the ribbon. All manufacturing companies have quality control techniques for preventing this "unknown change" problem in their production. Treat the printing of bar code symbols as a manufacturing process.

Print quality of the printed bar code symbols should be evaluated with precisely the same care as the manufacturing of product. Based upon the lot size of the labels printed at one time, a statistically significant sample should be taken to ensure that the printed symbols are within the established printing specifications. Further, when ribbons, plates, inks, toner, or label stock is changed, the symbols should be evaluated to ensure that the printed symbols are within the established printing specifications.

Printing specifications should be in accordance with the U.P.C. Symbol Specification Manual or ANS X3.182-1990. There are several manufacturers of Bar Code Verification devices conforming with the standards of ANS X3.182-1990 and the U.P.C. Symbol Specification, such as the one shown in Figure 10.1. If a system design calls for printing bar code symbols, then an ANS X3.182-1990 and U.P.C. Symbol verification device should be used regularly to inspect print quality. It may also be desirable for the user of verifiers to incorporate an audit trail of symbol print quality should any questions arise about adherence to print quality guidelines.

ANS X3.182-1990 addresses each of the elements of print quality mentioned in the list above. Basically, ANS X3.182-1990 evaluates the symbol over four categories (symbol contrast, modulation, defects, and decodability) to which grades of A, B, C, D, or F are assigned. Three other categories (minimum reflectance, minimum edge contrast, and decode) are evaluated as either "Pass" (Grade "A") or "Fail" (Grade "F"). Ten scans of the symbol are taken over the Inspection Band, as illustrated in Figure 10.2, assigning grades as described above. The grades of the ten scans are averaged to determine the Overall Profile Grade of the symbol.

Figure 10.3 shows a typical scan profile from the output of a bar code scanner reading a good quality symbol (Grade = A).

Application standards need to identify three variables to determine whether the symbol in question meets the need of the specific application. These variables include light source

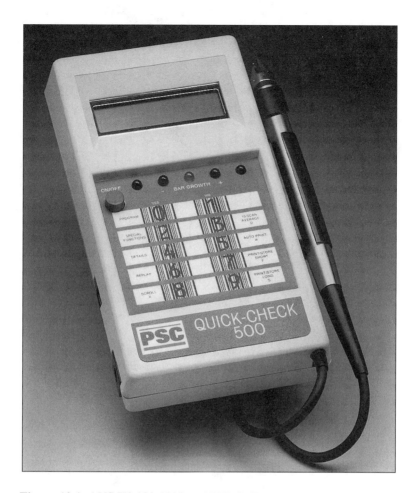

Figure 10.1: ANS X3.182-1990 and U.P.C. Symbol Verification Device

Units such as this check symbols for compliance with a given symbology's specifications. Audit trails can be created through output of details measured by the verifier to an appropriate computer database.

wavelength (what wavelength scanner is going to be employed in the application), evaluation aperture size (based upon the "X" dimension of the symbols in question, and acceptable grade.

Symbol quality is specified by a string of the form "Q/X/Λ" where "Q" is the quality grade (A . . . F), "X" is the aperture number, and Λ is the wavelength of the scanner's light.

I recommend adherence to the ANS MH10. 8M (1991 -Draft) specification of C/10/660, interpreted as a minimum symbol quality of "C," with an "X" dimension of 0.013 to 0.025 inch, and a light source wavelength of 670 nm. Suppliers of printed bar code symbols should endeavor to provide a symbol quality of B/10/670, and recipients of symbols should endeavor to receive C/10/670 as a minimum. There are two exceptions to the C/10/670 grade. The first is when verifying a U.P.C. or EAN symbol. In this case the grade should be C/06/670, which will provide what the UCC hopes to be a better quality symbol. The sec-

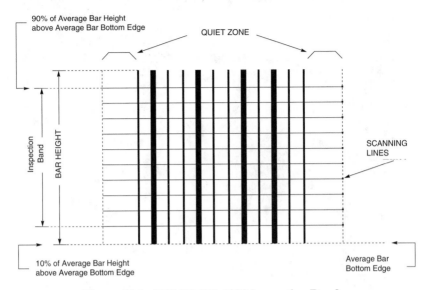

Figure 10.2: ANS X3.182-1990 Inspection Band

This is the scanning pattern used to evaluate the quality of a typical bar code symbol with a verifier. The verifier performs 10 scans of the "inspection band" across the symbol being checked, and evaluates the quality of the symbol based on the reflectance measured. A typical verifier reflectance profile is shown in Figure 10.3 with significant features annotated.

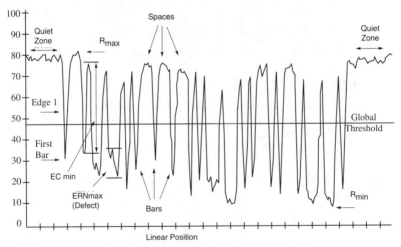

Figure 10.3: Typical Scan Profile

The reflectance signal derived from a verification scan across a symbol might look like this. The profile is a measure of reflectance (0% to 100%) measured along the scan line. The global threshold is a value of reflectivity separating the judgment of black (< threshold reflectivity) from white (> threshold reflectivity). R_{min} and R_{max} are measures of the range of reflectivity found in the verification scan. The annotations are based on the X3.182-1990 Bar Code Print Quality specification.

ond is when verifying symbols directly printed on corrugated. In this case the minimum grade should be D/20/670, to reflect the larger "X" dimension when printing on corrugated as well as the reduced grade "D," which takes into account the variability in the surface of corrugated stock. Where "D" quality symbols are encountered it is expected that a multiple scan path reader, e.g. a laser scanner, would be used to read the symbol.

The best technique to control the quality of the bar code printing operation and to prevent an unknown change is to audit the process on a regular basis.

- Establish the useful inking (toner/ribbon) life for the intended application.
- Audit bar code print quality regularly.
- Use a verifier capable of testing against ANS X3.182-1990 Print Quality Guidelines to audit the quality of the symbol.

Whenever the bar code audit reveals a problem, it will be necessary to identify and correct the problem quickly to prevent a widespread shipment of symbols with readability problems.

C H A P T E R 11

Data Collection Technology

The concept underlying bar code technology as well as electronic data interchange (EDI) is "Once data is entered into a computer system, that data should never have to be key-entered again." Bar code technology and EDI are integral elements of what we know as advanced electronic systems. The components of these electronic systems are:

- Source Data Capture
- Source Data Collection
- Database Management Systems
- Electronic Data Interchange (EDI)
- Graphic Presentation Systems

Source Data Capture is the use of bar code symbols to replace the traditional forms of key-entry. Bar code scanning is fast, and bar code data collection is far more accurate than key-entry when you consider that key-entry realizes one error in 300 characters entered while bar code scanning takes that error rate to better than one error in a million characters entered. Chapter 13 looks at issues of transactional identification systems. To capture transactions by bar code symbols in a fully integrated data collection system we need:

- Symbols on incoming product
- Symbols on work-in-process
- Symbols on finished goods
- Location tags and employee identification
- Scannable menus
- Scannable work orders

Source Data Collection involves communicating from the bar code symbol through the reader back to the applications software in the computer system. Source data collection technical areas to address include:

- Host computer communications to and from the work center
- Processor communications to and from portable/mobile terminals
- Issues of matching an application to scanner technology
- RF and batch terminals
- Data collection software
- Data entry time stamps

Database Management Systems (DBMS) permit the collected data to be organized in a manner that can be manipulated by computers. As shown in Figure 11.1, a computer must be able to recognize various "aliases" assigned to the same item. These databases must be able to:

- Handle "relationships"
- Provide data import and export ("integrated")
- Provide a query language
- Provide local report generation

Query languages provide the means of structuring an interaction between databases and users. One early database query language was the "Structured Query Language (SQL)" introduced with IBM database software for mainframe computers. With the advent of mini-computers, then personal computers, versions of SQL, like versions of other programming languages, have proliferated as various database software packages have been introduced.

While warehouse management may think of a product as a "stock item" or stock keeping

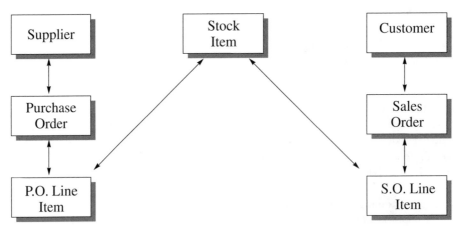

Figure 11.1: Database Structure

This diagram illustrates a typical database, such as an EDI supplier/customer data-base. The basic object is the Stock Item. At the customer side of the transactions, the details are contained in the sales order. At the supplier side of the transactions, the details are contained in the purchase order. When manufacturing and shipping of the items in the stock keeping unit are tracked at various stages using portable data terminals and bar code technology, this type of database is typically queried and updated at suppli-er and customer sites.

unit, the supplier thinks of that item as a purchase order line item, and the typical receiving system is designed to view a customer as a sales order line item. These aliases form relationships back to the stock keeping unit and need to be handled accordingly. The data import and export issues deal with how easily one can extract data from a host computer system's database and later update the same. Local work center databases need to have the ability to be specifically queried about the status of a specific transaction as well as be able to provide a screen or written report on a set of common transactions.

Most database software has some form of query language, often an SQL dialect, to permit this type of local manipulation.

The advent of restricted English-like applications oriented query languages provides for database access and manipulation without an in-depth understanding of the highly stylized Structured Query Language dialects associated with most database software. Unless someone in the work center area is familiar with the dialect of SQL used with local database software of an application, it is highly recommended that one of these newer applications query languages be installed on top of the normal database query language software to permit a more friendly human-machine interface to the database.

Electronic Data Interchange (EDI) is discussed in Chapter 12. Most often bar code technology and electronic data interchange are combined to aid in:

- Just-In-Time communications between suppliers and manufacturers
- Quick-Response communications between suppliers and retailers

EDI is standardized in the American National Standards Institute (ANSI) ASC X12 and UN/EDIFACT standards and most commonly communicates these business documents:

- Purchase Order (X12 Transaction Set 850/EDIFACT Message ORDERS)
- Invoice (X12 Transaction Set 810/EDIFACT Message INVOIC)
- Advance Ship Notice/Manifest (X12 Transaction Set 856/EDIFACT Message DESADV)
- Inventory Advice (X12 Transaction Set 846/EDIFACT Message INVRPT)
- Price Sales Catalog (X12 Transaction Set 832/EDIFACT Message PRICAT)

Today, we are seeing increasing evidence of management wanting more from computer systems than just reports beneficial for the data processing department. Existing data processing systems are collecting more information than management can possibly assimilate. The recently introduced technology of *Graphic Presentation Systems* often provides this additional management tool. Use of bar codes and transactional data collection systems will increase the availability of data in geometric proportions. Management needs methods of dealing with the output of these data collection systems. Executive information systems using graphic presentation technologies are emerging to provide graphic analysis of all of the data that is being collected. Taking collected data from the databases and providing information in a graphic presentation system makes sense because:

- Management prefers pictures to wading through printouts
- It is easier to see trends in pictures
- An executive information system (EIS) provides powerful "what if . . ." modeling
- Less middle management is needed when an EIS can do the reporting

But before we begin looking at the various devices that can provide input to these electronic systems, it will be helpful to understand some of the underpinnings of data communications and the way terminals talk to computers.

Data Communications

Binary Data

Computers process data and communicate with terminals and one another in a binary language composed of bits (**binary digits**). Just as our decimal system is based on the digits 0 through 9, binary systems are based on 1s and 0s. In decimal we have, from right to left, the ones place, tens place, hundreds place, thousands place, etc. In binary we have, from right to left, the ones place, twos place, fours place, eights place, etc. In Table 11.1 we show how the digits 0 to 9 are converted from decimal to binary.

Decimal Digit	Corresponding Binary Digits			
	8	4	2	1
0	0	0	0	0
1	0	0	0	1
2	0	0	1	0
3	0	0	1	1
4	0	1	0	0
5	0	1	0	1
6	0	1	1	0
7	0	1	1	1
8	1	0	0	0
9	1	0	0	1

Table 11.1: Decimal to Binary Conversion

Computers deal with binary encoded information, typically in 8-bit bytes. Each byte of data contains a set of binary digits with corresponding decimal weightings by powers of 2. As an example, we show the simple case of binary coded decimal, where 4-bit binary numbers are used to represent the decimal digits. In the more general case of the ASCII code, 7 bits are used to represent the decimal digits plus upper/lowercase letters, numerous special graphic characters and various non-printable control codes.

There are two basic ways to move and manipulate binary data: in serial data form (one bit at a time) or in parallel data form (eight bits—one byte—or more at a time). In the more general cases of ASCII (the typical 7-bit code of modern personal computers) and EBCDIC (the 8-bit code traditionally used on IBM and other mainframe computers), the same sort of serial versus parallel conventions apply.

Serial Data Transmission

Serial data transmission is the most common method of sending data from one computer or terminal to another. In the EIA RS-232c serial communications specifications, there are—formally—two types of equipment with two variations on cable wiring, denoted by two 3-digit mnemonics: DTE and DCE. Data terminal equipment (DTE) was originally the designation used for a terminal such as a CRT display terminal or Teletype. Data communications equipment (DCE) was originally the designation used for a modem. In modern practice, the wiring and setup specifications of any given hardwired connection need to be analyzed. Data is sent out in a stream, one bit at a time, over one channel. The most common of these serial coding structures, ASCII (American Standard Code for Information Interchange), EBCDIC (Extended Binary Code Decimal Interchange Code), and International Standards Organization 646 International Reference Version (IRV), are shown in Table J.4. When a computer is instructed to send data to another computer or terminal on a serial channel, the parallel data within the computer must pass through a serial interface to exit as serial data. Then it passes through ports, cables, and connectors that link the various devices. The boundaries (physical, functional, and electrical) shared by these devices are called interfaces.

Modems

A "modem" (MOdulator/DEModulator) serves as the interface between devices that need to share data using an audio channel such as a telephone line (or audio signals on an RF or fiber optic channel), and generally consists of a transmitter and a receiver. A modem transmits data from a computer or terminal at one site to another modem connected to a computer or terminal at the other end of the telephone line.

At the sending end, a modem prepares data for transmission by changing the data's characteristics to an audio signal so that it is compatible with the telephone channel. At the receiving end, a modem reconfigures the signal into the original data format used by the computer (see Figure 11.2).

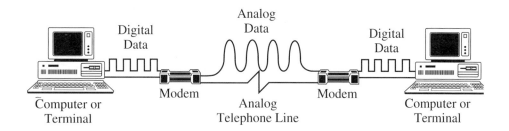

Figure 11.2: Modem Operation

The steps involved in the most common form of data communication are depicted symbolically here. A computer or terminal generates a time-varying serial sequence of binary data bits which is sent to a modem. The modem transforms this serial digital data stream into a serial analog data stream compatible with the communications channel, shown here as a telephone line. At the other end of the phone line, the receiving part of the modem transforms the serial analog form of the data into a regenerated digital data stream that is in turn interpreted by the receiving computer system.

To link two computers together via a telephone line, a modem must also perform format conversion. It must be able to convert data back and forth between the digital ("1s" and "0s") format used by the computers and the modulated analog format used over the telephone channel.

Terminals

Traditional data entry has been accomplished by people recording data manually with clipboard, pencil, and printed form. These source documents are then hand-carried, mailed, or phoned to a key-entry center where the data is then input to the computer. Many data processing departments expend 25 percent and more of their budget just in the wages of key-entry personnel. Bar codes and data entry terminals transfer the source data capture from key-entry personnel out to the people who actually do the work. This transfer of data entry responsibility is viewed as causing additional labor at the point where productivity is of utmost concern. But scanning the information instead of writing it onto a form actually will reduce the time for data entry. Additionally, once the data exists in the computer system, it never needs to be key-entered again. Within the realm of data collection technology we have on-line systems and batch systems. On-line systems can be either hardwired or wireless. Both on-line and batch systems can be either fixed-position or portable.

Hardwired Terminals
Hardwired Wedges

A wedge provides a seamless link between the scanner and the host computer, and often is physically connected either between the terminal display and its keyboard or to its EIA RS-232C or SCSI (small computer system interface) port. This type of reader interface between scanner and computer minimizes the amount of software modification necessary to capture scanned data. Wedges often have options to permit the transmission of certain ASCII control characters, e.g., Carriage Return, Line Feed, Horizontal Tab, Vertical Tab, to further minimize operator key strokes after reading the bar code symbol. It should be remembered that "wedges" require CRTs, and it may not always be possible, desirable, or cost effective to place a CRT everywhere data needs to be captured. Several suppliers provide keyboard emulation, permitting their devices to communicate directly with many microcomputers and mid-range computers, as well as mainframe processors. However, this fixed-position arrangement limits portability of the scanning activity to the length of the cord connecting the scanner to the wedge.

Hardwired Satellite Terminals

Satellite terminals are limited-function terminals, providing either an audible tone to permit the user to know when a bar code symbol is successfully read or a set of status lights (signifying system busy, good read, re-read the symbol, etc.), and are generally networked systems with the ability to link either an individual scanner or several scanners to a host computer. Such devices generally are without the benefit of full-character displays or memory. Typical applications for these devices might be in situations where brief messages are transmitted to the computer system from a variety of locations, e.g., central filing, work-in-process data entry, and time and attendance. One variety of a hardwired satellite terminal is a slot reader intended to read a bar code symbol on a thin rigid surface, such as an employee badge, patron card, etc. These devices generally employ a limited-distance, fixed-beam scanner, positioned to read a bar code symbol when the card is drawn through the slot of the reader.

Hardwired, Full-Featured, Fixed-Position Terminals

Full-featured, fixed-position terminals with character displays and keyboards may serve as a low-cost and smaller footprint alternative to full CRT implementations. Some of these devices may have limited editing capabilities. They often have extensive programmability in order to implement application-oriented data collection features. These terminals may transmit information immediately when scanned or collect several transactions before transmitting data to a host. Files from the computer system can be downloaded and uploaded to the intelligent terminal and can serve as a work center terminal with bar code reading equipment attached. These devices often have integrated keyboards, displays, and printers. In addition to programmability and store-and-forward capability, full-featured terminals provide the benefit of a display for operator prompting and the ability for limited key entry of non-scanned data, such as quantity or data from an unreadable bar code symbol.

Protection from magnetic fields, electrostatic charges, and power line transients should be considered for all hardwired systems. Clean and consistent power supplies are important in any data collection system. Wherever possible, uninterruptible power sources and line conditioning equipment should be employed.

Wireless Terminals

A serious consideration that needs to be given to the above terminal configurations concerns the word "hardwired." When you calculate the cost of these types of terminals, do not forget the cost of wire and connectors. Standard 7 conductor EIA RS-232C cabling (pins 2 through 4, 6 through 8, 20 connected) costs about $0.25 per foot. EIA RS-232C limits the distance of the cable to 50 feet to remain within its specifications. Similar extended distance shielded RS-232 cables, permitting distances of up to 500 feet, cost $0.39 per foot and up. These extended distance cables are not within the EIA RS-232 specifications, but are widely used. Additionally, installation and connectors may bring the cost to about $2 per installed foot. Add to this the cost of conduit for the cabling and electrical power wiring and you can easily see how the cost of hardwired systems mounts.

In addition to the cost associated with wired terminals, another consideration is the location of the symbol in relation to the terminal. It is often necessary to physically bring the item with the bar code symbol to the wired terminal. The distance between terminal and symbol is limited by the length of cord between the reader and the terminal.

Wireless technology permits the elimination of the input/output cord. Wireless communications exist not only for portable terminals but also as a replacement for some wired local area networks.

Portable Terminals

We are able to eliminate the power cord through battery power supplies and eliminate the input/output cords by either storing data internally within the terminal (a batch terminal) or transmitting the data from the terminal back to the computer in "real time" via a wireless, radio-frequency link. Figure 11.3 shows data entry by use of bar code equipped terminals without the interim data entry and handling steps. Portable data entry terminals commonly have a display, keyboard, memory, scanners, and batteries.

Displays are generally either LEDs (light emitting diodes) or LCDs (liquid crystal displays). LEDs are good for dimly lit environments but tend to wash out in direct sunlight. LEDs also have high power consumption—an issue which may need to be considered in battery powered applications. LCDs are good for brightly lit environments but may be

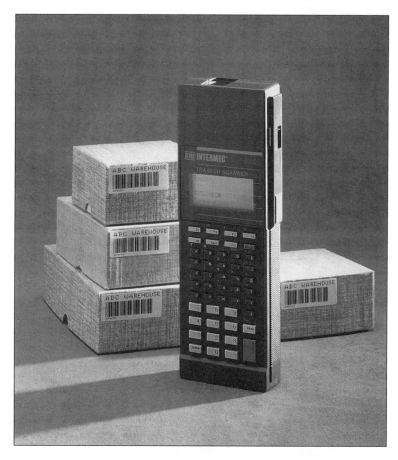

Figure 11.3: A Portable Data Entry Terminal

difficult to see in dimly lit environments. Many suppliers of portable data entry terminals solve this problem through backlighting the display. Displays are usually referred to as "n" characters long by "m" lines long. It is common to find 2- and 4-line displays 16 characters in length. Some suppliers of portable data entry terminals also incorporate the scrolling of displays which permits reviewing data where the number of characters in the field is longer than the display. Some terminals have longer displays as well as more lines in the display. A rule of thumb is that the number of characters in the display should fully display all operator prompts and all collected fields of information.

Portable data entry terminal *keyboards* permit key entry of data that is not intended to be scanned or that is not scannable. These keyboards are either numeric, numeric with special characters, alphanumeric, or alphanumeric plus special characters. Keyboard arrangements can be horizontal (typewriter-like) or vertical (calculator-like). Keyboards should be able to support all characters that are also normally scanned. For example, if key-entry is required of normally scanned data and the bar code contains alphabetic data, it is difficult to enter this data on a numeric-only keyboard. Further, one should evaluate the size of the keys in order to match key size to the operational environment. If a material handler is going be wearing gloves or has large fingers, it may be counter-productive to utilize keys spaced at $3/8$ inch center to center. Another issue regarding keyboard design is whether extensive "shifting" is required to enter all of the data required. Some keyboards may require shifting between alphabetic, numeric, and special characters. This shifting may lead to miskeyed data and operator frustration.

Memory is usually divided into three categories: program memory, buffer memory, and data memory. Historically, program memory was coded in ROM (Read Only Memory) or EPROM (Erasable Programmable Read Only Memory). ROMs are generally coded by the semi-conductor manufacturer and cannot be reused. EPROMs are programmed by the terminal manufacturer; the component is erased by extended exposure to ultra-violet (UV) light and is programmed electrically. More recently, programs have been coded into EEROM (Electrically Erasable Read Only Memory). This type of program memory can be coded by the terminal supplier or by the using organization. The benefit of ROM, EPROM, and EEROM is that once the program is coded in the semiconductor component, the data is not erased if power is removed from the unit. Buffer memory, on the other hand, is generally volatile RAM (Random Access Memory), which requires that power be available to memory to retain data. If power is removed and then reapplied to the unit, the buffer is cleared, removing the data. Buffer memory accepts keystrokes from the keyboard prior to writing the same to data memory. Buffer memory is also employed in data communications and scanning. Data memory is often RAM, ranging from memory sizes of 8K (8,192 characters) up to 1 megabyte (1,048,576 characters). Removal of power can wipe out the collected data, requiring the information to be recaptured. Some manufacturers of batch terminals provide a 10-year lithium power cell to retain buffer memory in the event of removal and replacement of the terminal's system batteries or when the batteries lose their charge. Some suppliers offer data memory in EEROM which prevents the loss of data in case of power loss.

Batteries employed within portable data entry terminals can be rechargeable nickel-cadmium (NiCad), single-use alkaline, or single-use lithium. Rechargeable lithiums are on the horizon. To avoid frequent replacement of single-use batteries, many organizations have opted to use rechargeable batteries. A word of caution to those anticipating the use of rechargeables: Rechargeable batteries—whether on portable data entry terminals, battery-powered cellular phones, or hedge clippers—develop a memory for how long the charge will last. Rechargeables need to be fully discharged before they are recharged. A terminal supplier may claim that a unit will function for eight hours. If that terminal has an initial charge good enough for eight hours but is repeatedly placed on a recharger after two hours of use, the effective life of the battery will become two hours. Battery reconditioners are available to bring battery life back to its original charge duration, but to keep from having to continually recondition the batteries, you are well advised to use the terminal until a low battery condition exists and then replace the battery with one that is fully charged.

Scanners can be either peripheral to the portable data entry terminal or functionally integrated with the portable data entry terminal. Most portable data entry terminals can be equipped with handheld laser scanners, wand scanners, or charge-coupled devices plugged directly into them. Each terminal supplier has its own unique connections between scanner and terminal. Most scanner manufacturers can support the popular portable data entry terminals. Figure 11.4(a) shows the scanner as a peripheral to a portable

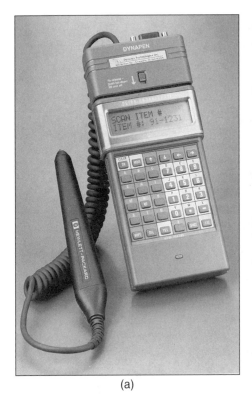

(a)   (b)

Figure 11.4: Some Portable Data Entry Terminal/Scanner Options.

(a) shows a scanner used as a peripheral unit plugged into the portable data entry terminal. (b) shows another option, where the scanner can be functionally integrated with the portable data entry terminal.

data entry terminal; Figure 11.4(b) shows a functionally integrated unit combining bar code reader and portable data entry terminal.

Batch vs. On-Line (Real-Time) Terminals

The basic difference between the two major classes of date entry terminals—batch and on-line (real-time)—is whether the terminal serves as an electronic clipboard (batch) or is actually on-line with a local database in real time.

With very few exceptions, some modification of the host computer software will need to be effected before multiple data entry terminals can load data to the host. In all cases, additional software may be required to permit the downloading of data files or application programs from the host to the portable data entry terminal.

Data entry terminals also require software programming at the terminal level for application programs. Application programs can be written by the supplier, a value-added reseller, or the end-user organization. Each supplier offers its own variety of software development language. This language generally operates only on the equipment of that specific supplier. Prior to the implementation of data entry terminals, several issues need to be clear to members of the using organization.

204

- What is the cost of the software development language?
- What is the annual maintenance for the software development language?
- What type of computer does the development language need to be developed on? If developed on a PC, can the language be supported on PCs already in the organization?
- How long does it take to learn the development language?
- How long does it take to develop an application program of moderate complexity?
- What other customers of the supplier have used this development language? What is their experience with the language?
- If the organization is going to develop its own application programs, are the resources available to accomplish the programming?

Some suppliers offer terminals that are programmable in BASIC. In this case, it is necessary to establish whether the "variety" of BASIC needed for programming supports all of the extensions and ROM BIOS of the BASIC that the organization is already familiar with. Some terminals are programmable in "C" or PASCAL. Do not accept the supplier's statement regarding how long it will take to develop these "C" or PASCAL programs. Go to one of the supplier's customers and establish how long it took to develop their application.

Batch terminals are simply electronic clipboards, recording the entered data in a manner that can later be uploaded to the work center or host computer. Generally, these devices are not intended to be downloaded with extensive databases for table lookup or editing functions. These batch terminals do not need high-speed (expensive) microprocessors inside. Generally, the processors are much slower than what is traditionally thought of as a microprocessor. Before deciding to implement systems that have substantial files downloaded to the terminals, establish how long it takes to download typical files and how long it takes to accomplish searches of information that has been randomly received. Also test to establish how long it takes to upload the data once it has been received.

Generally speaking, I recommend batch terminals only in cases where you would not have access to an on-line link. Such applications may exist in field sales order entry, direct store delivery, and package delivery applications. By the time you add in the cost of the additional memory for the terminal to accept a download of functional databases, it may often be as inexpensive to employ on-line portable data entry terminals using RF links.

Some suppliers of batch/on-line terminals will attempt to explain that their terminals will be able to continue to capture data if the RF or hardwired link is lost. At first blush this sounds like the best of both worlds. However, the distinction needs to be reiterated: Batch devices are only reporting systems, and on-line terminals are part of real-time control systems. If you are operating in an on-line mode in a shipping application and the link goes down, the system will continue to capture data in a batch environment for an hour until the link is reestablished. Of what good is it, once the link is reestablished, to inform the operator that the truck that was loaded 30 minutes ago and has since departed, contained an order that was shipped incomplete? A second issue regarding hybrid terminals is that involving what happens once the link is reestablished. How long will it take to put out onto the communications link the data that was previously captured? What happens to other terminals on the link while the hybrid is uploading its data?

Radio Frequency Portable Data Entry Terminals
For true "on-line communications" radio frequency (RF) portable data entry terminals

Figure 11.5: Several Variations on RF Data Communications

(a) shows a functionally integrated RF data collection terminal with scanner. (b) is an example of a vehicle-mounted RF data collection terminal with scanner. In this variation, a frequent requirement is the ability for the operator to be able to scan a label at a long distance while sitting in the driving seat. (c) shows a functionally integrated RF and scanning terminal. At (d) is a discrete component radio, scanner, and terminal combination.

should be seriously considered. These terminals are linked directly back to a work center or host processor, permitting on-line inquiry and updating of records and files. There are now about a dozen suppliers of these terminals, and these product offerings are becoming increasingly impressive. Where batch "store-and forward" terminal offerings may have functionally integrated the data collection terminal and the scanner, some RF portables functionally integrate the scanner, radio, and terminal. Likewise, some manufacturers may have three distinct components in the system for the operator to handle. Figure 11.5 shows several forms of RF portable data entry terminals.

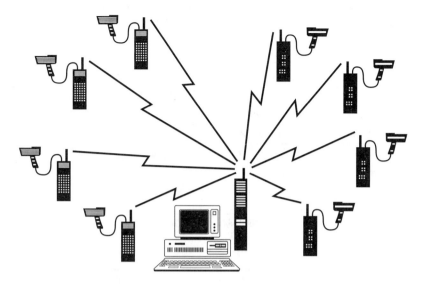

Figure 11.6: A Typical RF Terminal Configuration

This diagram shows a typical configuration of an RF base station serving as a multiplexer of multiple RF linked terminals for a work center's processor. The nodes addressed by the base station multiplexer are shown symbolically as terminals with handheld laser scanners, a common choice of hardware.

A typical RF terminal configuration would include portables (handhelds) and/or mobiles (forklift mounted) transmitting and receiving at a specified frequency with a base station/multiplexer connected to a work center processor, as shown in Figure 11.6.

The multiplexer serves as a "traffic cop," directing the communications between the base station and specific radio frequency terminals. The base station handles communication protocols and transmission speed from the RF terminals to the host work center.

RF terminals communicate data over specific wavelengths with the electromagnetic spectrum (EMS). This spectrum includes the wavelengths shown in Table 11.2.

In Table 11.2 specific attention should be given to the UHF frequencies between 300 MHz and 3 GHz. This is the frequency at which most radio-frequency (RF) terminals operate today. While traditional data communication is conveyed over some physical medium of wires or cables, RF communication exists in free space.

One of the most common forms of radio communication is AM radio (using amplitude modulation). In AM systems a carrier signal transmitted at a specific frequency has its amplitude varied linearly by some message signal. A disadvantage of AM is the presence of interference and static (noise), which may be experienced over the entire spectrum.

With frequency modulation (FM), the amplitude of the RF modulated wave remains constant while its frequency is varied at a rate determined by the frequency of the information transmitted. As with AM signals, there is some amplitude modulation of the FM carrier due to noise. However, the receiver is sensitive only to the frequency of the carrier so the AM noise is ignored. Because the transmitted information is a function of the rate at which the carrier is deviated from its center frequency, and not dependent upon variations in carrier amplitude, there is no degradation of the signal due to the superimposed amplitude noise.

EMS Region	Frequency	Wavelength	Typical Uses
Electromagnetic Radiation Bands (Radio)			
Extremely Low Frequency (ELF)	20 to 300	$1.5 \times 10^7 - 1.0 \times 10^6$ m	AC Power/Telegraphy
Voice Frequency (VF)	300 to 3,000	$1.0 \times 10^6 - 1.0 \times 10^5$ m	Human Speech
Very Low Frequency (VLF)	3,000 to 30,000	$1.0 \times 10^5 - 1.0 \times 10^4$ m	Timing Signals
Low Frequency (LF)	30 KHz to 200 KHz	$1.0 \times 10^4 - 1.5 \times 10^3$ m	Radio Telegraphy
Medium Frequency (MF)	200 KHz to 2 MHz	1500–150 m	AM Radio/LORAN
High Frequency (HF)	2 MHz to 30 MHz	150–10 m	Telemetry, Communications
Very High Frequency (VHF)	30 MHz to 300 MHz	10 to 1 m	TV (Ch 2-13)/FM Radio
Ultra High Frequency (UHF)	300 MHz to 3 GHz	1 to .01 m	RF Terminals/TV (Ch 14-83)
Super High Frequency (SHF)	3 GHz to 30 GHz	.01 to .001 m	Satellite/Microwave
Extremely High Frequency (EHF)	30 GHz to 300 GHz	.001 to .0001 m	Radar
Optical Radiation Bands			
Infrared	300 GHz to 428 THz	1000 nm to 701 nm	IR LEDs/IR Laser Diodes
Visible	428 THz to 750 THz	701 nm to 400 nm	Human Vision
Red	428 THz to 492 THz	701 nm to 610 nm	VR LEDs/HeNe gas lasers
Orange	492 THz to 501 THz	610 nm to 599 nm	
Yellow	501 THz to 527 THz	599 nm to 569 nm	
Green	527 THz to 600 THz	569 nm to 500 nm	
Blue	600 THz to 660 THz	500 nm to 455 nm	
Violet	660 THz to 750 THz	455 nm to 400 nm	
Ultraviolet (UV)	750 THz–30,000 Thz	400 nm to 100 nm	Bactericidal Applications
Nuclear Radiation Bands			
X-Ray	$3.0 \times 10^{16} - 1.0 \times 10^{19}$	$1.0 \times 10^{-8} - 3.0 \times 10^{-11}$ m	X-Ray Spectroscopy
Gamma	$1.0 \times 10^{19} - 5.0 \times 10^{20}$	$3.0 \times 10^{-11} - 6.0 \times 10^{-13}$ m	Astrophysical /nuclear transition radiation
Cosmic	$5.0 \times 10^{20} - 1.0 \times 10^{22}$	$6.0 \times 10^{-13} - 3.0 \times 10^{-14}$ m	Astrophysical /nuclear transition radiation

1 Kilohertz (KHz) = 1,000 (10^3) Hertz
1 Megahertz (MHz) = 1,000,000 (10^6) Hertz
1 Gigahertz (GHz) = 1,000,000,000 (10^9) Hertz
1 Terahertz (THz) = 1,000,000,000,000 (10^{12}) Hertz
1 Nanometer (nm) = 1/1,000,000,000 (10^9) Meter

Table 11.2: Electromagnetic Spectrum

Frequency modulation requires a greater bandwidth than AM. Consequently, it must operate higher in the electromagnetic spectrum. Most of today's RF terminals operate with frequency modulated signals.

Handheld radio frequency terminals are typically land-mobile terminals operating at a specified frequency assigned by the Federal Communications Commission (FCC).

Operating between 450 MHz and 470 MHz for business communications or between 402 MHz and 420 MHz for government communications, they are referred to as narrow-band radio frequency terminals. (Spread-spectrum RF terminals will be discussed later in this chapter.) In the 450-470 MHz band, these terminals typically operate at two watts of power for portables (handhelds) and five watts of power for mobiles (truck mounts).

A one-watt radio in these bands will transmit about one mile on flat land. Doubling the output power increases the range by about one-third. Therefore, a two-watt radio transmits 1.3 miles on flat land. Land is seldom flat, however, and without hills, buildings, trees, corrugated boxes, shelving, walls, and the like. Since the FCC limits the output power of handheld RF terminals to two watts, an alternative to increasing power is to increase the antenna gain. An antenna with a six dB (decibel) gain will double the effective coverage area. Another option is to increase the height of the antenna. Doubling the antenna height increases its range by about one-half.

In all types of transmission there is some amount of background noise. Noise can be divided into two categories: sky noise and man-made impulsive noise. Sky noise is naturally occurring noise typically derived from atmospheric, galactic, solar, or precipitation sources. Impulsive noise is caused by auto ignitions, power lines, fluorescent lighting, electrical equipment, and the like. Each communication system has a specified signal-to-noise ratio. Below a specified point where the noise is excessive to the amplitude of the signal, errors are introduced into the transmission of data. The further the distance an RF terminal is located from its base antenna, the lower the signal power transmitted from one to the other. If the noise background stays constant, a lower signal-to-noise ratio results and the higher the probability of error introduction.

A common error of communication terminology is often made by those who do not understand communication theory. A baud is a unit of signaling speed, while bit per second is a data transfer rate. Multiple bits can be transmitted in a single baud. Today's 450-470 MHz radio frequency terminals transmit at speeds from 1,200 to 9,600 bits per second (typically at 2,400 bits per second). At 2,400 bits per second a single bit is transmitted in 0.000417 seconds (0.4μsec) and at 9,600 bits per second a single bit is transmitted in 0.000104 seconds (0.1μsec). Therefore, a noise spike of 0.1μsec may introduce an error in a 9,600 bits per second transmission and not introduce the error in a transmission of 2,400 bits per second. The further the distance an RF terminal is located from its base antenna, the lower the transmission speed should be to minimize errors.

Because of the communication protocols in most data communication systems, transmitted data is seldom introduced into the computer. At the end of each transmission block one or more check characters are appended to ensure that the data has not been corrupted by an error. If the check sum(s) calculated at the receiving end agree with the check sum(s) appended to the transmission block, an "ACK" (positive acknowledgment) is transmitted back to the sender and the next block is then transmitted. If the check sum(s) calculated at the receiving end do not agree with the check sum(s) appended to the transmission block, a "NAK" (negative acknowledgment) is transmitted back to the sender and the same block is retransmitted. Most RF terminal systems will retransmit the same block a specified number of times prior to shutting down due to a noisy communications channel.

The Federal Communications Commission (FCC) licensing procedure is intended to provide a specific narrow-band radio-frequency transmission path for a specific user in a specific location. The FCC and support organizations such as the National Association of

Business and Educational Radio keep track of the frequencies that have been issued in specific locations.

An applicant for an FCC license for narrow-band transmission (450-470 MHz) must complete FCC Form 274 for each location. The information required on this application to the FCC includes the number of units (portables/mobiles plus base), distances involved, location of the site, physical address of site, contact person, applicant name and mailing address, number of frequencies requested, and nearest metropolitan area and distance to it. Generally, the radio frequency terminal supplier will take the required information and the signed FCC Form 274 from the applicant and help the applicant to complete and submit the application.

Of the information required in an FCC application, the most difficult to secure will probably be the specific latitude and longitude of base station location. This information is commonly available through city/county planning or engineering departments. The application fee for a narrow-band RF license is less than $200. Once the application is submitted, a five-year license is received for that location in four to six weeks. This license is issued at a specific frequency, for example, 467.77500 MHz. If an organization changes address or telephone number, an application for modification of the existing license should be submitted.

If an organization anticipates the implementation of numerous sites throughout the country, a nationwide license may be considered at the time of license application. The rationale behind a nationwide license lies in the need for spare equipment. The terminals and matching base stations have a common frequency. If a nationwide license is granted, all equipment within the organization is programmed with the same frequency. In the case of equipment failure, spare equipment in one location can be rushed to the location where the equipment failed. A note of caution, however, is in order. Each terminal has its own terminal identity, usually under dip switch control. If the failed terminal had a terminal identity of "08," the replacement terminal should also be set locally to a terminal identity of "08." If two terminals in the same system had the same identity, messages intended for one of the terminals would be sent to both—creating confusion for the applications software controlling the terminals.

Suppliers of RF terminal equipment must be type-accepted by the FCC in the United States, or national counterparts in other parts of the world, for each particular model of equipment. Under FCC rules the equipment should deviate no more than ±5 KHz from the authorized frequency and should have a frequency stability over the operating range of the equipment of better than 5 parts per million. Additionally, the equipment must transmit its station identification at the end of each transmission or at least once every 30 minutes.

Frequency control is supplied by a crystal-controlled oscillator or by a frequency synthesizer. Older crystal-controlled systems have a tendency to alter their transmitting characteristics over time and changes in temperature. Crystal-controlled systems should be tested and, if necessary, recalibrated at least once per year. It is not unusual for crystal-controlled systems to begin deviating (drifting) from their prescribed frequencies by as much as 500 KHz—100 times the acceptable level under FCC rules. As more organizations employ RF terminals, it will be increasingly important that authorized frequencies and allowable deviations be observed, lest the FCC find an offending transmission and require the licensee to cease operation until the frequency transmissions are within licensed limits. Frequency-synthesized systems seldom need recalibration but should be tested each year.

Data Communication Protocols

A communication system includes transmitting device(s), receiving device(s), one or more communication media (which may be a cable, telephone line, radio frequency channel, etc.), and a set of rules which describe how communications are effected (communication protocols). The International Standards Organization (ISO) has developed a seven-level Reference Model of Open Systems Interconnection to guide in the development of standard communication protocols.

Protocols within the ISO model are generally considered at the session layer (level 5). Protocols generally can be broken down into various constituent parts that dictate how the media is accessed by devices with transmission requirements, how the beginnings and ends of messages are indicated, how sender and intended receiver of messages are identified (addressing), how data and timing information (needed by the receiver to decode the incoming signal) are communicated, and how errors that may occur in transmission can be detected and corrected prior to the data reaching the application program.

In communication systems where a number of devices share a single medium or channel, the rules governing channel access are often the dominant factor in determining how well a particular system performs. Channel access protocols can be categorized into one of three types: polled, in which units are sequentially queried by individual addresses; contention, in which units with information compete or contend for use of the channel; and hybrid protocols which contain elements of both polled and contention-based approaches.

Polled Protocols

Polled protocols are easiest to implement and have performance advantages in certain situations. In polled systems a master unit (base station/system communication controller) initiates a communication session with an individual slave unit (terminal) by transmitting a poll or prompt identifying the unit by its unique address. The unit polled then responds with any data that is ready to transmit or with a message indicating that it has no data to send. In some systems, the lack of a return transmission is used to signify that the unit has no message to send. Reception of a message at the master unit is usually followed by a positive acknowledgment ("ACK") or negative acknowledgment ("NAK") back to the polled unit depending on whether or not errors were detected in the transmission.

When the base station has a message for a particular unit, the poll is modified to include the message—and the unit polled transmits the ACK/NAK message in response. At the conclusion of the communication session, the base station moves on to poll the next address in succession. After all units have been polled, the polling sequence is repeated.

The efficiency of polling is dependent on the respective number of units with messages to send and those without messages. Polling of units that do not require service results in wasted time, lower data throughput, and longer response time for units that have data to transmit. Adaptive polling techniques can be used to increase the efficiency of polled systems. In adaptive polling a history is maintained on each terminal, and those that have been recently transmitting data are polled more frequently than those that have been inactive.

Polling is best suited to systems with small numbers of terminals that all generate approximately equal message traffic. In the extreme case where all terminals have near-continuous transmission requirements, polling is one of the more efficient types of protocols.

Contention Protocols

The basic assumption behind contention protocols is that although the number of units operating in the communication system may be large, the number of units with transmission requirements at any one time is likely to be small. Rather than polling through the addresses of many units with no transmission requirements to find the few that do require transmission, contention schemes allow terminals with transmission requirements to compete for use of the channel.

In a pure contention mode, units transmit messages as soon as they are ready. If no other unit is transmitting data traffic at that time, the message gets through. If one or more other units require transmission during the same time interval, a collision occurs, and none of the messages gets through. Because of the possibility of collision, pure contention protocols are seldom used.

Modified contention protocols seek to address the issue of collision by providing a means of retransmitting lost messages and in some cases by incorporating measures to control their occurrence. Commonly used protocols include ALOHA, which is a pure contention scheme with retransmission; slotted ALOHA, ALOHA with added collision control; and CSMA which also includes collision control and retransmission features. (The ALOHA protocol was developed in radio packet switched network experiments at the Univeristy of Hawaii in the 1970s.)

One other important aspect of radio network design that should be stressed prior to further discussion of contention protocols is the phenomenon of *capture*. Instances where two or more units are transmitting simultaneously do not always result in collisions. In cases where the signal received from one of the transmitting units is significantly stronger than the others, the receiver will lock onto or capture the stronger signal, and the weaker signals will not be detected. Capture provides both an advantage and a disadvantage in systems design. Capture reduces the incidence of collision, but promotes what is referred to as a near-far imbalance, where units that are operating at a significant distance from the base station exhibit longer access delays than closer units.

ALOHA

ALOHA is a pure contention protocol with collision recovery. In an ALOHA system, units transmit as soon as they have a message to send. Collisions are assumed if a response is not received within a specified period of time. After a collision is detected, a waiting time is randomly selected prior to retransmitting the data. Two or more units that may have collided will most likely select different waiting periods, not to collide during retransmission. Retransmissions continue at random intervals until the message is acknowledged.

Slotted ALOHA

A major disadvantage of ALOHA is that collisions can occur anywhere in a message. For example, Unit A begins transmission of a 200-character message. After 180 characters have been transmitted, Unit B begins transmission of a 200-character message. The resulting collision destroys two messages, though only 20 characters of data were lost in each transmission.

Slotted ALOHA seeks to remedy this problem by forcing all transmissions to fall within slots or frames. A slot consists of a timing marker, which signifies when a transmission must begin, and a maximum message length, which defines the interval between timing markers. Use of slotted ALOHA with 200-character slots in the example above would have reduced the transmission time lost due to collision from 380 characters to 200 characters. The main disadvantage of slotted ALOHA is that it becomes much less efficient if message lengths are not constant. A 20-character ACK message which may follow a 200-character transmission does not make efficient use of a 200-character-wide slot.

CSMA

CSMA is the abbreviation for Carrier Sense Multiple Access. CSMA works like ALOHA, except that units with messages to transmit monitor the channel for other transmissions (sense carrier), and begin transmission only when the channel clears. In theory, a collision occurs only when two units begin to transmit simultaneously, making collisions much less likely than in ALOHA systems. Collisions in CSMA systems are generally handled in the same way as ALOHA and slotted ALOHA systems. Unlike slotted ALOHA, CSMA allows variable message lengths with no loss of transmission efficiency.

The low number of collisions and variable message length make CSMA one of the best of the modified contention protocols. Unfortunately, in local area radio networks CSMA suffers from one very severe problem. Typically, RF system coverage requirements in large installations dictate central location of the base station. As a result, while the base station is able to communicate with all terminals in the system, terminals may be unable to detect all transmissions from other terminals. This results in far more collisions than would be expected in a CSMA system, reducing system efficiency.

Hybrid Protocols

Some hybrid protocols are specifically designed to perform in the local area data system environment. Units with transmission requirements are identified in a contention channel access phase. Because the length of transmission required to identify units is short and of known length, collisions that do occur result in little lost transmission time. The length of the contention period is dynamically adjusted to match demands on the system. When traffic is light, the contention period is shortened; when it increases, so does the contention phase. The contention phase is also designed to reduce the issue of near-far imbalance, providing near equal access for units operating at substantial distances from the base station.

Units identified in the contention phase are subsequently polled by address during a communication phase. Only units that have transmission requirements are polled. Message lengths can be variable. Outbound messages from the base to portable units are routed directly to the address and are not subject to collision.

Response Time

Many vendors will claim that their radio frequency networks support large numbers of terminals, like 128 or 256 terminals per channel. No one with experience in communications engineering would ever hang 128 or 256 terminals on one communication port lest they experience substantial delays in response from the host computer. I suggest that no more than 32 terminals be connected on one channel—whether the medium is hardwired or an RF link—except in extremely low transmission volume situations.

Response time should be targeted at approximately two seconds and should not exceed five seconds. The response time of a communication system is a function of many different variables. First, the transmission speed—9,600 bits per second without errors and retransmission—is faster than 2,400 bits per second without errors (although 9,600 bits per second with frequent retransmission is slower than 2,400 bits per second without retransmission).

Some RF terminals incorporate a feature whereby transmission occurs at higher speeds, 9,600 bits per second, for example—unless frequent retransmissions occur, at which time the radio may reduce its transmission speed. All radio systems have a radio key-up delay. If the terminal has been inactive for some period of time, it may require a second or so to be reactivated. The number of transmitted characters per block, both from the base to the portable unit and from the portable unit to the base, also affects response time, with shorter messages taking less time than longer ones. Some RF terminal suppliers have a stored form option, permitting the transmission of prompt sequence when a communications session is begun or altered, minimizing the number of characters which are transmitted from the base station to the portable unit. This also permits only the variable data to be sent to the base from the portable unit, while the prompts remain stored in buffer memory within the portable unit. Each communication protocol also has a number of overhead characters which define the beginning and end of the block and the sequence number, and provide error detection. Some systems may offer forward error correction to minimize the number of retransmitted blocks, but this is usually accomplished by extensive redundancy of data in the initial transmitted block, negating many of the benefits of forward error correction.

By far the single greatest culprit in long response times is the host response time back to the RF communication channel. Included within host response are disk access time, time to move through several application layers of the host operating system and programs, computational time, clear-to-send delay, and the data transfer rate. Of these, disk access and wading through numerous application layers to get to the right program are the primary offenders. If excessive response times are encountered, one technique to minimize such delays involves executing data collection programs out of extended memory systems, which is nothing more than storing host data collection programs in memory, as opposed to on disk. Typical disk access speeds are quantified in milliseconds (10^{-3} seconds), while random access memory access speeds are quantified in nanoseconds (10^{-9} seconds). One issue that is paramount in the utilization of a processor's volatile memory is the availability of uninterruptible power supplies. Random access memory is volatile, and power outages may lose all collected data. An uninterruptible power supply ensures that power stays on to the volatile memory, thus preserving the data.

Spread Spectrum

In 1985 the Federal Communications Commission approved three spread-spectrum bands of frequencies for industrial, scientific, and medical data communications. These radio frequency bands are 902 MHz to 928 MHz, 2400 MHz to 2483.5 MHz, and 5725 to 5850 MHz.

The spread-spectrum approach originated in World War II as a way for military communications to minimize interception and jamming. Instead of rising above noise levels with a strong signal requiring FCC license (UHF at two to five watts of power), spread spectrum can transmit beneath the noise level ($\leq$ one watt of power). Spread spectrum transmits data faster than narrow-band radio frequency, and only spread-spectrum receivers can decipher such transmission from noise. Spread spectrum can help reduce eavesdropping and interference sources such as electrical motors and factory machinery. Spread spectrum also resists other wireless data transmission interference and doesn't affect other sensitive equipment such as that found in a hospital, airport, or lab environment.

Contemporary spread-spectrum digital communication was introduced in 1989 as an RF Terminal communications scheme. New terminology is also introduced with spread-spectrum transmission. A given bit of information is transmitted numerous times with each transmission of the same bit referred to as a *chip*. Under FCC rules it is necessary to have more than 10 chips per bit. Further, the transmitted bandwidth of spread-spectrum modulation is much wider (2 MHz) than for UHF narrow-band (25 KHz). This permits the bandwidth to be subdivided into discrete frequencies. To provide encryption of data, each successive chip can be transmitted on a different frequency. For example, with 11 chips per bit and 11 channels, each bit could be transmitted once on each channel, though there would be no encryption—only redundancy of data, since each bit would appear on each frequency once and the message could be reassembled. If the chip rate and number of channels were not the same, a predetermined pattern of *frequency-hopping* with each chip could provide encryption. Because of the greater bandwidth it is also possible that one transmitter/receiver combination may have the capability of transmitting over more than the number of frequencies employed in frequency-hopping. Under *dynamic frequency selection*, if interference is detected on one of the frequencies, both transmitter and receiver could select a replacement frequency over which to transmit. An example of a contemporary spread-spectrum terminal is shown in Figure 11.7.

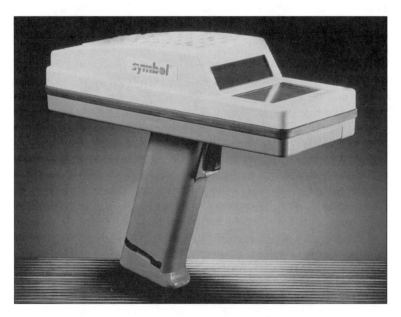

Figure 11.7: Functionally Integrated Scanning Spread-Spectrum Terminal

The coverage for one receiver is less for spread spectrum than for UHF, due to the lower transmit power. Typically, in an enclosed environment, the transmit distance is limited to 500 feet from the receiver, providing a coverage of over 785,000 square feet (coverage = πR^2) in an unobstructed environment. Since environments are seldom unobstructed, a terminal could move from cell to cell—each cell having its own receiver—and maintain communications. When the signal strength from a terminal is greater at one receiver than another, the receiver receiving the stronger signal processes the data. Spread spectrum does not transmit well through walls, and so may require several cells to provide adequate coverage.

One problem associated with spread spectrum as opposed to UHF narrow-band is that the frequencies are open to any transmitting device that is type-accepted to transmit narrow band. Paging systems and vehicle surveillance systems, such as Lo-Jack, transmit at much higher power in the same 902 MHz to 928 MHz band (several hundred watts at 915 MHz with return response at 902 MHz to 912 MHz). Electronic article surveillance systems also use the 915 MHz and 902 MHz to 905 MHz frequencies. Consequently, spread-spectrum systems should utilize frequencies at 916 MHz to 928 MHz when being utilized in areas where competing transmissions exist. The ability to utilize frequency-hopping and dynamic frequency selection should minimize potential interference.

Spread spectrum is currently a new technology for radio frequency terminals, though a number of RF terminal suppliers have announced products utilizing the technology. UHF communications has a much longer proven track record and in some applications may prove superior to spread spectrum. Other devices continue to exploit the spread-spectrum transmission spectrum. Several local area network (LAN) suppliers have announced products and received type-acceptance by the FCC for the manufacture of spread-spectrum devices. LAN applications will be particularly popular where users may be able to avoid the costly stringing of wire and cable to effect LAN communications. Spread spectrum is a technology well worth consideration by potential users of RF terminals. As with any new application of technology, potential users should proceed carefully and with full understanding of likely pitfalls.

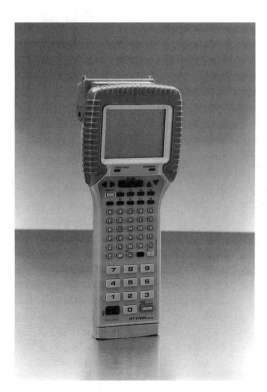

Figure 11.8: Modular Radio Data Terminal

This flexible data terminal can incorporate either UHF or Spread Spectrum radio modules, as well as integrated CCD or laser scanning modules.

Environmental Issues

RF terminals have environmental issues shared by all portable devices, as well as environmental issues unique to radio frequency. Common issues include those of withstanding adverse conditions of rain, humidity, salt fog, sand/dust, shock, and vibration. Potential buyers of terminal equipment to be used in an industrial environment should be sure their suppliers conform to the requirements of MIL-STD-810D for industrial devices. The address to secure MIL-STD-810D is contained in Appendix A, under the heading for U.S. Government.

Another environmental issue is that of temperature under which the terminal is expected to operate. As noted earlier, crystal-controlled oscillators have a tendency to alter their transmission characteristics over temperature extremes. Further, liquid crystal displays (LCDs) shut down at high temperatures and freeze at very low temperatures. Batteries also have a shorter charge life at low temperatures.

Generally, RF terminals radiate their signal from an antenna in all directions. This means that some of the signals may be absorbed by various materials such as paper, corrugated, and wood, and others will be reflected by materials such as metal and glass. This permits multiple paths for the radio signal to reach the receiver. Multipathing can create engineering challenges for RF terminal suppliers since a reflected signal may take longer to get to the receiver than a direct one. This causes the same information to reach the receiver at different times. The better terminal suppliers have various timing mechanisms to minimize adverse effects of multipathing.

Some applications may require that the RF terminal be rated as "intrinsically safe." The basic idea behind an intrinsically safe rating is that the equipment itself is incapable of releasing sufficient electrical or thermal energy to cause ignition of a specific hazardous atmospheric mixture. This differs from other methods of providing safety such as containing the equipment in explosion-proof enclosures or using some form of purge system to remove the ignitable mixture from the hazardous area.

In the United States, the basis for testing and certification of equipment as intrinsically safe is Article 500 of the National Electrical Code. Code enforcing authorities usually accept or approve the use of equipment that has been evaluated and labeled by Factory Mutual Corporation (FM) or Underwriters' Laboratories (UL).

The National Electrical Code defines intrinsically safe equipment as being incapable of releasing sufficient electrical or thermal energy under normal or abnormal conditions to ignite a specific hazardous atmospheric mixture. It can be used in either a Division 1 or Division 2 location (see classifications below). Non-incendiary equipment differs from intrinsically safe equipment in that operation under abnormal conditions is excluded, resulting in a lesser rating and restricting its use to Division 2 locations.

The examination for intrinsic safety and a non-incendiary rating determines whether or not the radio contains circuitry that can generate a spark or, through thermal effects, ignite a flammable or combustible material in the air. In the case of intrinsic safety, the evaluation is done with specific safety factors and fault conditions. For example, a higher voltage than that supplied by the battery is used for a safety factor, and the unit remains safe even though some components have faulted, such as a capacitor or transistor shorting.

In the case of a non-incendiary rating, components are considered to operate under normal conditions and without defects. No safety factor is used to take into account abnormal operation. For example, a normally operating switch is evaluated to determine that it won't ignite a hazardous atmosphere. If the switch fails, however, a hazard may be present.

Since the intrinsic safety rating is considerably more stringent than, and inclusive of, all non-incendiary requirements, intrinsically safe equipment can be used in a non-incendiary area, but not the reverse.

In the case of dust approval, the radio is examined for dust entry and must meet intrinsically safe requirements. For this reason, all radios with a dust listing also have an intrinsically safe listing: A non-incendiary rating is inadequate.

For both intrinsic safety and non-incendiary approvals the radio is tested for maximum obtainable temperature since hazardous materials can be ignited by thermal effects. Because of the large number of materials involved and the fact that the number continues to increase, and because of the variation in ignition temperature among materials, it has become impractical to incorporate temperature in the group rating. Therefore, each product is marked with the maximum temperature so users can determine if the device is appropriate for their particular requirements. As with the selection and implementation of any piece of equipment, some knowledge on the part of the user is required. The overall subject area is quite complex, and if any doubt exists, a safety expert should be consulted.

Classification

The following classifications of location, material grouping, and minimum ignition temperatures are summarized for explanation purposes only.

Class I locations are those in which flammable gases or vapors are or may be present in the air in quantities sufficient to produce explosions or ignitable mixtures. The gases and vapors have been classified into four groups, A, B, C, and D, based on their hazardous characteristics.

Class II locations are those that are hazardous because of the presence of combustible dust. Like gases and vapors, dusts have been classified into three groups, E, F, and G, based on their characteristics.

Division 1 refers to locations where particular hazardous materials are present in the air in potentially flammable concentrations continuously, frequently, or intermittently, under normal operating conditions.

Division 2 locations are those that might become hazardous in the event of a mechanical breakdown, accidental failure, or the abnormal operation of equipment.

RF terminals that are approved by Factory Mutual or Underwriters' Laboratories can be used in applications requiring reliable two-way, RF terminals in specific hazardous atmospheres. Not all manufacturing and processing operations require the same approval category, so a careful examination should be made to ensure that all radio frequency terminal and communications equipment has the proper approval. Factory Mutual publishes a yearly catalog of approved equipment and accessories, along with details of testing methods. This catalog can be ordered from:

Factory Mutual Engineering & Research
Training Resource Center—Order Processing Section
1151 Boston-Providence Turnpike
PO Box 688
Norwood, MA 02062

Factory Mutual and Underwriters' Laboratories test *specific configurations* of radio frequency terminal equipment (an RF terminal and base station, for example). They may also test the equipment with specific accessories, such as a specific variety of bar code scanner. An RF terminal system with a wand scanner, for example, may have FM or UL approval as intrinsically safe. Equipping the same terminal with a handheld laser, however, necessitates a separate intrinsically safe rating. At this writing no moving-beam bar code scanner has an intrinsically safe rating, though two vendors were in the process of attempting to secure one.

If a data collection system is going to be utilized in a hazardous-atmosphere environment, such as a chemical, mining, or grain-processing facility, intrinsically safe issues should be carefully explored.

Site Surveys

It may be quite straightforward to implement an RF system out-of-doors where towers can be constructed to whatever height is required to provide the coverage required. With all of the variables that exist in enclosed areas, the only way to truly engineer an inside radio frequency system is with a site survey once the vendor of the equipment is established. In my experience, some environments have required fairly sophisticated communications engineering, but no enclosed location has been found where RF communications was not a practicable solution. A site survey will enable the RF terminal supplier to recommend the proper antenna and antenna location for optimum coverage, eliminating any potential "dead spots" where communications may be more difficult. Many suppliers also provide a "coverage guarantee": If after installation an area in the facility previously deemed within the coverage area is no longer able to effect communications back to the base station, the vendor will correct the situation at no cost to the using organization. One word of caution is in order, however: Site surveys should be conducted in a live worst-case setting. It does no good to perform a site survey when no equipment that may cause interference is operational. In the case of a warehouse, the site survey should be conducted when the warehouse is full, since corrugated absorbs radio frequency signals. The more corrugated within a facility, the better the communications engineering needs to be.

While the development of systems requirements definitions (SRDs) and requests for quotations (RFQs) for all data collection systems are addressed in depth in Chapter 12, those preparing systems requirement definitions and requests for quotations for RF terminal systems should consider the following:

SRDs and RFQs for RF Terminals

Application Requirements
- Define how the RF terminals will be used.
- Identify the specific vehicle-mounted, handheld, and table-top applications required.
- Describe the areas that require RF coverage, specifying square footage, building structures, internal layout, and the material or equipment occupying each area.
- Define the environmental requirements.
    Operating temperature range
    Storage temperature range
    Chemical vapor conditions
    Dust conditions
    High humidity, moisture, or rain protection
    Ambient lighting conditions which might affect the readability of the terminal display
- Quantify usage in terms of hours per shift and shifts per day.

- Identify the need for flexibility to expand the system.
  Additional terminals
  Additional buildings
  Additional host computers per base station

Hardware Considerations
- RF Terminals—General Issues
  Specify display requirements—number of lines and number of characters per line.
  Identify the auxiliary devices required, i.e., wand scanner, moving-beam laser (long-range and normal-range), RF tag reader, printers, etc.
  Specify the bar code symbologies to be read.
  Identify keys needed to support the host application, i.e., alpha keys, numeric keys, and/or special function keys.
  Identify the preferred keyboard layout, i.e., QWERTY vs. ABC for alpha keys, and telephone vs. calculator layout for numeric keys.
  Specify the average message length and the number of messages per terminal per hour.
  Specify the required response time for RF communications. This should be the maximum acceptable time for the RF system to transmit a message to or from the host work center when the specified number of terminals is active.
- Handheld RF Terminals
  Specify the number of terminals required, including spares.
  Identify necessary holding accessories, i.e., shoulder strap, belt holster, etc.
  State drop-test/durability requirements.
  Specify how recharging will be accomplished, the operating time per battery charge, desired recharging time, and the number of chargers required.
  Consider the need for battery analyzer(s) and conditioner(s).
- Vehicle-mounted RF Terminals
  Specify the number of terminals required, including spares.
  Specify the voltage input to the terminal and the permissible current draw.
  State applicable shock and vibration standards.
- Table-top RF Terminals
  Specify the number of terminals required, including spares.
  Specify the voltage input to the terminal and the permissible current draw.
  State applicable shock and vibration standards.
- RF Base Stations
  Specify the base station to host/work center communications interface (electrical interface) and communications protocol.
  Considering every terminal that will be in use, quantify the total data throughput per hour (average message length times average number of messages per hour).
  Consider redundant base station hardware if 100 percent availability is required.
  Consider the need for an uninterruptible power supply.

Vendor Considerations
- Delivery, Warranties, Training, and Post-Sales Support
  Identify vendor lead time.
  Identify whether vendor services are available.

220

For site surveys

To assist in obtaining FCC license (if required)

For installation

Identify training needs and the ability of the vendor to meet these needs.

Application programmers

System supervisors

Operators

Maintenance staff

Identify vendor warranties.

Equipment

RF Coverage

Define post-sale maintenance requirements.

Vendor turnaround time and cost for repairs and service

Availability and cost of a maintenance contract

Availability of spare parts

System Acceptance
- Define an acceptance test plan that addresses system performance.

Application Software Considerations
- Host/Work Center Computer System Design—The performance and reliability of the host/work center computer directly impacts the response times and system availability experienced by the RF terminal users. When the host/work center computer is pre-existing, it should be determined whether pre-existing systems will satisfactorily support the RF application. Where necessary, a work center or larger computer may be needed to attain the desired results.
- Existing Application Software—In many situations, existing host-resident application software serving CRT users can without modification also serve RF terminal users. Existing application software should be reviewed in light of the RF application to identify its compatibility or shortcomings.
- Procurement of New Application Software—The procurement of application software involves separate though related considerations involved in RF data communications. Procurement of application software should follow those practices identified in Chapter 12.
- RF Communications Driver—In certain computer systems the communications interface between the base station and host computer may be such that the host/work center requires an RF communications driver. Some RF data communications suppliers offer such drivers. These products can relieve the need to develop the driver on its own and can increase the certainty of a smooth and predictable project.

RF portables provide the opportunity to:
- Reduce paperwork,
- Provide work direction,
- Verify the work performed,
- Immediately update a local work center computer, and
- Improve productivity.

The marriage of RF terminals and bar code readers presents some very promising opportunities for receiving, breakdown, put-away, picking, packing, shipping, transfers, physical inventory, and cycle counting. From the picking/cycle count side, let us examine a scenario presently in place at several Fortune 500 companies. A material handler scans a bar code marked employee identification badge. The system displays, "Good morning, Craig," and directs the handler to storage location 123. Upon arriving, the handler scans the shelf tag at storage location 124 and is corrected by the computer system. Scanning shelf tag 123, the operator is prompted to pick 12 of product ABC against work order 789. After the 12 ABCs are scanned, the system prompts the operator to enter the number of ABCs remaining at shelf location 123. The operator keys in "23." The system compares this amount to the amount present in its database and finds a discrepancy, that 24 of the item should be left at location 123.

The computer asks the operator to recount and enter the amount. The operator again counts 23, enters that number, and the computer prints an exception report at the warehouse manager's office noting the count discrepancy at location 123, who found it, and what time it was found. Warehouse management may then revisit the location and make whatever adjustments would be made in the case of count variances discovered through other means. These systems can perform a cycle count with each "pick" without the associated paperwork. Further, the easiest time to count the number of items at a given location is when there are few or none in the location. It is easier to count three of an item than to count 86 of the same item. In addition to typical ABC Inventory Analysis for cycle counting, systems designers for warehouse operations may wish to provide a cycle count at zero or a specified minimum quantity.

One problem that currently exists in manual cycle-count methodologies makes the use of this inventory method quite difficult. The basis of cycle counting is to count periodically the amount of product in a given location. An "A" item might be counted monthly, a "B" item quarterly, a "C" item semiannually, and "D" items yearly. In today's cycle-count methodology, approximately two hours before a given set of locations is to be counted, a material flow cutoff must be instituted, curtailing all inventory movement of those items. This is done because in most inventory systems, material is relieved from inventory when it is shipped or billed, not when it is picked. If a count of an inventory item is instituted, all product that has already been picked must be given the opportunity to reach the shipping/billing area so that none of the item to be counted continues to exist in the pipeline between picking and relieving the item from inventory.

But if a warehouse, for example, has a stock locator system resident within the same environment where the RF data collection is taking place, the stock locator system is instantly updated regarding the movement of product from receiving, to breakdown, to put-away, to picking, to packing, to shipping, and all location transfers in between. This makes cycle counting much easier, eliminating the need for a material flow cutoff and the associated follow-up reconciliations.

These types of systems can improve inventory accuracy levels to 99+ percent, eliminating the need for periodic physical inventory procedures. With auditors happy to achieve 95 to 97 percent inventory accuracy, the opportunities available with bar code technology and RF terminals are phenomenal.

CHAPTER 12

Electronic Data Interchange (EDI)

V arious markets currently are in the process of developing a series of "conventions" in order to standardize the transmission of electronic documents between distributors/resellers, their suppliers, and customers. The objective of this article is to explain the basics of this technology and to help the reader understand how this technology may be of benefit.

Many industries have already established EDI standards. The retail industry has standards issued by VICS (Voluntary Inter-industry Communication Standards). The electronics industry has standards issued by EIDX (Electronics Industry Data Exchange). The electrical industry has standards issued by EDX (Electrical Data Exchange). The chemical industry has standards issued by CIDX (Chemical Industry Data Exchange). The microcomputer industry has standards issued by ABCD—The Microcomputer Industry Association. What with established standards, why do other industries as well as end-users require their own? Why cannot an organization or industry simply embrace these other standards? In fact, most standards have marked similarities to those of other industries. However, there are types of information that are needed within one industry that are not relevant to others. Mass market retailers may look for product replenishment based on product sale (Quick Response). The chemical industry may need information, such as hazardous materials and Material Safety Data Sheets. The microcomputer industry may look for information on warranty registration, warranty claim, and spare parts. Each of these differences give rise to a requirement for an industry-specific EDI conventions.

The basic concept of EDI and its companion, bar code technology, is that once data is entered into a computer system, that data should never have to be key-entered again! The computer system in question may be yours, that of your customer, or that of your supplier. Each time data is key-entered into a computer system, the probability of error is approximately 1 character error in 300 characters keyed. With the cost of the errors conservatively estimated at $75 per error, minimizing redundant key entry should be a high organizational priority. If an industry ever expects truly to realize some of the efficiencies available with Just-In-Time (JIT), Total Quality Control (TQC), and Quick Response (QR), standardization among and close communications between trading partners is required. These efficiencies are referred to as Quality Response, which embodies the simple concepts of getting:

- The Right Product
  - To The Right Place
    - At The Right Time
      - At The Right Cost.

Fertile environments for EDI include those where a company buys or sells large volumes of stock items that can be described by a product code, where the product requires careful tracking and reporting, where the business transaction represents a tremendous amount of paperwork, where the company or industry finds itself in a very competitive market, or where there is a requirement for rapid processing and delivery of goods.

The laundry list of why an industry should be using EDI looks, quite literally, like most company's long range strategic plans.

Why Use EDI?

- To Increase Productivity
- To Reduce Overhead Costs
- To Reduce Data Keying
- To Reduce Inventory Cost
- To Improve Customer Service
- To Reduce Receivables Float
- To Improve Product Return Procedures
- To Improve Spare Parts Availability
- To Identify Product Availability

- To Reduce Business Paper
- To Reduce Error Rates
- To Improve Forecast Accuracy
- To Reduce Order Lead Time
- To Improve Vendor Relations
- To Enhance Customer Support
- To Improve Product Registration
- To Reduce Spare Parts Cost
- To Enhance Product Introduction Timing

In 1991 Arthur Anderson conducted a study to look at the use of technology in the distribution channels. This study revealed that EDI with major customers and suppliers was the top technology distribution organizations felt they will be required to implement in order to do business within the next five years. Furthermore, bar code standards with customers and suppliers were listed immediately following the EDI requirements.

Yet another study had financial managers within distribution organizations conservatively estimate the cost savings that they felt could be realized by using electronic communications. Including documents such as purchase orders, invoices, and shipping documents, this savings averaged over $5.25 per document. Other studies have shown industry averages for the costs of processing purchase order transactions range from $49 manually to $4.74 electronically.

What is EDI?

Electronic Data Interchange or EDI, is the intercompany, computer-to-computer comunication of data which permits the receiver to perform the function of a standard business transaction and is in a standard data format. EDI is the use of a standard communications convention with standard formats and agreed upon abbreviations that permit trading partnerships to communicate electronically. EDI is not facsimile, nor electronic mail, nor overnight mail, nor the exchange of tapes or disks.

Like any technology, EDI has a set of terms with which the organization implementing the technology needs to be familiar. If we think of EDI as "standard business transactions," we are really simply saying the types of documents which are exchanged between the buyer and seller of a product or service. Most industries utilize the American National Standards Institute (ANSI) ASC X12 Standard as the base document from which industry conventions are developed. In an international framework the equivalent of X12 is the UN/EDIFACT standards.Each year a new release of the X12 standards are published. Every three years X12 publishes a new version. In reality releases are not American National Standards, though they are implemented when issued by thousands of companies. The current version and Releases which are active in the X12 standards include:

- Version 2, Release 1 (002001) Issued 8/87
- Version 2, Release 2 (002002) Issued 8/88
- Version 2, Release 3 (002003) Issued 4/89
- Version 2, Release 4 (002040) Issued 12/89
- Version 3, Release 1 (003010) Issued 12/90
- Version 3, Release 2 (003020) Issued 12/91
- Version 3, Release 3 (003030) Issued 12/92
- Version 3, Release 4 (003040) Issued 12/93

Implementors of EDI would be well advised to work out a version migration schedule with their trading partners, so as not to have to maintain all releases of all versions on their system. At no time should more than 4 releases and versions of the X12 standards be supported.

An *Industry Convention* is a family of documents for an industry, e.g., ABCD, CIDX, VICS, EIDX, based on the available transactions from ASC X12.

A *Transaction Set* is one such document, e.g., Purchase Order, Invoice, Warranty Claim. Few industries employ all of the available X12EDI transactions. Typical transaction sets/messages include (ASC X12 Transaction Set Number in parenthesis and UN/EDI-FACT Message in all capital letters):

- Purchase Order (850)
  ORDERS
- Purchase Order Change (860)
  ORDCHG
- Price Sales Catalog (832)
  PRICAT
- Inventory Inquiry/Advice (846)
  INVRPT
- Order Status Inquiry (869)
- Invoice (810)
  INVOIC
- Ship/Notice Manifest (855)

- Ship/Billing Notice (857)
- Receiving Advice (861)
- Motor Carrier Information (204)
  IFTMIN
- Material Safety Data Sheet (848)

- Purchase Order Acknowledgement (855)
  ORDRSP
- Purchase Order Change
  Acknowledgement (865)
- Product Transfer & Resale Report (867)
- Product Data Activity (852)
  SLSRPT
- Order Status Report (870)
- Remittance Advice (820)
  REMADV/PAYORD
- Functional Acknowledgement (997) -
  This transaction set is sent by the DESADV
  recipient of the EDI transaction back to
  the sender. Transaction 997 does not
  indicate that the recipient will take any
  action, it only acknowledges receipt of
  the sender's EDI message.
  CONTRL

A *Data Segment* is a group of related data, e.g., Line Item, Ship To, F.O.B. Related Instructions. No industry employs all of the available segments within any X12EDI transaction set. Each transaction set shows an ordered arrangement of segments. The segment in an incoming message would appear:

ACT*098756*QEDbSYSTEMSN/L

A *Data Element* is one piece of data in a segment, e.g., Product Code, Number of Items Ordered. Each segment shows an ordered arrangement of data elements (Reference Designator). The ASC X12 Data Element Dictionary shows the possible code values for the data element and is arranged in the numeric order of the Data Element Reference Numbers. Standardized Codes are agreed upon abbreviations required to represent data elements. Standardized codes are also found in the ASC X12 Data Element Dictionary.

For one company's shipping system to communicate with another company's receiving system, a combination of hardware and software must be in place at the computer site of both trading partners. Company A's shipping system data would be "mapped" (the logical association of data between an application data format to an EDI standard data format) to the appropriate data element from any of numerous commercially available translator packages. The mapping process is the most difficult of the technological issues associated with EDI. The translator is a program or group of programs that encode/decode, format, and provide protocol conversion of EDI messages. The translator may provide mapping capabilities. In 1993, the marketplace will see several "mapping programs," that will permit the user to display an incoming data file and an application program's data file, point and click a mouse on the data element of the incoming file, and by pointing and clicking on the data element in the application data file "map" one data element to the other.

The data communications vehicle is traditionally a modem which provides linkage between Company A's computer system and the computer system of Company B. Commonly used modem speeds include 2400 bps (bits per second), 4800 bps, 9600 bps, 14,400 bps, and 38,400 bps. The most common communications protocols for the exchange of EDI data is IBM 2780/3780 Point-to-Point Binary Synchronous Communications (BSC) and SNA/SDLC, which can exist on either the public switched telephone network or on private leased lines. Increasingly, these transmissions are occurring at higher speeds (9,600, 14,400, and 38,400 bps) and with internationally recognized error control protocols, such as CCITT V.42.

By far, the easiest way to get up and working with EDI is by contracting with a Value Added Network (VAN) to provide communications from your computer system to that of your trading partner.

In a typical example, the companies QED and ABC are subscribers to a given value-added network. ABC may wish to issue a Purchase Order to QED, connects with the VAN and leaves that Purchase Order (Transaction Set 850) in the QED "mailbox." Later in the day, QED connects to the VAN and looks in its mailbox, finds the Purchase Order, and communicates the mailbox contents to the QED computer system. After the services called for in the Purchase Order have been completed, QED can connect with the VAN to leave an Invoice (Transaction Set 810) in the ABC mailbox. When ABC interrogates its mailbox and finds the Invoice, it can pull the Invoice to the ABC computer system. The VAN has an agreement with both ABC and QED to support the communication protocols, coding structures, and speeds needed by the subscriber's respective computer systems. Such an arrangement requires less coordination between the subscribers to be able to affect the electronic exchange of business documents.

VANs offer around-the-clock access seven days a week except a few hours weekly that are necessary for maintenance and backup. Most VANs are capable of store-and-forward services, in which they dial out to one trading partner for the other. All VANs can store and receive. VANs are capable of receiving transmissions from virtually all commercially available modems and can adapt to basically all communication protocols and line speeds. VANs also protect against electrical storms, power outages and other disasters. They use error-correcting software with rigid security subject to external audits.

VANs can provide audit trails, transmission, recovery, and redundancy. Lines are continuously monitored by sophisticated equipment and experienced personnel. VANs also offer Inter-Networking. If one trading partner will work only through a specific VAN, most networks enable you to communicate with that trading partner through a connection to the trading partner's VAN. Many companies, however, have found it to be less costly to connect to multiple VANs as opposed to paying interconnect fees.

Regrettably, there are many VANs. Oftentimes, large organizations choose a specific VAN to bring their trading partners up to speed with EDI. These larger companis are referred to as HUBs while each of the trading partners is referred to as a SPOKE. This way, the HUB company can influence their trading partners' selection of a specific network. One reason this is done is to reduce the overall cost of EDI communications. Most VANs charge an interconnect fee to connect to another VAN, driving up the cost of EDI communications when a company's trading partners are on different VANs. Some larger organizations, who have not yet decided to direct connect with their trading partners, elect to subscribe to multiple VANs, so as to minimize interconnect fees.

ASC X12 and UN/EDIFACT

EDIFACT is an acronym for EDI For Administration, Commerce, and Trade. The United Nations administers EDIFACT, thereby the name UN/EDIFACT. In North America the EDIFACT organization is the Pan American EDIFACT Board (PAEB) administered by the same organization that administers ASC X12, namely, Data Interchange Standards Association (DISA). Translators that handle X12 can also handle EDIFACT, though they would require separate mappings of the data. This is because the structure, syntax, and coding of EDIFACT is substantially different from that of X12. EDIFACT is more generic so that most of the segments used in one message (transaction set) is also used in most other messages.

Those just getting into EDI would be well advised to ensure that their translation and mapping software could handle both X12 and EDIFACT. This is because EDI outside of North America already is EDIFACT. Also, ASC X12 has voted to cease publication of the X12 syntax after 1997. What this will ultimately mean is that by the year 2000 many previously X12 committed users of EDI will be then committed to EDIFACT.

PDF417 and EDI

There are certain situations where communicating electronically with EDI does not deliver the expected benefits. It may be that as a result of being a high volume customer, one or more of a company's suppliers decide to locate a regional distribution center in the same locale as the customer company.

The nature of EDI today is one where companies utilize electronic mailboxes as described above. It is not uncommon for electronic mailbox users to pull down messages from the mailbox four times per day. This means that messages are received every two hours.

A second issue is that while there may be 50,000 EDI user companies in 1993, very few of these companies have "functionally integrated EDI." Functional integration is where one company's application software messages communicate directly with the recipient's application software. In reality, however, over 50 percent of EDI users in 1993 do not have functionally integrated EDI. What they do have is an EDI translator which spools the incoming messages to a printer. The incoming messages are then taken from the printer and re-keyed to the recipient's application programs. Fondly referred to as "Sneaker-Net" or "Rip and Tear EDI," these implementations delay the receipt of incoming messages to a point where, when combined with the suppliers located in the same community as the EDI recipient, it is highly likely that shipments may arrive at a receiving dock well before the EDI ship notice/manifest is available at the receiving dock.

In 1993, several companies are piloting a solution to this dilemma. Imagine if one could use a 2D symbology, such as PDF417, to encode a complete manifest/packing list (856/DESADV) or Motor Carrier Information (204/IFTMIN), and print this symbol on the shipping paper/packing list that would accompany the shipment. Since the PDF417 symbol's data would be in the exact syntax, structure, and coding as the EDI message, if the output of the scanner looked identical to the output of a modem, and if that output was then input to an EDI translator, a "plug and play" solution would exist to solve this dilemma. The receiving dock would getting the shipping paper, scan the PDF417 symbol, and have the data available at the same time as the shipment. This same type of printed EDI could have tremendous impact for the chemical industry, which requires that material safety data sheets (MSDSs) accompany all chemicals. Since an MSDS exists in ASCX12 as Transaction Set 848, this could be the solution to matching MSDSs with an actual container of chemicals buy labeling the container with a PDF417 848. It is not expected that 2D symbols will replace EDI, but more likely serve as a supplement to EDI transmitted data.

EDI Benefits

EDI can be thought of as providing competitive advantages, strategic benefits, and operational benefits. EDI can provide product or service differentiation from the user's competition, by the higher quality of EDI data. This higher quality service can be provided with lower costs than manual systems. EDI permits the user to penetrate new markets, some of whom already require EDI communications. From the competitive advantage perspective, it is also easier to do business with an EDI partner.

Strategic benefits include lower cost structures, improved asset productivity, increased operational efficiency, and improved information flow. EDI provides enhanced financial and managerial control by forcing a process alignment between trading parts and provides a mechanism to exchange information that could not be easily supported in a paper environment. EDI provides stronger trading partner relationships.

Operational benefits include increased responsiveness to customers, decreased product order/pay cycles, lower clerical costs, improved delivery of goods and services, reduced inventory, and eliminated redundant effort.

Since the format of data in one organization's computer is different from that in another, a common "language" is required for the interchange of data between the two computers. The conversion from paper documents to an electronic interchange involves internal considerations for each trading partner, external issues affect the other trading partner, as well as other issues and considerations concerning the joint relationship."

Internal Considerations

These issues and considerations should be resolved within the organization planning to implement the standards.

- Talk with experienced EDI users.
- Gain commitment of management, business units, and support.
- Establish an EDI Implementation Team and define each person's responsibility.
- Determine electronic data interchange objectives.
- Enlist the assistance of experienced consultants and third parties.
- Designate EDI business and technical contacts.
- Secure the appropriate reference material.
- Determine the application to be utilized (Purchase Order, Invoice, Test Results, etc.).
- Identify appropriate products with which to start.
- Educate user personnel about why the company is implementing the standards and its impact on current procedures.
- Explain the benefits of using a standards format for electronic data interchange.
- Explain why ASC X12 standards were chosen.
- Initiate an implementation schedule.
- Make certain the required data is available on existing systems, considering the extent to which internal systems are suitable for EDI.
- Review all documents to be interchanged and identify each data element with the X12 formats to ensure that all pertinent information will be included.
- Establish a liaison with all functional areas within your organization that may be affected.
- Identify hardware requirements.
- Conduct a communication/equipment survey.
- Determine the method of achieving translation interface: Develop software internally, purchase or lease software, or utilize a third-party service provider. Carefully weigh using PC software for data entry and high transaction volumes.
- Security precautions taken by electronic data interchange applications within an organization's computer center should be at least as good as those for the most secure existing application with which EDI is to be used. Authentication and encryption may be added to completely secure contents of the message. The security functions may also be included as part of the organization's existing data transport services.
- Provide an EDI training program (including training on EDI standards) for users.
- Publicize EDI benefits internally.

External Considerations

These issues should be resolved with the trading partner prior to exchanging data electronically, using the standard.

- Get involved with industry associations and standards organizations.
- Conduct a trading partner survey to identify potential business trading partners, selecting as pilot partners companies with experience in EDI.
- Begin with partnerships where transaction volumes are high.
- Define terms of exchange and establish agreement between partners.
- Agree on the version/release of the standards that will be implemented with each trading partner.
- Determine what optional product information will be employed.
- Determine what partnership identification scheme will be used.
- Verify that sufficient information is available for trading partners to correctly interpret the data.
- Ensure that the trading partner has adequate translation interface.
- Send sample data to trading partners for their evaluation (this does not need to be done in the same medium in which interchange will occur in actual operation).
- Limit initial effort to a few partners and transactions.
- Have frequent progress discussions with partners.
- If applicable, be sure links exist to allow transmissions to flow between third parties.

Other Considerations

Contingency plans should be made to address the following situations:

- Backup procedures: establish a fall-back position (e.g., mail delivery, etc.) in the event of system failure.
- Error recovery: establish a maximum number of attempts to retransmit following a text transmission error, thus minimizing communications costs for bad connections.
- Security: agree on passwords; a general review of tax, audit, and legal issues may also be desirable. Letters of agreement and terms and conditions that exist on physical business documents should be discussed with each trading partner and whatever arrangement is deemed necessary worked out on an individual basis.
- Network response time: establish a reasonable time frame for response (functional acknowledgment) to message receipt.
- Error reporting/contact support: names and telephone numbers of transmission partners and hardware and software vendors should be accessible. Some vendors provide diagnostic error routines to isolate failure prior to contact. If available, these routines should be attempted prior to contact to minimize service charges.

Start-up Checklist

- Network availability;
- Network communications (line type and speed);

- Line protocol, transmission mode;
- Install hardware and translation software that will allow interface to ASC X12 formatted data with present internal operating system;
- Test interface software under current environment using internal data;
- Develop required internal edits and controls;
- Establish a "go-live" date while running parallel (existing) systems for "x" amount of time;
- Document troubleshooting procedures;
- Establish date to drop parallel system;
- Fine-tune existing system and upgrade to new versions of standards, hardware, etc.;
- Integrate electronic data interchange with existing systems; and
- Add other applications and standards users.

Electronic data interchange requires a strategic commitment by the implementing organization's management. EDI achieves little immediate payback when implemented with only one trading partner. Employing both EDI and manual systems is more costly than using just the manual system. High transaction volume trading partners should be implemented first, using the "80 percent of transaction volume occurring from 20 percent of trading partners" rule. It will require several years of continuing effort for EDI to become the standard way of doing business as opposed to the exception. Stick with it: Once the majority of trading partners are EDI partners, the benefits will far outweigh the costs. But be patient—electronic data interchange is not an instant payback endeavor.

The combination of bar code technology, RF terminals at shipping and receiving, and EDI communications between trading partners can make the recording, delivery, and tracking of material and transactions a much more efficient process than manual recording, printed reports, printed purchase orders, printed invoices, printed manifests, and manual checking of information. This type of marriage of technology is doable, and many organizations have already implemented these systems with their trading partners.

The challenges industry faces today are that human resource costs are rising while the availability of critical skills is falling. We need to be able to increase business volumes without increasing headcount. The EDI solution permits eliminating manual, repetitive clerical tasks freeing up critical human resources to manage exceptions and to deal directly with customers. The EDI solution permits orders to be processed faster, product to be shipped sooner, and the streamlining of the invoicing and payment process. The EDI solution gives the user an opportunity to rethink outdated processes, such as individual "terms and conditions" with each purchase order and manually "receiving" each item on incoming shipments. The EDI solution provides reduced transaction costs through automated data entry, avoiding costly keystroke errors.

To those who adopt EDI and its companion, bar code technology, competitive advantage over their competition will result. However, all competitive advantages based in technology are ephemeral — for once everyone adopts the technology it no longer provides the competitive advantage. In 1993, bar codes and EDI can provide precisely such a competitive advantage. By 1996, they will be a survival strategy.

CHAPTER 13

Implementation

The use of bar code technology has been widely discussed in numerous publications whose audiences represent diverse elements of an organization. These publications may target executive management, materials handling, distribution, transportation, manufacturing, quality control, sales and marketing, office automation, data processing, customer service, or personnel management. Consequently, bar code technology implementations arise in the three following contexts:

- Customer Driven—A customer or group of customers has stated that bar code markings have become a cost of doing business with that customer. The objective here becomes one of meeting the customer's requirements in the least costly manner and/or in a manner in which internal benefit can accrue to the organization.
- Senior Management Down—Senior management has decided that bar code technology may provide substantial benefits to the organization and wishes to quantify the costs and benefits associated with the use of the technology within the organization.
- Middle Management Up—A departmental manager realizes that the use of bar code technology can improve the department's operations and seeks funding of a specific project.

In each of these three contexts a tremendous opportunity exists to improve the overall operations of an organization. Quite often, however, in the first context—Customer Driven—the organization may be concerned only with how to "meet the needs of the trade" without concern for internal applications of the technology. When an external force provides the impetus for applying bar code technology, senior management should be apprised that the requirement for bar code markings can offer opportunities to the organization as well.

The Senior Management Down and Middle Management Up scenarios require that the manager assigned to the project become familiar with the needs and applications of various departments within the organization. It is quite conceivable that within any organization, managers of several functional areas have each come to the conclusion that their individual area should embark upon implementation of bar code technology to solve a problem unique to their area. A manager in Office Automation may have developed an idea for the tracking of file folders; a manager in Personnel could develop a concept for time and attendance; a manager in Distribution might want to use bar codes as a base for cycle counting; a manager in Sales could use bar code marked order books; a manager in Manufacturing could explore W-I-P tracking; and a Quality Control manager might desire to implement statistical quality control and believe that bar codes are just the ticket. Each may have come upon the idea independently, without the knowledge of what others in the same organization are considering. Were they all to implement their own ideas independently, the organization might suffer "islands of automation"—where none of these applications would have the ability to communicate with the other, thereby squandering corporate resources.

Corporate Bar Code Task Force

A "champion" must arise from within senior management. The term "champion" is used since the team leader should be one who is already convinced that bar code technology will be of significant benefit to the organization. It is this champion who assumes the responsibility of resolving interdepartmental conflicts. The champion must be an internal corporate resource—not an external consultant or vendor representative—who understands the company functions, both internal and external. The champion also should have a good understanding of the corporate data processing environment. The champion should understand bar code technology activities being undertaken in the industry or industries served by the organization. The champion should have, or be able to secure, management approval to define and implement bar code data collection programs. Finally, the champion needs to be a salesman—able to sell superiors, peers, and, more importantly, subordinates on program concepts and requirements.

Reporting to the champion would be the Project Manager (or Bar Code Coordinator) who would have continuing responsibility for the day-to-day activities of the program. Eventually, the Bar Code Coordinator will serve as the corporate resource for bar code technology.

The first step in implementation is for senior management to call a meeting to be attended by a representative of each department within the organization. The attendees should include those representing operations, coprorate management, and engineering, typically including:

• Champion	• Manufacturing	• Raw Materials
• Project Manager	• Production Records	Warehousing
• Sales/Marketing	Administration	• Distribution
• Customer Service	• Manufacturing	• Packaging
• Finance	Engineering	• Purchasing
• Personnel	• Plant Engineering	• Quality Control
• Information Systems	• Finished Goods	• Industrial Engineering
• Software Engineering	Warehousing	

At least two weeks prior to the first *Corporate Bar Code Task Force* meeting, the initiator should provide to all identified Task Force members a copy of:

- The Project Objective.
- The name of the Project Manager.
- The identity of all Task Force Members.
- An agenda of the meeting, identifying
    —Meeting location and time;
    —Stated purpose of the meeting; and
    —The general time frame in which the initial purpose is to be accomplished.
- A statement indicating that the Project Manager will be contacting participating departments or agencies soon about the organization of the project.
- Copies of magazine articles and newsletters—along with a copy of this book— which address some of the potential applications for bar code technology.
- The identity and credentials of any outside speaker who is to attend.

At this initial meeting all team members should receive both an in-person and written background on bar code technology and its potential applications. It is suggested that this presentation be made by an experienced educator/consultant who is familiar with bar code reading, printing, data collection, and computer technology, as well as the specific needs of the organization's industry.

Following the presentation on the family of technologies involved and the applications in place within other organizations, the Task Force should begin to identify potential applications within the organization. All suggested applications should be recorded, along with the identity of the suggester. No application should be considered too frivolous for consideration. Someone may suggest that bar codes be used for parking lot control or to log in entrants at the annual company picnic sack race. While these applications may not have top corporate priority, they may stimulate thought and should be considered and recorded. From this initial list of applications a set of six applications should be identified and prioritized as those to receive initial attention. The initial application may be, "How do we meet the labeling requirements of the customer?" which should be rephrased, "How can we benefit in areas of cost containment and revenue enhancement while providing labeling requirements of the customer?"

Once the Project Manager has been installed, this individual will be responsible for the organization and establishment of future meeting dates, times, and agendas. Future meetings should be scheduled to:

- Select the specific initial application,
- Review operational evaluations,
- Define system requirements,
- Define the data element format,
- Assess available technology,
- Develop specifications,
- Evaluate vendors and bids,
- Develop internal training and an implementation plan,
- Review operations, and
- Plan the technology transfer.

It is suggested that the pilot application be one with a high degree of visibility within the organization, as well as one where current operations are deemed to be adequate (though not exemplary). Too often task forces are tempted to select an application area that is currently fraught with problems in the hope that the automation of this area will solve the problems. It is important that all task force members understand that "the automation of inefficiencies only causes those inefficiencies to occur more quickly." Selection of a highly visible area within the organization that is currently run in an acceptable manner lessens the risk associated with the pilot. All who are involved in the pilot application have a vested interest in making certain that the pilot is brought on-line within the identified time frame and within budget, and that it is identifiable to management as a successful application.

The team leader must also develop a comprehension of the technology, its component parts, and the applicable industry standards. It would be well-advised for the team leader to publish a set of approved corporate standards for both internal and external markings. Once agreed upon, this standard should be published and made available to the team members, the organizational heads of each department, and corporate management.

It may be a good idea for the project manager or champion to develop a close working relationship with a consultant/systems designer having proven expertise in data collection technology. The consultant will require a focal point within the organization in order to recommend internal applications, equipment suppliers, and providers of software services to support the various implementations within the organization. The champion or the consultant will need to identify various operational elements within the organization, including though not limited to:

- Specification of the existing information system to include the communications interface to the existing system;
- Identification of current and proposed operations in each of the functional areas within the organization;
- Identification of present statistics of manufacturing, order entry, receiving, storage, distribution, inventory control, and returns processing;
- Specification of labeling requirements; and
- Identification of existing and proposed product-numbering systems.

Simply stated, the role of the project manager is guiding on a project-by-project basis the implementation of each project and then transferring the technology and the lessons learned to subsequent projects.

Quite often when bar code systems are considered, little attention is given to how these systems will impact other organizational activities. Often, simply preparing for the implementation of bar code markings will effect a net savings to the organization. In most organizations, product packaging is specified by a product or brand manager, without regard for the existing packaging employed with other products. When the organization begins to consider bar code marking on all product packaging, an audit of product packaging often discloses that significant savings could be realized through the consolidation of packaging and label sizes across product lines. One midwestern health care supplier was ordering 43 different label sizes (4 of which were being purchased for product no longer being manufactured). Results of this packaging audit disclosed that three label sizes would suffice for all products. Similarly, packaging sizes were consolidated as well. The combined savings generated in packaging consolidation alone was able to totally offset the cost of the company's bar code marking program.

Changes in packaging will undoubtedly affect the packaging department. Instead of only human-readable data on the packaging, bar codes must now be included. This may require the development of a working relationship between a film master maker and printing plate manufacturer. Lead times must be considered to receive the bar code printing plates. Packaging quality control will also be affected, since it must now validate the the "in-spec" printing of the bar code symbols.

Beyond packaging issues, the implementation of bar code marking impacts other departments in the organization as well. Incorporation of bar codes may cause the distribution department to take advantage of these markings in put-away, picking, packing, shipping, returns processing, inventory control, and cycle-counting operations.

If the implementation of bar code markings is one that embraces the UPC Symbol and Code, the entire product-numbering system of the organization may be impacted. Since the product may become known by the bar code marking, the organization may wish to use this numbering system in lieu of existing product-numbering systems. If this is the case, data processing will need to incorporate the new numbering system or cross-reference the new codes to the old.

New numbering systems and the incorporation of bar code markings may cause the organization to reconsider its methods of order entry. Many organizations have found it advantageous to use bar codes in order entry procedures, where catalogs include not only traditional information, but also an associated bar code. To order a product, the customer has only to scan the bar code and identify the quantity ordered (which may be inherent in the symbol scanned). The customer can use a supplier-provided portable data entry terminal and accomplish computer-to-computer communications without electronic data interchange as described in Chapter 12.

Incorporating bar code markings can provide immeasurable benefit to an organization, providing the opportunity to scan information into a computer where the data formerly would be keyed.

Bar codes, by themselves, do nothing. It is the combination of symbol, reader, terminal, communications, and computer software that permits most bar code implementations to achieve a positive return on investment in less than one year. Many industries have standardized around the fixed-length, fixed-format, and numeric-only UPC code and symbology for units of sale, while using an extended format (though still fixed-length, fixed-format, and numeric-only) Interleaved 2 of 5 symbology on shipping containers with Application Identifiers for secondary identification. Other markets, including the manufacturing of custom product, have adopted the variable-length Code 39 symbology with FACT Data Identifiers. The rationale behind these standards is to foster the enhancement of existing industry software packages and promote the introduction of new ones that will serve the needs of the marketplace as defined by the marketplace. This is becoming increasingly important in the standardization of mini- and micro-sized computer systems.

Often a client suggests connecting data collection equipment directly to the mainframe. A quick way to defuse this suggestion might be to ask the client what the existing inquiry response time is for the mainframe. Even in traditional modes, response times measure 5 seconds, 10 seconds, and even 30 seconds or more. With such extended response times, collecting bar code data in real time is likely to bring the mainframe to its knees. Data capture in real time probably will entail time-stamping the entry, accessing associated data on disk, and then transmitting the data found back to the data collection terminal. A moderate to high level of data collection transactions may cause data to begin building up in queues, preventing more data from being captured. Further, both the mainframe and its communication links go down on occasion. When the system is down in mainframe-dependent designs, data can no longer be collected. The rationale for automated data collection is to come closer to a paperless environment. However, when data cannot be collected and a paper-based backup system is not immediately available, production must be interrupted. The need for consistent production and reduced cost in data collection has given rise to fault-tolerant, on-line transactional processing computer systems. Such systems may be configured as mainframes, like Tandem or Stratus, but not without substantial added cost. With devices such as work center processors (mini- or microcomputers) enhanced with coprocessor boards to permit faster clock speeds, multiuser, and multitasking environments, it is now possible to network two or more of these systems to provide the redundancy (or fault tolerance) required for electronic data collection in operational environments. Work center processors further permit fault tolerance at a substantially reduced cost compared to the mainframe solution.

The use of minis and micros on the factory floor permits faster implementation as well. Turning to corporate or institutional management and information systems departments for software support frequently means being confronted with three choices:

- Wait two years for the program to be coded;
- Replace an existing high priority project from the same department with the new project; or
- Use operations department budgets to hire additional programming staff.

Minis and micros can often be provided within six months, including the custom software needed to support bar code data collection, local operations management, and an interface to the mainframe which emulates existing data-entry methods. Microcomputer users and suppliers have a tremendous opportunity facing them with bar code technology and radio frequency data collection techniques.

Transactional Identification

For the most part, bar code technology is thought of as a method of identifying *things,* using a stock keeping unit (SKU), a catalog number, or an airbill. The adage, "If it moves—bar code it!", has caused many to overlook some even greater opportunities that exist in recording transactions. Physical "things" are not the only things that move: Information should move as well. Often, however, operational data moves far too slowly to meet the needs of effectively managing a business entity. In today's environment it behooves corporate management to work with information as current as can be obtained, and if at all possible, in real time.

Transactional identification technologies permit the capture of information in real time, through bar code identification of the essential elements of a transaction. These transactional elements are **WHO, WHAT, WHICH GROUP, WHICH ONE, HOW MANY, WHEN, WHERE, HOW,** and **WHY.** Elaborating further by means of example:

WHO may identify the individual recording the transaction. Such identity is conventionally secured from a bar code marked employee identification card, though successful operational examples exist where the employee identification is contained on some other form of bar code marked medium. **WHO** might identify either an operator or a recipient.

WHAT may be the identity traditionally thought of when considering bar code technology as an item identification technology, namely, the SKU number, the catalog number, or airbill number. Alternately, such an identity can describe a function or series of functions such as a work order number or quality test report number.

WHICH ONE may identify a specific item by means of a unique product serial number.

WHICH GROUP may identify a specific group of items by means of a unique lot, batch, run, or heat.

WHICH BOX may identify a specific container by means of a unique package License Plate.

HOW MANY may identify the quantity of **WHAT** being recorded.

WHEN may identify the time at which a transaction has occurred or when it is to occur. Recording the **WHEN** of a transaction is frequently accomplished by the computer's time-stamping the data at the time it is entered. **WHEN** could also direct an employee as to the time or within what sequence a transaction is to be accomplished. (In the case of recording statistical process control data, for example, a set of bar code symbols could identify the sequence of recording the data.)

WHERE may identify the location where the transaction occurred. Just as the computer can post a time to a transaction, it is possible for that computer system to maintain an "address" for each data entry terminal, appending that address to the transaction. Additionally, **WHERE** could be a bar code marked location sticker affixed to the data entry terminal or to a physical location such as a storage shelf, a warehousing location, or a room.

HOW may identify the steps taken or, if you will, the nature of the transaction. A straightforward example of **HOW** would be in a simple time and attendance setting. Bar code symbols representing MORNING CLOCK-IN, TO BREAK, FROM BREAK, and EVENING CLOCK-OUT could serve the same function as a time clock without the need to process the time cards. Each data entry is immediately posted to an employee's hourly record. Only marginal benefit exists to record time and attendance in this fashion, however. This concept is easily expanded to provide labor standards reporting based upon specific tasks. The tasks can be encoded in a bar code symbol generated in a semi-permanent fashion where only a predefined, limited set of tasks will occur at a given location (a "menu"—see Figure 13.1(a)), or task definition could be secured from a document that would travel with the **WHAT**s unique to the prescribed task (a "traveler"—see Figure 13.1(b)). In a quality-control environment, the tasks might be included within an Operations Manual whose pages would contain bar code symbols to represent specific tests and specific types of observations. In manufacturing, time and attendance can be assigned to specific manufacturing orders and tasks by *symbolizing* Standard Operating Procedures and Practices on the work order in bar code form.

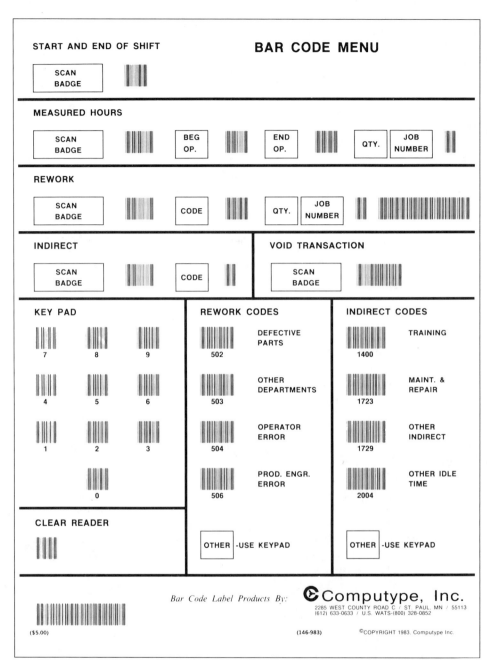

Figure 13.1: Bar Code Menu

240

WHY may identify the reason a specific activity is undertaken. Such identity may come from a work order or purchase order. **HOW** identifies the process or procedure and **WHY** identifies the authority for the process or procedure.

The implementation of any bar code system requires close attention to various issues of program management and technology. These areas include:

- Initial Requirements
- Project Management Plan
- Systems Requirements Definition
- Request for Quotation
- Organizational Bar Code Specification
- System Hardware Definition
- System Software Definition
- Installation Schedule
- Training Documentation

Initial Requirements

We discussed earlier the issues relating to the champion, project manager, and project task force. Four other issues are quite paramount to the consideration of initial requirements. Possibly the most important to any system development is the people issue. For any new endeavor in an organization to be successful, it is important that those who have to use the system buy in to the design and to the solution implemented. Beyond the training and education components discussed later, it is imperative that the systems design phase include identifying the needs of the people who are doing the work. Their insights may point out needs not readily identified by managerial personnel, provide issues that would render a specific solution unworkable, and suggest an elegant simplicity for the solution of other issues. But more importantly, their involvement in all stages of implementation will often be the deciding factor as to whether the project is a success or failure.

A second initial requirements issue is that of ensuring that the objectives of the program match the organization's strategic plan. In many cases, senior management may have certain hot buttons, issues such as "World Class Company," "Total Quality Control," "Productivity Enhancement," "Paperwork Reduction," and "Error Reduction." Knowledge of these key issues and framing project definitions which address these key issues may provide for faster top-management buy-in to projects.

The third and fourth initial requirements issues have to do with the personnel involved in the task force. It is quite important that both information systems and finance departments be involved early on. Bar code data collection is an information technology, and the information systems part of the organization is that part chartered with applying information technology. It may be that the operational components of an organization have a better understanding of bar code data collection than do the information systems personnel. To make the system work, management and information systems people must be involved and buy in to the project. Finance is just as important since the company has available only finite resources to pursue any activity. Working with finance personnel throughout the project may lessen resistance to certain funding requests by exposing the finance representatives to the wide-ranging benefits of bar code data collection systems.

It is the finance side of the house who will be able to explain to top management the benefit of cost savings. Which makes the most economic sense to the bottom line of the organization: a new contract for a million dollars or cost savings of $50,000. Go through the math to determine what the organization's pretax margin is on the million dollar contract. The adept systems designer will soon see that the cost savings makes a greater contribution to the company's bottom line than will the new contract. The finance folks can make this argument well.

Project Management Plan

The Project Management Plan begins with a Statement of Purpose charted by the original management project announcement or the organization's strategic plan. A scope statement is required, using a **WHO** will do "it," **WHAT** will they do, **WHEN** will they do "it" perspective—**WHO** and **WHAT** forming the base for one matrix and the **WHAT** and **WHEN** forming the base for the second. The **WHO** and **WHAT** framework, properly structured, will give the project manager a responsibility matrix for completing individual tasks. Defining **WHO** is responsible for **WHAT** gives the project manager a way to personalize task completion. The act of assembling an agreed-upon **WHO** and **WHAT** structure will give the project manager the commitment required from those who must support the project.

Managing a project can be simplified if the focus of the project manager's efforts is on managing only the aspects of a project he or she needs to worry about, namely, its problems. There are three kinds of project problems: Cost, Schedule, and Performance. For analysis, each one must be reduced to a cause and effect relationship. Once done, the impact one has on the others must be assessed and evaluated. Project problems exist only if you have Cost, Schedule, or Performance issues that are contrary to those that were established at the time the project was initiated. They should be dealt with using the "problem—impact—solution—I recommend" approach to get the objective approved. This kind of approach is usually the most effective one because cost, schedule, and performance problems usually have to be approved by the program champion.

Once the project's responsibility matrix is assembled, the schedule can be completed. Three considerations are paramount:

- that the focus of the schedule be event-oriented;
- that the schedule key on whatever constraints will dominate project decision-making; and
- that the schedule be structured in a way to emphasize the impact of a problem on the project's completion date.

Many projects that are reported as 90 percent complete are never finished. Percent complete is often defined by the beholder but not accepted by the project recipient. Focusing on events completed, reinforced by a statement of what is yet to be done relative to the project's time line, is a more realistic way of stating: "We are here and will meet our scheduled completion date." If the completion date will be affected in some way, an effort should be made to dramatically show how this new situation will affect the schedules and event. Negotiating an acceptable schedule should be the project manager's last organizational step prior to managing ongoing project objectives.

Costs and schedules are controlled by the scope of the project. Sometimes the scope of a project will change from what was originally proposed. It is imperative that any time the scope of a project changes, regardless of how minor the change, all parties agree to a formal Economic Impact Statement and Schedule Impact Statement prior to the implementation of the change.

The Project Management Plan must address the specific objective of the completed system. This objective may come from the Project Announcement, but should be more detailed. The system objective basically identifies what the proposed data collection system is supposed to do. Without a system objective, it will be impossible to know whether the system design meets the users' needs. Examples of such system objectives are:

- Currently the organization experiences a rate of five to eight percent shipping errors. An objective of the proposed system is to provide an error rate of less than 0.1 percent. Recommendation: No system is perfect. Never commit to totally eliminating errors. 99.9 percent accuracy is achievable—100 percent is not.
- Raw materials inventory accuracy is 82 percent. An Objective of the proposed system is to provide an accuracy of 99.9 percent.
- Labor reporting is currently a labor-intensive and error-prone process. An objective of the proposed system is to virtually eliminate the need for key-entry of labor data while providing timely reporting of labor statistics for management.

The costs and benefits of the proposed system need to be clearly defined. Prior to agreeing to funding the acquisition of hardware and software, management needs to feel comfortable that the dollar is being wisely spent, specifically that:

- The system meets investment criteria;
- Return on investment has been adequately quantified;
- The technology involved is well understood; and
- The technical and people skills required for the system are in place.

While the specifics of costs and benefits may be secured in the Systems Requirements Definition phase of the project, the Project Manager needs to be able to convince management that the above issues are addressed. Quite often benefits are deemed to be intangible. For example, how much is improved customer service worth? It may not be possible to precisely define the value of improved customer service, but it is still possible to provide "guesstimates" of improved market share, not losing market share, cost of handling customer complaints, and the like. It is important that no benefit be termed an intangible. If confronted by such a benefit, you should go to the departments involved and ask the question, "What do you think _____ is worth?" Such numbers may not be so precise as reducing shipping claims to 0.1 percent, but by securing the "value" from the concerned department, you reduce the chance of benefit numbers being challenged.

Few systems impact only the department implementing the system. The value of more accurate and more timely data may well influence other departments as well. As described in the task force members discussion earlier in this chapter, all of the members should be asked what impact the system development will have on their operation. Once the impact is described by the task force member, the follow-up question should always be, "What do you think _____ is worth?" They may need to get back to the project manager with a specific "value," but soliciting their input to the development of the system increases the buy-in throughout the entire organization.

An important part of the impact on other departments is that of the impact on the management and information systems (MIS) group. Below is a list of some of the issues that may impact MIS.

1. *What computer will the bar code application run on?* A PC? A mini? The corporate mainframe? Many applications today are PC based. This makes interfacing with the bar code equipment easier, but makes accessing the necessary databases, which invariably will be on another computer, more difficult.

2. *Will the bar code application adversely affect other departments or computer users?* Resolve any conflicts for computer resources or personnel early. Using a stand-alone PC for driving the bar code equipment can still impact others when databases are uploaded or downloaded.

3. *Is a stand-alone PC going to be used?* If so, is downloading and/or uploading data to other computers required? How will that be accomplished? Via telephones and modems? Via a network? Via direct-wired remote job entry link? Manually by operators carrying floppy disks from a PC to another computer? Automatically by programs started by remote computers or the PC itself? Will the host computer call the PC to establish whether any data needs to be uploaded or will the PC call the host? When will it happen? (Days of the week and time.) Will those resources be available then?

4. *How will changes to software—both application and operating system—be handled?* It is important to budget for ongoing support of the computer vendor's operating software upgrades. These periodic releases fix known software problems, add new features, and may create new and different software problems. Also be sure the bar code team is notified of all mini/mainframe software upgrades *before* they are installed.

5. *Are real-time programs required?* If so, does the computer support real-time programs? Will there be any conflicts (i. e., priority problems) with existing real-time applications? Does that pose a problem with current procedures or applications?

6. *If real time, what response times are needed?* Can the computer handle real time? Are there possible conflicts with other programs? What will happen if the response time is not met? Is it catastrophic?

7. *What commonly available high-level language(s) will be used?* Assembler, Fortran, Cobol, Pascal, C, or ??. Are programmers available with the necessary language expertise? Caution should be exercised when using a machine-oriented language like the C language. It's a popular and powerful language, but you should at least *triple* the time in-house programming staff says it will take to learn that language from scratch. Will programmers be available when needed? Are there company policy constraints on computer languages that can be used? Will this be a problem? For example, is the organization a "COBOL-only" shop?

8. *What language does the bar code equipment use?* Is it a minor variation of a language available on larger computers? What's the learning curve to become proficient in this language? (Don't take the vendor's word for this: Borrow the equipment and the manuals and let one of your programmers experiment to get the feel.) Are these languages compatible with the database?

9. *Number and kind of databases required?* Do they already exist or are you creating new ones? Or is it a combination of old and new? Where are the databases located?

10. *How much computer memory will the bar code application require?* Does that capacity currently exist? If not, can more memory be added?

11. *How much disk space will be needed?* Is it available? If not, can the computer system handle more disks? Would more disks reduce contention problems or be use-

ful in case of a disk crash? Should one disk be provided for actual file handling and another for mirroring of collected data?

12. *Degree of traceability required?* What audit trail information is needed? Are audit reports or statistics needed? Are programs to recover lost data from the audit files needed? How much audit data is kept? For how long? How is it archived? Will special programs be required to access archived data?

13. *What system software drivers are required?* Standard asynchronous ASCII or is a special handler required?

14. *What are the ramifications of "What if _____ goes down?"* As in: What if *the computer* goes down? What if *the bar code reader* goes down? What if *the port concentrator* goes down? What if *the remote job entry link to the mainframes* goes down? What if *the network server* goes down? What if *the power* goes down? Vendors of uninterruptible power sources may recommend a standby capacity of many hours. Is such capacity needed? Who is working when the lights are out? Often, all that is required is 15 to 30 minutes so that files can be closed and the system brought down in an orderly manner.

15. *Phase-in procedures?* Will the new bar code application run in parallel with the existing system? If so, for how long? Who verifies the parallel data?

16. *Fallback procedures?* Can the old system still be used? Will it be possible to merge the newly collected data into the old system?

17. *Will batch portable data entry terminals be used?* If so, will special software be required on the host computer to upload data and download programs? Once again, don't take the vendor's word on this. Borrow the equipment and experiment.

18. *Does the bar code equipment require downloaded programs?* If so, what languages? What's the learning curve? On what computer is the developmental programming completed? Is it available?

19. *Will there be read/write conflicts with the database?* Will two programs be trying to access the database at the same time? Will the database allow that?

20. *Using a laser printer?* Can it handle bar codes? As a special character font that is downloaded? Or as a special language subset for the printer? Or is a special program required to generate the bar codes and print them as graphics on the laser?

21. *Using a special purpose bar code printer?* That may mean yet another language to learn.

22. *Is date and time stamping of the data required?* Can the reader handle that? Or will the computer do it? What accuracy is needed? Closest minute? Closest second? Even more stringent than that? If the reader handles date and time stamping, how can you be sure that the computer and all of the readers have the same time?

23. *How many computer ports are required?* Are they available? If not, can the computer support the new requirement?

24. *Type of port protocol needed?* RS-232, RS-422, by-synch. It should be intuitively obvious to even the most casual observer that the bar code equipment and host computer must be able to talk to each other in the same protocol or that a protocol converter would be required.

25. *Baud rate(s) required?* Once again, be sure the bar code equipment and computer are compatible. Baud rates also must be considered when you have two computers talking to each other.

26. *Are any of the readers located remotely from the host computer?* Can modems be used for data transfer? Will the readers allow use of modems? Will they be dial-ups or hardwired? Is dialing a problem? Can they be polled automatically and remotely by the computer?

27. *What security is required in the access to terminals, local computer system, and host system?* Who has access to modify the database? From a remote terminal? From a computer terminal? Can employee identification cards be utilized? Are passwords necessary?

28. *What operator skills are required for system operation?* Will they be available when needed?

System Requirements Definition

The System Requirements Definition (SRD) is a document intended to describe how the operation works today and how the system is proposed to work when completed. The objectives of the system should be restated in the system requirements definition and compared to the original objectives set forth in the initial project funding request. While the objectives of the system may have grown by the SRD phase, it is important that all of the original objectives are still intact or a rationale provided as to why an item from the original has been added, modified, or dropped. SRDs can be completed by internal resources or by experienced consultants/systems designers having experience in the system requirements definition process.

The first part of the SRD is a description of how the process is presently being completed. Completed forms in use today should be attached as an appendix to the system requirements definition with ample reference in the SRD as to who is completing the form, when the form is completed, with what frequency the form is generated, and the process involved in entry and verification of the data on the form. Also detailed is what happens to the form after it is completed and how long it takes for the data on the form to be entered into the computer system. The movement of forms (information), people, product, and equipment should be documented in terms of who does it, where they do it, when they do it, what they do, what equipment is used to do it, how long it takes, and how frequently it is done. Blueprints and equipment layouts of the existing operations should be secured. Flow charts showing existing procedures will be helpful when comparing existing to proposed procedures.

Examination of existing procedures provides an excellent opportunity to identify the problems people have with the way things are done today and to solicit suggestions from operational personnel for improvememts. A brief explanation should be given as to the type of technology being considered—for example, bar codes with scanners attached to wireless terminals communicating to a local computer system—and feedback should be requested regarding the users' feelings about such a system. Early buy-in from operational personnel is key to the ultimate success of the system.

A word of caution, however: Operational personnel will inevitably ask when the system will be in place. Be conservative with time frame estimates. If workers expect a system to be in place in March and it is not up and working until September, false expectations were built which may damage their perception of the system.

Following the documentation of current operations is the need to design how the system will operate. Each step must be clearly and concisely defined, for it is this document that will ultimately be used as the Request for Quotation that is sent to system and equipment suppliers. Their bids will be submitted to management for capital appropriations. Failure to

246

precisely define the system may result in substantially higher final costs from suppliers. A suggested format for the SRD, which I have used in the past, is:

- Section I—Introduction: stating the goals and objectives of the proposed system.

- Section II—Company Overview: describing who the company is, what they do, where they do it, and desired direction for the future of the company by management personnel. Identify the major focus of the project, major problems currently being experienced, goals of the system, and other system requirements.

- Section III—Operational Overview: describing the current operations of the organization that are targeted to use the system. Identify the size of the facility, volume in terms of pieces, shipments, line items and transactions, product type, and how the material is moved. Again, this should be accomplished on an operation-by-operation basis, noting not only what is supposed to happen, but also what happens if things are not the way they are supposed to be—exception handling.

- Section IV—Design Narrative: describing how the system should operate. Concepts to be introduced in the design narrative include how bar codes and the associated data collection equipment are intended to be used. The design narrative should then provide a global design diagram of how data, material, and documents will flow in the system.

  Often, data will be downloaded from a host processor to a work center computer system which will drive the terminals employed by the user. File layouts—identifying fields, field length, whether numeric or alphanumeric, in what sequence, and how one field is delimited from another—must be precisely defined. The frequency of downloading data and the length of time required for the download from the host require careful consideration. Attention must also be given to communications between the host and the work center: communications protocol, speed, and the like.

  Each step of each data collection process should be carefully detailed, identifying the procedure in terms the user will understand, what prompts (and of what character length) the user will receive from the terminals being employed, the data to be scanned or keyed into the terminal (and of what character length), in what order, and whether the data is numeric or alphanumeric.

  Just as data was downloaded from the host to the work center, the collected data must be uploaded from the work center to the host. It is frequently less difficult to capture information for the host computer than to update the host processor. As with downloads, file layouts identifying the fields, of what length, whether numeric or alphanumeric, in what sequence, and how one field is delimited from another must be precisely defined for upload data. The frequency of uploading data and the length of time required for the upload from the work center require careful consideration. As before, attention must be given to communications between the host and the work center: communications protocol, speed, and the like. Further, the databases and files to be updated within the host system should be clearly delineated.

- Section V—Equipment Considerations: What type of bar code printing, reading, verification, and data collection equipment is envisioned? How many are needed? What amount of spare equipment is needed (10 percent spares)? Are the printers being used strictly for bar codes or for reports as well? Are there any environmental considerations existing for the printers? Will the printers employed be able to meet the print quality required? What is the size of the X dimension? How far away will the symbols be from the readers? Will the readers function at that distance with the specified X dimension? Is the equipment able to read the printed symbols? What types of terminals will be employed: wedges, hardwired data collection terminals, batch portables, radio frequency portables? To what will the terminals communicate—PC, LAN, parallel processors, host mainframe? What level of fault tolerance is needed? Are uninterruptible power supplies needed? Are spare batteries needed? How long does it take to charge the batteries? How will the batteries be charged? What will the terminals be doing while charging is occurring? What is the computer system and/or LAN topology anticipated?

Who within the organization is being charged with specific tasks both prior to system implementation and once the system is operational? What recovery procedures need to be in place when the system fails, and how will collected data be archived? What constitutes system completion, and what is the acceptance process for system completion?

• Section VI—Anticipated Benefits: Management requires economic benefits to offset the costs of the proposed data collection system. Benefits need to be quantified by process or how one process leads to benefits in another. Benefits should not be deemed as intangibles but as real dollars, even if those dollars are simply "guesstimates." These benefits should show return on investment over the period of time normally deemed acceptable by the organization. Where these benefits can provide for a faster positive cash flow, they need to be accentuated.

• Section VII—Reports and Inquiries: A precise definition of the printed and work center screen reports is required. A precise definition of the database structure for work centers and query methods of the database should be included within the system requirements definition.

• Section VIII—Appendices: Copies of the completed forms that will be replaced. Copies of reports that will be replaced by computer screens and operator input. Anticipated design of reports to be generated by the system. Blueprints and equipment layouts of the facility. An organizational bar code specification (described below) should also be included. Samples should be included of bar code symbols which may be used on employee badges, product labels, pallet labels, shipping labels, storage locations, forms, menus, files, assets, and the like. A definition of the FACT Data Identifiers and/or UCC/EAN-128 Application Identifiers to be employed in the data collection system. Check character calculations employed within various code structures to be printed in bar code symbols. The schedule that the organization wishes to proceed with, including:

—Project start date,
—System requirements definition sign-off,

—Requests for quotations released,
—Response date for requests for quotations,
—Employee education,
—Award of software development contract date,
—Equipment purchase order release date,
—Delivery schedule for equipment,
—Delivery schedule for software externally provided,
—Delivery schedule for software internally provided,
—Implementation date,
—Parallel system operation,
—Training, and
—Post-implementation review.

Once the SRD is completed, it should be signed off by the project manager and champion to ensure that the system being designed is truly what the organization desires.

Request for Quotation

After the system requirements definition has been completed and signed off, the document may be reformatted with very little modification into a Request for Quotation to be sent to likely vendors. The request for quotation should mention that by the date specified in the request for quotation (formerly the system requirements definition) the respondent should provide a firm quotation for the designed system, including identification of the manufacturers, software vendors, pricing, and, where applicable, model numbers for hardware, recommended spare equipment, software, installation, training, ongoing maintenance, warranty, payment terms, cost of additional licenses for software, and the cost basis for future modifications of the software. Potential software suppliers should also be evaluated in terms of protection against potential financial problems that the software supplier may have in servicing the needs of the customer. This can often be done with an escrow account for the software which is updated at any time the customer's software is updated. In the event that the software supplier is unable to service the needs of the customer, the source code in the escrow account becomes the property of the customer. Agreement should also be reached between the software supplier and the customer regarding whether or not the software supplier can resell the software whose development was paid for by the customer.

Organizational Bar Code Specification

Within the organization the position of Bar Code Coordinator (sometimes called UPC Coordinator) must be established. This individual is the contact for external, as well as internal, inquiries. The Bar Code Coordinator should have a library of all applicable standards for the organization. A minimum library would include:

• Organizational Bar Code Standard
• All UCC Manuals
• FACT Data Identifier Standard (ANS/FACT-1-1991)
• Print Quality Standard (ANS X3.182-1990)
• ANSI Standard for Transport Packages and Unit Loads (ANS MH10.8M-199X)
• AIM-USA-USA's USS-39
• AIM-USA's USS-128

• This book

The switchboard of the organization should have readily available the telephone number of the Bar Code Coordinator and have it cross-referenced to "U.P.C. Coordinator."

The Organizational Bar Code Standard should identify the reason the standard is being published, namely, to provide direction for bar code markings for raw materials receipt, internal applications, and finished goods marking. This standard should further address the impact of various industry standards, U.P.C. Manufacturer Identification Code, item coding, packaging of multipacks, print quality, coding for supplier markings, and coding for internal applications. It is strongly recommended that FACT Data Identifiers be used for all non-U.P.C. bar code symbols. Issues of bar height, label location and orientation, label size, adhesive, symbol protection, X dimension, and wide-to-narrow ratio (where applicable) should be included.

Today, many organizations are being bombarded with requests for bar code marking. Unfortunately, many requestors are asking that suppliers provide bar code marking of the customer's product code not only on shipping labels but also on individual items. The part of the organization that initially deals with the customer is often the sales department. The customer states that a condition of doing business is for the supplier to apply bar code symbols on incoming product. To secure the sale, the salesperson will invariably say "yes." However, it is not the sales budget that carries bar code marking costs: It is the operations, packaging, or distribution department that must incur this cost.

It is recommended that the organization develop its bar code standard to mark individual items with the supplier's manufacturer identification code assigned by the UCC and with the supplier's item code. If the product will ever be sold in a retail environment, the symbol must be the U.P.C. symbol. If the product is not being sold at retail, it is recommended that either the ANSI Common Label or the UCC/EAN formats be employed for individual items using the UCC Manufacturer Code and the Supplier's Item Code. When designing databases for U.P.C./EAN and ITF-14 structures it is recommended that the product code be a 14-digit field. And like numeric fields the data should be stored Right Hand Justified Zero Filled To The Left. This will provide worldwide unique identification for all item packs and multipacks of the same product.

The organization should make this standard available to all personnel, especially sales, identifying the organization's philosophy of bar code marking. The organizational standard should have language to the effect: "The organization has received and continues to receive numerous requests to mark product with coding structures unique to that customer. The organization endeavors to provide bar code markings consistent with reasonable industry standards. The organization will make available to any customer the bar code markings and coding structures that uniquely identify the organization's product. A customer requesting marking unique to that customer should be apprised of the organization's cost of marking product specifically for that customer. These costs include the additional cost for handling, labels, ribbons, amortization of equipment, label application, and profit margin. It is recommended that when product marking is provided as a service to the customer, this service be considered a value-added service and that the customer be charged for the cost of this value-added service." Alternately, the cost of unique marking could come from the organization's sales budget.

The reason that most customers want their product code on the incoming product is that their computer databases are designed to recognize that coding structure—not the supplier's. When presented as a value-added service, the choice becomes a simple one: What will cost less, changing the receiving database to accept supplier marking or continuing to incur the cost of value-added marking from suppliers? While packaging departments generally applaud this approach, it is important to recognize that almost all companies are both suppliers and customers. This means that the organization's database for incoming product needs to accept its supplier's markings, consistent with applicable industry standards, as well. No one organization is the "center of the universe," and bar code markings are least costly when applied by the supplier. Supplier markings are least costly when employed at the packaging line with UCC identity of the supplier and the supplier's item code.

Training and Education

Training and Education are critical at all levels within the organization. Training teaches "how." Education teaches "why." Senior management people need education since they are responsible for leading and directing the program. Middle and lower management also need this education since they must develop and then execute the programs. And last, but certainly not least, the users must be educated. The difference between successful systems and those that have failed is most often seen in the education and training provided to the end users. This is the "people" part of systems implementation. Users must be able to view the program with confidence, to see that they are making a contribution to the overall success of the program, and to consider the use of bar code technology as a friendly tool. The design of the program and close attention to issues such as print quality, symbol X dimension, reader aperture size, and symbol aspect ratio will ensure that the operator is easily able to achieve a good scan 85 to 90 percent of the time. Lower "first-read rates" will frustrate the user, destroying the confidence that may already exist. Many clerks in the larger national mass merchandiser chains totally lost confidence in early Optical Character Recognition (OCR) systems. This loss of confidence caused them to abandon the technology in favor of error-prone key-entry methods. And while it is highly unlikely that bar code reading will ever suffer the negative performance associated with early systems, careful attention to system design will improve the level of confidence in the program. The user must also be able to see his or her contribution to this program. The contribution may be as simple as a suggestion about where a terminal should be located. Involvement by the users during system design helps to improve their acceptance of the program after implementation.

Finally, the users must see bar code technology as a friendly tool, not as a form of automation that will replace them. Bar code technology makes information available more quickly and more accurately. It improves cash flow and is able to assist in lowering inventory levels. Like most automation, it does not create wholesale layoffs in personnel. Failure to automate is more likely to create layoffs than is automation. Lower head counts can be absorbed through attrition and filling parallel transfer or vacancies in other departments. Instead of seeing the bar code program as a threat, the user should be advised that successful use of the technology will substantially reduce paperwork. No one likes to fill out the paperwork associated with labor reporting, scheduling, and materials usage. Bar code technology can substantially reduce these irritants.

It is recommended that equipment and software to be used in the system be exposed to the user community as system cutover draws near. This may often be accomplished by bringing the equipment into a break room or common area within the organization, affording the future users an opportunity to "play" with the equipment. Bring in products with bar codes, allowing them to scan various codes at different times in the application demonstration. They will soon see that errantly scanning the wrong symbol will not cause the system to go down.

Documentation

To summarize, each system design requires specific documentation to ensure its success. These include:

- Project Management Plan
- System Requirements Definition
    - —System Usage Operating Procedures
    - —System Hardware Definition
    - —System Software Definition
    - —Installation Schedule
- Organizational Bar Code Specification
- Training Documentation
    - —Terminal Operation, Care, and Maintenance
    - —Reader Operation, Care, and Maintenance
    - —Printer Operation, Care, and Maintenance
    - —Computer Operation, Care, and Maintenance
    - —System Software Operation
    - —Archiving Procedures
    - —Recovery Procedures
    - —System Log

Some Final Thoughts on Implementation

The chosen method of implementation should be a phased implementation, where the bar code program has been planned by the task force, piloted in a visible application area, measured against pre-bar code costs and efficiencies, modified (if necessary) to embrace what was learned in the pilot, and expanded to other areas of the organization. The visible application area should be one that can be observed by many in the organization, while at the same time providing a reasonable degree of risk. If this is the project manager's first bar code project, choose something modest—for the project manager has a vested interest in the success of the project. With regard to the "modify" part of the phased implementation scheme, such modifications should not occur until the system has had a chance to settle. Certainly, if the program is inoperative, it should be modified to become operational. But if the modification is an enhancement, it should not be implemented until at least 90 days after the pilot goes live.

Some organizations have established numbering systems based upon group technology. While flexible manufacturing systems may benefit from group technology, bar code identification and marking does not. Numbering systems can be thought of as descriptive, or as a license plate. As was stated in Chapter 4, fixed-length nonsignificant numbers will best serve the organization for product coding and license plates. Code 39, the dominant bar code symbology in industrial applications, has 26 alphabetic and 10 numeric characters available in each character position. One character position gives 36 possible permutations; two characters permit 1,296; three—46,656; four—1,679,616; and five—60,466,176 unique codes. The license plate approach provides much flexibility in numbering, with the computer system maintaining descriptive and bill of materials data, while at the same time providing a small code structure. Numbering schemes become important in bar code technology, since the number of digits in the symbol affects the size of the printed symbol, the cost of the printed symbol, the time required to print the symbol, and the accuracy with which the symbol can be read by a given type of scanner.

When looking at the implementation of bar code systems, people often ask which comes first, the symbol or the reader. Customers are quick to state that they would be happy to buy bar code readers if only there were symbols to scan. And on the other side, suppliers quickly note that they would be happy to apply symbols if their customers only had readers. Symbols always come before readers. When implementing bar code data collection systems, scanning requires symbols. It is incumbent upon system designers to begin requiring bar code symbols on product well in advance of acquiring readers. Inventory that currently exists in raw materials and finished goods is not marked. That inventory needs to be labeled or flushed from inventory prior to scanning-based data collection. Though inventory may turn many times in a year, most inventory includes items that have been there for years. It is recommended that labeling requirements be implemented at least six months before scanning begins.

A quick review of the costs associated with system implementation includes:

Startup Costs
  • System Design
  • Orientation and Training of Personnel
  • Label Redesign
  • Packaging Changes
  • Printer Hardware
  • Bar Code Reading Hardware
  • Terminal Hardware
  • Verification Tool Hardware
  • Applicator Hardware (if employed)
  • Work Center Computer Hardware
  • Work Center Computer Software
  • Host Computer System Change Cost

Ongoing Costs
  • Manual Application (if no applicator)
  • Labels and Supplies
  • Hardware Maintenance
  • Software Maintenance

And a quick review of the benefits associated with sytem implementation includes:

Better Information
  • Standardized Information
  • More Timely Information
  • Eliminate Manual Errors
  • Accurate Product/Service Identification
  • Improved Operations
  • Rapid Collection of Data

- Automated vs. Manual Data Collection
- Less Manual Error Correction
- Streamlined Materials Handling

Finally, in the implementation of your system, you should:

- Design a total system
- Ensure that the expectations are realistic
- Use U.P.C. structures or Code 39 with FACT Data Identifiers or UCC/EAN-128 with UCC/EAN-128 Application Identifiers
- Consider the ease of use from the operator's viewpoint
- Select a medium and print technology conducive to quality printing
- Establish a complete pilot test
- Phase the final implementation to ensure continuity
- Organize for success
- Train all groups using bar code systems
- Conduct continuous performance reviews to fine-tune the system.

CHAPTER **14**

Applications Review

Today, bar codes are used in a variety of manufacturing, distribution, sales, and end-user functions. For trading partners, bar codes have a wide range of potential uses including receiving, breakdown, put-away, order picking, product reordering, cycle counting, product sortation, shipping, transportation, pallet and container management, labor reporting, point of sale, warranty tracking, and inventory control. All these applications offer significant productivity improvement opportunities throughout all channels of distribution. A review of these applications follows:

Automated Receiving

Problem

The adoption of Just-In-Time inventory procedures within many manufacturing facilities requires timely, product-specific data.

- Need to identify supplier, product, lot/batch, serial number, purchase order, and date;
- Need a means to quickly and positively identify product;
- Need to have the correct product on hand at the right time;
- Need to move the right product to the correct location at the right time;
- Bottlenecks occur within stored goods distribution;
- Facility suffers downtime due to shortages.

Solution
- Bar code labels identifying
    — Supplier
    — Product Code
    — Reference Number
    — Lot/Batch Code or Serial Number
    — Quantity
- Download open purchase order file from host to work center, scan all incoming product, compare to work center database, upload receipt to host, divert to subassembly area.

- X12EDI Purchase Order (TC 850);
- X12EDI Advance Ship Notice/Manifest (TC 856);
- X12EDI Inventory Advice (TC 846);
- X12EDI Price Sales Catalog (TC 832);
- X12EDI Warranty Claim (TC 142).

Possible Data Elements Employed
- U.P.C./EAN and ITF-14 (Supplier/Product ID)
- UCC/EAN-128 "00" (Serial Shipping Container Symbol)
- FACT DI - 2V (Supplier ID)
- FACT DI - 1P (Product ID)
- FACT DI - 7Q (Quantity with Unit of Measure)
- FACT DI - T or UCC/EAN-128 "10" (Lot/Batch Code)
- FACT DI - S or UCC/EAN-128 "21" (Serial Number)
- FACT DI - 17S (Combined Supplier ID/Serial Number)
- FACT DI - L (Location Code)
- FACT DI - K or UCC/EAN-128 "400" (Purchase Order)
- FACT DI - 2K (Bill of Lading)
- FACT DI - 6K or UCC/EAN-128 "95" (Carrier PRO#)
- FACT DI - 1H (Employee ID)
- FACT DI - 1R (RMA Code)
- FACT DI - 9S (Internal "License Plate")
- System Date/Time Stamp
- UCC/EAN-128 "90" (FACT DI follows)

Benefits
- Products are routed in a timely, cost-effective manner;
- Production time is decreased due to the correct product being delivered to the right location in a timely manner;
- Generation of local reports showing real-time data pertaining to day's activities.

Product Identification

Problem

Products must be identified and accounted for in numerous manufacturing production cycles. The product may need to be counted or diverted; an alarm, sounded; or the assembly line, shut down.

- Individual items are not properly identified;
- Work in process (WIP) sits idly on the shop floor without identification;
- Manually handling unidentified items is costly;
- Manual marking of product is labor intensive;
- Customer service is not aware of product status in the production cycle.

Solution
- All products marked with bar codes:
  — Product ID Number,

— Quantity,
— Date;
- All components and finished goods tracked with bar codes during process;
- Data Collection system reads bar code, verifies product, and uploads to host;
- X12EDI Purchase Order (TC 850);
- X12EDI Inventory Advice (TC 846);
- X12EDI Price Sales Catalog (TC 832);
- X12EDI Warranty Claim (TC 142);

Possible Data Elements Employed
- U.P.C./EAN and ITF-14 (Supplier/Product ID)
- UCC/EAN-128 "00" (Serial Shipping Container Symbol)
- FACT DI - 2V (Supplier ID)
- FACT DI - 1P (Product ID)
- FACT DI - 7Q (Quantity with Unit of Measure)
- FACT DI - T or UCC/EAN-128 "10" (Lot/Batch Code)
- FACT DI - S or UCC/EAN-128 "21" (Serial Number)
- FACT DI - 17S (Combined Supplier ID/Serial Number)
- FACT DI - L (Location Code)
- FACT DI - W (Work Order)
- FACT DI - 3W (Combined Work Order/Operation Sequence Number)
- FACT DI - 1H (Employee ID)
- FACT DI - 9S (Internal "License Plate")
- System Date/Time Stamp
- UCC/EAN-128 "90" (FACT DI follows)

Benefits
- Maintains the integrity of product databases;
- Manual identification and human misinterpretation of data are
  eliminated;
- Defective products are quickly identified, diverted, and recorded;
- Reporting generated locally by any designated category;
- Line shutdowns and delays eliminated.

Product Inventory

Problem

Computer inventory does not match shelf inventory, creating turmoil in shipping, production, and inventory control. Bottlenecks develop, shrinkage occurs, and filling orders becomes a real challenge.

- Physical inventory is inaccurate;
- Location of inventory unknown;
- Shrinkage level through pilferage or damage is unknown;
- Lack of perpetual inventory information;
- Cycle counting may not be feasible;
- More frequent inventory taking required;

- Increased overhead for maintaining inventory;
- Manual logging of data with interpretation errors.

Solution

Implementation of bar code scanning of all finished goods, WIP inventory, raw materials, and stores inventory.

- X12EDI Inventory Advice (TC 846);
- X12EDI Price Sales Catalog (TC 832).

Possible Data Elements Employed
- U.P.C./EAN and ITF-14 (Supplier/Product ID)
- FACT DI - 2V (Supplier ID)
- FACT DI - 1P (Product ID)
- FACT DI - 7Q (Quantity with Unit of Measure)
- FACT DI - T or UCC/EAN-128 "10" (Lot/Batch Code)
- FACT DI - S or UCC/EAN-128 "21" (Serial Number)
- FACT DI - 17S (Combined Supplier ID/Serial Number)
- FACT DI - L (Location Code)
- FACT DI - W (Work Order)
- FACT DI - 3W (Combined Work Order/Operation Sequence Number)
- FACT DI - 1H (Employee ID)
- FACT DI - 9S (Internal "License Plate")
- System Date/Time Stamp
- UCC/EAN-128 "90" (FACT DI follows)

Benefits
- Inventory logging is much easier and not manual; cycle counting, a reality;
- New products can be quickly uploaded to inventory;
- Elimination of human interpretation errors;
- Portable units can be used to track perpetual inventory;
- Put-away and pick data is used to update inventory levels, create shipping and invoicing data;
- Real-time report generation.

Product Verification

Problem

Customers and suppliers need positive verification of what is put into containers. The need exists to verify products, lot/batch codes, packages, and the distribution of the package contents.

- Products packaged in wrong containers;
- Orders get mixed;
- Customers become dissatisfied;
- Additional time required in shipping (checking);
- Wrong items routed to subassembly areas;

258

- Excessive use of floor space for inventory;
- Real-time data not available.

Solution

Implementation of bar codes on all packages and cartons for verification purposes provides substantial security in getting a product to market. Bar codes keep track of what product and lot/batch are shipped, the contents of cartons, and whether parts are available for assembly.

- X12EDI Purchase Order (TC 850).

Possible Data Elements Employed
- U.P.C./EAN and ITF-14 (Supplier/Product ID)
- UCC/EAN-128 "00" (Serial Shipping Container Symbol)
- FACT DI - 2V (Supplier ID)
- FACT DI - 1P (Product ID)
- FACT DI - 7Q (Quantity with Unit of Measure)
- FACT DI - T or UCC/EAN-128 "10" (Lot/Batch Code)
- FACT DI - S or UCC/EAN-128 "21" (Serial Number)
- FACT DI - 17S (Combined Supplier ID/Serial Number)
- FACT DI - L (Location Code)
- FACT DI - K or UCC/EAN-128 "400" (Purchase Order)
- FACT DI - 1H (Employee ID)
- FACT DI - 9S (Internal "License Plate")
- System Date/Time Stamp
- UCC/EAN-128 "90" (FACT DI follows)

Benefits
- Real-time information is available;
- Less space is required for inventory;
- Greater productivity with wireless or unattended scanning;
- Wrong parts or products quickly identified and diverted;
- Product recalls can be streamlined;
- Subassembly area space maximized;
- Proper parts sent for orders.

Work in Process (WIP) Tracking

Problem

Tracking product is a significant factor in an automated material handling environment. The need to know an item's location within workstations and other areas of the plant becomes a prerequisite to shop floor data collection and computer-integrated manufacturing (CIM).

- Customer is unsure of delivery date;
- 75 percent of WIP sits idly on plant floor, out of production;
- Parts, subassemblies, and products are not routed to the proper areas;

- Decreased productivity;
- Projects fall behind schedule;
- No integrity of statistics for report generation;
- Over-production of inventory goods (on hand).

Solution

Use of bar code based data collection systems results in timely movement and tracking of products. Database is updated so products can be monitored during routing.

- X12EDI Purchase Order (TC 850).

Possible Data Elements Employed
- U.P.C./EAN and ITF-14 (Supplier/Product ID)
- FACT DI - 2V (Supplier ID)
- FACT DI - 1P (Product ID)
- FACT DI - 7Q (Quantity with Unit of Measure)
- FACT DI - T or UCC/EAN-128 "10" (Lot/Batch Code)
- FACT DI - S or UCC/EAN-128 "21" (Serial Number)
- FACT DI - 17S (Combined Supplier ID/Serial Number)
- FACT DI - L (Location Code)
- FACT DI - W (Work Order)
- FACT DI - 3W (Combined Work Order/Operation Sequence Number)
- FACT DI - 1H (Employee ID)
- FACT DI - 9S (Internal "License Plate")
- System Date/Time Stamp
- UCC/EAN-128 "90" (FACT DI follows)

Benefits
- Unfinished goods can be tracked throughout the plant;
- Similar parts from different vendors can be tracked;
- Customer service can monitor items from start to finish.

Item Sorting

Problem

With high-speed inspection and conveyor lines, the need to identify a product, sort, and divert it to other lines is a critical, time-related problem. Products of unlike types and wrong quantities (along with the mixing of wrong products) creates confusion in material handling environments.

- Increased order turnaround time;
- Wrong product placement for forklift pickup or delivery to production line;
- Delayed shipments due to manual sorting;
- Lost tags which render products unusable;
- Manual sorting too slow for high speed applications and mistakes in sorting;
- High employee turnover due to mundane tasks;
- Decreased production.

Solution

Most feeder lines convey a multitude of items to be sorted and packaged. Systems must be capable of identifying an item and routing it properly. Bar code based data collection system permit items to be identified and tracked through sorting to final packaging or assembly.

Possible Data Elements Employed
- U.P.C./EAN and ITF-14 (Supplier/Product ID)
- UCC/EAN-128 "00" (Serial Shipping Container Symbol)
- FACT DI - 2V (Supplier ID)
- FACT DI - 1P (Product ID)
- FACT DI - 7Q (Quantity with Unit of Measure)
- FACT DI - T or UCC/EAN-128 "10" (Lot/Batch Code)
- FACT DI - S or UCC/EAN-128 "21" (Serial Number)
- FACT DI - 17S (Combined Supplier ID/Serial Number)
- FACT DI - L (Location Code)
- FACT DI - 9S (Internal "License Plate")
- System Date/Time Stamp
- UCC/EAN-128 "90" (FACT DI follows)

Benefits
- Minimized inventory space due to proper staging and routing;
- Sorting may be done by weight, quantity, destination, order, etc.;
- Bar code symbols permit specific product to be properly diverted to various staging areas.

Tool Crib Checking

Problem

Tool cribs are most often run with a paper-based system of tracking who has which tool. Tools are kept in places that the attendant thinks appropriate. Most requested items are kept close; in other systems they are stored alphabetically; and in yet other systems, by size or type. Tool cribs quickly become disorganized.

- Misplaced tools;
- Lost paperwork;
- Unreturned tools;
- No periodic calibration;
- Tools returned to incorrect locations within crib.

Solution

Bar code label attached to each tool. Database created on work center listing tool number, description, crib location, and calibration data. Each time a tool is checked out or in employee identity is entered along with tool ID. System has clock to record time checked out and to report tools remaining out for extended periods of time.

  - FACT DI - S or UCC/EAN-128 "21" (Serial Number)
  - FACT DI - 17S (Combined Supplier ID/Serial Number)
  - FACT DI - L (Location Code)
  - FACT DI - W (Work Order)
  - FACT DI - 3W (Combined Work Order/Operation Sequence Number)
  - FACT DI - 10S (Tool ID Code)
  - FACT DI - 1H (Employee ID)
  - FACT DI - 9S (Internal "License Plate")
  - System Date/Time Stamp
  - UCC/EAN-128 "90" (FACT DI follows)

Benefits
  - Reporting of all tools signed out;
  - Reporting of those tools out for an extended period of time;
  - Reporting of all tools needing periodic maintenance;
  - Stock locator system within tool crib identifies location of all tools;
  - Duplicate tools in other cribs are able to be cross-referenced.

Quality Control

Problem

Recording of quality control data is labor intensive and error prone. Delays in getting information entered may result in lost production time due to product not being released as available or rework of product which does not meet quality control requirements.

  - 60 percent of quality engineer's time spent as clerk;
  - Delays in releasing received material can slow down production by not having material at the right location in a timely manner;
  - Delays in releasing finished goods can slow down customer billing;
  - Statistical process control needs real-time data collection from source.

Solution

Bar code labels on all product or batches of product (containers, etc.). Quality control reporting employs on-line terminal (possibly wireless), bar code menus to denote test conducted, and bar code menus to denote recorded attribute of product as tested. Upload of QC data from work center to host allows quicker product release. On-line reporting to work center allows statistical process control data to be immediately available.

Possible Data Elements Employed
  - U.P.C./EAN and ITF-14 (Supplier/Product ID)
  - UCC/EAN-128 "00" (Serial Shipping Container Symbol)
  - FACT DI - 2V (Supplier ID)
  - FACT DI - 1P (Product ID)
  - FACT DI - 7Q (Quantity with Unit of Measure)
  - FACT DI - T or UCC/EAN-128 "10" (Lot/Batch Code)
  - FACT DI - S or UCC/EAN-128 "21" (Serial Number)

- FACT DI - 17S (Combined Supplier ID/Serial Number)
- FACT DI - L (Location Code)
- FACT DI - W (Work Order)
- FACT DI - 3W (Combined Work Order/Operation Sequence Number)
- FACT DI - 1H (Employee ID)
- FACT DI - 9S (Internal "License Plate")
- System Date/Time Stamp
- UCC/EAN-128 "90" (FACT DI follows)

Benefits
- Earlier release of received product to production;
- Earlier release of finished goods for shipping;
- Less time required for quality engineer entry of quality control data;
- Uniformity of quality control reporting;
- Statistical process control data immediately available from checkpoint to statistical process control processor and back.

Work Order/Traveler Tracking

Problem

Recording of production data is labor intensive and error prone. Delays in getting information entered may result in lost production time due to arrival of subassemblies without production operation or wrong operation performed on subassemblies requiring rework.

- Production delay to get production procedure;
- Rework of product due to incorrect or incomplete production procedures;
- Lack of reporting relating to status of work order at each workstation;
- Lack of timely data for shop floor data collection.

Solution

Bar code labels on all product or batches of product (containers, etc.). Bar code marked work orders to match product with operation, sequencing of operations, and identity of operation for shop floor data collection;

- X12EDI Purchase Order (TC 850).

Possible Data Elements Employed
- U.P.C./EAN and ITF-14 (Supplier/Product ID)
- UCC/EAN-128 "00" (Serial Shipping Container Symbol)
- FACT DI - 2V (Supplier ID)
- FACT DI - 1P (Product ID)
- FACT DI - 7Q (Quantity with Unit of Measure)
- FACT DI - T or UCC/EAN-128 "10" (Lot/Batch Code)
- FACT DI - S or UCC/EAN-128 "21" (Serial Number)
- FACT DI - 17S (Combined Supplier ID/Serial Number)
- FACT DI - L (Location Code)
- FACT DI - W (Work Order)

- FACT DI - 3W (Combined Work Order/Operation Sequence Number)
- FACT DI - 1H (Employee ID)
- FACT DI - 9S (Internal "License Plate")
- System Date/Time Stamp
- UCC/EAN-128 "90" (FACT DI follows)

Benefits
- Improved flow of production;
- Less rework;
- Better sequence control of production operations;
- More timely and more accurate data from the shop floor;
- Less labor required for production data entry.

Labor Reporting/Time and Attendance

Problem

Time and attendance and labor reporting are manual, error-prone, and labor-intensive processes. Compliance with labor standards is difficult to measure.

- Time and attendance time cards mechanically generated and subsequently key-entered;
- Labor standards data is often specious;
- Unable to easily identify labor component of incorrectly produced product;
- Shop floor data collection clerical tasks paid for at production or supervisory wage rates.

Solution

Bar code marked employee badges at clock-in, clock-out, interrupt, and shop floor/materials management/quality control data collection steps. Time stamp of data entry at work center provides accurate labor reporting data.

Possible Data Elements Employed
- FACT DI - S or UCC/EAN-128 "21" (Serial Number)
- FACT DI - 17S (Combined Supplier ID/Serial Number)
- FACT DI - L (Location Code)
- FACT DI - W (Work Order)
- FACT DI - 3W (Combined Work Order/Operation Sequence Number)
- FACT DI - 1H (Employee ID)
- FACT DI - 9S (Internal "License Plate")
- System Date/Time Stamp
- UCC/EAN-128 "90" (FACT DI follows)

Benefits
- Lower cost for payroll data entry:
- Lower cost for shop floor data entry;
- Better identity of employee/procedure;
- Better management reporting of labor.

Packaging and Staging

Problem

The throughput bottleneck in most production operations is located in the packaging facility. This operation is very labor intensive.

- Location records are lost and mislabeled;
- Inaccurate stock quantities;
- Manual, visual inspections, causing excessive hold areas;
- Increased turnaround time for customer orders and changes causing delayed inventory and billing;
- Container inventory to support Just-In-Time process;
- Shipping shortages, delays, and area congestion;
- Parts in wrong containers.

Solution

Automated product packaging using bar codes, fixed unattended scanners, object detect sensors, print/apply systems, PLCs, and automatic packaging machines linked with work center processor to increase throughput and updates to host.

- X12EDI Purchase Order (TC 850);
- X12EDI Advance Ship Notice/Manifest (TC 856).

Possible Data Elements Employed

- U.P.C./EAN and ITF-14 (Supplier/Product ID)
- UCC/EAN-128 "00" (Serial Shipping Container Symbol)
- FACT DI - 2V (Supplier ID)
- FACT DI - 1P (Product ID)
- FACT DI - 7Q (Quantity with Unit of Measure)
- FACT DI - T or UCC/EAN-128 "10" (Lot/Batch Code)
- FACT DI - S or UCC/EAN-128 "21" (Serial Number)
- FACT DI - 17S (Combined Supplier ID/Serial Number)
- FACT DI - L (Location Code)
- FACT DI - K or UCC/EAN-128 "400" (Purchase Order)
- FACT DI - W (Work Order)
- FACT DI - 3W (Combined Work Order/Operation Sequence Number)
- FACT DI - 1H (Employee ID)
- FACT DI - 9S (Internal "License Plate")
- System Date/Time Stamp
- UCC/EAN-128 "90" (FACT DI follows)

Benefits

- Package sequences and instructions by work center;
- Print/Apply and Wrap under PLC/work center control;
- Product carton/label data updates work center;
- Wrong parts or products quickly diverted;
- Product verification, no-reads rejected;

- Streamlined packaging reduces mislabeling;
- System identifies, tracks, and diverts to proper location for weighing, palletizing, and inventory.

Shipping

Problem

Bottlenecks in shipping department. Lack of sufficient storage space can slow production. Even with abundance of product, it cannot be sold until delivered. Without sufficient funds from delivered goods, product cannot be produced.

• Delays;	• Delayed billing;
• Lost products;	• Slowed production;
• Overstocking;	• Shortages;

- Wrong products shipped;
- Manual inspections and checking;
- Extra space required for staging products prior to shipping.

Solution

- Products scanned in and out of shipping area;
- Host download of data to shipping for last minute changes;
- Scanned data compared to open purchase order file to ensure correct shipment;
- X12EDI Purchase Order (TC 850);
- X12EDI Invoice (TC 810);
- X12EDI Advance Ship Notice/Manifest (TC 856).

Possible Data Elements Employed

- U.P.C./EAN and ITF-14 (Supplier/Product ID)
- UCC/EAN-128 "00" (Serial Shipping Container Symbol)
- FACT DI - 2V (Supplier ID)
- FACT DI - 1P (Product ID)
- FACT DI - 7Q (Quantity with Unit of Measure)
- FACT DI - T or UCC/EAN-128 "10" (Lot/Batch Code)
- FACT DI - S or UCC/EAN-128 "21" (Serial Number)
- FACT DI - 17S (Combined Supplier ID/ Serial Number)
- FACT DI - L (Location Code)
- FACT DI - K or UCC/EAN-128 "400" (Purchase Order)
- FACT DI - 2K (Bill of Lading)
- FACT DI - 6K UCC/EAN-128 "95" (Carrier PRO#)
- FACT DI - 1H (Employee ID)
- FACT DI - 9S (Internal "License Plate")
- System Date/Time Stamp
- UCC/EAN-128 "90" (FACT DI follows)

Benefits

- Increased throughput and customer satisfaction, fewer returns;
- Real-time data for accurate invoicing;
- Minimization of manual inspection and checking;

- Operations streamlined due to automated checking;
- Less inventory storage space required for staging products.

Customer Service

Problem

The ordering, availability, shipment, and receipt of product requires timely, product/order-specific data.
- Need to process customer orders quickly;
- Data entry is slow, costly, and error prone;
- Delivery dates subject to knowing product availability;
- Customers receiving wrong product/quantities;
- Customers looking for Just-In-Time and Quick Response.

Solution
- Scannable sales order entry books for salesmen/customers and order entry device:
  — Identity of customer, — Product Code, — Economic Order Quantity;
- Transmit order telephonically in computer-readable format; or,
- X12EDI Purchase Order (TC 850);
- X12EDI Advance Ship Notice/Manifest (TC 856);
- X12EDI Inventory Advice (TC 846);
- X12EDI Price Sales Catalog (TC 832);
- X12EDI Warranty Claim (TC 142);
- Order status available on-line.

Possible Data Elements Employed
- U.P.C./EAN and ITF-14 (Supplier/Product ID)
- UCC/EAN-128 "00" (Serial Shipping Container Symbol)
- FACT DI - 2V (Supplier ID)
- FACT DI - 1P (Product ID)
- FACT DI - 7Q (Quantity with Unit of Measure)
- FACT DI - T or UCC/EAN-128 "10" (Lot/Batch Code)
- FACT DI - S or UCC/EAN-128 "21" (Serial Number)
- FACT DI - 17S (Combined Supplier ID/Serial Number)
- FACT DI - K or UCC/EAN-128 "400" (Purchase Order)
- FACT DI - 2K (Bill of Lading)
- FACT DI - 6K (Carrier PRO#)
- FACT DI - 1H (Employee ID)
- FACT DI - 9S (Internal "License Plate")
- System Date/Time Stamp
- UCC/EAN-128 "90" (FACT DI follows)

Benefits
- Lower cost for order entry;
- Reduced errors in order taking and shipment;
- Better forecasting for MRP and DRP;

- Just-In-Time and Quick Response product;
- Better interdepartmental communication;
- Improved customer service.

Point of Sale

Problem

The sale of product requires timely, product-specific data.
- Need to quickly process customer sales;
- Keying product data at point of sale is error prone;
- Pricing errors erode retailer's margins;
- Impossible to track customer demographics or promotion data;
- Inventory adjustments made manually.

Solution
- Scannable product at point of sale;
- Price file lookup;
- Inventory adjustment at point of sale.

Possible Data Elements Employed
- U.P.C./EAN and ITF-14 (Supplier/Product ID)
- FACT DI - 2V (Supplier ID)
- FACT DI - 1P (Product ID)
- FACT DI - 7Q (Quantity with Unit of Measure)
- FACT DI - S (Serial Number)
- FACT DI - 17S (Combined Supplier ID/Serial Number)
- FACT DI - K or UCC/EAN-128 "400" (Purchase Order)
- FACT DI - 1H (Employee ID)
- System Date/Time Stamp
- UCC/EAN-128 "90" (FACT DI follows)

Benefits
- Lower cost checkout;
- Reduced pricing errors;
- Better data for inventory control;
- Less cost for shelf pricing versus product pricing;
- Better margins;
- Improved customer service.

14.1 - Federal Express

This application example is adapted from one written by Craig K. Harmon for Reading Between the Lines *(2nd Edition, Helmers Publishing, 1984) and the article "The Overnight Success Story" by Kevin Sharp which appeared in the April 1990 issue of* ID Systems *magazine.*

Possibly the largest single user of bar code technology and recipient of the 1990 Malcolm Baldrige Award is Federal Express. Founded in 1973, Federal Express directly serves virtually every U.S. community (with 598 city stations, 458 business centers, and 368 drive-through locations) and 127 foreign countries (with 220 city stations); its revenues have eclipsed the $8 billion level. Federal Express handles 1.7 million packages per night and 77.2 million pounds of heavy freight per month.

The concept for an overnight package delivery system was presented in a paper written by entrepreneur Fred Smith for a Yale economics class. The assignment got a "C," but the resulting company, Federal Express, became the first American company ever to achieve annual revenues of $1 billion in ten years without mergers.

Fred Smith's concept has grown into an icon. Today, the term "Fed Ex" means more than just a company. It is commonly used as a verb, as in, "Would you Fed Ex those documents to me right away?" The story of how Federal Express attained its current position is a story of strategic planning and of knowing what you want even before it is available.

Essential to the growth of Federal Express has been its commitment to the concept of positive tracking or knowing the location of a shipment at all times. To accomplish positive tracking of shipments, Federal Express uses a bar code marked bill of lading, called an airbill. Functionally integrated scanning data collection terminals record the movement of each package from its origin to its destination.

The value of using bar codes to track a package from pickup to delivery should be obvious. The cost savings arising from on-line comparison of desired package destination with actual vehicle loading are also clear.

In the 1990s, the public assumes that this type of package tracking technology is a requirement for any serious package delivery company. This assumption is exactly the point: Federal Express used bar code technology as a strategic tool.

No shipper today would trust an express package to a courier service that could not track packages throughout the handling process. Federal developed a capability none of its competition possessed and created a marketplace that demanded the technology. Developing a unique capacity and exploiting it is the essence of strategic planning.

One of Federal's strategic planning goals is the use of information systems. To Federal Express, information is more than just a tool to save money. According to David Dietzel, manager of strategic integrated systems, "We knew for a long time that information about a shipment was as important as the shipment itself. We use information as a weapon."

If you take the responsibility of delivering a $20 pipe fitting that is required to get a $100 million chemical plant back in service, you'd better not put the part on the wrong truck, or if you do, you'd better find out about it soon enough to fix the problem and deliver the package on time.

The Federal Express airbill has a 12-digit Codabar bar code symbol. Nine of the 12 digits are sequentially numbered to uniquely identify the shipment. The tenth digit is a check digit used to ensure the integrity of keyed data if the airbill cannot be scanned. The eleventh and twelfth digits are package numbers, always 01 on the original airbill. The airbills are printed on continuous web presses that have sequential bar code numbering towers. Each copy of the five-part airbill is printed and numbered with a bar code symbol. These copies are collated with patterned carbon paper. An area of the carbon paper is stripped of its ink to prevent smudging of the bar code symbol on the airbill. Codabar was selected because of its inherent data security, and because it is a discrete symbology, wider than normal intercharacter spaces could be employed to support the actuating pawls which advance the numbering machine for sequential numbering. Today, Federal Express realizes a data accuracy rate of 99. 9999997 percent, and errors that do occur are generally traceable to keyed errors and not scanning errors. Each shipment of the bar code marked airbills is statistically sampled and verified for scannability of 98 percent on all copies marked with symbols. The shipments that fall below the 98 percent scannability test are further sampled and tested prior to shipment acceptance by Federal Express and subsequent delivery to the field.

Federal Express has over 1000 handheld terminals in city stations across the United States and Canada. Each terminal is equipped with 64K of RAM, 24K of ROM/EPROM, a 15-segment, 16-character LED display, real-time clock, NiCad batteries, and a 39-key alphanumeric keyboard. The bar code scanner is a 6-mil, infrared wand scanner.

During each delivery, five scans take place to update the status of package movement. These scans occur three times at the originating locations for various purposes, once at the hub in Memphis, and once at the destination location. As a result of this package tracking, customers can contact Federal Express and be advised of the status of their shipments. The record available to the call center personnel includes when the package left the origin location and when it went out for delivery at the destination location. Any mishaps along the way are noted and if something goes awry, remedial action can be taken, rather than waiting for the customer inquiry in a late delivery.

The original portable data-entry terminals and system were designed by Tom Bullion of Federal Express and Craig K. Harmon. These portable data-entry terminals are programmed to prompt the operator through each data-entry function. The terminals and prompting system were developed with painstaking thought given to the "human friendliness" needed in the operation. A minimum number of abbreviations was used in the prompts, and the abbreviations that were employed were ones the portable terminal operators were familiar with through other Federal Express operations. The data entry is carefully checked to avoid misentry of keyed data. The portable terminal's flexibility and potential allows it to be used wherever information must be captured.

The airbill's design, created by Tom Mitchell of Graphic Systems, and the quality of the billions of forms that have been printed are deemed exceptional by any standard. The pioneering efforts of Codabar numbering machines on web presses combined with superior forms design make the Federal Express form the most functional of any bill of lading.

On January 26, 1981, the Federal Express COSMOS (Customer Oriented Service and Management Operating System) went into operation, and within the first year of operation over $10 million was saved in billed revenue that had previously gone unbilled. Federal Express began developing an information infrastructure designed to automatically track every package from the time a courier picked it up to the time it was delivered. The ultimate goal was to prevent as many handling errors as possible and prevent the rest from becoming service failures.

The first part of the Federal Express strategic information system was station-to-station tracking. A package was tracked from the time it entered the Federal Express facilities until it was loaded on a van for delivery. This tracking system, internally called COSMOS IIA, allowed the company to monitor every package during most of its route, but that still wasn't enough for Federal.

Problems in the operation of the wand scanners were encountered when the wand scanners connected to the original terminals were subjected to environmental extremes (the lens became fogged when taken from a cold to warm environment) battery life was shorter than desired (resulting from operator idiosyncrasies and the nature of early NiCads), and numbering wheel engravings were received that rendered the airbill scannable only from right to left. The numbering wheels had to be replaced more frequently, due to the carbon content of the printing inks. Each of these situations, though not anticipated in the original systems design, has since been resolved.

What Federal wanted was a portable computer small enough and tough enough to work in the hands of couriers. A field trial showed the feasibility of such a tracking system. Bar codes placed on packages could be read at various stages of package handling, and the resulting information could catch errors before they led to misdirected parcels. At the time, however, available portable bar code scanning devices were not small enough or rugged enough to satisfy courier tracking demands.

Federal continued to push prospective vendors to get the product they needed to fill their strategic information needs. While they worked with terminal manufacturers, they proceeded to install the first phase of the information infrastructure that would use the data collected by the portable terminals they were determined to get.

Federal Express did not give up its desire to extend package tracking into the courier's hands. It took three years and a lot of work by Federal Express and its suppliers, but the company was finally able to put a portable, bar code reading computer in the hands of every courier.

The reader that finally gave Federal the tracking capability at the courier level they wanted was the Micro-Wand from Hand Held Products. In Federal Express parlance, the Micro-Wand is a "Supertracker," and it is standard issue equipment for every Federal courier throughout the world.

The Supertracker accepts information from the courier and from bar codes placed on every Federal Express package. The Supertracker shown in Figure 14.1 houses 356K of RAM and 40K of EPROM. It contains software to ensure that the courier enters all the information required about an operation, and that it makes sense. It goes so far as to automatically place the period after the first initial of the recipient of every package.

Software in the Supertracker is automatically updated when required. The update occurs when the courier connects the portable terminal scanner to the communication pod that broadcasts the collected information to Federal's central computer network.

With the addition of the Supertracker to the already established Federal information system, every package handled by the company can be tracked through every handling operation. Within minutes, Federal Express customer service agents can tell a customer where a package is or if it has already been delivered. If it has been delivered, Federal knows who received it, when they got it, and whether the package was delivered to a lobby or a mail room.

The latest challenge for Federal comes from fax machines. Electronic capability in the form of information systems helped drive the growth of Federal Express, but fax machines are changing the entire nature of business communication.

Figure 14.1: Federal Express Supertracker

The Supertracker, designed for Federal Express and manufactured by Hand Held Products, is used to extend package tracking into the courier personnel's hands. This hand-held device is a combination of a wand bar code scanner and a computer with application programming for the tracking task. When placed back into its truck-mounted charger/cradle, it is able to communicate with Federal Express's central database via RF communications links.

According to an article in the *Journal of Commerce*, in late 1988, fax machines had cut almost 30,000 deliveries per day from the Federal Express growth curve. Business was in no way falling, but it wasn't rising as fast as it had in the past. Partly due to the continuing growth in fax installations and partly due to the acquisition of the Flying Tigers air freight company, in 1989 Federal Express saw, for the first time in its life, a larger growth in nondocument business deliveries than in document deliveries.

The change in revenue mix has coincided with Federal's heated battle for the lucrative international express market. Again the capabilities of Federal's information infrastructure may make the difference.

International shipments mean moving packages across national borders, and borders mean customs. To a company that built a reputation around delivery by 10:30 a.m., a few hours makes a big difference.

Electronic Data Interchange (EDI) is a technique used to automatically move information from one organization's computer to another's. In the international shipping business, is used to help speed shipments through customs. Electronic messages about package shipments are relayed to customs officials before the packages even arrive at a port of entry. By the time the package is unloaded, in most cases customs has already cleared it.

If history holds any clues, Federal will continue to use information as a competitive tool and will drive technology suppliers to develop the products it thinks are necessary in the international market. Federal's advantage in international competition is the company's experience at developing strategic capabilities and its ability to exploit competitive advantages.

14.2 - Labor Accounting at Tillotson-Pearson

This application example was edited from "Tillotson-Pearson Builds—and Runs—a Tight Ship" by Paul Susca from the June 1990 issue of ID Systems *magazine.*

Based in Warren, Rhode Island, Tillotson-Pearson, Inc. (TPI), is a well-known manufacturer of cruising and performance sailboats, sport-fishing power boats, windmill blades, and exercise swimming pools. TPI makes about 40 boats per month ranging in size from 20 to 44 feet and in price from $12,000 to $300,000. The recent installation of a bar code system to keep track of labor costs in the manufacture of TPI's boats has buoyed the spirits of the cost accounting department, virtually eliminated tiffs between foremen and accountants, and put the company on firmer footing when preparing cost estimates. TPI plans to expand its use of bar code technology as a result.

Before the implementation of the bar code system, record keeping was "a heavy burden on the foremen," according to Lee Gadoury, controller of TPI. Every day, each foreman filled out a summary sheet indicating how much time each worker spent on each job. The assembly department foreman had it easy; because workers tend to spend large blocks of time on assembly operations, the foreman spent about one hour per day filling out the forms. At the same time, each of the carpentry shop's three foremen spent at least two hours a day on paperwork. "After running around all day assigning the workers to the jobs, the foreman would have to recall what he had each man work on that day," Gadoury says. "A lot of it was 'guesstimates.' So the information was inaccurate, and it had a tendency to be fudged."

The problem did not end there. The labor data was a continuing source of friction between the foremen and the cost accounting department. To begin with, it typically took a week to compile and distribute the totals back to the foremen. By the time the data was compiled, Gadoury says, it was hard to tell if it was correct, since the numbers were collected and compiled manually. The foremen then disagreed with the cost department over the figures, "instead of concentrating on manufacturing the boats." TPI managers say they need to compile the information sooner and to place the responsibility for gathering the information with the foremen.

When TPI's new executive vice president Tom Pietraszek came on board in early 1989, he began to look for a better way to handle the daily labor reporting. He knew of large users of bar code systems, but he was also aware that few bar code system suppliers were geared toward mid-range systems such as TPI's DEC MicroVAX. Ultimately he found the Bar Code Data Collection Division of ASA International Ltd., which had the added advantage of being located in nearby Massachusetts.

System installation began in May 1989, with TPI planning to use the bar code system in parallel with the existing paperwork, bringing individual departments on-line for labor reporting. Gadoury explains that TPI's strategy was to begin implementing the system in the "simpler" departments, such as assembly, where workers spend larger blocks of time on each operation, and then move on to the "more difficult" departments where the labor-recording task is more involved. "A worker in the assembly department," Gadoury says, "may be doing his operation for 4 to 16 hours, installing the engine and the other mechanical components surrounding the engine. At the other extreme, in the carpentry shop, you get to a point where the job is making pieces, and it may take them 20 minutes to make 20 pieces for 20 different boats." The mold department is also unique in that workers are often assigned in groups so that their time is charged as groups of up to eight workers.

By early 1990, after several months of parallel testing, all departments had switched over to the bar code system for labor reporting, and TPI was planning to implement the system for time and attendance in April. In the interim, hours from the bar code system were compared to time clock hours, discrepancies had to be corrected, and the workers were paid according to the time clock. When the system is fully implemented, workers will be paid according to the bar code system.

Now foremen use the bar code system to sign workers onto a job. Signing a worker on automatically signs him off the previous job. This prevents blocks of unassigned time. The bar code system also allows foremen to do "batch coding," which entails assigning a worker to multiple jobs simultaneously, such as when the worker is making pieces in the carpentry shop. When the worker is signed onto the next job, the computer calculates the time spent on the batch job and divides the time evenly among each of the jobs in the batch.

Because TPI's operations are housed in a single building and work areas overlap, terminals are not dedicated to separate departments. Sixteen terminals are located around the perimeter of the building, and the foremen use whichever terminal is closest. Four of the 16 terminals are "intelligent units," and are located at the entrances. When the host MicroVAX is down, the smart units can store labor reporting data for later uploading to the host.

Each foreman interacts with the system by following prompts displayed on the terminal's 32-character screen. He scans the job number from the work order for each job, the worker's time clock card number from a laminated menu near each terminal, and the operation number from another laminated menu. When the system is implemented for time and attendance, each worker will have a bar code marked time card that foremen will use instead of the laminated menu to scan the worker identification numbers.

As an indication of the complexity of the labor reporting system, Gadoury says that although TPI has approximately 80 boats in various stages of manufacture at any one time, he estimates that 400 to 500 jobs are active in the system at any one time, and about 250 of those jobs are worked on in any given day. Within each job, the system keeps track of labor devoted to each of the 16 different assembly operations, including molding, patching molds, electrical work, rigging, joining, quality control, and inspection.

A few adjustments to ASA's software had to be made along the way. "With the original system you had to sign a person off a job and then reassign him to a new job," Gadoury said. "We had ASA change the programs so that when you assign a man to a new job it automatically signs him off the old job." Other modifications included one that, at the beginning of the day, assigns workers into the projects they were working on at the end of the previous day.

A second modification involved batch coding of jobs. The system originally allowed batching of up to five jobs; it was modified to accept up to 20. The third problem involved the intelligent terminals; they did not automatically increment the date from one day to the next. That, too, was changed. One ongoing modification was an effort to make report generation more user friendly and keep labor reporting systems users out of the VAX system level.

The total price for the system was $37,000, including about $20,000 for hardware. Hardware included 12 Intermec 9450 terminals and four Intermec 9550 intelligent terminals with 64K of memory. Using Code 39, both models are keyless and ruggedized and have a 2-line by 16-character display to prompt the user to scan the next field of data with the terminal's bar code wand. Each of the 16 readers is connected by RS-232 cable to an Intermec controller which appears to the VAX host as a DEC terminal server via an RS-232 port. Hence, the bar code reader/host interactions are terminal/host interactions.

The bar code system saves about 14 foreman-hours per day, Gadoury estimates, and he expects that to translate into better quality and better cost estimates. Foremen now spend five to ten minutes reviewing printouts from the previous day; they give the summary their OK or pass along corrections to the cost department manager. Predictably, Gadoury sees the greatest savings of foreman time in the carpentry shop. "They don't have to spend the time in the office; they can spend it out on the floor with the men. So they're giving more attention to the manufacturing," he says. Other benefits include improved accuracy of labor accounting and reduced bickering between foremen and the cost department. "The foremen no longer complain as they used to, because they're the ones who are responsible for putting the hours into the system," he says, "so they're responsible for its accuracy."

14.3 - Construction Site Labor Reporting

This application example is edited from "Bar Codes Tally Construction Crews" by Paul Susca, which appeared in the October 1990 issue of ID Systems *magazine.*

Using a custom-designed bar code system to clock employees on and off job sites, BE&K Construction Company is saving money for its customers and headaches for its employees. BE&K builds industrial facilities primarily for the pulp and paper industry and has used the bar code based time and attendance system on seven job sites since 1988.

BE&K's bar code marked identification cards replaced a system that used brass tokens, explains Diana Luther, BE&K paymaster at a job site in Port Wentworth, Georgia. When workers reported to the job site, they would pass by a window and call out their identification numbers. A clerk would retrieve each worker's "brass" from a large peg board and hand it to the worker. At starting time, the clerk would check to see which brass tokens were still on the board; everyone else would be logged in as on time. Those who reported late would be logged in when they appeared to pick up their tokens. Workers needed their "brass" to check out tools during the work day, and they turned in their "brass" when they left the site. Logs based on the brass records were compared with foremen's reports and used for payroll processing.

Ron Cain, manager of field administrative services at BE&K's offices in Birmingham, Alabama, recalls that BE&K's interest in bar codes began in late 1986 with the participation of the company's president in a program sponsored by the Construction Industry Institute dealing with automatic identification systems. "We chose to apply the technology to time and attendance control because we felt that it would be the easiest way to learn what the technology could do for us," says Cain.

Cain began to explore automatic identification options through several seminars in late 1986 and early 1987. "At that time there were very few companies in the construction industry that were applying bar code technology to time and attendance control," he says. Conversations with those companies convinced Cain that bar codes would work for BE&K. BE&K looked to a large computer vendor to bid on the system, but the vendor chose not to bid because it did not have an off-the-shelf time and attendance software product. The computer company referred BE&K to Compsee, a manufacturer and distributor of optical data collection systems.

By June 1988 BE&K was provided with a specification for a time and attendance control system. "At that time, we had a major construction project for Southeast Paper Company that was just coming out of the ground in Dublin, Georgia," Cain recalls, "so we suggested that we use this location for our initial bar code application.

The bar code system at the Dublin installation cost roughly $25,000, compared to an estimated $75,000 if the time and attendance recording had been done manually, according to Cain. "As it turns out, everyone involved with the project is convinced we obtained at least a $50,000 savings because of the reduced number of time-keeping clerks we used on that project," he reports.

Each of the BE&K systems consists of a Compu-Add 286 PC with a 40MB hard drive, a Data Net DNC 5000 network controller card, a number of Data Net DNT 250 slot reader terminals with a two-line display, and an uninterruptible power supply. The slot reader terminals are daisy-chained together with twisted-pair wiring, with a single twisted pair running back to the network controller card in the PC.

Some sites also use battery-operated Mars MEQ 130 wand readers for remote locations and Mars MEQ 1600 thermal printers to generate Code 39 labels for identification cards. Sites without label printers use labels that are laser-printed off-site.

One concern with the first installation was the need to train the construction workers to contend with the automated system. "It turned out to be not nearly as difficult as we feared it would be," Cain recalls. "In our experience it was difficult enough to get the cooperation of the work force with the manual system, and we envisioned problems with having the workers maintain possession of the identification cards, keep them in readable condition, and cooperate enough to pass their cards through readers as they come in and leave every day. But problems with lack of cooperation turned out to be almost nonexistent.

"Since then," Cain reports, "we have installed systems at another six locations, with continued success." Cain says BE&K has saved money for the customer on every project where it has used the system, with at least two other projects providing savings of the magnitude of the Dublin, Georgia, project.

The financial savings of the bar code systems are realized by BE&K's customers rather than by the construction firm itself, since the projects are contracted on a time-and-materials basis. BE&K benefits as well because the systems make life easier for administrative employees. At the end of the day, foremen's reports are compared to the time-keeping records, discrepancies are reconciled, and the edited records go straight to payroll on a floppy disk. This eliminates the process of manually totalling and key-punching weekly hours into the payroll system.

Another benefit for BE&K is the improved accuracy of record keeping. "We now have a system that records entry and exit times with a complete and accurate record, whereas when you record it on a manual basis, there's a chance of human error," Cain says. He roughly estimates that inaccuracies have been reduced from three to five percent with the manual system down to about one percent with the bar code system.

As each employee passes by the slot reader terminal, the display prompts him to run his card through the slot. After checking the worker's identification against an on-board file of workers assigned to that shift, the terminal normally activates a green light and displays a message that the clock-in is accepted. Some workers will be instructed, because of "blocking factors" entered into the system beforehand, to report to security, personnel, the medical office, or the paymaster, depending on their circumstances.

The slot reader terminal's on-board 128K RAM stores all clock-in and clock-out transactions until it is polled by the network controller. The number of slot readers at each job site is based on the number needed to store all transactions for a 24-hour period in the event that the PC is down. In any case, if a terminal fills up before it is polled, it displays a message that the employee should go to another gate. A site of up to 3,000 employees uses seven slot reader terminals.

One consideration in the selection of the industrial grade slot reader terminal was the harsh environment of the construction sites. In addition to the dust generated by pulp and paper operations, the equipment is exposed to dust by traffic as well as extremes of weather. At most sites, the readers are set up in open-air alleyways where the only shelter is a roof to keep out rain. Cain says that what they bought has functioned very well in their environment. "From time to time we have a problem with dust or moisture accumulating, but we've had very minimal equipment problems," he adds.

BE&K currently uses the bar code system at five southern sites from Georgia to Texas and one in Minnesota to monitor approximately 5,000 employees. The number of employees has at times been as high as 6,500. BE&K has dealt with the bitter cold Minnesota winters by housing the scanners in a heated trailer, more for the comfort of the employees when removing gloves than for the terminals.

Cain reports that the bar code system has been very beneficial for BE&K, but that they have not come up with many other applications. They are working on an application to replace the "brass" system still being used for tool control. Because of the rough handling that tools receive and the often corrosive environments in which they are used, Cain says, one option that he is exploring is to use a bar code menu tool catalog rather than placing bar code labels directly on the tools. Nevertheless, Cain reports that BE&K is "on the verge" of implementing bar code labels for tool control within the company's Birmingham warehouse even though a catalog approach may be required for field use.

14.4 - Using RF/ID In Dairy Operations

This application example is edited from "RF/ID Manages the Dairy" by Peter C. Doyle which appeared in the April 1990 issue of ID Systems *magazine.*

For over 10 years, dairy farmers have used radio frequency identification (RF/ID) of cows to monitor the milking process and to control feeding. The farmers save on labor and grain purchase costs, and benefit from data supplied by automated feeding systems' computers.

Most dairy farmers probably don't think of their operation as one of process control, but in essence it is. The products are milk and calves, the producing unit is the cow, and the raw materials that keep the cow producing milk are grain, silage, and hay. The bottom line is that if a cow is not producing, the farmer cannot afford to keep her.

To understand the process control with which the dairyman operates, one must understand the cow's cycle, from breeding, calving, and producing milk to preparing to deliver her next calf.

The cow's cycle begins when she has a calf or, in farming terminology, freshens. At that point, lactation starts and she begins to be milked. After about 60 days, the farmer looks for signs indicating the onset of estrus. This is the time when the cow comes into heat and will have to be rebred. About 100 days after breeding, the cow will be checked and generally found to be pregnant. Gestation averages 283 days. The cow will continue to be milked until about 305 days from when she last calved. At that time, milking is stopped and the cow is "dried off" before she calves again.

The non-farmer might be startled to learn just how much milk dairy cows actually produce. Herd averages for large, black and white Holsteins show that each will produce from 20,000 to 22,000 pounds of milk yearly. Individual cows have produced over 30,000 pounds in one year.

RF/ID systems help dairy farmers operate more efficiently. Each cow wears a heavy-duty collar that holds a radio frequency transponder. As the cow bellies up to an individual feeder to get her grain, a radio receiver next to the feeder sends a signal that energizes the transponder. The transponder then transmits a coded signal containing the cow's identification number. This is received by the transceiver and passed along to the computer that controls the entire system.

The cow at the feeder is immediately identified, and the computer starts the motors controlling the feeder's auger drive. Most dairies using automated feeding have two grain silos. One silo, for example, would contain grain with a protein content of 30 percent, while the other would hold grain with 18 percent protein. Because the computer knows what stage of lactation the cow is at and the cow's weight, it will blend the correct amount of each grain to produce the right percentage protein.

If the cow leaves the feeder before consuming her complete grain ration, it will shut off immediately. She may, however, return for the balance of her ration during the same feeding time period.

Most larger dairies use a freestall system where cows are free to roam about a large yard. At milking time, the cows are identified as they file into the milking parlor, and the amount of milk they produce is recorded. The amount each cow delivers is measured by weighing the jar into which milk is pumped or with a flow meter. The information is automatically collected by the computer.

A computer-controlled feeder is also available for those farms that do not have a milking parlor and where cows are kept in stanchions. Robert Engle, farm systems engineer for Agway, Inc., in Syracuse, New York, said, "We are marketing feeders for the tie-stall barn, where the feeder travels to the cow. It uses the same computer and identification system. The cart is on a track, which we put down around the barn. You set the computer, and every three to four hours, the cart goes around the barn and gives each cow so much grain. The amount for each cow is set in the computer.

"Because milk production levels have increased significantly over recent years, in order to maintain that level, we have to get more protein in the cows. So, if a farmer only feeds them twice a day and pours more grain at once, it doesn't do them that much good. It goes straight through them," Engle said. The farmer's alternative, he said, is to "grain them at noontime and again around 10 at night, in addition to during morning and evening milking."

This requires a very large amount of labor. Automatic feeding "reduces the labor expense, and the more frequent feedings result in improved milk production," said Engle.

A key factor in feeding is that each cow does not get the same amount of grain. It depends upon where she is in her cycle. Therefore, the farmer can't get just anyone to grain the cows and expect to get good results. If the farmer is feeding by hand, unless he has a reliable helper, he may have to do it all himself, 365 days a year.

Moreover, said Agway's Engle, "The automatic system takes the sentimental value out of feeding the cows. Typically the operator will give a bit more grain to a particularly nice cow, or the one that seems more hungry."

At the end of each milking time, the computer will print out a list that tells the farmer the order in which the cows were milked and how much milk they produced. If a pattern changes, the dairyman is alerted to a possible health problem.

Another indication of health is the amount of grain consumed. The grain feeding program records the amount each cow eats over a 12-hour period. At the end of the time period, it will print an "Attention List" of those cows that consumed less than 90 percent of their allotment.

The computer also tracks when a cow should be coming into estrus, the date she calved, and which cows are scheduled to be seen on the veterinarian's next visit.

Looking at the economy of installing an automated milking and feeding system, Bob Heidecker, director of research and development for Babson Brothers, said, "The systems become economical on farms with from 50 cows on up. It also depends on how well the dairyman is running the operation to begin with. Usually, there are just not enough hours in the day, so this helps him to feed his cows efficiently and see how much milk they are giving."

A key element of the system is the transponder. Heidecker explained that the electronic portion of each unit costs only a couple of dollars. The real expense comes from encapsulating each unit and securely attaching it to a sturdy collar. It must withstand abuse from a cow who has an itch where the transponder happens to be. It also must be sealed against moisture and work in temperatures down to –40°.

Most available transponders are attached to collars or necklaces and cost up to $35 per unit. Manufacturers have also investigated implanting them under the cow's skin. According to Agway's Engle, the major change in transponders might come with placing them in ear tags. This will mean greater miniaturization, and the hope is that it will lower costs.

"Everybody is looking for a better transponder, one that is less costly and very permanent," said Engle. "The large dairies, with 500 or more cows, have not gone to these identification systems very readily. It is quite involved keeping the necklaces on the cows."

According to Mark Juett, marketing manager for Alfa-Laval, his company commercially made the transponder controlled feeder for cows in 1976. Alfa-Laval's present system "has a passive transponder, without batteries. Because of our volume, we were able to commit to the manufacture of a custom-integrated circuit chip by Texas Instruments. It's in the transponder, which has fewer components, and that means greater reliability and cost-effectiveness.

"The unit charges itself when it comes near an identifier (transceiver). The transceiver gives off a one-second charge pulse and listens for one half second. This goes on 24 hours a day, whether a cow is present or not. For parlor identifiers, we use a different antenna on the transceiver, which works much faster. The cows can move through quite fast, about 15 feet per second, and be identified," said Juett.

Juett estimates that in the United States 120,000 to 125,000 farms have dairy herds with more than 30 cows, from 9.2 to 9.5 million cows in all. About 40,000 farms use milking parlors and about 80,000 farms have stanchion barns. Of the 40,000 parlor barns, only about 17 percent are equipped with RF/ID systems.

14.5 - Electronic Point-of-Sale at Pamida Stores

This application example is edited from "The EPOS Advantage" by Joe Taglia, which appeared in the January 1990 issue of ID Systems *magazine.*

The mass merchandising market is increasingly competitive. In a retailing environment where merchandisers carry the same products and where that product selection is continually growing, any advantages in stock turnover, as well as a better understanding of customer purchasing patterns, can mean the difference between success and bankruptcy. To gain these advantages, merchandising managers need effective computer-based information systems.

Pamida Stores, a 166-store general merchandiser headquartered in Omaha, Nebraska, recently installed an electronic point-of-sale (EPOS) system to maintain its position as a leading retailer in the Midwest. Working with systems integrators, Pamida purchased an EPOS system that provides complete, updated sales information, allows rapid data communications between headquarters and all branch stores, and remains reliable even under 24-hour use.

Pamida's electronic point-of-sale system consists of an IBM 4680 hardware platform combined with IBM's General Sales Applications software. The operating system used is FlexOS, a real-time multitasking system from Digital Research, Inc., along with Cornell-Mayo's Kwikprice software for price file lookups. Each store communicates with the headquarters mainframe via modems, with back office systems via a Token Ring local area network (LAN), and with handheld terminals used in the stores for inventory counts via RS-232 ports.

Pamida, already known for good customer service, is using timely information from its new EPOS system to track customer purchasing patterns more closely, so it can adjust its merchandise mix to meet shifting customer demand. Quick, accurate sales information also helps the retailer speed inventory turnover for even greater profitability.

Pamida is able to continually track consumer purchases and overall buying trends by using price lookup capabilities of its EPOS system. Handheld laser scanners (Symbol LS 7000) are used to read the Universal Product Code (U.P.C.) on product packages. These UPCs are then translated into an internal code based on the Voluntary Inter-industry Communication Standard. Once this translation has occurred, the Kwikprice software can be used for price lookups as well as for the production of daily sales reports, which include discounts and markdowns, and which guide Pamida's merchandising managers in their future buying as well as in the rapid clearance of old inventory.

The company uses handheld terminals that allow clerks to walk the aisles and capture U.P.C. data while keying in inventory counts at the same time. Using handheld terminals speeds up the company's inventory process and eliminates potentially costly errors that occur through data entry mistakes.

The operating system, FlexOS, provides Pamida's electronic point-of-sale system with the real-time and multitasking capabilities required for delivering fast, accurate information. FlexOS allows the average of 10 checkout terminals (IBM 4683 Models 1 and 2) per store to run simultaneously. It also permits the company's EPOS system to process large amounts of data throughout the entire 166-store system. The store checkout terminals use Metrologic MS-260 bar code scanners, receipt printers, numeric readouts, cash drawers, and credit card scanners, many of which are requesting price lookups of the EPOS system. At the same time that price lookups are being executed, the electronic point-of-sale system is also tracking customers' purchases and maintaining a complete discounting structure that includes accurate merchandise markdown reports.

The ability of Pamida's individual stores to exchange information quickly and easily both with headquarters and with each other is vital to the company's retailing success. Getting information where and when it is needed contributes to better customer service and makes store and parent company internal operations more efficient.

Frequent information exchange is an integral part of Pamida's electronic point-of-sale system. At the end of each business day, the individual stores communicate with the mainframe at headquarters via modems. Each store's master system uploads that day's sales to the mainframe, while at the same time receiving any new sales information it needs—including markdowns and special buys—from headquarters. Within individual stores, communication is enhanced by connecting the EPOS system to the store's back office system with a Token Ring network. This allows stores to produce sales reports and to place orders.

The information stored on Pamida's computers is critical to its day-to-day operations, so a systems "crash" with the potential for destroying this operating information cannot be tolerated. In view of this need, the company's EPOS system is configured to protect its vital data.

Back-up systems in both the software and hardware portions of the electronic point-of-sale system provide security from data-threatening crashes. A "master and slave" controller configuration consisting of a PC or minicomputer master and networked terminals as slaves keeps all data, such as price lookups, continually updated to the slave disk to ensure duplicate information. If the master system goes down, the slave takes over its function and then updates the master when it is brought back up. In the event of a complete system failure, data loss is limited by daily back-up.

Pamida is continuing to add capabilities to its EPOS system, enabling the organization to maintain a critical edge over competition. The company will be eliminating individual product pricing, instead providing customers with shelf and check-out register pricing. This will save Pamida the cost of tagging each product as well as the cost of handling pricing mistakes.

With its new electronic point-of-sale system, Pamida is satisfying its customers as well as its own internal needs in a highly efficient manner—all of which positions the company for success in an increasingly tough retailing environment.

14.6 - Factory Data Collection at Teledyne

This application example is edited from "Creating the Less-Paper Factory" by Blake Park, which appeared in the June 1990 issue of ID Systems *magazine.*

The idea of creating a paperless workplace has intrigued managers for years, but the concept remains little more than a dream for most companies. Teledyne Systems, a major southern California aerospace company, has made significant strides in reducing its paperwork, and the experience gained by that company offers insight for others wanting to reduce paperwork and increase plant efficiency.

One reason Teledyne succeeded in implementing its system hinges on the fact that Teledyne defined its goal not as creating a "paperless" factory, but as establishing a "less-paper" factory. "What was pursued was increased efficiency," explained Ron Beria, project manager for computer integrated manufacturing (CIM) at Teledyne. "Reducing paperwork was a means, not an end in itself, to make us more efficient and productive."

Teledyne's initial project was designed to tackle an especially troublesome area in the company, tracking primary parts from the receiving dock through inspection to placement in stock for the manufacturing process. Its manual system, although workable, posed several drawbacks that dampened the factory's efficiency. First, the system generated tremendous amounts of paperwork. The tracking process required 9 to 20 copies of each purchase order to be distributed manually to various departments, such as Finance and Material Planning. In addition, it lacked the flexibility needed to deal with several common situations. For example, the system did not indicate the specific location of a particular box of goods when it was received. As a result, if a box was placed in front of another on a shelf, the initial box might be lost for weeks, forcing the company to spend valuable time and resources recovering it.

The system's imprecision led its users to develop inconsistent procedures for dealing with work flow. The lack of uniformity created quality control and status-tracking problems, with errors occurring that had to be corrected later. Another shortcoming of the original paper log system was its inability to automatically locate and update the status of a received item as it was routed through receiving, inspecting, and stocking processes. The most serious problem, however, was that the system for receiving goods dramatically limited the firm's capacity to grow. "Our backlog got bigger—not our output," noted a senior Teledyne official.

Teledyne intends to automate the entire factory, but management recognized that worker acceptance of factory automation required an incremental approach. They concluded that establishing a bar code system for the receiving function would provide the company with an excellent introduction to the automation process. "We understood the basics of bar code technology," explained Bob Giardini, Teledyne's director of product assurance and operations systems and the driving force behind the "dock-to-stock" system, "but our knowledge stopped at automating the pencil. We wanted more."

Teledyne realized that adopting a tracking system did not require Buck Rogers technology: Existing technology could be applied to their factory. "We did not want to reinvent the wheel," commented an upper level manager involved with the project. At the same time, Teledyne's management did not want to take separate data collection components and create a new automated system. Instead, they wanted a turnkey system.

After considering 30 different companies, Teledyne chose ShopTrac Data Collection

Systems to design, implement, and maintain the system.

The guiding principle for the system's development centered on encouraging worker acceptance. "Too many programs fail because they ignore the people expected to use the system," explained the manager coordinating its introduction. This issue was addressed by placing the people issue as the "nucleus" of the system. It was realized that the bar code was only an input medium. It helps the technology to become transparent to the user, but it was necessary to develop a system—not just an input.

At the same time, the firm faced the added challenge of developing the system while minimizing disruption at the Teledyne plant. Since several satellite data collection applications already operated outside the company's mainframe, the tracking system needed to complement rather that compete against or replace existing systems. To answer this need, the new dock-to-stock system utilized standard system architecture with on-line interfaces to existing applications running in other areas of the corporation, allowing the system to communicate with Teledyne's mainframe.

Automating the first phase of the system was straightforward in design and implementation. As products arrive at the receiving dock, workers must identify the component received and its vendor. The original packing slip typically provided this identification information. Now, the operator enters the purchase order number at a workstation in the receiving area. By using the purchase order files supplied by Teledyne's mainframe, the new system immediately provides a CRT display of the purchase order to confirm the item received. This eliminates the laborious task of searching through racks of purchase order files.

At the terminal, the operator moves the cursor to the line item received, presses the return button, and is prompted to enter the quantity received. This data entry is the last piece of information manually entered into the system.

After the quantity received is entered, the CRT displays a formatted label containing a system-assigned control number along with appropriate product, lot, and receipt information. The control number then serves as the basis for tracking the material while at the factory. As the operator approves the label's data, the system generates bar code labels that are affixed to the package and/or components. Simultaneously, the system updates Teledyne's control number log and allows status updates for various departments through Teledyne's local area networks. A final record is transmitted to update the company's mainframe, thereby eliminating multiple copying and manual handling of each receiving document.

Developing a successfully integrated dock-to-stock tracking system required the integrator to become familiar with Teledyne's information needs. ShopTrac conducted an extensive plant-flow analysis prior to designing the system for Teledyne. The resulting communication between the two companies led to a high degree of trust, according to the Teledyne official, which helped the project come to fruition. "Trust was absolutely essential to the success of the project," noted the official, since everyone involved needed to be "open-minded to addressing our company's needs."

To understand how the system could benefit Teledyne, extensive employee participation in the development of system parameters was insisted upon. Potential users of the system were interviewed at the factory to identify areas in which workers and managers wanted information. An implementation team of Teledyne managers and workers was created, with members from all disciplines that would directly or indirectly come in contact with the system. The firm then took advantage of its existing software applications and prototyped the system, allowing users to test the input screens and reports, as it was developed. Existing application knowledge, software flexibility, and the ability to communicate to the mainframe provided the basis for the successful implementation of the bar code-based tracking system.

The system was designed around the needs of its particular users so each would benefit from using it and would be discouraged from bypassing it. However, management worried that workers might resist the new system since the company had experienced trouble in previous attempts to automate parts of the plant. Complicating matters was the fact that the system was to be implemented in areas of the company unaccustomed to computer terminals. In fact, most of the system's users had no previous experience with computers. Still, worker acceptance of the automated system has been "phenomenal," noted the project manager.

The reason for such rapid acceptance is simple, according to the project manager. First because it uses bar code technology as the principal input means, the system is easy to use. Second, users are rewarded with information previously difficult, if not impossible, to gain.

An examination of the way workers use the system demonstrates its benefits. Employees responsible for checking each component in a shipment find that the new system does not require learning entirely new terminology. Each workstation screen displays prompts written in words that the inspector is accustomed to from the original tracking system. The difference is the use of computer terminals and bar code readers. Even the challenge of entering a request is diminished by the menu-driven software. Consequently, though most of the users possessed no previous computer experience, acceptance of the system has been rapid. One initially skeptical worker noted his pleasure using the system since it "won't let me make a mistake; the computer tells me if I entered something wrong and makes recommendations on what I should enter (to correct my error)."

The terminals used in this system have PC compatibility and are designed and built by ShopTrac. All terminals are equipped with Welch-Allyn Digital LED Scanners and Hewlett-Packard HBSCS 7000 Digital Slot Readers.

"Quality compliance demands good inspection procedures, but efficiency requires knowledge of which inspection tests are needed, and then accurately conducting and recording their results," noted an upper-level manager. Accomplishing that task is the second major goal of the automated system. To reduce error and increase plant efficiency in the inspection area, steps were developed to make sure all inspectors follow a uniform procedure that requires less time than the old system. As a product comes into the inspection area, its movement between departments is noted as the mover scans the control number bar code. No added data input is needed.

When one of 20 inspectors takes a product off the inspection waiting racks, he returns to his work area and begins the inspection process by scanning the control number. His CRT displays vendor and purchase order information and instructions on inspection steps to be taken. Although the actual detail inspection documents still reside in printed manuals, the system directs the inspector to the correct documentation. A scheduled enhancement will display inspection documentation and capture results electronically. The current version of the system requires the inspector to note electronically the completion of each step and allows him to include appropriate comments.

What is essential, stressed Teledyne's project manager, is not only to provide value to the immediate users, but also to publicize those benefits to the rest of the plant so acceptance will grow as the system grows. Another manager added that publicizing the system's success is "the first move en route to a paperless factory; its visibility makes it the cornerstone of the (automation) process."

The benefits are not limited to those entering data into the system. The production planning and production control departments now know the status and location of needed components and the quantity available for manufacturing. Also, the shipping/receiving manager no longer has to send out expeditors to find misplaced packages or remaining parts for a partially completed package. As a result, interruptions have been reduced since the inspectors, engineers, and others can learn the status of particular projects electronically. In addition to reducing the number of interruptions, the receiving manager can use his time to do his primary job, increasing the efficiency of receiving goods.

The new system also benefits the management information systems (MIS) department since the tracking system's design stresses system integration. It communicates with databases already running at Teledyne and eventually will send status reports to various departments, such as Finance or Accounts Payable. MIS, therefore, gains from the accuracy of input and ease of transfer of the new system-generated data. Teledyne also avoids additional data processing support burdens since the new stand-alone system has its own backup and maintenance utilities. The final advantage comes from its ability to provide managers with extensive audits of where each processed item went, who handled it, and how long each step took.

"A real benefit of the system comes from how it encourages a horizontal flow of information. Information is beginning to flow across the organization—an impossibility prior to installing the system," explained Norman Wolstein, manager of production engineering.

If products are rejected in the inspection process, they are moved to holding or returns areas. Their locations are entered into the system by scanning the control numbers. Accepted products move to a staging area to be recorded in Teledyne's existing stocking system. "Before installing the automated dock-to-stock system, we had to manually input all of the details on every item into the mainframe all over again for stock," said Giardini. "We copied papers in the beginning and used our people for clerical entry at the end." Now the stocking personnel enter only the location data once a space for the product is determined. The new system updates all other Teledyne systems, decreasing paperwork and virtually eliminating the chance for data entry error.

The new system offers flexibility and expandability so it will not be made obsolete by Teledyne's expansion or by the addition of new satellite systems. The initial dock-to-stock application will be expanded by adding other data collection modules such as time and attendance, labor allocation, and work-in-process.

Current users of the new system find themselves able to do their jobs rather than having to continually track down misplaced boxes and chase paper. The system also reduces errors by preventing employees from taking shortcuts that might lead to inconsistencies and problems. These improvements in tracking the flow of jobs translate to improved efficiency and productivity. As a result, Teledyne is better able to control price and time. According to Bob Giardini, "We are becoming a more versatile and flexible company, but with better controls we are also becoming more competitive. . . . We need the automated dock-to-stock tracking system to stay competitive in the 1990s. We would not be able to survive the next decade without it."

14.7 - Manufacturing, Inventory, and Shipping Control at a Paper Manufacturer

This application example is edited from "On a Roll with Bar Code" by Phyllis Zaiger, which appeared in the January 1990 issue of ID Systems *magazine.*

Hollingsworth and Vose, an East Walpole, Massachusetts, manufacturer of specialty paper products, has enjoyed substantial success over the past year in its efforts to maximize control of finished goods moving through manufacturing to inventory; streamline shipping procedures; and simplify periodic inventories. Operations include eight plants spread over the U.S., Mexico, and England. Hollinsworth and Vose paper goods, used in a wide variety of applications, account for annual sales well in excess of $100 million.

The key to improved plant management is a bar code based data collection system. The system's success is due, in part, to a customized version of a bar code and labeling software system called generalized bar code and labeling software system from Integrated Software Design (ISD). The new system has established better inventory control over Hollingsworth and Vose's manufacturing operations.

Hollingsworth and Vose's initial priority was to develop a basic finished goods tracking system that could report, on demand, the resting place in inventory. The final system ensures complete accountability of finished goods consigned to inventory. The program also provides consistent product turnaround by managing inventory on a "first-in/first-out" basis.

The previous manual approach had resulted in a laborious method of stock entry and withdrawal for outgoing shipments. Manual methods also led to lengthy inventory holdovers for some rolls, product spoilage, scrapping, and related overhead losses.

Presently, product identification begins with assignment of manufacturing lot number to empty reels on paper making machines. After full reels are cut into rolls, each unit is given a unique identification number. Thus, a roll can be traced to the original parent reel in the event that a quality problem is later uncovered. At this point, production entry bar code labels are produced by an on-site PC computer—one of six IBM XT or PS/2 Model 30 satellite units at key locations throughout the plant. Printronix dot matrix printers are used at each station as well.

The two labels that are applied to the outside and inner core of each roll carry eight elements of production: roll number, paper grade, caliper (paper thickness), width, quantity, quality control factor, and roll weight with information on breaks. These identification labels are preprinted by A/L Systems on 70-pound, white, pressure-sensitive backed stock.

At the preinventory wrapping station, each roll is weighed by the press of a button for an accurate weight figure, wrapped by machine, palletized, and, finally, assigned a specific inventory location. All of these operations are PC controlled.

For finished rolls that are diverted to one or more conversion operations—coating, slitting, edge treatment, combining to expand roll lengths—the handling process is computer tracked. Each additional step is transmitted to the inventory PC for final bar code label recording. The system always knows where a roll has come from, how it has been processed, and where it stands in inventory.

Should a roll, for example, be returned to manufacturing from inventory for additional specialty conversion, the unit is monitored by computer and the added processing steps are recorded. A new bar code label, containing the updated data, is printed at the inventory station prior to the roll's reentry into inventory.

If laboratory testing indicates quality problems, the paper can be traced by lot number and roll number wherever it may be in the system. Should it be scrapped, an accounting by pounds is recorded. If it is saved in part or whole by conversion, this new information is retained as well.

Upon the roll's entry into inventory, the PC at this location transmits finished roll information to a local area network (LAN) server, which is the heart of ISD's internal software control system. The server, a 3COM Model 3S/200 housed within the shipping department, is connected to all six satellite computers receiving and assimilating production and inventory data for each roll produced on a three-shift per day schedule.

Although Hollingsworth and Vose envisioned a substantially less sophisticated tracking system at the outset, its requirements grew to what can be described best as a highly integrated, computerized finished goods tracking system.

From inventory, the installation of a packing list software system followed. Still another of the system's satellite PCs is located in the company's shipping department where it is wired to the LAN server and Wang VS mainframe, which also serves other facets of the company's operation.

Orders are downloaded into the shipping PC, which pulls the orders into the packing list system. The software system directs the shipping PC to search inventory to select "first-in" rolls that match order requirements. Once done, a packing list is printed, indicating roll production data and designating inventory locations of the desired rolls. At the same time, the PC directs printing of shipping labels for the same order.

The packing list data is next downloaded to a portable terminal, a Panasonic Data Partner Model JT-770, that is carried on-site to the inventory area where the appropriate paper rolls are located. Bar code labels are scanned for verification using Symbol Technologies Model 8110 handheld laser scanners. The order is then consolidated for shipment.

Built into the shipping software program is a provision for item override in the event a substitute roll that matches the order must replace an original order item. Substitutions are entered into the portable terminal and uploaded into the shipping PC. A discrepancy report is printed out to account for any changes that might occur between actual shipment items and rolls listed on the original packing list. Upon supervisor approval of the revision(s), the packing list is closed, and final details of the shipment are transmitted to the company's host computer where the input is automatically prepared for invoicing and adjustments are made to the inventory database.

The result of the computerized shipping system is that time-consuming paper preparation and error-prone manual handling in product selection from inventory has been eliminated. Packing lists and shipping labels are accurately and efficiently prepared, and outgoing product is now moving from inventory on a strictly systematic first-in/first-out basis.

The initial software program developed for Hollingsworth and Vose took about one and a half years to place on line. The final program, which covered reorganization of Hollingsworth and Vose's physical inventories, required two months to develop and install.

Hollingsworth and Vose's previous inventory method was to organize teams to manually sift through as many as 7,000 different rolls of paper held in the main inventory area or in conversion holding stations. An inventory summary was then prepared from these team reports and entered into the host computer. This data produced a record of inconsistencies that was reconciled to develop a current inventory database for the company.

Today, the system uses portable terminals and scanners, reducing inventory time to a fraction of the time required under the old system. The bar code labels on the rolls in inventory are scanned, and the information is stored in the portable terminals. This data is uploaded to the shipping PC and a printout of discrepancies follows. The company is now able to reconcile the inventory database with far less effort, far greater speed, and considerably higher reliability.

In early 1990, Hollingsworth and Vose was in the process of installing similar handling systems in its New York plant. Although the basic virtues of the parent plant system are incorporated in New York, some variations were required because of the essential differences in the types of papers produced. The New York plant tested its program to determine what revisions might work better for it. Similar handling, shipping, and physical inventory plans are set for other Hollingsworth and Vose locations.

Implementation of these new computerized handling systems has permitted Hollingsworth and Vose operations personnel to concentrate on other facets of production. Bar code technology has speeded product handling through the plant, firmed shipping procedures, and introduced new levels of accuracy in the company's inventory system. These benefits have already turned up notable savings in overhead costs as well.

Reports produced by the system's PC computers have been invaluable to supervisors operating on the plant floor in establishing up-to-date information on product flow and product locations when this is a requirement.

14.8 - RF Data Collection at James River

This application example is edited from "The Real-Time Payoff" by Paul Susca, which appeared in the February 1990 issue of ID Systems *magazine.*

The paper industry can be very demanding on automation equipment. Even specialty paper mills produce 15 to 20 tons of paper each hour, 24 hours a day, 7 days a week. System failures cause production stoppage, which can cost companies hundreds of thousands of dollars per hour in lost profits.

In late 1988, the James River Corporation installed a $1.4 million system that captures orders; schedules paper machines, coating machines, and other production steps; keeps track of work in process; and generates shipping and invoicing documents. Relying on a system of mobile bar code terminals linked by radio frequency (RF) to the system's mainframe, the production Management System is estimated to save $750,000 per year for the user.

James River operates a 350- to 400-ton-per-day specialty paper mill in Parchment, Michigan. Because the mill processes many small (40,000- to 80,000-pound) orders, keeping track of work in process with a manual system was often cumbersome.

The Code 39 label on each roll of James River paper encodes a nine-digit number, the content of which is specified by the Technical Association of the Pulp and Paper Industry (TAPPI). Using a bar code marked TAPPI standard roll number to identify each roll, the new tracking and scheduling system has ensured accuracy of loading, reduced labor requirements, reduced trim losses due to better scheduling of equipment, and cut work-in-process inventory by $300,000, according to Mark Nelson, industrial systems engineer for James River. James River's customers also can use the label to scan each roll into their own inventory, but the TAPPI number is more than a serial number. Those nine digits include the mill identifier, month, day, and machine it came from, reel, set number, and roll position.

"Reel," "set," and "roll" all have specific meanings in the paper industry, Nelson explained. A reel of paper is wound up directly on the paper machine. The reel is usually the full width of the paper machine and may be four to ten feet in diameter. The reel is then placed in a winder and cut down to customer specifications. For example, a customer may order 40-inch diameter rolls, 35 inches in width. A reel 56 inches in diameter will contain two sets of 40-inch diameter rolls. A set of paper may contain four 35-inch rolls if the width of the machine is 140 inches. For quality tracking purposes, the reel, the set, and the position the roll came from in the set are contained in the TAPPI roll number.

Because paper conditions change slightly during a production run, the user—a printing company, for example—may wish to use the paper in the order in which it came off the machine, so that the printing presses have to be adjusted only gradually to accommodate slight variations in such parameters as paper caliper and moisture content. Using the TAPPI code, the customer can tell where the rolls came from on the original reel, in what order they were produced, and which ones are most alike.

The printer's decision making is aided by the TAPPI roll number and other roll characteristic information printed out on the label. The printer can also use a peel-off tab that has the roll number printed on it to control inventory and production.

In the future, Nelson said, the production management system will be tied to on-line sensing equipment on the paper machines and quality information from the company's laboratories. This will allow instant access to moisture information, basis weight, and caliper profiles of the reel, set, and individual rolls produced. Nelson foresees the time when technical and quality control representatives, when responding to customer complaints, will take laptop PCs into customers' plants and obtain quality information via telephone lines from James River's minicomputer.

The use of bar codes begins at the winders, where paper comes off the machines and is first wound into rolls, and a TAPPI-standard roll number is applied. Nine Zebra Z-130 printers generate the bar code tags. Fixed-mount CRT terminals with Symbol Technologies LS 7000 laser scanners read the tags as the rolls go through the production equipment and when they are moved from the production machines to the wrap line. When rolls reach the wrap line they get a second label, generated by a Printronix P 600, applied on the outside of the wrapping, with the bar code marked and human-readable TAPPI roll number along with human-readable customer information.

That's where the LXE radio frequency terminals take over. There are hardwired terminals throughout the mill, but as the rolls move to different locations, they don't always go to another piece of machinery. They may go to small storage areas, and it's physically impossible to wire up enough terminals in enough locations throughout the mill to be able to record the movement of the rolls. In addition, the people who need to record the movement of the rolls are themselves mobile.

The radio frequency portion of the system is used to track rolls of paper from the production line to the loading dock. The RF system comprises a redundant LXE 120 RFU/CIU (radio frequency unit/computer interface unit), antenna and base station, and 12 mobile/portable units. Seven of the remote units are LXE 1140 terminals equipped with "chiclets" keyboards and 4-line by 40-character displays, mounted on lift trucks. The five portable units are handheld LXE 2140 terminals with Symbol LS 8500 laser scanners.

The mobiles (forklift mounted terminals) do not use bar codes. The reason truck operators do not use the scanners, Nelson said, is because the units have a maximum range of three feet, given the maximum size bar code that may appear on the package. "It's very difficult to scan rolls while you're sitting on a lift truck," he said. "If they had one that scans ten feet, we'd be all set."

Lift truck drivers type into the system where they are located. In real time, just as though the operator were using a fixed CRT terminal, the system checks to see which roll has been sitting there the longest. The 4-line by 40-character display on the terminal then tells the truck operator which nearby rolls need to be moved, based on a first-in/first-out algorithm. Drivers have the option of accepting the instructions or changing them to move rolls that are more accessible, for example. The truck operator will move the rolls and type in where he has moved the rolls to, using a three-character code or "bay location" that corresponds to a department, warehouse, and specific area.

The handheld terminals are mainly used by loadsmen in the shipping department. "The loadsman will have a couple of drivers loading for him," Nelson explained. "He will have his pick list of where the orders are located. He will type his load plan into his handheld terminal and begin scanning rolls, because he knows they're all in bay Z-4, for example."

In addition to shipping and moving inventory within the mill, the radio terminals are also used to scan rolls when workers are searching for a missing roll. "We see a roll lying around somewhere, and we don't know what it's for. We just scan it (to find out) where it's supposed to be," Nelson said. The system tells much more than where the roll belongs: It also displays the customer name, the width, diameter, weight, quality status, and production state of the roll.

The automated inventory tracking system was several years in coming, according to Nelson. James River started around the beginning of 1987 with the concept for the system. After a survey of possible vendors, company analysts "hit the problem hard" in mid-1988, drawing up a design and specifications for the system. The mainframe was installed in August of that year, Nelson said, and a detailed design for the bar code system followed. In October, LXE arrived to install the RF system and train the workers. "The LXE equipment came in really fast," Nelson said. "Within two weeks we were up and running."

Rather than implementing the new system in phases, the systems integrator cut it over in one day in December 1988, and it has been running non-stop since then. James River ran the old, manual system concurrently with the new system for about a week, but quickly dropped the manual system because it was such a headache to reconcile the two systems, since the manual system was three days behind the computer.

One challenging aspect of implementing the all-new tracking system was training the mill's 200 workers who would use the system. Of those, about 60 workers were trained to use the bar code system. To prepare for training, James River set up the new equipment a month and a half before cutting over the system to encourage workers to play with the equipment and become familiar with it. The formal phase of training involved small classes of four to five workers at a time, with individuals averaging about six hours in classes. Some workers picked up the new system quickly, having PCs of their own at home, and many workers were already familiar with information flows through the mill. Aspects of the system that required additional training included conserving batteries in the handheld units, replacing and recharging batteries, and using the right motion when scanning tags.

Nelson has been pleased with how LXE's RF equipment has held up. There were some minor problems early on such as blown fuses, but LXE repaired or replaced the units within two or three days, he said.

Other problems with the handheld terminals, also limited to the shakedown period, were attributed to rough treatment of the units. The only major item that failed was a computer interface unit which was replaced within a week. Still, the CIU failure did not disrupt the system because of its totally redundant architecture.

Each major part of the system is installed in pairs. Mobile units are linked by radio frequency to a pair of identical RFUs. Both RFUs are hardwired to both CIUs, which are connected to the computer. The computer is a Stratus fault-tolerant mainframe. If any component fails, the computer automatically switches over to the backup part and telephones the factory for a replacement.

The systems integrator said, "Every time we put in one of these systems it tends to be a heart-stopping event just because cutover has to be very quick and concise, and there's no going back. You just pick the day and an hour and say as of that moment we're running on the new system."

The LXE portion of the $1.4 million system cost around $80,000. Besides saving James River an estimated $750,000 annually, $50,000 of which is the avoided carrying cost of reduced inventories, there have been other, less quantifiable benefits of the tracking system.

"For one thing, we are becoming aware of more (preexisting) problems now, just because it's a real-time system," Nelson said, "whereas with a manual system the problems just got buried, and three days later the crisis was over." Another benefit is that the mill's various departments have learned to work together better because they are all on the same system.

14.9 - RF Data Collection at Arkwright

This application example is edited from an article provided by the author and Norand Data Systems.

A manual warehouse inventory system at Arkwright—maker of specialty films for imaging devices—resulted in unnecessary ordering of raw materials and increased operating costs due to excess inventory and time spent tracking down misplaced inventory.

Because inventory at the Fiskeville, Rhode Island, company was often posted in an untimely fashion, double-posted, or not posted at all, the system had an accuracy rate of only about 65 percent.

In 1989, the company replaced its manual-entry computer system and implemented an inventory control system. Within the first year of use, Arkwright achieved a 98 percent inventory accuracy, reduced inventory costs, and reduced response time to fulfill manufacturing's requests for raw materials. Greater operating efficiencies resulted in better allocation of manpower, without the addition or elimination of any jobs.

Using Symbol Technologies LS 7000 II and LS 8100 laser scanners, purchase orders are scanned at the receiving dock for purchase order number, product code, quantity, and vendor's lot code; the information is input directly into the inventory control system designed by Q.E.D. Systems via Norand RT 2210 radio frequency (RF) terminals.

The on-line, portable RF terminals provide real-time data communications, directing employees to open locations for incoming materials, generating paperless pick lists, and transferring materials from warehouse to manufacturing inventories.

Arkwright, a wholly owned subsidiary of the giant Oce' Van Der Girten N.V., stocks about 4,500 different products, and all of them are tracked with the RF system. "The RF system provides an accurate record and a handle on what we have in our raw materials warehouse," says Joe Raviele, distribution and warehouse manager.

Under the old system, employees wrote up inventory sheets on the warehouse floor, and later keyed the information on the inventory sheets into the Honeywell DPS-4 mainframe computer. The two-day lag between the written reports and computer entry, as well as entry errors, reduced accuracy and lowered response time to manufacturing's demand for raw materials.

Now, after the inventory is received, a Code 39 trace label is attached to each pallet. The bar codes are printed on a Monarch Marking thermal-transfer printer, Model 9440, on label stock purchased from Image Scan. The labels are a 2-mil polyester matter film which is then printed and over-laminated with a 2-mil clear polyester film.

The trace code stays with the pallet until all the inventory on that pallet has been dispersed. When the product is moved into the warehouse, the operator scans the trace code and the location code, updating the information via the RF terminal.

The terminals are linked via Ultra-High Frequency (UHF) radio waves to a Norand RB2212 base station, which serves as a receiver/transmitter. The base station is plugged into a Norand RM2216 communications multiplexer which directs the traffic to and from each user's RF terminal. The multiplexer connects via cable to an Acer 386 Model 1100/25 personal computer. An RF driver program in the PC generates terminal prompts and updates the database file in real time, as the user inputs responses on his terminal.

Before the manufacturing scheduler releases orders to the factory floor, he checks the inventory for material availability. The supervisor then determines what quantities of materials are needed in the next 24 hours. Using the RF system, he is able to order specific inventory for each line, indicating whether he wants the inventory delivered in the morning or afternoon.

Materials are allocated on a first-in/first-out basis, and the computer-generated pick list selects products according to the most efficient travel route through the warehouse. Each pick list is assigned a requisition number.

When an employee takes the requisition number and signs on to the RF terminal, he is directed through the warehouse, making picks that the computer has selected. At the same time, a paper pick list is printed out on an NEC Pinwriter P5300 printer connected to the Acer PC.

If the material selected by the computer requires a substantial amount of material handling, employees have the option of overriding a computer pick. An exception report is printed in the supervisor's office, alerting the supervisor to any inventory discrepancies, the fact that the employee overrode the computer-directed pick, or other problems. To double-check accuracy, the system also requires a random cycle count on every tenth pick.

Arkwright also has improved response time to manufacturing requests for materials. "Because of inaccurate inventory records, employees would have to walk the warehouse looking for missing product. It could take as long as two hours to locate a requested product that wasn't where our records said it was," explains Raviele. "Now, we can solve a problem in about 20 minutes."

Another problem Arkwright faced was product package obsolescence with the private-label products it manufactures for other firms. "Any time a company wanted to change its package graphics, we needed to supply it with an accurate count of inventory on hand. Often, we would have more, or less, product on hand than what inventory records showed.

"Now, when packaging changes occur, we can give the company an accurate count of what we have in stock."

Before purchasing the Norand system, Raviele and other company officials considered a batch system. Arkwright retained the author and his firm, Q.E.D. Systems of Cedar Rapids, Iowa, as consultants, who recommended purchasing an RF system because of the added benefit of real-time data collection and the ability to provide "control systems" with real-time software versus "reporting systems" available in batch terminal configurations. The recommended hardware was from Norand. The software and data collection configurations were designed and supplied by Q.E.D. Systems.

Q.E.D. Systems also recommended contacting all of Arkwright's suppliers to inform them that Arkwright desired to utilize bar code technology and that future shipments to Arkwright should have bar codes on the packaging, using FACT data identifiers, and in a Code 39 symbology. Many of Arkwright's suppliers were large chemical and film companies, much larger than Arkwright, and it was a concern that such large companies would not be receptive to marking product for Arkwright. Suppliers were asked to provide markings in industry and national standards formats, ANS MH10.8M and FACT-1, and it turned out that response was positive and quick.

"In addition to having up-to-date information all the time, we liked the idea that the RF system allows information to be available to everyone who needs it," says Raviele.

Prior to installation, employees were given a four-hour group training session provided by Q.E.D. Systems. They also had follow-up sessions after they began using the equipment. "They were very willing to learn about the system," says Raviele. "They were very receptive to the new equipment, and recognized it as an improvement over the old system of keying the information manually."

The inventory control system has been in place for several years, and the company is planning to expand the system into the product distribution center later this year. Arkwright plans to upgrade the warehouse system to include the Norand RT3210 hand-held terminals for the warehouse to track drums and bags of chemicals used to produce its polyester film coating.

The current expansion plans are part of a three-year program to implement bar code technology plant-wide. The next installation is planned for the work-in-process area, followed by the coating area, which will have hardwired fixed units. The third phase will bring the final packaging area and the physical distribution center on-line. "The goal is to have the entire factory—receiving, manufacturing, and shipping—on-line with bar code technology by 1992," says Raviele.

Bar code technology has many applications, but Raviele recommends starting small. "Take an area where you can install a pilot system. If your first implementation goes well, then you know you're going to have the support, dollars, and acceptance across the board from everyone. Then you can go ahead and look at other applications."

14.10 - EDI keeps Trading Partners Talking
...with International Jensen

This application example is edited from "EDI Keeps Trading Partners Talking" by James Bert, which appeared in the March 1990 issue of ID Systems *magazine.*

In 1985, a consumer electronics firm was buried by its daily flow of paperwork. The problem was severe enough to compromise the company's customer relations and internal operations. But by converting much of that paperwork into electronic data, loudspeaker manufacturer International Jensen of Chicago found a solution to its "paper chase" problems.

Using electronic data interchange (EDI), which replaces paper purchasing and invoicing documents with comparable computer-based records sent via networks, Jensen was able to make significant customer service and operations gains. These included reduced trading document errors; a substantial annual decrease in inventory costs; and better anticipation of, and ability to fulfill, customer needs.

Jensen, founded over 60 years ago, has a high volume of sales transactions—each requiring numerous training documents. The company's sales come from two major market areas, retail and automotive, each with subsets. Jensen sells its retail line to mass merchandisers, audio installers, and automotive sound shops, and its OEM loudspeaker line to auto manufacturers and automotive sound shops.

Five years ago, Thomas Bihun, Jensen's management information systems director, started looking at how his organization was doing business and how it could be improved. Bihun's chief concern was that the large amount of routine trading paperwork—particularly purchase orders and advance shipping notices—was hurting Jensen's customer relations and internal efficiency. With 20 years of industry background in production and inventory management, Bihun is an expert in overhauling manufacturing activities.

At the time Bihun was studying Jensen's operations, electronic data interchange was limited primarily to large mass merchandisers and auto manufacturers and a few key suppliers, known as trading partners. Jensen was selling to Kmart, one of the early EDI users, and Bihun noticed a repeated paperwork crunch with this particular customer. Each quarter, Kmart placed 2,000 loudspeaker orders for a store-wide promotion with Jensen, and each quarter Jensen was backlogged entering these orders into its computer. To break the purchase order logjam, Bihun decided to try EDI. Transferring all of Kmart's purchase orders onto the new system required Jensen to write proprietary EDI management software to handle the task of receiving and translating data coming from Kmart's mainframe computer over a network into Jensen's IBM System/38, Model 700. However, once the EDI software was written, Jensen was able to reduce the onerous order-entry process from as much as 10 days to less than one day, as well as virtually eliminating the costly errors associated with this high volume task.

Bihun could see the time and error-saving benefits of the Kmart conversion immediately, so he began to expand Jensen's EDI links to other customers. Ford was added, and again Jensen developed specialized software to accommodate the customer's hardware and network requirements.

This second EDI software development effort made it clear that reinventing the wheel for each customer's purchase order conversion was costly. So when the American

National Standards Institute's X12 standard governing EDI trading documents and software was published, Bihun began the search for an off-the-shelf software package that would support the new standards and meet his company's EDI needs.

After reviewing the software available for mini-computers, Bihun consulted his counterpart at Samsonite (both were subsidiaries of Beatrice Companies, Inc., at that time). Samsonite was successfully using EDI software for its mid-range computers from ACS Network Systems. Paper use at Samsonite's Denver headquarters had been cut by two-thirds, largely because of the company's use of EDI. Based on Samsonite's experience, Bihun purchased the ACS EDI software.

The EDI software runs on Jensen's IBM System/38 and serves its Lincolnshire, Illinois, headquarters; three manufacturing plants in the East; and the Midwest, East Coast, and West Coast distribution warehouses.

The electronic data interchange software (EDI/38) provides Jensen with the ability to send and receive trading documents in electronic form on a variety of EDI networks, such as OrderNet, McDonnell Douglas, and Sears. It also translates incoming documents from the ANS X12 standard into language that Jensen's System/38 can understand and handles the reverse translation process for outbound documents. In short, it serves as the interface for Jensen to the entire EDI process.

In addition, Jensen's EDI management software instantly updates all customer purchase order and advance shipping notice information to the company's manufacturing resources planning application. EDI-transmitted orders, once picked up from Jensen's trading partners, are entered into the manufacturing resources planning customer order file automatically, without the need to rekey.

According to Mark Carlile, Jensen's programmer who works daily with EDI, "The combination of the ACS software, our System/38 hardware, and the ANSI standards has made EDI easy for us. The EDI/38 software allows us to set up new trading partners quickly, with a minimum of programming. As a programmer without any formal background in EDI technology, I have been able to accomplish daily transmissions and tracking with ease."

Carlile also finds many ease-of-use features inherent in the EDI software. For example, setting up data communications within applications can be complicated. With the EDI software there are just a few variables to define, and those are explained at each step in the process. Carlile also likes the way the EDI software offers dual display of data after an EDI document has been received. He finds that since the data can be displayed in untranslated ANSI standard as well as in the translation for Jensen's own system and applications, it allows for easy document tracking and problem solving.

Carlile noted that referring to published standards—in Jensen's case, ANS X12, VICS (Voluntary Inter-industry Communications Standards), and AIAG (Automotive Industry Action Group)—has been extremely helpful in getting his organization up and running in the electronic data interchange environment. Some of these organizations also sponsor annual seminars and conferences that Jensen personnel have attended for further technical information.

Once the EDI software was implemented, Jensen began to realize the full benefits of the program. These advantages have become clear as Bihun has monitored the conversion of nine customers to EDI over the past five years.

According to Bihun, "One of the most dramatic savings from our use of EDI was faster shipping turnaround time, going from 10 days to one. This saved us an average five days of inventory carrying costs."

EDI also helped Jensen prevent lost sales and at the same time improved customer relations. Through the instantaneous receipt of customer purchase orders via EDI, the manufacturer gained more lead time to anticipate and satisfy sudden changes in customer requirements. Electronic data interchange further enhanced Jensen's customer relations by literally putting more personnel into this area. When customer purchase order data entry was eliminated through EDI, two people previously engaged in that job were reassigned to customer service.

Jensen experienced another advantage due to its shift from hard copy to computer records. Bihun found that errors that came with rekeying information nearly disappeared due to the direct communication inherent in EDI. This saved Jensen headaches on two fronts: explaining errors and remedies to customers, and the actual cost of tracking down and fixing mistakes.

In adopting an ANSI standard software package, Jensen also had cost savings in retraining. Before using the ACS software, which not only addresses current standards, but also includes ongoing upgrades as standards evolve and new ones appear, Jensen had different EDI software for each trading partner. These software differences required expensive training of data processing personnel on each software package and lowered productivity due to the constant shift between programs. Now Jensen data processing personnel get very familiar with one EDI package. The result is that they are more efficient in their use of the software and relieved to be off an endless software learning curve.

Bihun's opinion of the direction EDI will take is upbeat. He said, "At this point, relatively few organizations know about EDI and its benefits. EDI is where bar code technology was five years ago. It's about to take off because the technology is getting faster and cheaper. When people realize this is the way to do business, and as more organizations adopt [advanced computer technology], we'll see companies putting their customers and transactions in EDI."

Where does Jensen fit into this picture of the future? Bihun plans to pursue the conversion of other trading documents, starting with the transmission of invoices, to EDI. He has already started the process with Jensen's electronic trading of advance shipping notices in the auto industry. He figures he should save his company invoicing costs of over $15,000 per year as well as increase Jensen's cash flow through faster payments. Jensen's customers will welcome electronic advance shipping notices, too, since this speeds up their advance shipping notice/physical shipment matching task and increases matching accuracy from the 80 percent range to 99+ percent.

Other possibilities for replacing paper with bytes at Jensen include the company sending its purchase orders to suppliers via EDI, and both sending and receiving all payments electronically using an EDI subset, electronic funds transfer.

With the ANS X12 standards in effect, Jensen will be converting its first EDI customer, Kmart, along with others, from proprietary EDI software to the less demanding standardized software.

Bihun summed up Jensen's gains from electronic data interchange with a single comment, "EDI has contributed to the growth of our business." And as it becomes the accepted way to trade, Jensen's early entry into paperless transactions will doubtless continue to help fuel its corporate growth and give Jensen a competitive edge.

...with Ford Motor Company

In early 1989, Ford Motor Company decided to implement electronic data interchange as part of its first experimental Just-In-Time plant in Lorain, Ohio. Just-In-Time's stellar reputation within American management circles comes from its extensive use in Japanese manufacturing operations, where inventory costs are driven down by the last-minute arrival of materials. Ford, seeking greater competitiveness, has led America's auto industry in adopting Just-In-Time.

When Ford opened its Just-In-Time plant, it needed the speed that EDI lent to supplier transactions to meet its rigorous new scheduling requirements. Working with Ford, Jensen modified its normal EDI operations. Since Ford's Just-In-Time plant runs with only four hours of line inventory, it required Jensen to transmit advance shipping notices—documents treated as invoices by automakers—within an hour of shipment (normal transmittal time is within 12 hours). The quick shipment advice facilitates the automaker's tight inventory time needs and saves Jensen considerable time with invoicing.

Other automakers will soon follow Ford's lead, if not in full Just-In-Time manufacturing, at least in requiring that their numerous material and component suppliers use EDI. And Jensen, having electronic trading relationships that also include Chrysler, Mazda, and Honda, is an EDI leader in its own right to the auto industry.

EDI Savings by Industry

Below is a list of estimated cost savings for selected industries that use EDI. These numbers are likely conservative since electronic data interchange affects many areas, such as improved customer service and internal communications, which are difficult to quantify yet streamline operations.

- Automotive: $200 per car, according to General Motors. Potential savings if the entire U.S. auto industry adopted EDI are estimated at $2 billion per year, based on postage/Telex and error reduction savings.
- Transportation: Navistar International Transportation Corporation reduced its rapid freight payments by 90 percent for annual savings of $4.5 million. The company also reduced its inventory by $167 million in the first 18 months of EDI usage.
- Retailing: Service Merchandise, a discount retailing chain, reduced its cost per purchase order by $25.
- Computer Industry: Hewlett-Packard returns 40 percent fewer raw material shipments.

14.11 - EPA Puts Paper in Its Place

This application example is edited from "EPA Puts Paper in Its Place" by Arthur Donner, which appeared in the October 1990 issue of ID Systems *magazine.*

Before the Environmental Protection Agency's Office of Pesticide Programs developed its own bar code-based tracking system, staff members were unable to immediately locate as many as 30 percent of their 50,000 pesticide registration documents.

The documents, heavy paper folders that each contain essential correspondence about a specific EPA-approved pesticide registration, are used to make regulatory decisions. Nine project management teams were responsible for them, and each team had its own method for filing their assigned documents. The files filled over 100 revolving cabinets, allotted to different work groups at four to six per group and located mostly in one room. Security was a problem since virtually anyone had access to these documents.

With this decentralized system, few documents could be located in a timely manner, even though many had to be retrieved quickly. Although the documents were supposed to be stored in order of their registration numbers, many were shelved out of order, and multiple volumes of the same document were numbered poorly or physically split apart and shelved randomly. When a document was needed, a staff member sometimes had to search through each of the cabinets, document by document, to find it. Since the documents were not systematically tracked, they were easily misplaced when they were circulated between different work groups and support data entry contractors. Sometimes it could take months to locate a document—if it was ever found.

Efforts to correct this problem through the normal fiscal budget planning process were unsuccessful. However, in 1987, former EPA administrator Lee Thomas initiated an agency-wide productivity improvement competition. At stake was a maximum $50,000 award to finance projects with a minimum payback of five percent. As head of the administrative processing section, Arthur Donner proposed creating a centralized library operation to make documents available to authorized users on demand. After consideration of alternative approaches, bar code technology proved the most cost-effective solution.

The total cost for the first year of the Pesticide Registration Document Tracking System (PRDTS) would be $120,000—$50,000 to come from the EPA competition and $70,000 from pesticide program funds. This estimate included equipment, software, furniture, preprinted bar code labels, labor for moving the large revolving cabinets, custom-made file folders, contract programming services, and support staff salaries. A net cost-avoidance savings of $150,000 over five years was projected, and at least a ten percent reduction in the current backlog of work. A panel of top EPA officials selected the bar code project as one of several proposals with high projected returns, and project go-ahead was received at the end of January 1988. All funds for the project's equipment, supplies, and materials had to be spent by September 1988.

For numerous reasons, it was determined that it would be more manageable and cost-effective to develop the document tracking system in-house. A formidable list of tasks and system requirements evolved both during and after implementation. The tracking system would be required to: associate a bar code number with a registration number, retrieve location information when a bar code is scanned, determine whether the user requesting the document is authorized to check it out, add and delete records to and from the database, periodically back up information during daily operations, implement recovery procedures in the event of system failure, conduct routine file cabinet audits, reserve documents in the file room for a defined or undefined period of time, and flag a checked-out document to note that a requestor is awaiting its return.

A project milestone chart was used to organize activities in order of priority and to set dates for completing them. The milestone chart was particularly beneficial when organizing concurrent tasks and determining what tasks were contingent on the completion of the preceding ones. The chart served to identify, along with the tasks, the organizational units responsible for them. Without the planning and organization provided through the milestone chart, the conversion and implementation would undoubtedly have met with delays, conflicts, and obstacles. User suggestions and wide involvement during the project were encouraged. Openness, patience, and sharing responsibilities went a long way toward quickly and efficiently solving problems.

To develop PRDTS, systems analyst Reza Beheshti used Blaise Computing C Tools Plus/5.0, Fair Com C-Tree, and Roundhill Panel/QC. Utility software packages Advanced Norton Utilities and Fastback Compression Software are used routinely. Several software packages make up the engine of the document-tracking system: Ashton-Tate's dBase III+, Nantucket's Clipper, Microsoft's C Optimizing Compiler, and Quick C Version 2.0. Worthington Data Solutions' Label-RIGHT software is used to produce on-demand dot-matrix impact bar code labels and laser bar code labels on a Hewlett-Packard Laser Jet II printer. Data Document Systems furnished the preprinted bar code labels.

Several vendors were interviewed, and Intermec's bar code products were settled on since they offered the technical capability the system required. An Intermec 9570 bar code wedge reader was installed between the keyboard and an Epson Equity III+ personal computer equipped with a 30MB Seagate internal drive and a 56MB external drive. Three Intermec Model 9440 portable terminals equipped with 512K of RAM, high capacity NiCad battery packs, high density bar code wands, carrying cases, and Intermec's PC-IRL programming software were purchased.

Conversion began with three months of in-house programming support, but competing and higher priority demands on the programmer stretched the completion time to August 1989, about one year from the project's inception. Estimated time for the initial three library staff members to convert the 50,000 documents that were currently in-house was a year.

In December 1988, Congress established an annual pesticide registration maintenance fee, with the first fees due on March 1, 1989. Companies did not pay maintenance fees for about 21,000 registrations, and as a result they were cancelled. In June 1989, management decided that it made both program and economical sense to simultaneously retire the 21,000 documents and convert the remaining 29,000 documents to the automated tracking system. Completion of the software, retirement of the 21,000 canceled documents, converting, shelving, and inventorying of the 29,000 remaining documents, uploading of the system, staff training, and formal operation of PRDTS was required to be completed by August 1989.

With management and staff help, converting documents to the new system took seven weeks: two weeks of planning, three weeks of converting and refiling documents, and two weeks to tie up loose ends and load data. The file room was closed, and most operations were limited or suspended for about two weeks. Approximately 100 staff members were recruited for the accelerated implementation of PRDTS.

Personnel searched through the file room cabinets and personal office cabinets and desk drawers to identify documents for retirement or retention. The 21,000 retired documents were sent to the Federal Record Center for final storage. Staff members then affixed preprinted bar code labels to the custom-made document folders and transferred the contents of the retained documents to the bar code marked folders. Bar code labels were also added to the employee badges of authorized users. Each of the cabinet shelves was partitioned into three sections, and each section was assigned a bar code label.

Because staff members had become unable to access their documents for almost three weeks, pressure existed to start operations, and the library opened two weeks early on August 15, 1989. For a few weeks, the staff maintained both manual and automated systems. As demand and dependence on the automated tracking system increased, significant system bugs surfaced. On opening day, the computer system was missing several features and was not fully tested. However, each of the battery-powered portable terminals had enough memory and could assume basic transactions when the PC-based system failed. The software is now stable, and the system is fully functioning.

It now takes only a few minutes to key a document number into the system, print out the location information, retrieve the document from a cabinet shelf, and update PRDTS. If the documents have already left the room, the system reports back instantly with the name and telephone number of the user that has the document checked out.

Users now leave written requests for documents with the library staff, and the librarians fill requests in the order received, except for those that are emergency/health-hazard related—those requests are filled immediately.

To locate a document on the file room shelves, a library worker keys its regulatory case number into the system. PRDTS then produces a printout with the bar code numbers of the regulatory case and the shelf it is stored on, plus a brief description or message. When the requested documents are pulled from the shelves, they are held in the library until requestors, who have been summoned by telephone, can pick them up—usually within a couple of hours of submitting the requests.

Users, who are required to have a proper clearance and a bar code label affixed to their EPA badges, must present their badges when picking up their documents. The librarian selects the check-out function on the PC menu and scans the document and badge bar code labels. The PC database is verified and updated before the documents are released to the requestors.

In like manner, when a user wishes to transfer a document to another authorized staff person or contractor, he or she completes a written transfer request and gives it to the library staff along with the folder. The user to whom the file is transferred must present his badge when picking up the document. The librarian selects the document transfer function on the PC menu and scans the document and badge bar codes to update the database.

When a document is returned to the library, the librarian selects the check-in function from the PC menu. The document bar code and the bar code of a temporary storage location (a book cart) are scanned, and the temporary location information is updated on the PC. When the cart is full, the documents are reshelved randomly wherever shelf space is available. The librarian then uses the portable terminal to scan the document and the shelf location bar code labels. The information stored in the portable terminal is transferred to the PC via a cable, and a menu command on the PC initiates the update of the database.

PRDTS maintains a database of 29,824 documents, and staff members process over 1,000 document in/out transactions per day. The capabilities of PRDTS have been expanded since installation. Enhanced features include the ability to generate bar code labels from the system's menu, restore and reindex files automatically, create an ASCII file from the different category types to upload and compare to mainframe records, a "flag" feature to identify requested documents as they are returned to the file room, and the ability to generate additional management reports.

To verify PRDTS data, each of the 65 cabinets is inventoried once a month using the portable terminals. The inventory function is selected from an opening menu displayed on the portable's screen, and the bar code labels on the document folders and on their shelf are scanned. When the portable reaches its capacity (495 records), the data is uploaded to the database. The inventory, which takes about 34 hours each month, would not have been possible before conversion to PRDTS.

A document "checked out" verification report is periodically prepared by the system and distributed to each staff person who currently holds documents from the file room, listing only the documents held by that staff person, and how long they have been checked out.

Efforts are under way to move the system to a recently installed IBM Token Ring LAN. Users will eventually be able to request documents from terminals at their workstations. To access PRDTS, a user will scan the bar code label on his identification badge with a bar code reader at his terminal.

Excluding the salaries for library staff, one-time project cost was about $75,000. Presently four library staff members are employed at a cost of about $85,000 per year. Their duties have recently been expanded to include document maintenance activities.

The in/out rate of documents has increased significantly since the conversion to PRDTS. Documents can now be located readily and are immediately accessible for checkout to a user. Only authorized personnel are permitted access to the file room, improving security and decreasing the chance that documents will be lost or misfiled. Based on experiences to date, productivity has been improved in many operating areas and staff morale is up.

Receiving the $50,000 award was critical to the success of PRDTS, not only because it helped to finance the project, but because it guaranteed management commitment. A lot of people invested a great deal of effort in the conversion, but it was management support that turned it into a case study in successful productivity improvement.

14.12 - Hospital Uses Bar Codes for Fast, Accurate Test Results

This application example is edited from "Bar Code Assures Error-Free Blood Tests" by Rick Gregory, which appeared in the April 1991 issue of ID Systems *magazine.*

At Baltimore's Good Samaritan Hospital, a fully automated clinical chemistry laboratory system frees technologists from the drudgery of paperwork, eliminates error, and at the same time cuts turnaround time for reporting tests results almost in half. Beginning when tests are ordered, through identification of the sample, to reporting the results, the entire information flow has been automated.

"Bar coding and the bidirectional interface are the keys to full lab automation. Together they guarantee quick, accurate specimen identification and communication of test results that no manual system could possibly match," said Dr. Sheldon Glusman, chief pathologist. "The techs' work here used to be paper-pushing," admitted Glusman. "Now they're able to follow up on specimens, concentrate on the data, and evaluate it. They're finally able to do what technologists are supposed to do."

At the heart of the change are the hospital's two Kodak Ektachem 700XR analyzers and a lab computer system from Rubicon Corporation, complete with a bidirectional interface that software vendor Rubicon and the hospital developed together.

The route a sample takes these days is virtually error-free. A nurse orders a battery of tests for a patient by logging the order into the hospital's main computer system. The hospital information system downloads that information to the lab computer. It, in turn, generates a bar code label that identifies the patient, the sample, the tests to be run, and whether the request is STAT or routine. Three Zebra 130 thermal transfer demand printers—one in the lab and two at remote phlebotomy stations—are used to print the labels using both Code 39 and Codabar.

For routine testing, the labels are held in queue for batch draws by phlebotomists every two hours beginning at dawn. For STAT tests, the label is immediately turned over to a phlebotomist who draws the patient sample and returns it to the lab for testing.

When the sample reaches the lab, a clerk verifies specimen receipt by the lab in the computer and double checks the specimen number, which automatically downloads testing data for that sample to the analyzers. "We used to have to enter all that information manually," explained Janet Miller, systems manager for the lab. "Now the clerk just centrifuges the sample and puts it on the analyzer."

The Ektachem analyzer reads the Code 39 bar code label on a tube using a built-in infrared scanner and immediately matches its ID with a list of tests to be completed. It completes a routine chemistry profile of 17 tests in under 10 minutes, then uploads the results to the lab's computer. The technologist reviews the results, checks for unusual values, and releases them to the main hospital computer. They immediately become available for viewing on computer terminals throughout the hospital.

In addition, lab personnel call the appropriate nursing station to warn about "panic" values. For STAT tests, the system prints results at the nursing station where the test was ordered within three minutes after releasing results.

The hospital has also acquired a Sysmex NE 8000 hematology analyzer which reads Codabar bar codes using a photographic reader. Both Code 39 and Codabar are printed by the Zebra printers on one label packet for one patient order.

The most important benefit of the system is accuracy. "Our new system eliminates the transcription errors that have always plagued clinical laboratories," said Dr. Glusman.

In addition to the computer communication links, two factors make that possible. The first is positive sample identification—achieved in this case through bar coding. From the time the computer generates a bar code label for a particular sample, only that label identifies the sample; neither nurses nor lab personnel need to key in a number or name again. The bar code label that is applied to a sample at the patient's bedside by the phlebotomist identifies the sample during its entire trip through the lab.

The success of positive sample identification depends in turn on another feature, primary container sampling (PCS). In other words, the container in which a sample is collected is the same container a technologist loads into the analyzer for testing. PCS eliminates most aliquoting, which is pipet transfer of serum or plasma to another test tube. "Prior to our current analyzers, every sample had to be aliquoted and labeled for primary chemistry analysis," noted Astrida Eramanis, technical coordinating supervisor in the lab. "All the STATs were aliquoted too, because we sent them to a separate STAT lab."

Now, she said, primary containers are loaded directly into the analyzer for both the STAT and the routine tests. The hospital has eliminated the STAT lab; today it can process STATs just as quickly on the main laboratory's analyzers. In addition, because the analyzers consolidate tests that were previously run on five different instruments, samples rarely need to be split in the lab. Those few samples that require testing on another instrument may still not need to be aliquoted, thanks to the lab's speedier handling.

"We'll share a tube rather than an aliquote because the Ektachem analyzer handles it so quickly," explained Ermanis. "Even with our large batch draws in the morning, specimens that arrive in the lab by 7 a.m. have been run by 8:30."

Equally important is the speed at which the automated data transfer takes place. Bidirectional communications between the laboratory information system and analyzer allow results to be uploaded immediately after completion of the test. Thanks to yet another communications link, the lab computer posts STAT results on the mainframe computer for terminal viewing three minutes after the technologist reviews and releases them.

The lab now guarantees STAT results in an hour, but more often they are available in 20 to 30 minutes. Routine results are available on computer terminals in under two hours, or roughly half the pre-bar code turnaround time.

"Faster turnaround permits the physician to make judgments about other tests he or she may want to order in light of the information just received, and it allows that to occur during the same day, maximizing the value of the time the physician spends in the hospital," said Glusman.

Glusman envisions "reflex test ordering" as the next step. An abnormal test result would automatically trigger the running of a second test or battery of tests, usually from the same sample, and possibly while the sample is still in the analyzer. "Such automatic decision loops for ordering tests will accelerate diagnosis and decision making even more," he said. "Improvements like these go beyond simply improving convenience and efficiency. They ultimately mean we can provide better care."

14.13 - Bar Codes and Natural Resource Management

This application example is edited from "Bar Codes and Natural Resource Management" by Kimberly Hymas, which appeared in the May 1991 issue of ID Systems *magazine.*

> By conducting a national biodiversity inventory and disseminating its information, we will be the first tropical country to deliberately set out to put its native biological wealth to intellectual and economic work for society. As we pursue the project, we will develop local abilities that we will share with other neighboring tropical regions. In this manner, we confront the gravest threat of this and the next century—the potential loss of the extraordinary biodiversity of the tropics. Simultaneously, we promote the growth of a society whose ethical and moral values are rooted in respect for nature and the wise management of natural resources."
>
> Dr. Daniel Janzen

What began as a pastime for two people over 10 years ago is now a project involving several countries, employing dozen of workers, and shaping the future biological wealth of a country.

Dr. Daniel Janzen, a professor and researcher at the University of Pennsylvania, and his wife Winnie Hallwachs, began collecting moths as a pastime while working in Costa Rica in 1978. As their part-time project grew, Janzen and Hallwachs decided to collect more moths and track the entire moth fauna in their area. Their work eventually involved the assistance of taxonomists from museums all over the country. Many of these professionals urged them to increase the scope of the project and include the entire moth fauna of Costa Rica to help understand the country's ecosystems.

"Ecosystems are made of species and their interactions, and species come from genes," says Janzen. "These genes, species, and ecosystems are all parts that depend on each other. We must be concerned with each of the parts—and how they interact—if the ecosystems are to form a viable part of the national and international resource management scheme for Costa Rica."

Tropical Costa Rica, with its varied topography and geology, and its seasonal and rainforest climates, is extremely rich in species and habitats—among the richest in the world for its small size. Spread among the major tropical habitats of Costa Rica are at least a half million species.

"Almost all of this biological wealth has been conserved in 25 percent of the country in national parks and equivalent reserves," says Janzen. "However, we understand only a minute fraction of the species. What they eat, what they make, how they do what they do, how they can fit into the agroecosystem diversification that Costa Rica must sustain—all of these things are unopened books, written in strange languages. For Costa Rica's socioeconomic survival, and for Costa Rica's mutualism with the world, the books need to be opened and the language learned. Only in this way can we protect, manage, and develop the social benefits of Costa Rica's conserved wildlands."

With funding from the National Science Foundation, Janzen's project eventually grew.

"It became evident in 1989 that the question of understanding in Costa Rica required an institutional home," says Janzen. "Out of this came the National Biodiversity Institute."

For years, national and private institutions have been engaging in efforts to understand biodiversity. The National Biodiversity Institute (INBio), located in San Jose, Costa Rica, was established to help in its understanding and disseminate that information. The INBio is now working to unite the efforts and resources of these individual factions to create a national biodiversity. The organization anticipates a national inventory within ten years through major funding and ongoing organization and dissemination of this valuable information.

Information gathered from the INBio research is shared with various groups including government and natural resource planners, educational institutions, agriculture and forestry planners, ecotourism representatives, scientific researchers, medical researchers, biochemical professionals for commercial application, public information service representatives, and museum curators.

In order to disseminate the information the National Biodiversity Institute was gathering, a process for tracking this unique inventory had to be established. "In 1989 we were standing in a Philadelphia supermarket watching the checkout process," says Janzen. "We decided at that time that bar code data collection was what we needed to track our growing inventory of insects." Dr. Janzen's lab assistant, Julie Papp, contacted Intermec Corporation and began the process.

Intermec had previously aided in the development of the well-known pollination research honeybee tracking solution, so a request for tracking an insect inventory seemed almost routine. Figure 14.4 shows examples of this use of bar codes.

"When we started the labeling portion of the bar code project, we had two criteria for the labels," said Janzen. "The first was the label had to be absolutely indestructible. The second was that the label had to fit on the insect. With 5 million insects to track, we do not have extra room for labels that are larger than the insects."

While Janzen was visiting with colleagues from the National Museum, he realized that plant specimens around the world were also being tracked with bar code labels, not that the various systems being used were to be compatible. None of the numbering systems had a prefix to identify which museum the samples came from. Janzen realized that would lead to potential difficulties should these institutions need to share information in the future. "I questioned how a computer would recognize the difference between the insect and plant identification numbers—and the museums as well," says Janzen.

Code 49 provided the labeling answer Janzen was looking for. It allowed for the encoding within a bar code of 9 digits, 6 alpha codes, the option for an additional row if needed, and both a numeric and machine-readable prefix. Janzen's requirement for an indestructible label was met with a polyester label. "I took the sample label and did everything possible to destroy it," says Janzen. "The polyester label withstood my testing and proved to be exactly what we needed."

Janzen's order was the largest single-shipment, preprint order Intermec had ever had with a total cost for hardware and preprinted tags for 1.5 million labels of less than $20, 000. The solution proved to be a very cost-effective way to track such a large inventory.

Questions of the correct physical size and configuration, symbology, density, and human-readable content still had to be addressed. Many proofs were printed and tested in the process. The result was a tag that met all aspects of the customer's system requirements.

For Janzen, the importance of having an accurate tracking system was critical. "Unlike a product from a manufacturing environment, the information entered on the insects cannot be corroborated by the end users, so there is no way of knowing whether or not an error has been made when recording the data," says Janzen. "The system is set up so that there will never be a duplicate number. We have been programming the computer to record data blocks that are the same, while assigning a different number for each specimen. It saves a great deal of time when you have 5,000 insects with some data characteristics that are the same."

Inventory for the collection is gathered from national park workers throughout Costa Rica. Back at the institute in San Jose, the insects are labeled. "We hired local people who were doing assembly-line work. Now they are labeling insects," says Janzen.

Janzen and his colleagues rarely do any typing when entering new data. They simply call up a block of information and add that to the new specimen they are entering into inventory. According to Janzen, the system works like a social security card. "The number is the license plate; it is constant. Gradually, information is added to the database as it corresponds to the identification number."

Although the research project is broad in scope and complicated, the data collection program is simple. Synthetic photosensitive Code 49 labels house the alphanumeric code in a space 20mm by 8mm. Intermec laser scanners held in document stands read the bar code data. A special Macintosh wedge with a Code 49 chip was designed and built by Intermec to allow an Apple Mac SE to receive data, whether typed or scanned.

As Janzen's work continues to gain attention from museums and research institutions around the world, he hopes to create the foundation for establishing worldwide standards for tracking such valuable inventory.

"My anticipation is that the world's big collections will have to make a unified effort," says Janzen. "Such an undertaking would take time because each museum has its own system for tracking inventory. However, I can't see any other way than bar code for tracking those collections."

14.14 - Los Alamos National Laboratory

This application example is edited from "Los Alamos: Where Critical Research Relies on Bar Codes" by Elise M. Fletcher, which appeared in the October 1990 issue of ID Systems *magazine.*

In 1943, a small group of physicists headed by J. Robert Oppenheimer established Los Alamos to produce the world's first atomic weapon. Today, the laboratory spans 43 square miles, employs nearly 8,000 people, and is home to scientific discoveries that include one of the first developments of the computer, the development of the Rover nuclear reactor, and the first successful use of pion irradiation to treat cancer.

Given the significance of the laboratory's research, data management is critical, and automatic identification technologies are used to maintain tight control of materials. Bar codes track critical lab samples, information, and inventory with precision and accuracy that could not have been foreseen in Oppenheimer's day.

At the Los Alamos National Laboratory Robotics Section, some of the brightest minds in science are part of an international effort to determine the structure of DNA and thus map the human genome. This project is funded through the Office of Health and Environmental Research by Benjamin J. Barnhart, Sc.D., manager of the Human Genome Project of the Department of Energy.

The human being has 46 chromosomes: the "X" and/or "Y" chromosomes, and 22 chromosome pairs. Each chromosome contains unique genetic information within its DNA. By studying DNA construction, biologists can better understand the beginning and progression of genetic disorders that cause diseases like Hodgkin's, cancer, and Alzheimer's. When they successfully map the human genome, it may be possible to treat or suppress defective genes with drugs before the onset of disease.

In one effort, Los Alamos scientists are mapping chromosome 16. They extract microscopic DNA samples and place them in a specially formulated enzyme, which fragments the DNA. Chromosome 16 contains 100 million nucleotides, or base pairs; at Los Alamos, scientists divide DNA samples into approximately 2,500 sections and place them into cosmid libraries, which each contain about 40,000 base pairs. Los Alamos uses automatic identification to track the cosmid libraries.

Robotic project team members Tony J. Beugelsdijk, Robert M. Hollen, and Ken T. Snider worked with Innovative Products and Peripherals in their application. The bar code printing system from Zebra Technologies included a Z-130 thermal transfer printer, Poly-Trans 7A label stock, and type 5097 thermal transfer ribbon.

The biologists grow DNA clones in petri dishes and place them in trays known as microtiter plates. Each plate contains a grid of 96 wells, which are about 0.25 inch in diameter (see Figure 14.5).

The laboratory needs about 2,500 cosmid clones to rebuild one chromosome. Since this process requires overlap of these clones, Los Alamos biologists use 28,800 colonies to construct an array, or primary library. To safeguard the experiment, the scientists copy and store the primary library and use the secondary library to reconstruct the original DNA molecule.

"It is extremely critical that we track the DNA clones with 100 percent accuracy," said

Beugelsdijk.

To achieve this level of control, scientists print and apply a 0.5-inch by 2-inch bar code label to every plate in the array. Each label contains a five-digit Code 39 bar code that uniquely identifies that tray. By looking up a plate number in a database file, biologists can trace each of the 96 samples back to its original petri dish location.

The lab stores the bar code marked primary and secondary libraries in a cryocooler at 110°F and thaws them for use. Thus, the labels must withstand the subzero cryocooler temperatures and moisture.

"This on-site system meets our requirements for quality, reliability, and ease of use," said Hollen. "The polyester Poly-Trans 7A labels retain their initial high tack and scannability after being cycled in and out of the cryocooler as many as 15 times."

Because Los Alamos biologists have mastered the construction of DNA cosmid libraries, they make "filter arrays" for other laboratories, universities, and private foundations that do genetic research. To construct a filter array, samples from the secondary microtiter plates are placed in a grid-like dot pattern on a nylon sheet. If done by hand, this procedure is extremely tedious, low density, and open to error. Consequently, Los Alamos scientists have pioneered the first use of bar code labels, readers, and robotics to array DNA samples.

The laboratory's robotic workcell consists of a NUTEC single arm robot connected to an IBM PC XT. A Keithly 575 Measurement and Control System drives two automated microtiter plate dispensers via the PC. A Symbol Technologies LS6120 laser scanner is mounted at the bottom of the input plate dispenser.

First, a scientist stacks 30 microtiter plates from the secondary library in the dispenser. As a tray feeds into the robotic workstation, the scanner reads the bar code marked label and transmits the data to the PC. The robotic arm, equipped with a custom-designed gripper, places the plate on a holding station, picks up a 96-tip plastic gridding tool and dips it into the microtiter tray to remove DNA samples. Next, the arm deposits the samples on a 10-inch square nylon membrane in a grid-like pattern, producing a 96-dot array. The arm disposes of the gridding tool, picks up the microtiter tray, and places it on a retriever for restacking.

"Depending on user instructions, the robot may cycle through this procedure up to 16 times to produce an extremely dense 4-inch by 6-inch array with 1,536 dots. In all, one sheet of nylon can hold six complete arrays, or 9216 DNA samples," said Beugelsdijk.

When the array is complete, the host computer calculates the coordinates of each dot on the membrane and stores the addresses within a database. From this point, the laboratory's customized software determines which microtiter plate—and even which petri dish—each dot came from. Scientists require this information to rebuild the chromosome.

Scientists use a technique called hybridization to reconstruct the original chromosome. They wash the filter array with a radioactive solution, or "probe," and place an X-ray film over the array. The radioactivity darkens the areas on the film where sections should overlap. Using the dots' "x" and "y" coordinates, the computer references the corresponding database files to determine the structure of the DNA sections. This procedure is repeated until all 2,500 sections of the chromosome are ordered.

"By using an automated identification system and a powerful database, we have the advantage of easy, reliable tracking of hybridization patterns. We are able to produce a grid of much higher density. With the high-density grids, we can send a great deal of information in a very small package, something we would not be able to easily accomplish without this system," said Hollen.

A large portion of the Los Alamos energy program concentrates on the study of nuclear energy. Each year, chemists analyze approximately 6,000 hazardous nuclear material samples, which include plutonium and uranium. Although they receive some samples from outside sources, they generate the majority at the laboratory's on-site plutonium processing facility.

Technicians seal plutonium metal pieces in bar code marked master vials and deliver them to the Los Alamos Analytical Chemistry Group for analysis and testing. Depending on what type of experimentation needs to be done with a sample, lab technicians may cut it into as many as ten pieces for distribution to several task areas.

Since plutonium is radioactive and must be safeguarded, the laboratory wanted a system that would track samples with complete accuracy. To protect technicians from radioactivity, the laboratory cuts and analyzes the samples within hermetically sealed gloveboxes.

A Zebra Z-60 printer is employed due to its ease of label loading, reliability, and size, since all operations and maintenance need to be accomplished within the glovebox to prevent radioactive contamination of personnel. In addition to the printer, the glovebox contains a balance, cutting tools, empty vials, and other supplies. The sealed master vials and supplies feed into the glovebox through a tube.

While technicians work with a sample, their hands are gloved and inside the glovebox. Since this arrangement makes keyboard data entry difficult, they wear a headset connected to an IBM PC AT, which accepts data via automatic voice recognition technology.

To begin with, the technician reads the identification number from the master vials label. The PC transmits the data to the Laboratory Information Management System (LIMS). LIMS retrieves the sample's unique database file, and a monitor displays the information to the technician. This record details the scheduled tests for a particular sample.

The technician cuts the plutonium according to the instructions displayed on the monitor, weighs the individual pieces, and places them into smaller vials. To track the newly cut samples, the Z-60 prints a 2.25-inch by 1.375-inch bar code label for each vial. Since the technician's hands must remain within the glovebox, data is transmitted to the Z-60 by voice through LIMS.

The labels typically include master sample identification code, the sample's weight, a code specifying what type of analysis should be made, a section number indicating the task center where the sample will be analyzed, and a hazard code. A rotated seven-digit Code 39 symbol prints on the label's edge indicating where the sample originated. The first five digits refer to the original master sample, and the second two digits specify the sample's position within the original block. A LazerData Model 300 fixed-mount laser scanner, which interfaces to the PC through a modified Barcode Industries MaxiBar dual RS-232 wedge reader, reads the bar code through the glovebox's leaded glass and enters the sample into the laboratory's database.

A technician removes the cut and labeled samples from the glovebox and takes them to the appropriate task areas for analysis and testing or places them in a vault for temporary storage. While samples are in the vault, the laboratory sometimes needs to inventory them quickly and accurately. To accomplish this, technicians read the bar code labels with Computer Identics 530 portable bar code readers. The data is downloaded to the database via an auxiliary RS-232 port on the MaxiBar wedge. The MaxiBar's dual processor architecture enables the simultaneous download of data from the portables without interfering with the fixed-mount scanning operation.

At present, technicians must dissolve the plutonium samples by hand before testing and analysis. The laboratory plans to implement a unique robotics system in early 1991 to automatically cut the plutonium metal pieces, place them in vials, dissolve the metal in hydrochloric acid, and apply a bar code label.

The project team has stated that bar code technology helps guarantee optimum safety. Each time a vial moves to a new location, the bar code is scanned, providing complete accountability for every sample.

On a typical day, up to 300 items are delivered to the laboratory's central receiving center and distributed throughout 200 locations. During busy periods, up to 600 orders may be received daily.

"Without a bar code system in place, only 95 percent of the items delivered to the laboratory made their way to their recipients without special handling. The other five percent, representing approximately 16,000 items annually, required time-consuming investigatory work before they could be processed and delivered," said Edward Stuart, a group leader in Materials Management. Consequently, Stuart turned to bar code technology for better control of incoming goods.

In 1989 the laboratory's Material Management and ADP groups installed a receiving system with the assistance of Innovative Products that features several Zebra Z-130 thermal transfer printers, Zebra's Z-Ultimate labeling system, Symbol Technologies LS8500 scanners, and MaxiBars.

When the laboratory receives goods, a Z-130 prints a 4-inch by 6-inch Z-Trans 1A paper bar code label. The label is applied to the corresponding package and scanned to record the receipt of the order at the warehouse. To track the items, workers scan the labels, either with portable ScanStars or at MaxiBar scanning stations, when they load the goods on the Los Alamos delivery trucks, as shown in the example in Figure 14.6.

The laboratory has printed and permanently mounted 4-inch by 6-inch bar code location labels at each of the laboratory's 200 receiving docks, known as Designated Central Delivery Points; a Code 39 symbol encodes the building number and location code. Since most labels adhere to building exteriors, Stuart required a print technology and label material to withstand rain as well as the heat and ultraviolet radiation of the scorching Southwest sun. To meet these harsh environmental requirements, the Z-Ultimate labeling system was selected.

When workers deliver goods to a drop point, they use ScanStar portables to scan each package label, drop-point identification label, and the recipient's bar code marked badge to record the exact delivery date, time, location, and recipient. At the end of a shift, the workers upload the data from the portables to the mainframe to close the corresponding purchase orders. This virtually paperless system has helped the laboratory's delivery crew achieve a 99.9+ percent accuracy rate. "There is no doubt that these systems will serve as models for future research programs," said Hollen.

APPENDIXES

Bar Code, Data Collection & EDI Specification Sources

ABCD: THE MICROCOMPUTER INDUSTRY ASSOCIATION
450 E. 22nd Street • Suite 230
Lombard, IL 60148-6158
Telephone: 708.268.1818
Telefax: 708.278.1384
- ABCD Bar Code Labeling Guidelines (UCC/EAN & Code 39/FACT DIs)
- ABCD Bar Code Label Print Quality & Label Specification (ANS X3.182-1990)
– ABCD Manufacturers Bar Code Guidelines (UCC/EAN & Code 39/FACT DIs)
- ABCD Resellers & Distributors Bar Code Guidelines (UCC/EAN & Code 39/FACT DIs)
- ABCD Guidelines for Electronic Data Interchange
- ABCD Conventions for Electronic Data Interchange
    - Price/Sales Catalog (X12EDI 832-Final Draft)
    - Inventory Reporting (X12EDI 846-Issue 3010)
    - Purchase Order (X12EDI 850-Issue 3010)
    - Purchase Order Acknowledgement (X12EDI 855-Issue 3010)
    - Purchase Order Change (X12EDI 860-Issue 3010)
    - Purchase Order Change Acknowledgement (X12EDI 865-Issue 3010)
    - Product Transfer & Resale (X12EDI 867-Issue 3010)
    - Order Status Report (X12EDI 870-Final Draft)
    - Functional Acknowledgement (X12EDI 997-Issue 3010)
    - Ship Note/Manifest (X12EDI 856-Initial Draft)
    - Invoice (X12EDI 8510-Pre Draft)
    - Product Registration (X12EDI 140-Pre Draft)
    - Warranty Claim Response (X12EDI 141-Pre Draft)
    - Warranty Claim (X12EDI 142-Pre Draft)
    - Product Service Notification (X12EDI 143-Pre Draft)

AEROSPACE INDUSTRIES ASSOCIATION OF AMERICA (AIAA)
1250 Eye Street, NW
Washington, DC 20005
Telephone 202.371.8432
    Telephone: 206.234.1404
    Telefax: 206.234.5775

AIM-USA (see Automatic Identification Manufacturers)

AIR-CONDITIONING & REFRIGERATION INSTITUTE
1501 Wilson Blvd, Suite 600
Arlington, VA 22209
Telephone: 703.524.8800
- HVACR Bar Code Guidelines - Code 39

AIR DISTRIBUTION INSTITUTE (ADI)
4415 W. Harrison Street • Suite 242C
Hillside, IL 60162
Telephone: 708.449.2933

AIR TRANSPORT ASSOCIATION OF AMERICA
1301 Pennsylvania Avenue
Washington, DC 20004
Telephone: 202.626.4000
Telefax: 202.626.4264

ALUMINUM ASSOCIATION, INC
900 19th Street, NW
Washington, DC 20006
Telephone: 202.862.5100
- Bar Code Symbology Standard for Code 39 (1985)
- Bar Code Package Identification Standard
- Metals Industry Implementation Guidelines for EDI for use with ANS X.12 Standards

AMERICAN APPAREL MANUFACTURERS ASSOCIATION (AAMA)
2500 Wilson Blvd • Suite 301
Arlington, VA 22201
Telephone: 703.524.1864
- TALC Activities

AMERICAN ASSOCIATION OF BLOOD BANKS
117 North 19th Street • Suite 600
Arlington, VA 22209
Telephone: 703.528.8200

AMERICAN BLOOD COMMISSION (ABC)
1600 Wilson Boulevard • Suite 905
Arlington, VA 22209
Telephone: 703.525.1191
- Committee for Commonality in Blood Banking Automation (CCBBA) Report
- Guideline for the Uniform Labeling of Blood and Blood Components - Codabar

AMERICAN FURNITURE MANUFACTURERS ASSOCIATION (AFMA)
223 South Wrenn Street • P.O. Box HP-7
High Point, NC 27261
Telephone: 919.884.5000
Telefax: 919.884.5303
- Furniture Industry Bar Code (FIBC) Standard (Code 39/FACT DIs)
- Furnishings Bar Code Standard (FBCS) (Code 39/FACT DIs)

AMERICAN GAS ASSOCIATION (AGA)
1515 Wilson Boulevard
Arlington, VA 22209-2470

Telephone: 703.841.8400
- For Material Shipped to Natural Gas Utilities Label Format A A.G.A Guidelines

AMERICAN HARDWARE MANUFACTURERS ASSOCIATION (AHMA)
931 North Plum Grove Road
Schaumburg, IL 60173-4796
Telephone: 708.605.1025
Telefax: 708.605.1093
- Hardlines Industry Guidelines on Bar Coding (1989) (UCC/EAN)

AMERICAN MANAGEMENT ASSOCIATION (AMA)
135 West 50th Street
New York, New York 10020
Telephone: 212.586.8100

AMERICAN MEDICAL RECORDS ASSOCIATION
875 N. Michigan Avenue • Suite 1850
Chicago, IL 60611
Telephone: 312.787.2672

AMERICAN NATIONAL STANDARDS INSTITUTE (ANSI)
11 West 42nd Street
New York, NY 10036
Telephone: 212.642.4900
Telefax: 212.302.1286
The principal standards development body in the United States. ANSI is a non-profit, non-governmental body supported by over 1000 trade organizations, professional societies, and companies. It is the United States' member body to ISO (International Standards Organization)
- ANS FACT-1-1991 - Data Identifiers (New ANS FACT-1 out in 1994)
- ANS MH10.8M-1983 - Specifications for Bar Code Symbols on Transport Packages & Unit Loads - Code 39, Interleaved 2 of 5, Codabar (New MH10.8M out in 1993)
- ANS X3.2-1970 - Print Specifications for Magnetic Ink Character Recognition
- ANS X3.111-1986 - Optical Character Recognition Matrix Character Sets for OCR-MA
- ANS X3.17-1981- Character Set for Optical Character Recognition (OCR-A)
- ANS X3.49-1975 - Character Set for Optical Character Recognition (OCR-B)
- ANS X3.62-1987 - Optical Character Recognition (OCR) Paper Used in OCR Systems
- ANS X3.86-1980 - Optical Character Recognition (OCR) Inks
- ANS X3.93M-1981 - Optical Character Recognition (OCR) Character Positioning
- ANS X3.99-1983 - Optical Character Recognition (OCR) Print Quality, Guideline for
- ANS X3.182-1990 - Bar Code Print Quality
- ANS X9.1-1984 - Magnetic Stripe Data Content for Track 3
- ANS/ISO 4909-1987 - Bank Cards - Magnetic Stripe Data Content for Track 3
- ANS/ISO 7811/2-1985 - Identification Cards - Recording Technique Part 2: Magnetic Stripe
- ANS/ISO 7811/4-1985 - Identification Cards - Recording Technique Part 4: Location of Read-only Magnetic Tracks - Tracks 1 and 2
- ANS/ISO 7811/5-1985 - Identification Cards - Recording Technique Part 4: Location of Read-Write Magnetic Tracks - Track 3
- ANSI/NISO Z39.21-1988 - Book Numbering
- ISO 646-1983 ISO 7-bit Coded Character Set for Information Interchange
- ISO 1004-1977 Magnetic Ink Character Recognition - Print Specifications
- ISO 1073/1-1976 - Alphanumeric Character Sets for Optical Recognition - Part I: Character Set OCR-A Shapes and Dimensions of the Printed Image
- ISO 1073/2-1976 - Alphanumeric Character Sets for Optical Recognition - Part II: Character Set OCR-B Shapes and Dimensions of the Printed Image
- ISO 1831-1980 - Printing Specifications for Optical Character Recognition
- ISO 3166-1974(E) - Codes for Representation of Names of Countries

- ISO 4217-1st Ed.-1978-06-15 Codes for Representation of Currencies and Funds
- ISO 7816/1-1987 - Identification Cards - Integrated Circuit(s) with Contacts - Part I: Physical Characteristics
- ISO 8484-1987 - Magnetic Stripes on Savings Books
- International Standard ISO 646 — Information Processing - ISO 7-Bit Coded Character Set for Information Interchange, ISO, Second Edition 1983-0701
– U.S. Distribution for All ISO & CCITT Standards

AMERICAN PAPER INSTITUTE (API)
260 Madison Avenue
New York, NY 10016
Telephone: 212.340.0660
- Bar Coding: Voluntary Guidelines for Printing & Writing Papers and Newsprint (Code 39)

AMERICAN SOCIETY FOR HOSPITAL MATERIALS MANAGEMENT (ASHMM)
840 North Lake Shore Drive
Chicago, IL 60611
Telephone: 312.280.6155

AMERICAN SUPPLY & MACHINERY MANUFACTURER'S ASSOCIATION (ASMMA)
1300 Sumner Avenue
Cleveland, OH 44115
Telephone: 216.241.7333
Telefax: 216.241.0105

AMERICAN SUPPLY ASSOCIATION
20 N. Wacker Drive • Suite 2260
Chicago, IL 60606
Telephone: 312.236.4082
- Guideline for the Electronic Transmission of Purchase Orders (10/87)

AMERICAN TEXTILE MANUFACTURERS INSTITUTE (ATMI)
1101 Connecticut Ave, NW • Suite 300
Washington, DC 20036
Telephone: 202.862.0544
- TALC Activities

AMERICAN TRUCKING ASSOCIATIONS (ATA)
2200 Mill Road
Alexandria, VA 22314-4677
Telephone: 703.838.1721
Telefax: 703.836.0751
- Standard for Automatic Equipment Identification (Draft) RF
- Motor Carrier Industry Guide to EDI Implementation and Conventions

ArrayCode
ArrayTech Systems
#21 - 2544 Dunlevy Street
Victoria, BC V8R 5Z2 Canada
Telephone: 604.592.9525
Telefax: 604.592.9529

ASSOCIATION OF AMERICAN RAILROADS
c/o Railinc
50 F Street, NW

Washington, DC 20001
Telephone: 202.639.2325

ASSOCIATION OF HOME APPLIANCE MANUFACTURERS (AHAM)
20 North Wacker Drive
Chicago, IL 60606
Telephone: 312.984.5847
Telefax: 312.984.5823
- AHAM Preliminary Guidelines on Bar Coding/Automatic Identification (Code 39, UCC/EAN)

ASSOCIATION OF MICROCOMPUTER DISTRIBUTORS (AMD)
35 E. Wacker Drive • Suite 3202
Chicago, IL 60601
Telephone: 312.558.9114
Telefax: 312.558.1069

AUTOMATED VISION ASSOCIATION
900 Victors Way • P.O. Box 3724
Ann Arbor, MI 48106
Telephone: 313.994.6088
- Marking & Label Specifications for Electronic Component A15.09N (3/89)

AUTOMATIC IDENTIFICATION MANUFACTURERS (AIM-USA)
634 Alpha Drive
Pittsburgh, PA 15238-2802
Telephone: 412.963.8588
Telefax: 412.963.8753
- Uniform Symbol Specification for Code 39 (1986)
- Uniform Symbol Specification for Interleaved 2 of 5 (1986)
- Uniform Symbol Specification for Codabar (1986)
- Uniform Symbol Specification for Code 93 (1986)
- Uniform Symbol Specification for Code 128 (1986)
- Uniform Symbol Specification for Code 49 (1990)
- Uniform Symbol Specification for Code 16K (1990)
- Uniform Symbol Specification for PDF417 (1993)
- Uniform Symbol Specification for DataMatrix (1993)
- Uniform Symbol Specification for UPS Code (1993)
- Symbology Identifiers (1990)

AIM Europe
The Old Vicarage
Haley Hill, Halifax HX3 6DR
West Yorkshire, England
Telephone: 011.44.0.422.59161
Telefax: 011.44.0.422.55694

AT&T Network Services
185 Monmouth Parkway Room 2C125
West Long Branch, NJ 07764
Telephone: 908.870.7923
Telefax: 908.870.7923
- AT&T Shipping & Receiving Bar Code Label Specification - Code 39
- AT&T Product Packaging Bar Code Label Specification - Code 39 & Code 11

AUTOMOTIVE INDUSTRY ACTION GROUP (AIAG)
26200 Lahser Road, Suite 200

Southfield, MI 48034
Telephone: 313.358.3570
Telefax: 313.358.3253
- ARF-1 - General Parameters for Automotive Radio Frequency Identification Systems
- B-1 - Bar Code Symbology Standard (1988)
- B-2 - Vehicle Identification Number Label Application Standard
- B-3 - Shipping/Parts Identification Label Standard
- B-4 - Individual Part Identification Application Standard
- B-5 - Primary Metals Identification Tag Application Standard
- B-6 - Data Identifier Dictionary Standard (withdrawn 1993)
- B-7 - Vehicle Emissions Application Standard
- B-8 - Bar Code Evaluation Guidelines
- B-9 - Gas Cylinder Identification Label
- B-10 - AIAG Shipping Label (1993 Draft)
- C-27 - Standard for the Transmission of Application Advice (1988)
- EDI Implementation Guidelines (11/88)
- Functional Model for Application Data Exchange (11/87)

AUTOMOTIVE PARTS & ACCESSORIES ASSOCIATION
5100 Forbes Boulevard
Lanham, MD 20706
Telephone: 301.459.9110

BEARING SPECIALISTS ASSOCIATION (BSA)
800 Roosevelt Road • Building C, Suite 20
Glen Ellyn, IL 60137
Telephone: 708.858.3838
Telefax: 708.790.3095
- Recommended Bar Code Standards (individual parts only) for the Power Transmission, Bearing, and Related Industries (12/87) (UCC/EAN & Coce 39/FACT DIs)

BLACK BOX CORPORATION
P.O. Box 12800
Pittsburgh, PA 15241
Telephone: 412.746.5530
Telefax: 800.321.0746
- Block Box Catalog - Computer Communication Products
- Black Box LAN Catalog - LAN and Inter-networking Products

BOOK INDUSTRY STUDY GROUP, INC (BISG/BISAC)
160 Fifth Avenue
New York, NY 10010
Telephone: 212.929.1393
Telefax: 212.989.7542
- Machine-Readable Coding Guidelines for the U.S. Book Industry - UCC/EAN
- Serial Issue Identification: Code & Symbol Guidelines - Code 128
- Guidelines for Shipping Container Codes and Symbols for the U.S. Book Industry

BOOK MANUFACTURERS' INSTITUTE
111 Prospect Street
Stamford, CT 06901
Telephone: 203.324.9670
- Machine-Readable Coding Guidelines for the U.S. Book Industry - UCC/EAN
- Serial Issue Identification: Code & Symbol Guidelines - Code 128
- Guidelines for Shipping Container Codes and Symbols for the U.S. Book Industry

CANADIAN STANDARDS ASSOCIATION
178 Rexdale Blvd
Rexdale, Ontario, Canada M9W 1R3
Telephone: 416.747.2670

CHEMICAL INDUSTRY DATA EXCHANGE (CIDX)
1701 Nottingham Way
Trenton, NJ 08619
Telephone: 609.393.7088
Telefax: 609.588.8252
- CIDX Electronic Data Interchange
- CIDX Bar Code Convention - Code 39

CODABAR
Welch-Allyn, Data Collection Division
Jordan Road
Skaneateles Falls, NY 13153
Telephone: 315.685.8945
- Codabar

CODABLOCK
I.C.S. Identcode
Deutschland GmbH
Langgasse 22, D-6392 Neu Anspach 1 GERMANY
Telephone: 49.06.817091
Telefax: 49.60.8141950
- Codablock A
- Codablock E
- Codablock F
- Codablock N

CODE 1, CODE 16K
Laserlight Systems, Inc.
900R Providence Highway
Dedham, MA 02026
Telephone: 617.329.3090
Telefax: 617.329.8706
- Code 1
- Code 16K

CODE 39, CODE 11, CODE 93, CODE 49
INTERMEC Corporation
6001 36th Avenue, West • P.O. Box 4280
Everett, WA 98203-9280
Telephone: 206.348.2600
- Code 49 - Micro Symbology for Small Space Applications
- Code 11
- Code 39
- Code 93

COMITE EUROPEEN DE NORMALISATION (CEN)
Secretariat: Nederlands Normalisatie-instituut (NNI)
Kalfjeslaan 2 • P.O. Box 5059
2600 GB Deift Nederlands
Telephone: 011.31.15.690.390
Telefax: 011.31.15.690.190

- N231 Draft prEN - Bar Coding Data Identifiers
- N183 Numbering of Symbology Standards
- N171 Draft prEN - Bar Coding - Symbology Specifications - EAN/UPC
- N170 Draft prEN - Bar Coding - Symbology Specifications - Codabar
- N169 Draft prEN - Bar Coding - Symbology Specifications - Code 128
- N168 Draft prEN - Bar Coding - Symbology Specifications - Interleaved 2 of 5
- N167 Draft prEN - Bar Coding - Symbology Specifications - Code 39
- N166 Draft prEN - Bar Coding - Symbology Identifiers
- N161 Draft prEN - Bar Coding - Test Specifications for Bar Code Symbols

COMPUTER & BUSINESS EQUIPMENT MANUFACTURERS ASSOCIATION (CBEMA)
311 First Street, NW • Suite 500
Washington, DC 20001
Telephone: 202.626.5725
Telefax: 202.638.4922Leona Epson, Administrative Assistant/Communications

COUNCIL FOR PERIODICAL DISTRIBUTOR ASSOCIATION (CPDA)
60 East 42nd Street, Suite 2134
New York, NY 10165
Telephone: 212.818.0234
- Magazine & Paperback Title & Issue Coding: UPC Symbol Location & Orientation Guidelines

COUNCIL OF LOGISITICS MANAGEMENT (CLM)
2803 Butterfield Road • Suite 380
Oak Brook, IL 60521-1156
Telephone: 708.574.0985
Telefax: 708.574.0989

DATAMATRIX (f.k.a. DataCode)
International Data Matrix, Inc.
28050 U.S. 19 North • Suite 100
Clearwater, FL 34621-2600
Telephone: 813.725.9000
Telefax: 813.725.9500
- Data Code (DataMatrix)

DATA INTERCHANGE STANDARDS ASSOCIATION (X12 DISA)
1800 Diagonal Road • Suite 355
Alexandria, VA 22314
Telephone: 703.548.7005
Telefax: 703.548.5738
   To Order Publications:
      EDI Support Services
      11443 Twin Mills Way
      Chardon, OH 44024
      Telephone: 216.286.6810
- ANS X12 Secretariat & Manager, Maintenance

DATA PROCESSING MANAGEMENT ASSOCIATION (DPMA)
505 Busse Highway
Park Ridge, IL 60068
Telephone: 708.825.8124

EAN INTERNATIONAL (EAN)

Rue Royale 29
B-1000 Bruxelles (Belgium)
Telephone: 011.32.2.218.76.74
Telefax: 011.32.2.218.75.85

EDI COUNCIL OF CANADA
5401 Eglinton Avenue • Suite 103
Etobicoke, Ontario, Canada M9C 5K6
Telephone: 416.621.7160

EDIFACT Board Secretariat Committee of the EC
DG XIII/D-4 (Arts/Lux 3/27)
Rue De La Roi 200
Brussels, Belgium B-1049
Telephone: 011.32.22363261

ELECTRICAL DATA EXCHANGE (EDX)
A group formed to coordinate EDI activities for the electrical industry. Secretariat for the group is
   the National Electrical Manufacturers Association (NEMA).
2101 "L" Street, NW • Suite 300
Washington, DC 20037
Telephone: 202.457.8400
Telefax: 202.457.8468

ELECTRONIC DATA INTERCHANGE ASSOCIATION (EDIA)
TDCC/EDIA
225 Reinekers Lane • Suite 550
Alexandria, VA 22314
Telephone: 703.838.8042

ELECTRONIC FUNDS TRANSFER ASSOCIATION (EFTA)
1421 Prince Street • Suite 310
Alexandria, VA 22314
Telephone: 703.549.9800

ELECTRONIC INDUSTRIES ASSOCIATION (EIA)
A standards organization in the United States specializing in the electronic and functional charac-
   teristics of interface equipment
2001 Pennsylvania Avenue, NW
Washington, DC 20006
Telephone: 202.457.4966
Telefax: 202.457.4985
- EIA-556 - Electronic Industries Association Outer Shipping Container Bar Code Label
   Standard (Code 39)
- EIA-556A- Electronic Industries Association Shipping and Receiving Transaction Bar Code
   Label Standard (Code 39/FACT DIs)
- EIA-/IS-61) - Electronic Industries Association - Consumer Electronics Group Product and
   Packaging Bar Code Standard for Consumer Electronic Retail Distribution (Draft) (UCC/EAN)
- EIDX Guidelines

FABRIC AND SUPPLIERS LINKAGE COUNCIL (FASLINC)
225 Reinekers Lane • Suite 550
Alexandria, VA 22314
Telephone: 703.838.8042
- FASLINC Book of Standards (1989)

324

GAS APPLIANCE MANUFACTURERS ASSOCIATION (GAMA)
1901 North Moore Street • Suite 1100
Arlington, VA 22209
Telephone: 703.525.9565

Graphic Communications Association (GCA)
100 Daingerfield Road
Alexandria, VA 22314-2804
Telephone: 703.519.8160
Telefax: 703.548.2867
- GCA Standard 101-1983 - Document Markup Language (GenCode™) and the Standard
        Generalized Markup Language (SGML)
- GCA Standard 102 (Reserved)
- GCA Standard 103-1985 - Specification EMBARC - Electronic Manifesting & Bar Coding of
        Paper Stock Shipments $120.00
- GCA Standard 104-1986 - ADIS: Address Data Interchange Standards for Computerized
        Mailing Tapes
- GCA Standard 106-1986 - GIBC: Graphics Industry Bar Code Labeling Specification
- GCA Standard 107-1988 - GDIP-1: Graphic Arts Data Interchange Specification
- GCA Standard 108-1989 - Specification Manual PASS: Package and Sack/Skid Sequencing
        for Publications Mailings
- GCA Standard 109-1989 - EMLOOP/Receiving Advice
- GCA Standard 110-1989 - EMLOOP/Usage Advice
- GCA Standard 111-1989 - EMLOOP/Inventory Status Advice
- GCA Standard 112-1989 - EMLOOP/Waste Advice
- GCA Standard 113-1989 - EMLOOP/Paper Properties
- GCA Standard 114-1989 - EMLOOP/Paper Performance
- GCA Standard 115-1989 - EMLOOP/Disposition Advice
- GCA Standard 116-1989 - Printing and Publishing Industry Roll Identifier Specification
- GCA Standard 117-1990 - Sheeted Papers Identifier Specification (Draft)

GROCERY MANUFACTURERS OF AMERICA, INC (GMA)
1010 Wisconsin Avenue, NW
Washington, DC 20007
Telephone: 202.337.9400
- Trade Practice Recommendations for the Grocery Industry: Couponing (UCC/EAN)

HEALTH INDUSTRY BUSINESS COMMUNICATIONS COUNCIL (HIBCC)
The group responsible for the admistration of the HIBCC Standards, number issuance, and control
        of the Labeler Identification Codes within the health care industry.
5110 North 40th Street • Suite 250
Phoenix, AZ 85018
Telephone: 602.381.1091
Telefax: 602.381.1093
- HIBC Supplier Labeling Standard (1989)
- HIBC Provider Applications Standard (1988)
- HIBC Guidelines
- EDI Guidelines Manual
- Invoice Transaction Set (810)
- Price and Sales Catalog Transaction Set (832)
- Purchase Order Transaction Set (850)
- Purchase Order Acknowledgement Transaction Set (855)
- Functional Acknowledgement Transaction Set (997)

HOME CENTER INSTITUTE (HCI)

770 North High School Road
Indianapolis, IN 46214-3798
Telephone: 317.248.1261
Telefax: 317.241.4515

INDUSTRIAL DISTRIBUTION ASSOCIATION (IDA)
Three Corporate Square • Suite 201
Atlanta, GA 30329
Telephone: 404.325.2776
Telefax: 404.325.2784

INDUSTRY BAR CODE ALLIANCE (IBCA)
24 Far View Road
Chalfont, PA 18914
Telephone: 215.822.6880
Telefax: 215.822.8109
- IBCA Bar Code Application Guidelines

INTERNATIONAL AIR TRANSPORT ASSOCIATION (IATA)
26 Chemin de Boinville
CH-1216 Cointrin (Geneva)
SWITZERLAND
Telephone: 011.41.22.98.33.66 Ext 465
- Passenger Services Conference Resolutions Manual - 2/5 (1988)
- Bar Coding of Airline Tickets - 1720a, Attachment H - 2/5 (1988)
- Bar Coding of Baggage Tags - ITF (1988)
- Automated Boarding Control - 1789 - BCD, Magnetic Stripe (1988)
- Cargo Services Conference Resolutions Manual - Code 39 (1987)
- Standard Specifications for Bar Codes and Bar Code Equipment to be Used in Cargo
        Applications - Code 39 (1987)

INTERNATIONAL FOODSERVICE MANUFACTURERS ASSOCIATION (IFMA)
321 North Clark Street • Suite 2900
Chicago, IL 60610
Telephone: 312.644.8989
Telefax: 312.644.8185
- UPC for the Foodservice Industry
- UCS for the Foodservice Industry

INTERNATIONAL SANITARY SUPPLY ASSOCIATION (ISSA)
7373 North Lincoln Avenue
Lincolnwood, IL 06046
Telephone: 708.982.0800
Telephone: 800.225.4772
Telefax: 708.982.1012

INTERNATIONAL STANDARD BOOK NUMBERING (ISBN)
U.S. Agency - Bowker/Martindale-Hubbell
121 Chanlon Road
New Providence, NJ 07974
Telephone: 908.665.6770
Telefax: 908.464.3553

International Agency
International Standard Book Number Agency
Staatsbibliothek Preussischer Kulturbesltz

Posdamer Strasse 33, D-1000 Berlin 30 F.R.G.
Telephone: 011.49.030.2661 Ext. 2338, 2498
- ISBN System Users' Manual

INTERNATIONAL STANDARD SERIAL NUMBER (ISSN)
National Serials Data Program
Library of Congress
Washington, DC 20540
Telephone: 202.287.6452

MATERIAL HANDLING INSTITUTE (MHI)
8720 Red Oak Blvd • Suite 201
Charlotte, NC 28217
Telephone: 319.364.0212 •
Telefax: 319.365.8814
- ANSI/MH10.8M-1983 - Bar Code Symbols on Unit Loads and Transport Packages
- ANSI/MH10.8M-1993 - Bar Code Symbols on Unit Loads and Transport Packages
- ANSI/FACT-1-1991

MOTOR & EQUIPMENT MANUFACTURERS ASSOCIATION (MEMA)
300 Sylvan Avenue • P.O. Box 1638
Englewood Cliffs, NJ 07632-0638
Telephone: 201.569.8500
- Automotive Aftermarket Individual Part Bar Coding Guidelines (1986)
- Automotive Aftermarket Ship Label Bar Coding Guidelines

NATIONAL ASSOCIATION OF ELECTRICAL DISTRIBUTORS (NAED)
45 Danbury Road
Wilton, CT 06897
Telephone: 203.834.1908
Telefax: 203.834.1555

NATIONAL ASSOCIATION OF MANUFACTURERS (NAM)
1331 Pennsylvania Avenue, NW • Suite 1500 N
Washington, DC 20003-1703
Telephone: 202.637.3102
Telefax: 202.637.3182

NATIONAL ASSOCIATION OF MANUFACTURING OPTICIANS
P.O. Box 866428
Plano, TX 75086-6428
Telephone: 214.484.8128

NATIONAL ASSOCIATION OF PURCHASING MANAGEMENT (NAPM)
2055 East Centennial Circle • P.O. Box 22160
Tempe, Arizona 85285-2160
Telephone: 602.752.6276 (800.888.6276) x401
Telefax: 602.752.7890

NATIONAL ASSOCIATION OF SERVICE MERCHANDISING
118 South Clinton Street • Suite 300
Chicago, IL 60606
Telephone: 312.876.9494

NATIONAL ASSOCIATION OF WHOLESALERS-DISTRIBUTORS (NAW)
1725 K Street NW • Suite 710
Washington, DC 20006
Telephone: 202.872.0885
Telefax: 202.785.0586

NATIONAL ASSOCIATION RETAIL DEALERS OF AMERICA (NARDA)
10 East 22nd Street
Lombard, IL 60148
Telephone: 708.953.8950
Telefax: 708.953.8957

NATIONAL BICYCLE DEALERS ASSOCIATION (NBDA)
129 Cabrillo Street • Suite 201
Costa Mesa, CA 92627
Telephone: 714.722.6909

NATIONAL COMMITTEE FOR CLINICAL LABORATORY STANDARDS (NCCLS)
771 East Lancaster Avenue
Villanova, PA 19085
Telephone: 215.525.2435

NATIONAL COUNCIL INTERNATIONAL TRADE DOCUMENTS
350 Broadway • Suite 205
New York, NY 10013
Telephone: 212.925.1400

NATIONAL CUSTOMS BROKERS & FORWARDERS ASSOCIATION
5 World Trade Center • Suite 9273
New York, NY 10048
Telephone: 212.432.0050

NATIONAL ELECTRICAL MANUFACTURERS ASSOCIATION (NEMA)
2101 "L" Street, NW • Suite 300
Washington, DC 20037
Telephone: 202.457.8400
Telefax: 202.457.8468
- Electrical Industry Bar Code Application Guidelines (1987) (New Std out in 1991)
  ○ NEMA (National Electrical Manufacturers Association)
  ○ NEMRA (National Electrical Manufacturers Representative Association)
  ○ NAED (National Association of Electrical Distributors)
- RN3 Product ID Numbers Metallic Tubular Conduit Products for Use with Bar Coding and Electronic Data Interchange

NATIONAL ELECTRONICS DISTRIBUTORS ASSOCIATION (NEDA)
35 E. Wacker Drive • Suite 3202
Chicago, IL 60601
Telephone: 312.558.9114
Telefax: 312.558.1069

NATIONAL FASTENER DISTRIBUTORS ASSOCIATION (NFDA)
1348 Haddon Road
Columbus, OH 43209
Telephone: 614.237.0252

NATIONAL FOREST PRODUCTS ASSOCIATION (NFPA)
1250 Connecticut Avenue, NW
Washington, DC 20036
Telephone: 202.463.2765
Telefax: 202.463.2785
- Bar Coding Guidelines for the Wood Products Industry

NATIONAL GROCERS ASSOCIATION (NGA)
1825 Samuel Morse Drive
Reston, VA 22090
Telephone: 703.437.5300

NATIONAL INDUSTRIAL TRANSPORTATION LEAGUE
1090 Vermont Avenue, NW • Suite 410
Washington, DC 20005
Telephone: 202.842.3870

NATIONAL OFFICE PRODUCTS ASSOCIATION (NOPA)
301 North Fairfax Street
Alexandria, VA 22314
Telephone: 703.549.9040
Telefax: 703.683.7552
- Supplemental Guidelines for UPC Implementation in the Office Products Industry
- NOPA's UPC Symbol Reduction Guidelines for Marking Intermediate Packs
- Furniture Industry Bar Code Standard (FIBC) (1988)
- Furniture Industry Print Quality Guidelines (Extracted for ANS X3.182-1990)

NATIONAL PAPER TRADE ASSOCIATION (NPTA)
111 Great Neck Road
Great Neck, New York 11021
Telephone: 516.829.3070
Telefax: 516.829.3074
- NPTA Bar Code Guidelines
- NPTA Guidelines for EDI

NATIONAL RETAIL FEDERATION INC. (NRF) formerly
NATIONAL RETAIL MANAGEMENT ASSOCIATION (NRMA)
100 West 31st Street
New York, NY 10001-3401
Telephone: 212.244.8780
Telefax: 212.594.0487
- Standard Color & Size Handbook (1988)
- ARTS Standard

NATIONAL RETAIL HARDWARE ASSOCIATION (NRHA)
770 North High School Road
Indianapolis, IN 46214-3798
Telephone: 317.248.1261
Telefax: 317.241.4515

NATIONAL SPORTING GOODS ASSOCIATION
1699 Wall Street
Mount Prospect, IL 60056
Telephone: 708.439.4000

NATIONAL WELDING SUPPLY ASSOCIATION (NWSA)
1900 Arch Street
Philadelphia, PA 19103
Telephone: 215.5643484
- Welding Supply Hardgoods Bar Coding Guidelines (1988)

NATIONAL WHOLESALE HARDWARE ASSOCIATION (NWHA)
1900 Arch Street
Philadelphia, PA 19103
Telephone: 215.564.3484
Telefax: 215.564.2175

NATIONAL COUNCIL INTERNATIONAL TRADE DOCUMENTS
350 Broadway • Suite 205
New York, NY 10013
Telephone: 212.925.1400

NORTHAMERICAN HEATING AND AIRCONDITIONING WHOLESALES ASSOCIATION (NHAW)
1389 Dublin Road • P.O. Box 16790
Columbus, OH 43216
Telephone: 614.448.1835

OPTICAL PRODUCT CODE COUNCIL
6055A Arlington Boulevard
Falls Church, VA 22044-2790
Telephone: 703.237.8433
- Optical Product Code (1989)

ORGANIZATION FOR DATA EXCHANGE BY TELE TRANSMISSION IN EUROPE (ODETTE)
Forbes House - Halkin Street
London SW1X 7DS (United Kingdom)
Telephone: 011 33 01 235.7000
Telefax: 011 33 01 235.7112
- Transport Label Standard (1991)

PETROLEUM EQUIPMENT INSTITUTE (PEI)
6514 East 69th Street
Tulsa, OK 74133-1719
Telephone: 918.494.9696

PDF417
Symbol Technologies, Inc.
116 Wilbur Place
Telephone: 516.244.4697
Telefax: 516.244.4645

PHILLIPS DOT CODE
Phillips Industrial Electronics B.V.
P.O. Box 218
5600 MD Eindhoven
The Netherlands
Telephone: 011.31.40.78.80.17
Telefax: 011.31.40.78.62.56

PLESSEY
DS Limited
7 Wessex Trade Center
Ringwood Road
Poole, Dorset BH12 3PF ENGLAND
Telephone: 011.44.202.738.040
- Marketing Specification Bar Code Printing

PLUMBING MANUFACTURERS INSTITUTE (PMI)
800 Roosevelt Road, Building C
Glen Ellyn, IL 60137
Telephone: 708.858.9172
Richard Church (3/90)

POWER TRANSMISSION DISTRIBUTORS ASSOCIATION (PTDA)
6400 Shafer Court • Suite 670
Rosemont, IL 60018-4909
Telephone: 708.825.2000
Telefax: 708.825.0953
- Recommended Bar Code Standards (individual parts only) for the Power Transmission,
  Bearing, and Related Industries (12/87)

PRODUCT CODE COUNCIL OF CANADA (PCCC)
885 Don Mills Road • Suite 301
Don Mills, Ontario M3C 1V9 CANADA
Telephone: 416.510.8039
Telefax: 416.510.8043

RECORDING INDUSTRY ASSOCIATION OF AMERICA (RIAA)
1020 19th Street, NW, Suite 200
Washington, D.C. 20036
Telephone: 202.775.0101
- UPC Guidelines for the Recording Industry

SERIALS INDUSTRY SYSTEMS ADVISORY COMMITTEE (SISAC)
160 Fifth Avenue
New York, NY 10010
Telephone: 212.929.1393

SIMPLIFICATION OF INTERNATIONAL TRADE PROCEDURES
26/28 King Street
Almack House, London, England UK SW1Y 6QW
Telephone: 01.930.0532

SOCIETY OF LOGISTICS ENGINEERS (SOLE)
8100 Professional Place, Ste 211
New Carrollton, MD 20785
Telephone: 301.459.8446 (800.695.7653)

SOFTSTRIP
Softstrip Systems
835 South Main Street
Waterbury, CT 06706
Telephone: 203.573.0150
Telefax: 203.597.9762

SOFTWARE PUBLISHERS ASSOCIATION (SPA)
1101 Connecticut Avenue, NW • Suite 901
Washington, DC 20036
Telephone: 202.452.1600
Telefax: 202.223.8756

SPECIALTY TOOLS & FASTENERS DISTRIBUTORS ASSOCIATION (STAFDA)
P.O. Box 44
Elm Grove, WI 53122
Telephone: 414.784.4774

STANDARD ADDRESS NUMBER (SAN) - U.S. SAN AGENCY
U.S. Agency - R.R. Bowker
121 Chanlon Road
New Providence, NJ 07974
Telephone: 908.665.6770

SUNDRIES AND APPAREL FINDINGS COUNCIL (SAFLINC)
American Apparel Manufacturers Association (AAMA)
2500 Wilson Blvd • Suite 301
Arlington, VA 22201
Telephone: 703.524.1864
- Product Identification; Unique Producer Identification (5/88)

TELECOMMUNICATIONS INDUSTRY FORUM
Exchange Carriers Standards Association (ECSA)
5430 Grosvenor Lane, Suite 200
Bethesda, MD 20814-2122
Telephone: 301.683.3000
Telefax: 301.683.5690
- TCIF Package or Shipping Container Transaction Bar Code Label Specification (5/88)
- TCIF Product Package Labeling
- TCIF Implementation Guide to Package Labeling
- TCIF EDI Specifications

TEXTILE APPAREL LINKAGE COUNCIL (TALC) (ATMI)
TDCC/EDIA
225 Reinekers Lane • Suite 550
Alexandria, VA 22314
Telephone: 703.838.8042
American Apparel Manufacturers Association (AAMA)
2500 Wilson Blvd • Suite 301
Arlington, VA 22201
Telephone: 703.524.1864
- Roll Identification (11/86)
- Getting Started with Piece Goods Linkage (9/88)
- TALC Handbook

UNIFORM CODE COUNCIL (UCC)
8163 Old Yankee Road • Suite J
Dayton, OH 45458
Telephone: 513.435.3870
Telefax: 513.435.4749
- UPC Coupon Code Guidelines - UPC (1989)
- UPC Film Master Verification Manual (1991)

- UPC Guidelines (1990)
- UPC Industrial & Commercial Guidelines (1991)
- UPC Marking Guidelines for General Merchandise and Apparel (1989)
- UPC Symbol Specification Manual (1986)
- UPC Symbol Location Guidelines (1986)
- UPC Shipping Container Code and Symbol Specification Manual - ITF-14 (1990)
- Application Specification for UCC/EAN-128 Serial Shipping Container Code (with Symbol and Shipping Label Guidelines) - UCC/EAN-128 (1992)
- UPC Data Communications Guidelines for General Merchandise and Apparel (1992)
- VICS Implementation Guidelines for EDI
- VICS Electronic Data Interchange Standard for the Department Store Industry (1987)
- UCC/EAN-128 Application Identifiers (1993)

UNITED STATES GOVERNMENT
Standardization Documents Order Desk
Bldg 4D
700 Robbins Avenue
Philadelphia, PA 19111-5094
Telephone: 215.697.2667
Telefax: 215.697.2978
LOGMARS COORDINATOR
AMCPSCC
Tobyhanna, PA 18466-5097
Telephone: 717.894.7146
- MIL-STD-1189B - Standard DoD Bar Code Symbology (Code 39)
- MIL-STD-129K Appendix F- Bar Code Markings for Packing Lists & DD Form 1348-1/-1A
- MIL-STD-129K Appendix G- Bar Code Markings for Ammunition
- MIL-STD-129K Appendix H- Bar Code Markings for Containers
- MIL-STD-129K Appendix I- Bar Code Markings for Military Shipping Label
- MIL-STD-130G - Identification Marking of U.S. Military Property
- MIL-L-61002 - Labels, Bar Coded, Pressure Sensitive Adhesive (1990)
- FED-STD-123E - Civil Standard Marking 123E for Shipment (Code 39)

UNITED STATES POSTAL SERVICE (USPS)
Marketing Department
Regular Mail Services Division
U.S. Postal Service HQ
475 L Enfant Plaza, SW • Room 5541
Washington, DC 20260-6336
- A Guide to Business Mail Preparation (Publication 25) (Postnet & FIM)

UNIVERSAL SPORT CODE - USC
c/o Smart, Inc.
26 Cricket Lane
Wilton, CT 06897
Telephone: 203.762.3279
UTILITY INDUSTRY GROUP (UIG)
400 South Tryon Street
Charlotte, NC 28201-1007
Telephone: 704.382.4164
Telefax: 704.382.4264.
- UIG EDI Guidelines
- UIG Bar Code Labeling Guidelines

UPSCODE (CODE 6)
United Parcel Service (UPS)

Research & Development
51-53 Kenosia Avenue
Danbury, CT 06810-7317
Telephone: 203.731.6399
Telefax: 203.731.6340

VERICODE
Veritec
21345 Lassen St.
Chatsworth, CA 91311
Telephone: 818.407.8765
Telefax: 818.407.8783

VOLUNTARY INTERINDUSTRY COMMUNICATIONS STANDARDS COMMITTEE (VICS) - EDI
(see UNIFORM CODE COUNCIL)

WAREHOUSING EDUCATION RESEARCH COUNCIL (WERC)
1100 Jorie Blvd Suite 170
Oak Brook, IL 60521
Telephone: 708.990.0001
Telefax: 708.990.0256

WHOLESALE STATIONERS ASSOCIATION (WSA)
1701 E. Woodfield Road • Suite 403
Schaumburg, IL 60173
Alexandria, VA 22314
Telephone: 708.240.1909
Telefax: 708.240.1834

SOURCES FOR ADDITIONAL MATERIAL ON DATA COLLECTION TECHNOLOGY

Helmers Publishing
174 Concord Street • P.O. Box 874
Peterborough, NH 03458-0874
Telephone: 603.924.9631
Telefax: 603.924.7408
- *ID Systems* magazine (monthly)
- *Sensors* (monthly)
- *ID Systems Buyers Guide* (annual)

Q.E.D. SYSTEMS
Craig K. Harmon, President
P.O. Box 2524 (52406) • 3963 Highlands Lane, SE (52403)
Cedar Rapids, IA
Telephone: 319.364.0212
Telefax: 319.365.8814
- Microcomputer Industry Standards
- Furniture Industry Standards
- Office Products Industry Standards
- Utility Industry Standards
- Two-Dimensional Symbol Standards
- EDI & Bar Code Standards Development
- Education, Consulting, Systems Design & Integration

A P P E N D I X B

Significant Dimensional Parameters For Selected Code 39 Message Sizes

In this appendix, we present lookup tables for Code 39 Symbol Widths, given selection of some significant dimensional parameters: Narrow Bar Width "X", Wide to Narrow Ratio "R", and the number of characters contained in the message, here enumerated for various message lengths.

We have arbitrarily divided this information into 5 tables covering Code 39 symbols of 4-7, 8-11, 12-15, 16-19, and 20-22 characters. Longer symbols are possible but are not recommended.

The left column of each table is the selected set of narrow bar widths in inches defining a group of rows. For each narrow bar width grouping, several Wide-to-Narrow ratios are shown on separate rows.

Once these two items are determined, the specification of Code 39 gives a minimum quiet zone width, and the number of characters determines the overall symbol length.

Table B.1
Significant Dimensional Parameters of Code 39 at Selected Narrow Bar Widths and Wide-to-Narrow Ratios (4 to 7 characters)

Narrow Bar ("X")	Wide-to-Narrow Ratio ("R")	Wide Bar ("W")	Bar Width Tolerance ("T")	Min Quiet Zone ("Q")	Symbol Length No. of Data Chars ("D") 4	Min Bar Height 15% ("H")	Symbol Length No. of Data Chars ("D") 5	Min Bar Height 15% ("H")	Symbol Length No. of Data Chars ("D") 6	Min Bar Height 15% ("H")	Symbol Length No. of Data Chars ("D") 7	Min Bar Height 15% ("H")
0.0075	2.20	0.0165	±0.0017	0.25	1.10	0.50	1.21	0.50	1.31	0.50	1.41	0.50
0.0100	2.50	0.0250	±0.0027	0.25	1.36	0.50	1.51	0.50	1.65	0.50	1.80	0.50
0.0100	3.00	0.0300	±0.0035	0.25	1.45	0.50	1.61	0.50	1.77	0.50	1.93	0.50
0.0115	2.50	0.0288	±0.0031	0.25	1.49	0.50	1.66	0.50	1.82	0.50	1.99	0.50
0.0115	3.00	0.0345	±0.0040	0.25	1.59	0.50	1.78	0.50	1.96	0.50	2.14	0.50
0.0130	2.50	0.0325	±0.0035	0.25	1.62	0.50	1.81	0.50	2.00	0.50	2.18	0.50
0.0130	3.00	0.0390	±0.0045	0.25	1.74	0.50	1.94	0.50	2.15	0.50	2.36	0.50
0.0150	2.50	0.0375	±0.0041	0.25	1.79	0.50	2.01	0.50	2.23	0.50	2.44	0.50
0.0150	3.00	0.0450	±0.0052	0.25	1.93	0.50	2.17	0.50	2.41	0.50	2.65	0.50
0.0170	2.50	0.0425	±0.0046	0.25	1.96	0.50	2.21	0.50	2.46	0.50	2.70	0.50
0.0170	3.00	0.0510	±0.0059	0.25	2.12	0.50	2.39	0.50	2.66	0.50	2.93	0.50
0.0250	2.50	0.0625	±0.0068	0.25	2.65	0.50	3.01	0.50	3.38	0.51	3.74	0.56
0.0250	3.00	0.0750	±0.0086	0.25	2.88	0.50	3.28	0.50	3.68	0.55	4.08	0.61
0.0400	2.50	0.1000	±0.0109	0.40	4.24	0.64	4.82	0.72	5.40	0.81	5.98	0.90
0.0400	3.00	0.1200	±0.0138	0.40	4.60	0.69	5.24	0.79	5.88	0.88	6.52	0.98
0.0550	2.50	0.1375	±0.0149	0.55	5.83	0.87	6.63	0.99	7.43	1.11	8.22	1.23
0.0550	3.00	0.1650	±0.0190	0.55	6.33	0.95	7.21	1.08	8.09	1.21	8.97	1.34

Table B.2
Significant Dimensional Parameters of Code 39 at Selected Narrow Bar Widths and Wide-to-Narrow Ratios (8 to 11 characters)

Narrow Bar ("X")	Wide-to-Narrow Ratio ("R")	Wide Bar ("W")	Bar Width Tolerance ("T")	Min Quiet Zone ("Q")	Symbol Length No. of Data Chars ("D") 8	Min Bar Height 15% ("H")	Symbol Length No. of Data Chars ("D") 9	Min Bar Height 15% ("H")	Symbol Length No. of Data Chars ("D") 10	Min Bar Height 15% ("H")	Symbol Length No. of Data Chars ("D") 11	Min Bar Height 15% ("H")
0.0075	2.20	0.0165	±0.0017	0.25	1.51	0.50	1.61	0.50	1.72	0.50	1.82	0.50
0.0100	2.50	0.0250	±0.0027	0.25	1.94	0.50	2.09	0.50	2.23	0.50	2.38	0.50
0.0100	3.00	0.0300	±0.0035	0.25	2.09	0.50	2.25	0.50	2.41	0.50	2.57	0.50
0.0115	2.50	0.0288	±0.0031	0.25	2.16	0.50	2.32	0.50	2.49	0.50	2.66	0.50
0.0115	3.00	0.0345	±0.0040	0.25	2.33	0.50	2.51	0.50	2.70	0.50	2.88	0.50
0.0130	2.50	0.0325	±0.0035	0.25	2.37	0.50	2.56	0.50	2.75	0.50	2.94	0.50
0.0130	3.00	0.0390	±0.0045	0.25	2.57	0.50	2.78	0.50	2.98	0.50	3.19	0.50
0.0150	2.50	0.0375	±0.0041	0.25	2.66	0.50	2.88	0.50	3.10	0.50	3.31	0.50
0.0150	3.00	0.0450	±0.0052	0.25	2.89	0.50	3.13	0.47	3.37	0.50	3.61	0.54
0.0170	2.50	0.0425	±0.0046	0.25	2.95	0.50	3.19	0.50	3.44	0.50	3.69	0.55
0.0170	3.00	0.0510	±0.0059	0.25	3.20	0.50	3.48	0.52	3.75	0.56	4.02	0.60
0.0250	2.50	0.0625	±0.0068	0.25	4.10	0.62	4.46	0.67	4.83	0.72	5.19	0.78
0.0250	3.00	0.0750	±0.0086	0.25	4.48	0.67	4.88	0.73	5.28	0.79	5.68	0.85
0.0400	2.50	0.1000	±0.0109	0.40	6.56	0.98	7.14	1.07	7.72	1.16	8.30	1.25
0.0400	3.00	0.1200	±0.0138	0.40	7.16	1.07	7.80	1.17	8.44	1.27	9.08	1.36
0.0550	2.50	0.1375	±0.0149	0.55	9.02	1.35	9.82	1.47	10.62	1.59	11.41	1.71
0.0550	3.00	0.1650	±0.0190	0.55	9.85	1.48	10.73	1.61	11.61	1.74	12.49	1.87

Table B.3
Significant Dimensional Parameters of Code 39 at Selected Narrow Bar Widths and Wide-to-Narrow Ratios (12 to 15 characters)

Narrow Bar ("X")	Wide-to-Narrow Ratio ("R")	Wide Bar ("W")	Bar Width Tolerance ("T")	Min Quiet Zone ("Q")	Symbol Length No. of Data Chars ("D") 12	Min Bar Height 15% ("H")	Symbol Length No. of Data Chars ("D") 13	Min Bar Height 15% ("H")	Symbol Length No. of Data Chars ("D") 14	Min Bar Height 15% ("H")	Symbol Length No. of Data Chars ("D") 15	Min Bar Height 15% ("H")
0.0075	2.20	0.0165	±0.0017	0.25	1.92	0.50	2.02	0.50	2.12	0.50	2.23	0.50
0.0100	2.50	0.0250	±0.0027	0.25	2.52	0.50	2.67	0.50	2.81	0.50	2.96	0.50
0.0100	3.00	0.0300	±0.0035	0.25	2.73	0.50	2.89	0.50	3.05	0.50	3.21	0.50
0.0115	2.50	0.0288	±0.0031	0.25	2.82	0.50	2.99	0.50	3.16	0.50	3.32	0.50
0.0115	3.00	0.0345	±0.0040	0.25	3.06	0.50	3.25	0.50	3.43	0.51	3.62	0.54
0.0130	2.50	0.0325	±0.0035	0.25	3.13	0.50	3.31	0.50	3.50	0.53	3.69	0.55
0.0130	3.00	0.0390	±0.0045	0.25	3.40	0.51	3.61	0.54	3.82	0.57	4.02	0.60
0.0150	2.50	0.0375	±0.0041	0.25	3.53	0.53	3.75	0.56	3.97	0.59	4.18	0.63
0.0150	3.00	0.0450	±0.0052	0.25	3.85	0.58	4.09	0.61	4.33	0.65	4.57	0.68
0.0170	2.50	0.0425	±0.0046	0.25	3.93	0.59	4.18	0.63	4.43	0.66	4.67	0.70
0.0170	3.00	0.0510	±0.0059	0.25	4.29	0.64	4.56	0.68	4.84	0.73	5.11	0.77
0.0250	2.50	0.0625	±0.0068	0.25	5.55	0.83	5.91	0.89	6.28	0.94	6.64	1.00
0.0250	3.00	0.0750	±0.0086	0.25	6.08	0.91	6.48	0.97	6.88	1.03	7.28	1.09
0.0400	2.50	0.1000	±0.0109	0.40	8.88	1.33	9.46	1.42	10.04	1.51	10.62	1.59
0.0400	3.00	0.1200	±0.0138	0.40	9.72	1.46	10.36	1.55	11.00	1.65	11.64	1.75
0.0550	2.50	0.1375	±0.0149	0.55	12.21	1.83	13.01	1.95	13.81	2.07	14.60	2.19
0.0550	3.00	0.1650	±0.0190	0.55	13.37	2.00	14.25	2.14	15.13	2.27	16.01	2.40

Table B.4
Significant Dimensional Parameters of Code 39 at Selected Narrow Bar Widths and Wide-to-Narrow Ratios (16 to 19 characters)

Narrow Bar ("X")	Wide-to-Narrow Ratio ("R")	Wide Bar ("W")	Bar Width Tolerance ("T")	Min Quiet Zone ("Q")	Symbol Length No. of Data Chars ("D") 16	Min Bar Height 15% ("H")	Symbol Length No. of Data Chars ("D") 17	Min Bar Height 15% ("H")	Symbol Length No. of Data Chars ("D") 18	Min Bar Height 15% ("H")	Symbol Length No. of Data Chars ("D") 19	Min Bar Height 15% ("H")
0.0075	2.20	0.0165	±0.0017	0.25	2.33	0.50	2.43	0.50	2.53	0.50	2.63	0.50
0.0100	2.50	0.0250	±0.0027	0.25	3.10	0.50	3.25	0.50	3.39	0.51	3.54	0.53
0.0100	3.00	0.0300	±0.0035	0.25	3.37	0.51	3.53	0.53	3.69	0.55	3.85	0.58
0.0115	2.50	0.0288	±0.0031	0.25	3.49	0.52	3.66	0.55	3.82	0.57	3.99	0.60
0.0115	3.00	0.0345	±0.0040	0.25	3.80	0.57	3.98	0.60	4.17	0.63	4.35	0.65
0.0130	2.50	0.0325	±0.0035	0.25	3.88	0.58	4.07	0.61	4.26	0.64	4.45	0.67
0.0130	3.00	0.0390	±0.0045	0.25	4.23	0.63	4.44	0.67	4.65	0.70	4.86	0.73
0.0150	2.50	0.0375	±0.0041	0.25	4.40	0.66	4.62	0.69	4.84	0.73	5.05	0.76
0.0150	3.00	0.0450	±0.0052	0.25	4.81	0.72	5.05	0.76	5.29	0.79	5.53	0.83
0.0170	2.50	0.0425	±0.0046	0.25	4.92	0.74	5.17	0.77	5.41	0.81	5.66	0.85
0.0170	3.00	0.0510	±0.0059	0.25	5.38	0.81	5.65	0.85	5.92	0.89	6.20	0.93
0.0250	2.50	0.0625	±0.0068	0.25	7.00	1.05	7.36	1.10	7.73	1.16	8.09	1.21
0.0250	3.00	0.0750	±0.0086	0.25	7.68	1.15	8.08	1.21	8.48	1.27	8.88	1.33
0.0400	2.50	0.1000	±0.0109	0.40	11.20	1.68	11.78	1.77	12.36	1.85	12.94	1.94
0.0400	3.00	0.1200	±0.0138	0.40	12.28	1.84	12.92	1.94	13.56	2.03	14.20	2.13
0.0550	2.50	0.1375	±0.0149	0.55	15.40	2.31	16.20	2.43	17.00	2.55	17.79	2.67
0.0550	3.00	0.1650	±0.0190	0.55	16.89	2.53	17.77	2.66	18.65	2.80	19.53	2.93

Significant Dimensional Parameters of Code 39 at Selected Narrow Bar Widths and Wide-to-Narrow Ratios (20 to 22 characters)

Narrow Bar ("X")	Wide-to-Narrow Ratio ("R")	Wide Bar ("W")	Bar Width Tolerance ("T")	Min Quiet Zone ("Q")	Symbol Length No. of Data Chars ("D") 20	Min Bar Height 15% ("H")	Symbol Length No. of Data Chars ("D") 21	Min Bar Height 15% ("H")	Symbol Length No. of Data Chars ("D") 22	Min Bar Height 15% ("H")
0.0075	2.20	0.0165	±0.0017	0.25	2.74	0.50	2.84	0.50	2.94	0.50
0.0100	2.50	0.0250	±0.0027	0.25	3.68	0.55	3.83	0.57	3.97	0.60
0.0100	3.00	0.0300	±0.0035	0.25	4.01	0.60	4.17	0.63	4.33	0.65
0.0115	2.50	0.0288	±0.0031	0.25	4.16	0.62	4.32	0.65	4.49	0.67
0.0115	3.00	0.0345	±0.0040	0.25	4.54	0.68	4.72	0.71	4.90	0.74
0.0130	**2.50**	**0.0325**	**±0.0035**	**0.25**	**4.63**	**0.70**	**4.82**	**0.72**	*5.01*	*0.75*
0.0130	**3.00**	**0.0390**	**±0.0045**	**0.25**	*5.06*	*0.76*	*5.27*	*0.79*	*5.48*	*0.82*
0.0150	**2.50**	**0.0375**	**±0.0041**	**0.25**	*5.27*	*0.79*	*5.49*	*0.82*	*5.71*	*0.86*
0.0150	**3.00**	**0.0450**	**±0.0052**	**0.25**	*5.77*	*0.86*	6.01	0.90	6.25	0.94
0.0170	**2.50**	**0.0425**	**±0.0046**	**0.25**	5.91	0.89	6.15	0.92	6.40	0.96
0.0170	**3.00**	**0.0510**	**±0.0059**	**0.25**	6.47	0.97	6.74	1.01	7.01	1.05
0.0250	2.50	0.0625	±0.0068	0.25	8.45	1.27	8.81	1.32	9.18	1.38
0.0250	3.00	0.0750	±0.0086	0.25	9.28	1.39	9.68	1.45	10.08	1.51
0.0400	2.50	0.1000	±0.0109	0.40	13.52	2.03	14.10	2.12	14.68	2.20
0.0400	3.00	0.1200	±0.0138	0.40	14.84	2.23	15.48	2.32	16.12	2.42
0.0550	2.50	0.1375	±0.0149	0.55	18.59	2.79	19.39	2.91	20.19	3.03
0.0550	3.00	0.1650	±0.0190	0.55	20.41	3.06	21.29	3.19	22.17	3.32

Notes for Tables B.1 through B.1:

Narrow Bar (or "X" Dimension) and all other dimensions shown in inches

Wide-to-Narrow Ratio ("R") values in Tables are ratios of the Wide Bar "W" to the Narrow Bar "X"

Bar Width Tolerance ("T") calculated at T = ± ((4/27)•(W − 667))•X. Tolerance is equal for narrow bars/spaces as well as wide bars/spaces.

Minimum Quiet Zone ("Q") is equal to 0.25 inch or 10 times Narrow Bar Width ("X"), whichever is greater

Symbol Length ("L") for No. of Data Characters ("D") includes the Start and Stop characters, e.g., in Table C.5 under "No. of Data Chars" 22 represents 24 characters when Start and Stop characters are added.

Symbol Length calculated where Intercharacter Space equals "1X" and Quiet Zones are added. Symbol Length formula: Symbol Length equals (((Number of Data Characters plus 2) multiplied by (3 times W plus 7) minus 1)) multiplied by the Narrow Bar Width. L = ((D+2)•(3•W+7)-1)•X•R

Minimum Bar Height ("H") values are 15% the symbol length or 0.5 inch, whichever is greater

Dimensions shown in bold fall within the ANSI Common Label physical dimensions. Dimensions in bold italics fit only on ANSI Common Labels which are either greater than or equal to 6" wide

Dimensions shown in bold underscore fit only on ANSI Common Labels equal to 6.5 inches wide.

APPENDIX C

Symbology Identifiers

I n 1990 AIM (Automatic Identification Manufacturers) adopted a set of symbology identifiers that decoders would pass to applications software to signal the software as to which bar code was read and with what options. Such identifiers would also enable applications software to determine whether the entry was scanned or key-entered. While these identifiers have not yet been widely adopted, it is expected that reader manufacturers will be incorporating symbology identifiers in the 1990s. The material that follows has been adopted by AIM-U.S.A. and submitted to CEN/TC225 as a European Standard.

When activated, This option transmits a three-character string preamble to the receiving instrument indicating the origin of the transmission. When data is transmitted to the receiving instrument (terminal, computer, etc.), the prefix format of the message is in the format "]cm"—where "]" is the symbology identifier flag character. The character "]" is a character in the ASCII character set known as ASCII 93. "c" is the Code Character and "m" is the Modifier Character.

Code Characters have been assigned to all popular bar code symbologies and some that are not so popular. These Code Characters are case sensitive (that is, a capital "A" is a different code character than a lower case "a"). All code characters not listed below are reserved for future use. Table C.1 shows the assigned Code Characters, Option Values used to calculate Modifier Characters, and the Option associated with the Option Value.

Table C.1
Code Character Assignments

Symbology	Flag Character	Code Character	Option Value	Option
Code 39	]	A	0	No Check Character or Full ASCII processing
			1	Reader has validated modulo 43 check character
			2	Reader has stripped modulo 43 check character
			4	Reader has performed Full ASCII character conversion
Code 128	]	C	0	Standard data packet. No Function code 1 in first or second character position after start character
			1	UCC/EAN-128-function code 1 in first symbol character position after start character
			2	Function code 1 in second symbol character position after start character
EAN/UPC	]	E	0	Standard packet in full EAN code format which is 13 digits for EAN-13, UPC-A, and UPC-E (does not include supplemental data)
			1	Two-digit supplemental data only (transmitted separately from 13-digit UPC/EAN data packet)
			2	Five-digit supplemental data only (transmitted separately from 13-digit UPC/EAN data packet)
			3	Combined data packet comprising 13 digits from EAN-13, UPC-A, and UPC-E symbol and 2 of 5
			4	EAN-8 data packet
Codabar	]	F	0	No options specified at this time. Always transmit "0"
			1	Reader has checked check digit
Code 93	]	G	0	No options specified at this time. Always transmit "0"
Code 11	]	H	0	Single modulo 11 check digit validated
			1	Two modulo 11 check digits validated
			2	All check digit(s) stripped before transmission

Interleaved 2 of 5	]	I	0	No check digit processing
			1	Reader has validated modulo 10 check digit
			2	Reader has stripped check digit before transmission
Code 16K	]	K	0	No special characters in first or second symbol character positions after start character
			1	Function Character 1 implied in first symbol character position after start character
			2	Function Character 1 in second symbol character position after start character
			4	Pad Character in the first symbol character position after start character
MSI	]	M	0	Single modulo 10 check digit validated
			1	Two modulo 10 check digits validated
			2	All check digit(s) stripped before transmission
Anker	]	N	0	No options specified at this time. Always transmit "0"
Plessey Code	]	P	0	No options specified at this time. Always transmit "0"
Straight 2 of 5	]	S	0	No check digit processing
2 bar start/stop			1	Reader has validated modulo 7 check digit
			2	Reader has stripped modulo 7 check digit before transmission
Code 49	]	T	0	No special characters in first or second data character positions
			1	Function Character 1 in first data character position
			2	Function Character 1 in second data character position
			4	Function Character 2 in second data character position
PDF417	]	L	0	No options specified at this time. Always transmit "0"
Other Bar Code	]	X	0 - 9	All option numbers assigned by the reader manufacturer
Non-Bar Code	]	Z	0	Keyboard
			1 - 9	All other option numbers assigned by the reader manufacturer

341

Table C.2
Option Value Conversion to Modifier Character

Sum of Option Values	Modifier Character	Sum of Option Values	Modifier Character
0	0	8	8
1	1	9	9
2	2	10	A
3	3	11	B
4	4	12	C
5	5	13	D
6	6	14	E
7	7	15	F

Example 1

Code 39
If a reader decoded a Code 39 symbol, checked the data with a check character and then stripped the check character prior to transmission, the symbology identifier is determined as follows.
The symbology identifier is of the form:
]cm

Where

] is the symbol identifier flag character
c is the Code Character
m is the Modifier Character

From Table C.1, the Code Character for Code 39 is "A". The Option Values, again from Table C.1, are now added to determine the Modifier Character "m"

	1	Reader has validated the modulo 43 check character
+	2	Reader has stripped the modulo 43 check character
	3	The Modifier Character is "3"

The entire symbology identifier preamble is
]A3

Example 2

UPC/EAN Symbol with five-digit supplemental code
UPC/EAN symbols with supplemental digits are treated as two separate symbols, first the standard UPC/EAN code, then the supplemental symbol. In transmitting the information, the bar code reader decoder shall transmit two separate data strings, one with a symbol identifier associated with the main UPC/EAN portion of the code, and another with a symbol identifier associated with the supplemental data.
If a reader decoded a UPC-A symbol with a five-digit supplement, the following symbology identifiers are used.
First determine the symbol identifier for the UPC-A symbol from Table C.1. The symbology identifier is of the form:
]cm

Where

] is the symbol identifier flag character

c is the Code Character
m is the Modifier Character

From Table C.1, the Code Character for UPC/EAN is "E". The Option Values, again from Table C.1, are now added to determine the Modifier Character "m":

0   Standard data packet in full EAN country code format which is 13 digits for UPC-A and UPC-E

The modifier character for the UPC-A symbol is "0".

The entire symbology identifier preamble for the UPC-A symbol is:
]E0

Now determine the symbol identifier for the five-digit supplement from Table C.1. The symbology identifier is of the form:
]cm

Where   ] is the symbol identifier flag character
c is the Code Character
m is the Modifier Character

From Table C.1, the Code Character for UPC/EAN is "E". The Option Values, again from Table C.1, are now summed to determine the Modifier Character "m":

2   Five-digit supplement data

Since there are no other special processing values associated with the five-digit supplement, the modifier character is "2".

The entire symbology identifier preamble for the UPC-A five-digit supplement is:
]E2

The full data transmission resulting from a successful scan of a UPC symbol with five-digit supplemental code consists of two separate communication strings. One string contains the standard UPC data packet, the other string contains the supplemental information. These two strings may be transmitted in either order, standard packet first or supplemental packet first. Thus the full transmission is:
]E0 {standard data}{terminator}]E2 {supplement}{terminator}
or
]E2 {supplement}{terminator}]E0 {standard data}{terminator}

From Table C.1, the Code Character for UPC/EAN is "E". The Option Values, again from Table C.1, are now summed to determine the Modifier Character "m":

3   Combined data packet comprising 13 digits from EAN-13, UPC-A and UPC-E symbol and 2 or 5 digits from supplementary data

The entire symbology identifier preamble for the UPC-A five-digit supplement may be:
]E3

APPENDIX D

Check Characters

An a priori purpose of all automated data collection is to improve data accuracy as well as to improve the availability of data collected for management review. Several instances exist where the data accuracy of scanned data can be improved:

1. When a specific format of collected data is known and the length of data field is known, received data can be edited to ensure that the correct number of characters or known values in specific character positions have been received.

2. Moving-beam scanners have the opportunity to sample a given bar code symbol multiple times before needing to transmit the data to the data collection processor. In these cases it is possible to enable the moving-beam scanner to transmit data to the data collection processor only in those cases where the output of two adjacent scanning attempts yields identical data.

3. Many bar code symbologies begin and end with a narrow bar. To prevent errant receipt of data in those cases where a diagonal scan through the symbol detects bar space patterns that could be interpreted as a start pattern, data, and stop pattern; a continuous perpendicular bar ("bearer bar") greater than or equal in width to a wide data element (bar) intersecting the top and bottom of the symbol can eliminate this "short read" phenomenon which may exist with symbologies such as Interleaved 2 of 5 and, to a much lesser extent, Code 39.

4. Many newer scanning systems permit the reader first to determine which, among a given set, bar code symbol is being read and then to decode the same. This feature of "autodiscrimination" should be programmatically limited to those symbols that can be expected to be presented in the reading application.

5. A check character can be included that is part of the bar code symbology, such as is found with the Modulus 10 Check Digit in UPC/EAN and the Modulus 103 Check Character found in Code 128, both of which are explained later in this appendix.

    a. In the UPC/EAN, human-readable interpretation of the bar code symbol the check digit appears as another data character.

    b. In Code 128, the Modulus 103 Check Character appears in the bar code symbol but not in the human-readable interpretation.

While it is presumed that when made available, bar code symbols will be scanned, it is also highly likely that some trading partners, unable to scan the data, may want to record the "code" that appears in the bar code symbol. To ensure the accuracy of data that is going to be manually keyed, trading partners may wish to consider the value of including a Check Character in the bar code symbol and human-readable interpretation and then testing for the computed value of the check character when the data is entered.

Check Character (or Check Digit)

General Description. A check character is a calculated value used to enhance the accurate capture of a data message. Characters within a data message are assigned values that are used to calculate a check character. The check character is appended to the data message when printed, and the identical calculation is performed later during capture. If the captured message does not calculate to the same value as printed, an error is indicated. There are many different methods used to calculate a check character's value. Each different method has strengths and weaknesses in detecting the four types of errors that may occur during data capture.

Types of data capture errors. All data capture errors fall into one of four categories:

SUBSTITUTION - The replacement of an intended character by any other, e.g., the intended message "ABC" is captured as "AB3". Both automatic and manual capture methods are capable of making this type of error.

TRANSPOSITION - The trading of positions of two characters in adjacent positions, e.g., the intended message "ABC" is captured as "ACB". Theoretically, only manual capture methods are capable of making this type of error.

DOUBLE TRANSPOSITION - The trading of positions of two characters across an adjacent position, e.g., the intended message "ABC" is captured as "CBA". Theoretically, only manual capture methods are capable of making this type of error.

RANDOM - The combination of any two or more of the above types of errors, or the occurrence of any error other than the above. Random errors include "coincident numbers", where a check character coincidentally calculates the same on an erroneous message as would have been calculated on the correct message. Both automatic and manual methods are capable of making this type of error.

Mechanical and Electronic Check Characters. A check character calculation can be broadly categorized as "mechanical" or as "electronic". The mechanical types can be printed by purely mechanical means. They tend to employ simple calculations and a limited number of characters (typically ten or less) which can represent the check character value. Mechanical check characters are most often used because of historical precedent within an end-user or printing industry, or because of the economy of mass production mechanical printing methods can offer. Despite their simple calculations, mechanical checks greatly enhance data security, particularly when the data capture method is automatic.

Figure D.1
Example Calculation of a Mechanical Check Character

Modulus 9 DR (Divide, Remainder)

Data message » 123456

Divide by the Modulus (9) » $123456 \div 9 = 13717$, remainder 3.

The remainder is used as the check digit:

Data + check » 1234563

Electronic check characters generally employ more complex calculations and/or more than ten characters that can represent a check character value. A "weighting" scheme is often used, where a predetermined multiplier is positionally applied to a character's value as one step in the calculation. A computer-controlled printing method is typically required for generation. Computer-controlled methods can be used to generate mechanical check characters as well as the electronically generated varieties.

Figure D.2
Example Calculation of an Electronic Check Character

Modulus 10 (2-1-2 Weighting) DSR (Divide Subtract Remainder)

Data message 123456

Starting at the right, weight each character alternately by 2 and 1, add the products, and divide the sum by the Modulus (10):

1	2	3	4	5	6	
x 1	x 2	x 1	x 2	x 1	x 2	$= 33 \div 10 = 3$, remainder 3.
1 +	4 +	3 +	8 +	5 +	12	

Subtract the remainder from the Modulus (10): $10 - 3 = 7$.

The difference between 10 and 3 is used as the check digit.

Data + check 1234567

Mandatory and Optional Check Characters. Some bar code symbologies have a mandatory check character as part of their basic structure. Examples would be Code 128 and UPC, which always require a Modulus 103 and a modulus 103 and a modulus 10 check character, respectively. Other symbologies do not require any check character as part of their structure, but may have a check character suggested for optional use or required by an industry standard. An example would be Code 39, which suggests an optional Modulus 43 check character for use when an application requires enhanced data security. It should be understood that an optional check character represents a data system commitment on the part of all printers and recipients of a message; optional does not mean a check character can be sporadically used in an application. An optional check character is either specifically used or specifically not used by all recipients in an application or where non-using recipients consider the check character as a data character, i.e., a catalog number is increased in length by one character (the check character).

Choice of an Optional Check Character. Selecting an optional check character is more than simply selecting a secure calculation. A partial list of considerations follows:

PRINTING METHOD - Mass production may be more economic if a mechanical printing method is used. Future quantities must be considered as well; an application can start with small quantities where on-site electronic printing is practical, then grow to a proportion where off-site printing may be considered. Although off-site printing vendors are typically capable of producing electronic as well as mechanical check characters, the greatest economy may result from purely mechanical production. A vendor or consultant should be consulted before check character selection if there is a possibility of the application growing beyond on-site capabilities.

DATA CAPTURE METHODS - Mandatory check characters are normally optimized for the intended data capture method. For example, Code 39's Simple-Sum Modulus 43 (electronic) is an established routine for a bar code scanner. It does a very good job of detecting the types of errors a scanner is capable of making. It does not, however, do a good job of catching all of the types of errors a human is capable of making. Every character within a data message can transpose with every other without affecting the outcome of the check character calculation, e.g., data ABC123 will calculate to the same check character as every other arrangement of the data such as A1B2C3, 321ABC, CAB231, etc. Although mechanical types of check characters are normally more secure for human data entry than the mandatory types, they too must be carefully considered. The Modulus 9 mechanical rou-

347

tine shown in Figure E.1 will not catch any rearrangement of the data, i.e., all arrangements of the data 123456 will yield the check character "3". When you are selecting a check character ,all capture methods within a system should be considered, and the strengths and weaknesses of the possible check character routines should be considered.

WHEN AND WHERE CHECKED - The most potentially secure system will test data integrity each time data is captured, transmitted, and retrieved. Mandatory check characters often do not lend themselves to this approach. For example, Code 128's mandatory Modulus 103 is transparent to the user, as it is checked by the bar code reader and stripped from the data before transmission. It cannot be used with manual capture methods. Similarly, when Code 39's optional Simple-Sum Modulus 43 is selected, it is typically stripped by the bar code reader. Even though the reader may have a keypad or keyboard incorporated for manual back-up, manual entry is not normally checked by a reader. When the checking of manual entry or the prevention of stripping the check character are priorities, it is normally possible to incorporate custom software either in a reader that supports a user program or in the host system to which that reader is attached. Portable readers should be the type that support user programs or operate in real time with the host.

SYSTEM SUPPORT - All components of the data system must be capable of supporting the check character selected. For example, portable readers may employ abbreviated keypads that do not have all the characters that will be generated by the check character calculation, preventing manual entry. Also, some users may want a restricted character set (such as eliminating Codabar's characters : / . + or Code 39's characters $ / + % . – ([space]) and not realize that those codes' respective Modulus 16 and Modulus 43 will generate these characters. Further, in the case of Code 39, the presence of a ([space]) as the check character might not appear obvious to the user unless a substitute character is used in lieu of the human-readable space, i.e., some industry standards employ the "#" character as the human-readable representation of ([space]) though the bar space arrangement for the character is that of ([space]). All parties to the data transaction must be consulted before selection of a check character; the minimum common system capability may define the selection.

The importance of a proper selection is emphasized by the fact that changing an in-place calculation is difficult. A change requires that strict data segregation take place, or a system must accept either of two different check character calculations for a period of time and be weakened accordingly.

Comparison of Error Detection Ability. There are many different check characters in use today. Additive structures such as Simple-Sum Modulus 43, Modulus 9 Sum of Digits, and Modulus 16 are susceptible to keyed adjacent transposition errors, whereby the data content is incorrect but the code passes the modulus check. Weighted structures such as Weighted Modulus 43, Weighted Modulus 36, Weighted Modulus 36, UPC Modulus 10, Weighted Modulus 10, Weighted Modulus 11, Modulus 47, and Modulus 103 eliminate the transposition error passing the modulus check. Divide structures such as Mod 7 DR and DSR, Modulus 9 DSR, and Modulus 11 also minimize transposition errors.

Modulus 11 systems provide for two value "Ø" ("Ø" and "1Ø"). Either 2:11 symbols go unchecked or 1:11 symbols are discarded after the print run.

Weighting schemes can be positional sequential (1, 2, 3, 4 . . .) or be positional alternating (1, 3, 1, 3, 1 . . .). Where positional alternating weighting schemes are employed it is recommended that the weighted values be prime numbers, (e.g., 1, 3, 5, 7, 11 . . .).

A few popular check characters and their relative ability to detect the four categories of errors are presented in Table D.1. For the purpose of calculating error detecting capability it was assumed that any type of error could be made in any data position.

348

Check Digit Type	Substitution	Single Transposition	Double Transposition	Random
Mod 7 DR mechanical	93.33%	93.33%	93.33%	85.71%
Mod 9 SOD mechanical	97.7%	0.0%	0.0%	88.88%
Mod 10 3-1-3 SOP DSR	100.0%	88.88%	0.0%	90.0%
Mod 10 2-1-2 SOP DSR	94.4%	100.0%	0.0%	90.0%
Mod 11 DR mechanical Note 1	100.0%	100.0%	0.0%	90.90%
Mod 11 3-1-3 SOP DSR Note 1	100.0%	100.0%	0.0%	90.90%
Mod 16 SS DSR (Codabar)	98.0%	0.0%	0.0%	93.75%
Mod 36 3-1-3 SOP DR	100.00%	100.0%	0.0%	90.90%
Mod 43 SS DR (Code 39)	100.0%	0.0%	0.0%	97.67%
Mod 43 AW SOP DR Note 2	100.0%	100.0%	100.0%	97.67%

Legend - DR (Divide, Remainder); DSR (Divide, Subtract Remainder); SOD (Sum of Digits); SOP (Sum of Products); SS (Simple-Sum); AW (Arithmetic Weight).

Note[1]: Mod 11 DR produces an invalid (more than one position) check character of "10" which is conventionally printed as an "X"; the above chart assumes that this value is checked by the system as unique from other values. A Mod 11 DSR routine can produce the two invalid "10" and "11" which may weaken data security.

Note[2]: A data message length less than 43 characters is assumed

Modulus 7 DR and DSR

Two forms of Modulus 7 (Mod 7) Check Character generation schemes exist. One is referred to as a Mod 7 DR (Divide-Remainder) and the other is a Mod 7 DSR (Divide-Subtract-Remainder).

In both cases the basic number is divided by 7. For example, the consecutive number 12345 divided by 7 equals 1763 with a remainder of 4.

In a **Mod 7 DR** check digit environment the remainder 4 is the check digit and the self-check number would be 123454.

In a **Mod 7 DSR** check digit environment the division remainder 4 is subtracted from the Modulus $(7 - 4 = 3)$; the subtraction remainder 3 is the check digit; and the self-check number would be 123453.

Modulus 9 Sum of Digits and DSR

There are several Modulus 9 systems in use. Two forms are Modulus 9 (Mod 9) Sum of Digits System and the Divide-Subtract-Remainder (DSR) System.

In a **Mod 9 Sum of Digits** check digit environment, the check digit is the number that, when added to the sum of the individual digits of the basic consecutive number, produces a multiple of 9. For example, using the basic number 12345, the sum of digits is $1+2+3+4+5 = 15$. The number 15 is subtracted from the next highest multiple of 9, which is 18, leaving a remainder of 3. The check digit is 3, and the self-check number is 123453. The check digit for 12346 is 2, and the self-check number is 123462.

In a **Mod 9 DSR** check digit environment the consecutive number is divided by 9 and the remainder subtracted from 9 giving the check digit. For example, using the basic number 12345, dividing by 9 equals 1371 with a remainder of 6. The number 9 minus 6 equals 3. The check digit is 3, and the self-checking number is 123453.

UPC Modulus 10

Both the UPC Symbol (unit-of-sale) and the UPC Shipping Container Symbol (USCS) employ a UPC Modulus 10 check character. The following example will illustrate the calculation for a UPC symbol (09875610001) having:

- Manufacturer Identification Number = 098756 (1st Digit "0" is Number System Digit)
- Item Code Number = 10001

Step 1: Starting at the left, add all the characters in the <u>odd</u> positions (that is, first from the left, third from the left, and so on), <u>starting with the number system character.</u>

(In this example, $0 + 8 + 5 + 1 + 0 + 1 = 15$)

Step 2: Multiply the sum obtained in Step 1 by 3

(In this example, $3 \bullet 15 = 45$)

Step 3: Again starting at the left, add all the characters in the <u>even</u> positions.

(In this example, $9 + 7 + 6 + 0 + 0 = 22$)

Step 4: Add the product of Step 2 to the sum of Step 3.

(In this example, $45 + 22 = 67$)

Step 5: The UPC modulus 10 check character value is the smallest number which when added to the sum of Step 4 produces a multiple of 10.

(In this example, $67/10 = 6$ with a Remainder of 7; the check character value is the remainder subtracted from 10, namely, $10 - 7 =$ "3")

The full UPC A Symbol with Check Character is encoded "098756100013".

EAN Modulus 10

Position	13	12	11	10	9	8	7	6	5	4	3	2	1
Full Size Version EAN-13	P1	P2	P3	X	X	X	X	X	X	X	X	X	C
Short Size Version EAN-8						P1	P2	P3	X	X	X	X	C

IMPORTANT: Digit positions are numbered from right to left in this algorithm (the check digit is in the first position; the P1 prefix is in the 13th position in EAN-13 and in the 8th position in EAN-8).

Step 1: Starting from position 2 of the number, add up the values of the digits in even-numbered positions.

Step 2: Multiply the sum obtained in Step 1 by 3.

Step 3: Starting from position 3 of the number, add up the values of the digits in odd-numbered positions.

Step 4: Add the product of Step 2 to the sum of Step 3.

Step 5: The check digit is the smallest number which when added to the sum of Step 4 produces a multiple of 10.

The following example illustrates the calculation for an EAN-13 number (427622135746 C):

	4	2	7	6	2	2	1	3	5	7	4	6	C	
Step 1:		2	+	6	+	2	+	3	+	7	+	6		= 26
Step 2:											• 3			= 78
Step 3:	4	+	7	+	2	+	1	+	5	+	4			= 23
Step 4:	78 (Step 2) + 23 (Step 3)													= 101
Step 5:	101/10 = 10 with a Remainder of 1 10 – 1													= 9 (Check Digit)

The full EAN-13 number with Check Digit is encoded "4276221357469".

The following example illustrates the calculation for an EAN-8 number (3714274 C):

	3	7	1	4	2	7	4	C	
Step 1:	3	+	1	+	2	+	4		= 10
Step 2:						• 3			= 30
Step 3:		7	+	4	+	7			= 18
Step 4:	30 (Step 2) + 18 (Step 3)								= 48
Step 5:	48/10 = 4 with a Remainder of 8 10 – 8								= 2 (Check Digit)

The full EAN-8 number with Check Digit is encoded "37142742".

Weighted Modulus 10

In the Modulus 10 system, the check digit is obtained by multiplying the odd number digits by a constant (for illustration purposes "2"), and adding the resultant numbers to the sum of the even numbered digits. The total is then subtracted from the next higher multiple of 10. For example, if the consecutive number is 123456: Start numbering digits from the right

Consecutive Number	1 2 3 4 5 6
Multiply by 2	4 8 12
Digits not multiplied	1 3 5
Add	1 + 4 + 3 + 8 + 5 + 1 + 2 = 24

NOTE: In the computation of the check digit, a two-digit number is broken down into units. In this example the 12 becomes 1 + 2 = 3.

Next higher multiple of 10	30
Subtract	– 24
Check Digit	6
Consecutive number with check digit is	1234566

Modulus 11

The basic consecutive number is divided by 11, and the remainder is the check digit. For example, using the basic number 12345, dividing by 11 equals 1122 with a remainder of 3. The check digit is 3 and the self-checking number is 123453.

NOTE: In Modulus 11 it is possible to have a two-digit remainder of 10. Since a check digit is a single digit only, an alpha figure such as X is substituted for 10, thus creating an invalid number. The computer can be programmed to accept invalid numbers but it cannot verify the number. In the case of forms and labels, units with invalid numbers are usually removed and not used.

Weighted Modulus 11

The true Modulus 11 check-digit system uses a weighting factor for each digit in the consecutive number. Digits of a consecutive number or account number are verified by using these "weights," namely, 2, 3, 4, 5, 6, and 7 starting from the right.

Each digit position of the consecutive number is assigned a "weighted" factor. To calculate the check digit manually, a weighting factor is placed below each digit starting at the right and working left. Each digit is then multiplied by its weighting factor. The resultant products are added, and the sum of the products is divided by 11. The remainder of this division is then subtracted from 11, and the resulting figure is the check digit. This example is a Divide-Subtract-Remainder formula (DSR). If the first remainder is used as the check digit, before subtracting from 11, the formula would be a Divide-Remainder (DR) formula.

For example, if the consecutive number is 21345678:

Consecutive Number	2	1	3	4	5	6	7	8	
Weight Factor	X3	X2	X7	X6	X5	X4	X3	X2	
Multiply and Add	6 +	2 +	21 +	24 +	25 +	24 +	21 +	16	= 139
Divide Sum by 11	139/11 = 12 with a remainder of 7								
Subtract	11 − 7 = 4								
Check Digit	4								
Consecutive Number with Check Digit	213456784								

See NOTE under **Modulus II** *above.*

Weighted Modulus 11 (ABC Codabar)

The ABC Symbol, employed in Blood Banking, uses a check digit called a Weighted Modulus 11 (ABC Codabar) Check Digit. This check digit scheme for all numbers containing 10 digits or less is expected to catch essentially all of the transposition and transcription errors. For numbers containing 11 digits or more, the efficiency of the check digit is reduced slightly. The check digit is calculated as shown below for the code "524032140".

The rule for calculating the Weighted Modulus 11 (ABC Codabar) Check Digit requires two sets of weighting factors defined as follows:

Code Position:	12	11	10	9	8	7	6	5	4	3	2	1
Set 1 Weighting:	6	3	5	9	10	7	8	4	5	3	6	2
Set 2 Weighting:	5	8	6	2	10	4	3	7	6	8	5	9

Note: Set 1 and Set 2 are related as a complement of 11 except where the weighting digit is a 10 in which case there is a 10 in both positions. The procedure for calculating the Weighted Modulus 11 (ABC Codabar) Check Digit involves the following five steps:

Step 1: Multiply each digit in the data to be checked by the appropriate weighting factor. The data in Code Position 1 is multiplied by the associated Set 1 Weighting Factor ("2"). The data digits in the subsequent code positions are multiplied by the associated Set 1 Weighting

Factors progressing from the rightmost position to the left until all data digits have been multiplied by their associated Set 1 Weighting Factors.

Step 2: Sum the products obtained in Step 1.

Step 3: Divide the resulting sum by the modulus "11".

Step 4: Observe the remainder in Step 3. If the remainder is "1", scrap what you have done so far and go through Steps 1 through 4 using Set 2 Weighting Factors. You should not get a remainder of 1 for both Set 1 Weighting Factors and Set 2 Weighting Factors.

Step 5: Subtract the remainder in Step 4 from the modulus "11" and the difference is the check digit. If the remainder is 10, the check digit becomes a "1". If the remainder is "0", the check digit is "0".

Example, for code "524032140":

Code Position:	12	11	10	9	8	7	6	5	4	3	2	1
Code Position:				5	2	4	0	3	2	1	4	0
Set 1 Weighting:	6	3	5	9	10	7	8	4	5	3	6	2

$$45 + 20 + 28 + 0 + 12 + 10 + 3 + 24 + 0$$
$$= 142/11 = 12 \text{ with a remainder of } 10$$

If the remainder is "10", the check digit becomes a "1"

Data Structure with Check Character:

5	2	4	0	3	2	1	4	0	1

Modulus 16 (Codabar)

A check character is seldom employed in Codabar symbols and no de facto standard format has arisen. The two largest users of Codabar are the Blood Banking Community using a Weighted Modulus 11 (ABC Codabar) and Federal Express using a Modulus 7 DSR, both shown above. Nonetheless, in other applications requiring enhanced data security, a Modulus 16 check character may be used. The Modulus 16 scheme is presented below.

When used, the check character is positioned immediately following the final data character, before the store character. The encoding of the Modulus 16 check character is determined as follows:

1. Each Codabar character is assigned a numerical value as shown in the table below:

Numerical Value Assignments for Computing the Codabar Modulus 16 Check Character

Character	Value	Character	Value	Character	Value	Character	Value
0	0	5	5	–	10	+	15
1	1	6	6	$	11	A	16
2	2	7	7	:	12	B	17
3	3	8	8	/	13	C	18
4	4	9	9	.	14	D	19

2. The numerical values for all the message characters including the start and stop characters (A, B, C, & D) are added together. This sum is then divided by the modulus "16", the quotient is discarded, and the remainder is used in Step 3.

3. The remainder is then subtracted from the modulus "16". The data character whose value is the difference between the remainder and the modulus is used as the check character.

This check character generation is illustrated by the following example:

Symbol Data Structure: A 0 9 8 7 5 6 B

Sum of values: 16+0+9+8+7+5+6+17 = 68/16 = 4 with remainder of 4

Subtract remainder for modulus: 16 – 4 = 12.

Character with value of difference: Value "12" = Character ":"

Data Structure with Check Character:

A   0   9   8   7   5   6   :   B

Weighted Modulus 36 (3-1-3-1) (Code 39)

The following values are established for associated characters assignments in generating a Weighted Modulus 36 (Remainder Method):

Table D.2
Modulus 36 Character Value Table

Value	Character	Value	Character	Value	Character
0	0	12	C	24	O
1	1	13	D	25	P
2	2	14	E	26	Q
3	3	15	F	27	R
4	4	16	G	28	S
5	5	17	H	29	T
6	6	18	I	30	U
7	7	19	J	31	V
8	8	20	K	32	W
9	9	21	L	33	X
10	A	22	M	34	Y
11	B	23	N	35	Z

To calculate the Weighted Mod 36 Check Character the FACT Data Identifier shall be included in the check character calculation and shall be key-entered. No spaces or special characters shall be included in the data or key-entry.

STEP 1: Starting from the left, add all the characters in the odd positions (i.e., first from the left, third from the left, etc.). Be sure to start with the first character in the FACT Data Identifier.

Assuming the FACT Data Identifier "9K" (R.O. Number), with an R.O. Number of 0123456789 yielding a complete structure of "9K0123456789", as an example, the odd values are:

$$9 + 0 + 2 + 4 + 6 + 8 = 29$$

STEP 2: Multiply the sum in Step 1 by 3. The product in this example is: $29 \cdot 3 = 87$

STEP 3: Again, starting at the left, add all the characters in the even positions.

In this example, the even values from the left are (note that the character "K" has a value of 20 in the above Character Value Table):

$$20 + 1 + 3 + 5 + 7 + 9 = 45$$

STEP 4: Add the product of Step 2 to the sum of Step 3

In this example, the sum is:

$$87 + 45 = 132$$

STEP 5: The Mod 36 check character is obtained by dividing the number in Step 4 by 36, and looking in the Character Value Table for the character with the remainder value.

In this example, when you divide 132 by 36, you get:
$$132 \div 36 = 3 \text{ with a remainder of } 24.$$

Looking in the Character Value Table, a value of 24 corresponds to the letter "O". Therefore, in this example, the check character is "O".

Arithmetic Weighted Modulus 36 (Code 39)

The values shown in Table D.2 are used in generating a Weighted Modulus 36 (Remainder Method).

To calculate the Weighted Mod 36 Check Character the Data/Application Identifier shall be included in the check character calculation and shall be key-entered. No spaces or special characters shall be included in the data or key-entry.

STEP 1: Starting with the character immediately preceding the check character, multiply the value by the weighting constant. The weighting constant is the numerical value from 1 to 36 depending upon the number of character positions in the code. Character position 37 assumes the value of 1, 38 the value of 2, etc. The placement of character weights is from right to left.

STEP 2: Add the result of this multiplication for all data characters.

STEP 3: The check character is that character whose numerical value is equal to modulus 36 of the sum obtained in Step 2 above.

Check character generation is illustrated by the following example:

Symbol Data Structure:	1		2		3		4		A		B		C		D
Values:	1		2		3		4		10		11		12		13
Weighting:	8		7		6		5		4		3		2		1
Summation:	8	+	14	+	18	+	20	+	40	+	33	+	24	+	13
	= 170													

Divide 170 by 36. The quotient is 4 with a remainder of 26. The Check Character is the character corresponding to the value of the remainder, which in this example is 26, or character "P". The complete Symbol data structure including Check Character, would therefore be:

1 2 3 4 A B C D P

Modulus 43

Some Code 39 data structures employ a Modulus 43 Check Character for additional data security. The Check Character is the Modulus 43 sum of all the character values in a given message, and is printed as the last character value in a given message, preceding the Stop Character. Start and Stop Characters (*) are not used in calculating the Check Character. Check Character generation is illustrated by the following example with the Table below:

Symbol Data Structure:	E		5		9		8		9		7		6		9		8		7		
Sum of values:	14	+	5	+	9	+	8	+	9	+	7	+	6	+	9	+	8	+	7	=	82

Divide 82 by 43. The quotient is 1 with a remainder of 39. The Check Character is the character corresponding to the value of the remainder (see Table below), which in this example is 39, or "$". The complete Symbol data structure including Check Character, would therefore be:

E 5 9 8 9 7 6 9 8 7 $

**Numerical Value Assignments for Computing
the Standard and Weighted Code 39 Check Characters**

0	0	A	10	L	21	W	32
1	1	B	11	M	22	X	33
2	2	C	12	N	23	Y	34
3	3	D	13	O	24	Z	35
4	4	E	14	P	25	–	36
5	5	F	15	Q	26	.	37
6	6	G	16	R	27	Space	38
7	7	H	17	S	28	$	39
8	8	I	18	T	29	/	40
9	9	J	19	U	30	+	41
		K	20	V	31	%	42

Weighted Modulus 43

Some Code 39 data structures employ a Weighted Modulus 43 Check Character for additional data security in scanning and key entry. The Weighted Modulus 43 check algorithm described below is not generally implemented in all available reading equipment and may require the user's computer to provide the check algorithm. The same value system used in the Regular Mod 43 Computation also applies in the Weighted Modulus 43 system. The procedure for computing the weighted check character follows:

1. Starting with the character immediately preceding the check character, multiply the value by the weighting constant. The weighting constant is the numerical value from 1 to 43 depending upon the number of character positions in the code. Character position 44 assumes the value of 1, 45 the value of 2, etc. The placement of character weights is from right to left.

2. Sum the result of this multiplication for all data characters.

3. The check character is that character whose value is equal to modulus 43 of the sum obtained in Step 2 above.

356

Check character generation is illustrated by the following example:

Symbol Data Structure:	1	2	3	4	-	A	B	C	D
Values:	1	2	3	4	36	10	11	12	13
Weighting:	9	8	7	6	5	4	3	2	1
Summation:	9 +	16 +	21 +	24 +	180 +	40 +	33 +	24 +	13
= 360									

Divide 360 by 43. The quotient is 8 with a remainder of 16. The Check Character is the character corresponding to the value of the remainder, which in this example is 16, or character "G". The complete Symbol data structure including Check Character, would therefore be:

$$1\ 2\ 3\ 4 - A\ B\ C\ D\ G$$

Modulus 47 (Code 93)

Every Code 93 symbol contains two check characters (referred to as "C" and "K") which immediately precede the stop character.

Check Character "C" is the modulo 47 sum of the data character values (see Table 5.3 in the text) and a weighting sequence, where the weights from right to left are in the sequence 1, 2, 3, 4, ...18, 19, 20, 1, 2, 3, 4, ...18, 19, 20, 1, 2, 3, ...

Check Character "K" is the modulo 47 sum of the data character values (see Table 5.3 in the text) and a weighting sequence, where the weights from right to left, beginning with the check character "C" are in the sequence 1, 2, 3, 4, ...13, 14, 15, 1, 2, 3, 4, ...13, 14, 15, 1, 2, 3, ...

This check character generation is illustrated by the following example:

Symbol Data Structure:	M	H	8	0	3	1	2	"C"	"K"
Data values:	22	17	8	0	3	1	2		
C Weights:	7	6	5	4	3	2	1		
K Weights:	8	7	6	5	4	3	2	1	

To obtain "C", calculate the sum of the products

Data values:	22	17	8	0	3	1	2
C Weights:	7	6	5	4	3	2	1
	154 +	102 +	40 +	0 +	9 +	2 +	2

= 309/47 = 6 with a remainder of 27 = Character "R"

To obtain "K", calculate the sum of the products

Data values:	22	17	8	0	3	1	2	27
K Weights:	8	7	6	5	4	3	2	1
	176 +	119 +	48 +	0 +	12 +	3 +	4 +	27

= 389/47 = 8 with a remainder of 13 = Character "D"

Data Structure with Check Character:

$$M\ H\ 8\ 0\ 3\ 1\ 2\ R\ D$$

Note that the Code 93 reader employs the check characters "C" and "K" for checking the decoded message, but does not transmit the check characters to the application program.

Modulus 103

The character immediately preceding the Stop Character is the Check Character. The Check Character is a Modulus 103 Checksum that can be calculated by summing the start code value plus the products of each character position (most significant character position = 1) and the character value of that position. (See Table 3.17). Divide the sum of the start code value and the products by 103. The remainder of the answer is the Check Character, expressed as the value of the encoded Check character.

$$\frac{\text{Start Code Value} + {}^n\Sigma \begin{array}{c}(\text{Position})(\text{Position Value}) \\ \text{Position=1}\end{array}}{103} \qquad \begin{array}{l}\text{Answer} + \\ \text{Remainder,} \\ \\ \text{Remainder,} \\ = \text{Check Character Value}\end{array}$$

Every encoded character is included in the calculation with the exception of the Stop and Check Characters. Weighting is calculated with the Start Character as a "1" and the first character of the data message as a "1". Weighting is continuous . . . ∞, with no return to "1" in any single symbol. In the case of the UPC Serialized Shipping Container Symbol (SSCS), the first data character is the FNC1 character. Remember in the SSCS to take the value of the *two-digit* interpretation of the printed bar code character.

Example 1:

Encoded Characters	StartA	C	O	D	E
Value	103	35	47	36	37
Weighting	1	1	2	3	4
Multiplied Product	103 +	35 +	94 +	108 +	148

= 394/103 = 3 with Remainder of 85 Check Character is "NAK (value 85)" not printed in human-readable but encoded in bar space pattern.

Example 2:

(UPC Serialized Shipping Container Symbol): 00 0 0012345 555555555 8

Encoded Characters	StartC	FNC1	00 00 01 23 45 55 55 55 55 58
Value	105	102	00 00 01 23 45 55 55 55 55 58
Weighting	1	1	2 3 4 5 6 7 8 9 10 11

Multiplied Product 105+102+0+0+4+115+270+385+440+495+550+638= 3104/103 = 30 with Remainder of 14 Check Character is ". (period — value 14)" not printed in human-readable but encoded in bar/space pattern.

Mapping FACT DIs to UCC/EAN AIs

The mapping below shows the association between FACT Data Identifiers (as identified in the 1 February 1994 Public Review Draft of ANSI FACT 1 MH 10.8.2-199x) and the Uniform Code Council's and EAN International's UCC/EAN Application Identifiers (AIs). Those cases where an asterisk (*) is followed by a date, e.g., (1/90) represent a Data Identifier addition to the original ANSE/FACT-1-1991 Data Identifier Standard and the date assigned, e.g., January 1990. The Application Identifiers shown in the mapping below represent those AIs assigned as of January 1994.

DEFINED CATEGORIES

Editor's Note: The usage of the term "number" below is not intended to be restricted to numeric characters only, but to generically refer to a code structure which may contain numeric and/or alphabetic data. The following Application and Data Identifiers are assigned to the usages described. The usage of any alphabetic, numeric, or special character in a leading position (as a "data identifier") not defined herein is reserved for future assignment by the body controlling these guidelines. Unless otherwise specified leading zeroes (Ø's) are nonsignificant and not to be employed (e.g., ØA, ØØA, ØØØA, Ø1A, Ø11A).

CATEGORY	Description	FACT DI	UCC/EAN FORMAT (AI) ("n/e" means no equivalent)
CATEGORY 1:	Reserved		
Allocation:		A - 999A	n/e
Assigned:			
Prior Assignment		A - 5A	n/e
Reserved		6A - 999A	n/e
CATEGORY 2:	Container Information		
Allocation:		B - 999B	n/e
Assigned:			
Container Type (internally assigned or mutually defined)		B	n/e
Returnable container identification code assigned by the container owner or the appropriate regulatory agency		1B	8003

(e.g., a metal tub, basket, reel, unit load device (ULD),
trailer, tank, or intermodal container)
(excludes gas cylinders See "2B")

Gas Cylinder Container Identification Code assigned by the manufacturer in conformance with U.S. Department of Transportation (D.O.T.) standards.	2B	n/e
Motor Freight Transport Equipment Identification Code assigned by the manufacturer in conformance with International Standards Organization (ISO) standards.	3B	n/e
Reserved	4B - 999B	n/e

CATEGORY 3: Field Continuation

Allocation	C - 999C	n/e
Assigned:		
Continuation of an Item Code (Category 16) assigned by Customer that is too long for a required field size	C	n/e
Continuation of Traceability Code (Category 2Ø) assigned by Supplier	1C	n/e
Continuation of Serial Number (Category 19) assigned by Supplier	2C	n/e
Continuation of Free Text (Category 26) mutually defined between Supplier/Carrier/Customer	3C	n/e
Continuation of Transaction Reference (Category 11) mutually defined between Supplier/Carrier/Customer	4C	n/e
Continuation of Item Code (Category 16) Assigned by Supplier *(12/90)	5C	n/e
Reserved	6C - 999C	n/e

CATEGORY 4: Date

Allocation:	D - 999D	n/e
Assigned:		
Format YYMMDDNote 2	D	n/e
Format DDMMYYNote 2	1D	n/e
Format MMDDYYNote 2	2D	n/e
Format YDDD (Julian)Note 2	3D	n/e
Format YYDDD (Julian)Note 2	4D	n/e
ISO format YYMMDD immediately followed by an ANSI X12.3 (Version 003000) Data Element Number 374 Qualifier providing a code specifying type of date (e.g., ship date, manufacture date)	5D	n/e
Production Date (YYMMDD)	5D...405	11
Expiration Date (YYMMDD)	5D...036	17
Packaging Date (YYMMDD)	n/e	13
Best Before/Sell By Date (Quality) (YYMMDD)	n/e	15
ISO format YYYYMMDD immediately followed by an ANSI X12.3 (Version 003000) Data Element Number 374 Qualifier providing a code specifying type of date (e.g., ship date, manufacture date)	6D	n/e
Format MMYYNote 2	7D	n/e
Reserved	8D	n/e
Date (structure and significance mutually defined)	9D	n/e
Format YYWWNote 2 *(8/9Ø)	1ØD	n/e
Format YYYYWWNote 2 *(8/9Ø)	11D	n/e
Format YYYYMMDDNote 2 *(8/9Ø)	12D	n/e
Reserved	13D - 999D	n/e

Note 2: Mutually Defined Significance

CATEGORY 5:	Reserved		
Allocation:		E - 999E	n/e
Assigned:			
Prior Assignment		E	n/e
Reserved		1E - 999E	n/e
CATEGORY 6:	Reserved		
Allocation:		F - 999F	n/e
Assigned:			
Prior Assignment		F	n/e
Reserved		1F - 999F	n/e
CATEGORY 7:	Reserved		
Allocation:		G - 999G	n/e
Assigned:			
Prior Assignment		G	n/e
Reserved		1G - 999G	n/e
CATEGORY 8:	Human Resources		
Allocation:		H - 999H	n/e
Assigned:			
Reserved		H	n/e
Employee Identification Code assigned by employer		1H	n/e
U.S. Social Security Number		2H	n/e
ID Number for non-employee (internally assigned or mutually defined) (e.g., contract workers, vendors, service, and delivery personnel)		3H	n/e
National Social Security Number *(8/9Ø)		4H	n/e
Reserved		5H - 999H	n/e
CATEGORY 9:	Reserved		
Allocation:		I - 999I	n/e
Assigned			
Exclusive Assignment (U.S. Vehicle Identification Number - VIN)		I	n/e
Reserved		1I	n/e
Abbreviated VIN Code *(2/9Ø)		2I	n/e
Not recommended for use due to similarity of "1" to "I"		3I - 999I	n/e
CATEGORY 1Ø:	Reserved		
Allocation:		J - 999J	n/e
Assigned:			
Reserved		J - 999J	n/e
CATEGORY 11:	Transaction Reference Used In Trading Relationships		
Allocation:		K - 999K	n/e
Assigned:			
Order number assigned by Customer to identify a Purchasing Transaction (e.g., purchase order number)		K	400
Order number assigned by Supplier to identify a Purchasing Transaction		1K	n/e
Bill of Lading/Waybill/Shipment Identification Code assigned by Supplier/Shipper		2K	n/e
Bill of Lading/Waybill/Shipment Identification Code assigned by Carrier		3K	n/e
Line number of the order assigned by Customer to		4K	n/e

identify a Purchasing Transaction
(See Appendix C.1Ø)

Reference number assigned by the Customer to identify a Shipment Authorization (Release) against an established Purchase Order	5K	401
PRO# Assigned by Carrier	6K	95
Carrier Mode in Free Text format mutually defined between Customer and Supplier (e.g., Air, Truck, Boat, Rail)	7K	n/e
Contract Number	8K	n/e
Generic Transaction Reference Code (internally assigned or mutually defined)	9K	n/e
Invoice Number	1ØK	n/e
Packing List Number	11K	n/e
Reserved	12K - 13K	n/e
Combined Order Number and Line Number in the format nn...nn+nn...n where a plus symbol (+) is used as a delimiter between the Order Number and Line Number.	14K	n/e
KANBAN Number *(2/9Ø)	15K	n/e
DELINS Number: code assigned to identify a document which contains delivery information *(2/9Ø)	16K	n/e
Check Number *(8/9Ø)	17K	n/e
Reserved	18K - 999K	n/e

CATEGORY 12:   Location Reference

Allocation:	L - 999L	n/e
Assigned:		
Storage Location* (2/93)	L	n/e
Location	1L	n/e
"Ship To:" Location code defined by an industry standard or mutually defined	2L	410
"Ship From:" Location code defined by an industry standard or mutually defined	3L	n/e
Bill To (Invoice To) Location Code Using EAN-13 or DUNS (Dun & Bradstreet) Number with Leading Zeros	n/e	411
Purchase From (Location Code of Party from Whom Goods are Purchased)	n/e	412
Country of Origin, two-character ISO 3166 country code	4L	n/e
"Ship For:" Location code defined by an industry standard or mutually defined	5L	n/e
Route Code assigned by the supplier to designate a specific transportation path *(2/9Ø)	6L	n/e
Reserved	7L - 19L	n/e

The following identifiers can be used to provide for Location identification which is different than or in addition to Location Reference provided by "L".

First Level (internally assigned)	2ØL	n/e
Second Level (internally assigned)	21L	n/e
Third Level (internally assigned)	22L	n/e
Fourth Level (internally assigned)	23L	n/e
Fifth Level (internally assigned)	24L	n/e
Reserved	25L - 5ØL	n/e

The following two identifiers are to be used for shipments within the jurisdiction of a single postal authority.

"Ship From:" - Location code defined by a postal authority (e.g., 5-digit and 9-digit ZIP codes identifying U.S. locations or 6-character postal codes identifying Canadian locations)	51L	n/e
"Ship To:" - Location code defined by a postal authority (e.g., 5-digit and 9-digit ZIP codes identifying U.S. locations or 6-character postal codes identifying Canadian locations)	52L	420
Reserved	53L	n/e

The following identifiers are to be used for shipments between locations governed by different postal authorities

"Ship From:" - Location code defined by a postal authority in the format: postal code (e.g., 5-digit ZIP codes identifying U.S. locations or 6- or 7-character postal codes identifying United Kingdom locations) followed by two character ISO 3166 country code (e.g., US or GB)	54L	n/e
"Ship To:" - Location code defined by a postal authority in the format: postal code (e.g., 5-digit ZIP codes identifying U.S. locations or 6- or 7-character postal codes identifying United Kingdom locations) followed by two character ISO 3166 country code (e.g., US or GB)	55L	n/e
"Ship To:" - Location code defined by a postal authority in the format: postal code followed by three digit ISO 3166 country code (e.g., a 5-digit ZIP codes identifying U.S. locations or 6- or 7-character postal codes identifying United Kingdom locations)	n/e	421
Reserved	56L - 61L	n/e
Reserved *(8/91)	62L	n/e
Reserved	63L - 64L	n/e
Reserved *(8/91)	65L	n/e
Reserved	66L - 999L	n/e

CATEGORY 13:   Reserved

Allocation:	M - 999M	n/e
Assigned:		
Prior Assignment	M	n/e
Reserved	1M - 999M	n/e

CATEGORY 14:   Industry Assigned Codes

Allocation:	N - 999N	n/e
Assigned:		
National/NATO Stock Number (NSN)	N	n/e
Product Characteristic Data defined by the Chemical Industry Data Exchange (CIDX)	1N	n/e
Reserved	2N	n/e
Coding Structure in Accordance with Format Defined by Electronic Industries Association Japan (EIA-J)* (4/93)	3N	n/e
Reserved	4N - 999N	n/e

CATEGORY 15:   Reserved

Allocation:	O - 999O	n/e
Assigned:		

Not recommended for use due to similarity of "Ø" (zero) to "O"	O - 999O	n/e

CATEGORY 16:   Item Information

Allocation:	P - 999P	n/e
Assigned:		
Item Identification Code assigned by Customer	P	n/e
Item Identification Code assigned by Supplier	1P	n/e
Code assigned to specify the revision level for an Item (e.g., engineering change level, edition, or revision)	2P	n/e
Combined manufacturer identification code/item code under the 12/13-digit UCC/EAN formats, plus supplemental codes, if any	3P	UPC/EAN
Roll products - Width, Length, Core Diameter, Direction, & Splices	n/e	8001
Item Code portion of UCC/EAN formats	4P	n/e
Freight Classification Item Number assigned by Carrier for purposes of rating hazardous materials (e.g., Motor, Freight, Air, Boat, Rail Classification)	5P	n/e
Combined supplier identification and item code (internally assigned or mutually defined)	6P	n/e
Common Language Equipment Identification (CLEI) assigned by the manufacturer to some telecommunications equipment	7P	n/e
14-digit UCC/EAN format for Shipping Container Symbol code structure	8P	01 or 14 digit Interleaved 2 of 5 format
Reserved	9P	n/e
Hazardous Material Code as defined by ANSI X12.3 (Version 003000) in the format Data Element 2Ø8 (1-character code qualifier) followed by Data Element 2Ø9 (Hazardous Material Code)	1ØP	n/e
Reserved	11P	n/e
Document Type (e.g., Pick List, Design Drawing, etc.) (internally assigned or mutually defined)	12P	n/e
VMRS System Code *(2/9Ø)	13P	n/e
VMRS System and Assembly Code *(2/9Ø)	14P	n/e
VMRS System, Assembly, & Part Code *(2/9Ø)	15P	n/e
VMRS System, Assembly, or Part Code (User Modified) *(2/9Ø)	16P	n/e
Combined UCC supplier identification and item code assigned by the supplier*(11/90)	17P	n/e
Combined VMRS supplier ID and supplier assigned part number *(6/91)	18P	n/e
Reserved	19P	n/e

The following five identfifiers can be used to provide for Item identification (Item ID) which is different than or in addition to Item ID provided by "P".

First Level (Customer Assigned)	2ØP	n/e
Second Level (Customer Assigned)	21P	n/e
Third Level (Customer Assigned)	22P	n/e
Fourth Level (Customer Assigned)	23P	n/e
Fifth Level (Customer Assigned)	24P	n/e
Reserved	25P - 29P	n/e

364

The following five identfifiers can be used to provide for Item identification (Item ID) which is different than or in addition to Item ID provided by "1P".

First Level (Supplier Assigned)	3ØP	240
Second Level (Supplier Assigned)	31P	n/e
Third Level (Supplier Assigned)	32P	n/e
Fourth Level (Supplier Assigned)	33P	n/e
Fifth Level (Supplier Assigned)	34P	n/e
Reserved	35P - 999N	n/e

CATEGORY 17:   Measurement

Allocation:	Q - 999Q	n/e
Assigned:		
Quantity, Number of Pieces, or Amount (numeric only) (unit of measure and significance mutually defined)	Q	30
Theoretical Length/Weight (numeric only)	1Q	n/e
Actual Weight (numeric only)	2Q	n/e
Unit of Measure, as defined by the two character ANSI X12.3 (Version 003000) Data Element Number 355 Unit of Measurement Code	3Q	n/e

Net Weight, Kilograms	7Q ... 58	310
Length or 1st Dimension, Meters	7Q ... MR	311 or 331
Width, Diameter, or 2nd Dimension, Meters	7Q ... MR	312 or 332
Depth, Height, or Thickness or 3rd Dimension, Meters	7Q ... MR	313 or 333
Area, Square Meters	7Q ... SM	314 or 334
Volume, Liters	7Q ... LT	315 or 335
Volume, Cubic Meters	7Q ... CR	316 or 336
Net Weight, Pounds	7Q ... PN	320
Gross Weight, Kilograms	7Q ... GT	330

Prior Assignment	8Q	n/e
Piece Weight: weight of a single item	9Q	n/e
Prior Assignment	10Q	n/e
Tare Weight: weight of an empty container	110	n/e
Monetary Value established by the Supplier in the format of: the value followed by an ISO 4217 data element code for representing unit of value of currencies and funds (e.g., 12Q2.5ØUSD) (2.5Ø Monetary Value in USA Dollars) significance mutually defined	12Q	n/e
# of # ("this is the nth piece of x pieces in this shipment"). Presented in the format "n/x", where the "/" (slash) is used as a delimiter between two values. See Appendix C.7.3 for further information	13Q	n/e
Beginning Secondary Quantity *(8/9Ø)	14Q	n/e
Ending Secondary Quantity *(8/9Ø)	15Q	n/e
Reserved	16Q - 999Q	n/e

CATEGORY 18:   Miscellaneous

Allocation:	R - 999R	n/e
Assigned:		
Reserved	R	n/e
Return Authorization Code (RMA) assigned by the Supplier	1R	n/e
Return Code assigned by the Customer	2R	n/e
Reserved	3R - 999R	n/e

CATEGORY 19:   Traceability Number for an Entity

Allocation:	S - 999S	n/e
Assigned:		
Serial number or code assigned by the Supplier to an entity for its lifetime, (e.g., computer serial number, traceability number, contract tool identification)	S	21
Additional code assigned by the Supplier to an entity for its lifetime (e.g., traceability number, computer serial number)	1S	n/e
Electronic Serial Number for Cellular Mobile Telephones	n/e	8002
Advance Shipment Notification (ASN) Shipment ID corresponds to ANSI ASC X12 Data Element 396	2S	n/e
Unique Package Identification assigned by Supplier (lowest level of packaging which has a package ID code; shall contain like items)	3S	n/e
Package Identification assigned by Supplier to master packaging containing like items on a single customer order	4S	n/e
Package Identification assigned by Supplier to master packaging containing unlike items on a single customer order	5S	n/e
Package Identification assigned by Supplier to master packaging containing like items over multiple customer orders	6S	n/e
Package Identification assigned by Supplier to master packaging containing unlike items over multiple customer orders	7S	n/e
Supplier ID/Unique Container ID presented in the data format specified by the UCC/EAN Serial Shipping Container Code *(12/90)	8S	00
Package Identification, Generic (mutually defined)	9S	n/e
Machine, cell, or tool ID code	1ØS	n/e
Fixed asset ID code	11S	n/e
Document Number (internally assigned or mutually defined)	12S	n/e
Container Security Seal	13S	n/e
4th Class Non-identical parcel post manifesting	14S	n/e
Serial Number Assigned by the Vendor Entity, that can only be used in conjunction with "13V"* (4/93)	15S	n/e
Reserved	16S	n/e
Combined UCC supplier identification and unique package identification assigned by the supplier* (11/90)	17S	n/e
Reserved	18S	n/e
Combined Dun & Bradstreet supplier identification and unique package identification assigned by the supplier *(12/92)	19S	n/e
Traceability code for an entity assigned by the customer *(2/9Ø)	2ØS	n/e
Combined U.S. D.O.T. Tire Manufacturer Plant Code and unique tire identification assigned by the supplier *(12/92)	21S	n/e
Electronic Serial Number for Cellular Mobile Telephones *(4/93)	22S	8002
Reserved	23S - 29S	n/e
Additional traceability code for an entity assigned by the supplier in addition to or different from the traceability code(s) provided by "S" or "1S" *(2/9Ø)	3ØS	250
Beginning Serial Number for serial numbers in sequence	31S	n/e
Ending Serial Number for serial numbers in sequence	32S	n/e
Reserved	33S - 999S	n/e

CATEGORY 2Ø: Traceability Number for Groups of Entities

Allocation:	T - 999T	n/e
Assigned:		
Traceability Number assigned by the Customer to identify/ trace a unique group of entities (e.g., lot, batch, heat)	T	n/e
Lot Number (Transitional Use)	n/e	23
Traceability Number assigned by the Supplier to identify/ trace a unique group of entities, (e.g., lot, batch, heat)	1T	10
Prior Assignment	2T	n/e
Exclusive Assignment (U.S. EPA vehicle identification for emissions testing)	3T	n/e
Reserved	4T - 19T	n/e

The following five identfifiers can be used to provide for identification of a group of entities which is different than or in addition to identification provided by "T".

First Level (Customer Assigned)	2ØT	n/e
Second Level (Customer Assigned)	21T	n/e
Third Level (Customer Assigned)	22T	n/e
Fourth Level (Customer Assigned)	23T	n/e
Fifth Level (Customer Assigned)	24T	n/e
Reserved	25T - 29T	n/e

The following five identfifiers can be used to provide for identification of a group of entities which is different than or in addition to identification provided by "1T".

First Level (Supplier Assigned)	3ØT	n/e
Second Level (Supplier Assigned)	31T	n/e
Third Level (Supplier Assigned)	32T	n/e
Fourth Level (Supplier Assigned)	33T	n/e
Fifth Level (Supplier Assigned)	34T	n/e
Reserved	35T - 999T	n/e

CATEGORY 21: Reserved

Allocation:	U - 999U	n/e
Assigned:		
Reserved	U - 999U	n/e

CATEGORY 22:   Party To The Transaction

Allocation:	V - 999V	n/e
Assigned		
Supplier Code assigned by Customer	V	n/e
Supplier Code assigned by Supplier	1V	n/e
6-digit Manufacturer ID as assigned by the Uniform Code Council (UCC)	2V	n/e
Fabricator Code as assigned by the appropriate EAN - International (EAN).	3V	n/e
Carrier Identification Code assigned by an industry standard mutually defined by the Supplier, Carrier, and Customer	4V	n/e
Financial Institution Identification Code (mutually defined)	5V	n/e
Manufacturer's identification code (mutually defined)	6V	n/e
Code assigned to a party which has financial liability for an entity or group of entities (e.g., owner of inventory) (mutually defined)	7V	n/e

Customer code assigned by the customer	8V	n/e
Customer code assigned by the supplier	9V	n/e
Reserved	1ØV	n/e
Organization with budget responsibility for an entity, process, or procedure (e.g., shop, division, department)(internally assigned)	11V	n/e
DUNS number identifying manufacturer *(3/9Ø)	12V	n/e
DUNS number identifying supplier *(3/9Ø)	13V	n/e
DUNS number identifying customer *(3/9Ø)	14V	n/e
Carrier-assigned shipper number *(6/91)	15V	n/e
VMRS Supplier ID *(11/93)	16V	n/e
U.S. DoD CAGE Number *(11/93)	17V	n/e
Reserved	18V - 999V	n/e

CATEGORY 23:   Activity Reference

Allocation:	W - 999W	n/e
Assigned:		
Work Order Number (e.g., "Production Paper") (internally assigned)	W	n/e
Operation Sequence Number	1W	n/e
Operation Code/Work Code - the type of work to be performed (internally assigned or mutually defined)	2W	n/e
Combined Work Order Number and Operation Sequence Number in the format nn...n+nn...n where a plus symbol (+) is used as a delimiter between the Work Order Number and the Operation Sequence Number	3W	n/e
Status Code (internally assigned or mutually defined)	4W	n/e
Reserved	5W - 999W	n/e

CATEGORY 24:   Reserved

Allocation:	X - 999X	n/e
Assigned:		
Prior Assignment	X	n/e
Reserved	1X - 999X	n/e

CATEGORY 25:   Internal Applications

Allocation:	Y - 999Y	n/e
Assigned:		
Never to appear on item/document which leaves a closed system environment	Y - 999Y	n/e

CATEGORY 26:   Mutually Defined

Allocation:	Z - 999Z	n/e
Assigned:		
Mutually Defined between Customer and Supplier	Z	n/e
Mutually Defined between Carrier and Supplier	1Z	n/e
Mutually Defined between Customer and Carrier	2Z	n/e
Free Text	3Z	99
Mutually Defined between Carrier and Trading Partner *(1/94)	4Z	n/e
Reserved	5Z - 9Z	n/e
Structured Free Text (Header Data)	1ØZ	n/e
Structured Free Text (Line 1-89 Data)	11Z - 99Z	n/e
Reserved	1ØØZ - 999Z	n/e

APPENDIX F

EDI Transaction Sets

859	Freight Invoice
860	Purchase Order Change
861	Receiving Advice
862	Shipping Schedule
863	Report of Test Results
864	Text
865	Purchase Order Change Acknowledgement
866	Production Sequence
867	Product Transfer and Resale Report
868	Electronic Form Structure (Draft)
869	Order Status Inquiry
870	Order Status Report
997	Functional Acknowledgement

140
Product Registration (Draft)

The Product Registration transaction set can be used for warranty registrations, other product registrations, extended warranties and service contracts. A warranty is a specific instance of a service contract. That is, a warranty is a subset of a service contract. The Product Registration transaction set can specify the manufacturer, seller, secondary warranter, and purchaser or lessee of the product. It can specify the date the product was sold, delivered, and placed in service as well as identify the product model and serial numbers. It can specify the class of service expected from this individual sale, for example, industrial, commercial, or household. The data from this transaction should form the basis of a database so that the data will not have to be repeated in the warranty claim. It can be used to submit many Product Registrations at one time to one receiving organization.

A service contract or warranty can apply equally well to product's subassembly as to the product itself. For example, in a heavyduty truck the engine, transmission, axles, etc., are all subassemblies that have individual product registrations.

This product registration transaction set is not the vehicle for collecting nonproduct related marketing research data.

The information required for the product registration transaction is usually a complete or partial by-product of creating the sales ticket. The computer application program used for the sales ticket should also create the product registration transaction, asking only for that data that is not part of the sales ticket. Both the sale of a product and a service contract require a sales ticket so the program can accommodate both situations.

141
Warranty Claim Response (Draft)

The Warranty Claim Response transaction set provides for the transmission of the information providing the response with regard to warranty claims. It can specify the status of a claim and the items accepted and rejected for payment from the warranty claim. It may be used to trigger the payment for the aggregate of separate claim submissions. Each claim submission could have represented the repair of several individual products and each repair could have consisted of several repair actions involving parts and labor.

142
Warranty Claim (Draft)

The Warranty Claim transaction set provides for the transmission of the information from the claimant as to the cause of a warranty claim on a product being serviced, the subsequent servicing actions, labor times, parts used, associated servicing costs, basis for the product being in warranty, and the names of the product manufacturer, product owner, and servicing organization.

370

The Warranty Claim transaction set can specify the servicing organization, claimant, manufacturer, seller, and purchaser of the product. It can specify the product's current usage, date the product was sold, delivered, and placed in service as well as identify product model and serial numbers and serial numbers of any subsequent subassemblies. However, if this information was specified in the product registration transaction set, it should not be necessary to repeat it in this Warranty Claim transaction set. The Warranty Claim transaction set can specify a malfunction or recall condition, service performed, labor, parts, and any other associated costs. It can show the costs of repair and the date service was requested and when it was available to be placed back in service. The data obtained from this transaction can be used in a service record data base for the product to be able to establish failure mechanisms and typical repair actions.

143
Product Service Notification (Draft)

The Product Service Notification transaction set provides for the transmission of the information when a product has been recalled or cited for service. It can be used both for a mandatory government recall and a voluntary recall. While the recall transaction could be sent to the consumer, it is more likely to be sent to a servicing organization to provide its notice of the recall and to establish its authority to service the items specified in the recall notice. It could be sent to the seller if they are required to notify the purchaser, and it could be sent to an owning organization where they are capable of receiving EDI transactions, such as to a large fleet owner of automobiles. The notice also can be a service bulletin which could specify a repair to a product the next time that product is being serviced or it could be a recall from the distribution channel of a children's toy. One recall notice is limited to one set of items sharing the possibility of the same problem.

810
Invoice

The purpose of the Invoice transaction set is to provide for customary and established business and industry practices relative to the billing for goods and services provided.

819
Operating Expense Statement

The purpose of the Operating Expense Statement transaction set is to provide for the periodic transmittal of expense details from the operator of an asset to the various owners of that asset (e.g., the operation of a petroleum lease or property having multiple owners).

820
Payment Order/Remittance Advice

The Payment Order/Remittance Advice transaction set can be used for three different purposes: (1) to order a financial institution to make payment to payee(s) on behalf of the sending party, (2) to report the completion of a payment to payee(s) by the financial institution, and (3) to give advice to the payee by the payor on the application of a payment made with the payment order or by some other means. The Payment Order/Remittance Advice transaction is not designed for exception reporting from the financial institution to either party.

821
Financial Information Reporting

The Financial Information Reporting transaction set can be used to report balances, detail and summary financial transactions, and other related account information. It can be used by financial institutions and their agents to report to their clients.

822
Customer Account Analysis

The Customer Account Analysis transaction set is used to transmit detailed balance, service charge, and adjustment detail primarily from a bank to its corporate clients. However, this transaction set can also be used between and within corporations.

823
Lockbox

The Lockbox transaction set can be used to transmit lockbox (incoming payments) information and totals from a bank or any other lockbox service provider to a company.

824
Application Advice

The Application Advice transaction set provides the ability to report the results of an application system's data content edits of transaction sets. The results of editing transaction sets can be reported at the functional group and transaction set level, in either coded or free-form format. It is designed to accommodate the business need of reporting the acceptance, rejection, or acceptance with change of any transaction set. The Application Advice should not be used in place of a transaction set designed as a specific response to another transaction set (e.g., purchase order acknowledgement sent in response to a purchase order).

826
Tax Information Reporting (Draft)

The Tax Information transaction set can be used to exchange tax information between federal and state taxing agencies. This transaction set will support Individual and Business Master Files, Individual and Business Returns Transaction Files, and the Gift Tax Data Extract Exchange Program of the Federal/State Exchange Program.

827
Financial Return Notice

The Financial Return Notice transaction set is used to report to the originator the inability of the financial institution to have the Payment Order/Remittance Advice transaction set (820) processed.

829
Payment Cancellation Request

The Payment Cancellation Request transaction set is used to cancel a previously transmitted electronic payment between an originating company and its originating financial institution before funds are released.

830
Planning Schedule with Release Capability

The Planning Schedule with Release Capability transaction set provides for customary and established business practices relative to the transfer of forecasting/material release information between organizations.

The Planning Schedule with Release Capability transaction set may be used in various ways or in a combination of ways, such as: (1) a simple forecast; (2) a forecast with the buyer's authorization for the seller to commit to resources, such as labor or material; (3) a forecast that is also used as an order release mechanism, containing such elements as resource authorizations, period-to-date cumulative quantities, and specific ship/delivery patterns for requirements that have been represented in "buckets", such as weekly, monthly, or quarterly. The order release forecast may also contain all data related to purchase orders, as required, because the order release capability eliminates the need for discrete generation of purchase orders.

832
Price/Sales Catalog

The Price/Sales Catalog transaction set provides for customary and established business and industry practices relative to furnishing or requesting the price of goods or services in the form of a catalog. *The Price/Sales Catalog transaction set may also be used to furnish specific detail of a supplier's product offerings (e.g., the product's item code, quantity of an item in various packaging configurations, and description of the product).*

836
Contract Award

The Contract Award transaction set can be used by the buyer to notify the seller or other interested parties of the award of a contract which contains some indefinite features, such as delivery schedule, location, and/or quantities. This transaction set is intended to be the notification of the award of a requirements type of contract.

840
Request for Quotation

The Request for Quotation transaction provides potential buyers with the ability to solicit price, delivery schedule, and other items from potential sellers of goods and services.

841
Specifications/Technical Information

The Specifications/Technical Information transaction set can be used to transmit specifications or technical information between trading partners. It can be used to allow EDI trading partners the ability to exchange a complete or partial technical description of a product, process, service, etc., over the same path as any other EDI transaction. The detail area can include graphic, text, parametric, tabular, image, spectral, or audio data. A transmission includes identification information to assist the receiver in interpreting and utilizing the information included in the transaction.

Further action as a consequence of the receipt and initial processing of the specification or other technical data may or may not require human intervention. The transmission and receipt of the data may require private agreements between the trading partners to automate the receipt of the data.

The total transaction must be in the general form of all ASC X12 transactions so that an EDI computer system will be able to automatically recognize it as a Specification/Technical Information transaction set and pass it on for processing of the data itself. The transaction set is not media dependent.

The detail area of the Specification/Technical Information transaction set provides a structure that allows for the exchange of a variety of specification information. For example, if the transaction contains information describing a complete assembly, it would be necessary to include the assembly model, the models for each of the individual parts, and the associated specifications. In the case of a process it may be necessary to transmit the specification of the product along with the specifications of the process and raw materials. This transaction set can also be linked to other transaction sets.

The transaction set is not limited to a specific transmission protocol and uses other standards as applicable where they do not conflict with these requirements for specification transaction.

842
Nonconformance Report

The purpose of the Nonconformance Report transaction set is to report products and processes that do not fulfill specifications or requirements. The Nonconformance Report transaction set provides the ability for the sender to report the nonconformance at the level of detail that is required. It also provides the ability to report the specific nonconformances of a component/part while identifying the assembly as the product that is in nonconformance. The Nonconformance Report transaction set may be used to report, initiate, or request actions related to the nonconformance being reported.

843
Response to Request for Quotation

The Response to Request for Quotation transaction set provides potential buyers with price, delivery schedule, and other terms from potential sellers of goods and services, in response to a request for such information.

844
Product Transfer Account Adjustment

The Product Transfer Account Adjustment transaction set can be used to transmit specific data in the form of a debit, credit, or request for credit relating to preauthorized product transfer actions.

845
Price Authorization Acknowledgement/Status

The Price Authorization Acknowledgement/Status transaction set is used by a vendor or manufacturer to transmit specific data relative to the status of or changes to outstanding price authorizations.

846
Inventory Inquiry/Advice

The Inventory Inquiry/Advice transaction set may be used in the following ways: (1) for a seller of goods and services to provide inventory information to a prospective purchaser, with no obligation to the purchaser to acquire these goods or services; (2) for one location to supply another location with inventory information; and (3) for an inquiry as to the availability of inventory with no obligation on the seller of goods and services to reserve that inventory.

849
Response to Product Transfer Account Adjustment

The Response to Product Transfer Account Adjustment transaction set can be used to transmit a detailed or summary response to a party requesting an accounting adjustment relating to a preauthorized product transfer.

850
Purchase Order

The Purchase Order transaction set provides for customary and established business and industry practices relative to the placement of purchase orders for goods and services. This transaction set should not be used to convey purchase order changes or purchase order acknowledgement information.

852
Product Data Activity

The Product Data Activity transaction set allows a distributor, warehouse, or retailer to advise a trading partner of inventory, sales, and other product activity information. Product activity data enables a trading partner to plan and ship, or propose inventory replenishment quantities, for distribution centers, warehouses, or retail outlets.

The receiver of the transaction set will maintain some type of inventory/product movement records for its trading partners to enable replenishment calculations based on data provided by the distributor, warehouse, or retailer.

855
Purchase Order Acknowledgement

The Purchase Order Acknowledgement transaction set provides for customary and established business and industry practices relative to a seller's acknowledgement of a buyer's purchase order.

856
Ship Notice/Manifest

A Ship Notice/Manifest transaction set lists the contents of a shipment of goods as well as additional information relating to the shipment, such as order information, product description, physical characteristics, type of packaging, marking, carrier information, and configuration of goods within the transportation equipment. The Ship Notice/Manifest transaction set enables the sender to describe the contents and configuration of a shipment in various levels of detail and provides an ordered flexibility to convey information.

The sender of this transaction set is the organization responsible for detailing and communicating the contents of a shipment, or shipments, to one or more receivers of the transaction set. The receiver of this transaction set can be any organization having an interest in the contents of a shipment or information about the contents of a shipment.

858
Shipment Information

The Shipment Information transaction set provides the sender with the capability to transmit detailed bill-of-lading, rating, and/or scheduling information pertinent to a shipment.

859
Freight Invoice

The Freight Invoice transaction set provides the sender with the capability to transmit an invoice, including charges, allowances, and details, for the transportation services rendered.

860
Purchase Order Change

The Purchase Order Change transaction set provides the information required for customary and established business and industry practices relative to a purchase order change. This transaction can be used: (1) by a buyer to request a change to a previously submitted purchase order or (2) by a buyer to confirm acceptance of a purchase order change initiated by the seller or by mutual agreement of the two parties.

861
Receiving Advice

The Receiving Advice transaction set provides for customary and established business and industry practices relative to the notification of receipt of goods and services.

862
Shipping Schedule

The Shipping Schedule transaction set provides the ability for a customer to convey precise shipping schedule requirements to a supplier, and is intended to supplement the Planning Schedule transaction set (830). The Shipping Schedule transaction set will supersede certain shipping and delivery information transmitted in a previous Planning Schedule transaction set, but it does not replace the 830 transaction set. The Shipping Schedule transaction set shall not be used to authorize labor, materials, or other resources.

The use of this transaction set will facilitate the practice of Just-In-Time (JIT) manufacturing by providing the customer with a mechanism to issue precise shipping schedule requirements on a more frequent basis than with the issue of a Planning Schedule transaction set, e.g., daily shipping schedules versus weekly planning schedules. The Shipping Schedule transaction set also provides the ability for a customer location to issue shipping requirements independent of any other customer locations when Planning Schedule transactions are issued by a consolidated scheduling organization.

863
Report of Test Results

The Report of Test Results transaction set can be used to transmit the results of tests performed to satisfy specified product or process requirements. This includes, but is not limited to, test data such as inspection data, certification data, and statistical process control measurements.

864
Text

The Text transaction set provides users with the capability to electronically move messages, contracts, explanations, and other one-time communications. It is the intent of this transaction to provide electronic communication (messages) for people, not for computer processing. The use of the Text transaction set to transmit quasi or unique transaction set standards is discouraged.

The use of the Text transaction set demands of the sender certain detailed information about the recipient. The Text transaction set's purpose is to provide communication to the recipient in some human-readable form. The recipient's network will dictate what capabilities are available for delivery of the information. It is the responsibility of the sender to obtain this information and include it in the transmission.

865
Purchase Order Change Acknowledgement

The Purchase Order Change Acknowledgement transaction set can be used: (1) by the seller to acknowledge or convey acceptance of changes to a previously submitted purchase order or (2) by a seller to notify the buyer of changes initiated by the seller to a previously submitted purchase order.

866
Production Sequence

The Production Sequence transaction provides for the receiver of goods to request the order in which shipments of goods arrive, or to specify the order in which the goods are to be unloaded from the conveyance method, or both. This specifies the sequence in which the goods are to enter the materials handling process, or are to be consumed in the production process, or both. This transaction set shall not be used to authorize labor, materials, or other resources. This transaction set shall not be used to revise any product characteristic specification.

867
Product Transfer and Resale Report

The Product Transfer and Resale Report transaction set may be used in the following ways: (1) to report information about product that has been transferred from one location to another; (2) to report sales of product from one or more locations to an end customer; or (3) to report sales of a product from one or more locations to an end customer, and demand beyond actual sales (lost orders).

868
Electronic Form Structure (Draft)

The Electronic Form Structure transaction set provides a structure for transfer of EDI standards, or portions thereof in an electronic form. These EDI standards include, but are not limited to: ANSI X12 standards, approved ASC X12 draft standards for trial use, UN/EDIFACT standard messages, and industry EDI conventions and guidelines. It is intended to provide users with the following:
- The ability to send and receive EDI standards data which can be used to update application or translator software.
- The ability to exchange data maintenance information with trading partners about transaction sets, segments, elements, and codes that will be used for EDI transmissions.
- The ability to transmit complete or partial EDI standards or conventions.

869
Order Status Inquiry

The Order Status Inquiry transaction set provides the ability to request all pertinent information relative to an entire purchase order, selected line items on a purchase order, or selected products/services on a purchase order. Inquiry can also be made for all or a selected portion of the customer's unshipped items, or all or a selected portion of the customer's shipped items.

870
Order Status Report

The Order Status Report transaction set provides the ability to report on the current status of an entire purchase order, selected line items on a purchase order, or selected products/services on a purchase order, or purchase orders for a specific customer in their entirety or on a selection basis. The report format allows for the inclusion of "reasons" relative to the status of the purchase order(s). This transaction set may also be used to update the supplier's scheduled shipment or delivery date(s). This transaction set can result from either an inquiry (via the Order Status Inquiry transaction set [869]) or a prearranged schedule agreed to by the trading partners.

997
Functional Acknowledgement

The purpose of the Functional Acknowledgement transaction set is to define the control structures for a set of acknowledgements to indicate the results of the syntactical analysis of the electronically encoded documents. The encoded documents are the transaction sets, which are grouped in functional groups, used in defining transactions for business data interchange. The Functional Acknowledgement transaction set does not cover the semantic meaning of the information encoded in the transaction sets. *A Functional Acknowledgement transaction set is transmitted by the recipient of each business data interchange to acknowledge that the transmission was received in the proper form (sender's transaction set). The Functional Acknowledgement transaction set acknowledges only receipt of data, not an agreement to abide by the specific content of the sender's transaction set.*

Bibliography

- ABCD — The Microcomputer Industry Association Bar Code Label Print Quality & Label Specification, ABCD/QED, 1989.

- ABCD — The Microcomputer Industry Association Bar Code Labeling Guidelines, ABCD/QED, 1990.

- Ackley, H. Sprague (INTERMEC), Letter to the Editor, AID News, 16 May 1990.

- AIAG-B-1 Bar Code Symbology Standard, Automotive Industry Action Group, 1984.

- AIAG-B-2 Vehicle Identification Number Label Standard, Automotive Industry Action Group, 1985.

- AIAG-B-3 Shipping/Parts Identification Label Standard, Automotive Industry Action Group, 1984.

- AIAG-B-4 Individual Part Identification Label Standard, Automotive Industry Action Group, 1986.

- AIAG-B-5 Primary Metals Identification Tag Application Standard, Automotive Industry Action Group, 1984.

- Allais, David C. (Applied Tactical Systems), Letter to the Editor, AID News, 21 May 1990.

- American National Standard — Book Numbering, ANSI/NISO Z39.21-1988.

- American National Standard for Electronic Data Interchange (ASC X12 Version 3 Release 1), DISA, 1990.

- American National Standard for Materials Handling - Bar Code Symbols on Unit Loads and Transport Packages (ANS MH10.8M-1983), ANSI, 1983.

- American National Standard for Materials Handling - Bar Code Symbols on Unit Loads and Transport Packages (ANS MH10.8M-199X), ANSI, 1991 (Draft).

- American National Standard Guidelines for Bar Code Print Quality (ANS X3.182-1990), ANSI, 1990.

- Angerbauer, George J., Electronics for Modern Communications, Prentice-Hall, 1974.

- Application Specification for UCC-128 Serial Shipping Container Code (with Symbol and Shipping Label Guidelines), Uniform Code Council (UCC), 1989.

- Bar Code Package Identification Standard, Aluminum Association, 1985.

- Bar Code Symbology Standard for Code 39, Aluminum Association, 1985.

- BLACK BOX Catalog, May, 1991.

- BLACK BOX LAN Catalog, February, 1991.

- Commercial and Industrial Application of the Uniform Industrial Code, Uniform Code Council (UCC), 1989.

- Committee for Commonality in Blood Banking Automation (CCBBA) Report, American Blood Commission (ABC), 1977.

- Corrigan, Patrick H. & Guy, Aisling, "Choosing LAN Hardware," LAN Times 1990-91 Buyers Guide, McGraw-Hill, 1990.

- Direct Thermal Printing, AIM USA, 1989.

- EDI & Bar Code Implementation Guidelines, CIDX, 1990.

- EIA-556 - Electronics Industries Association Outer Shipping Container Bar Code Label Standard, ANSI/EIA, 1988.

- EIA-556A (Draft) - Electronics Industries Association Outer Shipping Container Bar Code Label Standard, ANSI/EIA, 1991.

- EIA/IS-61 - Electronics Industries Association - Consumer Electronics Group Product and Packaging Bar Code Standard for Consumer Electronic Retail Distribution, EIA/CEG, 1990 (Interim Standard).

- Federation of Automated Coding Technologies (F.A.C.T.) Common Label Standard, FACT/AIM, 1990 (Draft).

- Federation of Automated Coding Technologies (F.A.C.T.) Data Identifier Standard, ANSI/FACT-1, 1991.

- Flexographic Printing, AIM USA, 1989.

- General EAN Specifications, International Article Numbering (EAN), 1987 (updated February 1989, October 1989, and June 1990).

- General Specifications for the Article Symbol Marking, International Article Numbering (EAN), 1977.

- GIBC: Graphics Industry Bar Code Labeling Specification, GCA, 1986.

- A Guide to Business Mail Preparation (USPS Publication 25), (USPS), 1988.

- Guidelines on Symbology Identifiers, AIM USA, 1990.

- Guidelines for Shipping Container Codes and Symbols for the U.S. Book Industry, Book Industry Study Group, 1989.

- Harlow, Frank A., Justifying a Change - Productivity Gains Justify the Effort, AIM/Scan-Tech 90, 1990.

- Harmon, Craig K., Bar Code Technology - Applications in Health Care, American Hospital Association, July, 1984.

- Harmon, Craig K., Bar Code Technology, Handbook of Medical Device Packaging - Drugs in the Pharmaceutical Sciences, Marcel Dekker, 1989.

- Harmon, Craig K., Bar Code Technology, National Office Products Association (NOPA), 1987.

- Harmon, Craig K., Data Collection (Manufacturing), Datapro Research Corporation, 1988.

- Harmon, Craig K., Data Collection (Minicomputers), Datapro Research Corporation, 1988.

- Harmon, Craig K., Inter-industry Bar Code & EDI — ID Expo '91, Q.E.D. Systems, 1991.

- Harmon, Craig K., Myths, Legends, and Realities of Customer Service — The Magic of Electronics, Q.E.D. Systems, 1990.

- Harmon, Craig K., Reading Between the Lines — an Intensive Introduction to Bar Code and Data Collection Technology, Q.E.D. Systems, 2nd Edition, 1990.

- Harmon, Craig K., Using Bar Codes in Warehousing & Distribution, Q.E.D. Systems, 15th Edition, 1991.

- Harmon, Craig K. & American Furniture Manufacturers Association (AFMA), Furnishings Bar Code Standard, AFMA/Q.E.D. Systems, 1989.

- Harmon, Craig K. & Bar Code/EDI Task Force of ABCD — The Microcomputer Industry Association, ABCD — The Microcomputer Industry Association Bar Code Labeling Guidelines, Q.E.D. Systems, 1990.

- Harmon, Craig K. & Furniture Industry Task Force, The Furniture Industry Bar Code (FIBC) Standard, National Office Products Association (NOPA), 1988.

- Harmon, Craig K., and National Business Forms Association (NBFA), Bar Codes, NBFA, 1985.

- Harmon, Craig K. & Wahoski, Martha, Supplemental Guidelines for Universal Product Code Implementation in the Office Products Industry, National Office Products Association (NOPA), 1988.

- Harmon, Craig K. & Wahoski, Martha, NOPA's UPC Symbol Reduction Guidelines for Marking Intermediate Packs, National Office Products Association (NOPA), 1988.

- Harmon, Craig K. & Wahoski, Martha, <u>Questions & Answers About the Universal Product Code and the Office Products Industry</u>, National Office Products Association (NOPA), 1987.

- <u>HIBC Supplier Labeling Standard</u>, HIBCC, 1989.

- <u>Integrated Systems and Controls - Guidelines for Preparing An RFP or RFQ for Radio Frequency Data Terminals</u>, The Material Handling Institute (MHI), 1989.

- <u>International Article Numbering Association E.A.N. Annual Report 1989</u>, International Article Numbering (EAN), 1989.

- <u>International Article Numbering Association E.A.N. Annual Report 1990</u>, International Article Numbering (EAN), 1990.

- <u>International Standard ISO 646 — Information Processing - ISO 70-Bit Coded Character Set for Information Interchange</u>, ISO, Second Edition, 1983-0701.

- <u>Ion Deposition Printing</u>, AIM USA, 1989.

- <u>Laser Printing</u>, AIM USA, 1989.

- Laserlight Systems, Inc., <u>Code 16K</u>, 1989.

- <u>Letterpress Printing</u>, AIM USA, 1989.

- <u>Machine-Readable Coding Guidelines for the U.S. Book Industry</u>, Book Industry Study Group, 1987.

- <u>Matrix Impact Printing</u>, AIM USA, 1989.

- Morgan, Joe, FLEXcon, <u>Pressure-sensitive Label Components Must Stick Together</u>, 1991.

- National Electrical Manufacturers Association, <u>Electrical Industry Bar Code Application Guidelines</u>, NEMA, 1987.

- Palmer, Roger C., <u>The Bar Code Book</u>, Helmers Publishing, 2nd Edition, 1991.

- Pavlidis, Theo & Wang, Ynjiun P., <u>Two-Dimensional Bar Codes</u>, presented to IEEE Industrial Automation Conference, Toronto, 1990.

- Pavlidis, Theo, Swartz, Jerome, & Wang, Ynjiun P., <u>Fundamentals of Bar Code Information Theory</u>, Symbol Technologies, Computer, IEEE, 1990.

- Payne, Robert, <u>Requirements of an EDI Network</u>, EDI — Spread The Word, EDI Green Pages, 1990.

- Pierce, John R., <u>Signals - The Telephone and Beyond</u>, W.H. Freeman and Company, 1981.

- Porter, Phillip T., <u>Land-Mobile Radio Communications Networks</u>, Electronics Engineers' Handbook, 2nd Edition, McGraw-Hill, 1982.

- Pramstellar, Michael E., National Business Forms Association (NBFA), <u>Bar Codes</u>, NBFA, 1985.

- Sellberg, Charles W., Diagraph Corporation, " Specifying Large Character Ink Jet Printing Systems," Journal of Packaging Technology, June/July 1989.

- Sokol, Phyllis K., EDI - The Competitive Edge, McGraw-Hill, 1989.

- Specification EMBARC - Electronic Manifesting & Bar Coding of Paper Stock Shipments, GCA, 1985.

- Specification for Postal Numeric Encoding Technique (Postnet), (USPS), 1980 Rev 2. 1981.

- Stamper, Bonney, A Guide to Barcoding, Bar Code Systems, 1988.

- Stamper, Bonney & American Hardware Manufacturers Association (AHAM), Hardlines Industry Guidelines to Bar Coding, AHAM, 1989.

- Stultz, D.C., Harris Corporation, Fifty Bar Code Questions You Might Forget to Ask, AIM/Scan-Tech 90, 1990.

- Swartz, Jerome, Pavlidis, Theo, and Wang, Ynjiun P., Fundamentals of Bar Code Information Theory, Symbol Technologies, 1989.

- TCIF Implementation Guide to Package Labeling, TCIF, 1989.

- TCIF Package or Shipping Container Transaction Bar Code Label Specification, TCIF, 1989.

- TCIF Product Package Labeling, TCIF, 1989.

- The EDI Handbook - Trading in the 1990s, Blenheim Online Publications, 1988.

- Universal Product Code Industrial & Commercial Guidelines Manual (Draft), Uniform Code Council (UCC),1991.

- UPC Coupon Code Guidelines Manual, Uniform Code Council (UCC), 1989.

- UPC Guidelines Manual, Uniform Code Council (UCC), 1990.

- UPC Industrial Code Guidelines Manual, Uniform Code Council (UCC), 1984.

- UPC Shipping Container Code and Symbol Specification Manual, Uniform Code Council (UCC), 1990.

- UPC Symbol Location Guidelines, Uniform Code Council (UCC), 1986.

- UPC Symbol Specification Manual, Uniform Code Council (UCC), 1986.

- VICS Retail Industry Conventions and Implementation Guidelines for EDI, Uniform Code Council (UCC), 1989.

- Wang, Ynjiun P. & Bravman, Richard, PDF417, A Two-Dimensional Bar Code System, Symbol Technologies, 1990.

- Weiland, Norman R. (Monarch Marking Systems), <u>Code 16K</u>, FACT Two-Dimensional Code Seminar, 1990.

- <u>Zebra Media Selection Guide,</u> Zebra Technologies, 1991.

- <u>Zebra — The Label's The Thing,</u> Zebra Technologies, 1991.

- <u>Zebra — What Quality Ribbons Are All About,</u> Zebra Technologies, 1991.

Glossary of Terms

This glossary contains an alphabetic list of terms relevant to the automatic identification field and the related fields of data communications, electronic data interchange, and local area networks. Where a term's explanation is given with respect to conventional usage in data communications, the abbreviation "DataComm" is noted in parentheses after the terms. Similarly, electronic data interchange terms have the notation "EDI," and local area network terms have the notation "LAN." Terms without these specific notations are explained either in a general sense as they are understood in computer applications and/or automatic identification (bar code) technology and applications. Names and addresses of organizations relevant to automatic identification are found in Appendix A.

ABC symbol — the symbol of the American Blood Commission, developed in 1977 by the Committee for Commonality in Blood Banking Automation (CCBBA) as a bar code standard for automated systems in the blood service community. The symbology used in the ABC symbol is Codabar.

achieved width — the calculated element width based on measurements.

ACK — (DataComm) an "acknowledgement" character, sent to the source of a transmission after a message has been received without detected errors.

acoustic coupler — (DataComm) a portable device that couples its model to the telephone line without a hardwired connection.

active device — in current loop applications, a device capable of supplying the current for the loop.

address — (LAN) a unique sequence of bits, a character, or a group of characters that identifies a network station, user, or application; a unique designation for the location of data; used mainly for routing purposes.

alphanumeric — a character set that contains alphabetic characters (letters), numeric digits (numbers), and usually other characters such as punctuation marks.

analog — (DataComm) in communications, transmission employing variable and continuous waveforms to represent information values, compare with *digital*. Digital data is converted to an analog signal by a modem.

angle of incidence — the angle between an incident ray and the normal to a surface at the point of incidence; the angle at the symbol being read. If the reader is perpendicular to the plane of the code, the angle of incidence is zero degrees.

anilox roll — a textured-surface roll, achieved by engraving or ceramic coating, suitable for carrying ink in microscopic cells from a press metering point to the printing plate.

ANSI X12 Data Element Dictionary — (EDI) ANSI document that contains definitions and attributes of all data elements of ANSI X12 transaction sets plus code list values for all elements requiring them.

ANSI X12 Segment Directory — (EDI) ANSI document that contains definition and layouts of all segments used in the ANSI X12 transaction sets.

aperture — the physical opening in an optical system that establishes the field of view.

aperture diameter — the effective diameter of the optical system aperture.

API (application program interface) — (LAN) a set of formalized software calls and routines that can be referenced by an application program to access underlying network services.

APPC (advanced peer-to-peer communications) — (DataComm) also called Logical Unit (LU) 6.2; a network architecture definition by IBM, specified as featuring high-level program interaction capabilities on a peer-to-peer basis.

AppleTalk — (LAN) a proprietary computer networking standard promulgated by Apple Computer for use in connecting Macintosh computers and peripherals.

application format — (EDI) the specific file format generated by a computer program or expected as input to a computer program.

application layer — (DataComm) the highest layer of the seven-layer OSI model structure; contains all user or application programs; in the IBM SNA, the end-user layer.

application link software — (EDI) program developed to act as a link between an application program and a predefined data format.

application software — a system of programs running in a computer and designed to accomplish some operational task or tasks.

application-to-application — (EDI) transference of data generated by a computer program directly to another computer program.

architecture — (DataComm) the parameters by which computer or communications systems are defined.

ARP (address resolution protocol) — (LAN) a Transmission Control Protocol/Internet Protocol (TCP/IP) process that maps IP addresses to Ethernet addresses; required by TCP/IP for use with Ethernet.

ARQ (automatic request for retransmission) — (DataComm) a communications feature whereby the receiver asks the transmitter to resend a block or frame, generally because of errors detected by the receiver.

ASCII (American Standard Code for Information Interchange) — a system used to represent alphanumeric data; a 7-bit-plus-parity character set established by ANSI and used for data communications and data processing; ASCII allows compatibility among data services; ASCII is normally used for asynchronous transmission.

aspect ratio — in a bar code symbol, the ratio of bar height to symbol length.

asynchronous — (DataComm) data transmission that is not related to the timing, or a specific frequency, of a transmission facility; transmission characterized by individual characters, or bytes, encapsulated with start and stop bits.

asynchronous transmission — (DataComm) a data coding structure where each character transmitted is preceded by a start signal and followed by a stop signal.

attenuation — (DataComm) the deterioration of signal strength, measured in decibels; opposite of *gain*.

audit trail — record of transactions created as a by-product of data processing runs or mechanized operations.

authentication — (EDI) procedure to insure that data cannot be tampered with without being detectable by the receiver. key).

authentication key — (EDI) a group of characters used to initiate the authentication process.

autodiscrimination — the capability of a scanning algorithm to decode any of several types of bar code symbologies without operator interaction.

automatic identification system (AIS) — the application of various technologies, such as bar code recognition, image recognition, voice recognition, and RF/MW transponders, for the purpose of data entry to a data processing system, by-passing the key-entry component of traditional data entry.

average background reflectance — expressed as a percent, it is the simple arithmetic average of the background reflection readings from at least five different points on a sheet.

average edge — an imaginary line dissecting the irregularities of the character edge.

backbone network — (DataComm) a transmission facility designed to interconnect low-speed distribution channels or clusters of dispersed user devices.

back-end processor — a small computer attached to a larger computer as a standard data processor for some processing after the main application processing.

background — the area surrounding a printed symbol. See *substrate*.

background reflectance — measurement of the brightness of the substrate that a bar code is printed on.

bandwidth — (DataComm) the range of frequencies available for signaling; the difference between the highest and lowest frequencies of a band, expressed in hertz (Hz).

bar — one of two types of elements comprising a bar code symbol. An element of a bar code symbol whose reflectance is less than the global threshold.

bar code density — the number of characters that can be represented in a lineal inch.

bar code scanner (or **reader**) — a device used to identify and decode a bar code symbol.

bar code symbol — an array of rectangular bars and spaces arranged in a predetermined pattern following specific rules to represent elements of data that are referred to as characters. A bar code symbol typically contains a leading quiet zone, start character, data character(s) including an optional check character, stop character, and a trailing quiet zone.

bar height (bar length) — the bar dimension perpendicular to the bar (element) width.

bar reflectance — the smallest reflectance value in a bar.

bar width — the thickness of a bar measured from the edge closest to the symbol start character to the trailing edge of the same bar.

bar width ratio — the ratio of the widest to the narrowest width within a bar code symbol.

bar width reduction — reduction of the nominal bar width dimension on film masters or printing plates to compensate for systematic errors in some printing processes.

base line — a reference line used to specify the desired vertical position of characters printed on the same line.

baseband — (DataComm) a signal frequency below the point when the signal is modulated as an analog carrier frequency.

batch processing — (DataComm) a data-processing technique in which data is accumulated and processed in batches.

baud — unit of signaling speed. The speed in baud is the number of discrete conditions or events per second. If each event represents only one bit condition, a rate in baud is identical to a rate in bits per second (bps). When each event represents more than one bit, as is the case with various coding methods, the rate in baud does not equal bps.

bearer bar — Bearer bars are bars that are located on the perimeter of some bar code symbols, but do not carry any information. As a minimum, two bearer bars (measuring at least four times the width of the narrow element) are located along the length of the code, each touching the ends of the bars. These bearer bars are used to eliminate problems of partial scans which could result in incorrect data being decoded.

Bell 212 — (DataComm) an AT&T specification of full-duplex, asynchronous or synchronous, 300- or 1200-bps data transmission for use on the public telephone network.

bidirectional — relating to the characteristic of some bar codes that allows decoding of their contents whether scanned in one direction or the reverse direction.

bilevel code — a coding technique in which data bits are presented in two parallel rows.

bill of lading (BoL) — a transaction that is sent by a supplier to a carrier that describes shipment content and delivery details of an order awaiting pickup.

binary — the number system that uses the base 2, with two distinct characters, usually "1" and "0."

binary code — a code that expresses data as binary numbers.

binary digit (bit) — The fundamental unit of a digital computer's memory store. A bit can take one of two defined values, usually denoted "0" (zero) or "1" (one).

bisynchronous protocol — (DataComm) set of conventions controlling synchronous transmission that defines the controlling start and end characters and the error checking performed.

bisynchronous transmission (BSC) — (DataComm) a byte- or character-oriented IBM communications protocol which has become an industry standard.

bit error rate/block error rate testing (BERT/ BLERT) — (DataComm) an error-checking technique that compares a received data pattern with a known transmitted data pattern to determine transmission-line quality.

bits per second (bps) — (DataComm) the number of bits that pass a given point in a communication line per second. The basic unit of measure for serial data transmission capacity;

Kbps for kilo (thousands of) bits per second; Mbps for mega (millions of) bits per second; Gbps for giga (billions of) bits per second; Tbps for tera (trillions of) bits per second.

bridge — (LAN) a device that connects different local area networks at the data-link layer. Similar to a gateway, however, it does not support protocol conversion.

broadband — (DataComm) describing transmission equipment and media that can support a wide range of electromagnetic frequencies; typically, the technology of CATV transmission, as applied to data communications, that employs coaxial cable as the transmission medium and radio frequency carrier signals in the 50- to 500-MHz range; sometimes used synonymously with *wideband.*

broadcast — (LAN) a method of transmitting messages to two or more stations at the same time.

buffer — a temporary storage allocation in a computer or a temporary storage device used to compensate for a difference in data rate or data flow between two devices or processes.

bus — (LAN) a transmission path or channel; an electrical connection, with one or more conductors, by which all attached devices receive all transmissions at the same time.

byte — (DataComm) a unit of memory (data storage) capacity in computers consisting of 8 bits (by current convention).

CAD (computer-aided design) — capability of a computer to be used for industrial design through visual devices.

calibration mark or bar — a code bit that provides the scanner with contrast, speed, or code position information, as required.

caliper — a measure of a paper's thickness expressed in thousandths of an inch (mils).

carbon copy routing — (EDI) transmission of a duplicate data stream to another receiving location or trading partner.

carrier sheet — the backing material on which printing plates are mounted.

CCD (charge-coupled device) — an array (linear or matrix) of photosensitive elements wherein packets of electrons are set in each element as a result of the quantity of light received during an exposure interval, and where these packets are recovered from the array in the form of a pulse height-modulated electric signal.

central office — (DataComm) the building in which common carriers terminate customer circuits (also known as central exchange).

centralized processing — a system of handling data concentrated at a single location or by a single computer application.

character — the smallest group of elements which represents one or more numbers, letters, punctuation marks, or other information. A standard 8-bit unit representing a symbol, letter, number, or punctuation mark; generally means the same as *byte*.

character density — the dimension, in linear inches, required to encode one character; measured in characters per inch (cpi).

character-oriented — (DataComm) describing a communications protocol or a transmission procedure that carries control information encoded in fields of one or more characters (or bytes).

character parity checking — a self-checking feature of some bar codes which relies upon parity values being assigned to the various widths of bars and spaces within a bar code representation of a given character. The presence of character parity checking adds security to the bar code.

character set — those characters available for encodation within a particular bar code symbology.

characteristic impedance — (DataComm) the impedance termination of an (approximately) electrically uniform transmission line that minimizes reflections from the end of the line.

check character (check sum/check digit) — the total of a group of data items or a segment of data that is used for error-checking purposes. Both numeric and alphabetic fields

can be used in calculating a check sum, since the binary content of the data can be added. Just as a check digit tests the accuracy of a single number, a check sum serves to test an entire set of data which has been transmitted or stored. See also *modulo check character(s)*.

clamping voltages — (DataComm) the "sustained" voltage held by a clamp circuit at some desired level.

clear area — a clear space, containing no dark marks, that precedes the start character of a symbol and follows the stop character. The clear area of a bar code should be 10 times the size of the narrowest bar in the code or .250 inch, whichever is greater. Also called *quiet zone*.

clock — (DataComm) an oscillator-generated signal that provides a timing reference for a transmission link.

clock mark/clock bar — a timing mark or bar used in certain codes, such as the timing track of bar/half bar codes like Postnet.

closed system — a system in which a single authority has control over all elements, e.g., data content, bar code printing, bar code scanners; opposite of an *open system,* with voluntary published standards for such elements.

coaxial cable — (LAN) a popular transmission medium usually consisting of one central wire conductor (two, for twinaxial cable) surrounded by a dielectric insulator and enclosed in either a wire mesh or an extruded metal sheathing; common Community Antenna Television (CATV) transmission cable, typically supporting RF frequencies from 50 to about 500 MHz; also called "coax."

Codabar — a bar code format in which four bars and three spaces are used to represent the digits 0 through 9 and certain special characters. The code is characterized by four unique start/stop codes, variable intercharacter spacing, and code density of up to 10 characters per inch.

Code 11 — a code that contains 11 different characters (0 through 9 and -). Each character has three bars and two intervening spaces, for a total of five elements. Of these five elements, two are wide and three are narrow, except for the 0, 9, and - characters, which have only one wide element and four narrow elements. Nominal bar code density is 15 characters per inch.

Code 16K — A stacked multirow bar code symbology utilizing an inverse form of the Code 128 encodings, intended for high density labeling of small objects. A Code 16K symbol has 1 to 16 uniquely numbered row bar codes, stacked vertically with solid separator bars.

Code 39 (3 of 9 Code) — a variable-length, bidirectional, discrete, self-checking, alphanumeric bar code widely used in industry. Its data character set contains 43 characters: 0-9, A-Z, –, ., $, /, +, , and Space. The name (also known as "Code 3 of 9") derives from the method of encodation — each character has nine elements, three of which are always wide.

Code 49 — A stacked multirow bar code symbology, intended for high density labeling of small objects. A Code 49 has two to eight uniquely numbered row bar codes stacked vertically with solid separator bars.

Code 93 — a code that includes a character set that is identical to Code 39. Each character is constructed from nine modules arranged into three bars with adjacent spaces. Nominal bar code density is 13.9 cpi.

Code 128 — a variable-length, bidirectional, continuous, self-checking, alphanumeric bar code. Its data character set contains 105 characters in each of three unique subsets. Each character consists of three bars and three spaces consuming 11 modules of width. Bars and spaces may be one, two, three, or four modules wide. The name Code 128 derives from the capability of encoding the full ASCII 128 character set. Adopted symbology for UCC/EAN-128.

code medium — the material used to construct a machine-readable code. Such materials may be retroreflective, luminescent, magnetic, opaque, transponder, or conductive.

codeword — a given sequence of the elements of a code alphabet. In bar code technology codewords are arrangements of bars and spaces used to communicate one or more data characters.

codify — (EDI) generate a code to identify a narrative message or parameter.

common carrier — (DataComm) a private data-communications utility company that furnishes communications services to the general public.

communication board — (DataComm) usually an electronic printed circuit board that allows a computer to perform communications via telephone line.

communication medium — (EDI) the tecnnology and means by which data is communicated. EDI standards and practices provide the message format; communication software provides the communication procedures.

communications server — (LAN) an intelligent device (a computer) providing communications functions; an intelligent, specially configured node on a local area network designed to enable remote-communications access and exit for LAN users.

compatibility — (DataComm) the characteristic of computers, communication devices, and software to accept and process data prepared by another computer system or another component of one computer system without a conversion utility process or code modification.

composite link — (DataComm) the line or circuit connecting a pair of multiplexers or concentrators; the circuit carrying multiplexed data.

compression — (DataComm) any of several techniques that reduce the number of bits required to represent information in data transmission or storage (thus conserving bandwidth and/or memory), in which the original form of the information can be reconstructed; also called "compaction."

computer-to-computer — transference of data generated by one computer to another computer.

concentrator — (DataComm) any communications device that allows a shared transmission medium to accommodate more data sources than there are channels currently available within the transmission medium.

conditioning — (DataComm) extra-cost options that allow improved line performance with regard to frequency response and delay distortion.

contact scanner — a bar code scanner that requires physical contact between the code medium and the scanner.

contention — (DataComm) in communications, the situation when multiple users compete for access to a transmission channel.

continuous bar code symbol — a bar code symbology where all spaces within the symbol are parts of characters, e.g., ITF. There is no intercharacter space in continuous codes.

continuous ink jet — a method of printing that uses print heads that spray a continuous stream of charged ink droplets at the paper. One of two ink jet technologies, the other being drop on demand. Continuous ink jet can give a finer line with greater control of registration of the applied ink. Also called Hertz technology.

contrast — amount of difference in reflectance between the dark bars and the light spaces of a bar code.

control envelope — (EDI) the beginning and ending segments of an interchange or functional group in a standard data format.

control number/reference number — (EDI) number used to identify an entity.

converter — a general class of manufacturers who convert plastic and paper stock for a variety of end uses including corrugated boxes, labels, forms, and tickets.

core — (LAN) the central region of an optical fiber wave guide through which light is transmitted.

CPU (central processing unit) — central processor of a computer, containing the main storage and arithmetic computation unit.

CRC (cyclic redundancy check) — (DataComm) a basic error-checking mechanism for link-level data transmissions; a characteristic link-level feature of (typically) bit-oriented data communications protocols.

cross-industry standard — (EDI) a data standard that has cross-industry application. ANSI X12 is such a standard, with broad participation from many industries and a requirement of public review prior to becoming a standard.

crossed pinning — (DataComm) configuration that allows two DTE devices or two DCE devices to communicate.

crossover — (DataComm) conductor that runs through the cable and connects to a different pin number at each end.

CRT (cathode ray tube) — computer terminal that may be for display only or may be fully interactive with a keyboard.

CTX (corporate trade exchange) — (EDI) process of effecting electronic funds transfer by use of EDI transaction sets.

current loop — (DataComm) method of interconnecting terminals and transmitting signals.

cut sheet — form delivered as individual sheets. Distinguished among bar code printers from *continuous form.*

data — a general term (plural) for the basic elements of information that can be processed or produced by a computer.

data acquisition — the process by which data are moved from the site of an event to an environment in which the data can be processed into meaningful information.

data availability — (EDI) describes those data elements accessible to a computer application for purposes of generating an EDI data transmission.

data character — an element of data (letter, number, symbol, or byte of information).

data collection system — a system that consists of input devices located at points where data are created. Once captured, the data may be immediately transmitted, by cable, telephone line, or radio signal, to a central location, usually in or near a computer room for automatic recording. Or the data may be transmitted to a storage medium, such as a tape, disk, or semiconductor memory for later transfer to a host computer application program.

data communications — (DataComm) the transmission, reception, and validation of data.

data element — **1.** a specific item of information appearing in a set of data. **2.** (EDI) a group of characters that specifies an item at or near the basic level.

data element delimiter character — (EDI) a character that marks the end of information contained in a variable length data field.

data element reference number — (EDI) the number that identifies each element found in a standard segment with its corresponding definition in the data element dictionary.

data element separator character — (EDI) a character that separates the various data elements within a standard segment.

data flow path — the route taken by data at each step in the procedures of a system or business area.

data identifier (flag character) — A character (or set of characters) within a bar code symbol that defines the general category or specific use of the data that is encoded in the same bar code symbol.

data integrity — a performance measure based on the rate of undetected errors maintaining the identical data stream as transmitted by sending party.

data link — (DataComm) any serial data-communications transmission path, generally between two adjacent nodes or devices and without intermediate switching nodes.

data message — (DataComm) an arrangement of data characters with appropriate communications overhead, e.g., check characters.

data stream — (DataComm) all data transmitted through a channel in a single transmission.

data type — (EDI) the characteristic of a data element that describes whether it is numeric, alphabetic, or alphanumeric.

database — a collection of related data which may be utilized to serve one or more functions. The data are independent of the programs that utilize them.

datagram — (LAN) a finite-length packet with sufficient information to be independently routed from source to destination.

deauthentication — (EDI) performing the same authentication process at the receiving site of a transmission as that performed at the sending site.

debug — to locate and correct any errors in a computer program.

decimal — the number representation system with a radix of 10.

DECNET — (LAN) Digital Equipment Corporation's proprietary network architecture that works across all of the company's machines.

decodability — a measure of printing accuracy as would be perceived by a bar code reader using the symbology reference decode algorithm.

decode — determine the information represented by a bar code symbol.

decoder — the portion of a bar code reading system that performs the decode function; the electronics package that receives the signals from the input device and performs the algorithm to translate the signals into meaningful data.

dedicated line — (DataComm) a dedicated circuit, a non-switched channel; also called a private line. See *leased line*.

delay — (DataComm) in communications, the time between two events. See *propagation delay* and *response time*.

delimiter — an item of lexical information whose form or position in a format or program denotes the boundary between adjacent syntactic components of the format or program.

delta code — one of two fundamental ways (see *width code*) of encoding information in a one-dimensional medium. An interval is subdivided into *modules* each of which is assigned the value of "one" or "zero." Modules with "ones" form the bars while "zeros" correspond to the spaces. A single bar or space may contain many modules. UPC, Code 128, Code 93, Code 49, and PDF417 are delta codes.

demand printer — a printer that creates individual documents one at a time, as directed.

depth of field — the difference between the minimum and maximum horizontal distance from the aperture of the bar code reader throughout which the bar code can be read.

DES (data encryption standard) — (DataComm) a scheme approved by the National Bureau of Standards that encrypts data for security purposes.

destination field — (LAN) a field in a message *header* that contains the address of the station to which a message is being directed.

detector — a sensor that converts optical energy to electrical energy, such as a PIN photodiode.

diagnostic verifier — a device that automatically evaluates the quality of a film master or a printed code. Measures the quality of the symbol against the proper specification for the printing of the symbol.

dial-up link — (DataComm) dialed-up link over the switched telephone network.

diffuse reflection — the component of reflected light that emanates uniformly in all directions from the reflecting surface.

digit — any of a set of "n" characters assigned to the possible values of a number expressed in the notation of a base "n" number system. In binary coded decimal (base 10) notation, the digits may be any of the 10 numeric characters 0 (zero) through 9 (nine).

digital — (DataComm) pertaining to data in the form of digits. In signals, digital refers to a signal that assumes one of a predetermined set of binary values, as opposed to a signal that may assume any value over a continuing range of values, such as an analog signal.

digital transmission — (DataComm) transmission of a series of discrete signal pulses representing coded values.

direct product coding — a type of coding in which the code is marked or printed on the article without using an additional substrate.

dirt — refers to the presence of relatively nonreflective foreign particles embedded in or on a bar code symbol's substrate.

discrete bar code symbol — a bar code symbol in which the intercharacter space is not part of the code and is allowed to vary dimensionally within wider tolerances than those specified for bars and spaces, e.g., Code 39.

disk/file server — (LAN) a mass-storage device that can be accessed by several computers; enables the storage and sharing of files.

distributed processing — having multiple sites/computers within a company that perform processing of similar transactions.

DLC (data link control) — (LAN) the set of rules (protocol) used by two nodes, or stations, on a network to perform an orderly exchange of information.

DMA (direct memory access) — a method of moving data from a mass storage device to random access main memory.

DOS (disk operating system) — a set of programs that instructs a disk-based computing system to manage resources and operate related equipment.

dot matrix — a system of printing where individual dots are printed in a matrix forming bars, alphanumeric characters, and simple graphics.

download — the transfer of data or programs from a large computer to a smaller computer.

downtime — the period during which computer

or network resources are unavailable to users because of a failure.

driver — (DataComm) a software module that, under control of the processor, manages an I/O port to an external device, such as a serial port to a modem.

DSD/UCS (direct store delivery of UCS data) — (EDI) standard data transactions to be used by the direct store delivery segment of the grocery industry, specifically those transactions having to do with a particular transaction used at the receiving location (back door) of the retailer.

DSR (data set ready) — (DataComm) an RS-232 modem interface control signal that indicates the terminal is ready for transmission.

EAN — International Article Numbering, the international standard bar code for retail food packages.

EAROM (electrically alterable read only memory) — a type of PROM that can be altered by electronic techniques under control of software. This form of PROM is typically used in computer terminals, bar code scanners, modems, and other products to retain configuration settings which are part of installation.

edge contrast (EC) — the difference between the space reflectance (R_s) and the adjoining bar reflectance (R_b).

EDI (electronic data interchange) — intercompany, computer-to-computer communication of data that permits the receiver to perform the function of a standard business transaction and is in a standard data format.

EDI "gateway" — (EDI) the logical location of entry or exit of EDI data into/out of a company. A device having output and input channels through which EDI communication of EDI data is effected.

EDIFACT (EDI for administration, commerce, and trade) — (EDI) the acronym for the international data standard of business transactions.

EFT (electronic funds transfer) — (EDI) computerized systems that process financial transactions and information about financial transactions between two parties.

electronic invoice — (EDI) invoice transaction in standard data format.

electronic mail (e-mail) — (EDI) system that provides the ability to deliver user-generated messages to any and all defined locations (addresses) on the system. Often an intracompany capability in human-readable format.

electrostatic — a method of printing using a special paper or a charged drum, either of which attracts toner to the charged area.

element edge — the location where the scan reflectance profile intersects the midpoint between the space reflectance (R_s) and bar reflectance (R_b) of adjoining elements. Visual measuring techniques will generally locate the element edge closer to the center of the bar.

element reflectance nonuniformity (ERN) — the reflectance difference between the highest peak and lowest valley within each element and quiet zone. Where an element consists of a single peak or valley, its reflectance nonuniformity is zero.

element width — the thickness or width of a bar or space.

EMI (electromagnetic interference) — (DataComm) a device's radiation leakage that couples onto a transmission medium, resulting (mainly) from the use of high-frequency-wave energy and signal modulation; reduced by shielding; minimum acceptable levels are detailed by the FCC based on type of device and operating frequency.

EMI/RFI (electromagnetic interference/radio frequency interference) filtering — (DataComm) protection from "background noise" that could alter or destroy data transmission.

emulation — (DataComm) the imitation, performed by a combination of hardware and software, of all or part of one device, terminal, or computer by another, so that the imitating device accepts the same data, performs the same functions, and appears to other network devices as if it were the imitated device.

emulsion side — the image-bearing side of a film master. Can be identified visually by the slightly raised image. The non-emulsion side is called the base side.

encoded area — the total area consumed by all characters of a code pattern, including start/stop and data.

encoding/decoding — (DataComm) the process of organizing information into a format suitable for transmission, and then reconverting it after transmission.

encryption — procedure of scrambling data through a series of calculations starting with a secret key, that makes it indecipherable without the secret key. The receiver of such data must perform the same calculations from the same key to get the data back to its original form.

encryption key — a group of characters used to initiate the encryption process.

end-user — the person who uses the terminal equipment on an information processing system.

EPROM (erasable programmable read only memory) — a type of integrated circuit PROM which can be erased in bulk through its cells' sensitivity to ionizing radiation provided by exposure to ultraviolet light through a quartz window in its package, or through exposure to X rays penetrating a UV-opaque package.

error detecting protocol — (DataComm) a communications protocol having a procedure in place to detect when data received is not identical to that sent.

Ethernet — (LAN) a popular local area network design, the product of Xerox Corp., characterized by 10-Mbps baseband transmission over a shielded coaxial cable and employing CSMA/CD as the access control mechanism; standardized by the IEEE as specification IEEE 802.3; referring to the Ethernet design or as compatible with Ethernet.

even parity — (DataComm) a single bit error detection method in which each character must have an even number of "on" bits, supported by a parity bit which is "off."

exclusive assignment — data identifier that has been assigned to an exclusive agency.

extraneous ink — ink in a scan area that is not intended to be there, such as tracking and splatter.

facestock — The medium onto which printing is applied to create a label.

FCS (frame check sequence) — (DataComm) in bit-oriented protocols, a 16-bit field that contains transmission-error checking information, usually appended at the end of a frame.

feasibility study — a document generated out of investigation into the economic environment, internal and external pressures, systems, procedures, and communication capability in a business area within a firm; an integral part of a corporate implementation plan.

feature extraction — a method of image recognition in which a processed image is compared in terms of mathematical transformations of features of the message. Optical images are recognized in OCR; vocal images are recognized in voice recognition. Compare with *templating.*

FEP (front-end processor) — (DataComm) a dedicated computer linked to one or more host computers or multiuser minicomputers; performs data-communications functions and serves to off-load the attached computers of network processing.

fiber optics — (DataComm) transmission technology in which modulated light wave signals, generated by a laser or LED, are propagated along a (typically) glass or plastic medium, and then demodulated to digital electrical signals by a light-sensitive receiver.

field — any group of characters defined as a unit of information. This differs from a line because one line may contain several fields.

field of view — the lineal dimension defining the length of a code that can be read in one scan, particularly significant in moving beam and CCD-array sensor technologies.

field separator — a printed mark or symbol that identifies the boundary between fields to the scanner; also referred to as field mark. See also *delimiter.*

file server — (LAN) in local area networks, a station dedicated to providing file and mass data storage services to the other stations on the network.

film master — a precise negative or positive film transparency of a specific bar code symbol from which a printing plate is made.

filter — a medium that attenuates electrical or optical energy signals of some frequencies more than others. A filter may transmit one band of frequencies and reject all other frequencies.

firmware — a computer program or software stored permanently in PROM or ROM or semi-permanently in EPROM.

first-read rate — the proportion, expressed as a percentage, of the number of successful decodes to the number of scan attempts.

fixed-beam scanner — either a visible light or laser bar code scanner reading a fixed spot in a plane through which a bar code symbol is moved. Requires a more exact positioning of a bar code symbol than with a moving beam scanner.

fixed-length (code and field) — referring to a symbol or code in which the data elements must be of a specific length.

fixed reader — a bar code reader that is mounted in a stationary fashion to intersect the plane of a bar code symbol passing before the reader. Often employed in conveyor and transport systems.

flag — (DataComm) in communications, a bit pattern of six consecutive "1" bits (character representation is 01111110) used in many bit-oriented protocols to mark the beginning (and often the end) of a frame.

flexography — a method of direct rotary printing using resilient, raised image printing plates, affixed to variable repeat plate cylinders, inked by a roll or engraved metal roll that is wiped by a doctor blade, carrying fluid or paste-type inks to virtually any substrate.

flow control — (DataComm) the procedure or technique to regulate the flow of data between two devices; prevents the loss of data once a device's buffer has reached its capacity.

flux — a measure of the power (energy per unit time) of electromagnetic radiation transmitted or received. Visible light energy is called luminous flux, and is measured in lumens, a measure of the power transmitted or received by radiation at the wavelengths of visible light from 390 to 770 nanometers. Radiant flux is the more general term applying to total power found in an electromagnetic signal.

format — the geometric construction rules that define a particular bar code or symbol.

formed character printing — an impact printing method similar in nature to an office typewriter. The bars and spaces are engraved or etched in reverse on a rotating drum, type chain, or type band. Paper, vinyl, or mylar label stock and a dry carbon ribbon pass between the drum and the hammer operated by an electromagnet. The hammer forces the paper and ribbon against the drum, causing the image to be transferred from the ribbon to the label. Each hammer stroke forms a complete character or bar. This technology is used primarily in discrete bar codes.

four-level code — a bar code that uses four different element widths in its structure.

framing — (DataComm) a control procedure used with multiplexed digital channels, such as T1 carriers, whereby bits are inserted so that the receiver can identify the time slots that are allocated to each sub-channel; framing bits may also carry alarm signals indicating specific alarm conditions.

frequency-division multiplexer (FDM) — (DataComm) a device that divides the available transmission frequency range into narrower bands, each of which is used for a separate channel.

FTP (file transfer protocol) — (LAN) an upper-level TCP/IP service that allows copying of files across a network.

full duplex (FDX) — (DataComm) simultaneous, two-way, independent transmission in both directions.

functional acknowledgment — (EDI) an ANSI X12 transaction set generated by the receiver of EDI data and transmitted to the sender.

functional group — (EDI) a group of like EDI transaction sets being sent from one party to another.

functional group header segment — (EDI) a standard data format segment defined as the start of a functional group. It contains group type, group identifier, sender and receiver codes, and version of the standard used.

functional group trailer segment — (EDI) a standard data format segment defined as the end of a functional group. It contains the group identifier and the number of transaction sets contained in the group.

gain — (DataComm) increased signal power, usually the result of amplification.

gallium arsenide (GaAs) light emitting diode — an infrared LED in which most of the material's energy is given up in the form of radiant energy. With forward bias, the diode emits a narrow wavelength of around 900 nanometers.

gateway — (LAN) a conceptual or logical network station that serves to interconnect two otherwise incompatible networks, network nodes, subnetworks, or devices; performs a protocol-conversion operation across numerous communications layers.

gateway application — (EDI) a computer program or group of programs that receives EDI data directly after being translated from the standard data format or that sends data directly to be translated into the standard data format.

generic standard — (EDI) a data standard with cross-industry application such as ANSI X12.

GHz (gigahertz) — one thousand million (10^9) cycles per second, unit of frequency.

gloss — a phenomenon related to the specular reflection of incident light. The effect of gloss is to reflect more of the incident light in a specular manner, and to scatter less. It occurs at all angles of incidence and should not be confused with the grazing angle which is specular reflection often referred to as sheen.

global threshold (GT) — the reflectance level that discriminates bars from spaces in a scan reflectance profile. The reflectance value is determined by dividing the symbol contrast (SC) by 2 and adding the minimum reflectance, R_{min}.

group addressing — (DataComm) in transmission, the use of an address that is common to two or more stations; on a multipoint line, where all stations recognize addressing characters, but only one station responds.

guard bars — the bars at both ends and center of a UPC and EAN symbol to provide reference points for scanning.

half-duplex (HDX) — (DataComm) transmission in either direction, but not carried out simultaneously.

haloing — a shadow effect around the entire printed segment or around the leading edge of a printed segment, caused by excessive pressure between the printing plate and the printed surface.

handheld scanner — a scanner held and operated by a human, thus enabling the scanner to be brought to the symbol. May be a contact (wand) scanner or a noncontact (laser or CCD) scanner.

handshaking — (DataComm) the required exchange of predetermined signals between two devices establishing a connection. Usually part of a communications protocol.

hardware — the electric, electronic, and processing equipment used for processing data; any piece of automatic data processing equipment, such as computer, communication device, printer, or other computer peripheral. Contrast with *software*.

head end — (DataComm) a passive component in a broad-band transmission network that translates one range of frequencies (Transmit) to a different frequency band (Receive); allows devices on a single cable network to send and receive signals without interference.

helium-neon (He-Ne) laser — the type of gas laser commonly used in bar code scanners. It emits coherent red light at a wavelength of 632.8 nanometers.

HIBC symbol and code — the format and symbology for automated data entry within the health industry.

hickey — a black mark or area where there should be no ink. Hickeys can interfere with the scanning of bar codes, since they may cause a space to scan as a bar.

hot stamp printing — a printing technology that uses a dry carbon ribbon or foil to transfer an image from a specific printing plate. Bar widths for this technology rarely go below 0.01 inch; the print quality is excellent. Hot stamping is a marginal technology costwise and is mainly used for very high quality multicolor labels.

human-readable — referring to the representation of the contents of a bar code symbol characterized by alphabetic and numeric characters, as well as special symbols that can be read and understood by a human.

Hz (hertz) — the international unit of frequency, equal to one cycle per second.

image orientation — orientation of the image on a film master; can be emulsion up or emulsion down.

impact printing — any printing system where a microprocessor-controlled hammer with graphic pattern impacts against a ribbon and a substrate.

incident irradiation — incidence is the amount of flux per unit area that is normal (perpendicular) to a surface or detector. If the flux is not normal (not perpendicular), then the normal component of the angular flux is the incidence. In radiometric terms, incidence is called radiant incidence or irradiance. Irradiance (Ee) is measured in watts per square meter using the formula $Ee = W/m2$.

industry-specific standard — (EDI) a data format containing transaction sets and data elements that are designed to specifically fill the business needs of a particular industry group.

information density — information density is calculated by raising the character density to a power equal to the number of characters in a character set. Assuming an inch as the given unit length of space and a character density of 5 cpi, a numeric coding structure of 10 characters has an information density of 10 to the 5th power, i.e., 100,000 units, and an alphanumeric coding structure of 36 characters has an information density of 36 to the 5th power, i.e., 60,466,176 units.

Infrared — the band of light wavelengths too long for response by a human eye. This band is represented by waves between 750 and 4 million nanometers in length. Photodiodes operating with light in this band are usually manufactured at a peak response of around 900 nanometers.

ink fill-in — expansion of a mark beyond specified tolerances.

ink fountain — the ink pan or trough on a flexo press.

ink jet — a method of printing using liquid ink projected a drop at a time against a substrate.

inspection band — an area of the bar code symbol where measurements are to be taken, spanning from 10 percent to 90 percent of the average bar height.

integrated applications — (EDI) a series of applications designed so that output of one application can be automatically fed into the next application with no modifications or human intervention.

integrated services digital network (ISDN) — (DataComm) based on digital transmission, a network that will allow voice and data traffic to utilize the same digital links and exchanges.

intelligent terminal — a programmable terminal.

intensity — the amount of radiant or luminous flux per unit solid angle that is diverging from a light source. Also called **flux density**.

interactive processing — (DataComm) describing time-dependent (real-time) data communications; a user enters data and then awaits a response from the destination before continuing; also, conversational. Contrast with *batch processing*.

interchange — (EDI) all data coming from one party and going to one party in a single transmission. In a standard data format, an interchange begins with an interchange header segment and ends with an interchange trailer segment.

intercharacter space — the space between the last bar of one character and the first bar of the next which separates the two adjacent characters. Also called **intercharacter gap**.

interconnection — (EDI) transferring data from one third party service to another via communication link.

interelement spaces — the spaces between bars in bar codes that use only the bars to encode binary data.

interface — (DataComm) a shared boundary; a physical point of demarcation between two devices, where the electrical signals, connectors, timing, and handshaking are defined; the procedures, codes, and protocols that enable two entities to interact for a meaningful exchange of information.

interleaved bar code — a bar code in which characters are paired together, using bars to represent the first character, spaces to represent the second, bars the third, etc.

Interleaved 2 of 5 — a bar code symbology encoding the ten digits zero through nine. The name Interleaved 2 of 5 is derived from the method used to encode two adjacent characters. In the symbol, two characters are paired, using bars to represent the first character and the interleaved spaces to represent the second character. Each character has two wide elements and three narrow elements for a total of five elements. For any appreciable degree of data security the application in which the symbol is to be read should define a fixed length for the symbol, and the symbol should employ bearer bars. Most commonly represented in the UPC Shipping Container Symbol. See *USCS*.

internal edits — validation of data elements as found within computer application programs.

internet — (DataComm) (LAN) a large network comprised of several smaller networks. Not to be confused with the research network called "Internet."

interpretation — (EDI) reading and understanding the meaning of EDI data that has been received from a trading partner.

invoice — document containing a record of the transaction between buyer and seller (a bill for merchandise) prepared by the seller.

I/O — (DataComm) input/output.

IP (internet protocol) — (LAN) used in gateways to connect networks at the OSI network layer (layer 3 and above).

item code — **1.** a code identifying an item. **2.** an identifying code by which a single part of material purchased, manufactured, and/or distributed is known. See also *serial number*.

JIT manufacturing schedules — schedule of manufacturing tasks such that each task is dependent on conclusion of the previous task toward development/assembly of a complete product. See *just-in-time*.

jitter — (DataComm) the slight movement of a transmission signal in time or phase that can introduce errors and loss of synchronization in high-speed synchronous communications.

joule — a unit of energy expended when a force of one newton (metric system) moves the point of application one meter in the direction of the force.

just-in-time (JIT) — manufacturing philosophy of receiving parts from suppliers at the manufacturing site just in time to be used in a manufacturing process. This requires very fast turnaround of orders and shipment of goods.

Kelvin (K) — the unit of temperature in the metric system measured such that the freezing point of water is approximately 273°K. A "color temperature" of a light source, expressed in Kelvin, is the temperature of peak emission of a perfect "black body" equivalent to the source. The higher the temperature of the source, the more violet the light as the peak of radiation shifts to shorter wavelengths.

key mark/trigger — a code bit that tells the scanner when the code is in position to be read.

KHz (kilohertz) — one thousand (10^3) cycles per second, unit of frequency.

kilo (K) — literally 1000 units, as in the electrical engineering usage of 1K ohms for resistance. In information processing 1K conventionally equals 1,024 or 2^{10}, as in 1K bytes of data or 1K bits per second.

labeler code — NDC/HRIC number assigned by the Food and Drug Administration identifying the manufacturer of a product.

labeler identification code — a four-character alphanumeric identification in the HIBC System of the labeler of health care products.

ladder code —a bar code printed in a vertical position.

LAN — see *local area network.*

Laser (light amplification by the stimulated emission of radiation) — a coherent, monochromatic, electronically controllable source of light with a narrow cone of divergence. The optical properties of lasers make them well suited for bar code scanning as explained in the main text. There are many basic laser types at various power levels including crystal (as in "ruby") lasers, gas lasers, liquid lasers, free electron lasers, and semiconductor lasers. The higher power varieties are used industrially and in cases where optical power must be projected long distances; bar code uses of high power lasers are seen in the preparation of laser etched metal tags and other labels. Low power (milliWatt and microWatt) laser types most commonly used in bar code laser scanners are heliumneon gas lasers and semiconductor lasers. Output power and safety considerations of lasers are regulated by the FDA Agency Center for Devices and Radiological Health, particularly under 21 CFA 1040 and ANSI Standard Z-136,1-1980.

laser diode — a light producing semiconductor capable of producing coherent light.

laser marking — etching of data by medium to high power lasers directly onto marking surfaces such as metal, wood, and fiberboard.

laser printer — a printer employing a pulsed or rastered laser light source to positively charge an image on a dielectric cylinder of electrostatic printing mechanism.

laser scanner — an optical bar code reading device using a low energy laser light beam as its source of illumination. Can be either handheld or fixed position.

latency — (DataComm) the interval between the time a network station seeks access to a transmission channel and the time access is granted or received; equivalent to waiting time.

layer — (DataComm) in the OSI reference model, one of seven basic layers, referring to a collection of related network processing functions; one level of a hierarchy of functions.

LED (light-emitting diode) — a semiconductor device that accepts electrical signals and converts the energy to a visible light or invisible infrared light signal.

letterpress — a printing process that employs a relief, or raised, inked image which comes into direct contact with the material being printed. Letterpress printing can be performed from metal type or plates, or rubber or plastic plates, using a rotary, flatbed, or platen press.

levels of security — (EDI) the various degrees of access to data in order to assure protection of computer-stored data.

license plate — see *serial number.*

light-emitting diode (LED) — a semiconductor that produces light at a frequency determined by its chemical composition when a voltage is applied. The light source commonly used in wand type readers.

light pen — an alternative name for a handheld wand scanner, a contact bar code reader where the operator moves the wand (the light pen) across every bar of the bar code symbol.

light source — light energy is emitted in straight lines from one of two source types, the point source and the extended source. The point source is ideally a single point. The extended source of light energy illuminates a point in space from an extended area of uniform brightness. Light sources for bar code reading equipment are typically infrared (900 nanometers peak), visible red (630 to 720 nanometers), and incandescent (400 to 900 nanometers). The source wavelength of He-Ne laser light is precisely 632.8 nanometers. Due to the size of the emitting area, lasers and LEDs approximate point sources unless optical techniques are used to produce the effect of an extended source.

line driver — (DataComm) a signal converter that conditions a digital signal to ensure reliable transmission over an extended distance.

line turnaround — (DataComm) the reversing of transmission direction from sender to receiver or vice versa when a half-duplex circuit is used.

linear array — a row and series of sensor elements (one for each pixel) able to convert the quantity of light received to individual electrical signals. Distinguished from a matrix array.

lithography — a printing process in which both the image and nonimage areas are on the same plane. It is based on the principle that oil (ink) and water do not mix. The image is first transferred to a rubber blanket cylinder and then to paper.

local area network (LAN) — a network with limited geographical coverage, often a single building, interconnecting different types of computers and terminals, with moderate to high data rates (100 Kbps to 50 Mbps). The area served may consist of a single building, a cluster of buildings, or a computer-type arrangement. The network uses some type of switching technology, and does not use common carrier circuits although it may have gateways or bridges to other public or private networks.

local line, local loop — (DataComm) a channel connecting the subscriber's equipment to the line-terminating equipment in the central office. Usually a two-wire or four-wire circuit.

lockbox — (EDI) a post office or electronic box in which customer payments are deposited.

logistics — the science of planning and carrying out the movement and maintenance of operations of an organization. For the U.S. Department of Defense LOGMARS purposes, those aspects of military operations that deal with the design and development, acquisition, storage, movement, distribution, maintenance, evacuation, and disposition of material.

LOGMARS (logistic applications for marking and reading symbols) — a Department of Defense program to place Code 39 symbols encoding specific data on all federal items. For specifications see MIL-STD-1189.

loopback — (DataComm) type of diagnostic test in which the transmitted signal is returned to the sending device after passing through all or part of a data-communications link or network. A loopback test permits the comparison of a returned signal with the transmitted signal.

looping — (EDI) the repetition of a group of segments in a standard data format transaction set.

LU 6.2 — (DataComm) in systems network architecture, a set of protocols that provides peer-to-peer communications between applications.

MAC (macro authentication code) — (EDI) a character string computed as a result of an authentication of an EDI data stream. The MAC is appended to the original stream and transmitted along with the data. After performing the identical computations at the receiving location, the receiver must verify that the computed MAC is identical to that sent. If not, the user knows that the data has been tampered with during transmission.

machine-readable — that characteristic of printed information that permits the direct transfer of information from a printed surface to a data processing system without operator intervention. Bar code and optical character recognition are technologies of machine reading, as is that of image cameras. Data contained in predefined locations (fields) within a data stream that can be interpreted by a computer program.

magnetic code reader — a computer peripheral that reads and identifies by the detection of the presence or absence of a magnetic field.

magnetic ink character recognition (MICR) — the machine recognition of characters printed with ink that contains particles of a magnetic material. Commonly used in check printing within the banking and financial community.

magnetic medium — any data-storage medium and related technology, including disks, diskettes, and tapes, in which different patterns of magnetization represent bit values.

magnification factor (MF) — a term used in the UPC and UCS/TCS specifications identifying the size of a printed bar code compared to a standard (nominal) size. A magnification factor of 1.00 (100 percent) is nominal.

mailbox — (EDI) a logical file area of data storage in which all data sent to a particular recipient is stored until retrieved by that recipient. Mailboxes are provided as a service by third party EDI service and e-mail.

make-ready — the preparation and correction of the printing plates, before starting the print run, to ensure uniformly clean impressions of optimum quality; all preparatory operations preceding production.

managed data network (MDN) — (EDI) sometimes called third party network or VAN, where network owner sells spare network capacity to interested parties. Additional network services are often available.

Manchester encoding — (LAN) digital encoding technique (specified for the IEEE 802.3 Ethernet baseband network standard).

mandatory data element/segment — (EDI) a data element or segment within a standard data format in which information must be contained.

manufacturer identification code — a property of an entity, not of a transaction. The manufacturer identification code is a six-digit number assigned by the Uniform Code Council (UCC). Should be stored in computer records as a seven-digit code to accommodate International Article Numbering (EAN) coding authorities.

manufacturer identification number — in the UPC system, the six-digit number assigned to

a manufacturer by the Uniform Code Council. This number appears as the left half of the UPC number. See *item code*.

map — (EDI) the logical association of one set of values with values in another set. In EDI, moving data element values in an EDI data stream from one format to another.

mark — (DataComm) presence of signal. In telegraph communication, a mark represents the closed condition or current flowing. A mark impulse is equivalent to a binary 1.

mark reading — automatic optical reading of printed marks. Often used in test scoring of multiple-answer questions.

mark sensing — machine reading of marks by using the conductive properties of the marks themselves, such as those made by number 2 pencil.

mass storage — computer peripherals that store data in a less accessible form than main memory, most frequently as a record in magnetic media such as hard disk, diskette, or tape. Media such as tape or diskette is usually removable; hard disk mass storage is either removable or permanently mounted.

material release — (EDI) a transaction set used by the automotive industry which acts as a release for product against an annually negotiated purchase order.

material requirements planning (MRP) — a production scheduling process, usually computer-based, which arranges for the placement of materials and components where and when they are needed.

materiel — equipment, apparatus, and supplies used by an organization.

matrix array — a set of rays and columns of transductive elements able to convert the quantity of light received to a relatively sized modulated electrical signal. Distinguished from a linear array.

matrix printing — a method of printing that employs a print head to produce a series of dots in a pattern that forms characters or bars. On some printers the head is fixed and the label stock moves. On others the head moves and the stock is fixed. Technologies employing matrix printing include dot-matrix impact, ink jet, thermal, electrostatic, and thermal transfer printing.

MAU (multistation access unit) — (LAN) a wiring concentrator used in local area networks.

maximum element reflectance nonuniformity (ERN_{max}) — the largest element reflectance nonuniformity in a scan reflectance profile.

maximum reflectance (R_{max}) — the largest reflectance value in a scan reflectance profile.

megabyte (MB or M) — 2^{20} = 1,048,576 bytes, equivalent of 1024 kilobytes; basic unit of measurement of mass storage.

menu-driven — computer programs whose functionality can be accessed by a user via on-line, preformatted screens presenting various "menus" of options.

message — a group of characters encoded in the bar code symbol. A transmitted series of words or symbols designed and intended to relay information.

message code — a user-specific meaning ascribed to a bar code or other message, including message format restrictions and check characters.

message length — the number of characters encoded in the bar code symbol or other message.

MHS (Message Handling System) — (DataComm) the standard defined by the CCITT as X.400 and by the ISO as Message Oriented Text Interchange Standard (MOTIS).

MHz (megahertz) — one million (10^6) cycles per second, unit of frequency.

micro channel — a proprietary bus developed by IBM for its PS/2 family of computers' internal expansion cards; also offered by Tandy and other vendors. Compare with *EISA bus.*

microcomputer — a general term referring to a complete, tiny (usually but not always desktop) computing system consisting of hard-

ware and software.

micron — a unit of measure equal to one millionth of a meter, or about 0.00004 inch; 25.4 microns equal 0.001 inch (one mil).

microprocessor — an electronic integrated circuit, typically a single-chip package, capable of receiving and executing coded instructions. For example, Zilog Z80, Intel 8088, and Motorola 68000 are popular microprocessors.

mil — a dimensional unit equal to 0.001 inch in the English system of measure, commonly used to refer to the width of bar code elements, e.g., 0.013 inch would be expressed as 13 mils.

mini-MAP (mini-manufacturing automation protocol) — (LAN) a version of MAP consisting of only physical, link, and application layers, intended for lower-cost, process-control networks. With mini-MAP, a device with a token can request a response from an addressed device; unlike a standard MAP protocol, the addressed mini-MAP device need not wait for the token to respond.

minimum edge contrast (EC_{min}) — the smallest edge contrast in a scan reflectance profile.

minimum reflectance (R_{min}) — the smallest reflectance value in a scan reflectance profile.

minimum reflectivity difference — the difference between the smallest minimum space reflectance value and the largest maximum bar reflectance value as measured across the entire symbol. Bar, space, and MAD reflectances can be expressed as percentages or in decimal form. If the reflectance of the bars is determined to be 2 percent, and the reflectance of the spaces is determined to be 90 percent, then the MAD equals 88 percent.

MIPS (millions of instructions per second) — a general comparison gauge of a computer's raw processing power.

misalignment — misorientation of the label from its normal position.

miscoding or misencodation — occurs when the characters to be represented in symbol form are not correctly encoded in the bars and spaces; for example, when the desired number is 1-2-3-4 and the number encoded in the symbol is 1-2-5-4.

misread — see *substitution error.*

modem (modulator-demodulator) — (Data-Comm) a device used to convert serial digital data from a transmitting terminal to a signal suitable for transmission over a telephone channel, or to reconvert the transmitted signal to serial digital data for acceptance by a receiving terminal.

modem eliminator — (DataComm) a device used to connect a local terminal and a computer port in replacing the pair of modems that they would ordinarily need; allows DTE-to-DTE data and control signal connections otherwise not easily achieved by standard cables or connectors.

modulation (MOD) — the ratio of minimum edge contrast (EC_{min}) to symbol contrast (SC). MOD = EC_{min}/SC.

module — the narrowest nominal bar or space in the bar code symbol. Wider bars and spaces are often specified as multiples of one module. Also known as *X dimension.*

module width encoding — a method of bar encoding in which narrow elements represent binary zeros and wide elements represent binary ones.

modulo check character(s) — a means of assuring message accuracy through the use of check character(s) that represent the remainder obtained when the summation of character values assigned by the code to the message contents is divided by the number of available encodable characters.

moving beam scanner — a scanning device where scanning motion is achieved by mechanically moving the light beam through the bars and spaces of a bar code symbol.

MS-DOS (Microsoft disk operating system) — microcomputer operating system developed for the IBM PC and, hence, a de facto industry standard; referred to as PC-DOS, primarily by IBM.

MS OS/2 LAN Manager — (LAN) the multi-user network operating system co-developed by Microsoft and 3Com. LAN Manager offers a wide range of network management and control capabilities unavailable with existing PC-based network operating systems.

MTBF (mean time between failures) — a stated or published period of time for which a user may expect a device to operate before a failure occurs.

MTTR (mean time to repair) — the average time required to perform corrective maintenance on a failed device.

multicode reader — also called an autodiscrimination reader. A bar code reader possessing the software or firmware capable of decoding various types of bar codes, such as Code 39, UPC/EAN, Interleaved 2 of 5, and Codabar. Two varieties of multicode readers exist. A switch-selectable, or firmware-based, system permits the selection of the desired code based on switch position (on or off). An auto-discrimination, or software-based, system is capable of distinguishing between and decoding any of a specific set of codes automatically, without operator intervention.

multifont — an OCR reader capable of recognizing more than one type font automatically, such as OCR-A and OCR-B, or various letter-quality printer fonts.

multimedia EDI — (EDI) the passing of data electronically via any combination of batch, interactive, print, and electronic mail methods.

multimode fiber — (DataComm) an optical fiber designed to carry multiple signals, distinguished by frequency or phase, at the same time. Compare with *single mode.*

multiple font — a firmware-based reader capable of recognizing more than one type of font, but only one at a time.

multiple routing — (DataComm) the process of sending a message to more than one recipient, usually when all destinations are specified in the header of the message.

multiplexer — (DataComm) a device used for division of a transmission facility into two or more subchannels of lower speeds, either by splitting the frequency band into narrower bands (frequency division) or by allotting a common channel to several different transmitting devices one at a time (time division).

multipoint line — (DataComm) a single communications line or circuit interconnecting several stations supporting terminals in several different locations. This type of line usually requires some kind of polling mechanism, each terminal with a unique address. Also called a multidrop line.

multitasking — the concurrent execution of two or more tasks or applications by a computer; may also be the concurrent execution of a single program that is used by many tasks.

N (wide-to-narrow ratio) — in symbologies with two element widths, the wide-to-narrow ratio of elements is calculated by summing the average wide bar width and average wide space width and dividing the sum by two times the average narrow element width. Intercharacter gaps, if applicable, are not included.

NAK (DataComm) — a "negative acknowledgement" character, sent to the source of a transmission after a message has been received with one or more errors, indicating a request for a retransmission of the message.

nanometer (nm) — one billionth of a meter; a unit of measure used to define the wavelength of light, equal to 10^{-9} meters.

nanosecond — one billionth of a second (10^{-9} second).

national stock number (NSN) — a 13-character number assigned uniquely to each item of procurement of the U.S. government.

NCC (network control center) — (DataComm) any centralized network diagnostic and management station or site, such as that of a packet-switching network.

NDC/NHRI (National Drug Code/National Health Related Items Code) — a ten-digit code number assigned and administered by the Food and Drug Administration. In the UPC implementation, these numbers use the UPC number system character 3 as the first

digit, instead of 0 used by regular grocery items. NDCs can appear in a 4-4-2, 5-4-1, or 5-3-2 format, with the first set of digits representing the manufacturer identification number and the second set of digits representing the item code. NHRICs can appear in a 4-6 or 5-5 format.

NDIS (network driver interface specification) — (DataComm) a standard established by Microsoft for writing hardware-independent drivers.

NETBIOS (network basic input/output system) — (LAN) software developed by IBM; provides the interface between a PC's operating system, the I/O bus, and the network; a de facto network standard.

network — (DataComm) an interconnected group of nodes; a series of points, nodes, or stations connected by communications channels; the assembly of equipment through which connections are made between data stations.

network architecture — (DataComm) a set of design principles, including the organization of functions and the description of data formats and procedures, used as the basis for the design and implementation of a network (ISO). Reference used for the definition and development of protocols and products for internetworking between data processing systems, often used to define a hierarchy of communication function layers.

network interface controller — (LAN) electronic circuitry that connects a workstation to a network, usually in the form of a card that fits into one of the expansion slots inside a personal computer. It works with the network software and computer operating system to transmit and receive messages on the network; also, network interface card.

network layer — (LAN) layer 3 in the OSI model; the logical network entity that services the transport layer; responsible for ensuring that data passed to it from the transport layer is routed and delivered through the network.

network topology — (LAN) the physical and logical relationship of nodes in a network; the schematic arrangement of the links and nodes of a network.

NEX/UCS — (EDI) network exchange of UCS data; standard data transactions to be used in office-to-office EDI transmissions in the direct store delivery segment of the grocery industry.

NFS (network file server) — (LAN) an extension of TCP/IP that allows files on remote nodes of a network to appear locally connected.

nm (nanometer) — see *nanometer.*

node — **1.** (DataComm) a computer or switching device situated at the point where two or more communications lines meet with both input and output circuits. **2.** (LAN) a point where one or more functional units interconnect transmission lines; a physical device that allows for transmission of data within a network; includes host processors, communications controllers, cluster controllers, and terminals.

noncontact — a method of bar code reading typified by fixed- or moving-beam scanners that can read bar code symbols without actually contacting the symbols.

non-read — the failure of a bar code scanner to recognize or decode a bar code symbol after a scanning attempt. This may be due to bar code symbol defects, scanner defects, or operator error, e.g., incomplete scan of a symbol.

non-return-to-zero (NRZ) encoding — a method of bar code encoding in which binary zeros and ones are represented by reflective and non-reflective modules, respectively; a series of four binary zeros, for example, represented by a nonreflective area four modules in width.

null modem — (DataComm) a device that connects two DTE devices directly by emulating the physical connections of a DCE device.

number — a set of characters that refer to a code structure, not restricted to numeric digits. In this document the term "number" is used synonymously with the term "code." See also *numeric code.*

number system character — the first, or left-hand, digit in a UPC number; identifies different numbering systems. Regular supermarket items carry a 0, 6, or 7; random weight items such as meat and produce that are marked at the store carry a 2; NDC/NHRIC items carry a 3; retailers may use a 4 for in-store marking, coupons carry a 5; and number systems 1, 8, and 9 are not defined for use at this time. Only number system 0 is valid for the six-digit UPC Version E symbol.

numeric code — a code that contains only numeric characters, the digits (zero) through 9 (nine).

OCR — optical character recognition.

OCR-A — an abbreviation commonly applied to the character set contained in ANSI standard X3.17-1981. Consists of 26 alphabetic characters, 10 numerals, 60 other graphic shapes, plus the space character. OCR-A was initially chosen as the official symbology of the National Retail Merchants Association (NRMA) and the Canadian Standard Product Code for wine, beer, and liquor items. OCR-A is more stylized than the OCR-B font.

OCR-B — an abbreviation commonly applied to the character set contained in ANSI standard X3.49-1975. Consists of 26 alphabetic characters, 10 numerals, 60 other graphic shapes, plus the space character. OCR-B has been adopted by the Uniform Code Council as the human-readable portion of the UPC symbol. The less stylized and more human-readable of the two OCR fonts.

odd parity — (DataComm) a single bit error detection method in which each character must have an odd number of "on" bits, supported by a parity bit which is "on."

OEM — original equipment manufacturer.

off-line — (DataComm) condition in which a user, terminal, or other device is not connected to a computer or is not actively transmitting via a network, or the operations performed on such equipment.

omnidirectional — refers to a code format that can be read regardless of orientation in a given plane, such as a bullseye code, or a reader or scanner with the ability to read a bar code symbol from any angle.

on-line — (DataComm) condition in which a user, terminal, or other device is actively connected with the facilities of a communications network or computer; opposite of off-line. As pertaining to an application, requiring input by a human.

opacity — the property of a substrate material that minimizes show-through from the back side on the next sheet. The ratio of the reflectance with a black backing to the reflectance with a white backing. Ink opacity is the property of an ink that prevents the substrate from showing through.

opacity value — the calculated value of a material by means of two reflectance measurements, R1 and R2. The first measurement, R1, is taken on a sample of a blank material, backed with enough layers of the same material so that doubling the number of layers does not change the measured value of reflectance. The second measurement, R2, is taken of the same blank material sample except that a black backing is placed behind the material sample instead of the multiple layers. The reflectance value of the black backing should not exceed five percent. The calculation of the opacity value is as follows: opacity value = $1.00 - (R1-R2/R1) = R2/R1$.

open network — (EDI) a service provided by a third party EDI service provider which allows a customer to transmit data to or receive data from a noncustomer. Noncustomers receive the data through an autodial feature, having no mailbox on the network.

open system — a system that specifies standards and can therefore be readily connected to other systems that comply with the same standard.

open systems interconnection (OSI) — (DataComm) agreed standard procedures for information exchange between previously incompatible systems.

open systems interconnection model — (DataComm) reference model for the definition of OSI. Developed by the International Telephony and Telegraphy Consultative Committee (CCITT) and the International Standards Organization (ISO). A logical structure (model) for network operations standardized within the ISO; a seven-layer network architecture being used for the definition of network protocol standards to enable any OSI-compliant computer or device to communicate with any other OSI-compliant computer or device for a meaningful exchange of information (the layers are: physical, data link, network, transport, session, presentation, application).

operating system — the software of a computer that controls the execution of programs, typically handling the functions of input/output control, resource scheduling, and data management.

operational "window" — (EDI) a predefined number of hours per day and days per week in which normal business can be transacted. In EDI, those hours when data can be transmitted to a company directly.

optical character reader — an information processing device that accepts prepared forms and converts data from them to computer output media via optical character recognition.

optical character recognition (OCR) — the machine identification of printed characters by optical sensors and software.

optical disk — a very-high-density information storage medium that uses light to read and write digital information.

optical distortion — change in appearance of objects when viewed through transparent material, adding certain defects such as waviness of surface.

optical fiber — (DataComm) any filament or fiber made of dielectric materials that is used to transmit laser- or LED-generated light signals.

optical throw — the horizontal distance from the aperture of a bar code reader to the leading vertical plane of the depth of field; the minimum distance a bar code symbol can be away from the scanner and still be successfully read.

optional data element/segment — (EDI) a data

element or segment within a standard transaction set in which data can, but does not need to, be present.

order processing application — a computer program or group of programs accepting a validated order from an order entry application, evaluating it in terms of available inventory, and generating an internal staging order for stock items with inventory availability and an internal order to a manufacturing or assembly location for stock items with no inventory availability.

orientation — the alignment of the symbol's scan path. Two possible orientations are "horizontal" with vertical bars and spaces (picket fence) and "vertical" with horizontal bars and spaces (ladder).

orientation bar — a code bar that provides the scanner with start and stop reading instructions, as well as code orientation.

OS/2 — the operating system developed by IBM and Microsoft for use with the Intel 80286 and 80386 microprocessor. Unlike its predecessor (PC MS-DOS), OS/2 is a multitasking operating system. OS/2 also refers to operating software that will run on the Personal System/2. OS/2 Standard Edition is a joint Microsoft and IBM development, while OS/2 Extended Edition is the IBM proprietary extension to include communications and database managers.

OSINET — (DataComm) a test network, sponsored by the National Bureau of Standards (NBS), designed to provide vendors of products based on the OSI model a forum for doing interoperability testing.

overall profile grade — the lowest grade received by any of the following parameters: edge determination, overall profile reflectance grade, decode, and decodability defined in ANS X3.182-1990.

overhead — **1.** in a bar code system, the fixed number of characters required for start, stop, and checking in a given symbol, e.g., a symbol requiring a start, stop, and one check character contains three characters of overhead. Therefore, to encode four characters, seven characters are required to be printed. **2.** (DataComm) in communications, all information, such as control, routing, and error-checking characters, that is in addition to user-transmitted data; includes information that carries network status or operational instructions, network routing information, and retransmissions of user data messages that are received in error.

over-laminate — a coating or material placed over a bar code symbol for protection against dirt, wear, and/or abrasion.

packet — (DataComm) a group of bits (including data and call control signals) transmitted as a whole on a packet-switching network. Usually smaller than a transmission block. A sequence of data, with associated control information, that is switched and transmitted as a whole; refers mainly to the field structure and format defined with the CCITT X.25 recommendations.

packet access device (PAD) — (DataComm) an interface between a terminal or computer to a packet-switched network by converting usual data flow to and from packets, setting up calls and addressing packets.

packet switching — (DataComm) the switching of data in individual packets ensuring acceptance by the network and subsequent delivery. Packet sequence and destination is determined by control information passed from the originating terminal and the network.

paper bleed — an optical phenomenon that causes the bars to appear larger and the spaces narrower than they are actually printed. It is caused by the scattering of incident light rays within the paper media.

parallel processing — concurrent or simultaneous execution of two or more processes, or programs, within the same processor, as contrasted with serial or sequential processing.

parallel transmission — (DataComm) transmission mode that sends a number of bits simultaneously over separate lines (e.g., eight bits over eight lines) to a printer. Usually unidirectional.

parity — a system for encoding characters with odd or even bar code patterns. Even parity characters have an even number of binary ones in their structure, while odd parity characters have an odd number of binary ones in their structure. Parity is used to provide a self-checking feature in bar codes and other data transmission techniques.

parity bit/bar/module — a bit that is set at "0" or "1" in a character to ensure that the total number of 1 bits in the data field is even or odd.

pass-through — (LAN) the ability to gain access to one network element through another.

passive device — (DataComm) in current loop applications a device that must draw its current from connected equipment.

PBX (private branch exchange) — (DataComm) a manual, user-owned telephone exchange.

PC (personal computer) — a generic term for a single-user microcomputer; PC also refers to the IBM Personal Computer, the first microcomputer to be widely accepted in business and a de facto standard for compatibility.

peak — the graphical pattern on a scan reflectance profile that looks like an upside down "U" or "V." Within a profile a peak represents a "space." One or more peaks could also be found within an element, representing a reflectance change within an element.

periodic binary code — a binary code format using the same amount of space for each bit; narrow bars are zero and wide bars are one.

permanent code — a code that is reused indefinitely in a system.

phase modulation — (DataComm) one of three ways of modifying a sine wave signal to make it "carry" information. The sine wave or "carrier" has its phase changed in accordance with the information to be transmitted.

photocell / photoelectric cell / photo-sensor — a solid-state, photosensitive, electronic device in which use is made of the variation of current-voltage characteristics as a function of incident radiation (light). In conveyor and transport systems, a photocell may serve as a presence sensor, identifying when an item is in view and ready to be scanned.

photocomposition — the process of setting type copy photographically, as opposed to using the method of inking and proofing lead type characters.

photodiode array (linear) — the grouping of many photodiodes (usually as an integrated circuit chip called a CCD) in a line that detects photon energy (light) from the radiation that strikes a surface and changes the reflected light into electrical current which can be measured. Each photodiode in the array is sampled by the electronics and converted to a bit value which is decoded by a microprocessor.

photodiode array (matrix) — a video sensor; similar to a linear photodiode array, except composed of multiple lines in an array of "n" rows of "m" electronically scanned photosensors, each capturing one pixel of an image of the symbol to be decoded. Matrix array (video) scanning techniques employ software to explicitly incorporate vertical redundancy of bar codes, excluding the effects of localized printing defects. The images captured by matrix array sensors can—with appropriate software—provide two-dimensional optical character recognition as well as enhanced one-dimensional (bar code) optical character recognition.

photoengraving — a metal plate prepared by the photochemical process, from which the matrix or rubber mold is reproduced.

photopolymer — a polymer made so that it undergoes a change on exposure to light.

pick instructions — instructions to a warehouseman that describe what and how much product to remove from storage in order to stage a shipment.

picket fence code — a bar code printed horizontally, with individual bars that look like pickets in a fence.

pitch — rotation of a bar code symbol about an axis parallel to the direction of the bars.

pixel (picture element) — smallest unit of a graphics or video display or memory image; light characteristics (color and intensity) are often associated with each pixel of an image in a graphic system, but bar code scanners typically deal with a binary (dark versus light) pixel value.

planning schedule transaction — (EDI) a transaction set used in the automotive industry containing information describing a customer's forecasted manufacturing requirements.

pneumatic code reader — a code reader that reads and identifies codes by detecting the presence or absence of pneumatic flow, such as reading perforations in keypunch cards by means of air flow.

point-of-sale (POS) data entry system — a system in which actual transactions are recorded by terminals operating on-line to a central computer, such as supermarket registers. These systems frequently employ optical scanning as a means of capturing data.

polarity — (DataComm) any condition in which there are two opposing voltage levels or changes, such as positive and negative.

polling — (DataComm) a means of controlling devices on a multipoint line.

polymer — a compound formed by the linking of simple and identical molecules having functional groups that permit their combination to proceed to higher molecular weights under suitable conditions.

port — (DataComm) a point of access into a computer, a network, or other electronic device; the physical or electrical interface through which one gains access; the interface between a process and a communications or transmission facility.

portable data entry terminal — a microprocessor-based, handheld terminal capable of capturing data by taking the data capture device to the product as opposed to taking the product to the data capture device. Portable data entry terminals can be either batch oriented, where the data is captured remotely and later transmitted to a computer, or on-line, which immediately transfers captured data to the computer through a radio frequency (RF) or microwave (MW) link. Features of portable data entry terminals include the number or characteristics of data entry keys, the attachment of scanning peripherals, program memory, data memory, the number of characters displayed, the method of display, and data transmission techniques.

predefined fixed file — (EDI) a file defined as input or output of an application program containing records whose data elements are each of a fixed length. In EDI, this type of file may be defined by a third party service provider as input to an in-network translation capability.

preformatted screen — a user-friendly screen that may offer menu options or act as a data entry medium.

preprinted symbol — a symbol that is printed in advance of application either on a label or on the article to be identified.

presence sensor — a device, often photoelectric, used in conveyor and transport systems to tell the system that an item is in view and ready to be read.

presentation layer — (DataComm) layer 6 of the ISO reference model; provides standards for restructuring data into the required format, character set, or language.

print contrast signal (PCS) — a comparison between the reflectance of the bars and spaces of a bar code symbol; the bar reflectance expressed as a percentage of the space reflectance.

print gain — gain in bar width in the final printed bar code symbol, compared to the original precision film master; influenced by platemaking and ink spread during printing. Film masters are made with an appropriate amount of bar width reduction (BWR) to allow for print gain.

print quality — the measure of compliance of a bar code symbol to the requirements of accuracy, defects, modulation, and symbol contrast as described in ANS X3.182-1990.

print server — (LAN) an intelligent device used to transfer information to a printer selected from a set of one or more printers.

print tolerance — an absolute measurement of deviation from a nominal print width, expressed as being plus or minus (+ or −) so many thousandths of an inch.

printability gauge — a printer's tool used to determine the amount of print gain under given printing conditions.

printability range — the range of print gain found under actual working conditions, based on press sheets selected at random during a press run.

printing plate — the printing image carrier used on rotary presses, which accepts ink in the image area for printing.

product code — a code uniquely identifying product. It may contain components of price, manufacturer, stock number, and product category. See *item code*.

production mode — in data processing, automatic job scheduling and execution; occurs after programs have been debugged during test mode.

PROM (programmable read only memory) — 1. a random access memory region of a computer fabricated from one of a number of technologies (EPROM, PROM, EAROM, Flash Memories) which allow non-volatile data patterns to be stored in semiconductor devices. 2. The first programmable read only memory integrated circuit technology developed, employing "fusible links" to represent the bits of patterns permanently stored in the chip.

propagation delay — (DataComm) the time it takes a signal composed of electromagnetic energy to travel from one point to another over a transmission channel; usually most noticeable in communicating with satellites; normally, the speed-of-light delay.

proprietary company standard — a standard data format developed and owned by a company to handle transactions between that company and its trading partners. Most often developed by a major customer company.

proprietary inquiry system — (EDI) a program or group of programs developed and owned by a supplier, which is offered to its customers to handle inventory and order status inquiries. Usually, such a system is interactive.

proprietary ordering system — (EDI) a group of programs developed and owned by a supplier, which is offered to its customers to handle ordering. Usually, such a system is interactive.

protocol — (DataComm) formal set of rules governing the format, timing, sequencing, and error control of exchanged messages of a data network; may be oriented toward data transfer over an interface, between two logical units directly connected, or on an end-to-end basis between two users over a large and complex network. Simple protocols define only hardware configuration; more complex protocols define timings, data formats, error detection, and correction techniques.

protocol conversion — (DataComm) for computers with different protocols to understand each other, meaningful conversation needs to take place. Many VANS are equipped to allow conversations between different "tongues."

public network — (DataComm) a network operated by common carriers or telecommunications administrations for the provision of circuit-switched, packet-switched, and leased-line circuits to the public.

public switched network — (DataComm) any switching communications system—such as Telex, TWX, or public telephone networks—that provides circuit switching to many customers.

pulse code modulation — (DataComm) the method of transmitting analog speech and data in a digital form.

purchase-pay cycle — (EDI) period of time from generation of a purchase order, through receipt of ordered product, and to payment for that product.

purchasing transaction — (EDI) one of many transactions containing information relating to the purchase of a product or service. For example, purchase order, purchase order change, purchase order acknowledgment.

Q.E.D. — *quod eratus demonstrandum.* Latin for "that which has been proven."

qualifier code — (EDI) a piece of information

placed in a data element which is related to a second element and is used to identify how to interpret the data in the second element.

quality control — the systematic planning, measurement, and control of a combination of people, materials, metrology, and machines, with the objective of producing a product that satisfies the quality and profitability of the enterprise.

queue — (DataComm) any group of items, such as computer jobs or messages, waiting for service.

queueing — (DataComm) sequencing of batch data sessions.

quick response (QR) — retail philosophy, developed by VICS, of receiving goods from suppliers at the retail site based upon the sales of the supplier's goods that are transmitted to the supplier on a periodic basis. Sales are generally recorded using bar codes; transmission between retailer and supplier occurs through the use of X12EDI.

quiet zone — the area immediately preceding the start character and following the stop character and which contains no markings that would attenuate or interfere with the scanning of the bar code symbol.

radiant power — the time rate of flow of energy as electromagnetic radiation (light, radio, etc.), measured in watts (W).

radiation pattern — the optical pattern of light that leaves the media surface, as described by the radiated light intensity at various angles.

radio frequency (RF) / microwave (MW) / transponder — a technology of automated identification systems that operates on the same principle as security tags placed on clothing. The tag signals an alarm if it passes through an antenna field, which is usually located at the door of the establishment. Passive devices are commercially available that will encode and transmit information back to a computer system when in proximity to its associated antenna.

RAM (random access memory) — semiconductor read/write memory. Usually volatile, i.e., data stored is lost if power is turned off.

randomly accessed file — a data file whose units of information can be accessed in any order using an address or key.

read area — area covered by a scanner; especially important in material handling applications, such as scanners reading cartons on a conveyor line. Bar codes must reliably pass through the read area with the length of the symbol parallel to the scan plane.

reader — a device used for machine reading of bar codes; typically consists of a scanner, a decoder, and a communications interface.

real-time — computer functions carried out at a time demanded by the user—usually refers to present time. Operating mode that allows immediate interaction with data as it is created, as in a process-control system or computer-aided design system.

redundancy — (DataComm) in data transmission, the portion of a message's gross information content that can be eliminated without losing essential information; also, duplicate facilities.

reflectance — the ratio, usually expressed as a decimal, of the amount of light reflected from a surface to the amount incident on that surface, usually detailed under a given set of illumination conditions. (Standards are defined in the document "ANS X3.182-1990, Reference Reflectivity Measurements.")

reflectance, absolute — the ratio of the total reflectance by a document to the total light incident on that document.

reflectance, diffuse — reflected light at angles other than the angle of incidence of the illuminating light, such as in reflection from a rough surface.

reflectance, specular — reflected light whose angle of reflection is equal to the angle of incidence of the illuminating light, such as in reflection from a mirror.

relational data base — a file of information in normalized form, i.e., a flat file that has been inverted.

release liners — in pressure sensitive label stock, the component that functions as a carrier for the label. Prior to label application, it protects the adhesive; at the time of application, it is readily separated from the label.

repeat lengths — in printing presses, the circumference of the printing cylinders in the printing section. A 22-inch press has a repeat length of 22 inches and within that one repeat length could print one 22-inch form, two 11-inch forms (with two images on the printing plate), three 7.33-inch forms (with three images on the printing plate), etc., before the cylinder's cycle is repeated.

resolution — the ability of a bar code reader to read narrow bars in a bar code; optically reproducing fine detail.

response time — (DataComm) the elapsed time between the generation of the last character of a message at a terminal and the receipt of the first character of the reply. It includes terminal delay and network delay.

retroreflective — refers to a characteristic of material, causing it to reflect light back to its source, regardless of the angle of incidence.

reverse image — a symbol in which the normally dark areas are represented by the material substrate and the light areas are represented by the inked portion of the symbol.

RF scanner — that variety of portable data entry terminals possessing the capability of a radio-frequency data link back to a computer system.

right-hand justified zero filled — a common data processing convention for the storage of variable-length numeric data in fixed-length memory locations. When data are input that are of shorter length than the maximum length of the storage location field, the data are shifted to the right so that the last significant character of the input appears in the last reserved memory location of the storage medium. The memory locations preceding the first character of the field being input are unused and filled with zero characters (ASCII hex 30). A convention used for numeric fields.

ring network — (LAN) a network topology in which each node is connected to two adjacent nodes.

RISC (reduced instruction set computing) — internal computing architecture where processor instructions are pared down so that most can be performed in a single processor cycle, theoretically improving computing efficiency.

ROM (read-only memory) — a specialized form of integrated circuit memory that is manufactured with a fixed pattern of data that cannot be altered in the field except by replacing the ROM memory chip itself.

router — (LAN) a network device that examines data addresses, determines the most efficient pathway to the destination, and routes the data accordingly.

routing — (DataComm) the process of selecting the correct circuit path for a message.

RS-232 — (DataComm) interface between DTE and DCE, employing serial binary data interchange, commonly used for terminals and modems. EIA standard.

scan reflectance profile — a record of the reflectance measured using the reference reflectivity method (standards are defined in the document "ANS X3.182-1990") as a function of distance across the entire bar code symbol.

scanner — a device that examines a spatial pattern, one part after another, and generates analog or digital signals corresponding to the pattern. Scanners are often used in mark sensing, pattern recognition, character recognition, and bar code recognition. The scanner converts bar code symbols to electrical signals for input to a bar code reader decoder for processing and subsequent output through a data communications interface.

segment — (EDI) in a standard data format, a unit of a transaction set made up of related data elements.

segment delimiter character — (EDI) a character that marks the end of information contained in a variable-length segment.

segment diagram — (EDI) as related to a standard data format, a diagrammatic representation of a segment in terms of all of its data elements.

segment identifier — (EDI) as related to a standard data format, the code that uniquely identifies a segment, contained in the segment as the first data field.

segment terminator — (EDI) as related to a standard data format, the character that defines the end of a data segment.

self-checking bar code — a bar code in which a single printing defect will not cause the character with the defect to be transposed into another valid character within that symbology.

self-clocking — a characteristic of bar code symbologies in which timing information necessary for decoding is derived from actual reflectance data as scanned. Self-clocking codes can be read and decoded with a single aperture handheld wand reader or fixed-beam, fixed-mount reader over a range of velocities, with reasonable allowances for changes in velocity during the scan.

sequential file — a data file organized in such a way that its information must be accessed in sequential order from first to last record.

serial number — the number appearing on an entity as assigned by the manufacturer or product user to uniquely identify that entity from all other like and unlike entities.

serial transmission — (DataComm) the most common transmission mode; in serial, information bits are sent sequentially on a single data channel.

session layer — (DataComm) layer 5 of the OSI reference model; provides protocols for assembling physical messages into logical messages.

shipping transaction — (EDI) one of several transaction sets containing information on shipment of product.

short-haul modem — (DataComm) a signal converter that conditions a digital signal to ensure reliable transmission over DC continuous private-line metallic circuits, without interfering with adjacent pairs of wire in the same telephone.

show-through — the generally undesirable property of a substrate that allows underlying markings or materials to affect reflectance.

single mode fiber — (DataComm) an optical waveguide designed to propagate light of only a single wavelength and perhaps a single phase; essentially, an optical fiber that allows the transmission of only one light beam, or data-carrying light-wave channel, and is optimized for a particular light-wave frequency. Compare with *multimode*.

skew — rotation of a bar code symbol about an axis parallel to the symbol's length.

SKU — see *stock-keeping unit*.

slot scanner — the scanning portion of a point-of-sale system embedded within the retail checkout lane counter. Traditionally a helium-neon laser is employed, reflecting the light beam by a series of mirrors to create a pattern that reads UPC symbols. The symbol is drawn across the scanner window so that at least one beam of light intersects the entire UPC symbol.

SNA (systems network architecture) — (DataComm) the IBM network architecture for communications among IBM devices, and between IBM and other machines.

software — a set of computer programs, procedures, and the associated documentation concerned with the operation of a data processing system, such as compilers, library routines, manuals, and circuit diagrams. Contrast with *hardware*.

source data collection — methods of recording data at its source in machine-readable form that can be reused to produce other records without rewriting the original data.

source marking — the bar code marking of a specific item at the point of initial production of the item; refers to supplier marking of a product with the supplier's manufacturer identification code and the supplier's item product code.

space — one of two types of elements comprising a bar code symbol. The element of a bar code symbol whose reflectance is greater than the global threshold. (DataComm) Absence of signal. In telegraph communications, a space represents the open condition

414

or no current flowing. A space impulse is equivalent to a binary 0.

space encoding — in bar code technology, the use of the spaces between the bars to carry encoded information. See *continuous code.*

space reflectance — the largest reflectance value in a space or quiet zone.

special symbol/character — in a character set, refers to a character that is not a numeral, a letter, or a blank, such as –, *, $, /, +, and %.

spectral band — a specific range of wavelengths (or equivalent frequencies) of electromagnetic radiation from a minimum to a maximum, often named after a central value. Thus, the spectral band B633 includes those wavelengths ±5% of the 633 nanometer peak. B900 includes those wavelengths ±10% of the 900 nanometer peak.

spectral response — the variation in sensitivity of a reading device to light of different wavelengths.

specular reflection — the mirror-like reflection of light from a surface. Reflection of light from a surface at an angle equal, but opposite to, the angle of incidence.

SPOOL (simultaneous peripheral operation on-line) — a program or piece of hardware that controls data going to an output device.

spot size — the diameter of the focused image of the emitter in scanners that use apertured optical systems.

standard business transaction — (EDI) a business procedure between trading partners that accomplishes a specific purpose, for example, relaying the intent to purchase goods. Many transactions are characterized by the paper document that was developed to communicate the data requirements to the trading partner, i.e., the purchase order.

standard data format — (EDI) a machine-readable data format, predefined and agreed to by trading partners, that can accomplish a standard business transaction.

standard DOD symbology (SDS) — MIL-STD-1189 defines Code 39 as the standard

U.S. government symbology for marking unit packs, outer containers, and selected documents.

standard syntax rules — (EDI) the rules governing structure in a standard data format.

star topology — (LAN) the point-to-point wiring of network elements to a central node.

start/stop characters or patterns — distinct characters or patterns used at the beginning and end of each bar code symbol that provide initial timing references and direction-of-read information to the decoding logic.

station — (DataComm) any DTE that receives or transmits messages on a data link, including network nodes and user devices.

stationary scanner bar code reader — see *fixed reader.*

stepladder code — a bar code printed in a vertical position.

stock-keeping unit (SKU) — an internal number generated by a company to uniquely identify a product, as opposed to the UPC code, which is a universal numbering system.

store and forward — (DataComm) communication systems in which messages are received at intermediate routing points and recorded (stored) if immediate retransmission is not possible, then forwarded to a further routing point or to the ultimate recipient when routing is available.

striation — a fine, streaky pattern of parallel lines, usually in the direction of the web of a printing press.

stroke analysis — in OCR, a technique of recognition in which each character is analyzed as a connected set of strokes, the straight lines and simple curves descriptive of the character. Matching to templates is done on the basis of this abstract topological information, rather than on the pixel values of the character's unprocessed image.

subset of a standard — (EDI) a selected group of transaction sets, segments, and data elements from a data standard such as ANSI X12 or UCS.

substitution error — in bar code scanning, the replacement of a character with an erroneous character, usually traceable to poor quality printing, decoding logic error, human input error, or any combination of these.

substitution error rate (SER) — the ratio of the number of invalid or incorrect characters entered into the data base to the number of valid characters entered.

substrate — the material (paper, plastic, metal, etc.) upon which a bar code symbol is "printed" or reproduced.

switched network — (DataComm) shared network where users have the potential to communicate over the network with each other at any time.

switching — (DataComm) allows the routing of data to the necessary recipient over communications networks.

symbol contrast (SC) — the difference between the largest and smallest reflectances in a scan reflectance profile.

$$SC = R_{max} - R_{min}$$

symbol density — the number of characters per lineal inch; limited by the width of the narrowest bar or space.

symbol grade — the simple average of all the overall profile grades (standards are defined in the document "ANS X3.182-1990") using the standard weighting 4.0 = A, 3.0 = B, 2.0 = C, 1.0 = D, and 0.0 = F. The symbol grade may be stated as a decimal or converted to a letter grade. A symbol grade has meaning only when the measuring aperture is also specified. The format for denoting the symbol grade is: "Symbol Grade" followed by "Measuring Aperture Number" followed by a slash ("/") followed by the wavelength(s) in nanometers.

symbol length — the physical length of a bar code symbol, including quiet zones.

symbology — a discrete set of characters used to represent and transmit information; a set of rules for encoding information in a bar code symbol. Examples of bar code symbologies include: Code 39, UPC/EAN, Interleaved 2 of 5, Code 128, Code 49, Code 16K, and PDF417.

symbology reference decode algorithm — a decoding algorithm that may be found in a particular application and/or symbology specification.

systematic error — errors introduced by the printer, reader, or other system elements that are consistent for all bars or all spaces.

systems architecture — the defined arrangement of the various components to provide a working computer system.

T carrier — (DataComm) a time-division-multiplexed, digital transmission facility, typically telephone-company supplied, usually operating at an aggregate data rate of 1.544 Mbps and above.

tack — the stickiness of an adhesive.

TCP/IP (transmission control protocol/internet protocol) — (LAN) a layered set of protocols that allows sharing of applications among computers in a high-speed communications environment. Because TCP/IP's protocols are standardized across all its layers, including those that provide terminal emulation and file transfer, different vendors' computing devices (all running TCP/IP) can exist on the same cable and communicate with one another across that cable. Corresponds to layers 4 (transport) and 3 (network) of the OSI reference model.

telecommunication port — (DataComm) entry channel through which data is communicated. A port is part of a central computer system.

telecommunications — (DataComm) a term encompassing transmission or reception of coded signals, writing, sounds, or intelligence of any nature by wire, radio, light beam, or any other electromagnetic means.

Telepen — a continuous code developed by S.B. Electronics that encodes the full ASCII character set of 128 characters. Each alphanumeric character is represented by 16 modules and two bar widths.

TELNET — (LAN) a virtual terminal service available through the TCP/IP protocol suite.

templating — a technique of image recognition that compares the image read or an analyzed abstraction of the image (stroke analysis) to a template stored in software to establish the identity of the image as a character.

terminal — (DataComm) point in a network at which data can either enter or leave; a device, usually equipped with a keyboard, often with a display, capable of sending and receiving data over a communications link; generically the same as data terminal equipment (DTE).

terminal server — (LAN) a device that allows one or more terminals or other devices to connect to an Ethernet.

terminated line — (DataComm) a circuit with a resistance at the far end equal to the characteristic impedance of the line, so no reflections or standing waves are present when a signal is entered at the near end.

text — (DataComm) in communications, transmitted characters forming the part of a message that carries information to be conveyed; in some protocols, the character sequence between start-of-text (STX) and end-of-text (ETX) control characters; information for human, as opposed to computer, comprehension, intended for presentation in a two-dimensional form.

thermal printing — a printing system where dots are selectively heated and cooled and drag upon a heat-sensitive substrate. The substrate turns dark in the heated areas. Also called *direct thermal.*

thermal transfer printing — a printing system like thermal except a one-time ribbon is used and common paper is used as a substrate. Eliminates the problems of fading or changing color inherent in direct thermal.

THz (terahertz) — one million million (10^{12}) cycles per second, unit of frequency.

tilt — rotation of a bar code symbol about an axis perpendicular to the substrate.

time-division multiplexer (TDM) — (Data-Comm) a device that accepts multiple channels on a single transmission line by connecting terminals, one at a time, at regular intervals, interleaving bits (bit TDM) or charac-

ters (character TDM) from each terminal.

time-sharing — (DataComm) a method of computer operation that allows several interactive terminals to use one computer. Although the terminals are actually served in sequence, the high speed of the computer makes it appear as if all terminals were being served simultaneously.

token bus — (LAN) a LAN standard that uses a token-passing media access method on a bus configuration.

token ring — (LAN) a data signaling scheme in which a special data packet (called a token) is passed from one station to another along an electrical ring. When a station wants to transmit, it takes possession of the token, transmits its data, then frees the token after the data has made a complete circuit of the electrical ring.

TOP (technical and office protocols) — (LAN) a Boeing version of the MAP protocol suite, aimed at office and engineering applications.

traceability number — a number assigned by a controlling authority to provide unique identification to an entity or group of entities to permit tracking of the movement of that entity or group of entities from point to point through a series of transactions.

trading partners — all members within the channels of distribution of an industry (e.g., customers, suppliers, carriers, banks).

transaction set — (EDI) a collection of information required by the receiver to perform a standard business transaction. In a standard data format, a transaction set contains a predefined group of segments in header, detail, and summary areas.

transaction set detail area — (EDI) segments that contain information relating to the line items within the transaction set.

transaction set diagram — (EDI) a diagram of the segments in a transaction in the order in which they are valid in that transaction.

transaction set header area — (EDI) segments that contain information relating to the entire transaction set.

transaction set summary area — (EDI) segments that contain information relating to transaction set totals.

transaction set trailer segment — (EDI) a segment that defines the end of a transaction set.

transceiver — (DataComm) a device that can both transmit and receive.

transient — (DataComm) an abrupt change in voltage of short duration (e.g., a brief pulse caused by the operation of a switch).

transition point — the edge of a space or bar where continued movement to an adjacent and complementary module causes a photodetector to reverse its bias from dark current to saturation and vice versa.

translation software — (EDI) a program or group of programs that decode, format, provide for protocol conversion, and may map data between an application data format or a predefined fixed-field data format to another data format.

transport case symbol (TCS) — the European nomenclature for the recommendations of the DSSG.

transport layer — (DataComm) layer 4 in the OSI reference model; provides a logical connection between processes on two machines.

transport package — a package intended for the transportation and handling of one or more articles, smaller packages, or bulk material.

tree — (LAN) a LAN topology that recognizes only one route between two nodes on the network. The "map" resembles a tree or the letter T.

trigger mark — a code bit that provides the scanner with the instruction that the code is in position to be read. Same as *key mark*. See also *presence sensor*.

truncation — decreasing the length of the bars to reduce the height of the bar code symbol to below the normal UPC specification. Truncation decreases a symbol's ability to

be read omnidirectionally and should be avoided.

TSR (terminate stay resident) — a software program that once executed remains operational within a single-tasking, single-user computer system. Often used as an interface program permitting microcomputers to communicate to mainframes.

two-level code — a bar code that uses two element widths, wide and narrow, in its structure. Code 39 is a two-level code.

2 of 5 Code — a numeric discrete character bar code in which each decimal digit is represented by five bars, two wide and three narrow, corresponding to the ones and zeros of a binary representation. An early, successful bar code developed by the Nieaf Company in the Netherlands, it can achieve densities of 15 numeric characters per inch. In practice, this code has been superseded by the denser Interleaved 2 of 5 Code.

UDP (user datagram protocol) — (LAN) the TCP/IP transaction protocol used for applications such as remote network management and name-service access; lets users assign a name, such as "VAX 2," to a physical or numbered address.

unidirectional code — a code format that permits reading in only one direction.

uniform container symbol (UCS) — a bar code symbol designed for printing on corrugated board; a result of DSSG.

unit — a module or segment; the smallest width of bars and spaces in a bar code. See *module*.

unit load — one or more filled transport packages or other items held together by one or more means such as pallet, slip sheet, strapping, interlocking, glue, shrink wrap, or net wrap, making them suitable for transport, stacking, and storage as a unit.

Unix — a multiuser/multitasking operating system originally designed by AT&T for communicating multiuser, 32-bit minicomputers; has come into wide commercial acceptance because of its predominance in academia and its programming versatility. AT&T System V Version 3 and Berkeley System Development Version 4.3 are currently popular.

unloaded line — (DataComm) a line with no loaded coils that reduce line loss at audio frequencies.

UPC (universal product code) — most commonly a numeric 12-digit bar code pattern adopted by the U.S. grocery industry (and subsequently by other retail industries), composed of a six-digit manufacturer number assigned by the UCC, a five-digit product code assigned by the manufacturer, and a modulo 10 check digit as the twelfth digit.

upload — to transfer data from a front-end processor to a large computer.

USCS (UPC shipping container symbol) — a bar code structure and symbol administered by the UCC designed for printing on corrugated board. The code is an extension of the coding structure employed in UPC; the symbology used is Interleaved 2 of 5.

valley — the graphical pattern on a scan reflectance profile that looks like a "U" or "V." Within a profile a valley represents a "bar." One or more valleys could also be found within an element representing a reflectance change within the element.

VAN (value-added network) — (EDI) a network whose services go beyond simple switching, providing communication services such as line speed conversion and protocol matching.

variable length code — a code that can be of any length within a range of lengths, commonly with a maximum length specified and frequently with a minimum length also specified.

variable length field — a data field or data element that may vary within a prescribed minimum and maximum.

variable length symbology — a symbology whose format is not fixed beyond basic requirements for overhead characters, such as start/stop codes. For example, UPC is a fixed-length, numeric symbology that supports only six characters (Version E) or 10 characters (Version A). Code 39 is a variable length alphanumeric code that can support any data length from one character up to a maximum dictated by the reading system employed, typically 32 or more characters.

verification — the technical process by which a symbol is evaluated to determine whether it meets the specification for that specific symbol. Verification can be accomplished by semiautomated means, with elements measured by a microscope and contrast established by a densitometer. Verification can also be accomplished by automatic means with a device that measures width of elements, contrast, and reflectance, and establishes decodability.

verifier — a device that makes measurements of the bars, spaces, quiet zones, and optical characteristics of a symbol to determine if the symbol meets the requirements of a specification or standard.

vertical redundancy — the availability of more than one scan path through the elements of a bar code symbol.

virtual circuit — (DataComm) in packet-switching, a network facility that gives the appearance to the user of an actual end-to-end circuit; a dynamically variable network connection where sequential data packets may be routed differently during the course of a "virtual connection"; virtual circuits enable transmission facilities to be shared by many users simultaneously.

voice-grade line — (DataComm) a channel that is capable of carrying voice-frequency signals.

voice recognition — a process by which a computer or control mechanism can accept data input by spoken command with no intermediate key entry.

void(s) — unwanted light areas wholly contained within the dark elements of a positive bar code symbol. When such areas lie along the element's edge, they are considered as edge irregularities.

volatile memory — a storage medium that loses all data when power is removed.

wand scanner — a handheld scanning device

used as a contact bar code or OCR reader.

wavelength — a fundamental measure of electromagnetic radiation, proportional to the inverse of the radiation's frequency.

web — the paper, foil, film, or other flexible material that comes from a roll as it moves through a machine in the process of being formed, converted, or printed.

wedge — a device that usually plugs between a keyboard and a CRT terminal or personal computer that allows data to be entered either by keyboard or scanner.

wide area network (WAN) — (DataComm) national or international network connecting points of wide geographical coverage.

wide-to-narrow ratio (N) — the ratio between the width of the wide elements and narrow elements in a bar code having two widths.

width code — one of two fundamental ways (see *delta code*) of encoding information in a one-dimensional medium. Each bit is assigned to a bar or space: If the element is wide the bit value is "1," and if narrow the bit value is "0." Code 39 and Codabar are width codes. Also referred to as a *binary code*.

width error — the difference between bar (or space) widths, calculated from the scanner's digital output and the optically measured bar (space) widths.

WINS — (EDI) warehouse information network standard.

wiring closet — (DataComm) central location for termination and routing of on-premises wiring systems.

X12 — (EDI) the accredited subcommittee of the American National Standards Institute whose mandate is to develop standard data formats for business transactions with cross-industry application.

x-axis — one of three coordinate directions relating to the orientation and movement of a symbol on a conveyor or transport system. The x-axis is parallel to and in the same direction as the movement of the conveyor or transport system; symbol *pitch* is rotation of the symbol about the y-axis in the plane formed by the x-axis and z-axis.

X dimension — the intended width of the narrow elements dictated by the application and/or symbology specification. See also *module*.

X-ON/X-OFF (transmitter on/transmitter off) — (DataComm) control characters used for flow control, instructing a terminal to start transmission (X-ON) and end transmission (X-OFF).

y-axis — one of three coordinate directions relating to the orientation and movement of a symbol on a conveyor or transport system. The y-axis is horizontal and at a right angle to the x-axis; symbol *roll* or *tilt* is rotation of a symbol about the x-axis in the plane formed by the y-axis and the z-axis.

z-axis — one of three coordinate directions relating to the orientation and movement of a symbol on a conveyor or transport system. The z-axis is vertical and at a right angle to the x-axis; symbol *yaw* or *skew* is rotation of a symbol about the z-axis in the plane formed by the x-axis and y-axis.

Z dimension — to evaluate a bar code symbol's compliance to a specified bar/space width tolerance, one may need to utilize achieved element widths since the nominal or intended values may be unknown. This Z dimension is defined as an average of two averages: the average of all the narrow bar element widths and the average of all the narrow space element widths, excluding intercharacter gaps.

zero suppression — the technique used to shorten UPC codes by omitting certain zeros from the bar code.

Index

302–306
Text Characters Within a Matrix Grid, 162
Thermal Paper, 175
Thermal Printing, 117, 158, 162, 174
Thermal Transfer Ribbons, 158, 176
Thermal Transfer, 40, 141, 158–160, 162, 175–179, 181, 183, 186, 305, 310, 313
Time & Attendance, 59–60, 65–66, 68–69, 113–115, 122, 126, 130, 132–133, 136, 138, 196, 198–201, 204–205, 210–214, 220–222, 234–239, 242, 244–249, 251–253, 255–277, 279–280, 282–287, 289–290, 292–295, 297–300, 302, 305–306, 308–309, 313
Tool Crib Checking, 261–262
Training and Education, 241, 251
Transaction Set, 69, 106, 197, 225–228
Transactional Identification, 195, 238
Translation Software, 231
Translator, 226, 228
Transponders, 2, 5, 280
Traveler, 131, 239, 263
Truncation, 19, 135
Two-Dimensional Symbols, 14, 114
U.P.C. Character Construction, 21
U.P.C. Modulus 10, 21, 345–358
U.P.C. Symbol Location, 16, 19
U.P.C. Version E, 21–24, 31, 33, 46
Uniform Code Council (UCC,) 9, 14–17, 19–20, 22–23, 25–29, 32, 41–44, 46, 48, 54–57, 59–60, 68–70, 87, 105–106, 109–112, 116, 248–251, 254, 256–268, 332
Underwriters Laboratories, 217–218
Uniform Plumbing Code, 15
Uniform Symbology Specification, 41, 72
United Parcel Service (UPS), 103
United States Postal Service (USPS), 9, 76–77
Universal Product Code (U.P.C.) 9–10, 12–34, 36–38, 40–49, 54–55, 57, 59–61, 64, 69–71, 84–86, 88, 106, 109–110, 112–113, 115, 129, 135–137, 185, 188–191, 250, 254, 256–263, 265–268, 282
University of Victoria, 98
Vericode, 96–98, 102–103
Verifying the Quality of the Printed Symbol, 185–193
Veritec, 97–98, 102–103
VICS, 16, 223, 225, 298
Visible Laser Diode (VLD), 140
Voice Recognition, 4–5, 7, 312
Voting Algorithm, 116, 133
Wal-Mart, 17
Wang, Ynjiun, vi
Weighted Modulus, 62, 87, 345–358
Width Codes, 13, 84–86
Williams, Ted, 50
Wireless Terminals, 201, 246

Woolf, Gerry, 38
Wright, George, 29
X Dimension, 10, 19–20, 41, 50, 63, 72, 86, 113, 122, 128–129, 131, 137, 142–143, 149, 155–156, 178, 183, 191, 193, 248, 250–251
X12 Transaction Set, 197, 225
Zebra Technologies, 159, 310
ZIP Code, 76, 78